Lecture Notes in Computer Science 2297

Edited by G. Goos, J. Hartmanis, and J. van Leeuwen

T0241437

Springer
Berlin
Heidelberg
New York
Barcelona
Hong Kong
London
Milan
Paris
Singapore
Tokyo

Roland Backhouse   Roy Crole
Jeremy Gibbons (Eds.)

Algebraic and Coalgebraic Methods in the Mathematics of Program Construction

International Summer School and Workshop
Oxford, UK, April 10-14, 2000
Revised Lectures

 Springer

Series Editors

Gerhard Goos, Karlsruhe University, Germany
Juris Hartmanis, Cornell University, NY, USA
Jan van Leeuwen, Utrecht University, The Netherlands

Volume Editors

Roland Backhouse
University of Nottingham, School of Computer Science and IT
Jubilee Campus, Wollaton Road, Nottingham NG8 1BB, United Kingdom
E-mail: rcb@cs.nott.ac.uk

Roy Crole
University of Leicester, Dept. of Mathematics and Computer Science
University Road, Leicester LE1 7RH, United Kingdom
E-mail: roy.crole@mcs.le.ac.uk

Jeremy Gibbons
Oxford University Computing Laboratory, Wolfson Building
Parks Road, Oxford OX1 3QD, United Kingdom
E-mail: jeremy.gibbons@comlab.ox.ac.uk

Cataloging-in-Publication Data applied for

Die Deutsche Bibliothek - CIP-Einheitsaufnahme

Algebraic and coalgebraic methods in the mathematics of program construction ;
international summer school and workshop, Oxford, UK, April 10 - 14, 2000 ;
revised lectures / Roland Backhouse ... (ed.). - Berlin ; Heidelberg ; New York ;
Barcelona ; Hong Kong ; London ; Milan ; Paris ; Tokyo : Springer, 2002
    (Lecture notes in computer science ; Vol. 2297)
    ISBN 3-540-43613-8

CR Subject Classification (1998): D.2, D.3, F.3, F.4

ISSN 0302-9743
ISBN 3-540-43613-8 Springer-Verlag Berlin Heidelberg New York

Springer-Verlag Berlin Heidelberg New York
a member of BertelsmannSpringer Science+Business Media GmbH

http://www.springer.de

© Springer-Verlag Berlin Heidelberg 2002
Printed in Germany

Typesetting: Camera-ready by author, data conversion by DA-TeX Gerd Blumenstein
Printed on acid-free paper   SPIN 10846432   06/3142   5 4 3 2 1 0

Preface

Program construction is about turning specifications of computer software into implementations. Doing so in a way that guarantees correctness is an undertaking requiring deep understanding of the languages and tools being used, as well as of the application domain. Recent research aimed at improving the process of program construction exploits insights from abstract algebraic tools such as lattice theory, fixpoint calculus, universal algebra, category theory, and allegory theory. This book provides an introduction to these mathematical theories and how they are applied to practical problems.

The book is based on the School on *Algebraic and Co-algebraic Methods in the Mathematics of Program Construction* held in April 2000 at the University of Oxford. The School, which was sponsored under the Mathematics for Information Technology initiative of the Engineering and Physical Research Council in the UK, had the goal of introducing this research area to new PhD students in a way that would provide a sound and broad basis for their own research studies. The lecturers were chosen on the basis of a combination of a distinguished track record of research contributions in this area and an ability to present difficult material in a comprehensible way without compromising scientific rigor.

The students that attended the School had varied backgrounds to which due account was given by the lecturers in preparing their material. The experience and feedback gained during the School has been used in preparing this major revision of that material. The lecture material has also been augmented by an introductory chapter giving a detailed overview of the remaining chapters. We hope that this chapter will prove useful in allowing readers to select the chapters most relevant to their own research and to plan their further reading.

Our thanks go to all those involved in making the School a very enjoyable and successful event. Particular thanks go to the EPSRC and the London Mathematical Society for their generous financial support, to the students for their enthusiasm and positive feedback, to the lecturers for their unstinting hard work, and to Springer-Verlag for making the publication of this book possible.

January 2002

Roland Backhouse
Roy Crole
Jeremy Gibbons

Contributors

Peter Aczel: Departments of Mathematics and Computer Science, University of Manchester, Manchester M13 9PL, England. petera@cs.man.ac.uk, http://www.cs.man.ac.uk/~petera/.

Roland Backhouse: School of Computing and Information Technology, University of Nottingham, Nottingham NG8 1BB, England. rcb@cs.nott.ac.uk, http://www.cs.nott.ac.uk/~rcb/.

Richard Bird: Oxford University Computing Laboratory, Wolfson Building, Parks Road, Oxford OX1 3QD, England. richard.bird@comlab.ox.ac.uk, http://www.comlab.ox.ac.uk/oucl/work/richard.bird/.

Roy Crole: Department of Mathematics and Computer Science, University of Leicester, University Road, Leicester LE1 7RH, England. roy.crole@mcs.le.ac.uk, http://www.mcs.le.ac.uk/~rcrole/.

Henk Doornbos: EverMind, Westerkade 15/4, 9718 AS Groningen, The Netherlands. henk.doornbos@evermind.com, http://www.evermind.com.

Jeremy Gibbons: Oxford University Computing Laboratory, Wolfson Building, Parks Road, Oxford OX1 3QD, England. jeremy.gibbons@comlab.ox.ac.uk, http://www.comlab.ox.ac.uk/oucl/work/jeremy.gibbons/.

Bart Jacobs: Department of Computer Science, University of Nijmegen, P.O. Box 9010, 6500 GL Nijmegen, The Netherlands. bart@cs.kun.nl, http://www.cs.kun.nl/~bart/.

Burghard von Karger: Christian-Albrechts-University of Kiel, Institute of Computer Science and Applied Mathematics, Olshausenstrasse 40, D-24098 Kiel, Germany. burghard.von.karger@gmx.de, http://www.informatik.uni-kiel.de/~bvk/.

Shin Cheng Mu: Oxford University Computing Laboratory, Wolfson Building, Parks Road, Oxford OX1 3QD, England. shin-cheng.mu@comlab.ox.ac.uk, http://www.comlab.ox.ac.uk/oucl/work/shin-cheng.mu/.

Hilary Priestley: Oxford University Mathematical Institute, 24–29 St Giles', Oxford OX1 3LB, England. hap@maths.ox.ac.uk, http://www.stannes.ox.ac.uk/college/members/priestley.ha.html.

Table of Contents

Chapter 1
Introduction

Roy Crole

Department of Mathematics and Computer Science, University of Leicester

1 Preliminaries

This volume is an up-to-date introduction to developments in the calculational construction of computer programs, with particular emphasis on the use of algebraic and coalgebraic datatypes. By including introductory chapters on the relevant mathematical foundations alongside more advanced chapters describing applications, the contents are designed to be accessible to a broad spectrum of readers — from computer practitioners with little or no knowledge of the area seeking a basic introduction, to researchers with an active interest wishing to broaden and deepen their understanding.

The purpose of this introduction is to allow readers to determine which of the various chapters are relevant to their own interests and on the best order to read the chapters, dependent on their own current knowledge and background. In particular, we

- state what we assume of our readers;
- give a very broad overview of the main subject themes;
- provide an informal account of the mathematics which unifies and underpins the computing applications; and
- outline the chapter contents, and the relationships to the underpinning mathematics.

This volume will interest anyone wishing to learn more of the theory of Computer Science, especially the sort of theory which has immediate application to practical computing problems. In particular we hope that it will be be useful for computing practitioners who want to learn about calculational methods for program construction.

1.1 Assumed Knowledge

We assume that the reader has some acquaintance with programming, and programming languages. The main styles of programming which feature here are imperative (such as Algol, Pascal, C etc), functional (such as ML, Scheme, Haskell etc) and object oriented (such as Smalltalk, Java, C++ etc). Any reader who knows something of at least one language from one of these paradigms will be able to benefit considerably from this volume. It is not necessary to be a skilled programmer who writes sophisticated software; but understanding how to write

R. Backhouse et al. (Eds.): Algebraic and Coalgebraic Methods ..., LNCS 2297, pp. 1–19, 2002.
© Springer-Verlag Berlin Heidelberg 2002

short programs which involve key programming concepts in at least one real language will be essential. For an excellent overview of programming concepts see for example [17]. For a more comprehensive account of programming pragmatics, from high-level concepts to low-level machine detail, see for example [16].

Much of the mathematics in this volume requires knowledge of naive set theory, including relations and functions, and simple discrete mathematics. The material found in a good introduction to discrete mathematics will provide a very solid foundation. Gries and Schneider's calculational presentation of discrete mathematics [6] is the most in tune with the style of presentation in this volume. We also assume an understanding of very basic logic to a similar level. Some of the material in this volume is based upon *category theory*. The basic definitions are all self-contained and the introduction contains an informal discussion. For more details please see [2,3,4,7,10].

1.2   Volume Overview

Having described our intended audience, we now give a broad explanation of the volume title, *Algebraic and Coalgebraic Methods in the Mathematics of Program Construction*. We will be studying *programs*, or more precisely computer programs. Sometimes specific programming languages are studied, and we will be concerned with programs written in a fixed language. At other times, programming styles, or methodologies, such as *functional programming* or *object oriented programming*, are studied at a suitable level of generality (if the reader is familiar with only one language, then this language is likely to embrace just one programming style). Scientific results and advances will then apply to a range of different but none-the-less similar programming languages, each conforming to a particular programming style.

So, what aspects of computer programs are we interested in? A key aim is to develop methods and tools for *program construction*. For example, a method might show how to *construct* a program by transforming a high level description of what the program should do, its *specification*, into an actual program which will often be written in a particular language.

The starting point is a specification and the finish point is an efficient implementation. The steps in between must guarantee that the final implementation does indeed satisfy the initial specification. In order to provide such a guarantee the transformation rules are founded on *precise* mathematical laws that are provably correct with respect to the semantics of the implementation and specification languages. In order that the transformations are practical, the laws must be *simple* and *concise* so that they can be applied straightforwardly without error. In this way, we develop programs from their specifications *hand-in-hand* with a guarantee of their correctness.

The calculational style we advocate is reminiscent of the simplifications used when calculating with arithmetic expressions. Arithmetic expressions obey certain equational rules such as commutativity, distributivity and so on. Such rules can be viewed as a calculus with which we may simplify algebraic expressions.

We see how to develop analogous equational rules which hold between programs and can be used in calculation and simplification.

Examples of algebras to be found in mathematical texts are groups, rings and fields. Datatypes such as natural numbers and finite lists are also examples of (computational) algebras. In each case one has a set (for example the set of natural numbers) together with operations (zero and successor) whose inputs come from the set—all algebras have this kind of structure. Although there are many examples of algebras, it turns out that it is possible to describe them in a very general way. In fact there are mathematical frameworks within which the above algebras can be seen as examples of just one definition—such frameworks are said to be *unifying*. Two subjects which provide such frameworks are *universal algebra* and *category theory*. Originally, both of these subjects arose, in part, through attempts to extract common key ideas from apparently diverse areas of mathematics. However, it turns out that many technical methods which appear in the mathematics of program construction can also be defined using methods from these subjects. In particular, category theory provides us with a very general notion of an *algebra* of which groups, rings, natural numbers and lists are examples. It is this notion that embodies our so-called *algebraic methods*. Many computing concepts, not just natural numbers and lists, are instances of algebras.

In category theory every definition has a so called "dual" or "opposite", and thus we can "dualize" the notion of algebra. This gives rise to the idea of a *coalgebra*, and to *coalgebraic methods*. We leave a definition of algebras and coalgebras until later on; for the time being we whet the reader's appetite by mentioning that many apparently diverse concepts such as finite and infinite datatypes, different algorithms, operational behaviours of languages can all be seen as instances of algebras and coalgebras. These latter two concepts unify many other subjects, so that each may be seen within a common framework.

2   A Mathematical History Tour

We give an outline of the underpinning mathematical topics. The intention is not to concentrate on applications, but to present a coherent mathematical overview with emphasis on examples and minimal technical detail. In particular, we present developments chronologically, beginning with some of the original mathematics used in program construction, and culminating with quite recent material.

2.1   Fixed Points

First we recall the idea of a fixed point of a function. If $f : X \rightarrow X$ is an endofunction on X, then $x \in X$ is a *fixed point* if $f(x) = x$. If the set X is ordered, by $\leq$ say, then x is a *least* fixed point if it is least in the set of all fixed points. For example, if $X = \{ 1, 2, 3, 4 \}$ ordered as usual, and f is $1 \mapsto 2$, $2 \mapsto 3$, $3 \mapsto 3$, $4 \mapsto 4$, then 3 and 4 are fixed points and 3 is the least fixed point.

The topic of fixed points is pervasive throughout this volume, and further details can be found in Chapter 2. The original interest of computer scientists in fixed points can be traced, very roughly, to the sixties and early seventies. There is a considerable body of theory which was developed by mathematicians before this period; we look at how this has been adapted and advanced by computer scientists. Fixed points arise within two important but distinct and intimately connected topics in computing, namely syntax and semantics. First we look at syntax, where we assume that readers have some knowledge of formal grammars.

During the very late fifties and early sixties, computer scientists developed the first "high-level" programming languages. These provide the programmer with a language whose concepts are close to mathematical thinking and do not (necessarily) involve the "low level" machine details associated with machine and assembly code. During the evolution of the first high-level languages, it was realized that a rigorous method was required for writing down a formal description of the programming syntax. Recall that a *context-free grammar* is just one variety of formal language which had already been developed by mathematicians. Backus [1] developed a special notation for describing context-free grammars, which was ideally suited to the description of programming languages. In fact this notation was used in the definition of the programming language Algol 60 [1,9] which was the vehicle for the introduction of block structured programming. Due to the contributions of both Backus and Naur, a language definition is said to be in Backus Naur Form (BNF) if written in this notation. In fact one can understand such language definitions as fixed points, which we illustrate by example. Here is a very simple BNF grammar

$$E ::= z \mid v \mid (E + E)$$

where z ranges over the integers $\mathbb{Z}$, v over a set of variables, and E over a set of arithmetic expressions. A typical expression is $(^-3 + (x + 88))$. However, the set of expressions defined by such a grammar can be seen to arise as a fixed point of a function. Each expression is regarded as a finite tree. Integers and variables have one labelled node, and $(E + E')$ has root node $+$ with immediate subtrees E and E'. Let $\mathcal{P}(S)$ be the set of subsets of a set S. If $\mathcal{T}$ is the set of all rooted binary trees, we can define a function $\Phi : \mathcal{P}(\mathcal{T}) \to \mathcal{P}(\mathcal{T})$ which maps a subset S of $\mathcal{T}$ to the set consisting of all integers, all variables, and all those finite trees with root $+$ and immediate subtrees belonging to S. Let us write $\mathcal{E}$ for the set of all expressions. Given the definition of Φ, we would expect that $\Phi(\mathcal{E}) \subseteq \mathcal{E}$, because if $\xi \in \Phi(\mathcal{E})$, then ξ is either an integer, or is of the form $(E + E')$ with $E, E' \in \mathcal{E}$. We call such an $\mathcal{E}$ a *prefixed point* of Φ. However, we only wish to build expressions out of integers and variables, and $\mathcal{E}$ should contain nothing else. In other words, $\mathcal{E}$ should be the smallest or *least* prefixed point of Φ—that is the least subset $\mathcal{E}$ of $\mathcal{T}$ such that $\Phi(\mathcal{E}) \subseteq \mathcal{E}$. In fact it turns out that for such an $\mathcal{E}$, $\Phi(\mathcal{E}) = \mathcal{E}$, that is $\mathcal{E}$ is actually a genuine fixed point. So, what have we achieved?

– We have given an informal example which illustrates that languages specified by a BNF grammar can be defined as fixed points;

- we will be able to manipulate and calculate with such languages using a calculus of fixed points to be introduced in Chapter 4; and
- we will see that we can dualize the definition of least prefixed point to obtain new and useful tools.

We move on to semantics. In the early sixties, there had already been considerable engineering advances made in the implementation of the first high-level languages such as Lisp and Algol 60. Computer scientists and engineers had a reasonable "informal" understanding of programming languages based in terms of the compilation of high-level expressions into low-level machine code. However, there was no semantic theory of languages that was in some sense independent of the instruction set architecture into which a language was compiled. The key advances in this area were made primarily by Dana Scott and Christopher Strachey, at Oxford University [11,12,13,14,15,18]. They developed a so-called *denotational semantics*. In such a semantics, an imperative program P is modeled by an element $[\![P]\!]$ of a mathematical set D. P is said to *denote* the element $[\![P]\!]$ in D. Such semantics give rise to fixed points in a natural way; we consider a small imperative programming language to give a simple illustration of why this is so. Consider a programming syntax defined by the grammar

$E ::= c$		Boolean or integer constant
$\mid l$		memory location
$\mid E\ op\ E$		$op \in \{+, -, *, \leq, <, =\}$
$P ::= l := E$		assignment
$\mid$ if E then P else P		conditional
$\mid$ while E do P		while loop
$\mid P\ ;\ P$		sequencing

The basic data types are integers and Booleans. The language consists of simple Boolean and arithmetic expressions, along with standard commands formed from assignments. A *program* consists of a program command P and a state s; a state is a finite partial function from memory locations to basic data, such as $s = \langle l \mapsto 4, l' \mapsto 5 \rangle$, which is defined on all locations in P.

We can give a semantics to the arithmetic expressions easily; any expression denotes the integer or Boolean given by looking up the values of locations in s, and then calculating the resulting expression. The denotation of $l+3$ is a function from the set of states S to the integers $\mathbb{Z}$; for s above, $[\![l + 3]\!](s) = 7$. How do we give a semantics to commands? When a command is executed, it either transforms a start state to a final state, or it may loop. For example, if we begin with state $\langle l \mapsto 4, l' \mapsto 5 \rangle$, running the command $l := 7$ yields the final state $\langle l \mapsto 7, l' \mapsto 5 \rangle$. And running if $2 < 3$ then $l := 7$ else $l := 8$ would yield the same final state. What about while T do $l := 6$? This command should loop, and not return a final state. So a command can be modeled by a partial function from S to S, or a total function $S \to S_\perp$, where $S_\perp = S \cup \{\perp\}$ is an ordered set and $\perp$ is a distinguished least element meaning "undefined". More precisely, if $e, e' \in S_\perp$, then $e \leq e'$ just in case $e = e' \in S$, or $e = \perp$. We shall write B for any Boolean expression.[1] Let us write $[\![B]\!] : S \rightarrow \{\, T, F \,\}$ for the semantics of a Boolean B, and $[\![P]\!] : S \rightarrow S_{\perp}$ for the semantics of a command P. The idea is that running P in state s terminates with state s' just in case $[\![P]\!](s) = s'$, and loops if $[\![P]\!](s) = \perp$.

What is the semantics of $W =$ while B do P? To run this command, we run B in a starting state s. If we obtain F the result is s. If we obtain T we would run P in s, which would either loop (in which case W loops) or we get a new state s'. In the latter case we run W again, but in state s'. Let us suppose that we know the semantics of the subprograms B and P. We can then define a new function Φ whose inputs are functions $w : S \rightarrow S_{\perp}$ and outputs are functions $S \rightarrow S_{\perp}$, by

$$
w \mapsto s \mapsto \begin{cases} s & \text{if } [\![B]\!](s) = F \\ \perp & \text{if } [\![B]\!](s) = T \text{ and } [\![P]\!](s) = \perp \\ w(s') & \text{if } [\![B]\!](s) = T \text{ and } s' = [\![P]\!](s) \neq \perp \end{cases}
$$

The informal argument amounts to saying that the semantics of W at s is $\Phi([\![W]\!])(s)$. But the semantics must also be $[\![W]\!](s)$. As this holds for any s, we take the semantics of W to be a[2] fixed point of Φ.

During the seventies and early eighties, the pioneering work of Scott and Strachey was continued by a variety of researchers, and the techniques for describing denotational semantics were extended and refined, as were the kinds of programming languages for which one could describe clean denotational semantics. As well as developing models of imperative languages, Scott also considered very elementary functional languages. In fact, in the first instance, he considered what it would mean to have a denotational model of the untyped lambda calculus. Scott's work led to the description of an equation whose *solution is a set* which arises as a fixed point. In such a denotational model, each term t of the lambda calculus denotes an element of a set D. But any term t can be applied to another term s to form the term $t\, s$. Thus, very roughly, t denotes not only an element of D, but also a function from D to D. This leads to the requirement that D and $D \rightarrow D$ are isomorphic, or put another way, that D is a solution to an equation of the form $X \cong X \rightarrow X$. If we define $\Phi(X) = X \rightarrow X$, then once again the solution to a problem in semantics is a fixed point (up to isomorphism) of a function Φ.

During the seventies and eighties, a great deal of work took place concerning language definitions; denotational semantics, operational semantics and their connections; and in particular program construction. The earlier program construction work concentrates on imperative languages (such as the calculation of loops from invariants) and also includes material on verification. In the late eighties and early nineties the first conferences on program construction took

---

[1] We do not give a formal definition of "Boolean expression" but rely on the reader's goodwill in believing that we could make this precise!

[2] It is possible to show that we should select the *least* fixed point with respect to a certain partial order, but the details are omitted.

place. Current work, as described in this volume, encompasses a variety of programming paradigms, and emphasizes the utility of *calculation* over *verification*.

2.2   Induction and Coinduction

The set of expressions defined by a BNF grammar is an example of an *inductive* definition. We recall that the formal definition of the set of expressions was the least fixed point of a function Φ. The "usual" inductive definition of $\mathcal{E}$ would be the smallest set which

- contains all of the integers and variables; and
- is such that given any two expressions E and E' in $\mathcal{E}$ so too is $(E + E')$,

and if one examines the description of the least prefixed point $\mu\Phi$ of the function Φ defined in Section 2.1, $\mu\Phi$ can be seen to correspond to the inductive "definition".

The use of inductive definitions to define languages for computation and programming has been widespread over the last thirty to forty years. Although the original BNF grammars were used to define fairly simple programming languages, inductive definitions in general have been used to specify sophisticated programming languages; type systems and type theories many of which are highly complex; the operational (run-time) behaviour of languages, and so on. In many of these situations, the calculus of fixed points described in this volume can be used to reason about programming definitions via their realizations as fixed points. A function $\Phi : \mathcal{P}(X) \to \mathcal{P}(X)$ is *monotone* if whenever $A, A' \in \mathcal{P}(X)$ and $A \subseteq A'$, then $\Phi(A) \subseteq \Phi(A')$. The set *inductively* defined by such Φ is the least fixed point $\mu\Phi$ of Φ. Monotonicity ensures that this exists. In the last decade, the dual notion of the set *coinductively* defined by Φ, namely the greatest fixed point $\nu\Phi$ of Φ, has been studied intensively and shown to arise in a variety of applications. We discuss the ideas briefly, because inductive and coinductive definitions yield simple examples of algebras and coalgebras, and the latter are equally prominent in the mathematics of program construction.

Possibly the first example of a coinductive definition in computer science was that of *bisimilarity* of processes (see for example [8]). Suppose that p and q are "processes", and we want to define when they have the same behaviour. Each process can perform an "action" and become a new process, written $p \leadsto p'$. For example p might be a vending machine, $\leadsto$ is the action of taking money and dispensing chocolate, and p' is the vending machine after the financial transaction and with one less chocolate bar. Informally, we might say that p and q have the same behaviour if whenever p performs an action so can q, and the resulting p' and q' also have the same behaviour, and vice versa. We will write $p \sim q$ to denote that p and q have the same behaviour, and call the (equivalence) relation *bisimilarity*. What is a formal definition of $\sim$? Let $\mathcal{B}$ be any binary relation on processes. Define a new binary relation $\Phi(\mathcal{B})$ by setting $p\ \Phi(\mathcal{B})\ q$ just in case whenever $p \leadsto p'$ then $q \leadsto q'$, or whenever $q \leadsto q'$ then $p \leadsto p'$, and in each case $p'\ \mathcal{B}\ q'$. If $\mathcal{B} \subseteq \Phi(\mathcal{B})$ (that is, $\mathcal{B}$ is a post fixed point) then whenever $p\ \mathcal{B}\ q$ it follows that $p\ \varPhi(\mathcal{B})\ q$. Thus $\mathcal{B} \subseteq \varPhi(\mathcal{B})$ is a formal statement that p and q have the "same $\mathcal{B}$ behaviour". Of course $\mathcal{B}$ captures a formal description of one particular pattern of behaviour. We want the relation $\sim$ to characterize "all possible behaviours". We can do this by taking $\sim$ as the *greatest* relation $\mathcal{B}$ which is a postfixed point of $\varPhi$, that is, bisimilarity $\sim$ is the set *coinductively* defined by $\varPhi$. In the last decade, many computer science definitions have been formulated coinductively, and coinduction has been a topic of intensive research.

2.3   Types and Categories

Types and categories play a crucial role in the mathematics of program construction. In this section we review some of the concepts of type theory, with which we assume readers have at least some knowledge from programming languages, and we also try to give a very brief and informal introduction to the notion of a category.

We begin with type theory. A crude definition of a *type* is a set, together with a collection of operations on the set. The key point is that from the programmer's point of view, a type σ should behave as a mathematical set, and the programmer should only be able to determine whether some code c has type σ or not. If c is of type σ, the programmer should only be allowed to apply certain operations to c— for example if c is a list, taking the head or tail. What should be hidden from the programmer is the actual *machine representation* of σ and consequently the ability to manipulate c through such knowledge. One might consider a type as protective armour for a set, which prevents ad-hoc use of arbitrary operations, but allows certain specified operations. For example, the Booleans should be a two-element set, with the usual logical operations, conditionals, etc. But just because a particular instance of a Boolean is stored as a bit-sequence, one should not be able to add the Boolean to an integer by applying high-level addition—a type error should be raised.

Category theory is a branch of mathematics which arose by abstracting key concepts from algebraic topology, which is the study of topology using algebraic techniques. Despite these origins, category theory itself has deep connections with computing concepts. We begin with an example of a category. Computer scientists often work with functions $f : X \to Y$ between sets X and Y. Notice that for any set X there is an identity function on X. Also, if $f : X \to Y$ and $g : Y \to Z$ are functions then so too is the composition $g \circ f : X \to Z$. Every category possesses this kind of structure. There is a collection of *objects* (in our example, the sets), a collection of *morphisms* (the functions), *identity* morphisms, and one can always *compose* morphisms of a suitable kind (note the matching target and source set Y of f and g). An example of a category of a rather different nature is an ordered set X in which the order is reflexive and transitive. Here, the objects are the elements of the underlying set, and there is a unique morphism from x to x' (where $x, x' \in X$) precisely when $x \leq x'$. Identities and composition exist because of the properties of the relation.

Suppose that $f : X \to Y$ is a function, and that $[X]$ and $[Y]$ are the sets of (finite) lists of elements of X and Y. One often has a list of elements of X,

say $[x_1, x_2, x_3]$, and wants to compute $[f(x_1), f(x_2), f(x_3)]$. There is of course
a function $g : [X] \to [Y]$ such that $g([x_1, x_2, x_3]) = [f(x_1), f(x_2), f(x_3)]$, and g
could be denoted by $[f]$ to show dependence on f (functional programmers will
recognise g as "*map f*"). Such a mapping of objects to objects ($X \mapsto [X]$) and
morphisms to morphisms ($f \mapsto [f]$) is an example of a *functor*. The key point
is that if $f : X \to Y$, then $[f] : [X] \to [Y]$—the image of the morphism f
under the functor is a morphism between the images of the source and target
of f. Some other conditions must be satisfied: the morphism mapping should
preserve identities ($[id] = id$) and composition ($[g.f] = [g].[f]$). Functors arise
throughout the study of categories, and some more examples appear below.

Having discussed categories and types separately, we explain briefly the connections between them, which underpin many of the applications in computing.
In fact there are very many different connections, and we just outline the ideas
which are most important for us.

- Types are often modeled as objects in a category. For example the type of
  natural numbers might be modeled as a set $\mathbb{N} = \{\,0, 1, 2, 3, \dots\,\}$. However, if
  one is interested in programs which output natural numbers, but may not
  terminate, the type might be modeled by an ordered set $\mathbb{N} \cup \{\perp\}$ in which
  $\perp$ is a least element meaning non-termination. Types arise in most of the
  chapters in this volume.
- Program expressions are often modeled as morphisms in a category. At its
  simplest, consider a program expression P of type τ in which a variable x
  of type σ occurs. Then $P.x : \sigma$, the expression together with a type environment, is modeled by a morphism $[P] : [\sigma] \to [\tau]$.
- Functors map objects to objects, and can be considered as models of type
  constructors. For example, given types σ and τ, a programming language
  may allow the product type $\sigma \times \tau$. In fact the mapping of (σ, τ) to $\sigma \times \tau$
  is part of the definition of a functor (where the types make up objects in
  a category). Similarly, in the category of sets and functions, given sets A
  and B, the Cartesian product $A \times B$ is a set. Mapping the pair (A, B) into
  $A \times B$ is part of the definition of a functor. These ideas are exploited in
  Chapter 5.

2.4 Algebras and Coalgebras

We often find type definitions in programming languages similar to the following
example

$$\mathsf{nats} = \mathsf{Zero} \mid \mathsf{Suc\ nats}$$

Here, the programming notation means that Zero is an expression of type nats,
and that $\mathsf{Suc} : \mathsf{nats} \to \mathsf{nats}$ is an injective function from nats to itself, with
$\mathsf{Suc}\ N$ not the same as Zero for any expression N of type nats.

Let's think about a model of this. We should have a set, $\mathbb{N}$, and two functions,
say $z : 1 \to \mathbb{N}$ and $s : \mathbb{N} \to \mathbb{N}$. We can then impose certain conditions on these
functions which ensure that the set $\mathbb{N}$ is indeed the natural numbers. (The details
need not concern us here, but the conditions which mathematicians often use are

the *Peano axioms*—see for example [5].) Computer Scientists often refer to such conditions (axioms) as a *specification*. The example we have here is an *algebraic specification*, and the set $\mathbb{N}$ together with z and s is an example of an *algebra*. Let's have another example. Here is an algebraic specification of a *group*. We are given

- a set G;
- a function $e : 1 \to G$ called the *identity*;
- a function $\iota : G \to G$ called *inverse* ;
- a function $m : G \times G \to G$ called *multiplication*;
- some equational axioms such as $\forall g \in G.m(g, \iota(g)) = e$ and

$$\forall g, h, k \in G.m(g, m(h, k)) = m(m(g, h), k)$$

The natural numbers are frequently used by programmers, and although groups are not, it is often possible to use "algebraic specifications" to give descriptions of types which are used by programmers. So, we might say that we can "construct" programmers' types using algebraic methods. This is one of the subjects of Chapter 7, where you will find further details of the example of groups, together with other examples which are more pertinent to computing science.

Each such algebraic specification is an example of a *(categorical) algebra*. There is a subclass of such algebras which is especially important. These are known as *initial* algebras, and we illustrate their properties by example. In fact we have already seen some initial algebras. Recall that any ordered set can be regarded as a category: the objects are the elements, and the morphisms are instances of the order relation. Suppose that $\Phi : X \to X$ is a monotone function. It is not difficult to see that Φ is an example of a functor from the category X to itself. Moreover, the least prefixed point has a special property, namely, given any other prefixed point $\Phi(x) \leq x$, there is a (necessarily unique) morphism from $\mu\Phi$ to x, namely $\mu\Phi \leq x$. We can picture this as a diagram

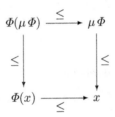

Note that the definition of $\mu\Phi$ implies that the morphism exists. Further, $\leq$ is transitive, and so $\Phi(\mu\Phi) \leq x$. Thus the "paths" around the diagram are "identical" and we say the diagram *commutes*.

In fact $\Phi(\mu\Phi) \leq \mu\Phi$ is an example of an *algebra*, and the existence of a single morphism $\mu\Phi \leq x$ with the commuting property makes the algebra *initial*. We do not give the (general) definitions of algebras and initial algebras here—we rely on the reader to look at the remaining examples, and then consult the articles in this volume for the definitions.

Algebras are usually defined in terms of categories and functors. They are useful because many *datatypes* of interest in computing have models which arise as *initial algebras*. An example is the set of natural numbers. Let $1 = \{*\}$ be a singleton set, and $+$ denote disjoint union of sets. Then using the Peano axioms, we can define a function $zs : 1 + \mathbb{N} \to \mathbb{N}$ which maps $*$ to 0 and n to $n + 1$, and which satisfies various properties which ensure that $\mathbb{N}$ is indeed the set of natural numbers. The Peano definition of $\mathbb{N}$ is equivalent to the following.

Suppose that $f : 1 + A \to A$ is any function. Then there is a unique function $\mathsf{fold}(f) : \mathbb{N} \to A$ for which the following diagram commutes

$$
\begin{array}{ccc}
1 + \mathbb{N} & \xrightarrow{\ zs\ } & \mathbb{N} \\
{\scriptstyle 1\,+\,\mathsf{fold}(f)}\Big\downarrow & & \Big\downarrow{\scriptstyle \mathsf{fold}(f)} \\
1 + A & \xrightarrow{\ f\ } & A
\end{array}
$$

where $1 + \mathsf{fold}(f)$ maps $*$ to itself, and n to $\mathsf{fold}(f)(n)$, which means that

$$\mathsf{fold}(f) \circ zs = f \circ (1 + \mathsf{fold}(f))$$

The reader should compare this diagram with the previous one, writing $\Phi(\xi)$ for $1 + \xi$, $\mu\Phi$ for $\mathbb{N}$, and x for A. The proof of the equivalence of these definitions is not immediate; see [5].

The information in the second definition is another example of a categorical initial algebra—we illustrate why it is relevant and applicable. In computer programming, we often have calculations which we want to repeat over and over again. Initial algebras provide a framework which captures this kind of process. Let's look at a very simple example. Suppose that we want to multiply a number n by -2. We can do this by adding up the number -2, n times. (In an elementary computer processor, circuits might be provided for addition, with multiplication implemented by the repeated use of these circuits.) Consider the following commutative diagram (as above with $A = \mathbb{Z}$)

$$
\begin{array}{ccc}
1 + \mathbb{N} & \xrightarrow{\ zs\ } & \mathbb{N} \\
{\scriptstyle 1\,+\,\mathsf{fold}(f)}\Big\downarrow & & \Big\downarrow{\scriptstyle \mathsf{fold}(f)} \\
1 + \mathbb{Z} & \xrightarrow{\ f\ } & \mathbb{Z}
\end{array}
$$

in which the function f maps $*$ to 0 and for any $n \in \mathbb{N}$ maps n to $n - 2$. Then it is an exercise for the reader to check that *if* $\mathsf{fold}(f)$ exists then we *must* have

- $\mathsf{fold}(f)(0) = 0$
- $\mathsf{fold}(f)(n + 1) = \mathsf{fold}(f)(n) - 2$

But this is a well defined definition of $\mathsf{fold}(f)$. Hence $\mathsf{fold}(f)$ exists and is unique. The reader should check that indeed $\mathsf{fold}(f)(n) = (-2)n$. Thus the function f models the calculation to be repeated (which we provide) and then the mediating function $\mathsf{fold}(f)$ models repeated calculations. We usually say that the function $\mathsf{fold}(f)$ is defined by *recursion*. In this example, the recursion can be seen as "traditional" recursion on the natural numbers. However, the algebraic framework gives a uniform setting in which many other forms of recursion can all be seen in the same light. General results about algebras can then be applied to all examples of recursion.

There is a notion of coalgebraic specification, analogous to that of algebraic specification. The details can be found in Chapter 7. There is also a notion of *categorical final coalgebra*, which we illustrate by example. Let $\mathbb{N}^\infty$ be the set $\mathbb{N} \cup \{\infty\}$ and $1 = \{\mathsf{HALT}\}$. Define a function $\sigma : \mathbb{N}^\infty \to 1 + \mathbb{N}^\infty$ by $\sigma(0) = \mathsf{HALT}$, $\sigma(p) = p - 1$ where $p \geq 1$, and $\sigma(\infty) = \infty$. Then $\sigma : \mathbb{N}^\infty \to 1 + \mathbb{N}^\infty$ is a final coalgebra because it has the following property.

Given any function of the form $f : A \to 1 + A$, there is a unique function $\mathsf{unfold}(f) : A \to \mathbb{N}^\infty$ for which the following diagram commutes

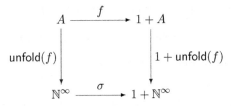

The reader should consider again the example of least fixed points as initial algebras, and try to formulate a similar picture for greatest post fixed points. You should aim to have a picture just like the diagram above, and to deduce that greatest post fixed points are examples of final coalgebras.

Computer Scientists often wish to study complex computer systems which have a *state*. The state is a description of the system at a particular time. For example, the state of a stand-alone computer might be defined to be the contents of its inboard memory. It turns out that coalgebras are useful models of "systems" which have a state that changes over time. Either the state will alter a finite number of times and the system halts, or the system loops forever. We can think of the (final) coalgebra as capturing the essence of this idea. The natural numbers represent finite time. The state can evolve forever, captured by the element ∞. The function σ "counts" changes of state. If the system is in a given state s, and evolves a finite number of times n before ending in a "halt" state, this is captured by repeated applications of σ which reduce n to HALT, with HALT representing the halt state.

Let us give an example. Consider the following imperative program

$$\mathsf{while}\ n \neq 1\ \mathsf{do}\ (n := n - 1\ ;\ x := n * x)$$

Our "system" is a computer which can run the program above. The system state at any given time is the pair (n, x) or HALT. If p is any positive integer, given a starting state of (p, p) then the system will halt, with the final state being $(1, !p)$ where $!p$ is the factorial of p. Given a starting state (p, x) with x any integer, then the system will halt. Given a starting state (r, x) where r is a non-positive integer, then the system will never halt.

We can model this example as a coalgebra. We take the set A to be $\mathbb{Z} \times \mathbb{Z}$. The function f captures the effect of the program above, and is defined by

$$f(n, x) = \begin{cases} (n - 1, x * (n - 1)) & \text{if } n \geq 2 \\ \mathsf{HALT} & \text{if } n = 1 \\ (n - 1, x * (n - 1)) & \text{if } n \leq 0 \end{cases}$$

Notice that for $n \geq 1$ there exists a $k \geq 1$ for which[3] $f^k(n, x) = \mathsf{HALT}$. For $n \leq 0$, no such k exists; the system will continue to evolve forever. What does the function $\mathsf{unfold}(f)$ do? We leave it as an exercise to check that the only possible definition of $\mathsf{unfold}(f)$ is

- $\mathsf{unfold}(f)(n, x) = n - 1$ for $n \geq 1$; and
- $\mathsf{unfold}(f)(n, x) = \infty$ for $n \leq 0$

and thus $\mathsf{unfold}(f)$ exists and is unique. We say that $\mathsf{unfold}(f)$ is defined by *corecursion*. Informally $\mathsf{unfold}(f)(n, x)$ is the number of state changes which take place before the HALT state is reached. If n is zero or below, there is an infinite number of state changes, that is, the program loops and HALT is never reached.

The key points are

- Programmers' types can be specified algebraically and coalgebraically.
- Such specifications can be modeled as categorical algebras and coalgebras.
- Algebras yield finite data; coalgebras yield possibly infinite data.
- (Co)algebras have a universal property yielding morphisms which model (co)recursive programs.
- (Co)algebras are defined as fixed points of functors; fixed points of monotone functions are simple examples.

3 Mathematics in ACMMPC

In this section we give a sketch of the contents of each chapter, and in particular we indicate where the underpinning mathematics described in the introduction will be used. The first two chapters describe fundamental mathematical theory. The remaining chapters cover applications.

---

[3] The notation f^k means repeated application of f. Of course $f : A \to 1 + A$, but whenever an image of f lies in A, say $f(a)$, we can apply f again to get $f^2(a) = f(f(a))$ and so on.

3.1   Chapter 2: Ordered Sets and Complete Lattices

This chapter provides a substantial part of the (pure) mathematical theory required to under-pin the topics which appear in the remaining chapters.

The chapter begins with some informal explanation of why ordered sets arise in Computing, from which various formal definitions of order relations are given. We see ways in which we can build new ordered sets from old, just as we can build up datatypes in programming languages from basic types.

Lattices are ordered sets with special properties that ensure the existence of fixed points. They first arose in Computer Science as examples of denotational models (see Section 2.2). Lattices are defined in detail, and a number of examples given. The first historical examples of lattices were based on powersets, and in fact we can *represent* any lattice as a collection of sets (the elements of the lattice are sets) with the subset order. It is often easier to reason about a lattice when it is presented in such a concrete way, and many examples of program models are based on similar representations [19].

Galois connections are defined, together with some basic theory. The key components of a Galois connection consist of two ordered sets, and two composable functions between the sets. Then given elements x and y, one from each set, one is able to check if one element x is below the other element y's image, by checking instead if x's image is below y. Galois connections constitute an important topic, and although the basic definition is very simple to state, a wealth of examples follow, many of which arise in connection with computing. There are a number of simple results about Galois connections, and many of them can be used to provide a "calculus" with which to reason about programming problems characterized by Galois connections.

We have already tried to show that fixed points are common in computing. The final parts of the chapter discuss fixed points in detail. If we are interested in solving fixed point equations, we need to know that solutions exist. In fact monotone functions over complete lattices always have fixed points. The functions described in Section 2 which arise naturally from computing examples are often monotone, and thus (for example) the corresponding inductive and coinductive sets exist. As well as lattices, there are other varieties of ordered sets and functions which always have fixed points; some motivation for the development of these ideas can be found in [11,13,14]. Least and greatest fixed points are discussed in detail, and have special roles in the mathematics of program construction—applications pervade the remaining chapters.

3.2   Chapter 3: Introducing Algebras and Coalgebras

Algebras *and* Coalgebras *are defined, and their basic properties are explained at length by example.*

This chapter concentrates on just two key examples, one algebra, and one coalgebra. These examples are based on the category of sets and functions. The algebra example leads to a precise definition of *finite trees* which are structures that are commonly used in the definitions of programming languages; and the coalgebra example leads to a precise definition of *infinite trees* which are structures that are becoming useful in the definitions of programming languages. These examples are used to give illustrations of fold(f) and unfold(f) functions, which are used extensively in Chapters 5 and 8.

3.3   Chapter 4: Galois Connections and Fixed Point Calculus

A calculus of fixed points is described, which provides methods with which one can reason about fixed points. The theory of Galois connections is re-visited and summarised, and relationships between Galois connections and fixed points are developed. Applications to program construction are given.

This chapter begins with Galois connections. In particular, a wide variety of examples is given, some of which show that simple definitions in arithmetic (such as the largest integer smaller than a given real) can be seen as Galois connections. Techniques for understanding when Galois connections arise are given; for example there are simple conditions which ensure that any function is (part of) a Galois connection.

As fixed points are so pervasive, it seems desirable to look for axioms and properties which they satisfy, so that we can use these to reason about them. To this end the *fixed point calculus* is introduced. This consists of a collection of axioms and derived rules for reasoning about the calculation, and properties, of fixed points.

Relationships between fixed points and Galois connections are drawn up, which help to clarify the ideas of the theory, and the ideas are applied to the formal construction of simple programming syntax. In fact the theory leads to a neat proof that two apparently different languages are in fact the same.

3.4   Chapter 5: Calculating Functional Programs

Algebras and coalgebras are used to give models of datatypes, and properties of algebras and coalgebras are used to calculate algorithms over such datatypes. This chapter makes heavy use of the material from Chapter 3.

This chapter concentrates on *functional programming*. In this programming style, there are no assignments, and hence no side-effects. Any program corresponds to a mathematical function, for which given any input there is a corresponding output (assuming termination), and the machine state is not (directly) known to or accessible by the programmer.

Categories and functors are introduced from the perspective of functional programming. In particular, we see that types and functions are modelled by objects and morphisms in a category, and that functors provide models of the type constructors found in functional programming. The equational properties of categories are used to derive useful algebraic equations which can be used for calculating, and thus often simplifying, functional programs.

Recursive datatypes pervade functional programming. We learn that as functors can be used to model datatype constructors, we can therefore model recursive datatypes as solutions up to isomorphism of fixed points of functors. In fact one can define a notion of least and greatest fixed point, and these yield initial and final coalgebras. Various examples of (models of) datatypes are given, all expressed as (co)algebras.

Equations useful for calculations are derived by using the special properties of fold(f) and unfold(f) functions. The equations for fold(f) can be applied to datatypes which are initial algebras, and the equations for unfold(f) to datatypes which are final coalgebras. However, there can be close connections between algebras and coalgebras. More precisely, if $s : FU \to U$ is an initial algebra, then sometimes $s^{-1} : U \to FU$ is a final coalgebra. This observation can be used to show that some fundamental algorithms over datatypes modelled by such U can be expressed using a combination of fold(f) and unfold(f) functions. In fact a number of apparently diverse sorting algorithms fit into this framework; compare the material to the final section of Chapter 6.

This chapter concludes with three applications to practical computing problems, including the definition of a simple compiler, and tree traversal search algorithms.

3.5   Chapter 6: Algebra of Program Termination

A theory of induction and well-founded relations is developed. Applications include the calculation of loops from invariants. Algebraic and coalgebraic methods are used to unify functional algorithms. The material builds heavily on Chapter 2 and Chapter 4, and extends some of the fixed point theory.

The calculus is applied to imperative programming. For example, one may wish to be clear that a process that is repeated over and over again in a program will eventually stop, and the mathematical tools built up in this chapter can be used to prove facts about program termination. Closely related is the notion of an invariant. It is well-known in imperative programming that a rigorous method for implementing a program specification is to construct an *invariant*, which is a property which remains unchanged through each cycle of a loop. We see that the techniques introduced can be used to help calculate the code for the loop. Many of the ad-hoc methodologies used by programmers wishing to construct loops all fit within the frameworks developed here.

The chapter develops further the theory of inductively defined sets, and shows the connections with well founded relations. The vertical order $<$ on the natural numbers $\mathbb{N}$ is well founded; its connection to induction is explained, and the ideas generalized.

The final section concentrates on functional programming. We see that commonly occurring functional programs can be defined as functions of the form fold(f) and unfold(f). This is useful, as not only can we apply general categorical results to reasoning about such programs, but a number of apparently diverse algorithms can be formulated in a common framework. Examples of sorting algorithms are presented. The material in this final chapter has some overlap with the second half of Chapter 5, and readers are urged to compare and contrast the approaches.

3.6   Chapter 7: Exercises in Coalgebraic Specification

The theory of coalgebraic specifications is presented. The examples illustrate that coalgebras arise as the models of computer systems which have potentially infinite state spaces (recall the example of Section 2.4), and that coalgebras form models of datatypes with potentially infinite elements (such as lazy lists). This chapter builds on Chapters 3 and 5.

The chapter begins with mathematical preliminaries, and illustrates algebraic specifications for groups and vector spaces. The datatype of potentially infinite binary trees is the first example of a coalgebraic specification. The example contains a lot of detail, and illustrates vividly the definition and properties of coalgebras. The style in which specifications are presented will be familiar to object oriented programmers.

The next topic concerns bisimilarity (introduced informally in Section 2.2). A general definition is given which is rather more abstract than that of Section 2.2, and the definition is applied to infinite binary trees. Connections are drawn with algebra. For example, a relation is defined to be a *bisimulation* if the coalgebraic operations preserve the relation. This mirrors the idea of algebraic congruence. If one has an algebra, together with operations on the algebra, a relation is said to be a *congruence* if the operations preserve the relation. (A typical example from computing concerns the relation of equivalence of programs; one shows that the operations which build up program code form a congruence for a particular equivalence, and thus one may reason about program equivalences using "standard" algebraic equations.)

The examples of coalgebras which concern state suggest connections with notions of time. A temporal logic for coalgebras is developed, and this is used to capture properties of computing systems which can not (easily) be expressed in the standard language of coalgebras. This material culminates in a coalgebraic description of Petersen's Mutual Exclusion algorithm. This algorithm describes a method in which computers with shared memory may run concurrently, avoiding memory requests which lead to simultaneous access of the same memory area. Techniques built up in the chapter are applied to yield a proof of the correctness of Peterson's algorithm.

3.7   Chapter 8: Algebraic Methods for Optimization Problems

A calculus of relations is developed within which programs can be specified and the specification refined to a functional program.

The (pure) functional programming style is often regarded as more abstract than (pure) imperative programming styles. A key reason is that pure functional programming does not allow assignments, and places emphasis on recursion. The result is that implementation details are often hidden from the user, with only the mathematical details of the function visible to the programmer. However, a functional program is still quite concrete in that it expresses an algorithm for the solution to a (programming) problem. But problems are often described as specifications which may be written in a language based on, say, logic, and the programmers task is therefore to *construct* a program which will match (solve) the specification. In this chapter we study the task of constructing programs from specifications within a special framework, and in particular there is a case study of an algebraic optimisation problem.

A problem often involves properties such as non-determinism or conjunction. For example, an optimisation problem might have different solutions, each of which fits the criteria for being optimal. Or a problem might state that condition *A and* condition *B* must be satisfied by a solution. However, these kinds of operators are not necessarily found in a programming language. They are perhaps better expressed in programming logics or so-called "specification" languages.

It is common to have such a specification language, and a separate programming language. One might then take a specification, and construct a program from it. The central idea of this chapter is to reason about programs using a language of relations. A function is indeed a relation, and moreover relations satisfy "logical" rules such as conjunction and disjunction.

In this chapter, a language and theory of relations is developed which is particularly suitable for specifying programs. The specifications can then be refined, using either calculational techniques or formal theorems, to yield functional programs. The final section gives a detailed solution to the so-called "bracketing problem", namely, given a tuple of integers, and a binary arithmetic operation, how can the integers be bracketed to ensure the result is as small or as large as possible. (For example, given the tuple of integers $(2, 3, 5)$, and subtraction as the operation, $2 - (3 - 5) = 4$ but $(2 - 3) - 5 = -6$.)

3.8   Chapter 9: Temporal Algebra

Temporal logics are reformulated as algebraic systems, and the resulting algebra is used for the verification of software systems.

Temporal logics have been used in the specification and verification of software systems. Well-known examples are the linear and interval temporal logics, and also the duration calculus. A key aim of this chapter is to give algebraic presentations of these logics which are amenable to calculations, and hence which can be used for program construction. Galois connections are used extensively in this chapter in order to provide a very succinct account of the axiomatic basis of temporal logic. This idea is captured by the notion of a Galois algebra and used as the basis for temporal algebra and sequential algebra. Variants of the former correspond to linear temporal logic; variants of the latter correspond to interval temporal logic and the duration calculus. In this chapter, a detailed theory of such algebras is presented, along with a few applications. For example, the "gas burner" of the duration calculus is revisited, and presented in an algebraic form.

References

1. J. Backus. The Syntax and Semantics of the Proposed International Algebraic Language of the Zurich ACM-GAMM Conference. In *International Conference on Information Processing*, pages 125–132, June 1959. 4

2. M. Barr and C. Wells. *Category Theory for Computing Science*. International Series in Computer Science. Prentice Hall, 1990. 2

3. R. L. Crole. *Categories for Types*. Cambridge Mathematical Textbooks. Cambridge University Press, 1993. xvii+335 pages, ISBN 0521450926HB, 0521457017PB. 2

4. P. J. Freyd and A. Scedrov. *Categories, Allegories*. Elsevier Science Publishers, 1990. Appears as Volume 39 of the North-Holland Mathematical Library. 2

5. R. Goldblatt. *Topoi : the categorial analysis of logic*. Amsterdam ; Oxford : North-Holland, 1984. ISBN: 0444867112. 10, 11

6. David Gries and Fred B. Schneider. *A Logical Approach to Discrete Math*. Springer-Verlag, 1993. 2

7. S. Mac Lane. *Categories for the Working Mathematician*, volume 5 of *Graduate Texts in Mathematics*. Springer Verlag, 1971. 2

8. R. Milner. *A Calculus of Communicating Systems*, volume 92 of *Lecture Notes in Computer Science*. Springer-Verlag, 1980. 7

9. P. Naur. Revised Report on the Algorithmic Language Algol 60. *Communications of the ACM*, 6(1):1–17, 1963. 4

10. B. C. Pierce. *Basic Category Theory for Computer Scientists*. Foundations of Computing Series. The MIT Press, 1991. 2

11. D. S. Scott. The lattice of flow diagrams. Technical Report 3, Programming Research Group, Oxford University Computing Laboratory, 1970. 5, 14

12. D. S. Scott. Towards a mathematical theory of computation. In *4th Annual Princeton Conference on Information Sciences and Systems*, 1970. 5

13. D. S. Scott. Continuous lattices. Technical Report 7, Programming Research Group, Oxford University Computing Laboratory, 1971. 5, 14

14. D. S. Scott. Datatypes as lattices. *SIAM Journal of Computing*, 5(3):522–587, 1976. 5, 14

15. D. S. Scott. Domains for denotational semantics. In *ICALP 1982*, volume 140 of *Lecture Notes in Computer Science*, pages 577–613. Springer-Verlag, 1982. 5

16. M. L. Scott. *Programming Language Pragmatics*. Morgan Kaufmann, 2000. 2

17. R. Sethi. *Programming Languages: Concepts and Constructs*. Addison-Wesley, 1989. 2

18. D. S. Scott and C. Strachey. Towards a mathematical semantics for computer languages. Technical Report 6, Programming Research Group, Oxford University Computing Laboratory, 1971. 5

19. G. Winskel and K. G. Larsen. Using information systems to solve recursive domain equations effectively. Technical Report 51, University of Cambridge Computer Laboratory, 1983. 14

Chapter 2
Ordered Sets and Complete Lattices
A Primer for Computer Science

Hilary A. Priestley

Mathematical Institute, University of Oxford

Abstract. These notes deal with an interconnecting web of mathematical techniques all of which deserve a place in the armoury of the well-educated computer scientist. The objective is to present the ideas as a self-contained body of material, worthy of study in its own right, and at the same time to assist the learning of algebraic and coalgebraic methods, by giving prior familiarization with some of the mathematical background that arises there. Examples drawn from computer science are only hinted at: the presentation seeks to complement and not to preempt other contributions to these ACMMPC Proceedings.

1 Introduction

Order enters into computer science in a variety of ways and at a variety of levels. At the most lowly level it provides terminology and notation in contexts where comparisons arise, of such things as

- size (of numbers),
- amount of information (after a number of steps of a computation, for example),
- degree of defined-ness (of partial maps).

Many areas of computer science use as models structures built on top of ordered sets. In some cases, only token familiarity with order-theoretic ideas is needed to study these, as is the case with CSP, for example. At the other extreme, domain theory uses highly sophisticated ordered structures as semantic domains (see for example Abramsky & Jung [2]). Indeed, the development of the theory of CPOs since the 1970s has led to new insights into the theory of ordered sets; see Gierz *et al.* [9] and, for a more recent perspective, Abramsky & Jung [2].

At an intermediate level come three notions exploited in computer science and closely linked to order-theoretic ideas: Galois connections, binary relations, and fixed points. A recurring theme here is the theory of **complete lattices**, and this account focusses on the way in which complete lattices can be described and their properties explored. Specifically we investigate the concepts in the diagram in Figure 1 and the arrows that link them. (An arrow pointing from A to B indicates that every object of type A gives rise, in a natural way, to an object of type B.

R. Backhouse et al. (Eds.): Algebraic and Coalgebraic Methods ..., LNCS 2297, pp. 21–78, 2002.

We are not claiming that this is done in such a way that all triangles in the diagram commute.) Some of the links are principally of mathematical interest, but discussion of them has been included to complete the overall picture. For a summary of the results, see 7.10.

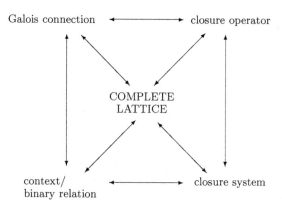

Fig. 1. A web of concepts

There is another, quite different, way in which order assists computer science. Category theory has established itself as a fundamental tool, and underpins much of the ACMMPC Workshop material. Ordered structures and the maps between them provide a wealth of examples of categories and functors. Equally importantly perhaps, every poset gives rise to a category in a natural way. Such categories are highly special (every set of arrows has at most one element) but very simple. As we hint in Section 9, elementary order-theoretic notions provide instances of more abstract categorical notions. For example, product, supremum, and infimum are instances of product, colimit, and colimit. Further, Galois connections between posets are instances of adjunctions between categories. Understanding categorical constructs in the special case of posets-as-categories can be helpful in cementing the general ideas.

As a final general comment on order in computer science we remark on the role of sets and powersets. Sets are a familiar concept and have accordingly been widely used, in such areas as the calculus of relations, for example. A powerset is ordered by its inclusion relation. As an ordered structure it possesses extremely nice properties, with infinitary disjunction and conjunction (union and intersection) available and interacting in a optimally well-behaved way. Powersets are too nice! Programs built on pure set models cannot capture all the behaviours that one might wish. Ordered set models are richer.

Probably some, but not all, of the ideas presented here will be familiar already to most readers. However, as befits concepts which have incarnations in a variety of disciplines, the concepts don different clothes in different settings.

These notes are written by a mathematician, and the style reflects a mathematician's approach. We have however followed, though not slavishly, the calculational proof style favoured by functional programmers. This formalism contrasts with and is complemented by the pictorial dimension to order theory which gives the latter much of its appeal.

No prior knowledge of lattices or ordering will be presupposed, but basic facts concerning sets, maps, and relations are assumed. Many subsections contain 'Mini-exercises'. These serve both to record elementary results needed later on and as an invitation to the reader to reinforce understanding of the immediately preceding material; most of the verifications are of the 'follow-your-nose' variety. More substantial exercises are interspersed through the text. A background reference is the text *Introduction to Lattices and Order*; chapter numbers given are those in the second (2002) edition. This will henceforth be referred to simply as ILO2. Chapters 1–4 and 7–10 contain the material of primary relevance to this survey.

2   From Binary Relations to Diagrams

2.1   A Fundamental Example: Powersets

Very many of the structures we consider are families of subsets of some given set X, that is, they are members of the **powerset** of X. This powerset carries a natural ordering, namely set inclusion, $\subseteq$. We denote the set of all subsets of X by $\wp(X)$, and always regard this as equipped with the inclusion order. Alternatively (though this may seem perverse at this stage), we might order the subsets of X by reverse inclusion, $\supseteq$. When we wish to use reverse inclusion we shall write $\wp(X)^{\partial}$. (See 3.4 for a more general occurrence of the same idea.)

A recurrent theme hereafter will be the way in which ordered sets can be depicted diagrammatically. Ahead of considering this in a formal way, we give some illustrative examples. Let us first consider $X = \{0, 1, 2\}$. We can give a representation of $\wp(X)$, as shown in Figure 2(a). In (b) we show an unlabelled diagram for $\wp(\{0, 1, 2, 3\})$.

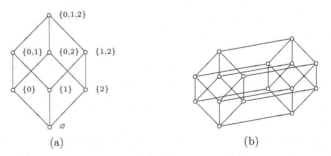

(a)   (b)

Fig. 2. Some powersets, pictorially

Mini-exercise

(i) Draw a labelled diagram of $\wp(\{0, 1, 2\})^{\partial}$.
(ii) Label the diagram in Figure 2(b), and indicate a connected sequence of upward line segments from $\{3\}$ to $\{1, 3, 4\}$.

Any collection of subsets of a set X—not necessarily the full powerset—is also ordered by inclusion. For an example, see the diagram in Figure 8(b).

Mini-exercise

(i) Draw a diagram for the family $\{\{3\}, \{1, 3\}, \{1, 3, 4\}\}$ in $\wp(\{1, 2, 3, 4\})$.
(ii) Draw a similar picture for the following family of sets in $\wp(\{A, B, C, D, E\})$:

$$\varnothing, \{E\}, \ \{A, E\}, \ \{D, E\}, \ \{C, D, E\}, \ \{A, D, E\},$$
$$\{A, B, E\}, \ \{A, C, D, E\}, \ \{B, C, D, E\}, \ \{A, B, C, D, E\}.$$

2.2   Input-Output Relations Pictorially

Consider a simple input-output relation with the inputs labelled by a, b, c, d, e and the outputs by A, B, C, D, E. The relation is indicated in the table in Figure 3. We may think of this as modelling a program which when started from a given input state p can terminate only in a output state Q for which $\times$ appears in position (p, Q) in the table. Note that the input state labelled e has no associated output states, and may be thought of as a way of capturing the possibility of non-termination.

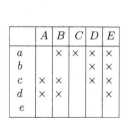
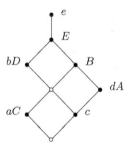

	A	B	C	D	E
a		×	×	×	×
b				×	×
c	×	×		×	×
d	×	×			×
e					

Fig. 3. An input-output relation and a diagram for it

To reach a prescribed output state we have the following sets of starting states:

$$A^{\triangleleft} = \{c, d\} \qquad C^{\triangleleft} = \{a\} \qquad E^{\triangleleft} = \{a, b, c, d\}$$
$$B^{\triangleleft} = \{a, c, d\} \qquad D^{\triangleleft} = \{a, b, c\}$$

We now take these five sets and all sets we can form from them by closing up under intersections. This adds to the original collection $\{c\}$, $\{b,c\}$, $\varnothing$, and the empty intersection (that is, the intersection of no sets); for example, $\{c\} = A^\lhd \cap D^\lhd$, indicating that c is the only input state from which it is possible to terminate in either A or D.

In a similar way we can write down the set of output states that can be reached from each input state:

$$a^\rhd = \{B,C,D,E\} \qquad c^\rhd = \{A,B,D,E\} \qquad e^\rhd = \{E\}$$
$$b^\rhd = \{D,E\} \qquad d^\rhd = \{A,B,E\}$$

Conjuring a rabbit out of a hat we exhibit the picture in Figure 3. Leaving aside for now how we derived the labelling, we can see rather easily how this encodes the information in the input-output table. To see which output states are attainable from a given input state, say p, simply locate the output states Q which lie above p, in the sense that there is a connected sequence of upward line segments from p to Q. For $p = a$, for example, this gives C and D as the possibilities for Q. Similarly, to find the input states from which it is possible to terminate in a given output state Q, look downwards along connected line segments to find the input states below Q.

Mini-exercise Carry out the procedure above for each of the input and output states, and so reconstruct the original input-output table from Figure 3.

Now consider the central unshaded point in Figure 3. Looking upward along line segments for points labelled with output states we find B, D, E and looking downward for points labelled with input states we see a, c. Observe that B, D and E are precisely the output states attainable from both the input states a and c, while a and c are exactly the possible initial states if the program is to be guaranteed to terminate in one of B, C, or D.

We make no claim that this diagrammatic way of viewing an input-output relation has any merits from a computer scientist's standpoint. Indeed quite the reverse might be said, since it goes counter to the philosophy of operating according to fixed calculational rules. However we shall with profit return to this very simple example later, and indicate that analysis of more complicated examples can yield information which is not otherwise easy to obtain.

2.3 Exercise

Analyse the input-output relation with table shown in Table 1. See if you can work out how to draw a labelled diagram encoding the input-output table, and interpret the diagram in the same way as in the example in 2.2.

Table 1. Input-output relation for Exercise 2.3

	A	B	C	D	E
a			×	×	
b	×		×	×	
c	×				
d	×	×	×		
e	×	×	×	×	

2.4 Binary Relations and Their Polars

Let G and M be sets, and let $R \subseteq G \times M$ be a binary relation. Changing the perspective from that we adopted in 2.2, we think of G as a set of **objects**, M as a set of **attributes** and the relationship $(g, m) \in R$ (sometimes written alternatively as gRm) as asserting that 'object g has attribute m'. We shall refer to the triple (G, M, R) as a **context**. The choice of letters G and M comes from the German (*Gegenstände* and *Merkmale*—the theory of concept lattices having been principally developed by R. Wille and his group at TH Darmstadt. From its beginnings 20 years ago this theory has evolved into a commercially applicable tool for data analysis through the TOSCANA software. The concept lattice associated with a context reveals inherent hierarchical structure and thence natural groupings and dependencies among the objects and the attributes. Introductory accounts of the theory, with illustrations, appear in ILO2 Chapter 3, and in Ganter & Wille [8].

Given the context (G, M, R) we define

$$A^{\triangleright} := \{\, m \in M : (\forall g \in A)\,(g, m) \in R \,\}, \quad \text{for } A \subseteq G,$$
$$B^{\triangleleft} := \{\, g \in G : (\forall m \in B)\,(g, m) \in R \,\} \quad \text{for } B \subseteq M,$$

called the **polars** of A, B, respectively. For singleton sets we drop the set brackets and write $g^{\triangleright}$ instead of $\{g\}^{\triangleright}$ and $m^{\triangleleft}$ instead of $\{m\}^{\triangleleft}$. The polar map $^{\triangleright}$ takes subsets of G to subsets of M—it takes a set A of objects to the set of attributes common to all the objects in A; likewise, $^{\triangleleft}$ maps subsets of M to subsets of G, taking a set of attributes B to the set of all objects which possess all of the attributes in B. Of course the bigger A is, the fewer attributes all its members will share and the bigger B is, the fewer objects will share all the attributes demanded by B. It is therefore natural to reverse the ordering on one side and to regard $^{\triangleright}$ as mapping from $\wp(G)$ to $\wp(M)^{\partial}$ and $^{\triangleleft}$ as mapping from $\wp(M)^{\partial}$ to $\wp(G)$. Flipping the order on $\wp(M)$ like this makes $^{\triangleright}$ and $^{\triangleleft}$ monotone (that is, order-*preserving*), rather than order-*reversing*). We also have

$$\begin{aligned}
A \subseteq B^{\triangleleft} &\iff (\forall g \in A)(\forall m \in B)(g, m) \in R && (\text{definition of } ^{\triangleleft}) \\
&\iff (\forall m \in B)(\forall g \in A)(g, m) \in R && (\text{predicate calculus}) \\
&\iff A^{\triangleright} \supseteq B && (\text{definition of } ^{\triangleright}).
\end{aligned}$$

Note the reversal, as expected, of the order. (Those already in the know will recognize that we have established that $(^{\triangleright}, {^{\triangleleft}})$ sets up a Galois connection between $\wp(G)$ and $\wp(M)^{\partial}$.)

The polars give rise to related notions. Write

$$g \dashv A \iff g \in A^{\triangleright\triangleleft} \quad (g \in G,\ A \subseteq G),$$
$$B \vdash m \iff m \in B^{\triangleleft\triangleright} \quad (m \in M,\ B \subseteq M);$$

$\dashv$ and $\vdash$ may be referred to as the **emulation** operator and the **semantic consequence** operator, respectively. For clarity we worked in 2.2 with the set of input states and the set of output states distinguished. Taking $G = M = S$ and $R \subseteq S \times S$ we may regard (S, S, R) as defining a (**non-deterministic**) **transition system** on S. Such systems provide a point of entry into the theory of coalgebras; see Rutten [16], and other papers by the same author.

Given $A \subseteq G$ and $B \subseteq M$ we call (A, B) a **concept** if

$$A = B^{\triangleleft} \quad \text{and} \quad A^{\triangleright} = B.$$

Concepts are ordered by inclusion on the first co-ordinate, reverse inclusion on the second (this is just the order inherited from the co-ordinatewise ordered product $\wp(G) \times \wp(M)^{\partial}$; see 3.7). The set of all concepts ordered in this way is denoted $\mathfrak{B}(G, M, R)$. What we have drawn in Figure 3 is a pictorial representation of $\mathfrak{B}(G, M, R)$ for the context given in 2.2.

2.5 Exercise

Let X be a set and let $R_{=}$ and $R_{\neq}$ denote $=$ and $\neq$ regarded as binary relations, that is, as subsets of $X \times X$.

(i) Consider the context $(X, X, R_{\neq})$. Identify the polars $A^{\triangleright}$ and $B^{\triangleleft}$ for $A, B \subseteq X$, and show that $\mathfrak{B}(X, X, R_{\neq}) = \{\, (A, X \backslash A) : A \subseteq X \,\}$.

(ii) Consider the context $(X, \wp(X), \in)$. Show that

$$\mathfrak{B}(X, \wp(X), \in) = \{\, (A, \{\, B \in \wp(X) : A \subseteq B \,\}) : A \subseteq X \,\}.$$

2.6 Summing Up So Far

Binary relations, and their associated contexts, are versatile creatures, with a wide spectrum of semantic interpretations. Any context has associated with it a pair of polar maps, forming what is known as a Galois connection. In a way we have yet fully to explore, these maps in turn give rise to an ordered set of objects we call concepts, and this encodes the original binary relation. But we are rushing ahead. Before we can make all this precise we need to know quite a lot about ordered sets.

3   Order, Order, Order, ...

We have mentioned order in an informal way in the preceding section, and have
made use of the inclusion and reverse inclusion orderings on a powerset. Now we
need to be more formal. What exactly do we mean by order? an order relation?
an ordered set?

3.1   Partial Order

Let us consider ordering in the context of some familiar datatypes:

(a) $<$ on the natural numbers, $\mathbb{N} = \{1, 2, 3, \ldots\}$, with $1 < 2 < 3 < \ldots$;
(b) $\subseteq$ ('is a subset of') on the powerset $\wp(X)$ of all subsets of a set X;
(c) the relation $\mathbf{F} < \mathbf{T}$ on the set of booleans $\{\mathbf{F}, \mathbf{T}\}$;
(d) the prefix order on binary strings—here $0110 < 011001100000$, for example;
(e) the relation 'is more defined than' on partial maps π from $\mathbb{N}$ to $\mathbb{N}$ (so the
    domain and range of π are subsets of $\mathbb{N}$); for example, for $\pi_k : \{1, \ldots, k\} \to \mathbb{N}$
    given by $\pi_k(n) = n + 1$ for $n = 1, \ldots, k$, we have π_k less defined than π_{k+1}
    for each k.

These examples confirm that order concerns comparison between pairs of objects: 1 is smaller than 2 in $\mathbb{N}$, etc. In mathematical terms, an ordering is a
binary relation on a set of objects.

Order relations are of two types: strict and non-strict. Outside mathematics,
the strict notion is more common. When comparing people's heights, the relation
'is taller than' is generally taken to mean 'is strictly taller than'. Mathematicians
usually allow equality and write, for instance, $3 \leqslant 3$ and $3 \leqslant 22/7$. We shall deal
mainly with non-strict order relations.

What distinguishes a strict order relation amongst binary relations? Firstly,
it is transitive. From the facts that $0 < 1$ and $1 < 10^{23}$ we can deduce that
$0 < 10^{23}$. Secondly, a strict order is antisymmetric: 5 is bigger than 3 but 3 is
not bigger than 5. Formally: a binary relation $<$ on a set P is a **strict partial
order** if it satisfies

(spo1) **antisymmetry**: for $x, y \in P$, if $x < y$ holds, then $y < x$ does not hold;
(spo2) **transitivity**: for $x, y, z \in P$, $x < y$ and $y < z$ implies $x < z$.

A (**non-strict**) **partial order**, $\leqslant$, on P is a binary relation satisfying

(po1) **reflexivity**: for $x \in P$, $x \leqslant x$;
(po2) **antisymmetry**: for $x, y \in P$, $x \leqslant y$ and $y \leqslant x$ imply $x = y$;
(po3) **transitivity**: for $x, y, z \in P$, $x \leqslant y$ and $y \leqslant z$ implies $x \leqslant z$.

Relaxing the conditions by dropping antisymmetry leads to what is known as a
pre-order or **quasi-order**.

Formally, a binary relation R on the set P is a subset of $P \times P$. With this
interpretation the equality relation, $=$, is $R_= := \{(x, x) : x \in P\}$. Given a partial
order $\leqslant$ on P, the associated subset of $P \times P$ is $R_\leqslant := \{(x, y) : x, y \in P, x \leqslant y\}$,

and likewise for $<$. Then $R_\leqslant = R_< \cup R_=$, the union being disjoint. This is a fancy way of expressing the way in which $<$ and $\leqslant$ are related.

A set P equipped with a partial order, strict or non-strict, is called in ILO2 an **ordered set**. Here we shall use the snappier term **poset**. Usually we shall be a little slovenly and say simply 'P is a poset'. When we wish to make the order explicit we write $\langle P; \leqslant \rangle$ and when working with more than one poset we shall sometimes write $\leqslant_P$ for the order on poset P.

Associated notation is predictable: $x \leqslant y$ and $y \geqslant x$ are used interchangeably, and $x \nleqslant y$ means '$x \leqslant y$ is false', and so on. Of course,

$$R_\geqslant = \{ (x,y) \in P \times P : (y,x) \in R_\leqslant \}$$

—the **converse** of $R_\leqslant$. Similarly, $R_\nleqslant = (P \times P) \setminus R_\leqslant$. Any subset Q of a poset P inherits P's ordering: $x \leqslant_Q y$ if and only if $x, y \in Q$ and $x \leqslant_P y$. Note that $R_{\leqslant_Q}$ is just $R_{\leqslant_P} \cap (Q \times Q)$. The usual orderings of $\mathbb{N}$, $\mathbb{Z}$ and $\mathbb{Q}$ of natural numbers, integers, and rationals are obtained in this way from the ordering of the real numbers $\mathbb{R}$.

In the ordering $<$ on $\mathbb{R}$, any two distinct real numbers can be compared. This comparability property is possessed by many familiar orderings, but it is *not* universal. It is important to realize that under a partial order (strict or non-strict) we may have mutually incomparable elements. As examples, note that the sets $\{2\}$ and $\{1,3\}$ in $\wp(\{0,1,2,3\})$ are not comparable and the strings 101 and 010 are incomparable in the prefix order. A poset in which any two elements are comparable is called a **chain**, and the associated order relation a **linear** or **total** order. Of particular importance is the 2-element chain $\mathbf{2} = \{0,1\}$ in which $0 < 1$: writing $\mathbf{F}$ (false) for 0 and $\mathbf{T}$ (true) for 1, we have the booleans, ordered by putting $\mathbf{F} < \mathbf{T}$. At the opposite extreme from a chain we have an **antichain**, in which $\leqslant$ coincides with $=$.

3.2   Information Orderings

We have already referred to binary strings and their prefix order. Strings may be thought of as information encoded in binary form: the longer the string the greater the information content. Let Σ^* be the set of all finite binary strings, that is, all finite sequences of 0s and 1s; the empty string is included. Adding the infinite sequences, we get the set of all finite or infinite sequences, which we denote by Σ^{**}. We order Σ^{**} by putting $u \leqslant v$ if and only if u is a prefix (that is, finite initial substring) of v. Given any string v, we may think of elements u with $u < v$ as providing approximations to v. In particular, any infinite string is, in a sense we later make more precise, the limit of its finite initial substrings.

The statement that some computed quantity r equals 1.35 correct to 2 decimal places may be re-expressed as the assertion that r lies in a particular closed interval in $\mathbb{R}$. We may accordingly treat the collection of all intervals $[\underline{x}, \overline{x}]$ (where $-\infty \leqslant \underline{x} \leqslant \overline{x} \leqslant \infty$) as defining a set P of approximations to the real numbers, with the intervals for which $\underline{x} = \overline{x}$ corresponding to exact values. The set P carries a very natural order: for $x = [\underline{x}, \overline{x}]$ and $y = [\underline{y}, \overline{y}]$ define $x \leqslant y$ if and only if $\underline{x} \leqslant \underline{y}$ and $\overline{y} \leqslant \overline{x}$. Then $x \leqslant y$ means that y represents (or contains) at least as much information as x. These very simple ideas underlie the recent development of a method for doing exact computations with real numbers (see A. Edelat, [7] for an introductory survey).

Now consider partial maps. Let A, B be (non-empty) sets and denote by $A \multimap\!\!\!\to B$ the partial maps from A to B. Thus each element of $A \multimap\!\!\!\to B$ is a map π with domain $\operatorname{dom} \pi \subseteq A$ and range $\operatorname{ran} \pi \subseteq B$: π may be regarded as a recipe which assigns an output $\pi(x)$ in $\operatorname{ran} \pi$ to each input x in $\operatorname{dom} \pi$. Alternatively, and equivalently, π is determined by its graph,

$$\operatorname{graph} \pi := \{ (x, \pi(x)) \, : \, x \in \operatorname{dom} \pi \},$$

a subset of $A \times B$. If $\pi \in A \multimap\!\!\!\to B$ is such that $\operatorname{dom} \pi = A$, then π is a map on X (or, for emphasis, a **total map**). Therefore $A \multimap\!\!\!\to B$ consists of all total maps from A to B and all partial determinations of them. This set is ordered in the following way: given partial maps π, σ, define $\pi \leqslant \sigma$ if and only if $\operatorname{dom} \pi \subseteq \operatorname{dom} \sigma$ and $\pi(x) = \sigma(x)$ for all $x \in \operatorname{dom} \pi$. Equivalently, $\pi \leqslant \sigma$ if and only if $\operatorname{graph} \pi \subseteq \operatorname{graph} \sigma$ in $\wp(A \times B)$. Note that a subset G of $A \times B$ is the graph of a partial map if and only if

$$(\forall s \in A) \, ((s, x) \in G \, \& \, (s, x') \in G) \implies x = x'.$$

The examples above illustrate ways in which posets can model situations in which the relation $x \leqslant y$ has interpretations such as 'y is more defined than x' or 'y is a better approximation than x'. In each case, we have a notion of a **total object** (a completely defined, or idealized, element). These total objects are the infinite binary strings in the first example, the 1-point intervals in the second, and the total maps in the third. The most interesting examples from a computational point of view are those in which the total objects may be realized as limits (in an order-theoretic manner) of objects which are in some sense finite. A finite object should be one which encodes a finite amount of information: for example, finite strings, or partial maps with finite domains. These issues are taken up briefly in Section 8.

3.3   Diagrams

As we have already suggested, an attractive feature of posets is that, in the finite case at least, they can be 'drawn'. The diagram of a finite poset P is drawn in such a way that $x < y$ in P if and only if there is a sequence of connected line segments moving upwards from x to y. For our purposes, common sense will suffice to indicate what constitutes a legitimate diagram; the formal rules governing diagram-drawing are set out in ILO2, 1.15. As an example: Figure 4 gives a diagram for the subset of Σ^* consisting of strings of length $\leqslant 3$.

The same poset may have many different diagrams. Two valid alternative diagrams for the cube are shown in Figure 5. The first comes from a computer science text (do some computer scientists have twisted minds?). The second,

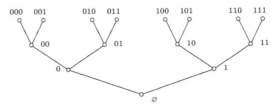

Fig. 4. Binary strings of length $\leqslant 3$ under the prefix order

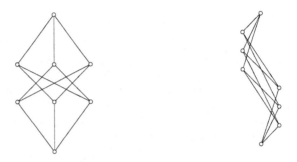

Fig. 5. Two 'bad' diagrams for a cube

while not having the maximal possible number of line-crossings **Mini-exercise**: prove that this number is 19) still serves to make the point that diagram-drawing is as much an art as a science. Good diagrams aid understanding.

3.4   Duality: Buy One, Get One Free

Given any poset P we can form a new poset P^{∂} (the **dual** of P) by defining $x \leqslant y$ to hold in P^{∂} if and only if $y \leqslant x$ holds in P. For P finite, we obtain a diagram for P^{∂} simply by 'turning upside down' a diagram for P. Figure 6 provides a simple illustration.

Poset concepts and results hunt in pairs. Any statement about a poset P yields a corresponding (dual) statement about P^{∂}, obtained by interchanging $\leqslant$ and $\geqslant$ and making consequential changes to all other symbols (replacing $\not\geqslant$ by $\not\leqslant$, and so on). This **Duality Principle** permits us to prove just one of any pair of mutually dual claims.

3.5   Bottom and Top

Let P be a poset. We say P has a bottom element if there exists $\bot \in P$ (called **bottom**) with the property that $\bot \leqslant x$ for all $x \in P$. Dually, P has a top element if there exists $\top \in P$ such that $x \leqslant \top$ for all $x \in P$. As a simple instance of the

P P^{∂}

Fig. 6. A pair of mutually dual posets

Duality Principle note that the true statement '$\perp$ is unique when it exists' has as its dual version the statement '$\top$ is unique when it exists'.

In $\langle \wp(X); \subseteq \rangle$, we have $\perp = \varnothing$ and $\top = X$. A finite chain always has bottom and top elements, but an infinite chain need not have. For example, the chain $\mathbb{N}$ has bottom element 1, but no top, while the chain $\mathbb{Z}$ of integers possesses neither bottom nor top. Bottom and top do not exist in any antichain with more than one element.

In the context of information orderings, $\perp$ and $\top$ have the following interpretations: $\perp$ represents 'no information', while $\top$ corresponds to an over-determined, or contradictory, element. None of the posets in 3.2 has a top element, except for $A \multimap B$ in very special cases. Each has a bottom element: $[-\infty, \infty]$ for interval approximations to real numbers, the empty string for Σ^{**} and the partial map with empty domain for $A \multimap B$. In each case $\perp$ is the least informative element. In modelling computations, a bottom element is also useful for representing and handling non-termination. Accordingly, computer scientists commonly choose as models posets which have bottom elements, but prefer these topless.

3.6   Lifting

It is tiresome that what may be thought of as the simplest posets of all, namely the antichains, fail to have bottoms (except in the 1-element case). Lack of a bottom element can be easily remedied by adding one. Given any poset P (with or without $\perp$), we form $P_{\perp}$ (called P 'lifted') as follows. Take an element $\perp \notin P$ and define $\leqslant$ on $P_{\perp} := P \cup \{\perp\}$ by

$$x \leqslant y \text{ if and only if } x = \perp \text{ or } x \leqslant y \text{ in } P.$$

For example, take the natural numbers $\mathbb{N}$ with the antichain order, $=$. Then $\mathbb{N}_{\perp}$ is as shown in Figure 7. $P_{\perp}$ is just $\{\perp\} \oplus P$. A poset of the form $S_{\perp}$, where S is an antichain, is called **flat**.

3.7   New Posets from Old: Sums and Products

Antichains and chains, and the lifting construction, are examples of constructing new posets from existing ones by forming suitable order-theoretic sums. Given

Fig. 7. Lifting

two disjoint posets P and Q we form their **linear sum** $P \oplus Q$ by stacking Q on top of P. Formally, we take $P \cup Q$ and order it by $x \leqslant y$ if and only if one of the following holds:

    (i) $x, y \in P$ and $x \leqslant_P y$,
    (ii) $x, y \in Q$ and $x \leqslant_Q y$,
    (iii) $x \in P$ and $y \in Q$.

    Given two disjoint posets P and Q we order their union $P \cup Q$ by setting $x \leqslant_{P \cup Q} y$ if and only if either (i) $x, y \in P$ and $x \leqslant_P y$ or (ii) $x, y \in Q$ and $x \leqslant_Q y$. The resulting poset is denoted $P \dot\cup Q$. Note that in the formation of linear sums and disjoint sums it is essential that the posets P and Q be disjoint.

    Given two posets P and Q, we can form their product $P \times Q$ by giving the set $P \times Q$ of all ordered pairs $\{ (p, q) : p \in P, q \in Q \}$ the co-ordinatewise order

$$(p_1, p_2) \leqslant_{P \times Q} (q_1, q_2) \iff p_1 \leqslant_P p_2 \text{ and } q_1 \leqslant_Q q_2.$$

See ILO2, 1.12, for comments on diagrams of products posets. A related **Mini-exercise**: what can you deduce from the diagram of $\wp(\{0, 1, 2, 3\})$ shown in Figure 2(b)?

    Mini-exercise Let X be a set with n elements. Prove that $\wp(X) \cong \mathbf{2}^n$ (here $\wp(X)$ has the usual inclusion order, and $\mathbf{2}^n$ denotes the n-fold product of $\mathbf{2}$ with itself. (If stuck, consult ILO2, 1.26.)

3.8   Maps between Posets

It should come as no surprise at all that along with posets we also consider suitable structure-preserving maps between posets. Let P and Q be posets. A map $F: P \to Q$ is said to be

    (i) **monotone** (or, alternatively, **order-preserving**) if $x \leqslant y$ in P implies $F(x) \leqslant F(y)$ in Q;
    (ii) an **order-embedding** if $x \leqslant y$ in $P \iff F(x) \leqslant F(y)$ in Q;
    (iii) an **order-isomorphism** if it is an order-embedding mapping P onto Q.

When there exists an order-isomorphism from P to Q, we say that P and Q are **order-isomorphic** and write $P \cong Q$. Order-isomorphic posets are essentially indistinguishable; in the finite case this happens if and only if they can be represented by the same diagram (see ILO2, 1.18). Frequently used properties of maps are contained in the next Mini-exercise.

Mini-exercise

(i) Any order-embedding is clearly monotone. Show that it is also one-to-one (you will need (po2), antisymmetry of $\leqslant$, in P). Show that not every one-to-one monotone map is an order-embedding (get an example using 2-element posets).

(ii) Let $F\colon P \to Q$ and $G\colon Q \to R$ be maps between posets P, Q, R. Show that if F and G are monotone (order-embeddings, order-isomorphisms) then so is the composite $G \circ F\colon P \to R$.

(iii) A monotone map $F\colon P \to Q$ is an order-isomorphism if and only if it has a monotone inverse $G\colon Q \to P$ (meaning that $G \circ F = \mathrm{id}_P$ and $F \circ G = \mathrm{id}_Q$). (Here $\mathrm{id}_S\colon S \to S$ denotes the **identity map** on S given by $\mathrm{id}_S(x) = x$ for all $x \in S$.)

The familiar poset $\wp(X)$ of subsets of a set X with its inclusion order is connected by an order-isomorphism to another important poset associated with X, namely the poset $\mathbb{P}$ of **predicates** on X. A **predicate** is a statement taking value $\mathbf{T}$ (true) or value $\mathbf{F}$ (false), or, more formally, a function from X to $\{\mathbf{T}, \mathbf{F}\}$; here we don't distinguish between different ways of specifying the same function. For example, the map $p\colon \mathbb{R} \to \{\mathbf{T}, \mathbf{F}\}$ given by $p(x) = \mathbf{T}$ if $x \geqslant 0$ and $p(x) = \mathbf{F}$ if $x < 0$ is a predicate on $\mathbb{R}$, which can be alternatively be specified by $p(x) = \mathbf{T}$ if $|x-1| \leqslant |x+1|$ and $\mathbf{F}$ otherwise. We order $\mathbb{P}(X)$ by implication: for $p, q \in \mathbb{P}(X)$,

$$p \Rightarrow q \text{ if and only if } \{\, x \in X \ : \ p(x) = \mathbf{T} \,\} \subseteq \{\, x \in X \ : \ q(x) = \mathbf{T} \,\}.$$

Then $F\colon \mathbb{P}(X) \to \wp(X)$ given by $F(p) := \{\, x \in X \ : \ p(x) = \mathbf{T} \,\}$ sets up an order-isomorphism between $\langle \mathbb{P}(X); \Rightarrow \rangle$ and $\langle \wp(X); \subseteq \rangle$. In the special case that X has just one element, $\mathbb{P}(X)$ is (isomorphic to) the poset of booleans.

3.9   Pointwise Ordering of Maps

Now let Q be a poset and X any set. Then the ordering on Q can be lifted, pointwise, to a partial order $\sqsubseteq$ on the set Q^X of all maps from X to Q: for $F, G\colon X \to Q$,

$$F \sqsubseteq G \iff (\forall x \in X)\, F(x) \leqslant G(x).$$

(We shall always use $\sqsubseteq$ rather than $\leqslant$ when ordering functions pointwise.) Thinking of predicates on X as maps from X into $\{\mathbf{T}, \mathbf{F}\}$ the pointwise order is just the implication order $\Rightarrow$. When X is itself a poset, P say, the subset of Q^P consisting of the monotone maps from P to Q inherits the order $\sqsubseteq$; we denote this poset by $\langle P \to Q \rangle$.

Mini-exercise (Currying) Prove that, for all posets P, Q and R,

$$\langle P \to \langle Q \to R \rangle \rangle \cong \langle P \times Q \to R \rangle.$$

3.10   Up-Sets: An Inbred Example

Let P be a poset.

(i) Let $x \in P$. Then define $\uparrow x := \{y \in P : y \geqslant x\}$.
(ii) Let $Y \subseteq P$. Then Y is an **up-set** of P if $x \in P$, $x \geqslant y$, $y \in Y$ implies $x \in Y$.

Note that $\uparrow x$ is an up-set for each $x \in P$ (by (po3), the transitivity of $\leqslant$). Denote the family of up-sets of P by $\mathcal{U}(P)$, and order it by inclusion. Thus $\mathcal{U}(P)$ is itself a poset. We shall shortly see that it is much more than this. In particular, an elementary calculation shows that if $\{A_i\}_{i \in I}$ is any subset of $\mathcal{U}(P)$ then $\bigcup_{i \in I} A_i$ and $\bigcap_{i \in I} A_i$ belong to $\mathcal{U}(P)$. **Mini-exercise**: check this statement (follow your nose). As an example, we show in Figure 8 a diagram of a poset P and of $\mathcal{U}(P)$.

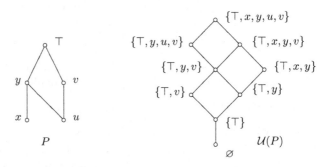

Fig. 8. A poset P and its poset $\mathcal{U}(P)$ of up-sets

Mini-exercise

(i) Prove that P is an antichain if and only if $\mathcal{U}(P) = \wp(P)$.
(ii) Analyse $\mathcal{U}(P)$ when P is (a) the chain $\mathbb{N}$, (b) the chain $\mathbb{R}$ (both with the usual order).

Mini-exercise Let P and Q be disjoint posets. Describe the up-sets of $P \dot\cup Q$ and prove that $\mathcal{U}(P \cup Q) \cong \mathcal{U}(P) \times U(Q)$.

3.11   Monotone Maps and Up-Sets

Let P be a poset and recall that $\mathbf{2} = \{0, 1\}$ is the 2-element chain ordered by $0 < 1$. Then there is an order-isomorphism between $\mathcal{U}(P)$ and $\langle P \to \mathbf{2}\rangle$ ordered as always by the pointwise order $\sqsubseteq$. Under this isomorphism an up-set U is associated to its characteristic function χ_U (which takes value 1 on U and 0 otherwise). **Mini-exercise**: Verify this assertion.

3.12   Exercise (More on Monotone Maps and Up-Sets)

Let P and Q be posets and $F\colon P \to Q$ a map.

(i) Prove that $F\colon P \to Q$ is monotone if and only if

$$F^{-1}(Y) := \{\, x \in P \,:\, F(x) \in Y \,\}$$

is an up-set in P whenever Y is an up-set in Q.

(ii) Assume $F\colon P \to Q$ is monotone. Then, by (i),
$F^{-1}\colon \mathcal{U}(Q) \to \mathcal{U}(P)$ is a well defined map.

(a) Prove that F is an order-embedding if and only if F^{-1} maps $\mathcal{U}(Q)$ onto $\mathcal{U}(P)$.

(b) Prove that F maps P onto Q if and only if $F^{-1}\colon \mathcal{U}(Q) \to \mathcal{U}(P)$ is one-to-one.

It is also instructive to re-formulate and re-work this exercise in a purely functional setting (see 3.11).

3.13   Down Is Nice Too

We can define down-sets of a poset P in just the same manner as we defined up-sets and form the poset down-sets, $\mathcal{O}(P)$, carrying the inclusion ordering. The symbol $\mathcal{O}$ is traditional here—$\mathcal{O}$ stands for 'order ideal', a synonym for 'down-set'.

Mini-exercise Formulate explicitly the analogues for down-sets of the definitions and Mini-exercise results in 3.10.

Mini-exercise Draw a labelled diagram of $\mathcal{O}(P)$ for the poset P in Figure 6.

Mini-exercise Let P be a poset. How do the down-sets of $P_\perp$ (as defined in 3.6) relate to those of P? Prove that $\mathcal{O}(P_\perp) \cong \mathcal{O}(P)_\perp$.

Mini-exercise Prove that the poset Σ^{**} of all binary strings is a **tree** (that is, a poset P with $\perp$ such that $\downarrow x$ is a chain for each $x \in P$).

3.14   Exercise (Turning Things Upside Down)

(i) For $Y \subseteq P$, prove that $Y \in \mathcal{O}(P)$ if and only if $P \setminus Y \in \mathcal{U}(P)$.

(ii) Prove that $\mathcal{O}(P) \cong \mathcal{U}(P)^{\partial}$.

(iii) Prove that $\mathcal{U}(P^{\partial}) \cong \mathcal{U}(P)^{\partial}$ and $\mathcal{O}(P^{\partial}) \cong O(P)^{\partial}$.

You might have doubts about how the orderings work out here. If so, refer to the example in Figure 8 and Mini-exercise 3.13.

3.15   The Down-Set Operator, $\downarrow$, and the Up-Set Operator, $\uparrow$

Let P be a poset and $x, y \in P$. Then we claim that the following are equivalent:

(a) $x \leqslant y$;
(b) $\downarrow x \subseteq \downarrow y$;
(c) $(\forall Y \in \mathcal{O}(P))\ y \in Y \implies x \in Y$.

This innocent little result says that the order $\leqslant$ on P is determined by the down-sets in P. The implication (a) $\implies$ (b) is needed in 5.6.

Mini-exercise Prove the claim. (a) $\implies$ (b) has already been noted; follow-your-nose for (b) $\implies$ (c). For (c) $\implies$ (a) take $Y := \downarrow y$. Note: you will need (po1) and (po3).

There is likewise an up-set operator, $\uparrow$, mapping each subset of P to the up-set it generates. Notice though that $x \leqslant y$ if and only if $\uparrow x \supseteq \uparrow y$ (check it!). This order reversal means that for many purposes down-sets and $\downarrow$ are more convenient to work with than up-sets and $\uparrow$. However up-sets relate better to monotone functions; see 3.11.

For any subset Y in a poset P there is a smallest down-set containing Y. This may be described in two equivalent ways:

(a) $\downarrow Y = \{\, z \in P\ :\ (\exists y \in Y)\, z \leqslant y \,\} = \bigcup\{\, \downarrow y\ :\ y \in Y \,\}$;
(b) $\downarrow Y = \bigcap\{\, Z\ :\ Z \in \mathcal{O}(P),\ Z \supseteq Y \,\}$.

Note that when $Y = \{x\}$, where $x \in P$, then $\downarrow\{x\}$, as defined in (a), is just $\downarrow x$ as defined in 3.10; we henceforth always write this down-set as $\downarrow x$. Observe that the operator $\downarrow\colon A \mapsto \downarrow A$ defines a map from $\wp(P) \to \wp(P)$ whose image is precisely $\mathcal{O}(P)$.

Mini-exercise Prove the equivalence of (a) and (b) above, by showing that each of the sets presented is contained in the other.

Exercise (Properties of the Operator $\downarrow$) Prove the following: for all $Y, Z \in \wp(P)$,

(i) $Y \subseteq \downarrow Y$;
(ii) $Y \subseteq Z \implies \downarrow Y \subseteq \downarrow Z$;
(iii) $\downarrow Y = \downarrow\downarrow Y$;
(iv) $Y = \downarrow Y$ if and only if $Y \in \mathcal{O}(P)$.

(Obviously, $\uparrow$ behaves analogously.)

3.16   Exercise (A Context Explored)

Let P be a poset and consider the context $(P, P, R_{\nleqslant})$. Let $^{\rhd}$ and $^{\lhd}$ be the associated polar maps.

(i) Show that $g^{\rhd} = P \setminus {\downarrow}g$ and $m^{\lhd} = P \setminus {\uparrow}m$ for $g, m \in P$.
(ii) For $A, B \subseteq P$ show that $A^{\rhd} = P \setminus {\downarrow}A$ and $B^{\lhd} = P \setminus {\uparrow}B$.
(iii) Show that $(A, B) \in \wp(P) \times \wp(P)^{\partial}$ is a concept if and only if $A \in \mathcal{O}(P)$ and $B \in \mathcal{U}(P)$, with $A = P \setminus B$.

3.17   Maximal and Minimal Elements

We next introduce some important special elements. Let P be a poset and let $S \subseteq P$. Then $a \in S$ is a **maximal** element of S if $a \leqslant x \in S$ implies $a = x$. We denote the set of maximal elements of S by $\operatorname{Max} S$. Note that $\operatorname{Max} S$ contains just one element if S (with the order inherited from P) has a top element, $\top_S$; in this case $\top_S$ is called the **greatest** element of S and denoted $\max S$. Note that then $\operatorname{Max} Y = \{\max S\}$. Note also that $x \in \operatorname{Max} P$ if and only if ${\uparrow}x = \{x\}$. A **minimal** element of $S \subseteq P$ and $\operatorname{Min} S$ and (where it exists) $\min S = \bot_S$ are defined dually, that is by reversing the order.

In general Y may have many maximal elements, or none. A subset of the chain $\mathbb{N}$ has a maximal element if and only if it is finite and non-empty. In the subset Y of $\wp(\mathbb{N})$ consisting of all subsets of $\mathbb{N}$ except $\mathbb{N}$ itself, there is no top element, but $\mathbb{N} \setminus \{n\} \in \operatorname{Max} Y$ for each $n \in \mathbb{N}$. The subset of $\wp(\mathbb{N})$ consisting of all finite subsets of $\mathbb{N}$ has no maximal elements. An important set-theorists' tool, **Zorn's Lemma**, guarantees the existence of maximal elements, under suitable conditions. Zorn's Lemma is discussed from an order theory viewpoint in ILO2, Chapter 10.

Referring to the examples in 3.2, we see that the maximal elements in Σ^{**} are the infinite strings and those in $A \longrightarrow B$ are the total maps. This suggests that when an order relation models information we might expect a correlation between maximal elements and totally defined elements.

Mini-exercise Let P be a *finite* poset and let $\emptyset \neq Y \subseteq P$.

(i) Prove that $\operatorname{Max} Y$ is a non-empty antichain.
(ii) Prove that Y is a down-set if and only if $Y = {\downarrow}\operatorname{Max} Y$.

3.18   Stocktaking

In connection with a poset P and its subsets we have now met

- **binary relations**: $\leqslant$, its converse $\geqslant$, and their complements $\nleqslant$, $\ngeqslant$;
- paired **polar maps**: $(^{\rhd}, ^{\lhd})$ between $\wp(P)$ and $\wp(P)^{\partial}$, associated with any relation $R \subseteq P \times P$ and in particular with the relations $\leqslant$, $\geqslant$, $\nleqslant$ and $\ngeqslant$;

- **families of sets** $\mathcal{U}(P)$ (**up-sets**) and $\mathcal{O}(P)$ (**down-sets**), and the family of **concepts** associated with the pair of polar maps $(^{\triangleright}, {}^{\triangleleft})$ associated with a relation $R \subseteq P \times P$, all themselves posets;
- the **down-set operator**, $\downarrow$, and the **up-set operator**, $\uparrow$;
- **diagrams** for posets, in particular for the poset of **concepts** of a context.

A number of points should be clear from our examples: that the notions above are closely interconnected, and that the families of sets arising have nice properties not possessed by posets in general.

Our next task is to pursue order-theoretic ideas further, in order to have available the vocabulary needed to define and explore complete lattices and their relationship to Galois connections and closure operators. Afficionados of Galois connections will need to be a little patient: we put in place the other pieces of the jigsaw before slotting in this key piece.

4   Lattices in General and Complete Lattices in Particular

Many important properties of a poset P are expressed in terms of the existence of certain upper bounds or lower bounds of subsets of P. Important classes of posets defined in this way are

- lattices,
- complete lattices,
- CPOs (complete partial orders).

These classes enter into different application areas to differing extents. Lattices, where we are dealing with *finitary* operations, are algebraic structures and their theory belongs to, and has a symbiotic relationship with, algebra. There are also close connections with logic. Complete lattices are the ordered structures of most interest to us in these notes. CPOs are more general, and provide an appropriate setting in which to study fixed point theorems; restricting somewhat to (Scott) domains, we have a much-studied class of semantic domains. Much of the motivation comes from the need to have semantic models supporting recursion.

4.1   Lattices

Consider the posets depicted in Figure 9. In (a) we have $\uparrow a \cap \uparrow b = \varnothing$. In (b) we find that $\uparrow a \cap \uparrow b = \{c, d\}$. Similar considerations apply to the down-set operator. For points x, y in a poset P there may be a point $z \in P$ such that $\downarrow x \cap \downarrow y = \downarrow z$, or this may fail either because the intersection is empty or because it is not of the form $\downarrow z$.

By contrast, if we look at a powerset $\mathscr{P}(X)$ we find easily that, for any subsets A, B of X, there exists $C \in \mathscr{P}(X)$, namely $C = A \cup B$, such that $\uparrow A \cap \uparrow B = \uparrow C$; and similarly for $\downarrow$.

Fig. 9. Thwarted suprema

Let L be a non-empty poset. Then L is a **lattice** if, for $x, y \in L$, there exists elements $x \vee y$ and $x \wedge y$ in L such that

$$\uparrow x \cap \uparrow y = \uparrow(x \vee y) \quad \text{and} \quad \downarrow x \cap \downarrow y = \downarrow(x \wedge y);$$

the elements $x \vee y$ and $x \wedge y$ are called, respectively, the **join** (or **supremum**) and **meet** (or **infimum**) of x and y. Formally, $\vee \colon L \times L \to L$ and $\wedge \colon L \times L \to L$ are binary operations on L. Note that L^{∂} is a lattice if and only if L is, with the roles of $\vee$ and $\wedge$ swapping.

Mini-exercise As a special kind of poset, a lattice is equipped with a partial order, $\leqslant$, as well as with the binary operations of join and meet. The link between $\vee$, $\wedge$ and $\leqslant$ (portentously called the **Connecting Lemma** in ILO2), is given by

$$x \wedge y = x \iff x \leqslant y \iff x \vee y = y$$

(note that this implies that either of $\vee$ and $\wedge$ determines $\leqslant$). Verify these implications.

Mini-exercise

(i) Show that any *finite* lattice possesses top and bottom elements.
(ii) Give an example of a poset with $\top$ and $\bot$ which is *not* a lattice.

Let L be a lattice. Then $(L; \vee, \wedge)$ may be viewed as an algebra, with $\vee$ and $\wedge$ satisfying certain laws (equations) capturing the properties that their order-theoretic ancestry gives them. For all $x, y, z \in L$,

(L1) $(x \vee y) \vee z = x \vee (y \vee z)$ (associativity)
(L2) $x \vee y = y \vee x$ (commutativity)
(L3) $x \vee x = x$ (idempotency)
(L4) $x \vee (x \wedge y) = x$ (absorption),

and their dual versions, $(L1)^{\partial}$–$(L4)^{\partial}$. It is an easy **Mini-exercise** to verify (L1)–(L3) and their duals. Note that only the absorption laws (L4) and $(L4)^{\partial}$ involve *both* $\vee$ and $\wedge$. These laws, of course, capture exactly what the Connecting Lemma demands. In the opposite direction, the lattice laws are set up in such a way that any (non-empty) structure $(L; \vee, \wedge)$ satisfying these laws gives rise to a poset $\langle L; \leqslant \rangle$: the partial order is (well-)defined by the equivalent conditions $x \leqslant y \Longleftrightarrow x \vee y = y \Longleftrightarrow x \wedge y = x$, and join and meet operations given by sup and inf are just the original $\vee$ and $\wedge$. This correspondence between lattice-as-algebra and lattice-as-poset is set out in more detail in Chapter 2 of ILO2.

The associative laws allow us unambiguously to define iterated joins and meets: if $F = \{a_1, \dots, a_n\}$ is a finite non-empty subset of a lattice L then we write $\bigvee F$ as alternative notation for $a_1 \vee \cdots \vee a_n$, and $\bigwedge F$ for $a_1 \wedge \cdots \wedge a_n$.

We have demanded that a lattice be non-empty, whereas we allow posets to be empty. This reflects customary practice: algebras are non-empty but relational structures, such as posets, are allowed to have an empty underlying set.

Mini-exercise Let P and Q be non-empty posets. Prove that $P \times Q$, with the usual co-ordinatewise order, is a lattice if and only if both P and Q are lattices.

Mini-exercise Let L be a lattice. Prove that for all $a, b, c, d \in L$

(i) $a \leqslant b$ implies $a \vee c \leqslant b \vee c$ and $a \wedge c \leqslant b \wedge c$;
(ii) $a \leqslant b$ and $c \leqslant d$ imply $a \vee c \leqslant b \vee d$ and $a \wedge c \leqslant b \wedge d$. (Note that this says precisely that the binary operations $\vee \colon L \times L \to L$ and $\wedge \colon L \times L \to L$ are monotone.)

4.2 Examples of Lattices

(1) Every non-empty chain is a lattice in which $x \vee y = \max\{x, y\}$ and $x \wedge y = \min\{x, y\}$. Thus the real numbers, $\mathbb{R}$, and the natural numbers, $\mathbb{N}$, are lattices under the usual orderings. Note that $\mathbb{R}$ lacks both $\top$ and $\bot$ and that $\mathbb{N}$ lacks $\top$.
(2) For any set X, the powerset $\wp(X)$ is a lattice in which $\vee$ and $\wedge$ are just $\cup$ and $\cap$. Dually, $\wp(X)^{\partial}$ is a lattice, with $\vee$ as $\cap$ and $\wedge$ as $\cup$.
(3) Now let $\varnothing \neq \mathfrak{L} \subseteq \wp(X)$. Then $\mathfrak{L}$ is known as a **lattice of sets** if it is closed under finite unions and intersections. In a lattice of sets $\mathfrak{L}$ we have $A \vee B = A \cup B$ and $A \wedge B = A \cap B$ for $A, B \in \mathfrak{L}$. This is not *quite* obvious; see 5.2. As examples, we see that, for any poset P, our old friends $\mathcal{U}(P)$ and $\mathcal{O}(P)$ are lattices of sets.

4.3 Distributive Lattices

In any powerset $\wp(X)$ we have, for $A, B, C \subseteq X$,

$$A \cap (B \cup C) = (A \cap B) \cup (A \cap C) \quad \text{and} \quad A \cup (B \cap C) = (A \cup B) \cap (A \cup C).$$

Therefore $\wp(X)$ satisfies the distributive laws: for all $x, y, z \in L$

(D) $x \wedge (y \vee z) = (x \wedge y) \vee (x \wedge z)$;
(D)$^{\partial}$ $x \vee (y \wedge z) = (x \vee y) \wedge (x \vee z)$.

More generally, any lattice of sets satisfies these laws, and in particular the lattices $\mathcal{O}(P)$ and $\mathcal{U}(P)$ of down-sets and up-sets of a poset P are distributive.

We may ask whether *every* lattice is distributive. It is far from transparent algebraically whether or not this is true, and it is well known that in the pioneering days of lattice theory more than a century ago it was 'proved' that all lattices are distributive. However it can be seen extremely easily that both the lattices in Figure 10 fail (D)—the pictorial approach demonstrates its power!

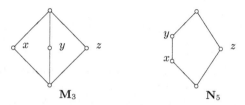

Fig. 10. A pair of non-distributive lattices

We remark that it can be shown that, globally in a lattice L, (D) holds if and only if $(D)^\partial$ does. On the other hand, locally, for particular triples of elements x, y, z, the two conditions are not equivalent. See ILO2, Chapter 4.

Mini-exercise Consider again the context $(X, X, R_=)$ in Exercise 2.5.

(i) Show that if $|X| = 3$ the poset $\mathfrak{B}(X, X, R_=)$ is isomorphic to the lattice $\mathbf{M}_3$ in Figure 10.

(ii) Convince yourself that for arbitrary X the poset $\mathfrak{B}(X, X, R_=)$ is a lattice and that this is not distributive.

4.4   Boolean Algebras

The best-known lattices of all are the powersets, and these come ready equipped with an extra unary operation, $'$, of complementation satisfying $x \vee x' = \top$ and $x \wedge x' = \bot$. Such an operation is not available in arbitrary distributive lattices with $\bot$ and $\top$. In the chain $0 < 1 < 2$, for example, 1 has no complement and, in a down-set lattice $\mathcal{O}(P)$, the only complemented elements are those which are up-sets in P as well as being down-sets. The distributive lattices possessing nullary operations $\bot$, $\top$ and a unary operation $'$ are the **Boolean algebras**.

4.5   Lattices in Logic

It is no coincidence that the symbols adopted for join and meet in a lattice are the same as those used for disjunction and conjunction in logic. Consider PROP, the propositions of classical propositional calculus: it looks as if these should form a lattice with 'or' and 'and' acting as the lattice operations; $\neg$ as $'$;

F ('falsity') as $\bot$ and **T** ('truth') as $\top$. We would then expect $\rightarrow$ ('implies') to play the role of $\leqslant$. This doesn't quite work: we can have distinct propositions α and β for which $\alpha \rightarrow \beta$ and $\beta \rightarrow \alpha$ both hold. Thus $\rightarrow$ defines a pre-order rather than a partial order. To get a partial order we don't distinguish α and β when $\alpha \leftrightarrow \beta$. With this identification, which can be formalized in terms of the relation of logical equivalence on PROP, we do get a Boolean algebra. A brief account of the theory of Boolean algebras, including an elementary treatment of the role of lattice theory in propositional calculus, is given in ILO2, Chapter 4.

One point about logic and lattices is well worth stressing. It is by no means always the case that logics have a classical, Boolean, negation. Logics of various different kinds are extensively used in computer science as a means of reasoning about programs. In such a setting we may wish to model negation in a less restrictive way, retaining the property that $P \wedge \neg P = \mathbf{F}$ ('not both of P and $\neg P$ are true'), but discarding the **Law of the Excluded Middle**, $P \vee \neg P = \mathbf{T}$, and substituting something weaker. This is done, for example in intuitionistic logic, where the implication operation behaves differently from that in classical logic; see 6.5.

We may also wish to allow truth values other than the booleans **F** and **T**: for example, we might want to accommodate a third value, **P**, representing 'possible' or 'not yet determined'. Or we might, as in probabilistic models and in fuzzy logic, wish to allow truth values lying in the interval $[0, 1]$. We may also, as in modal and temporal logic, wish to allow for additional operations, such that $\diamondsuit$ and $\square$. But, however we want our additional operations to behave, it is almost always the case that the usual laws will govern disjunction and conjunction, and then there will be an underlying distributive lattice associated with the logic. The study of logics from an algebraic point of view has benefitted from and driven forward the study of lattices, in particular of distributive lattices with additional operations. We do not have space to explore these ideas further here. For additional information see, for example, the article by Davey & Priestley [6] and Brink & Rewitzky [5].

4.6 Upper Bounds and Sups, Lower Bounds and Infs

So far we have discussed lattices, but not the complete lattices we have advertised. We now work towards remedying this omission. Let P be a poset and let $S \subseteq P$. We define

$$S^u := \{\, x \in P \,:\, (\forall s \in S)\, x \geqslant s \,\} \quad \text{and} \quad S^\ell := \{\, x \in P \,:\, (\forall s \in S)\, x \leqslant s \,\};$$

S^u and S^ℓ are, respectively, the sets of all **upper bounds** and all **lower bounds** of S. Notice that $\varnothing^u = \varnothing^\ell = P$. Now let $S \neq \varnothing$. Then it is easy to see that the sets of bounds can be alternatively described by

$$S^u := \bigcap \{\, \uparrow s \,:\, s \in S \,\} \quad \text{and} \quad S^\ell := \bigcap \{\, \downarrow s \,:\, s \in S \,\}.$$

In particular, for elements x, y of P,

$$\{x, y\}^u = \uparrow x \cap \uparrow y \quad \text{and} \quad \{x, y\}^\ell = \downarrow x \cap \downarrow y.$$

Accordingly, a lattice is a non-empty poset in which, for every pair of elements x, y, the set $\{x, y\}^u$ has a least (bottom) element and $\{x, y\}^\ell$ has a greatest (top) element.

For an arbitrary subset S of a poset P, we say that the **supremum** or **sup** (also known as the **least upper bound** or **join**), α, of S exists if

(sup1) $(\forall s \in S)\, s \leqslant \alpha$ (that is, $\alpha \in S^u$, so α is *an* upper bound of S);
(sup2) $(\forall x \in S^u)\, \alpha \leqslant x$ (that is, α is the *least* upper bound of S).

In this case we write $\bigvee S$ for α, or, when we need to keep track of the poset in which we are working, $\bigvee_P S$. When dealing with families of sets, we abuse notation slightly and write $\bigvee_{i \in I} A_i$ in place of $\bigvee \{ A_i \,:\, i \in I \}$, and similarly with other operators in place of $\bigvee$.

The supremum α of S is characterized by

(sup) $(\forall y \in P)((\forall s \in S)\, y \leqslant s \Longleftrightarrow y \leqslant \alpha)$.

This is slicker, and more in the spirit of an equational approach, but is less transparent until the two-step definition has been fully mastered.

Likewise, the **infimum** or **inf** (also known as the **greatest lower bound** or **meet**), *beta*, of S exists if

(inf) $(\forall y \in P)((\forall s \in S)\, y \geqslant s \Longleftrightarrow y \geqslant \beta)$.

and we write $\bigwedge S$ (or $\bigwedge_P S$) for β. Clearly sup and inf are dual notions, with sups in P translating into infs in P^∂.

Mini-exercise Let P be a poset, let $S, T \subseteq P$ and assume that $\bigvee S$, $\bigvee T$, $\bigwedge S$ and $\bigwedge T$ exist in P. Check the following oft-used elementary facts.

   (i) For all $s \in S, s \leqslant \bigvee S$ and $s \geqslant \bigwedge S$.
   (ii) Let $x \in P$; then $x \leqslant \bigwedge S$ if and only if $x \leqslant s$ for all $s \in S$.
   (iii) Let $x \in P$; then $x \geqslant \bigvee S$ if and only if $x \geqslant s$ for all $s \in S$.
   (iv) $\bigvee S \leqslant \bigwedge T$ if and only if $s \leqslant t$ for all $s \in S$ and all $t \in T$.
   (v) If $S \subseteq T$, then $\bigvee S \leqslant \bigvee T$ and $\bigwedge S \geqslant \bigwedge T$.

(Compare with Mini-exercise 4.1.)

4.7   Much Ado about Nothing, and about Everything

Let P be a poset and $S = \varnothing$. As noted earlier, $\varnothing^u = P$ and hence sup $\varnothing$ exists if and only if P has a bottom element, and in that case sup $\varnothing = \bot$. Dually, inf $\varnothing = \top$ whenever P has a top element.

It is easily seen that, if P has a top element, then $P^u = \{\top\}$ in which case sup $P = \top$. When P has no top element, we have $P^u = \varnothing$ and hence sup P does not exist. By duality, inf $P = \bot$ whenever P has a bottom element.

4.8 Complete Lattices

As we have already seen, in a lattice L, $x \vee y = \bigvee\{x, y\}$ and $x \vee y = \bigwedge\{x, y\}$. Further, $\bigvee F$ and $\bigwedge F$ exist for any non-empty finite subset of L, viewed either as iterated binary joins and meets or as an instance of sups and infs. We say that a non-empty poset P is a **complete lattice** if $\bigwedge S$ and $\bigvee S$ exist for all $S \subseteq P$. We do not exclude $S = \varnothing$ so that any complete lattice has $\top$ and $\bot$.

4.9 Completeness on the Cheap

Let P be a non-empty poset.

- (i) Assume that $\bigwedge S$ exists in P for every non-empty subset S of P. Then $\bigvee S$ exists in P for every subset S of P which has an upper bound in P; indeed, $\bigvee S = \bigwedge S^u$.
- (ii) The following are equivalent:
  - (a) P is a complete lattice;
  - (b) $\bigwedge S$ exists in P for every subset S of P;
  - (c) P has a top element, $\top$, and $\bigwedge S$ exists in P for every non-empty subset S of P.

Proof. (i) Let $S \subseteq P$ and assume that S has an upper bound in P; thus $S^u \neq \varnothing$. Hence, by assumption, $\beta := \bigwedge S^u$ exists in P. But this means that $\bigvee S = \beta$.

(ii) It is trivial that (a) implies (b), and (b) implies (c) since the inf of the empty subset of P exists only if P has a top element (see 4.7). It follows easily from (i) that (c) implies (a).   □

4.10 A Special Class of Complete Lattices

Any finite lattice L is automatically a complete lattice, because the supremum (infimum) of a non-empty subset is in fact an iterated join (meet) while the sup and inf of $\emptyset$ are $\bigwedge L$ and $\bigvee L$, respectively (see 4.7 and 4.8).

This completeness result extends to an important class of infinite posets. A poset P satisfies the **ascending chain condition**, (ACC), if given any sequence $x_1 \leqslant x_2 \leqslant \ldots \leqslant x_n \leqslant \ldots$ of elements of P, there exists $k \in \mathbb{N}$ such that $x_k = x_{k+1} = \ldots$. Any flat poset satisfies (ACC). As non-flat examples of posets satisfying (ACC) we present $\mathbb{N}^\partial$ and $\wp_{\mathrm{fin}}(\mathbb{N})^\partial$ (where $\wp_{\mathrm{fin}}(\mathbb{N})$ denotes the finite subsets of $\mathbb{N}$, ordered by inclusion). As an example of an infinite lattice in which (ACC) holds, take any infinite antichain with top and bottom adjoined.

Let L be a lattice satisfying (ACC). We assert that for $\varnothing \neq S \subseteq P$ there exists a finite subset F of S such that $\bigvee S = \bigvee F$ (which certainly exists). Consequently, if P is a lattice with $\bot$ which satisfies (ACC) then P is a complete lattice, by 4.9. The assertion that arbitrary suprema reduce to finite ones in the presence of (ACC) relies on an ancillary result of independent interest, stating that a poset P satisfies (ACC) if and only if $\mathrm{Max}\, S \neq \varnothing$ for $\varnothing \neq S \subseteq P$. The forward implication needs the Axiom of Choice; see 8.14 below.

4.11   Suprema, Infima, and Monotone Maps

Consider a little example. Let P be the linear sum $\mathbb{N} \oplus Q$, where $\mathbb{N}$ has its usual order and $Q = \{a, b\}$ is a 2-element chain with $a < b$. Note that $\bigvee_P \mathbb{N} = a$. Define $F \colon P \to P$ by letting F be the identity map on $\mathbb{N}$ and map both a and b to b. Then F is monotone. Also

$$F(\textstyle\bigvee_P \mathbb{N}) = F(a) = b > a = \textstyle\bigvee_P \mathbb{N} = \textstyle\bigvee_P F(\mathbb{N}).$$

The moral is that monotone maps need not preserve suprema (or, dually, infima) even when these exist.

On the other hand, any map between lattices preserving $\vee$ (or $\wedge$) is automatically monotone. To see this, let $F \colon L \to M$ be such that $F(x \vee y) = F(x) \vee F(y)$ for all x, y. Then, for $x, y \in L$,

$$
\begin{aligned}
x \leqslant y &\Longrightarrow x \vee y = y && \text{(by the Connecting Lemma, 4.1)}\\
&\Longrightarrow F(x) \vee F(y) = F(y) && \text{(by assumption)}\\
&\Longrightarrow F(x) \leqslant F(y) && \text{(by the Connecting Lemma).}
\end{aligned}
$$

All the more so, if F is a map between complete lattices P and Q such that $F(\bigvee_P S) = \bigvee_Q F(S)$ for any (non-empty) subset S of P, then F is monotone. Examining the argument above we see that all we have used is the fact that $F(\bigvee \{u, v\}) = \bigvee \{F(u), F(v)\}$ when u and v are comparable. Accordingly, any map preserving suprema of chains, when these exist, is monotone.

Although monotone maps need not preserve suprema or infima, we can, usefully, get half way: let $F \colon P \to Q$ be a monotone map between posets P and Q and let $S \subseteq P$. Then

$$F(\textstyle\bigvee_P S) \geqslant \textstyle\bigvee_Q F(S) \quad \text{and} \quad F(\textstyle\bigwedge_P S) \leqslant \textstyle\bigwedge_Q F(S)$$

whenever the sups and infs involved exist. To verify the first of these note that:

$$
\begin{aligned}
(\forall s \in S)\, s \leqslant \textstyle\bigvee_P S &\Longrightarrow (\forall s \in S)\, F(s) \leqslant F(\textstyle\bigvee_P S) && \text{(since F is monotone)}\\
&\Longrightarrow F(\textstyle\bigvee_P S) \in F(S)^u.
\end{aligned}
$$

For order-isomorphisms the situation is, not unexpectedly, better. To state the result we need a definition. Let P and Q be posets. A map $F \colon P \to Q$ is said to **preserve existing sups** if whenever $\bigvee_P S$ exists then $\bigvee_Q F(S)$ exists and $F(\bigvee_P S) = \bigvee_Q F(S)$. Preservation of existing infs is defined dually.

Mini-exercise   Assume that P and Q are posets and that $F \colon P \to Q$ is an order-isomorphism. Then F preserves all existing sups and infs. In particular, the image of a (complete) lattice under an order-isomorphism is a (complete) lattice. Further, an order-isomorphism preserves $\top$ and $\bot$ when these exist.

The pay-off from the elementary observations in this subsection comes when we consider Galois connections and fixed points in Sections 7 and 8.

5 Complete Lattices, Concretely: Closure Systems and Closure Operators

Once we have recorded one elementary technical fact we will be able to exhibit many examples of complete lattices.

5.1 A Useful Technical Remark

Let K be a non-empty subset, with the inherited order, of some complete lattice L. For $S \subseteq K$, we claim that

$$\bigvee_L S \in K \implies \bigvee_K S \text{ exists and equals } \bigvee_L S,$$
$$\bigwedge_L S \in K \implies \bigwedge_K S \text{ exists and equals } \bigwedge_L S,$$

leaving as a **Mini-exercise** the verification that the elements asserted to be the sup and inf really do serve as the least upper bound and greatest lower bound.

5.2 Complete Lattices of Sets

Applied in a powerset, 5.1 tells us that any non-empty family $\mathcal{L}$ of subsets of a set X is a complete lattice if it is such that $\bigcup_{i \in I} A_i$ and $\bigcap_{i \in I} A_i$ belong to $\mathcal{L}$ for any family of sets $\{A_i\}_{i \in I}$ in $\mathcal{L}$ is a complete lattice, in which $\bigvee_{\mathcal{L}}$ and $\bigwedge_{\mathcal{L}}$ are given by $\bigcup$ and $\bigcap$. A lattice of this type is known as a **complete lattice of sets**. Important examples are powersets and their duals, and the lattices $\mathcal{U}(P)$ and $\mathcal{O}(P)$ of up-sets and down-sets of a poset P.

5.3 Closure Systems

The down-set and up-set lattices $\mathcal{O}(P)$ and $\mathcal{U}(P)$ are defined within the powerset lattice $\mathcal{P}(P)$ by reference to the order relation $\leqslant$ on P. Likewise, there are many other situations in which structure on a set X naturally leads to consideration of subsets of $\mathcal{P}(X)$. Here are some mathematical examples, instructive for those with the requisite knowledge.

(1) Suppose that V is a vector space. Then Sub (V), the subspaces of V, form a subset of $\mathcal{P}(V)$. Let $U_1, U_2 \in$ Sub (V). Notice that the intersection $U_1 \cap U_2$ is always a subspace, but that the union $U_1 \cup U_2$ never is, unless either $U_1 \subseteq U_2$ or $U_2 \subseteq U_1$. (For an example, look at the vector space $\mathbb{R}^2$, with U_1 and U_2 distinct lines through 0: the sum of non-zero vectors, one from U_1 and one from U_2, is in neither U_1 nor U_2.) Thus Sub (V) is *not* a complete lattice of sets, as defined in 5.2, nor even a lattice of sets.

(2) The example in (1) is one of a family of examples of similar type: substructures of some given algebraic structure. We might look for example at subgroups of a group, subrings of a ring, ... In very many such cases we have closure under intersections, but seldom closure under unions.

(3) Let X be a set equipped with a topology $\mathfrak{T}$. Then the family of **closed** subsets of the topological space $(X, \mathfrak{T})$ is closed under arbitrary intersections but not in general arbitrary unions. If we look at the open sets, then the position is reversed: open sets are closed under arbitrary unions but not in general under arbitrary intersections. (We remark in passing that every poset P has an associated topology in which we declare the open sets to be the up-sets; taking complements, the closed sets are then the down-sets. In this case, the family of open sets is closed under intersections.)

In all the preceding examples we are half way to having a complete lattice of sets, but only half way. This is where 4.9 comes to the rescue. We do get complete lattices, but with only one of the operations $\bigwedge$ and $\bigvee$ as the set-theoretic one. Here's how.

5.4   Closure Systems

Let X be a set and let $\mathfrak{L}$ be a family of subsets of X, ordered as usual by inclusion, and such that

(cs1) $\bigcap_{i \in I} A_i \in \mathfrak{L}$ for every non-empty family $\{A_i\}_{i \in I} \subseteq \mathfrak{L}$, and
(cs2) $X \in \mathfrak{L}$.

Then $\mathfrak{L}$ is a complete lattice in which

$$\bigwedge_{i \in I} A_i = \bigcap_{i \in I} A_i,$$
$$\bigvee_{i \in I} A_i = \bigcap \{ B \in \mathfrak{L} : \bigcup_{i \in I} A_i \subseteq B \}.$$

Proof. By 4.9, to show that $\mathfrak{L}$ is a complete lattice for the inclusion order it suffices to show that $\mathfrak{L}$ has a top element and that the inf of every non-empty subset of $\mathfrak{L}$ exists in $\mathfrak{L}$. By (cs2), $\mathfrak{L}$ has a top element, namely X. Let $\{A_i\}_{i \in I}$ be a non-empty subset of $\mathfrak{L}$; then (cs1) gives $\bigcap_{i \in I} A_i \in \mathfrak{L}$. By 5.1, $\bigcap_{i \in I} A_i$ is the inf of $\{A_i\}_{i \in I}$ in $\mathfrak{L}$, that is,

$$\bigwedge_{i \in I} A_i = \bigcap_{i \in I} A_i.$$

Thus $\mathfrak{L}$ is indeed a complete lattice when ordered by $\subseteq$.

Since X is an upper bound of $\{A_i\}_{i \in I}$ in $\mathfrak{L}$, 4.9(i) gives

$$\begin{aligned}
\bigvee_{i \in I} A_i &= \left(\bigwedge_{i \in I} A_i \right)^u \\
&= \bigcap \{ B \in \mathfrak{L} : (\forall i \in I) \, A_i \subseteq B \} \\
&= \bigcap \{ B \in \mathfrak{L} : \bigcup_{i \in I} A_i \subseteq B \}. \quad \square
\end{aligned}$$

If $\mathfrak{L}$ is a non-empty family of subsets of X which satisfies conditions (cs1) and (cs2) above, then $\mathfrak{L}$ is said to be a **closure system** (called a **topped intersection structure** in ILO2) on X. If $\mathfrak{L}$ just satisfies (cs1), it is referred to as an **intersection structure**. Intersection structures arising in computer science are usually topless while those in algebra are almost invariably topped.

5.5 Examples

(1) Consider $A \multimap\!\!\rightarrow B$, where A, B are non-empty sets. From the observations in 1.6 we saw that the map $\pi \mapsto \operatorname{graph} \pi$ is an order-embedding of $A \multimap\!\!\rightarrow B$ into $\wp(A \times B)$. Let $\mathfrak{L}$ be the family of subsets of $A \times B$ which are graphs of partial maps. To prove that $\mathfrak{L}$ is closed under intersections, use the characterization given in 1.6: if $S \subseteq A \times B$, then $S \in \mathfrak{L}$ if and only if $(s, x) \in S$ and $(s, x') \in S$ imply $x = x'$. Thus $\mathfrak{L}$ is an an intersection structure. It is not topped unless B has just one element.

(2) Each of the following is a closure system and so forms a complete lattice under inclusion: the subspaces of a vector space, the subgroups, or normal subgroups, of a group, the congruence relations on an algebra, the convex subsets of the Euclidean plane, ... These families all belong to a class of intersection structures closely related to Scott domains.

(3) The closed subsets of a topological space are closed under finite unions and finite intersections and hence form a lattice of sets in which $A \vee B = A \cup B$ and $A \wedge B = A \cap B$. In fact, the closed sets form a closure system and consequently the lattice of closed sets is complete. Infs are given by intersection while the sup of a family of closed sets is not their union but is obtained by forming the *closure* of their union.

5.6 From a Complete Lattice to a Closure System

For any poset P, the map $x \mapsto {\downarrow}x$ from P to $\mathcal{O}(P)$ is an order-embedding (recall 3.15). So any poset P can be faithfully mapped into a complete lattice $\mathcal{O}(P)$. We can take this a bit further. Let L be an (abstract) complete lattice. We claim that L is isomorphic to a closure system.

Proof. Use $F\colon x \mapsto {\downarrow}x$ to map L into $\mathcal{O}(L)$. Then F maps L order-isomorphically onto $\mathcal{L} := \{{\downarrow}x \, : \, x \in L\}$. Now, $\mathcal{L}$ has top element ${\downarrow}\top$ and is closed under intersections:
$$\bigcap\nolimits_{i \in I} {\downarrow}x_i = \bigwedge\nolimits_{i \in I} {\downarrow}x_i$$
(see 5.1). □

5.7 Defining Closure Operators

Let P be a poset. Then a map $c\colon P \to P$ is called a **closure operator** (on P) if, for all $x, y \in P$,

 (clo1) $x \leqslant c(x)$,
 (clo2) $x \leqslant y \Longrightarrow c(x) \leqslant c(y)$,
 (clo3) $c(c(x)) = c(x)$.

An element $x \in P$ is called **closed** if $c(x) = x$. The set of all closed elements of P is denoted by P_c.

As examples of closure operators we have

(i) the operators $\downarrow$ and $\uparrow$ on the subsets of a poset, for which the closed sets are respectively the down-sets and the up-sets (3.15);

(ii) the operator of topological closure defined on any topological space.

In these examples the lattices of closed sets form closure systems, and so are complete lattices. This is true more generally.

5.8   New Complete Lattices from Old: From a Closure Operator to a Complete Lattice

Let P is a complete lattice and let $c\colon P \to P$.

(i) (The **Prefix Lemma**) Assume that c is monotone. Then $Q := \{\, x \in P : c(x) \leqslant x \,\}$ is a complete lattice.

(ii) Assume that c is a closure operator on P. Then

$$c(P) = P_c := \{\, x \in P : c(x) = x \,\}$$

is a complete lattice in which

$$\textstyle\bigwedge_{P_c} S = \bigwedge_P S \text{ and } \bigvee_{P_c} S = c(\bigvee_P S),$$

and $\mathsf{T}_{c(P)} = c(\mathsf{T}_P)$.

Proof. (i) To prove that Q is a complete lattice, it suffices, by 4.9, to show that arbitrary infs exist in Q. By 5.1, this happens if, for every $S \subseteq Q$, we have $\alpha := \bigwedge_P S \in Q$ (and then $\bigwedge_Q S = \alpha$). But

$$(\forall s \in S)\, s \geqslant \alpha \implies (\forall s \in S)\, c(s) \geqslant c(\alpha) \qquad \text{(by definition of } Q\text{, and (po3))}$$
$$\implies \alpha \geqslant c(\alpha) \qquad\qquad\quad \text{(by definition of } \textstyle\bigwedge\text{)}.$$

Now consider (ii). Note first that $y \in P_c$ implies $y = c(y) \in c(P)$ while if $y = c(x)$ for some $x \in P$, then $c(y) = c(c(x)) = c(x) = y$, by (clo3), and so $y \in P_c$. Thus $c(P) = P_c$, and by (clo3) this set is just the set Q in (i). From the proof above, P_c is a complete lattice, whose infs coincide with those in P. We must now establish the formula for sups. Let $\beta := c(\bigvee_P S)$ where $S \subseteq P_c$. Certainly $\beta \in c(P) = P_c$. Also

$$s \in S \implies s \leqslant \textstyle\bigvee_P S \qquad\qquad \text{(definition of } \textstyle\bigvee_P\text{)}$$
$$\implies s = c(s) \leqslant c(\textstyle\bigvee_P S) = \alpha \quad \text{(by (clo2))},$$

so β is an upper bound for S in P_c. Also, for any upper bound y for S with $y \in P_c$,

$$(\forall s \in S)\, s \leqslant y \implies \textstyle\bigvee_P S \leqslant y \qquad\qquad \text{(definition of } \textstyle\bigvee_P\text{)}$$
$$\implies \beta = c(\textstyle\bigvee_P S) \leqslant c(y) = y \quad \text{(using (clo2))},$$

so β is indeed the least upper bound. Finally, $\mathsf{T}_P = c(\mathsf{T}_P)$, by (clo1). $\qquad\square$

5.9 Closure Operators more Concretely

The most commonly occurring closure operators are those on powerset lattices. By specializing 5.8 we get (i) below. The proofs of (ii) and (iii) are straightforward.

(i) Let X be a set and C a closure operator on $\wp(X)$. Then the family

$$\mathfrak{L}_C := \{\, A \subseteq X \ : \ C(A) = A \,\}$$

of closed subsets of X is a closure system and so forms a complete lattice, when ordered by inclusion, in which

$$\bigwedge_{i \in I} A_i = \bigcap_{i \in I} A_i,$$
$$\bigvee_{i \in I} A_i = C\big(\bigcup_{i \in I} A_i\big).$$

(ii) Given a closure system $\mathfrak{L}$ on X the formula

$$C_{\mathfrak{L}}(A) := \bigcap \{\, B \in \mathfrak{L} \ : \ A \subseteq B \,\}.$$

defines a closure operator $C_{\mathfrak{L}}$ on X.

(iii) The relationship between closure systems and closure operators is a bijective one: the closure operator induced by the closure system $\mathfrak{L}_C$ is C itself, and, similarly, the closure system induced by the closure operator $C_{\mathfrak{L}}$ is $\mathfrak{L}$; in symbols,

$$C_{\mathfrak{L}_C} = C \quad \text{and} \quad \mathfrak{L}_{C_{\mathfrak{L}}} = \mathfrak{L}.$$

Of course, under the correspondence in (iii), the closure operator $\downarrow\colon \wp(P) \to \wp(P)$ corresponds to $\mathcal{O}(P)$, and $\uparrow$ to $\mathcal{U}(P)$, for any poset P.

6 Galois Connections: Basics

This section may profitably be read in parallel with the treatment of Galois connections in Chapter 4. The latter complements the mathematical discussion here by giving a detailed presentation of some computationally instructive examples and by recasting some core notions in a framework especially well suited to fixed point calculus. Galois connections are also explored both in Chapter 4 and in Chapter 9, with the emphasis in the latter being from the viewpoint of what are termed **Galois algebras**.

6.1 Introduction

Let P and Q be posets. A pair (F, G) of maps $F\colon P \to Q$ and $G\colon Q \to P$ is said to defines a **Galois connection** between P and Q if and only if

(Gal) $F(p) \leqslant q \iff p \leqslant G(q)$ for all $p \in P$, $q \in Q$,

Those familiar with maps between sets but less familiar with Galois connections may find it helpful to recognize that when $\leqslant$ is the equality relation $=$ then F and G are just set-theoretic inverses for each other: $F(p) = q$ holds if and only if $G(q) = p$, for $p \in P$, $q \in Q$. This set-theoretic example gives pointers to certain elementary facts about Galois connections. For example, just as invertible (bijective) maps $F_1 \colon P \to Q_1$ and $G \colon Q \to S$ compose to give an invertible map $G \circ F \colon P \to S$, so too can Galois connections be composed: if (F, G) is a Galois connection between P and Q and (H, K) is a Galois connection between Q and S, then $(H \circ F, K \circ G)$ is a Galois connection between P and S.

The symbols F and G don't actively assist one in remembering which map appears to the left of $\leqslant$ and which to the right. Accordingly, following the usage in ILO2, we shall in the first part of this section replace F and G by $\triangleright$ and $\triangleleft$ with these triangle maps written to the right of their arguments. In this notation, the Galois connection condition becomes

(Gal) $p^{\triangleright} \leqslant q \Longleftrightarrow p \leqslant q^{\triangleleft}$ for all $p \in P$ and $q \in Q$.

Just as there is no universally accepted notation for Galois connections there is also, regrettably, no uniformly adopted terminology, though generally nomenclature relates to the side of $\leqslant$ on which a map appears: we adopt the terms **lower adjoint** and **upper adjoint** for $\triangleright$ and $\triangleleft$, respectively; alternative terms are **left adjoint** and **right adjoint**. The notation in Gierz *et al.* [9]: d (for 'down') and g (for 'greater') seems, grammatically at least, a trifle odd.

We suggested at the start that ubiquitous concepts adopt different guises in different settings. Galois connections illustrate this all too well. There are two versions of the definitions: the one we adopt here, in which the paired maps are monotone (that is, order-preserving) and the other in which these are order-reversing. The literature seems to divide roughly equally between the two alternatives (for example, ILO2, Birkhoff [4] and Ganter & Wille [8] have order-reversing maps and Aarts [1] and Gierz *et al.* [9] order-preserving ones. Historically, and in algebra, there are arguments for order-reversal: Galois's own Galois connection between field extensions and subgroups of a Galois group is order-reversing. The two formulations are instances of, respectively, a categorical adjunction and dual adjunction. The difference is not significant: we can swap backwards and forwards between the two versions by swapping between Q and Q^{∂}.

6.2   Lattice Representation via Galois Connections

Assume that L is a lattice and let X be a subset of L which is **join-dense**, in the sense that every element of L is a (possibly empty) join of elements from X. Define $F \colon \mathcal{O}(X) \to L$ by $F(A) := \bigvee A$ and $g \colon L \to \mathcal{O}(X)$ by $G(a) := {\downarrow}a \cap X$. Then (F, G) is a Galois connection and it satisfies $G \circ F = \mathrm{id}_L$. **Mini-exercise**: verify these claims.

Now assume that L is finite. A natural choice for X here is $\mathcal{J}(L)$, the subset of L consisting of elements which are **join-irreducible**, that is, cannot be obtained as a (finite) join of strictly smaller elements. With this choice, more can be said about the Galois connection (F, G). If—and necessarily only if—L is distributive, it can be shown that we additionally have $F \circ G = \mathrm{id}_{\mathcal{O}(X)}$. Thus F and G set up an isomorphism between L and $\mathcal{O}(X)$. This is **Birkoff's representation theorem**. The theorem shows that every finite distributive lattice can be concretely represented as the down-set lattice of a finite poset.

Consider the special case of the above in which X has the equality order. Then we have $\mathcal{O}(X) = \wp(X)$ (by the dual of 3.10). This occurs precisely when L has a complementation operation, $'$, and so is a Boolean algebra (as a finite lattice, L certainly has $\bot$ and $\top$). In the concrete representation of L as a powerset this negation is captured by set complement (recall Exercise 3.14). What we have here is the finite version of Stone's famous representation of Boolean algebras.

There are two ways in which these representations may be extended to the infinite case. The link between the two approaches lies in the theory of canonical extensions, famously pioneered in the Boolean case by Jónsson & Tarski; see Jónsson [10], in particular §3.2.

The first approach captures the finitary nature of $\lor$ and $\land$ by adding a compact topology to the structure X. We pursue this a little further in Section 9. Alternatively, we may consider infinitary disjunctions and conjunctions, and replace join-irreducible elements by completely join-irreducible ones. An element is **completely join-irreducible** if it is not the supremum of strictly smaller elements. We obtain a Galois connection (F, G) satisfying $F \circ G = \mathrm{id}_{\mathcal{O}(X)}$ between L and $\mathcal{O}(X)$, where X is the set $\mathcal{J}^\infty(L)$ of completely join-irreducible elements of L. Assume that L is complete and distributive. Then a variety of different but equivalent conditions can be imposed on L to make F and G mutually inverse isomorphisms. These conditions include strong distributivity conditions involving arbitary disjunction, $\bigvee$, and arbitrary conjunction, $\bigwedge$. The results reduce in the Boolean case to well-known characterizations of powerset algebras as those Boolean algebras which are, equivalently, either complete and completely distributive or complete and atomic. A self-contained treatment of both the distributive and Boolean cases can be found in ILO2, Chapter 10.

6.3   Galois Connections from Binary Relations: Method I

Let $R \subseteq G \times M$ be a binary relation, do that (G, M, R) is a context. As we indicated in 2.4 the maps $^\triangleright : \wp(G) \to \wp(M)^\partial$ and $^\triangleleft : \wp(M)^\partial \to \wp(G)$ given by

$$A^\triangleright := \{\, m \in M \ : \ (\forall g \in A)\,(g, m) \in R \,\},$$
$$B^\triangleleft := \{\, g \in G \ : \ (\forall m \in B)\,(g, m) \in R \,\}$$

define a Galois connection. Two special instances are worth noting; both are of order-theoretic interest.

Example 1. Let P be a poset. Take the relation R as $\not\geqslant$. Then (Exercise 3.16) we have

$$A^\triangleright = P \setminus {\downarrow}A \quad \text{and} \quad A^\triangleleft = P \setminus {\uparrow}A$$

and $(^{\triangleright}, ^{\triangleleft})$ establishes a Galois connection between $\wp(P)$ and $\wp(P)^{\partial}$. Further, we have

$$A^{\triangleright\triangleleft} = P \setminus {\uparrow}(P \setminus {\downarrow}A) = P \setminus (P \setminus {\downarrow}A) = {\downarrow}A$$

(using the fact that $P \setminus {\downarrow}A$ is always an up-set). Dually, $A^{\triangleleft\triangleright} = {\uparrow}A$. $\supseteq$,

Example 2. Our choice of $\not\geqslant$ as the relation in the preceding example may have seemed a trifle perverse. Now consider instead the $\leqslant$ relation of a poset P. Then for $A, B \subseteq P$ we see that $A^{\triangleright}$ and $B^{\triangleleft}$ are respectively the sets of upper bounds of A and lower bounds of B:

$$A^u := \{\, y \in P \ : \ (\forall x \in A)\, x \leqslant y \,\},$$
$$B^{\ell} := \{\, y \in P \ : \ (\forall x \in B)\, y \leqslant x \,\}.$$

It is easy to see directly that $(^u, ^{\ell})$ is a Galois connection between $\wp(P)$ and $\wp(P)^{\partial}$:

$$A^u \supseteq B \Longleftrightarrow (\forall y \in B)((\forall x \in A)\, x \leqslant y)$$
$$\Longleftrightarrow (\forall x \in A)((\forall y \in B)\, y \geqslant x)$$
$$\Longleftrightarrow A \subseteq B^{\ell}.$$

6.4   Galois Connections and Algebras—A Fleeting Glimpse

Any algebra $(A; F)$ gives rise to a fundamental (order-reversing) Galois connection, via the maps Inv and Pol. These arise as the polar maps associated with the binary relation of preservation between the operations, F, and the finitary relations, R, on A. Specifically,

- Pol(R) denotes the family of all finitary functions $f \colon A^n \to A$ ($n \geqslant 1$) which preserve the relations in R (this is known as a **clone**);
- The set of all relations s which are invariant under all functions $f \in F$ is denoted by Inv(F).

For illustrative examples, see Mckenzie *et al.* [14], pp. 51–53.

6.5   Galois Connections by Sectioning

Galois maps can be viewed as unary operations. However many operations of importance in, for example, algebra and logic, are binary. Bringing such operations within the scope of the theory of Galois connections requires a well-worn trick: treat one argument as a parameter and the other as the variable on which $^{\triangleright}$ or $^{\triangleleft}$ is to act.

Just as Boolean algebras model classical propositional logic, so Heyting algebras model intuitionistic propositional logic. A distributive lattice L with $\perp$ and $\top$ is a **Heyting algebra** if, for every $a, b \in L$, there exists $a \to b \in L$ characterized by

$$c \leqslant (a \to b) \Longleftrightarrow a \wedge c \leqslant b.$$

Put another way, each map $\wedge_a \colon c \mapsto a \wedge c$ $(a \in L)$ has an upper adjoint, $b \mapsto (a \to b)$. Very many other examples of Galois connections arising by **sectioning** can be found in Chapters 4 and 9.

It is well known that, in a Heyting algebra,

$$a \to b = \max\{\, c \in L \, : \, a \wedge c \leqslant b \,\};$$

the existence of the maximum element in the set on the right-hand side is the condition for the existence of $a \to b$. This observation is not particular to this example. In 6.11 below, we give formulae for obtaining each of the maps $(^{\triangleright}, {}^{\triangleleft})$ in any Galois connection from the other.

6.6   Galois Connections from Binary Relations: Method II

It may be thought really tiresome that our way of constructing a Galois connection from a binary relation $R \subseteq G \times M$ has Galois maps between $\wp(G)$ and $\wp(M)^{\partial}$ and so involves an order reversal on $\wp(M)$. There is an alternative approach which avoids this, while retaining monotonicity of the Galois maps. Define maps $F_R \colon \wp(G) \to \wp(M)$ and $G_R \colon \wp(M) \to \wp(G)$ by

$$F_R(A) := \{\, m \in M \, : \, (\exists g \in A)\,(g,m) \in R \,\}, \text{ and}$$
$$G_R(B) := \{\, g \in G \, : \, (\forall m \in M)\,\big((g,m) \in R \Rightarrow m \in B\big) \,\},$$

for all $A \subseteq G$ and $B \subseteq M$. Then (a straightforward **Mini-exercise**)

(i) (F_R, G_R) is a Galois connection between $\wp(G)$ and $\wp(M)$;

(ii) Conversely, given any Galois connection (F, G) between the powersets $\wp(G)$ and $\wp(M)$, define $R \subseteq G \times M$ by

$$R := \{\, (g,m) \in G \times M \, : \, m \in F(\{g\}) \,\}.$$

Then $(F, G) = (F_R, G_R)$.

We have already seen in particular instances how a context $(G.M, R)$ or, in other parlance, a binary relation $R \subseteq G \times M$, gives rise to a complete lattice. We seek to expose the relationship between Galois connections and complete lattices in general. But first we need to have available the fundamental properties of Galois connections.

6.7   Galois Connections: Basic Properties

It is immediate from the definition that $(^{\triangleright}, {}^{\triangleleft})$ is a Galois connection between P and Q if and only if $({}^{\triangleleft}, {}^{\triangleright})$ is a Galois connection between Q^{∂} and P^{∂}. Consequently we have a 'buy one, get one free' situation, and only need below to prove one from each pair of mutually dual assertions. The names attached to properties (Gal1) and (Gal3) derive from their interpretation in the case that $\leqslant$ is the relation $=$.

Assume $(^\triangleright, {}^\triangleleft)$ is a Galois connection between P and Q. Then

(Gal1) **Cancellation Rule:** $p \leqslant p^{\triangleright\triangleleft}$ for all $p \in P$ and $q^{\triangleleft\triangleright} \leqslant q$ for all $q \in Q$.

(Gal2) **Monotonicity Rule:** $^\triangleright$ and $^\triangleleft$ are both monotone.

(Gal3) **Semi-inverse Rule:** $p^{\triangleright\triangleleft\triangleright} = p^\triangleright$ and $q^{\triangleleft\triangleright\triangleleft} = q^\triangleleft$ for all $p \in P$ and $q \in Q$.

Proof. Throughout, p, p_1, p_2 and q denote elements of P and Q, respectively.
(Gal) $\implies$ (Gal1):

$$p \in P \implies p^\triangleright \leqslant p^\triangleright \qquad \text{(by (po1))}$$
$$\iff p \leqslant p^{\triangleright\triangleleft} \qquad \text{(by (Gal) with } q = p^\triangleright).$$

(Gal) $\implies$ (Gal2):

$$p_1 \leqslant p_2 \implies p_1 \leqslant p_2^{\triangleright\triangleleft} \qquad \text{(by (Gal1), (po3))}$$
$$\iff p_1{}^\triangleright \leqslant p_2{}^\triangleright \qquad \text{(instance of (Gal)).}$$

(Gal) $\implies$ (Gal3):

$$p \in P \implies p^\triangleright \leqslant p^{\triangleright\triangleleft\triangleright} \qquad \text{(instance of (Gal1))}$$

and

$$p \in P \implies p^{\triangleright\triangleleft} \leqslant p^{\triangleright\triangleleft} \qquad \text{(instance of (po1))}$$
$$\iff p^{\triangleright\triangleleft\triangleright} \leqslant p^\triangleright \qquad \text{(instance of (Gal)).}$$

Hence, by (po2), $p^\triangleright = p^{\triangleright\triangleleft\triangleright}$. $\qquad\qquad\qquad\qquad\qquad\qquad\square$

Note that (Gal 3) may be stated as $\mathrm{id}_P \sqsubseteq {}^\triangleright \circ {}^\triangleleft$ (in $\langle P \to Q \rangle$) and $\mathrm{id}_Q \sqsupseteq {}^\triangleleft \circ {}^\triangleright$ (in $\langle Q \to P \rangle$). In the special case that P and Q carry the antichain orders, the implication (Gal) $\implies$ (Gal3) is just a trivial fact about bijective maps.

Those who hanker after results stated in maximum generality may wonder how far the theory of Galois connections can be taken if posets are replaced by pre-ordered sets. Antisymmetry of $\leqslant$,(po2), was used above in the derivation of (Gal3) from (Gal). This signals that we could not expect more than a smattering of rudimentary properties still to hold in the wider setting of pre-ordered sets.

6.8 $^\triangleright$ and $^\triangleleft$ Have Isomorphic Images

Property (Gal3) in 6.7 deserves closer scrutiny. What it says is that, given a Galois connection $(^\triangleright, {}^\triangleleft)$ between posets P and Q, the map $^\triangleleft \circ {}^\triangleright$ acts as the identity when restricted to elements of the form $p^\triangleright$ for $p \in P$, and dually.

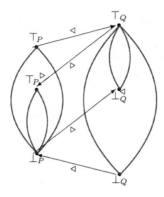

Fig. 11. Isomorphic images of Galois maps

Consequently the maps $^\triangleright$ and $^\triangleleft$ set up mutually inverse order-isomorphisms between the images

$$P^\triangleright := \{ p^\triangleright : p \in P \} \quad \text{and} \quad Q^\triangleleft := \{ q^\triangleleft : q \in Q \}$$

(recall Mini-exercise 3.8). Figure 11 illustrates the situation (for the case when P and Q have top and bottom elements, as they do in particular when these posets are complete lattices).

Look again at Example 1 in 6.3. In this case,

$$\wp(P)^\triangleright = \mathcal{U}(P)^\partial \quad \text{and} \quad (\wp(P)^\partial)^\triangleleft = \mathcal{O}(P),$$

and these are indeed isomorphic: recall 3.16. This example is atypical, in that not just the images but also the domains of $^\triangleright$ and $^\triangleleft$ (namely $\wp(P)$ and $\wp(P)^\partial$) are also order-isomorphic. Certainly Galois maps do not have to have isomorphic domains in general: indeed, as 6.3–6.4 confirm, this need not be the case.

6.9 Equivalent Definitions for Galois Connections

Let P and Q be posets and let $^\triangleright : P \to Q$ and $^\triangleleft : Q \to P$ maps. Then the following are equivalent:

  (i) $(^\triangleright, ^\triangleleft)$ is a Galois connection (that is, (Gal) holds) ;
  (ii) $^\triangleright$ and $^\triangleleft$ are monotone and $p \leqslant p^{\triangleright\triangleleft}$ and $q^{\triangleleft\triangleright} \leqslant q$ for all $p \in P$, $q \in Q$
      (that is, (Gal1) and (Gal2) are satisfied);
  (iii) $^\triangleright$ and $^\triangleleft$ satisfy the following:
      (a) $^\triangleright$ is monotone,
      (b) $q^{\triangleleft\triangleright} \leqslant q$ for all $q \in Q$,
      (c) $p^\triangleright \leqslant q \Longrightarrow p \leqslant q^\triangleleft$ for all $p \in P$ and $q \in Q$.

Proof. We have proved in 6.7 that (i) implies (ii). We now prove that (ii) implies (iii). For $p \in P$ and $q \in Q$ we have

$$p \leqslant q^{\triangleleft} \Longrightarrow p^{\triangleright} \leqslant q^{\triangleleft\triangleright} \qquad \text{(by (Gal2))}$$
$$\Longrightarrow p^{\triangleright} \leqslant q \qquad \text{(by (Gal1), (po3))}.$$

Finally, to prove that (iii) implies (i) we need to show that, when (a) and (b) in (iii) hold, then $p \leqslant q^{\triangleleft}$ implies $p^{\triangleright} \leqslant q$ for $p \in P$ and $q \in Q$. But

$$p \leqslant q^{\triangleleft} \Longrightarrow p^{\triangleright} \leqslant q^{\triangleleft\triangleright} \qquad \text{(by monotonicity of } {}^{\triangleright}\text{)}$$
$$\Longrightarrow p^{\triangleright} \leqslant q \qquad \text{(by (b) and (po3))},$$

as required.   □

A few comments on the relative merits of the alternative characterizations in 6.9 are desirable. The initial definition via (Gal) is the easiest to remember, but in handling Galois connections it is frequently the properties (Gal1) and (Gal2) that are invoked. The third, asymmetric, formulation is occasionally useful too; it obviously has a dual version (**Mini-exercise**: formulate this) which focusses on $\triangleleft$ instead of on $\triangleright$.

There are many more triangle-juggling games that can be played. Here is a sample.

Mini-exercise Assume that $({}^{\triangleright}, {}^{\triangleleft})$ is a Galois connection between P and Q. Prove the following are equivalent for $p_1, p_2 \in P$:

(a) $p_1^{\triangleright} \leqslant p_2^{\triangleleft}$;
(b) $p_1^{\triangleright\triangleleft} \leqslant p_2^{\triangleright\triangleleft}$;
(c) $p_1 \leqslant p_2^{\triangleright\triangleleft}$.

6.10   The Good (and Less Good) Behaviour of Galois Maps

One reason that Galois connections are so important is that they have preservation properties stronger than just monotonicity.

To motivate the general result, let us consider again Example 1 in 6.3. This example introduced the Galois connection on $\wp(P)$ associated with the binary relation $R_{\not\geqslant}$ of a given poset P. For any family $\{A_i\}_{i \in I}$ of subsets of P,

$$\bigcap_{i \in I} A_i^{\triangleright} = P \setminus \bigcup_{i \in I} {\downarrow} A_i = P \setminus {\downarrow}\left(\bigcup_{i \in I} A_i\right) = \left(\bigcup_{i \in I} A_i\right)^{\triangleright}$$

This tells us that ${}^{\triangleright} : \wp(P) \to \wp(P)^{\partial}$ preserves infs. Dually, $\triangleleft$ preserves sups. We cannot expect ${}^{\triangleright}$ to preserve sups or $\triangleleft$ to preserve infs. To see this, take P to be the poset $\{\bot, 0, 1\}$ as shown.

Then
$$\{0\}^{\triangleright} \cup \{1\}^{\triangleright} = (P \setminus \{\bot, 0\}) \cup (P \setminus \{\bot, 1\}) = \{1\} \cup \{0\}$$

whereas
$$(\{0\} \cap \{1\})^{\triangleright} = \emptyset^{\triangleright} = P.$$

In fact, the left and right adjoint maps of a Galois connection $(^{\triangleleft}, ^{\triangleright})$ formed by taking the polar maps associated with a binary relation R preserve infs and sups, respectively. What makes this happen is the universal quantifier in the definition of $^{\triangleright}$. Because of the reversal of the inclusion order on the domain of $^{\triangleleft}$, this map preserves sups rather than infs. Similarly, the existential and universal quantifiers in the definitions of F_R and G_R in 6.3 impart opposite preservation properties to these left and right adjoints.

In complete generality we have the following result:

Let $(^{\triangleright}, ^{\triangleleft})$ be a Galois connection between posets P and Q. Then $^{\triangleright}$ $(^{\triangleleft})$ preserves existing sups (infs) in the sense defined in 4.11.

Proof. We first define $\alpha := \bigvee_P S$ and show that $\alpha^{\triangleright}$ is *an* upper bound for $S^{\triangleright}$. By (Gal2),
$$(\forall s \in S)\, s \leqslant \alpha \implies (\forall s \in S)\, s^{\triangleright} \leqslant \alpha^{\triangleright}.$$

Now let q be any upper bound for $S^{\triangleright}$. Then
$$
\begin{aligned}
(\forall s \in S)\, s^{\triangleright} \leqslant q &\iff (\forall s \in S)\, s \leqslant q^{\triangleleft} && \text{(by (Gal))} \\
&\implies \bigvee_P S \leqslant q^{\triangleleft} && \text{(by definition of } \bigvee_P S\text{)} \\
&\iff \left(\bigvee_P S\right)^{\triangleright} \leqslant q && \text{(by (Gal))}.
\end{aligned}
$$

We conclude that $\alpha^{\triangleright}$ is the *least* upper bound of $S^{\triangleright}$.   □

6.11   Uniqueness of Adjoints: $^{\triangleright}$ from $^{\triangleleft}$ and $^{\triangleleft}$ from $^{\triangleright}$

We have seen that Galois connections, and equations and inequalities concerning them, come in pairs. We show next the important fact that in a Galois connection $(^{\triangleright}, ^{\triangleleft})$ between posets P and Q each of $^{\triangleright}$ and $^{\triangleleft}$ uniquely determines the other. This rests on the ultra-elementary fact that if a non-empty subset Q of a poset has a greatest element, then this greatest element provides $\bigvee_P Q$.

By (Gal), for any $p \in P$,
$$p^{\triangleright} \text{ is an upper bound for } S := \{\, q \in Q : p \leqslant q^{\triangleleft} \,\},$$

and $p^{\triangleright} \in S$, by (Gal3). Consequently
$$p^{\triangleright} = \min\{\, q \in Q : p \leqslant q^{\triangleleft} \,\}$$

and likewise
$$q^\triangleleft = \max\{\, p \in P : p^\triangleright \leqslant q \,\}.$$

(Recall that $\min S$, $\max S$ denote respectively the least, greatest elements of a subset S of a poset, when these exist.)

We have already met one instance of the latter formula, in 6.5. For another illustration, we return yet again to Example 1 in 6.3. For $A \in \mathscr{P}(P)$,

$$
\begin{aligned}
A^\triangleright \supseteq B &\iff P \setminus {\downarrow}A \supseteq {\uparrow}B && \text{(since the LHS is an up-set)} \\
&\iff {\downarrow}A \subseteq P \setminus {\uparrow}B && \text{(taking complements)} \\
&\iff A \subseteq P \setminus {\uparrow}B && \text{(since the RHS is a down-set)}
\end{aligned}
$$

and the largest set A satisfying the final condition is clearly $P \setminus {\uparrow}B$.

It is worth contrasting the formula for $^\triangleleft$ above with the formula in (iii) in the following exercise.

6.12 Exercise (Surjective and Injective Galois Maps)

Let $(^\triangleright, {}^\triangleleft)$ be a Galois connection. Prove that the following are equivalent:

(i) $^\triangleright$ is a surjective map;
(ii) $^\triangleleft$ is an injective map;
(iii) $q^\triangleleft = \max\{\, s \in P : s^\triangleright = q \,\}$;
(iv) $^\triangleleft \circ {}^\triangleright = \mathrm{id}_Q$.

(What we have here is what is known in order theory as a **retraction** of P onto Q with retraction map $^\triangleright$ and coretraction map $\triangleleft$. Retraction and coretraction pairs are however not Galois connections in general.)

Formulate also the dual statement.

6.13 A Look Ahead

Let P and Q be posets. A valuable strategy for showing that a map $F \colon P \to Q$ is inf-preserving is to show that it is the left adjoint of some Galois connection (F, G). We know from 6.11 that there is a unique candidate for G and from 6.10 that unless G preserves all existing sups then it cannot be a right adjoint. Monotonicity is also necessary (recall (Gal2)). This leads us to ask the question: does a monotone map preserving existing sups possess an upper adjoint (and dually)? We shall prove in 6.15 that the answer is affirmative provided the domain of the map is a complete lattice, so that *all* sups (and infs) exist. En route we give the order-theoretic version of the result we seek. The content of the assertion in (ii) is that $F^{-1}({\downarrow}q)$ has a *greatest* element; by the dual of 6.14 this inverse image is always a down-set.

6.14 Existence of Adjoints: A Technical Lemma

Let P and Q be posets and $F\colon P \to Q$ a monotone map. Then the following are equivalent:

(i) F is the lower adjoint in a Galois connection, that is, there exists a monotone map $F^{\sharp}\colon Q \to P$ such that both $F^{\sharp} \circ F \sqsupseteq \mathrm{id}_P$ and $F \circ F^{\sharp} \sqsubseteq \mathrm{id}_Q$;

(ii) for each $q \in Q$ there exists a (necessarily unique) $s \in P$ such that $F^{-1}(\downarrow q) = \downarrow s$.

Proof. Assume (i). We claim that $F^{-1}(\downarrow q) = \downarrow F^{\sharp}(q)$. We have

$$
\begin{aligned}
p \in F^{-1}(\downarrow q) &\iff F(p) \leqslant q \\
&\implies (F^{\sharp} \circ F)(p) \leqslant F^{\sharp}(q) \text{ (since } F^{\sharp} \text{ is monotone)} \\
&\implies p \leqslant F^{\sharp}(q) \qquad\quad \text{(from } F^{\sharp} \circ F \sqsupseteq \mathrm{id}_P \text{ \& (po3))} \\
&\iff p \in \downarrow F^{\sharp}(q).
\end{aligned}
$$

For the other direction, we have

$$
\begin{aligned}
p \in \downarrow F^{\sharp}(q) &\implies F(p) \leqslant (F \circ F^{\sharp})(q) \\
&\implies F(p) \leqslant q \\
&\implies p \in F^{-1}(\downarrow q).
\end{aligned}
$$

Therefore (ii) holds.

Now assume (ii). For each $q \in Q$ we have a unique element $s \in P$, depending on q, such that $F^{-1}(\downarrow q) = \downarrow s$. Define $F^{\sharp}(q) := s$. Restated, this means that

$$(\forall q \in Q)(\forall p \in P)\; F(p) \leqslant q \iff p \leqslant F^{\sharp}(q).$$

We now see that the pair $(F, F^{\sharp})$ is a Galois connection between P and Q, so that the properties in (i) follow from 6.7. □

6.15 Existence Theorem for Adjoints

Let P and Q be posets and $F\colon P \to Q$ be a map.

(i) Assume P is a complete lattice. Then F possesses an upper adjoint $F^{\sharp}$ (that is, $(F, F^{\sharp})$ is a Galois connection) if and only if F preserves arbitrary sups.

(ii) Assume Q is a complete lattice. Then G possesses a lower adjoint $G^{\flat}$ (that is, $(G^{\flat}, G)$ is a Galois connection) if and only if G preserves arbitrary infs.

Proof. We only need to prove (i). The forward implication comes from Proposition 6.10. For the backward implication, we shall use 6.14. Assume that F preserves arbitrary sups. Note first that F is monotone, by 4.11. Let $q \in Q$. We claim that

$$s := \bigvee{}_{P} \left\{\, p \in P\,:\, F(p) \leqslant q \,\right\} \left(= \bigvee{}_{P} F^{-1}(\downarrow q)\right)$$

is such that $F^{-1}(\downarrow q) = \downarrow s$. It is immediate that $F^{-1}(\downarrow q) \subseteq \downarrow s$. Since F preserves arbitrary joins,

$$F(s) = \bigvee_Q \left\{ F(p) \in P : F(p) \leqslant q \right\}$$

and hence $F(s) \leqslant q$. For any $p \in \downarrow s$, we have $F(p) \leqslant q$, because F is monotone and $\leqslant$ is transitive. Therefore $\downarrow s \subseteq F^{-1}(\downarrow q)$.   □

6.16   Postscript

Most of our concrete examples have been of Galois connections between power-sets and their duals. In the next section we complete the circle of ideas linking such Galois connections with closure operators, closure systems and complete lattices.

A different focus can be seen in Chapter 4. There the term **pair algebra**, is used for a binary relation $R \subseteq X \times Y$ such that

$$(x, y) \in R \iff F(x) \leqslant y \iff x \leqslant G(y),$$

with (F, G) a Galois connection between X and Y. Unlike the construction of a Galois connection via polars, this imposes restrictions on R: precisely those needed for the necessary sup- and inf-preservation properties to hold. There are however important cases in which a pair algebra arises from the restriction of a Galois connection from powersets to their singleton members.

7   Making Connections, Conceptually

We are now ready to wheel on the machinery of Galois connections and closure operators to develop the basic theory of concept lattices. In the opposite direction this provides a concrete framework within which to interpret the abstract ideas of the preceding section. We shall also thereby put in place the remaining connections between the notions in Figure 1.

7.1   From a Galois Connection to a Closure Operator

Once again, let $(^{\triangleright}, {}^{\triangleleft})$ be a Galois connection between posets P and Q. The composite maps $c := {}^{\triangleright} \circ {}^{\triangleleft}$ maps P to P and, by (Gal1)–(Gal3), it is a closure operator on P. Its closed sets are the members of

$$P_c := \left\{ p \in P : p^{\triangleright\triangleleft} = p \right\}$$

and, as a set, this is exactly $P^{\triangleright}$ (use (Gal3)). Note however that, while this is a complete lattice, suprema are *not* in general the restricted suprema from P; see 5.8. At this point we encounter a minor irritation. (Gal3) tells us that $q \geqslant q^{\triangleleft\triangleright}$ for all $q \in Q$. So the inequality is the wrong way round for $k := {}^{\triangleleft} \circ {}^{\triangleright}$ to be a closure operator (it is an **i**nterior operator instead). But we do have that

$$Q_k := \left\{ q \in Q : q^{\triangleleft\triangleright} = q \right\}$$

is a complete lattice, isomorphic to P_c, via the mutually inverse order-isomorphisms $\vartriangleleft$ and $\vartriangleright$. We see the closure operator, interior operator

By way of illustration, refer yet again to 6.3. In Example 1, we have $A^{\vartriangleright\vartriangleleft} = {\downarrow}A$, for $A \subseteq P$. So here the closure operator c is simply the down-set operator. Just as 5.8 leads us to expect, its image is indeed a complete lattice: it is just the family $\mathcal{O}(P)$ of down-sets, a complete lattice of sets. The up-set operator is also a closure operator on $\wp(P)$. But, when viewed on $\wp(P)^{\partial}$, it is an interior operator. All this fits with facts which are easy to establish directly.

Example 2 in 6.3, by contrast, shows that the theory of Galois connections may yield results which are not transparent. This theory tells us that $A \mapsto A^{u\ell}$ is a closure operator, c, on $\wp(P)$. The image of this closure operator is a complete lattice (by 5.8). In addition, this lattice contains the sets

$$\{p\}^{u\ell} = {\downarrow}p^{\ell} = {\downarrow}p \quad (\forall p \in P).$$

The map $p \mapsto {\downarrow}p$ is therefore an order-embedding of P into the complete lattice $c(P)$. This lattice is known as the **Dedekind–MacNeille completion** $\mathbf{DM}(P)$ of P. This construction is most familiar as one route by which the rationals can be extended to the reals (with $\pm\infty$ adjoined as top and bottom elements).

7.2 From a Closure Operator to a Galois Connection

In a somewhat contrived way we can recognize that every closure operator arises as the composite of the left and right maps of a Galois connection. To see this, let $c\colon P \to P$ be a closure operator. Define $Q := P_c$, $\vartriangleright\colon P \to P_c$ to be such that $p^{\vartriangleright} = c(p)$, and $\vartriangleleft\colon P_c \to P$ to be the inclusion map. Then $c = \vartriangleright \circ \vartriangleleft$.

7.3 Contexts and Concepts: Re-setting the Scene

Let us consider again a context (G, M, R). Let $(\vartriangleright, \vartriangleleft)$ be the associated Galois connection between $\wp(G)$ and $\wp(M)^{\partial}$:

$$A^{\vartriangleright} := \{\, m \in M : (\forall g \in A)\,(g, m) \in R\,\}, \quad \text{for } A \subseteq G,$$
$$B^{\vartriangleleft} := \{\, g \in G : (\forall m \in B)\,(g, m) \in R\,\} \quad \text{for } B \subseteq M.$$

We recall that, given $A \subseteq G$ and $B \subseteq M$, the pair $(A, B) \in \wp(G) \times \wp(M)^{\partial}$ is called a **concept** if

$$A = B^{\vartriangleleft} \quad \text{and} \quad A^{\vartriangleright} = B.$$

The set of all concepts is denoted by $\mathfrak{B}(G, M, R)$.

7.4 Ordering Concepts

The fewer objects we consider, the more shared attributes they are likely to possess. More precisely, for concepts $(A_1, B_1), (A_2, B_2)$,

$$
\begin{aligned}
A_1 \subseteq A_2 &\Longleftrightarrow A_1 \subseteq B_2^{\vartriangleleft} && ((A_2, B_2) \text{ a concept}) \\
&\Longleftrightarrow A_1^{\vartriangleright} \supseteq B_2 && (\text{by (Gal)}) \\
&\Longleftrightarrow B_1 \supseteq B_2 && ((A_1, B_1) \text{ a concept}).
\end{aligned}
$$

So we have:

$$(A_1, B_2) \leqslant (A_2, B_2) \text{ in } \wp(G) \times \wp(M)^\partial$$
$$\Longleftrightarrow A_1 \leqslant A_2 \text{ in } \wp(G) \Longleftrightarrow B_1 \leqslant B_2 \text{ in } \wp(M)^\partial.$$

As a by-product we have that, for concepts, $(A, B_1) = (A, B_2)$ if and only if $B_1 = B_2$ and, likewise, any concept is uniquely determined by its second component. Not surprising: recall 6.11.

7.5   Three for the Price of One: A Trinity of Complete Lattices

We define

$$\mathfrak{B}_G := \{\, A \in \wp(G) \ : \ (\exists B \subseteq M)\,(A, B) \in \mathfrak{B}(G, M, R) \,\},$$
$$\mathfrak{B}_M := \{\, B \in \wp(M)^\partial \ : \ (\exists A \subseteq G)\,(A, B) \in \mathfrak{B}(G, M, R) \,\}.$$

Note that 7.5 tells us that the natural projections $\pi_1 \colon \mathfrak{B}(G, M, R) \to \wp(G)$ and $\pi_2 \colon \mathfrak{B}(G, M, R) \to \wp(M)^\partial$ are order-embeddings.

The polar maps $^\triangleright$ and $^\triangleright$ take us to and fro between $\mathfrak{B}_G$ and $\mathfrak{B}_M$. Now 7.1 tells us immediately that, as sets,

$$\mathfrak{B}_G := c(\wp(G)), \quad \text{where } c := {}^\triangleleft \circ {}^\triangleright,$$
$$\mathfrak{B}_M := k(\wp(M)), \quad \text{where } k := {}^\triangleright \circ {}^\triangleleft,$$

and we have a commutative diagram

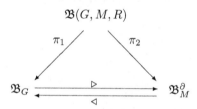

with the indicated maps setting up order-isomorphisms.

Further, 7.1 tells us that $\mathfrak{B}_G$ and $\mathfrak{B}_M$ are complete lattices. Explicitly we have

$$\bigwedge{}_{\mathfrak{B}_G} \{A_j\}_{j \in J} = \bigcap{}_{j \in J} A_j,$$
$$\bigvee{}_{\mathfrak{B}_G} \{A_j\}_{j \in J} = \left(\bigcup{}_{j \in J} A_j\right)^{\triangleright\triangleleft};$$
$$\bigvee{}_{\mathfrak{B}_M} \{B_j\}_{j \in J} = \bigcap{}_{j \in J} B_j,$$
$$\bigwedge{}_{\mathfrak{B}_M} \{\, B_j \ : \ j \in J \,\} = \left(\bigcup{}_{j \in J} B_j\right)^{\triangleleft\triangleright}.$$

This implies that the concepts $\mathfrak{B}(G, M, R)$ form a complete lattice, in which sups and infs are given by

$$\bigvee_{j \in J} (A_j, B_j) = \left(\left(\bigcup_{j \in J} A_j \right)^{\triangleright \triangleleft}, \bigcap_{j \in J} B_j \right),$$
$$\bigwedge_{j \in J} (A_j, B_j) = \left(\bigcap_{j \in J} A_j, \left(\bigcup_{j \in J} B_j \right)^{\triangleleft \triangleright} \right).$$

Our next objective is to see how the lattice $\mathfrak{B}(G, M, R)$ encodes G, M and R.

7.6   Manufacturing Concepts

For any sets A and B in G and M respectively, $(A^{\triangleright}, A^{\triangleright \triangleleft})$ and $(B^{\triangleleft \triangleright}, B^{\triangleleft})$ are concepts, by (Gal3). In particular, for each $g \in G$ and $m \in M$,

$$\gamma(g) := (g^{\triangleright \triangleleft}, g^{\triangleright}) \quad \text{and} \quad \mu(m) := (m^{\triangleleft}, m^{\triangleleft \triangleright})$$

are concepts, and we have maps $\gamma \colon G \to \mathfrak{B}(G, M, R)$ and $\mu \colon M \to \mathfrak{B}(G, M, R)$. Further, we can capture the relation R using these maps, as follows:

$$
\begin{aligned}
(g, m) \in R &\Longleftrightarrow g \in m^{\triangleleft} && \text{(definition of } ^{\triangleleft}) \\
&\Longleftrightarrow \{g\} \subseteq m^{\triangleleft} && \text{(set notation)} \\
&\Longleftrightarrow g^{\triangleright \triangleleft} \subseteq m^{\triangleleft \triangleright \triangleleft} && \text{(by (Gal2) for} \Rightarrow, \text{(Gal1) for} \Leftarrow) \\
&\Longleftrightarrow g^{\triangleright \triangleleft} \subseteq m^{\triangleleft} && \text{(by (Gal1))} \\
&\Longleftrightarrow \gamma(g) \subseteq \mu(m) && \text{(see 7.3).}
\end{aligned}
$$

7.7   Density: Generating all Concepts via γ or μ

For all $(A, B) \in \mathfrak{B}(G, M, R)$,

$$\pi_2 \left(\bigvee \gamma(A) \right) = \pi_2 \left(\bigvee_{g \in A} \gamma(g) \right) = \bigvee_{g \in A} g^{\triangleright} = \bigcap_{g \in A} g^{\triangleright} = \left(\bigcap_{g \in A} g \right)^{\triangleright} = A^{\triangleright} = B.$$

This shows that every element of $\mathfrak{B}_M$ is obtained by taking intersections of sets of elements of the form $g^{\triangleright}$. Dually, every element of $\mathfrak{B}_G$ is obtained by taking unions of sets of elements of the form $m^{\triangleleft}$. Expressed another way, this says that every element of $\mathfrak{B}(G, M, R)$ is generated from $\gamma(G)$ by taking sups and from $\mu(M)$ by taking infs. Note that the empty sup and inf are allowed here. They give, respectively, $\perp$ and $\top$ in $\mathfrak{B}(G, M, R)$ (recall 4.7).

We label $\mathfrak{B}(G, M, R)$ by giving a label g to each concept $\gamma(g)$ and a label m to each concept $\mu(m)$. Then to find $g^{\triangleright}$ we simply look for those M-labels in $\uparrow g$, and to find $m^{\triangleleft}$ we look for the G-labels in $\downarrow m$.

Now look back to the example in 2.2. By taking intersections of sets of the form $Q^{\triangleleft}$ for Q ranging over the output states and of the form $p^{\triangleright}$ for p ranging over the input states we were generating all the concepts, in two ways. What we drew in Figure 3 was, of course, the concept lattice, labelled in this way.

Table 2. Contexts for Mini-exercise 7.7

	A	B	C
a	×	×	×
b		×	×
c			×

(i)

	A	B	C
a		×	×
b	×		×
c	×	×	

(ii)

Mini-exercise Draw and label the concept lattices for the contexts shown in Table 2 (take care over the top and bottom elements):

The contexts in the preceding Mini-exercise are small enough for the concept lattices to be obtained quite easily. However for contexts which are sufficiently large for concept lattices to be of genuine benefit in analysing them, a systematic method for obtaining the lattices becomes necessary. Chapter 3 of ILO2 presents an algorithm for obtaining all the concepts of a context.

7.8   From a Complete Lattice to a Concept Lattice

To complete our circle of ideas, we note that the properties we have derived in the preceding subsections characterize concept lattices. Assume that L is a complete lattice and that $\gamma \colon G \to L$ and $\mu \colon M \to L$ are mappings such that $\gamma(G)$ is sup-dense and $\mu(M)$ is inf-dense in L and $R \subseteq G \times M$ is such that $(g, m) \in R$ if and only if $\gamma(g) \leqslant \mu(m)$. Then it can be proved that $\mathfrak{B}(G, M, R) \cong L$. We refer to ILO2, Chapter 3 or Ganter & Wille [8], pp. 21–22.

Given any complete lattice L, we can choose $G = M = L$ and $R = R_{\leqslant}$, with $\gamma = \mu = \mathrm{id}_L$. The conditions of the preceding paragraph are clearly satisfied and hence $L \cong \mathfrak{B}(L, L, R_{\leqslant})$. We conclude that *every* complete lattice can be regarded as a concept lattice.

Taking a poset P rather than a complete lattice L, $\mathfrak{B}(L, L, R_{\leqslant})$, or more conveniently its image under π_1 (recall 7.5) yields the Dedekind–MacNeille completion of P. The well-known fact that P order-embeds into its completion as a subset which is both sup- and inf-dense is an instance of general properties of concept lattices. On the other hand, the other important feature of the embedding, *viz.* that it preserves all sups and infs which exist in P, depends on properties particular to this context. For further details see ILO2, Chapter 7.

7.9   The Case for the Defence

A criticism that is sometimes levelled at concept analysis is that it lacks depth. As we have presented it here, it interacts in an illuminating way with Galois connections, closure operators and complete lattices on a theoretical level. But does it go deeper than pretty diagrams? Certainly good diagrams of big concept lattices reveal dependencies and relationships not visible at all from a context table: a nice example is provided in Ganter & Wille [8], pp. 28–30, concerning political groupings of more than 100 developing countries. The evangelists claim with justification that the analysis of data via the associated concept lattices goes beyond this. As a good piece of propaganda we draw attention to the analysis of binary relations to be found in Ganter & Wille [8], pp. 86–90. A list of properties of such relations is presented. Some of these (symmetric, reflexive, transitive, for example) appear frequently in mathematical and computer science contexts. Others have arisen in more detailed studies of relations, for example within measurement theory (see Schader [17]). Examples are connex (xRy or yRx for all $x \neq y$) and negatively transitive (xRy true and yRz false imply xRz false, for all x, y, z). The objective is to expose which implications between the various properties are universally valid and which are not. This is done by seeking a set of 'test' examples, on small sets, and taking these as the objects for a context, and a list of properties as the attributes. The objective is to set up this context in such a way that the lists of properties and attributes are, in a sense which can be made precise, complete and irredundant. This is achieved by the theory developed by Wille *et al.* for attribute exploration. The resulting concept lattice (Ganter & Wille [8]), p. 90) displays the implications between the properties and the examples which witness the non-implications. Concept analysis allows the measurement theorists' empirical treatment to be illuminated by an approach which is systematic and backed up by theory.

7.10   Summing Up

We have shown

- how every closure system is a complete lattice and how every complete lattice can be realized concretely as a closure system (5.4 and 5.6);
- how closure operators give rise to closure systems and vice versa (5.9);
- how Galois connections give rise to closure operators, and vice versa (7.1 and 7.2);
- how every context, or equivalently every binary relation, gives rise to a Galois connection via its polars (2.4).
- how every context, or equivalently every binary relation, gives rise to a complete lattice, its concept lattice (7.5);
- how every complete lattice can be realized as a concept lattice (7.8).

All the arrows in Figure 1 are now in place, some of them by transitivity.

8   The Existence of Fixed Points

Fixed points, especially as models of recursive programs, are so ubiquitous in computer science that it would be gratuitous to include here any discussion of their provenance. The study of fixed points may be regarded as having two aspects: (i) the existence of fixed points and (ii) calculus with fixed points (and prefix points). Since so many computational models have an underlying partial order, posets of suitably special kinds provide a natural setting in which to investigate fixed point theory. Here we concentrate on the existence of fixed points and highlight in particular two famous fixed point theorems:

- the Knaster–Tarski Fixed Point Theorem, in complete lattices, asserting that every monotone endofunction on a complete lattice has least and greatest fixed points;
- the Fixed Point Theorem for CPOs (with which the name of Park is frequently associated), asserting that a monotone endofunction on a CPO has a least fixed point, and which has a very simple, algorithmic, proof if F is continuous, in the sense of 8.10 below.

Lassez *et al.* [11] delve into the rather obscure and complicated history of the various fixed point theorems and their attributions.

8.1   Fixed Points and Least Fixed Points: Definitions

For completeness we record the following well-known definitions. Let P be a poset and let $F\colon P \to P$ be a map. We say $x \in P$ is a **fixed point** of F if $F(x) = x$, and a **prefix point** if $F(x) \leqslant x$. The set of all fixed points (prefix points) of F is denoted by $\operatorname{fix} F$ ($\operatorname{pre} F$); both carry the inherited order. The least element of $\operatorname{fix} F$, when it exists, is denoted by $\mu(F)$. In computational contexts it is usually the *least* fixed point of a map $F\colon P \to P$ which is the one sought. Very frequently the poset P is some CPO of partial maps $S_{\perp} \multimap S_{\perp}$ on a flat CPO $S_{\perp}$. For example, that favourite example of a recursive definition, the factorial function **fact**, arises as the least fixed point of the map $\pi \mapsto \overline{\pi}$, for π a partial map on the natural numbers (including 0), where $\overline{\pi}(0) = 1$ and $\overline{\pi}(k) = k\pi(k-1)$ for $k > 0$.

8.2   Characterizing Least Fixed Points via Least Prefix Points

Let P be a poset and let F be a monotone endofunction on P. Assume that F possesses a least prefix point $\mu_{*}(F)$. Then the least fixed point $\mu(F)$ exists and satisfies

$$F(x) \leqslant x \Rightarrow \mu(F) \leqslant x \qquad \text{(the \textbf{Induction Rule})}.$$

Indeed, $\mu(F) = \mu_{*}(F)$. This is the case whenever P is a complete lattice.

Proof. Assume that $\mu_{*}(F)$ exists. We want to show that $\mu_{*}(F) \in \operatorname{fix} F$. Since $\operatorname{fix} F \subseteq \operatorname{pre} F$ we must then have $\mu(F) = \mu_{*}(F)$.

As $\mu_{*}(F) \in \operatorname{pre} F$ by definition, we have $F(\mu_{*}(F)) \leqslant \mu_{*}(F)$. Applying the monotone map F we get $F(F(\mu_{*}(F))) \leqslant F(\mu_{*}(F))$, so that $F(\mu_{*}(F)) \in \operatorname{pre} F$. Since $\mu_{*}(F)$ is the *least* element of $\operatorname{pre} F$ we therefore have $\mu_{*}(F) \leqslant F(\mu_{*}(F))$. Hence, $\mu_{*}(F)$ is indeed a fixed point of F.

In case P is a complete lattice there is an obvious candidate for $\mu_{*}(F)$, namely $\bigwedge \operatorname{pre} F$. It follows easily from the monotonicity of F that $\bigwedge \operatorname{pre} F \in \operatorname{pre} F$.   □

8.3   The Knaster–Tarski Fixed Point Theorem

Let P be a complete lattice and $F\colon P \to P$ a monotone map. Then

$$\bigwedge \{\, x \in P \,:\, F(x) \leqslant x \,\}$$

is the least fixed point of F. Dually, F has a greatest fixed point, given by

$$\bigvee \{\, x \in P \,:\, F(x) \geqslant x \,\}.$$

Proof. This is immediate from 8.2 and its dual.   □

8.4   Exercise

Let P be a complete lattice and let $F\colon P \to P$ be a monotone map. Stated in the terminology of this section, the Prefix Lemma in 5.8 says that $\operatorname{pre} F$ is a complete lattice. Prove that $\operatorname{fix} F$ is a complete lattice. Specifically, for X a subset of P, define

$$Y := \{\, y \in P \,:\, (\forall x \in X)\, y \leqslant F(y) \leqslant x \,\}$$

and let $\alpha := \bigvee_P Y$. Prove that $\alpha = \bigwedge_{\operatorname{fix} F} X$ and then appeal to 4.9.

8.5   Exercise

Let P be a complete lattice and define $F\colon \wp(P) \to \wp(P)$ by $F\colon A \mapsto {\downarrow}\bigvee A$. Show that F is monotone and that $\operatorname{fix} F \cong P$. (Consequently, *every* complete lattice is, up to isomorphism, a lattice of fixed points—this last fact is actually a triviality (why?).)

8.6   From Complete Lattices to CPOs

The Knaster–Tarski Theorem is mathematically slick, but it has certain deficiencies as regards computer science. First of all, in a semantic domain a top element will represent an overdetermined, or inconsistent, state, and topless models are often to be preferred. Also, the Knaster–Tarski proof identifies a fixed point, but does not supply an algorithm for computing it.

Let P be a poset with $\bot$ and let $F\colon P \to P$ be a monotone endofunction. Then a natural way to try to construct a fixed point is to consider the sequence $\bot, F(\bot), F(F(\bot)), \ldots$ and to hope that 'in the limit' we arrive at a fixed point. To make this precise, we let, recursively, $x_0 = \bot$ and $x_{n+1} := F(x_n)$ for $n \geqslant 0$. Then an easy proof by induction shows that we have a chain

$$x_0 \leqslant x_1 \leqslant \ldots \leqslant x_n \leqslant x_{n+1} \leqslant \ldots,$$

each member of which is half way to being a fixed point. Make the assumptions

(a) $\alpha := \bigvee \{\, x_n \,:\, n = 0, 1, 2, \ldots \,\}$ exists, and
(b) $F(\bigvee C) = \bigvee F(C)$ for any non-empty chain C.

Then

$$F(\alpha) = \bigvee_{n \geq 0} F(x_n) \qquad \text{(by (b), with } C \text{ as } \{x_n\})$$

$$= \bigvee_{n \geq 0} x_{n+1} \qquad \text{(by definition of } x_{n+1})$$

$$= \bigvee_{n \geq 0} x_n \qquad \text{(since } x_0 = \bot)$$

$$= \alpha \qquad \text{(by definition of } \alpha).$$

So our assumptions allow us to assert that F has a fixed point. Note that infima play no role in the argument. The condition on F is stronger than monotonicity (recall 4.11); the condition on P is strictly weaker than lattice completeness (look at $\mathbb{N}_\bot$). This suggests that we should look at posets in which suprema exist for all chains (the supremum of the empty chain supplies $\bot$; see 4.7). It turns out to be no more restrictive, and in some ways more natural, to consider sets more general than chains.

8.7   A Sense of Direction

In the context of information orderings, an element is frequently the supremum of approximations below it: partial maps approximating total maps, finite strings approximating infinite strings, and so on. Take the example of a map $F \colon \mathbb{N} \to \mathbb{N}$. We may obtain F as the supremum of the partial maps which are the restrictions of F to finite subsets of $\mathbb{N}$. These approximations are mutually compatible, in the sense that any two of them give consistent information about F at any $k \in \mathbb{N}$ at which both are defined. Conversely, suppose we have a family D of elements of $\mathbb{N} \dashrightarrow \mathbb{N}$ with the property that, for any pair π_1 and π_2 in D, we have $\pi \in D$ with $\pi_1 \leqslant \pi$ and $\pi_2 \leqslant \pi$ in the ordering of $\mathbb{N} \dashrightarrow \mathbb{N}$ (so π extends both of π_1, π_2). Then the union of the graphs of the elements of D defines a partial map, which is $\bigvee D$.

Let S be a non-empty subset of a poset P. Then S is said to be **directed** if each pair of elements $x, y \in S$ has an upper bound lying in S. An easy induction shows that S is directed if and only if, for each non-empty finite subset F of S, there exists $z \in S$ such that $z \geqslant y$ for all $y \in F$, that is, $z \in F^u$. This definition should be compared with another which naturally arises in computer science contexts, namely that of a **consistent** set: S is consistent if for every non-empty finite subset F of S there exists $z \in P$ such that $z \, in \, F^u$.

Clearly any non-empty chain in a poset is directed. In a poset P satisfying (ACC) (as defined in 4.10) a non-empty subset D of P is directed if and only if D has a greatest element. We leave the easy verification as a **Mini-exercise**.

8.8   Exercise (Sups and Directed Sups Related)

Let P be a complete lattice. Assume that $\emptyset \neq S \subseteq P$. Prove that

$$\bigvee S = \bigsqcup \{ \bigvee F : \emptyset \neq F \subseteq S, \ F \text{ finite} \}.$$

8.9   CPOs

We say that a poset P is a **CPO** (an abbreviation for **complete partially ordered set**) if

(i) P has a bottom element, $\perp$,

(ii) $\bigvee D$ exists for each directed subset D of P.

We shall write $\bigsqcup D$ in place of $\bigvee D$ when D is directed, as a reminder of the directedness.

An appropriate setting for the fixed point existence proof in 8.6 can now be seen to be a CPO. The need for $\perp$ in that proof is clear. In other contexts posets in which directed sups exist, but which do not necessarily possess $\perp$, are important. Often, such a poset is called a **dcpo** (and a CPO given the name **dcppo**, the extra 'p' signifying 'pointed').

Here are some simple examples.

(1) Any complete lattice is a CPO.

(2) Let S be an antichain. Then $S_\perp$ is a CPO. In particular, $\mathbb{N}_\perp$ is a CPO. Indeed, this example is a motivation for the introduction of the lifting construction. More generally, any poset P with $\perp$ satisfying (ACC) is a CPO.

(3) Any closure system which is closed under directed unions is a CPO, with $\bigsqcup$ coinciding with $\bigcup$ (recall reflat-sets).

Our examples justify the introduction of directed sets. However it turns out, highly non-trivially, that a poset with $\perp$ is a CPO if and only if it is **chain-complete** (that is, $\bigsqcup C$ exists for every non-empty chain C).

8.10   Directed Sets and Continuity

It is natural to regard $\bigvee S$ as the limit of S precisely when S is directed. Accordingly a map F between CPOs preserving directed sups is called **continuous**: this means that $\bigsqcup F(D) = F(\bigsqcup D)$ for any directed set D. The following facts are elementary: if D is a directed subset in P and if F is monotone then the set $F(D)$ is directed and $\bigsqcup F(D) \leqslant F(\bigsqcup D)$ (see 4.11). Also, since $\{x, y\}$ is directed when $x \leqslant y$, it is easily seen that every continuous function is monotone.

Mini-exercise Define $F \colon \wp(\mathbb{N}) \to \wp(\mathbb{N})$ by

$$F(S) = \begin{cases} \varnothing & \text{if } S \text{ is finite,} \\ \mathbb{N} & \text{otherwise.} \end{cases}$$

Prove that F is monotone but fails to preserve the (directed) supremum of the family of finite subsets of $\mathbb{N}$. So not every monotone map is continuous.

Mini-exercise Prove that a monotone endofunction $F\colon P \to P$ is continuous whenever P satisfies (ACC).

The topological connotations of continuity are more than superficial analogies. The symbiotic relationship between topology and order has been extensively researched and exploited; see Gierz *et al.* [9], and Abramsky & Jung [2] and the references therein.

8.11   New CPOs from Old

A significant virtue of CPOs as a class in which to work is that it has excellent closure properties. Given CPOs P and Q the following are also CPOs:

$$(P \mathbin{\dot{\cup}} Q)_\perp, \qquad P \times Q, \qquad [P \to Q];$$

Here $[P \to Q]$ denotes the set of of all continuous maps from P to Q, with the customary pointwise ordering. There is an alternative to the **separated sum** above. We can also form the **coalesced sum**) by taking $P \cup Q$ and identifying $\perp_P$ and $\perp_Q$. The proofs that all these constructions do indeed yield CPOs are notation chases, of varying difficulty. See ILO2, Chapter 8, for guidance on the harder ones.

8.12   Fixed Point Theorem for a Continuous Function on a CPO

With the appropriate terminology in place we can record as a theorem what we proved in 8.6, and claim a bit more.

Let P be a CPO, let $F\colon P \to P$ be a continuous map and let

$$\alpha := \bigsqcup\nolimits_{n \geqslant 0} F^n(\perp).$$

Then the least fixed point $\mu(F)$ exists and equals α. **Mini-exercise**: prove the leastness assertion.

8.13   From Continuity to Monotonicity

Continuity is often an undesirably strong assumption. Relaxing continuity to monotonicity is feasible but requires more powerful mathematical machinery. One approach builds on the elementary proof in 8.6, using ordinals and transfinite induction. Several other approaches to proving that any monotonic endofunction on a CPO has a least fixed point have been devised, most notably the recent elegant proof obtained by D. Pataraia. This proof is presented, with Pataraia's permission, in ILO2. Unlike earlier proofs it does not rely on first proving the independently interesting result that a fixed point exists for any increasing endofunction on a CPO (F being **increasing** if $x \leqslant F(x)$ for all x). The method we adopt below is much simpler, but necessitates calling on a property of CPOs which we shall take as an axiom: it says that any CPO has a maximal element.

8.14   An Assumption: Zorn's Lemma (ZL), CPO Form

Let P be a CPO. Then $\operatorname{Max} P \neq \varnothing$.

To indicate that this is very plausible, we consider first the special case that the CPO P satisfies (ACC). Let $x_0 = \bot$. If $x_0 \notin \operatorname{Max} P$, pick $x_1 > x_0$. If $x_1 \notin \operatorname{Max} P$, pick $x_2 > x_1$, and so on. This process terminates, at a maximal element, because we cannot have an infinite strictly ascending chain in P; the maximal element is the largest element of our chain, and necessarily its supremum. Thus for CPOs satisfying (ACC) we cannot climb for ever strictly upwards via a chain. For a general CPO the existence of suprema for directed sets, and in particular for non-empty chains, suggests that every non-empty chain is 'capped' by a maximal element of P. Those content to accept (ZL) for CPOs may without detriment skip over the next paragraph.

Replacing the informal 'and so on' above by a rigorous argument requires invocation of what is known as the Axiom of Choice. This famous optional add-on to ZF set theory is one of a cluster of equivalent statements. One of these is Zorn's Lemma in the form it is most often stated, another is (ZL) for CPOs. We do not wish to digress to present this background material here. A self-contained account of the equivalences most useful in the context of posets and lattices is given in ILO2, Chapter 10. Mathematics, and in particular order theory and algebra, are considerably impoverished if we deny ourselves (AC) and (ZL). However it can be proved that a set-theoretic world in which the *negation* of (AC) operates is not internally inconsistent.

8.15   The Fixed Point Theorem
for a Monotone Endofunction on a CPO

Assume that P is a CPO and that $F \colon P \to P$ is monotone. Then F has a least fixed point.

Proof. (with (ZL); due to A.W. Roscoe, [15], p. 175) Let

$$Q := \{\, x \in P : x \leqslant F(x) \ \& \ (\forall y \in \operatorname{fix} F)\, x \leqslant y \,\}.$$

It is important to realize that in the definition of Q we are not claiming that F has a fixed point: The second clause in the definition is satisfied vacuously if $\operatorname{fix} F = \emptyset$. It serves to ensure that a fixed point of F in Q is the *least* fixed point of F.

We first claim that Q is a CPO (in the inherited order). Certainly $\bot_P \in Q$. Now let $D \subseteq Q$ be directed and denote $\bigsqcup_P D$ by α. Then, because $F(D)$ is directed and $\bigsqcup F(D) \leqslant F(\bigsqcup D)$ (recall the remarks in 8.9),

$$
\begin{aligned}
x \in D &\Longrightarrow x \leqslant F(x) && \text{(by the definition of } Q) \\
&\Longrightarrow x \leqslant \bigsqcup F(D) && \text{(the join existing as } F(D) \text{ is directed)} \\
&\Longrightarrow x \leqslant F\big(\bigsqcup D\big) = F(\alpha) && \text{(by (po3))).}
\end{aligned}
$$

Hence $\alpha \leqslant F(\alpha)$. Also

$$y \in F \implies (\forall x \in D)\, x \leqslant y \qquad \text{(since } D \subseteq Q\text{)}$$
$$\implies \alpha \leqslant y \qquad \text{(by definition of } \alpha\text{)}.$$

Therefore $\alpha \in Q$. This proves that Q is a CPO. (Compare this with the proof in 5.6).

By (ZL) for CPOs, Q has a maximal element, β say. By definition of Q we have $\beta \leqslant F(\beta)$. Clearly

(a) $F(\beta) \leqslant F(F(\beta))$ (since F is monotone), and

(b) $y \in \text{fix}\, F \implies \beta \leqslant y$, so that $F(\beta) \leqslant F(y) = y$.

Hence $F(\beta) \in Q$, so maximality of β gives $\beta = F(\beta)$. By the definition of Q, we must have $\beta = \mu(F)$.   □

8.16 Exercise

This exercise indicates a proof that the set of fixed points $\text{fix}\, F$ of a monotone endofunction F on a CPO P is itself a CPO; compare with 8.4).)

Let D be a directed set in $\text{fix}\, F$ and let $\alpha := \bigsqcup D$. Prove, with the aid of 8.2, that F maps $\uparrow\!\alpha$ to $\uparrow\!\alpha$. Deduce that G, the restriction of F to $\uparrow\!\alpha$, has a least fixed point, which is given by $\bigsqcup_{\text{fix}\, F} D$.

8.17 Exercise

We have used (ZL) for CPOs to prove the fixed point theorem in 8.15. This exercise gives another application of (ZL) within order theory. Let X be a set. Let

$$\mathcal{S} := \{\, R_< \in \wp(X \times X) : \, < \text{ is a strict partial order on } X \,\}.$$

   (i) Prove that $\mathcal{S}$ is a CPO.

  (ii) Prove that any maximal element of $\mathcal{S}$ is a linear order (that is, it makes X a chain).

 (iii) Deduce that any strict partial order is contained in a strict linear order.

(This is hard. Part (iii) is a well-known result from order theory (Szpilrajn's Theorem) whose proof requires Zorn's Lemma in some form.

8.18 Concluding Remarks

The theorems in 8.3 and 8.15 are in a sense optimal. The following converses exist. Both are difficult to prove; see Markowsky [13].

   (i) Let L be a lattice and assume that every monotone endofunction $F \colon L \to L$ has a fixed point. Then L is a complete lattice.

  (ii) Let P be a poset and assume that every monotone endofunction $F \colon P \to P$ has a least fixed point. Then P is a CPO.

9 Speaking Categorically

9.1 Categories

It is uncommon for a class of structures of a given type to be introduced without an associated class of structure-preserving maps following hard on its heels. Posets + monotone maps is one example. Others are complete lattices + maps preserving $\bigvee$ and $\bigwedge$, groups + group homomorphisms, topological spaces + continuous maps, etc., etc., etc. The recognition that an appropriate unit for study is a class of structures all of the same type, together with a class of structure-preserving maps between these, leads to category theory. Computer scientists have embraced this with such enthusiasm that it seems unnecessary to repeat the formal definitions here. Loosely, a **category** $\mathcal{C}$ consists of a collection $\mathrm{Obj}(C)$ of **objects** and a collection $\mathrm{Arr}(\mathcal{C})$ of **arrows** (also called **morphisms**). Each arrow $f \in \mathrm{Arr}(\mathcal{C})$ has a source $A \in \mathrm{Obj}(\mathcal{C})$ and a target B in $\mathrm{Obj}(\mathcal{C})$, and there is an operation of composition of arrows satisfying a rudimentary set of conditions demanding

(cat1) the existence of an **identity arrow** $\mathrm{id}_A \colon A \to A$ for each object A,

(cat2) arrows can be composed in the same way that maps between sets can be.

The set of arrows in $\mathcal{C}$ with source A and target B will be denoted by $\mathrm{Arr}(A, B)$. Commuting diagrams of objects and arrows expressing properties of categories and *their* structure-preserving maps (called **functors**) form the basis of category theory. Natural constructs within categories—products, limits, and so on—can be described in terms of commuting diagrams, with the philosophy 'everything is an arrow' perhaps sometimes taken to excess.

Every poset (or more generally pre-ordered set) P gives rise to a category we shall call $\mathcal{C}_p$: the objects are just the elements of P, and, for $p, q \in P$, there is an arrow from p to q if and only if $p \leqslant q$, and just such arrow; so we identify arrows with inequality statements. The existence of the arrow id_p for each p is just the reflexivity condition, (po1); the composition law on arrows is guaranteed by transitivity, (po3). Figure 12 indicates the interpretations in categories $\mathcal{C}_P$ of some fundamental categorical notions.

To illustrate, we consider the most complicated of these correlations: Galois connections as adjunctions. An adjunction is a symmetric relation between categories $\mathcal{A}$ and $\mathcal{X}$ set up by a pair of covariant functors $F \colon \mathcal{A} \to \mathcal{X}$ and $G \colon \mathcal{X} \to \mathcal{A}$ which are 'mutually inverse'. Explicitly, suppose that for each $A \in \mathcal{A}$ and each $X \in \mathcal{X}$ there are arrows

$$e_A \colon A \to GF(A) \quad \text{and} \quad \varepsilon_X \colon X \to FG(X).$$

It is said that $\langle F, G, e, \varepsilon \rangle$ sets up an **adjunction** between $\mathcal{A}$ and $\mathcal{X}$ if:

(adj1) for $u \colon A \to B$ in $\mathcal{A}$ and $\varphi \colon X \to Y$ in $\mathcal{X}$, the two square diagrams in Figure 13 commute;

P	$\mathcal{C}_P$
$\bot$	initial object
$\top$	terminal object
dual poset	opposite category
product	product
disjoint sum	coproduct
inf	limit
sup	colimit
monotone map	functor
order-embedding	monomorphism
Galois connection	adjunction
$(\forall p)\, p \leqslant p^{\triangleright\triangleleft}$	unit
$(\forall q)\, q^{\triangleleft\triangleright} \leqslant q$	counit
closure operator	monad

Fig. 12. From posets to categories

(adj2) for $A \in \mathcal{A}$ and $X \in \mathcal{X}$ there is a bijection between $\mathrm{Arr}_{\mathcal{A}}(A, G(X))$ and $\mathrm{Arr}_{\mathcal{X}}(X, F(A))$ associating u and φ as given in the two commuting triangle diagrams of Figure 13.

Of course, $\mathrm{id}_{\mathcal{A}}\colon \mathcal{A} \to \mathcal{A}$ and $GF\colon \mathcal{A} \to \mathcal{A}$ are covariant functors and the left-hand square of Figure 13 says precisely that $e\colon \mathrm{id}_{\mathcal{A}} \to GF$ is a **natural transformation**. Similarly for the right-hand square.

All this may look complicated to beginners. But in the special case of a Galois connection $(^{\triangleright}, ^{\triangleleft})$ between posets P and Q it just sums up the basic calculus for Galois connections: put

$$
\begin{array}{lll}
objects & arrows & functors \\
A := p_1 & u := p_1 \leqslant p_2 & F := {}^{\triangleright} \\
B := p_2 & F := q_1 \leqslant q_2 & G := {}^{\triangleleft} \\
X := q_1 & e_A := p_1 \leqslant p_1^{\triangleright\triangleleft} & \\
Y := q_2 & \varepsilon_X := q_1 \geqslant q_1^{\triangleleft\triangleright} &
\end{array}
$$

and relabel the diagrams!

Mini-exercise (For those more at home with categories than with posets)

(i) Convince yourself that disjoint sums in P correspond to coproducts in $\mathcal{C}_P$.
(ii) Convince yourself that the notion of supremum in a poset P corresponds to the notion of colimit in the category $\mathcal{C}_P$.

All this is well-trodden territory, mapped out in Maclane [12], for example. Less familiar is the way in which Table 9.1 can be extended by observing that the

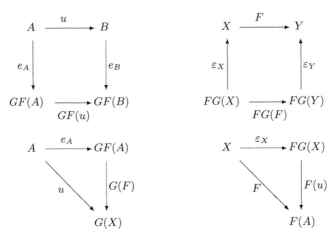

Fig. 13. An adjunction

poset concepts of prefix points and postfix points, match up in the categorical setting with algebras and coalgebras. Fixed point calculus in posets lifts to a fixed point calculus in categories whose calculational rules (the **Fusion Rule**, and so on) are highly useful in the context of coalgebras; Backhouse *et al.* [3] show how the transition from posets to categories can be made.

There is another way in which adjunctions enter into the theory of lattices. A particularly profitable kind of adjunction between categories $\mathcal{A}$ and $\mathcal{X}$ is one in which the categories $\mathcal{A}$ and $\mathcal{X}$ are of different types and we are able to use the adjunction as a tool for studying $\mathcal{A}$ by exploiting its properties as a category and the way that the adjunction mirrors these in $\mathcal{X}$. The most famous such adjunctions are dual adjunctions (set up by contravariant rather than covariant functors) and are dual equivalences rather than just adjunctions. They include those which set up dualities between

Boolean algebras	and	Boolean spaces	(Stone)
Finite distributive lattices	and	Finite posets	(Birkhoff; see 6.2)
Distributive lattices	and	Priestley spaces	(Priestley)

in each case with a natural class of morphisms. For the second of these, the functor from finite posets to finite distributive lattices is, on objects, simply the map taking a poset P to its up-set lattice $\mathcal{U}(P)$. Because of the way that distributive lattices with additional operations provide algebraic models for them, these dualities give a useful means of studying logics of various kinds; for a recent survey see Davey & Priestley [6].

References

1. C. J. Aarts. Galois connections presented calculationally. Master's thesis, Eindhoven University of Technology, 1992. 52
2. Samson Abramsky and Achim Jung. Domain theory. In *Handbook of Logic in Computer Science*, volume 3, pages 1–168. Oxford University Press, 1994. 21, 72
3. R. Backhouse, M. Bijsterveld, R. van Geldrop, and J. van der Woude. Categorical fixed point rules. http://www.win.tue.nl/pm/papers/abstract.htmlcatfixpnt, 1995. 77
4. G. Birkhoff. *Lattice Theory*. American Mathematical Society, third edition, 1967. 52
5. C. Brink and I. M. Rewitzky. Power structures and program semantics. Monograph preprint, 1997. 43
6. B. A. Davey and H. A. Priestley. Distributive lattices and duality. In G. Grätzer, editor, *General Lattice Theory*, pages 499–517. Birkhäuser Verlag, second edition, 1998. 43, 77
7. A. Edelat. Domains for computation, physics and exact real arithmetic. *Bulletin of Symbolic Logic*, 3:401–452, 1997. 30
8. B. Ganter and R. Wille. *Formal Concept Analysis*. Springer-Verlag, 1999. 26, 52, 66, 67
9. G. Gierz, K. H. Hofmann, K. Keimel, J. D. Lawson, M. W. Mislove, and D. S. Scott. *A Compendium of Continuous Lattices*. Springer-Verlag, 1980. 21, 52, 72
10. B. Jónsson. A survey of Boolean algebras with operators. In I. G. Rosenberg and G. Sabidussi, editors, *Algebras and Orders*, volume 389 of *ASI Series C*, pages 239–286. NATO, 1993. 53
11. J.-L. Lassez, V. L. Nguyen, and E. A. Sonenberg. Fixedpoint theorems and semantics: A folk tale. *Information Processing Letters*, 14:112–116, 1982. 68
12. Saunders Mac Lane. *Categories for the Working Mathematician*. Springer-Verlag, 1971. 76
13. G. Markowsky. Chain-complete posets and directed sets with applications. *Algebra Universalis*, 6:53–68, 1976. 74
14. R. N. McKenzie, G. F. McNulty, and W. E. Taylor. *Algebras, Lattices, Varieties*, volume I. Wadsworth & Brooks, 1987. 54
15. A. W. Roscoe. *The Theory and Practice of Concurrency*. Prentice-Hall International, 1997. 73
16. J. J. M. M. Rutten. A calculus of transition systems: Towards universal coalgebra. In A. Ponse, M. de Rijke, and Y. Venema, editors, *Modal Logic and Process Algebra*, volume 53 of *CSLI Lecture Notes*, pages 231–256. CSLI Publications, Stanford, 1995. 27
17. M. Schader, editor. *Analysing and Modelling Data and Knowledge*. Springer-Verlag, 1992. 67

Chapter 3
Algebras and Coalgebras

Peter Aczel

Departments of Mathematics and Computer Science, University of Manchester

1 Introduction

This chapter introduces the notion of a final coalgebra relative to an endofunctor and corecursion on a final coalgebra via the paradigm examples of a particular kind of tree. The notion is dual to the more familiar notion of an initial algebra and structural recursion on an initial algebra. The chapter starts with the paradigm syntactic examples of initial algebras, the term algebras.

Given a signature of function symbols the variable free terms form an inductively generated set and determine an initial algebra. Given a set of colours and a set of index sets there is a notion of tree, whose nodes are labelled with colours and where the children of any node are indexed by the elements of an index set. The set of such trees form a final coalgebra. These will be our paradigm examples. We will use these examples to introduce the ideas of recursion and corecursion. We will allow function symbols to be infinitary and allow index sets to be infinite so as to get a greater level of generality. We will enrich these examples by allowing terms and trees to depend on variables which can be substituted for. Substitution into terms and trees give us good examples of recursion and corecursion.

It will be convenient to introduce some notation and definitions. We shall make use of class terminology—however, readers familiar only with basic set theory will be able to understand the majority of this chapter. Classes are collections of objects (of the set theoretic universe) that may not themselves be objects of the set theoretic universe. The sets are just those classes that are such objects. Much of the set theoretic notation can usefully be carried over to classes.

If A is a set and X is a class then we write $f : A \to X$ if f is a function with domain A and range a subset of X. We let X^A be the class of such functions, which is a set when X is a set. Also, if $\mathcal{A}$ is a set of sets we write $f : \in\mathcal{A} \to X$ if $f : A \to X$ for some set A in $\mathcal{A}$ and write $X^{\in\mathcal{A}}$ for the class of all such functions, which is also a set when X is. Finally, for each class X, we let $Pow(X)$ be the class of all subsets of X, which is the powerset of X when X is a set.

If A, B are classes then A is a subclass of B, written $A \subseteq B$, if every object in A is an object in B. Classes are extensional; i.e. if classes A, B are subclasses of each other then they are equal. If A, B are classes then a subclass F of $A \times B$ is an **operator** $F : A \to B$ if for every $a \in A$ there is a unique $b \in B$ such that $(a, b) \in F$. This unique b will be written $F(a)$.

R. Backhouse et al. (Eds.): Algebraic and Coalgebraic Methods ..., LNCS 2297, pp. 79–88, 2002.

Let *Set* be the class of all sets. This class is partially ordered by the subset relation $\subseteq$. So we may naturally call *Set*, with $\subseteq$, a **poclass**. We call an operator $F : Set \rightarrow Set$ a **set operator**. It is a **monotone set operator** if, for all sets a, b, $a \subseteq b$ implies that $F(a) \subseteq F(b)$. A monotone set operator F is a **bounded set operator** if there is a set B of sets such that whenever $x \in F(a)$ there is a set $b \in B$ and a function $f : b \rightarrow a$ such that $x \in F(ran(f))$. One can prove

Theorem 1 *Every bounded set operator has a least fixed point.*

2   Terms

2.1   Variable-Free Terms

We assume given a signature consisting of a set sym of (function) **symbols**, each symbol p having an **arity** $|p|$, which can be any set. In the case when p is an ordinary predicate calculus function symbol its arity is $|p| = \{1, \ldots, n\}$ for some natural number n. When $n = 0$ so that $|p|$ is the empty set then p is an ordinary predicate calculus constant symbol.

Given the set sym we introduce the set T_{sym} as the set of objects called **terms** inductively generated using the following rule.

– If $p \in$ sym and t_i is a term for each $i \in |p|$ then $p[t_i]_{i \in |p|}$ is a term.

When $|p| = \{1, \ldots, n\}$ then $p[t_i]_{i \in |p|}$ can be written $p(t_1, \ldots, t_n)$ and just p when $n = 0$ as usual in the syntax of the predicate calculus. Note that there has to be at least one such symbol p, with $|p| = \emptyset$, in order to get generated any terms at all.

It is implicit in this inductive specification of the set of terms that every term must have been generated using the rule from previously generated terms. This is made explicit as the following principle.

Structural Induction *Let T be any set of terms such that for all $p \in$ sym,*

$$\text{if } t_i \in T \text{ for all } i \in |p| \text{ then } p[t_i]_{i \in |p|} \in T.$$

Then every term is in T.

It is also implicit in the inductive specification of terms that every term has the form $p[t_i]_{i \in |p|}$ in at most one way, so that the symbol p and the subterm t_i for each $i \in |p|$ are uniquely determined. This is made explicit as follows.

Structural Recursion *Let A be a set and let $\alpha^p : A^{|p|} \rightarrow A$ for each $p \in$ sym. Then there is a unique function $\pi : T_{\mathsf{sym}} \rightarrow A$ such that if $p \in$ sym and $t_i \in T_{\mathsf{sym}}$ for $i \in |p|$ then*

$$\pi(p[t_i]_{i \in |p|}) = \alpha^p(\{\pi(t_i)\}_{i \in |p|}).$$

Following the ideas of universal algebra we combine a set A with functions $\alpha^p :$ $A^{|p|} \to A$ for each $p \in$ sym to form a **sym-algebra** $\mathcal{A} = (A, \{\alpha^p\}_{p \in \text{sym}})$, where the notation $\{\alpha^p\}_{p \in \text{sym}}$ means the **family** of functions α^p indexed by $p \in$ sym. Moreover the set of terms can be made into a sym-algebra in a natural way. We let $\mathcal{T}_{\text{sym}} = (T_{\text{sym}}, \{\tau^p\}_{p \in \text{sym}})$, where for each $p \in$ sym we let $\tau^p : T_{\text{sym}}^{|p|} \to T_{\text{sym}}$ be given by

$$\tau^p(\{t_i\}_{i \in |p|}) = p[t_i]_{i \in |p|}.$$

This is the **term-algebra** for sym. By introducing the natural notion of homomorphism between sym-algebras we can express the principle of structural recursion on terms very concisely as follows.

For every sym-algebra $\mathcal{A}$ there is a unique homomorphism $\mathcal{T}_{\text{sym}} \to \mathcal{A}$.

This requires the following definition.

Definition 2 *If $\mathcal{A} = (A, \{\alpha^p\}_{p \in \text{sym}})$ and $\mathcal{B} = (B, \{\beta^p\}_{p \in \text{sym}})$ are sym-algebras then a function $f : A \to B$ is a **homomorphism** $f : \mathcal{A} \to \mathcal{B}$ if whenever $p \in$ sym and $a_i \in A$ for $i \in |p|$ then*

$$f(\alpha^p(\{a_i\}_{i \in |p|})) = \beta^p(\{f(a_i)\}_{i \in |p|}).$$

Exercise 3 *Show that the sym-algebras form the objects of a category, sym-Alg, whose maps are the homomorphisms between sym-algebras. Show that the principle of structural recursion gives a characterisation of the term algebra as the unique up to isomorphism initial sym-algebra, that is, the term algebra is an initial object of the category sym-Alg.*

2.2   Terms as Set Theoretical Objects

So far we have not needed to state exactly what object a term is. It will now be convenient to do so. We will take the term $p[t_i]_{i \in |p|}$ to be $(1, (p, \{t_i\}_{i \in |p|}))$. Then the inductive specification of T_{sym} becomes the definition of T_{sym} as the least fixed point of the bounded set operator F_{sym}, where for each set X we let

$$F_{\text{sym}}(X) = \{1\} \times \Sigma_{p \in \text{sym}} X^{|p|}.$$

This set operator can be made into a functor on the category SET as follows. If $f : A \to B$ in SET then we define $F_{\text{sym}}(f) : F_{\text{sym}}(A) \to F_{\text{sym}}(B)$ by

$$F_{\text{sym}}(f)((1, (p, \{a_i\}_{i \in |p|}))) = (1, (p, \{f(a_i)\}_{i \in |p|}),$$

if $p \in$ sym and $a_i \in A$ for $i \in |p|$.

Exercise 4 *Show that F_{sym} is indeed an endofunctor on SET.*

Any sym-algebra $\mathcal{A} = (A, \{\alpha^p\}_{p \in \text{sym}})$ can be made into a F_{sym}-algebra (A, α) by defining $\alpha : F(A) \to A$ so that

$$\alpha((1, (p, \{a_i\}_{i \in |p|}))) = \alpha^p(\{a_i\}_{i \in |p|})$$

for all $p \in \mathsf{sym}$ and $a_i \in A$ for $i \in |p|$. In particular the term-algebra $\mathcal{T}_{\mathsf{sym}} = (T_{\mathsf{sym}}, \{\tau^p\}_{p \in \mathsf{sym}})$ becomes the F_{sym}-algebra (T_{sym}, τ) where

$$\tau((1, (p, \{t_i\}_{i \in |p|}))) = p[t_i]_{i \in |p|}$$

for all $p \in \mathsf{sym}$ and $t_i \in T_{\mathsf{sym}}$ for $i \in |p|$. Moreover it is easy to see that every F_{sym}-algebra arises in a unique way from some sym-algebra.

Exercise 5 *Given* sym-*algebras* $\mathcal{A}$ *and* $\mathcal{B}$ *with corresponding* F_{sym}-*algebras* (A, α) *and* (B, β) *show that a function* $f : A \to B$ *is a map* $f : \mathcal{A} \to \mathcal{B}$ *of* sym-*Alg iff it is a map* $f : (A, \alpha) \to (B, \beta)$ *of* F_{sym}-*Alg.*

It follows from this exercise that the two categories, the category of sym-algebras and the category of F_{sym}-algebras, are essentially the same. From now on we will usually prefer to work with the notion of F_{sym}-algebra.

Summary

Associated with the set T_{sym} of variable-free terms we can associate the endofunctor $F_{\mathsf{sym}} : \mathsf{SET} \to \mathsf{SET}$. We can make the set T_{sym} into the F_{sym}-algebra $\mathcal{T}_{\mathsf{sym}} = (T_{\mathsf{sym}}, \tau)$, which can be characterised up to isomorphism as the initial F_{sym}-algebra; i.e. an initial object in the category F_{sym}-Alg. This characterisation encapsulates the method of definition by structural recursion for defining functions on the set T_{sym}.

2.3   Terms with Variables

So far we have only considered the set of variable-free terms for sym. We now want to consider terms that may have variables occurring in them. We introduce a flexible setting where any object x can be used as a (name of a) variable and will write $\langle x \rangle$ for the variable as a term. So for each set X we let $T_{\mathsf{sym}}(X)$ be the set of terms generated using the following rules.

- If $p \in \mathsf{sym}$ and t_i is a term for each $i \in |p|$ then $p[t_i]_{i \in |p|}$ is a term.
- If $x \in X$ then $\langle x \rangle$ is a term.

As before it is implicit in this inductive specification that every term is either generated from previously generated terms using the first rule or else is generated using the second rule. It is also implicit that which rule is used is uniquely determined, so that no term can have both the forms $p[t_i]_{i \in |p|}$ and $\langle x \rangle$ and if it has the first form then p and the t_i are uniquely determined and if it has the second form then x is uniquely determined. As with variable-free terms there is a principle of structural induction for $T_{\mathsf{sym}}(X)$. But it will be more important for us to focus on the principle of structural recursion on $T_{\mathsf{sym}}(X)$. First note that we can form the F_{sym}-algebra $\mathcal{T}_{\mathsf{sym}}(X) = (T_{\mathsf{sym}}(X), \tau)$, where $\tau : F(T_{\mathsf{sym}}(X)) \to T_{\mathsf{sym}}(X)$ is defined using the same equation as used when defining $\tau : F_{\mathsf{sym}}(T_{\mathsf{sym}}) \to T_{\mathsf{sym}}$ in $\mathcal{T}_{\mathsf{sym}} = (T_{\mathsf{sym}}, \tau)$. Also let $\eta_X : X \to T_{\mathsf{sym}}(X)$ be given by $\eta_X(x) = \langle x \rangle$ for all $x \in X$.

Structural Recursion *Let $\mathcal{A} = (A, \alpha)$ be an F_{sym}-algebra and let $\alpha_X : X \to A$. Then there is a unique map $\pi : T_{\mathsf{sym}}(X) \to \mathcal{A}$ of F_{sym}-Alg such that $\pi \circ \eta_X = \alpha_X$.*

In universal algebra terminology this principle characterises this term algebra up to isomorphism as the free **sym**-algebra with set X of (names of) generators. Once again we can capture these ideas using categorical terminology.

2.4   Initial (F, X)-Algebras

We generalise our previous discussion to any endofunctor F on an arbitrary category $\mathcal{C}$.

Definition 6 *Let $F : \mathcal{C} \to \mathcal{C}$ be an endofunctor on $\mathcal{C}$ and let X be an object of $\mathcal{C}$. An (F, X)-**algebra** is a pair $(\mathcal{A}, \alpha_X)$ where $\mathcal{A} = (A, \alpha)$ is an F-algebra and $\alpha_X : X \to A$ in $\mathcal{C}$. The category (F, X)-Alg of (F, X)-algebras is defined by defining a map $f : A \to B$ in $\mathcal{C}$ to be a map $f : (\mathcal{A}, \alpha_X) \to (\mathcal{B}, \beta_X)$ of (F, X)-Alg if $f : \mathcal{A} \to \mathcal{B}$ and $f \circ \alpha_X = \beta_X$.*

We can thus express the principle in category theoretic terminology as characterising $T_{\mathsf{sym}}(X)$ as forming an initial (F_{sym}, X)-algebra. Here such an algebra is a pair $(\mathcal{A}, \alpha_X)$ where $\mathcal{A} = (A, \alpha)$ is a F_{sym}-algebra and $\alpha_X : X \to A$.

Exercise 7 *Show that the above principle of structural recursion can be reformulated to state that $(T_{\mathsf{sym}}(X), \eta_X)$ is an initial object of the category (F_{sym}, X)-Alg of (F_{sym}, X)-algebras.*

2.5   Substitution

One of the main roles in syntax for a variable is to act as a marker of places in an expression where certain other expressions can be inserted to replace the variable. The operation of making such replacements is called a substitution. Given arbitrary sets X and Y we may use any function $s : X \to T_{\mathsf{sym}}(Y)$ to determine a substitution function $\hat{s} : T_{\mathsf{sym}}(X) \to T_{\mathsf{sym}}(Y)$. The idea is that if $t \in T_{\mathsf{sym}}(X)$ then $\hat{s}(t)$ should be the result of simultaneously replacing each occurrence of $\langle x \rangle$ in t by $s(x)$. We characterise this function as follows.

Substitution *If $s : X \to T_{\mathsf{sym}}(Y)$ then there is a unique homomorphism $\hat{s} : T_{\mathsf{sym}}(X) \to T_{\mathsf{sym}}(Y)$ such that $\hat{s} \circ \eta_X = s$. This is just the unique homomorphism from the initial (F_{sym}, X)-algebra $(T_{\mathsf{sym}}(X), \eta_X)$ to the (F_{sym}, X)-algebra $(T_{\mathsf{sym}}(Y), s)$.*

The following result generalises substitution on terms to our abstract setting.

Theorem 8 (Substitution Theorem) *Let F be an endofunctor on $\mathcal{C}$ and for each object X of $\mathcal{C}$ let $(T(X), \eta_X)$ be an initial object of (F, X)-Alg. Then for each $s : X \to T(Y)$ there is a unique map $\hat{s} : T(X) \to T(Y)$ of F-Alg such that $\hat{s} \circ \eta_X = s$.*

Proof. We define $\hat{s} : T(X) \to T(Y)$ to be the unique map $\hat{s} : (T(X), \eta_X) \to (T(Y), s)$ in (F, X)-Alg.

Definition 9 *Given an endofunctor F on a category $\mathcal{C}$, we call an assignment of an (F, X)-algebra $(T(X), \eta_X)$ to each object X of $\mathcal{C}$ a **substitution system** if for each map $s : X \to T(Y)$ there is a unique map $\hat{s} : T(X) \to T(Y)$ of F-Alg such that $\hat{s} \circ \eta_X = s$.*

3   Trees

3.1   Variable-Free Trees

We assume given a set col of **colours** and a set ind of **index sets**. We will be concerned with labelled trees of the following kind. As usual a tree will have a root node and associated with each node will be a set of its children nodes and there will be an edge from the node to each of its children nodes. A node that has no children nodes is called a leaf node. Each node of the tree will be labelled with a colour. The edges from a node to its children will be labelled with indices from an index set so that each index from the index set is used exactly once. We let $T_{(\mathsf{col}, \mathsf{ind})}$ be the set of such trees.

Each node of a tree determines the subtree consisting of the node itself as root and its descendents; i.e. its children, their children and so on. If t is a tree and i labels an edge from the root of t to one of its children then let t_i be the subtree determined by that child. If I is the index set of such indices and p is the colour of the root node then we will write

$$t = p[t_i]_{i \in I}.$$

Note the special case when the index set I is empty, when the tree consists only of its root node and we can write just $t = p$.

A finite or infinite sequence of nodes of a tree is called a **branch** of the tree if the sequence starts with the root node, continues with one of its children if there are any, followed by one of its children if there are any and so on, either ending with a leaf node when the branch is finite or else continuing indefinately when the branch is infinite. If a tree has no infinite branches then the tree is **well-founded**.

3.2   Representing Terms as Well-Founded Trees

From the notation that we have been using it should be clear how each term of T_{sym} can be represented as a well-founded tree of $T_{(\mathsf{col}, \mathsf{ind})}$ provided that every symbol $p \in \mathsf{sym}$ is a colour and $|p| \in \mathsf{ind}$ for each $p \in \mathsf{sym}$. But note that not all such trees will represent terms. In fact with this representation the set T_{sym} can be characterised as the least fixpoint of a function. Let $F : Pow(T_{(\mathsf{col}, \mathsf{ind})}) \to Pow(T_{(\mathsf{col}, \mathsf{ind})})$ where, for each set $T \subseteq T_{(\mathsf{col}, \mathsf{ind})}$, $F(T)$ is the set of trees

$$p[t_i]_{i \in |p|}$$

where $p \in \mathsf{col}$ and $t_i \in T$ for each $i \in |p|$. Note that F is a monotone function on the complete lattice $Pow(T_{(\mathsf{col}, \mathsf{ind})})$ so that the least fixed point does exist.

3.3   Corecursion

This is a method for specifying trees. More precisely it is a method to define a function π that associates a tree $\pi(a)$ with each $a \in A$, when given functions $\alpha_{\mathsf{col}} : A \to \mathsf{col}$ and $\alpha_{\mathsf{ind}} : A \to A^{\in \mathsf{ind}}$. The idea is that $\alpha_{\mathsf{col}}(a)$ should be the colour of $\pi(a)$ and if $\alpha_{\mathsf{ind}}(a) = \{a_i\}_{i \in I}$, where $I \in \mathsf{ind}$, then $\pi(a_i)$ should be the immediate subtree of $\pi(a)$ whose root is the child of the root of $\pi(a)$ given by index $i \in I$. So the nodes and edges of each tree $\pi(a)$ are built up starting with its root, the root's children, their children and so on, so that in the limit the whole tree $\pi(a)$ gets determined.

Corecursion Lemma *Let $\alpha_{\mathsf{col}} : A \to \mathsf{col}$ and $\alpha_{\mathsf{ind}} : A \to A^{\in \mathsf{ind}}$. Then there is a unique function $\pi : A \to T_{(\mathsf{col},\mathsf{ind})}$ such that for all $a \in A$*

$$\pi(a) = p[\pi(a_i)]_{i \in I}$$

where $\alpha_{\mathsf{col}}(a) = p$ and $\alpha_{\mathsf{ind}}(a) = \{a_i\}_{i \in I} \in A^I$.

As with structural recursion for terms we can package this result in a convenient way. We call a triple $\mathcal{A} = (A, \alpha_{\mathsf{col}}, \alpha_{\mathsf{ind}})$, as in the lemma, a $(\mathsf{col}, \mathsf{ind})$-**coalgebra**, and given another such triple $\mathcal{B} = (B, \beta_{\mathsf{col}}, \beta_{\mathsf{ind}})$ a **homomorphism** $f : \mathcal{A} \to \mathcal{B}$ is a function $f : A \to B$ such that for each $a \in A$, if $\alpha_{\mathsf{ind}}(a) = \{a_i\}_{i \in I}$, then

$$\beta_{\mathsf{col}}(f(a)) = \alpha_{\mathsf{col}}(a) \quad \text{and} \quad \beta_{\mathsf{ind}}(f(a)) = \{f(a_i)\}_{i \in I}.$$

The set $T_{(\mathsf{col},\mathsf{ind})}$ naturally forms a $(\mathsf{col}, \mathsf{ind})$-coalgebra

$$\mathcal{T}_{(\mathsf{col},\mathsf{ind})} = (T_{(\mathsf{col},\mathsf{ind})}, \tau_{\mathsf{col}}, \tau_{\mathsf{ind}})$$

where if $t = p[t_i]_{i \in I} \in T_{(\mathsf{col},\mathsf{ind})}$ then

$$\tau_{\mathsf{col}}(t) = p \quad \text{and} \quad \tau_{\mathsf{ind}}(t) = \{t_i\}_{i \in I}.$$

Exercise 10 *Show that the $(\mathsf{col}, \mathsf{ind})$-coalgebras and the homomorphisms between them form a category and show that the corecursion lemma characterises $\mathcal{T}_{(\mathsf{col},\mathsf{ind})}$ as the unique up to isomorphism final object in this category.*

3.4   Set Theoretical Representation of Trees

The set of well-founded trees can be represented in a similar way to the way we have used to represent terms. But this method will not work in axiomatic set theory for all trees including the non-well-founded trees unless we modify the set theory to allow for non-well-founded sets, see [1]. Another approach that keeps to the standard axiomatic set theory is to make a subtle change to the way that ordered pairs and functions are represented in set theory to define a modified bounded set operator having a largest fixed point that represents the set $T_{(\mathsf{col},\mathsf{sym})}$, see [3].

Here we follow yet another approach. We represent trees as functions $t : S \to \{1\} \times$ col where S is a non-empty prefix-closed set of finite sequences of indices. The elements of S are to be the nodes of the tree, with the empty sequence () being the root of the tree and if a sequence σ is a node and an index i labels an edge from that node to one of its children then $\sigma^\frown(i)$ is that child. So, for each node σ, $\{i \mid \sigma^\frown(i) \in S\}$ must be an index set; i.e. a set in ind. If $t(\sigma) = (1,p)$ then the node σ has the colour p.

Proposition 11 *Let $t : S \to \{1\} \times$ col be a tree. If p is a colour and $t_i : S_i \to \{1\} \times$ col is a tree for each $i \in I$, where I is an index set in ind, then $t = p[t_i]_{i \in I}$ iff*
both

$$S = \{()\} \cup \{(i)^\frown\sigma \mid i \in I \ \& \ \sigma \in S_i\}$$

and

$$\begin{cases} t(()) & = (1,p) \\ t((i)^\frown\sigma) = t_i(\sigma) \ \text{for all } i \in I \ \& \ \sigma \in S_i. \end{cases}$$

We have seen that the set of trees, $T_{(\mathsf{sym},\mathsf{col})}$, can be made into the $(\mathsf{col},\mathsf{ind})$-coalgebra $T_{(\mathsf{col},\mathsf{ind})}$. We now show how to represent $(\mathsf{col},\mathsf{ind})$-coalgebras as $F_{(\mathsf{col},\mathsf{ind})}$-coalgebras for a suitable endofunctor $F_{(\mathsf{col},\mathsf{ind})} : \mathsf{SET} \to \mathsf{SET}$. For each set A let

$$F_{(\mathsf{col},\mathsf{ind})}(A) = \{1\} \times (\mathsf{col} \times (A^{\in\mathsf{ind}}))$$

and if $f : A \to B$ in SET let $F_{(\mathsf{col},\mathsf{ind})}(f) : F_{(\mathsf{col},\mathsf{ind})}(A) \to F_{(\mathsf{col},\mathsf{ind})}(B)$ where, if $p \in$ col and $\{a_i\}_{i \in I} \in A^{\in\mathsf{ind}}$ then

$$F_{(\mathsf{col},\mathsf{ind})}(f)((1, (p, \{a_i\}_{i \in I}))) = (1, (p, \{f(a_i)\}_{i \in I})).$$

Given a $(\mathsf{col},\mathsf{ind})$-coalgebra $\mathcal{A} = (A, \alpha_{\mathsf{col}}, \alpha_{\mathsf{ind}})$ define $\alpha : A \to F_{(\mathsf{col},\mathsf{ind})}(A)$ as follows. If $a \in A$ let

$$\alpha(a) = (1, (\alpha_{\mathsf{col}}(a), \alpha_{\mathsf{ind}}(a))).$$

So we get an $F_{(\mathsf{col},\mathsf{ind})}$-coalgebra (A, α). In particular the $(\mathsf{col},\mathsf{ind})$-coalgebra $T_{(\mathsf{col},\mathsf{ind})} = (T_{(\mathsf{col},\mathsf{ind})}, \tau_{\mathsf{col}}, \tau_{\mathsf{ind}})$ determines the $F_{(\mathsf{col},\mathsf{ind})}$-coalgebra $(T_{(\mathsf{col},\mathsf{ind})}, \tau)$, where for each $t \in T_{(\mathsf{col},\mathsf{ind})}$, if $t = p[t_i]_{i \in I}$ then

$$\tau(t) = (1, (p, \{t_i\}_{i \in I})).$$

Moreover every $F_{(\mathsf{col},\mathsf{ind})}$-coalgebra (A, α) arises uniquely in this way. This means that instead of working with the category of $(\mathsf{col},\mathsf{ind})$-coalgebras we can work with the equivalent category of $F_{(\mathsf{col},\mathsf{ind})}$-coalgebras.

Summary

We can associate with the set $T_{(\mathsf{col},\mathsf{ind})}$ of trees the endofunctor $F_{(\mathsf{col},\mathsf{ind})} : \mathsf{SET} \to \mathsf{SET}$. We can make the set into an $F_{(\mathsf{col},\mathsf{ind})}$-coalgebra $T_{(\mathsf{col},\mathsf{ind})} = (T_{(\mathsf{col},\mathsf{ind})}, \tau)$, which can be characterised up to isomorphism as the final $F_{(\mathsf{col},\mathsf{ind})}$-coalgebra; i.e. a final object in the category $F_{(\mathsf{col},\mathsf{ind})}$-CoAlg. This characterisation encapsulates the method of definition by corecursion for defining functions into the set $T_{(\mathsf{col},\mathsf{ind})}$.

3.5 Trees with Variables

As with terms that may involve variables we want to extend our notion of tree to one that may involve variables; i.e. we want to allow trees to have a new kind of leaf node, called a **variable node** that is labelled with a (name of) a variable. As before we will write a tree whose root node is of the standard kind as $p[t_i]_{i \in I}$. Such a tree will be called a **colour tree**. We now also have trees that only consist of their root node that is also a leaf node of the new kind, labelled with a (name of) a variable x. Such a tree will be written $\langle x \rangle$ and called a **variable tree**. For each set X we write $T_{(\mathsf{col},\mathsf{ind})}(X)$ for the set of all such trees involving (names of) variables x only for $x \in X$. The trees t in $T_{(\mathsf{col},\mathsf{ind})}(X)$ will be represented set theoretically as the functions $t : S \to (\mathsf{col} + X)$, where S is a non-empty prefix-closed set of finite sequences such that for each $\sigma \in S$ if $t(\sigma) = (1, p)$ then $\{i \mid \sigma^\frown i \in S\}$ is an index set in ind and if $t(\sigma) = (2, x)$ then $\{i \mid \sigma^\frown i \in S\} = \emptyset$.

Theorem 12 (Corecursion) *Let F be the endofunctor $F_{(\mathsf{col},\mathsf{ind})} + X$ on the category* SET *and let $T = (T, \tau)$ where $T = T_{(\mathsf{col},\mathsf{ind})}(X)$ and $\tau : T \to F(T)$ is given by*

$$
\begin{cases}
\tau(p[t_i]_{i \in I}) = (1, (p, \{t_i\}_{i \in I})) & \text{if } p \in \mathsf{col}, I \in \mathsf{ind} \\
& \text{and } t_i \in T \text{ for } i \in I, \\
\tau(\langle x \rangle) \quad = (2, x) & \text{if } x \in X.
\end{cases}
$$

Then T is a final F-coalgebra.

3.6 Substitution

As with terms we have a substitution operation for trees. But the substitution functions $\hat{s}$ can no longer be defined by structural recursion. This is because the non-well-founded trees are not inductively generated. Nevertheless the substitution process for trees is highly intuitive. For example the result of substituting a tree t' for a variable x in a tree t is the tree obtained from t by replacing every variable node, labelled with x, with the tree t'.

Theorem 13 (Substitution) *Assigning the $(F_{(\mathsf{col},\mathsf{ind})}, X)$-algebra $(T(X), \eta_X)$ to each set X yields a substitution system, where $T(X) = (T(X), \tau^X)$ with $T(X) = T_{(\mathsf{col},\mathsf{ind})}(X)$ and $\tau^X : F_{(\mathsf{col},\mathsf{ind})}(T(X)) \to T(X)$ given by*

$$
\tau^X((1, (p, \{t_i\}_{i \in I}))) = p[t_i]_{i \in I},
$$

for $p \in \mathsf{col}$, $I \in \mathsf{ind}$ and $t_i \in T(X)$ for $i \in I$, and $\eta_X : X \to T(X)$ is given by $\eta_X(x) = \langle x \rangle$ for each $x \in X$.

3.7 Solution Property

A fundamental feature of trees that does not hold for terms is that suitable systems of equations have unique solutions. We explain the idea in the general context of a substitution system, $X \mapsto (\mathcal{T}(X), \eta_X)$, for an endofunctor F on a category $\mathcal{C}$ that has binary coproducts. Here, for each object X of $\mathcal{C}$ we have an F-algebra $\mathcal{T}(X) = (T(X), \tau^X)$ and a map $\eta_X : X \to T(X)$. In this context a **system of equations (soe)** is a map $e : X \to T(X + Y)$. The soe is **guarded** if it factors through the map

$$[\tau^{X+Y}, \eta_{X+Y} \circ in_2] : F(T(X+Y)) + Y \to T(X+Y);$$

i.e. $e = e_0 \circ [\tau^{X+Y}, \eta_{X+Y} \circ in_2]$ for some $e_0 : X \to F(T(X+Y))$. Here $in_2 : Y \to X + Y$ is the canonical injection. A **solution** to the soe e is a map $s : X \to T(Y)$ such that $s = \widehat{[s, \eta_Y]} \circ e$.

Definition 14 *A substitution system has the* **solution property** *if every guarded soe has a unique solution.*

Theorem 15 (Solution Theorem) *The substitution system given by theorem 12 has the solution property.*

The key to proving this result as well as the substitution theorem for trees is corecursion. In fact these results are instances of a very general category theoretic result about final coalgebras.

4   The Monad of a Substitution System

Recall that a substitution system, $X \mapsto (\mathcal{T}(X), \eta_X)$, for a functor $F : \mathcal{C} \to \mathcal{C}$ associates to each object X of $\mathcal{C}$ an algebra $\mathcal{T}(X) = (TX, \tau_X)$ for F and a map $\eta_X : X \to TX$ such that for each $s : X \to TY$ there is a unique algebra homomorphism $\hat{s} : (TX, \tau_X) \to (TY, \tau_Y)$ such that $s = \hat{s} \circ \eta_X$.

For those readers familiar with the notion of a monad we here observe the following result. A proof may be found in [2].

Theorem 16 *Every substitution system,* $X \mapsto (\mathcal{T}(X), \eta_X)$ *for a functor* $F : \mathcal{C} \to \mathcal{C}$ *determines a monad* (T, η, μ) *on* $\mathcal{C}$ *in the following way.*

1. *If* $f : X \to Y$ *then* $Tf : TX \to TY$ *is defined to be* $\widehat{\eta_Y \circ f}$. *This makes* T *into a functor and* η *into a natural transformation* $Id_{\mathcal{C}} \to T$.
2. *Let* $\mu_X = \widehat{id_{TX}} : T^2X \to TX$ *for each* X. *Then* μ *is a natural transformation* $T^2 \to T$ *and, for each* X, $\mu_X \circ \eta_{TX} = id_{TX} = \mu_X \circ T\eta_X$ *and* $\mu_X \circ \mu_{TX} = \mu_X \circ T\mu_X$.

References

1. Peter Aczel, *Non-well-founded Sets*, CSLI, (1988). 85
2. Peter Aczel, Jiri Adamek and Jiri Velebil, A Coalgebraic View of Infinite Trees and Iteration, in *Electronic Notes in Theoretical Computer Science* 44.1 (2001). See http://www.elsevier.nl/gej-ng/31/29/23/73/23/show /Products/notes/index.htt. 88
3. Larry Paulson, Final Coalgebras as greatest fixed points in ZF set theory, in *Mathematical Structures in Computer Science*, pp 545-567, (1999). 85

Chapter 4
Galois Connections and Fixed Point Calculus

Roland Backhouse

School of Computer Science and Information Technology, University of Nottingham

Abstract. Fixed point calculus is about the solution of recursive equations defined by a monotonic endofunction on a partially ordered set. This tutorial presents the basic theory of fixed point calculus together with a number of applications of direct relevance to the construction of computer programs. The tutorial also summarises the theory and application of Galois connections between partially ordered sets. In particular, the intimate relation between Galois connections and fixed point equations is amply demonstrated.

1 Introduction

1.1 Fixed Point Equations

Formulating and solving equations is a fundamental mathematical activity and whole areas of mathematics are devoted to the methods for solving particular classes of equations — think, for example, of the differential calculus developed in order to solve differential equations. This chapter is about a class of equations called *fixed point* equations that is particularly important in computing.

Fixed point equations have a very simple form, namely

$$x = f.x \ ,$$

where f is a given function and x is the unknown. A solution to the equation is called a "fixed point" of the function f because applying f to a solution leaves the value "fixed", i.e. unchanged.

1.2 Languages

In the literature on computing science, fixed point equations are most often called *recursive* equations because the unknown x "recurs" on the right side of the equation. Recursion was first used extensively in computing science in the now-classic Algol 60 report [18] which defined the programming language Algol 60. The Algol 60 report introduced so-called "Backus-Naur Form" to define the syntax of the language. Here is a small, simplified extract from the language definition.

$$\langle Expression \rangle ::= \langle Expression \rangle + \langle Expression \rangle \quad | \quad (\ \langle Expression \rangle \ ) \\ | \quad \langle Variable \rangle$$

R. Backhouse et al. (Eds.): Algebraic and Coalgebraic Methods ..., LNCS 2297, pp. 89–150, 2002.
© Springer-Verlag Berlin Heidelberg 2002

This defines (arithmetic) expressions by recursion. The symbol "$::=$" can be read simply as "is" or, indeed, as an equality symbol. The symbol "$|$" is read as "or". Terms enclosed within angle brackets (thus $\langle Expression \rangle$ and $\langle Variable \rangle$) are called "non-terminals" —these are the entities being defined— and the remaining symbols (here "$+$" and the two parentheses "(" and ")") are called the "terminal" symbols —these are the symbols that form words in the language being defined— . In this way the definition of $\langle Expression \rangle$ is read as:

An expression is either an expression followed by the symbol "$+$" followed by an expression, or a parenthesised expression, or a variable.

Assuming that x and y are variables, the following are examples of expressions:

$$x+y \quad , \quad (x) \quad , \quad x \quad , \quad x+x+y \quad , \quad y+(x+y) \quad .$$

The definition of $\langle Expression \rangle$ is an example of a fixed point equation in which the unknown x is $\langle Expression \rangle$ and the function f is a function from languages (sets of words) to languages. Language theory provides many good examples of fixed point calculus; we use it frequently as a source of examples.

1.3   Functions

Recursion is used extensively in mathematics for the definition of functions. An elementary example is the factorial function, which is specified by the equation in fac,

$$\begin{aligned} fac.0 &= 1 \\ fac.n &= n * fac.(n-1), \text{ for } n > 0. \end{aligned} \qquad (1)$$

The definition of the factorial function also has the form of a fixed point equation although this is not so easy to see as in the previous example. To verify that this is indeed the case we need to rewrite the definition in the form

$$fac = \cdots \quad .$$

Using the notation $\langle x: x \in \mathsf{Type} : \mathsf{Exp} \rangle$ for a function that maps a value x of type Type to the value given by expression Exp, we have:

$$fac = \langle n: n \in \mathbb{N} : \mathbf{if}\ n=0\ \mathbf{then}\ 1\ \mathbf{else}\ n*fac.(n-1) \rangle \quad .$$

Now, abstracting from fac on the right side of this equation, define the function $\mathcal{F}$ by

$$\mathcal{F} = \langle f: f \in \mathbb{N} \leftarrow \mathbb{N} : \langle n: n \in \mathbb{N} : \mathbf{if}\ n=0\ \mathbf{then}\ 1\ \mathbf{else}\ n*f.(n-1) \rangle \rangle \quad .$$

This defines $\mathcal{F}$ to be an endofunction[1] on functions of type $\mathbb{N} \leftarrow \mathbb{N}$, the type of the factorial function. That is, the function $\mathcal{F}$ maps a function to natural

---

[1] An *endofunction* is a function whose target and source are the same.

numbers from natural numbers to a function to natural numbers from natural numbers. For example, applying $\mathcal{F}$ to the successor function $\langle n::n+1\rangle$ we get

$$\mathcal{F}.\langle n::n+1\rangle \;=\; \langle n:: \textbf{if } n=0 \textbf{ then } 1 \textbf{ else } n*((n-1)+1)\rangle \;\;.$$

(For brevity we have omitted the type information on n.) Simplifying,

$$\mathcal{F}.\langle n::n+1\rangle \;=\; \langle n:: \textbf{if } n=0 \textbf{ then } 1 \textbf{ else } n^2\rangle \;\;.$$

The characteristic feature of the factorial function is that its definition demands that
$$fac = \mathcal{F}.fac \;\;.$$
That is, fac is a *fixed point* of $\mathcal{F}$.

1.4   Datatypes

Recursion is also used in the definition of datatypes in programming languages. A definition of, for example, lists in a functional programming language looks like the following:

$$\textsf{List } a \;\;=\;\; \textsf{Nil} \;\; | \;\; \textsf{Cons } a \; (\textsf{List } a)$$

This states that a list of a's (where a stands for an arbitrary type) is either $\textsf{Nil}$ or the operator $\textsf{Cons}$ applied to a value of type a and a list of a's.

The definition of $\textsf{List}$ is not strictly a fixed-point equation. Rather than expressing the equality of $\textsf{List } a$ and $\textsf{Nil} \; | \; \textsf{Cons } a \; (\textsf{List } a)$ (misleadingly suggested by the equals sign) the declaration expresses an *isomorphism* between the type $\textsf{List } a$ and the type $\mathbb{1}+a\times(\textsf{List } a)$, the disjoint sum ("$+$") of the unit type (a set containing exactly one element, here denoted by "$\mathbb{1}$") and the cartesian product ("$\times$") of the type a and the type $\textsf{List } a$.

1.5   Galois Connections

Fixed point calculus is only of value to computing science if many of the things we want to compute are specified by fixed point equations. Fortunately, this is very much the case. Indeed, many specifications are directly expressed in terms of the solution of a fixed point equation. Moreover, a large number of additional problems have specifications that involve a fixed point equation, albeit less directly. In such cases it is often the case that the specification can be transformed to one that expresses the solution to the specification directly in terms of a fixed point equation. The key to such transformations is the notion of a *Galois connection*.

Galois connections are of interest in their own right, even when not related to the theory of fixed point equations. Their typical use is to define one, relatively complex, function in terms of another, relatively simple, function. A number of the examples we present are of very elementary and well-known functions;

even so, readers not familiar with Galois connections may find our calculations delightfully refreshing!

The basic theory of Galois connections is discussed by Priestley elsewhere in this volume. Here we emphasise how the theory helps to identify instances of Galois connections. Galois connections are also basic to the fundamental notions of infimum and supremum. Section 4.1 discusses these notions; in particular, the notion of suprema and infima of a certain "shape" is discussed in detail.

1.6   Basic Assumptions

The simple form of a fixed-point equation means that it is a very general notion which captures a very broad range of computational problems. But a theory that is too general is usually also too weak to be of practical value. In developing a useful fixed-point calculus we need to impose some non-trivial mathematical properties on the fixed point equations we consider. Here we require two properties. The first property we demand is that the domain of solutions be a *complete lattice*. That is the domain of solutions is a partially ordered set such that suprema and infima of any shape always exist. This requirement clearly holds in the case of languages. When a language is being defined it is required that the "alphabet" of the language is clearly stated. The *alphabet* of a language is just a finite set of symbols, and *words* in the language are finite sequences of symbols in the alphabet. If Σ denotes an alphabet then Σ^* is the notation used to denote the set of all words in that alphabet (that is, the set of all finite sequences —including the empty sequence— of symbols in the alpahabet). A language is thus a subset of Σ^* and, as is well known, the set of all subsets of a given set is a complete lattice under the subset ordering.

Although there is no ordering relation explicitly mentioned in the definition of fac (other than the equality relation, which is pretty uninteresting as an ordering relation) the theory we develop still applies by the simple device of viewing functions as special cases of binary relations. A binary relation between two sets A and B is a subset of the cartesian product $A \times B$ and the set of all subsets of $A \times B$ forms a complete lattice. This will be our solution domain when solving a fixed-point equation that is intended to define a function to set A from set B.

The second requirement we impose is that the function f in the given fixed point equation be *monotonic* in the ordering on the solution domain. This requirement is also clearly met in the case of language definitions. The function $\langle X :: \{b\} \cup \{a\} \cdot X \cdot \{c\} \rangle$ is typical of the sort of functions that are used in language definitions. (A raised infix dot denotes the concatenation operator extended to sets.) It is the composition of three functions, the function $\langle X :: \{b\} \cup X \rangle$, which adds the word b to a language, the function $\langle X :: \{a\} \cdot X \rangle$, which concatenates a at the beginning of every word in a given language, and $\langle X :: X \cdot \{c\} \rangle$, which concatenates c at the end of every word in a given language. These functions are all clearly monotonic, and thus so is their composition.

1.7   Issues and Applications

An arbitrary fixed point equation may have no solutions, it may have exactly one solution, or it may have more than one solution. An important consequence of our two assumptions is that the fixed point equations we consider always have at least one solution. Indeed, the set of solutions is itself a complete lattice. In particular, a monotonic function on a complete lattice has a *least* and a *greatest* fixed point. Moreover, it has a unique fixed point if (and only if) the least and great fixed points coincide.

A major element of these lecture notes is how to manipulate fixed point equations. Finding out how to express the same quantity by different equations is important to understanding. Another important element is providing general, practical, sufficient conditions for a fixed point equation to have a unique solution. These foundational elements of fixed point calculus are discussed in depth in section 6.

An example of the sort of issue tackled in section 6 is the use of recursion to define a number of values simultaneously. The terminology "mutual recursion" is used. In the definition of Algol 60, for example, this is what the definition of $\langle Expression \rangle$ really looks like:

$$\langle Expression \rangle ::= \langle Expression \rangle + \langle Term \rangle \quad | \quad \langle Term \rangle$$
$$\langle Term \rangle \quad ::= \langle Term \rangle \times \langle Factor \rangle \quad | \quad \langle Factor \rangle$$
$$\langle Factor \rangle \quad ::= (\langle Expression \rangle) \quad | \quad \langle Variable \rangle$$

This is still a fixed point equation, but it is an equation in the triple of languages

$$(\langle Expression \rangle , \langle Term \rangle , \langle Factor \rangle) \ .$$

An important issue is whether a fixed point equation in a vector of values can be solved piecewise and, if so, how. This is the content of theorem 80.

Section 5.1 is introductory; section 5.3 is also introductory but, even so, considers an important application of fixed point calculus, namely Kleene algebra, which is the algebra of choice, composition and iteration, three indispensible ingredients of any programming language.

2   Galois Connections — Introductory Examples

This section begins our discussion of "Galois connections", a concept first introduced by Oystein Ore in 1944 [19].

The importance of Galois connections lies in their ubiquity and their simplicity. Mathematics and, in particular, computing science abounds with instances of Galois connections. Some simple examples are presented in subsection 2.1 whilst subsection 2.2 continues with a more detailed analysis of the floor and ceiling functions. Later sections discuss more abstract properties of Galois connections.

2.1   Simple Examples

A Galois connection involves two preordered sets[2] $(\mathcal{A}, \leq)$ and $(\mathcal{B}, \prec)$ and two functions, $F \in \mathcal{A} \leftarrow \mathcal{B}$ and $G \in \mathcal{B} \leftarrow \mathcal{A}$. These four components together form a *Galois connection* iff for all $x \in \mathcal{B}$ and $y \in \mathcal{A}$ the following holds

$$F.x \leq y \;\equiv\; x \preceq G.y \;. \tag{2}$$

This compact definition of a Galois connection was first introduced in [20]. We refer to F as the *lower adjoint* and to G as the *upper adjoint*. (Many texts use the names "left" and "right" where we use "lower" and "upper". Our terminology is in line with [8] which is a standard reference on the theory presented here.)

Lots of examples of Galois connections can be given. In the first instance, examples can be given by observing that two inverse functions are Galois connected. Suppose $\mathcal{A}$ and $\mathcal{B}$ are two sets and $F \in \mathcal{A} \leftarrow \mathcal{B}$ and $G \in \mathcal{B} \leftarrow \mathcal{A}$ are inverse functions. Then their being inverse can be expressed by the equivalence, for all $x \in \mathcal{B}$ and $y \in \mathcal{A}$,

$$F.x = y \;\equiv\; x = G.y \;.$$

This is a Galois connection in which we view $\mathcal{A}$ and $\mathcal{B}$ as ordered sets where the ordering relation is identical to the equality relation. (Two elements are ordered if and only if they are equal.)

That inverse functions are Galois connected is a useful observation — *not* because a study of Galois connections will tell us something we didn't already know about inverse functions, but because we can draw inspiration from our existing knowledge of properties of inverse functions to guide us in the study of Galois-connected functions.

Further examples of Galois connections are not hard to find although sometimes they are not immediately evident. One is the connection between conjunction and implication in the predicate calculus:

$$p \wedge q \Rightarrow r \;\equiv\; q \Rightarrow (p \Rightarrow r) \;.$$

Here p, q and r denote predicates and the connection is between the functions $(p \wedge)$ and $(p \Rightarrow)$. To be more precise, both sets $\mathcal{A}$ and $\mathcal{B}$ in the definition of a Galois connection are taken to be the set of predicates, and the ordering relation is implication $(\Rightarrow)$. The above formula describes a *family* of Galois connections, one for each instance of the variable p.

An interesting example is provided by negation (**not**) in the predicate calculus. We have:

$$\neg p \Rightarrow q \;\equiv\; p \Leftarrow \neg q \;.$$

The example is interesting because it involves two different orderings on the same set. Specifically, we can order predicates by implication $(\Rightarrow)$ or by the converse

---

[2] The pair $(\mathcal{A}, \leq)$ is a *preordered set* if $\leq$ is a binary relation on $\mathcal{A}$ that is reflexive (i.e. $x \leq x$ for all x) and transitive (i.e. $x \leq y \wedge y \leq z \Rightarrow x \leq z$ for all x, y and z).

ordering follows-from ($\Leftarrow$). *Predicates ordered by implication and predicates ordered by follows-from are quite different partially ordered sets.* The point is that there are four elements to the definition of a Galois connection: two ordered sets and two functions between the ordered sets. All four elements form an integral part of the definition and mistakes in the exploitation of the properties of Galois connections may occur if one is not clear about all four.

One elementary example of a Galois connection that is not immediately evident is afforded by the binary maximum operator, max, on real numbers. Denoting it by the infix operator $\uparrow$, we have:

$$x \uparrow y \leq z \;\equiv\; x \leq z \wedge y \leq z \;.$$

At first sight this doesn't look like a Galois connection principally on account of the conjunction on the righthand side of the equation. We can however identify it as such as follows. First note that max is a binary function, i.e. a function from the cartesian product $\mathbf{R} \times \mathbf{R}$ (the set of pairs of real numbers) to the set $\mathbf{R}$. Now $\mathbf{R}$ is ordered by the at-most relation ($\leq$), and this relation can be extended pointwise to an ordering relation on $\mathbf{R} \times \mathbf{R}$. Specifically, denoting the relation by $\leq^2$, we define

$$(u, v) \leq^2 (x, y) \;\equiv\; u \leq x \wedge v \leq y \;.$$

Finally, we define the *doubling function*, denoted by $\triangle$, by

$$\triangle z = (z, z) \;.$$

Having done so we can rewrite the definition of max as follows:

$$\mathsf{max}(x, y) \leq z \;\equiv\; (x, y) \leq^2 \triangle z \;.$$

Thus max is a function mapping $\mathbf{R} \times \mathbf{R}$, ordered pointwise by the relation $\leq^2$, to $\mathbf{R}$, ordered by the at-most relation ($\leq$), and is defined by a Galois-connection connecting it to the doubling function.

Many predicates are themselves adjoints in a Galois connection, but the fact is rarely recognised. An example is the predicate even on integers (which is true when its argument is divisible by 2). Specifically, the nonnegative integers are partially ordered[3] by the "is-divisible-by" relation, which we denote here by " $/$ " (so m / n should be read as "m is divisible by n " or, more precisely, as "there is an integer k such that $n \times k = m$ ") and, for all integers m and booleans b ,

$$\mathsf{even}.m \Leftarrow b \;\equiv\; m / (\textbf{if } b \textbf{ then } 2 \textbf{ else } 1) \;.$$

This is an instance of the general result that a predicate p on the elements of a poset ($\mathcal{A}$, $\leq$) with greatest element $\top$ is a lower adjoint in a Galois connection (between ($\mathcal{A}$, $\leq$) and (Bool , $\Leftarrow$)) if there is some constant a such that $p.x \equiv x \leq a$. Specifically, the Galois connection is, for all $x \in \mathcal{A}$ and $b \in$ Bool ,

$$p.x \Leftarrow b \;\equiv\; x \leq \textbf{if } b \textbf{ then } a \textbf{ else } \top \;.$$

---

[3] When extended to include all integers the ordering is a preordering.

It is quite surprising how many predicates fulfill this condition. The "is-empty" test on a set is an example (a set S is empty if $S \subseteq \phi$). Another example is the membership test on a set. Fix some value a in a universe of values and consider the predicate p that given a subset S of the universe returns the value of $a \in S$. Then, since $a \in S \equiv \{a\} \subseteq S$, the general result says that p is a lower adjoint in a Galois connection. Indeed,

$$a \in S \Leftarrow b \quad \equiv \quad S \supseteq \text{ if } b \text{ then } \{a\} \text{ else } \phi \ .$$

2.2   The Floor Function

This section discusses a simple but illuminating example of a Galois connection. The *floor* function from reals to integers is described in words as follows: for all real x we take $\lfloor x \rfloor$ (read "floor x") to be the greatest integer that is at most x. Formally, this is captured by a simple equivalence.

Definition 3 (Floor Function)   For all real x, $\lfloor x \rfloor$ is an integer such that, for all integers n,

$$n \leq \lfloor x \rfloor \equiv n \leq x \ .$$

☐

In the definition of the floor function we use the mathematical convention of *not* denoting the conversion from integers to reals. It is implicit in the inequality $n \leq x$ which seems to compare an integer with a real. In fact, what is meant is the comparison of the real value corresponding to n with the real value x. On the right side of the equivalence the at-most relation ("$\leq$") is between reals whereas on the left side it is between integers.

Making explicit both conversions, temporarily adopting a Java-like casting notation, reveals the two adjoint functions in a Galois connection. We have, for all real $\mathbf{x}$, $(\mathtt{floor})\mathbf{x}$ is an integer such that for all integers $\mathbf{n}$,

$$\mathbf{n} \leq (\mathtt{floor})\mathbf{x} \quad \equiv \quad (\mathtt{real})\mathbf{n} \leq x \ .$$

So the floor of x is defined by connecting it to the conversion from integers to reals in a simple equivalence.

The floor function is an instance of a common phenomenon, namely that many functions are defined to be adjoint to an embedding of one partially ordered set in another. The functions so defined are *closure operators*[4]. Examples include the reflexive closure, symmetric closure and transitive closure of a relation. These are adjoints of the embeddings of, respectively, all reflexive relations, all symmetric relations and all transitive relations in the ordered set of relations (of an appropriate type).

---

[4] Formally, it is not the adjoint that is a closure operator but the composition of the adjoint with the embedding function. This said, it is useful to adopt the mathematical convention of omitting explicit mention of the embedding function and this is what we do from now on.

Properties of Floor The first time that one encounters a definition like definition 3 it can be difficult to see how it is used. This section illustrates the basic techniques for exploiting Galois connections.

The first thing we can do is to try to identify some special cases that simplify the definition. Two possibilities present themselves immediately; both exploit the fact that the at-most relation is reflexive. The equation

$$n \leq \lfloor x \rfloor \equiv n \leq x$$

is true for all integers n and reals x. Also, $\lfloor x \rfloor$ is by definition an integer. So we can instantiate n to $\lfloor x \rfloor$. We get

$$\lfloor x \rfloor \leq \lfloor x \rfloor \equiv \lfloor x \rfloor \leq x \ .$$

The lefthand side that is obtained — $\lfloor x \rfloor \leq \lfloor x \rfloor$ — is true, and so the righthand side is also true. That is,

$$\lfloor x \rfloor \leq x \ .$$

This tells us that the floor function rounds down. It returns an integer that is at most the given real value.

The second possibility is to instantiate x to n. This is allowed because every integer is a real. Strictly, however, we are instantiating x to the real value obtained by converting n. We get

$$n \leq \lfloor n \rfloor \equiv n \leq n \ .$$

In this case it is the right side of the equivalence that is true. So we can simplify to

$$n \leq \lfloor n \rfloor \ .$$

Earlier we determined that $\lfloor x \rfloor \leq x$ for all real values x. Instantiating x to n, we get

$$\lfloor n \rfloor \leq n \ .$$

So, as the at-most relation is anti-symmetric, we have derived that for all integers n

$$\lfloor n \rfloor = n \ .$$

A good understanding of the equivalence operator suggests something else we can do with the defining equation: use the rule of *contraposition*. The contrapositive of the definition of the floor function is, for all integers n and real x,

$$\neg(n \leq \lfloor x \rfloor) \equiv \neg(n \leq x) \ .$$

But $\neg(n \leq m) \equiv m < n$. So

$$\lfloor x \rfloor < n \equiv x < n \ .$$

Equally, using that for integers m and n, $m < n \equiv m+1 \leq n$,

$$\lfloor x \rfloor + 1 \leq n \equiv x < n \ .$$

Now we can exploit reflexivity of the at-most relation again. Instantiating n with $\lfloor x \rfloor + 1$ and simplifying we deduce:

$$x < \lfloor x \rfloor + 1 \ .$$

Recalling that $\lfloor x \rfloor \leq x$, we have established

$$\lfloor x \rfloor \ \leq \ x \ < \ \lfloor x \rfloor + 1 \ .$$

In words, $\lfloor x \rfloor$ is the (unique) integer such that $\lfloor x \rfloor$ is at most x and x is less than $\lfloor x \rfloor + 1$.

We now ask whether the floor function is monotonic. That is, we want to show that

$$\lfloor x \rfloor \leq \lfloor y \rfloor \ \Leftarrow \ x \leq y \ .$$

Here we calculate:

$$\lfloor x \rfloor \leq \lfloor y \rfloor$$
$$= \qquad \{ \qquad \text{definition 3, } x,n := \lfloor y \rfloor , \lfloor x \rfloor \quad \}$$
$$\lfloor x \rfloor \leq y$$
$$\Leftarrow \qquad \{ \qquad \text{transitivity of } \leq \quad \}$$
$$\lfloor x \rfloor \leq x \leq y$$
$$= \qquad \{ \qquad \lfloor x \rfloor \leq x \quad \}$$
$$x \leq y \ .$$

Thus the floor function is indeed monotonic.

Rounding Off Let us now demonstrate how to derive more complicated properties of the floor function. In the process we introduce an important technique for reasoning with Galois connections called the rule of *indirect equality*.

The definition of the language Java prescribes that integer division rounds *towards* zero. This causes difficulties in circumstances when it is required to round *away* from zero. Had the definition been that integer division rounds *down* then it is easy to implement rounding *up*, *towards* zero or *away* from zero. Rounding up, for example, corresponds to negating, then rounding down, and then negating again. (See exercise 7(a).)

The problem is thus how to implement rounding up integer divisions supposing that our programming language always rounds down.

In order to express the problem we need the *ceiling* function. The definition is a dual of the definition of the floor function.

Definition 4 For all real x, $\lceil x \rceil$ is an integer such that, for all integers n,

$$\lceil x \rceil \leq n \equiv x \leq n \ .$$

□

We leave it as an exercise to the reader to derive properties of the ceiling function dual to the properties of the floor function derived in section 4.

Rounding down an integer division of positive numbers m and n is expressed by

$$\left\lfloor \frac{m}{n} \right\rfloor$$

where $\dfrac{m}{n}$ is the real division of m and n. Dually, rounding up is expressed by

$$\left\lceil \frac{m}{n} \right\rceil .$$

Implementing rounding up given an implementation of rounding down amounts to finding suitable values p and q so that

$$\left\lfloor \frac{p}{q} \right\rfloor = \left\lceil \frac{m}{n} \right\rceil .$$

The values p and q should be expressed as arithmetic functions of m and n (that is, functions involving addition and multiplication, but not involving the floor or ceiling functions).

The rule of *indirect equality* is

$$m = n \equiv \forall \langle k :: k \leq m \equiv k \leq n \rangle$$

where k, m and n all range over the same poset. Using this rule, we can *derive* suitable expressions for p and q. Specifically, for arbitrary integer k, we aim to eliminate the ceiling function from the inequality

$$k \leq \left\lceil \frac{m}{n} \right\rceil$$

obtaining an inequality of the form

$$k \leq e$$

where e is an arithmetic expression in m and n. We may then conclude that

$$\lfloor e \rfloor = \left\lceil \frac{m}{n} \right\rceil .$$

The first step in the calculation is perhaps the most difficult. This is because the definition of the ceiling function, definition 4, provides a rule for dealing with inequalities where a ceiling value is on the lower side of an at-most relation but not when it is on the higher side (which is the case we are interested in). However, recalling our discussion of the floor function, the solution is to consider the contrapositive of the defining equation. Specifically we have, by negating both sides of 4,

$$n < \lceil x \rceil \equiv n < x . \tag{5}$$

We can now proceed with the derivation:

$$k \leq \left\lceil \frac{m}{n} \right\rceil$$

$\equiv$ {   integer arithmetic   }

$$k-1 < \left\lceil \frac{m}{n} \right\rceil$$

$\equiv$ {   contrapositive of definition of ceiling (rule (5))   }

$$k-1 < \frac{m}{n}$$

$\equiv$ {   arithmetic, $n > 0$ }

$$n(k-1) < m$$

$\equiv$ {   integer inequalities   }

$$n(k-1)+1 \leq m$$

$\equiv$ {   arithmetic, $n > 0$ }

$$k \leq \frac{m+n-1}{n}$$

$\equiv$ {   definition of floor function: (3)   }

$$k \leq \left\lfloor \frac{m+n-1}{n} \right\rfloor .$$

Here k is arbitrary. So, by indirect equality, we get

$$\left\lceil \frac{m}{n} \right\rceil = \left\lfloor \frac{m+n-1}{n} \right\rfloor . \tag{6}$$

In Java, for example, if it is required to round up the result of dividing `m` by `n` one should compute `(m+n-1)/n` .

Exercise 7   *Prove the following properties.* (Hint: use indirect equality.)

(a) $-\lfloor x \rfloor = \lceil -x \rceil$,
(b) $\lfloor x+m \rfloor = \lfloor x \rfloor + m$,
(c) $\lfloor x/m \rfloor = \lfloor \lfloor x \rfloor /m \rfloor$ (assuming m is a positive integer),
(d) $\left\lfloor \sqrt{\lfloor x \rfloor} \right\rfloor = \lfloor \sqrt{x} \rfloor .$

□

3   Identifying Galois Connections

In order to exploit the theory of Galois connections it is necessary to be able to identify them. The different but equivalent formulations of the definition of a Galois connection discussed by Priestley elsewhere in this volume are particularly helpful. Here we will quickly summarise those formulations whilst discussing some additional examples in more detail.

3.1 Symmetric Definitions

In what follows we take $(\mathcal{A}, \sqsubseteq_\mathcal{A})$ and $(\mathcal{B}, \sqsubseteq_\mathcal{B})$ to be *partially* ordered sets. We assume that $F \in \mathcal{A} \leftarrow \mathcal{B}$ and $G \in \mathcal{B} \leftarrow \mathcal{A}$. For such an F and G we recall the following definition.

Definition 8 (Galois Connection) (F, G) is a Galois connection between the posets $(\mathcal{A}, \sqsubseteq_\mathcal{A})$ and $(\mathcal{B}, \sqsubseteq_\mathcal{B})$ means that, for all $x \in \mathcal{B}$ and $y \in \mathcal{A}$,

$$F.x \sqsubseteq_\mathcal{A} y \equiv x \sqsubseteq_\mathcal{B} G.y \ .$$

□

In order to make the formulae more readable, we will often drop the subscripts from the orderings. This can be confusing, even though it can usually be deduced which ordering is meant from type considerations. Thus, occasionally we will reintroduce the subscripts.

Recall also that F is referred to as the lower adjoint, since it is on the *lower* side of an ordering, and G as the upper adjoint, since it is on the *upper* side of an ordering.

Definition 8, proposed by J. Schmidt [20], is easy to remember since it contains only one clause, and lends itself to compact calculation. It is a form of "shunting rule": the game that one plays with it is to shunt occurrences of function F in an expression out of the way in order to expose the function's argument. After performing some manipulations on the argument, F is shunted back into the picture. (Or, of course, the other way around: function G is shunted temporarily out of the way.) It's an attractive strategy, requiring little creativity, that is particularly useful in inductive proofs.

An alternative definition, the one originally proposed by Ore [19], is captured by the following theorem.

Theorem 9 (F, G) is a Galois connection between the posets $(\mathcal{A}, \sqsubseteq_\mathcal{A})$ and $(\mathcal{B}, \sqsubseteq_\mathcal{B})$ iff the following two conditions hold.

(a) For all $x \in \mathcal{B}$ and $y \in \mathcal{A}$,

$$x \sqsubseteq G.(F.x) \quad \text{and} \quad F.(G.y) \sqsubseteq y \ .$$

(b) F and G are both monotonic.

□

Ore's definition is most useful when expressed at function level. Let us define the relation $\dot{\sqsubseteq}$ on functions of the same type by

$$f \dot{\sqsubseteq} g \equiv \forall \langle x :: f.x \sqsubseteq g.x \rangle \ .$$

Then we can eliminate the dummies x and y in the cancellation laws to obtain

$$I_\mathcal{B} \dot{\sqsubseteq} G {\bullet} F \quad \text{and} \quad F {\bullet} G \dot{\sqsubseteq} I_\mathcal{A} \ . \tag{10}$$

Schmidt's definition can also be lifted to function level and, in combination with (10), can be used to construct elegant theorems. Specifically, we have:

Lemma 11 (F, G) is a Galois connection between the posets $(\mathcal{A}, \sqsubseteq_\mathcal{A})$ and $(\mathcal{B}, \sqsubseteq_\mathcal{B})$ equivales, for all functions h and k with the same (arbitrary) domain, and ranges respectively $\mathcal{B}$ and $\mathcal{A}$,

$$F \bullet h \mathrel{\dot{\sqsubseteq}} k \equiv h \mathrel{\dot{\sqsubseteq}} G \bullet k \quad .$$

□

In words,

$$(F, G) \text{ forms a Galois connection} \quad \equiv \quad (F\bullet, G\bullet) \text{ forms a Galois connection.} \tag{12}$$

A property that is somewhat weaker but in a sense dual to this one is the following:

$$(F, G) \text{ forms a Galois connection} \quad \Rightarrow \quad (\bullet G, \bullet F) \text{ forms a Galois connection.} \tag{13}$$

(Take care to note the switch in the order of F and G.) Specifically, we have:

Lemma 14   If (F, G) is a Galois connection between the posets $(\mathcal{A}, \sqsubseteq_\mathcal{A})$ and $(\mathcal{B}, \sqsubseteq_\mathcal{B})$ then, for all *monotonic* functions h and k with the same range, and domains respectively $\mathcal{B}$ and $\mathcal{A}$,

$$h \bullet G \mathrel{\dot{\sqsubseteq}} k \equiv h \mathrel{\dot{\sqsubseteq}} k \bullet F \quad .$$

□

3.2   Universal Property

Standard mathematical definitions of functions like, for example, the floor function often do not take the form of either Schmidt's or Ore's definition even though a Galois connection is indeed involved. Rather, they correspond to a hybrid of the two. The hybrid definition is given in the following lemma.

Lemma 15 (F, G) is a Galois connection between the posets $(\mathcal{A}, \leq)$ and $(\mathcal{B}, \preceq)$ iff the following conditions hold.

(a) G is monotonic.
(b)   For all $x \in \mathcal{B}$, $x \preceq G.(F.x)$.
(c)   For all $x \in \mathcal{B}$ and $y \in \mathcal{A}$, $x \preceq G.y \Rightarrow F.x \leq y$.

□

The hybrid definition of a Galois connection is the least elegant of the three alternatives because the symmetry between the adjoint functions is hidden. An explanation for why it is nevertheless commonly used is that Galois connections are often used to define a function, F, in terms of a known function, G. The hybrid definition focuses on the requirements on F. Indeed, we can put the hybrid definition into words as follows.

Given a monotonic function G, the lower adjoint, F, of G is defined by the requirement that, for all x, $F.x$ is the least y such that $x \preceq G.y$.

(Note that requirement (b) in lemma 15 requires that $F.x$ be a y such that $x \preceq G.y$ and requirement (c) that it be the least such y.) The requirement "for all x, $F.x$ is the least y such that $x \preceq G.y$" is often referred to as the *universal property* of F.

Examples of this form of definition can be found in Gentzen's [7] formalisation of what he called "natural deduction". Gentzen defined the logical operators (conjunction, implication, etc.) systematically by giving *introduction* and *elimination* rules for each operator. An example is his definition of disjunction. There are two introduction rules, namely:

$$p \Rightarrow p \vee q$$

and

$$q \Rightarrow p \vee q \ .$$

There is one elimination rule for disjunction:

$$(p \Rightarrow r) \wedge (q \Rightarrow r) \ \Rightarrow \ (p \vee q \Rightarrow r) \ .$$

To see that Gentzen's rules conform to properties (a), (b) and (c) of lemma 15 we first rewrite the elimination rule in the same way as we did for maximum above. Doing so and comparing with requirement (c), we identify G as the doubling function and F as disjunction:

$$((p, q) \Rightarrow^2 (r, r)) \ \Rightarrow \ (\vee.(p, q) \Rightarrow r) \ .$$

(The relation $\Rightarrow^2$ is defined in just the same way as we defined $\leq^2$ earlier. That is, $(p, q) \Rightarrow^2 (r, s)$ equivales $(p \Rightarrow r) \wedge (q \Rightarrow s)$.) We now check that the required cancellation law ($x \sqsubseteq G.(F.x)$) corresponds to the introduction rules. Formally, it is:

$$(p, q) \Rightarrow^2 (p \vee q, p \vee q)$$

which is indeed the same as the conjunction of $p \Rightarrow p \vee q$ and $q \Rightarrow p \vee q$. Finally, it is obvious that the doubling function is monotonic.

3.3 Commutativity Properties

In our discussion of elementary examples of Galois-connected functions we observed that inverse functions are Galois connected. A vital property of inverse functions is that they have "inverse" algebraic properties. The exponential function, for instance, has as its inverse the logarithmic function; moreover,

$$\exp(-x) = \frac{1}{\exp x} \quad \text{and} \quad \exp(x + y) = \exp x \cdot \exp y$$

whereas

$$-(\ln x) = \ln\left(\frac{1}{x}\right) \quad \text{and} \quad \ln x + \ln y = \ln(x \cdot y) \ .$$

In general, if θ and ϕ are inverse functions then, for any functions f and g of appropriate type,

$$\forall\langle x:: \theta.(f.x) = g.(\theta.x)\rangle \;\equiv\; \forall\langle y:: f.(\phi.y) = \phi.(g.y)\rangle \;.$$

More generally, and expressed at function level, if (θ_0, ϕ_0) and (θ_1, ϕ_1) are pairs of inverse functions, then for all functions f and g of appropriate type,

$$\theta_0 \bullet f = g \bullet \theta_1 \;\equiv\; f \bullet \phi_1 = \phi_0 \bullet g \;. \tag{16}$$

In general, our goal is to try to predict algebraic properties of functions previously unknown to us. Many such properties have the form of "commutativity properties". Among such properties are, for example, the property $-(2{\cdot}x) = 2{\cdot}(-x)$ which expresses the fact that multiplication by 2 commutes with negation. In addition we include properties like $\ln\dfrac{1}{x} = -(\ln x)$ in which the order of application of the logarithmic function is "commuted" but in so doing a change occurs in the function with which it is commuted (in this case the reciprocal function becomes negation). In this way distributivity properties also become commutativity properties. For instance the property that $x{\cdot}(y{+}z) = (x{\cdot}y) + (x{\cdot}z)$ is a commutativity property of addition. Specifically, multiplication by x after addition commutes to addition after the function $(y, z) \mapsto (x{\cdot}y, x{\cdot}z)$.

In general, for a given function F we are interested in discovering functions g and h for which $F \bullet g = h \bullet F$. In the case that F is defined by a Galois connection we can often answer this question most effectively by translating it into a question about the commutativity properties of its adjoint — especially in the case that the adjoint is a known function with known properties, or a "trivial" function whose algebraic properties are easily determined. The latter is the case with the floor function: the adjoint function is the function embedding integers into reals.

The rule that is the key to this strategy is the following. Suppose, for numbers m and n, $0 \le m$ and $0 \le n$, and for all i, $0 \le i < m{+}n$, (F_i, G_i) is a Galois-connected pair of functions. Then, assuming the functions are so typed that the compositions and equalities are meaningful,

$$F_0 \bullet \ldots \bullet F_{m-1} = F_m \bullet \ldots \bullet F_{m+n-1} \;\equiv\; G_{m+n-1} \bullet \ldots \bullet G_m = G_{m-1} \bullet \ldots \bullet G_0 \;. \tag{17}$$

(Note that the cases $m = 0$ and $n = 0$ are included; the composition of zero functions is of course the identity function.) In particular, if for $i = 0..1$, (h_i, k_i) is a Galois-connected pair of functions and so too is (F, G) then

$$h_0 \bullet F = F \bullet h_1 \;\equiv\; k_1 \bullet G = G \bullet k_0 \;. \tag{18}$$

The rule (17) captures the strategy used to discover algebraic properties of an unknown function F, namely to translate to the discovery of properties of the adjoint function.

The proof of (17) is this: the m-fold composition $G_{m-1} \bullet \ldots \bullet G_0$ is an upper adjoint of $F_0 \bullet \ldots \bullet F_{m-1}$ and the n-fold composition $G_{m+n-1} \bullet \ldots \bullet G_m$ is an upper adjoint of $F_m \bullet \ldots \bullet F_{m+n-1}$. Thus, (17) is the statement that adjoint functions are unique.

Exercise 19 A property that combines (11) and (14) is the following. Suppose, for $i = 0, 1$, $(\mathcal{A}_i, \sqsubseteq_{\mathcal{A}_i})$ and $(\mathcal{B}_i, \sqsubseteq_{\mathcal{B}_i})$ are posets and $(F_i \in \mathcal{A}_i \leftarrow \mathcal{B}_i, \ G_i \in \mathcal{B}_i \leftarrow \mathcal{A}_i)$ are Galois-connected pairs of functions. Let $h \in \mathcal{B}_0 \leftarrow \mathcal{B}_1$ and $k \in \mathcal{A}_0 \leftarrow \mathcal{A}_1$ be arbitrary monotonic functions. Then

$$F_0 \bullet h \mathrel{\dot{\sqsubseteq}} k \bullet F_1 \equiv h \bullet G_1 \mathrel{\dot{\sqsubseteq}} G_0 \bullet k \ . \tag{20}$$

Prove this rule.

□

Exercise 21 A pattern that you may have observed in the properties of the floor function is that if f is an arbitrary function from reals to reals such that

- it is the upper adjoint in a Galois connection, and
- its (lower) adjoint maps integers to integers.

then f commutes with the floor function in the sense that, for all real x,

$$\lfloor f.x \rfloor = \lfloor f. \lfloor x \rfloor \rfloor \ .$$

Show how this is an instance of (17). In other words, state precisely how to instantiate m, n and the functions $F_0, \ldots, F_{m+n-1}$ and $G_0, \ldots, G_{m+n-1}$ in order to obtain the law.

□

4 Pair Algebras

In this section we delve deeper into the theory of Galois connections. The goal is to discuss a number of theorems that predict the existence of adjoint functions. These theorems are all intimately tied up with extremum preservation properties of functions, which in turn depend on the notions of supremum and infimum. There are four sections. Section 4.1 defines suprema and infima of a given "shape", section 4.2 then defines preservation properties and section 4.3 presents the existence theorems.

In order to better motivate what is to follow, let us begin with a brief outline. We recall that a Galois connection is a connection between two functions F and G between two posets $(\mathcal{A}, \sqsubseteq)$ and $(\mathcal{B}, \preceq)$ of the form

$$F.x \sqsubseteq y \equiv x \preceq G.y \ .$$

Typical accounts of the existence of Galois connections focus on the properties of these *functions*. For example, given a function F, one may ask whether F is a lower adjoint in a Galois connection. The question we want to ask is subtly different.

Note that the statement $F.x \sqsubseteq y$ defines a *relation* between $\mathcal{B}$ and $\mathcal{A}$. So too does $x \preceq G.y$. The existence of a Galois connection states that these two relations are equal. A natural question is therefore: under which conditions does an arbitrary (binary) relation between two posets define a Galois connection between the sets?

Exploring the question in more detail leads to the following question. Suppose R is a relation between posets $\mathcal{B}$ and $\mathcal{A}$ (i.e. $R \subseteq \mathcal{B} \times \mathcal{A}$). What is a necessary and sufficient condition that there exist a function F such that

$$(x, y) \in R \equiv F.x \sqsubseteq y \quad ?$$

Such a relation is called a *pair algebra*. If we know the answer to this question then we can answer the question of whether a given function G has a lower adjoint — by defining R to be the relation $x \preceq G.y$ on x and y. We can also answer the dual question of whether there exists a function G such

$$(x, y) \in R \equiv x \preceq G.y \quad .$$

If, for a given relation R, the answer to both these questions (the original and its dual) is positive, then the relation R clearly defines a Galois connection.

In order to simplify the question, we make an abstraction step. We are required to find —*for each* x— a value $F.x$ such that $(x, y) \in R \equiv F.x \sqsubseteq y$. Suppose we fix x and hide the dependence on x. Then the problem becomes one of determining, for a given predicate p, necessary and sufficient conditions guaranteeing that

$$p.y \equiv a \sqsubseteq y \tag{22}$$

for some a. If we can solve this simplified problem, we have also solved the original problem by defining $p.y$ to be $(x, y) \in R$ and $F.x$ to be a.

It is easy to identify a necessary condition for (22) to hold: a must be the *least* y satisfying p. That is, $p.a$ must hold (since $a \sqsubseteq a$) and for all y such that $p.y$ holds, $a \sqsubseteq y$. The question thus becomes: when is there a least element satisfying a given predicate p, and when does this least element a (say) satisfy (22) for all y?

The least element satisfying a given property (if it exists) is characterised by two properties. First, it itself satisfies the property and, second, it is the "infimum" of all values satisfying the property. Section 4.1 defines the notion of an infimum via a Galois connection. The dual notion of "supremum" is also discussed in this section. Infima and suprema are collectively called "extrema".

Among the properties of extrema that we study, the question studied in section 4.2 of whether a function preserves infima is particularly important. The question is of importance in its own right, but we shall also see that it is vital to answering our question about the existence of Galois connections. Indeed, the basic insight is that a predicate p on a (complete) poset preserves infima if and only if there is an a such that, for all y, $p.y$ is $a \sqsubseteq y$. We see in section 4.3 how this simple observation is the basis of the "fundamental theorem" (theorem 36) on the existence of Galois connections.

4.1 Infima and Suprema

Infima and Completeness In this section we formulate the notion of an *extremum* (an infimum or a supremum) of a certain "shape" (for example, the infimum of a finite set, or the infimum of a countably infinite set) via a Galois connection. The notions of completeness and cocompleteness, relative to a given shape, are also defined.

Suppose $(\mathcal{A}, \sqsubseteq)$ and $(\mathcal{B}, \preceq)$ are partially ordered sets and $f \in \mathcal{A} \leftarrow \mathcal{B}$ is a monotonic function. Then an *infimum* of f is a solution of the equation:

$$x :: \quad \forall \langle a :: a \sqsubseteq x \equiv \forall \langle b :: a \sqsubseteq f.b \rangle \rangle \quad . \tag{23}$$

As an example, consider the function $\langle b : c \sqsubseteq b : b \rangle$ where c is some given constant. This has infimum c since

$$\forall \langle a :: a \sqsubseteq c \equiv \forall \langle b : c \sqsubseteq b : a \sqsubseteq b \rangle \rangle \quad .$$

There are two ways in which this definition differs from the most common definition of an infimum. The first is that it is more common to define the infimum of a *set* rather than of a *function*. That the two notions are equivalent is not difficult to see. The infimum of a set is the infimum of the identity function on that set, and the infimum of a function can be thought of as the infimum of the range of the function. (The range of a function is a set.) Defining infima on functions is an elegant way of being able to talk about different kinds of infima as we shall see very shortly. The second difference is that an infimum is often defined as a *greatest lower bound*. That is, x is an infimum of f if it is a lower bound:

$$\forall \langle b :: x \sqsubseteq f.b \rangle \quad ,$$

and it is greatest among such lower bounds

$$\forall \langle a :: a \sqsubseteq x \Leftarrow \forall \langle b :: a \sqsubseteq f.b \rangle \rangle \quad .$$

This is entirely equivalent to (23), as is easily verified.

As mentioned, equation (23) need not have a solution. If it does, for a given f, we denote its solution by $\sqcap f$. By definition, then,

$$\forall \langle a :: a \sqsubseteq \sqcap f \equiv \forall \langle b :: a \sqsubseteq f.b \rangle \rangle \quad . \tag{24}$$

Suppose we fix the posets $\mathcal{A}$ and $\mathcal{B}$ and consider all functions of type $\mathcal{A} \leftarrow \mathcal{B}$. Suppose that there is a function $\sqcap$ mapping all such functions to their infima. Then we recognise (24) as a Galois connection. Specifically,

$$\forall \langle b :: a \sqsubseteq f.b \rangle$$

$\equiv \qquad \{ \qquad \bullet \quad$ define the function $\mathsf{K} \in (\mathcal{A} \leftarrow \mathcal{B}) \leftarrow \mathcal{A}$ by $(\mathsf{K}.a).b = a \qquad \}$

$$\forall \langle b :: (\mathsf{K}.a).b \sqsubseteq f.b \rangle$$

$\equiv \qquad \{ \qquad$ definition of $\dot{\sqsubseteq}$ (pointwise ordering on functions) $\qquad \}$

$$\mathsf{K}.a \dot{\sqsubseteq} f \quad .$$

Thus, our supposition becomes that there is a function $\sqcap$ that is the upper adjoint of the so-called "constant combinator" of type $(\mathcal{A}{\leftarrow}\mathcal{B}){\leftarrow}\mathcal{A}$ defined by

$$(\mathsf{K}.a).b = a$$

for all $a{\in}\mathcal{A}$ and $b{\in}\mathcal{B}$. That is, for all $a{\in}\mathcal{A}$ and $f{\in}\mathcal{A}{\leftarrow}\mathcal{B}$,

$$a \sqsubseteq \sqcap f \; \equiv \; \mathsf{K}.a \,\dot{\sqsubseteq}\, f \; . \tag{25}$$

If this is the case we say that the poset $\mathcal{A}$ is $\mathcal{B}$-*complete*. If a poset $\mathcal{A}$ is $\mathcal{B}$-complete for all $\mathcal{B}$ we say that it is *complete*.

Shape Posets   The poset $\mathcal{B}$ is called the *shape poset*. By varying $\mathcal{B}$ we can consider different "types" or "shapes" of infima. For instance, if we take $\mathcal{B}$ to be **2**, the two-point set $\{0,1\}$ ordered by equality, then the set of functions to $\mathcal{A}$ from $\mathcal{B}$ is in (1–1) correspondence with pairs of elements (a_0, a_1) (to be precise: $f{\mapsto}(f.0, f.1)$ and $(a_0, a_1){\mapsto}f$ where $f.0 = a_0$ and $f.1 = a_1$). Via this correspondence, the function K is the doubling function: $(\mathsf{K}.a).b = \triangle a = (a,a)$, and writing $f.0 \sqcap f.1$ instead of $\sqcap f$, the Galois connection (25) simplifies to

$$a \sqsubseteq x \sqcap y \; \equiv \; (a,a) \sqsubseteq (x,y) \; .$$

That is,

$$a \sqsubseteq x \sqcap y \; \equiv \; a \sqsubseteq x \wedge a \sqsubseteq y \; .$$

This is the Galois connection defining the infimum of a bag of two elements (of which the Galois connection defining the minimum of two numbers is a special case).

If $\mathcal{B}$ is the empty poset, ϕ, then there is exactly one function of type $\mathcal{A}{\leftarrow}\mathcal{B}$. The right side of (25) is vacuously true and, thus, for all $a{\in}\mathcal{A}$ and $f \in \mathcal{A}{\leftarrow}\phi$,

$$a \sqsubseteq \sqcap f \; .$$

In words, the poset $\mathcal{A}$ is ϕ-complete equivales $\mathcal{A}$ has a greatest element.

If $\mathcal{B}$ equals $\mathcal{A}$ then the set of functions of type $\mathcal{A}{\leftarrow}\mathcal{B}$ includes the identity function. The infimum of the identity function is a solution of the equation

$$x \; :: \; \forall\langle a :: a \sqsubseteq x \equiv \forall\langle b :: a \sqsubseteq b\rangle\rangle \; .$$

and thus, by instantiating a to x, a solution of

$$x \; :: \; \forall\langle b :: x \sqsubseteq b\rangle \; .$$

The infimum of the identity function is thus the least element in the set $\mathcal{A}$.

A final example is the case that $\mathcal{B}$ is $(\mathbb{N}, \geq)$ (the natural numbers ordered by the at-least relation). Functions in $\mathcal{A}{\leftarrow}\mathcal{B}$ are then in (1–1) correspondence with so-called (descending) *chains* — sets of elements a_i $(0 \leq i)$ such that $a_0 \sqsupseteq a_1 \sqsupseteq a_2 \sqsupseteq \dots$. To say that $\mathcal{A}$ is $(\mathbb{N}, \geq)$-complete is equivalent to all such chains having an infimum in $\mathcal{A}$.

Suprema and Cocompleteness The notion dual to infimum is "supremum" and the notion dual to completeness is "cocompleteness". Suppose $(\mathcal{A}, \sqsubseteq)$ and $(\mathcal{B}, \preceq)$ are partially ordered sets and $f \in \mathcal{A} \leftarrow \mathcal{B}$ is a monotonic function. Then a *supremum* of f is a solution of the equation:

$$x :: \quad \forall \langle a :: x \sqsubseteq a \equiv \forall \langle b :: f.b \sqsubseteq a \rangle \rangle \quad . \tag{26}$$

As for infima, equation (26) need not have a solution. If it does, for a given f, we denote its solution by $\sqcup f$. By definition, then,

$$\forall \langle a :: \sqcup f \sqsubseteq a \equiv \forall \langle b :: f.b \sqsubseteq a \rangle \rangle \quad . \tag{27}$$

The poset $\mathcal{A}$ is $\mathcal{B}$-*cocomplete* if there is a function $\sqcup$ that is the lower adjoint of the constant combinator of type $(\mathcal{A} \leftarrow \mathcal{B}) \leftarrow \mathcal{A}$. That is, for all $a \in A$ and $f \in \mathcal{A} \leftarrow \mathcal{B}$,

$$\sqcup f \sqsubseteq a \equiv f \mathbin{\dot{\sqsubseteq}} \mathsf{K}.a \quad . \tag{28}$$

If a poset $\mathcal{A}$ is $\mathcal{B}$-cocomplete for all $\mathcal{B}$ we say that it is *cocomplete*. It can be shown, using the techniques developed here, that completeness and cocompleteness of a poset are equivalent. So the term "cocomplete" (used without qualifying shape poset) is redundant.

The fact that extrema are defined via Galois connections immediately suggests a number of useful calculation properties. We mention just two. First, both extremum operators are monotonic. That is,

$$f \mathbin{\dot{\sqsubseteq}} g \Rightarrow \sqcap f \sqsubseteq \sqcap g \wedge \sqcup f \sqsubseteq \sqcup g \quad .$$

Second, instantiating a to $\sqcap f$ in (24) we get the *cancellation* property:

$$\forall \langle b :: \sqcap f \sqsubseteq f.b \rangle \quad .$$

In words, $\sqcap f$ is a lower bound on (the range of) f. Dually,

$$\forall \langle b :: f.b \sqsubseteq \sqcup f \rangle \quad .$$

That is, $\sqcup f$ is an upper bound (on the range of) f.

4.2   Extremum Preservation Properties

Suppose $\mathcal{A}$ and $\mathcal{B}$ are partially ordered sets and suppose $f \in \mathcal{A} \leftarrow \mathcal{B}$. An important consideration is whether f preserves infima (or suprema) of a certain shape. If f preserves infima of shape $\mathcal{C}$ we say that f is $\mathcal{C}$-inf-preserving. If f preserves suprema of shape $\mathcal{C}$ we say that f is $\mathcal{C}$-sup-preserving. The precise formulation that we use in calculations is as follows.

Definition 29   Suppose $\mathcal{A}$, $\mathcal{B}$ and $\mathcal{C}$ are partially ordered sets such that $\mathcal{B}$ is $\mathcal{C}$-complete. Then function $f \in \mathcal{A} \leftarrow \mathcal{B}$ is $\mathcal{C}$-*inf-preserving* if, for all functions $g \in \mathcal{B} \leftarrow \mathcal{C}$,

$$\forall \langle a :: a \sqsubseteq f.(\sqcap g) \equiv \mathsf{K}.a \mathbin{\dot{\sqsubseteq}} f \bullet g \rangle \quad . \tag{30}$$

Dually, suppose that $\mathcal{B}$ is $\mathcal{C}$-cocomplete. Then function $f \in \mathcal{A} \leftarrow \mathcal{B}$ is said to be $\mathcal{C}$-*sup-preserving* if, for all functions $g \in \mathcal{B} \leftarrow \mathcal{C}$,

$$\forall\langle a :: \ f.(\sqcup g) \sqsubseteq a \equiv f \bullet g \ \dot{\sqsubseteq}\ \mathsf{K}.a\rangle \ . \tag{31}$$

If $\mathcal{B}$ is complete, we say that f is *inf-preserving* if it satisfies (30) for all $\mathcal{C}$ and all g. *Sup-preserving* is defined dually.

□

The definition of inf-preserving does not require that $\mathcal{A}$ be complete. If that is the case, and we abuse notation by using $\sqcap$ to denote the infimum operator for both $\mathcal{A}$ and $\mathcal{B}$, then $f \in \mathcal{A} \leftarrow \mathcal{B}$ is inf-preserving if for all functions g with range $\mathcal{B}$

$$f.(\sqcap g) = \sqcap(f \bullet g) \ . \tag{32}$$

Although more complicated, we are obliged to use equation (30) if we want to establish properties of inf-preservation, whereas the less complicated equation (32) is the equation we will use when we want to establish properties of a function f that is known to be inf-preserving, and the posets concerned are known to be complete.

A predicate is a function with range Bool, the two element set with elements true and false. Ordering Bool by implication $(\Rightarrow)$ the infimum of a (monotonic) predicate p is the universal quantification $\forall p$ (that is $\forall\langle x :: p.x\rangle$). Also that predicate p is $\mathcal{C}$-inf-preserving means that $p.(\sqcap g) \equiv \forall(p \bullet g)$ for all functions g with range the domain of p and domain $\mathcal{C}$. Formally,

$$p \in \mathsf{Bool} \leftarrow \mathcal{B} \text{ is } \mathcal{C}\text{-inf-preserving}$$

$\equiv \qquad \{ \qquad \text{definition} \quad \}$

$$\forall\langle g: g \in \mathcal{B} \leftarrow \mathcal{C}: \forall\langle a: a \in \mathsf{Bool}: a \Rightarrow p.(\sqcap g) \equiv \forall\langle x:: a \Rightarrow p.(g.x)\rangle\rangle\rangle$$

$\equiv \qquad \{ \qquad \text{simplification using } \mathsf{true} \Rightarrow q \equiv q$

$\qquad\qquad \text{and } \mathsf{false} \Rightarrow q \equiv \mathsf{true} \quad \}$

$$\forall\langle g: g \in \mathcal{B} \leftarrow \mathcal{C}: p.(\sqcap g) \equiv \forall\langle x:: p.(g.x)\rangle\rangle \ .$$

That is, for predicate p with domain $\mathcal{B}$,

$$p \text{ is } \mathcal{C}\text{-inf-preserving} \ \equiv \ \forall\langle g: g \in \mathcal{B} \leftarrow \mathcal{C}: p.(\sqcap g) \equiv \forall\langle x:: p.(g.x)\rangle\rangle \ . \tag{33}$$

The dual of (33) is:

$$p \text{ is } \mathcal{C}\text{-sup-preserving} \ \equiv \ \forall\langle g: g \in \mathcal{B} \leftarrow \mathcal{C}: p.(\sqcup g) \equiv \forall\langle x:: p.(g.x)\rangle\rangle \ . \tag{34}$$

Just as for (co)completeness properties, various terminology exists for specific instances of $\mathcal{C}$. Taking $\mathcal{C}$ to be $(\mathsf{Bool}, \Rightarrow)$, the booleans ordered by implication, a $\mathcal{C}$-(inf or sup)-preserving function, f, is a function that maps values x and y such that $x \sqsubseteq y$ to values $f.x$ and $f.y$ such that $f.x \sqsubseteq f.y$. Thus a function is $(\mathsf{Bool}, \Rightarrow)$-(inf and/or sup)-preserving if and only if it is monotonic.

If $\mathcal{C}$ is the empty set then f is $\mathcal{C}$-sup-preserving means that f maps the least element of $\mathcal{B}$ to the least element of $\mathcal{A}$. The terminology that is often used in the computing science literature is "f is *strict*". Sometimes one says f is *bottom-strict*, "bottom" being a common name in the computing science literature for the least element in a set. "Top-strict" then means preserving the greatest element, i.e. empty set-inf-preserving.

If $\mathcal{C}$ is the set of natural numbers ordered by the usual at-most relation then $\mathcal{C}$-sup-preservation of a function is often called ω-*continuity*.

If $\mathcal{C}$ is a non-empty finite set then $\mathcal{C}$-inf-preservation of f is equivalent to f preserving binary infima (i.e. $f.(x \sqcap y) = f.x \sqcap f.y$). This is sometimes referred to as *positive inf-preservation* of f.

Several examples of finite preservation properties have already been discussed. All of these examples are instances of a fundamental extremum preservation property of adjoint functions which we present in the next section.

4.3   Existence Theorem

In this section we derive a fundamental theorem on the existence of Galois connections. To simplify matters we often make the assumption that we are dealing with complete posets, particularly in the beginning of the discussion. The section ends with a discussion of properties of adjoint functions when this assumption is not valid.

Pair Algebra Theorem   We are now in a position to answer the question posed at the beginning of section 4, namely, given a relation R, when is there a function F such that $(x, y) \in R \equiv F.x \sqsubseteq y$. This is followed by several examples.

Theorem 35 (Pair Algebras)   Suppose $\mathcal{B}$ is a set and $(\mathcal{A}, \sqsubseteq)$ is a complete poset. Suppose $R \subseteq \mathcal{B} \times \mathcal{A}$ is a relation between the two sets. Then the following two statements are equivalent.

- The function F defined by

$$F.x = \sqcap \langle y : (x, y) \in R : y \rangle$$

satisfies, for all $x \in \mathcal{B}$ and all $y \in \mathcal{A}$,

$$(x, y) \in R \equiv F.x \sqsubseteq y \ .$$

- For all $x \in \mathcal{B}$, the predicate $\langle y :: (x, y) \in R \rangle$ is inf-preserving.

$\Box$

A simple example of the pair-algebra theorem is provided by the membership relation. For all sets S and all x (in a given universe of which S is a subset) we have:

$$x \in S \equiv \{x\} \subseteq S \ .$$

This statement has the form

$$(x, S) \in R \equiv F.x \subseteq S$$

where the relation R is the membership relation. We thus deduce that the predicate $(x \in)$ is inf-preserving. That is, for all bags of sets $\mathcal{S}$,

$$x \in \cap \mathcal{S} \equiv \forall \langle S: S \in \mathcal{S}: x \in S \rangle .$$

A common way to exploit the pair algebra theorem is to take a function or relation and extend it to a relation between sets in such a way that the infimum and supremum preserving properties are automatically satisfied. In fact this is the basis of the so-called "Galois correspondence" between groups and fields put forward by Évariste Galois in 1832. That example involves too much background terminology to usefully include it here. A simpler example is the following.

Consider a relation R on two sets A and B. (Thus $R \subseteq A \times B$.) These sets need not be ordered. Define the relation $\overline{R}$ on subsets X and Y of A and B, respectively, by

$$(X, Y) \in \overline{R} \equiv X \times Y \subseteq R .$$

Now, the functions $\langle X :: X \times Y \rangle$ and $\langle Y :: X \times Y \rangle$ preserve arbitrary unions of sets, and hence so do the predicates $\langle X :: X \times Y \subseteq R \rangle$ and $\langle Y :: X \times Y \subseteq R \rangle$. Thus, by the pair-algebra theorem (taking care with the direction of the orderings) there are functions F_R and G_R such that for all subsets X and Y of A and B, respectively,

$$F_R.X \supseteq Y \equiv X \times Y \subseteq R \equiv X \subseteq G_R.Y .$$

In words, $F_R.X$ is the largest set Y such that every element of X is related by R to every element of Y. Similarly, $G_R.Y$ is the largest set X such that every element of X is related by R to every element of Y. The functions F_R and G_R are called *polarities*; F_R is the *left polar* and G_R is the *right polar* of relation R. This Galois connection is the basis of so-called *concept lattices* [3,10]. In this application area, the set A is a set of objects, and the set B is a set of attributes (or "concepts"). For example, we may take A to be the set of planets of the sun (Mars, Venus, Jupiter, etc.) and B to be attributes like "has a moon" and "is nearer to the sun than the Earth". The relation R is then "satisfies the predicate". We may then ask for all the planets that both have a moon and are nearer to the sun than the Earth.

A more substantial example of the pair-algebra theorem, that stands out in the computing science literature, is provided by conditional correctness assertions of program statements.

Suppose S is a program statement and p and q are predicates on the state space of S. Then, one writes $\{p\}S\{q\}$ if after successful execution of statement S beginning in a state satisfying the predicate p the resulting state will satisfy predicate q. In such a case one says that statement S is *conditionally correct* with respect to precondition p and postcondition q. ("Conditional" refers to the fact that satisfying predicate q is conditional on the termination of statement S.)

In this way each program statement S defines a relation on state predicates. This relation is such that, for all bags of predicates P,

$$\{\exists\langle p\colon p{\in}P\colon p\rangle\}S\{q\} \;\equiv\; \forall\langle p\colon p{\in}P\colon \{p\}S\{q\}\rangle \;.$$

That is, for each state predicate q the predicate $\langle p\colon\colon\{p\}S\{q\}\rangle$ preserves suprema in the poset of predicates ordered by implication (equivalently, preserves infima in the poset of predicates ordered by follows-from). Thus, by the dual of the pair-algebra theorem with implication as the ordering on predicates, for each statement S and predicate q there is a predicate $\mathsf{wlp}(S,q)$ satisfying

$$\{p\}S\{q\} \;\equiv\; p\Rightarrow\mathsf{wlp}(S,q) \;.$$

The abbreviation "wlp" stands for "weakest liberal precondition".

Before leaving this example, let us note that it is also the case that, for all bags of predicates Q,

$$\{p\}S\{\forall\langle q\colon q{\in}Q\colon q\rangle\} \;\equiv\; \forall\langle q\colon q{\in}Q\colon \{p\}S\{q\}\rangle \;.$$

There is thus also a predicate $\mathsf{slp}(S,p)$ satisfying

$$\{p\}S\{q\} \;\equiv\; \mathsf{slp}(S,p)\Rightarrow q \;.$$

Combining this equation with the equation for the weakest liberal precondition, we thus have the Galois connection: for all predicates p and q,

$$\mathsf{slp}(S,p)\Rightarrow q \equiv p\Rightarrow\mathsf{wlp}(S,q) \;.$$

The abbreviation "slp" stands for "strongest liberal postcondition".

The Existence Theorem Now that we have seen several concrete examples, let us state the fundamental theorem.

Theorem 36 (Fundamental Theorem)   Suppose that $\mathcal{B}$ is a poset and $\mathcal{A}$ is a complete poset. Then a monotonic function $G\in\mathcal{B}{\leftarrow}\mathcal{A}$ is an upper adjoint in a Galois connection equivales G is inf-preserving.

Dually, a monotonic function $F\in\mathcal{A}{\leftarrow}\mathcal{B}$ is a lower adjoint in a Galois connection equivales F is sup-preserving.

$\square$

We mentioned a couple of instances of theorem 36 immediately prior to its derivation. There are many other instances we could give. The predicate calculus is a source of several. We saw earlier that for all predicates p the function $(p\wedge)$ is a lower adjoint. Specifically,

$$(p\wedge q \Rightarrow r) \equiv (p\Rightarrow(q\Rightarrow r)) \;.$$

The supremum operator in the lattice of predicates ordered by implication is existential quantification since

$$(\exists\langle x :: p.x\rangle \Rightarrow q) \equiv \forall\langle x :: p.x \Rightarrow q\rangle \ .$$

Instantiating theorem 36 we thus conclude that $(p\wedge)$ commutes with existential quantification. That is,

$$p \wedge \exists\langle x :: q.x\rangle \equiv \exists\langle x :: p \wedge q.x\rangle \ .$$

The dual theorem is that $(p\Rightarrow)$ commutes with universal quantification:

$$(p \Rightarrow \forall\langle x :: q.x\rangle) \equiv \forall\langle x :: p \Rightarrow q.x\rangle \ .$$

A more enlightening example is afforded by negation. Recall that

$$(\neg p \Rightarrow q) \equiv (p \Leftarrow \neg q) \ .$$

Now, in order to instantiate the fundamental theorem we need to be very clear about the partially ordered sets involved: instantiate $\mathcal{A}$ to the predicates ordered by implication and $\mathcal{C}$ to the predicates ordered by follows-from. Observe that the supremum operator in $\mathcal{A}$ is existential quantification, and in $\mathcal{C}$ is universal quantification. Thus by application of the lemma:

$$\neg\forall\langle x :: p.x\rangle \equiv \exists\langle x :: \neg(p.x)\rangle \ .$$

This example illustrates why in general it is necessary to take great care with the precise definitions of the orderings on the posets $\mathcal{A}$ and $\mathcal{B}$ when applying theorem 36.

The above examples all illustrate the fact that, given a Galois connection, we can infer that the lower adjoint preserves suprema (and the upper adjoint preserves infima). The converse property is most often used to ascertain that a function is a lower adjoint (or is an upper adjoint) without it being necessary to know what the corresponding upper adjoint of the function is. Indeed it is often the case that the upper adjoint has a clumsy definition that one wishes to avoid using explicitly at all costs.

Exercise 37   Consider an arbitrary set $\mathcal{U}$. For each x in $\mathcal{U}$ the predicate $(x\in)$ maps a subset P of $\mathcal{U}$ to the boolean value true if x is an element of P and otherwise to false. The predicate $(x\in)$ preserves set union and set intersection. That is, for all bags $\mathcal{S}$ of subsets of $\mathcal{U}$,

$$x \in \cup\mathcal{S} \equiv \exists\langle P : P \in \mathcal{S} : x \in P\rangle$$

and

$$x \in \cap\mathcal{S} \equiv \forall\langle P : P \in \mathcal{S} : x \in P\rangle \ .$$

According to the fundamental theorem and its dual, the predicate $(x\in)$ thus has a lower and an upper adjoint. *Construct a closed formula for the upper and lower adjoints of $(x\in)$.*
□

Exercise 38   Consider the predicate $(\neq \phi)$ (where ϕ denotes the empty set) on subsets of a given set $\mathcal{U}$. *Construct a Galois connection in which the predicate is the lower adjoint.*

$\square$

5   Fixed Points

5.1   Prefix Points

We begin our study of fixed points by introducing the notion of a "prefix" point. As an instance of where the notion commonly occurs, consider the following example from language theory. The set $L = \{n: 0 \leq n: a^n b c^n\}$ over the alphabet $\{a,b,c\}$ is sometimes specified in the following way.

- The word b is in the set L.
- If w is in the set L then so is the word awc.
- Nothing else is in the set L.

Expressing the first two clauses in terms of set inclusion we see that L is required to satisfy the equation:

$$X :: \ \{b\} \subseteq X \wedge \{a\} \cdot X \cdot \{c\} \subseteq X \ ,$$

which is equivalent to the equation:

$$X :: \ \{b\} \cup \{a\} \cdot X \cdot \{c\} \subseteq X \ .$$

Now consider the function f mapping sets of words to sets of words defined by:

$$f.X = \{b\} \cup \{a\} \cdot X \cdot \{c\} \ .$$

Then the requirement is that L be a so-called "prefix point" of f, i.e. L should satisfy the equation:

$$X :: \ f.X \subseteq X \ .$$

What about the third clause: "Nothing else is in the set L"? Note that this clause is necessary to specify L since, for example, the set of all words over the alphabet $\{a,b,c\}$ is a prefix point of the function f. One way to understand this clause is as the requirement that L be the *least* prefix point of the function f. Thus the complete specification of L is the equation

$$X :: \ f.X \subseteq X \wedge \forall \langle Y: f.Y \subseteq Y: X \subseteq Y \rangle \ .$$

Here, the first conjunct is the requirement that X be a prefix point of f, and the second conjunct that f be at most all prefix points Y of f.

In this section we define the notions of least prefix point and least fixed point in a general setting, and we establish the most basic properties of these notions.

You are recommended to instantiate the properties we establish on the example just discussed as you read in order to confirm your understanding.

Suppose $\mathcal{A} = (A, \sqsubseteq)$ is a partially ordered set and suppose f is a monotonic endofunction on $\mathcal{A}$. Then a *prefix point* of f is an element x of the carrier set A such that $f.x \sqsubseteq x$. A *least prefix point* of f is a solution of the equation

$$x :: \ f.x \sqsubseteq x \ \wedge \ \forall \langle y: \ f.y \sqsubseteq y: \ x \sqsubseteq y \rangle \ .$$

A least prefix point of f is thus a prefix point of f that is smaller than all other prefix points of f. A *least fixed point* of f is a solution of the equation

$$x :: \ f.x = x \ \wedge \ \forall \langle y: \ f.y = y: \ x \sqsubseteq y \rangle \ . \tag{39}$$

Rather than study *fixed* points of f we are going to study *prefix* points of f since the latter are mathematically more manageable than the former.

Exercise 40   Relations are often defined by just saying which pairs are in the relation. Implicitly the relation in question is defined to be the least solution of a certain equation. (Recall that relations are sets of pairs and thus ordered by set inclusion.)

An example is the following definition of the "at-most" relation on natural numbers (denoted as usual by the infix operator $\leq$). The "at-most" relation is the least relation satisfying, first, that for all natural numbers n ,

$$0 \leq n$$

and, second, for all natural numbers m and n ,

$$m+1 \leq n+1 \Leftarrow m \leq n \ .$$

This defines the "at-most" relation as a least prefix point of a function from relations to relations. *What is this function?*

□

It is easy to see that a least prefix point of f is unique. Let x and x' be least prefix points of f. Then,

$$x = x'$$

$\equiv$ {   anti-symmetry   }

$$x \sqsubseteq x' \wedge x' \sqsubseteq x$$

$\Leftarrow$ { $\forall \langle y: \ f.y \sqsubseteq y: \ x \sqsubseteq y \rangle$ with the instantiation $y := x'$

                      $\forall \langle y: \ f.y \sqsubseteq y: \ x' \sqsubseteq y \rangle$ with the instantiation $y := x$ }

$$f.x' \sqsubseteq x' \wedge f.x \sqsubseteq x$$

$\equiv$ { x and x' are prefix points of f }

     true .

A similar argument establishes that a least fixed point of f is unique.

Nothing is lost by studying least prefix points rather than least fixed points since, by the following calculation, a least prefix point of a monotonic function f is a fixed point of f.

$$x = f.x$$

$\equiv$ $\qquad \{ \qquad \bullet \quad f.x \sqsubseteq x \quad \}$

$\qquad x \sqsubseteq f.x$

$\Leftarrow$ $\qquad \{ \qquad \bullet \quad \forall \langle y: f.y \sqsubseteq y: x \sqsubseteq y \rangle, \ y := f.x \quad \}$

$\qquad f.(f.x) \sqsubseteq f.x$

$\Leftarrow$ $\qquad \{ \qquad f \text{ is monotonic} \quad \}$

$\qquad f.x \sqsubseteq x$

$\equiv$ $\qquad \{ \qquad \bullet \quad f.x \sqsubseteq x \quad \}$

$\qquad$ true .

Since all fixed points are also prefix points it follows that a least prefix point of f is also a least fixed point of f.

Dual to the notion of least prefix point we can define the notion of "greatest postfix point": a *greatest postfix point* of endofunction $f \in (A, \sqsubseteq) \leftarrow (A, \sqsubseteq)$ is a least prefix point of the function $f \in (A, \sqsupseteq) \leftarrow (A, \sqsupseteq)$. Spelling this out in detail, a *postfix point* of f is an element x of the carrier set A such that $x \sqsubseteq f.x$ and a *greatest postfix point* of f is a solution of the equation

$$x :: \ x \sqsubseteq f.x \land \forall \langle y: y \sqsubseteq f.y: y \sqsubseteq x \rangle \ . \tag{41}$$

A *greatest fixed point* of f is a solution of the equation

$$x :: \ f.x = x \land \forall \langle y: f.y = y: y \sqsubseteq x \rangle \ .$$

Since a least prefix point is a least fixed point, we immediately have the dual result that a greatest postfix point is also a greatest fixed point. A simple but important corollary is that function f has a unique fixed point if and only if the least prefix point of f equals the greatest postfix point of f.

Let us summarise what has been learnt in this section. Introducing the notation μf for a solution of the equation (39) and νf for a solution of the equation (41) we have:

Theorem 42 (Least Prefix Point)   Suppose $(A, \sqsubseteq)$ is an ordered set and the function f of type $(A, \sqsubseteq) \leftarrow (A, \sqsubseteq)$ is monotonic. Then f has at most one least prefix point, μf, characterised by the two properties:

$$f.\mu f \sqsubseteq \mu f \tag{43}$$

and, for all $x \in A$,

$$\mu f \sqsubseteq x \ \Leftarrow \ f.x \sqsubseteq x \ . \tag{44}$$

Moreover, the least prefix point of f is a fixed point of f:

$$f.\mu f = \mu f \quad . \tag{45}$$

□

Note that least fixed points are characterised by the combination of (43) and (44) or (45) and (44). Because (43) is weaker than (45) it is usual to use the former characterisation when it is required to *establish* that a particular value is a least prefix point, and the latter characterisation when it is required to *exploit* the fact that a particular value is a least prefix point.

Theorem 46 (Greatest Postfix Point)   Suppose $(A, \sqsubseteq)$ is an ordered set. Suppose, also, that the function f of type $(A, \sqsubseteq) \leftarrow (A, \sqsubseteq)$ is monotonic. Then f has at most one greatest postfix point, νf, characterised by the two properties:

$$\nu f \sqsubseteq f.\nu f \tag{47}$$

and, for all $x \in A$,

$$x \sqsubseteq \nu f \ \Leftarrow\ x \sqsubseteq f.x \quad . \tag{48}$$

Moreover, the greatest postfix point of f is a fixed point of f:

$$f.\nu f = \nu f \quad . \tag{49}$$

□

Use of the rules (44) or (48) corresponds to using induction. We therefore refer to their use in calculations as *fixed point induction*. (Strictly we should say *least* fixed point induction or *greatest* fixed point induction but it will invariably be clear which of the two rules is meant.) Rules (45) and (49) are called *computation rules* because they are often used in programs as left-right rewrite rules, repeated application of which is used to compute a fixed point.

Both induction rules can of course be written as an implication rather than a follows-from. For example, (44) can be written as

$$f.x \sqsubseteq x \ \Rightarrow\ \mu f \sqsubseteq x \quad .$$

This is the way many would write the rule. We deviate from this practice because in almost all our calculations we will apply the rule from left to right in the form given in (44). This is independent of whether our goal is to *verify* a statement of the form $\mu f \sqsubseteq x$ or, given x, to *construct* an f satisfying $\mu f \sqsubseteq x$, or, given f, to *construct* an x satisfying $\mu f \sqsubseteq x$. The benefit of proceeding in this way is the replacement of complification steps by simplification steps.

Exercise 50   *Show that $\mu f \sqsubseteq \nu f$.*

□

5.2   A First Example

In this section we present a simple example of the Least Prefix Point theorem (theorem 42). The example illustrates why (44) really is an induction rule. It also illustrates the use of the computation rule (45) in a simple example of algorithm design.

Let L be the least solution of the equation

$$X :: \{a\} \cup \{b\} \cdot X \cdot X \subseteq X \ .$$

This corresponds to a grammar having two productions $X ::= a$ and $X ::= bXX$. We first use (44) to prove that, for all words w in L, the number of a's in w is one more than the number of b's in w.

Let M be the set of all words w such that the number of a's in w is one more than the number of b's in w. Let $\#_a w$ denote the number of a's in w, and $\#_b w$ denote the number of b's in w. We have to show that $L \subseteq M$. We use fixed point induction:

$$L \subseteq M$$

$\Leftarrow$ $\qquad \{ \qquad$ by definition $L = \mu f$ where $f = \langle X :: \{a\} \cup \{b\} \cdot X \cdot X \rangle$,

$\qquad\qquad\qquad$ induction: (44) $\quad \}$

$$\{a\} \cup \{b\} \cdot M \cdot M \subseteq M$$

$\equiv \qquad \{ \qquad$ set theory, definition of concatenation $\quad \}$

$$a \in M \ \wedge \ \forall \langle x, y \colon x \in M \wedge y \in M \colon bxy \in M \rangle$$

$\equiv \qquad \{ \qquad$ definition of M $\quad \}$

$$\#_a a = \#_b a + 1$$

$\wedge \ \forall \langle \qquad x, y$

$\qquad\qquad : \qquad \#_a x = \#_b x + 1 \ \wedge \ \#_a y = \#_b y + 1$

$\qquad\qquad : \qquad \#_a(bxy) = \#_b(bxy) + 1$

$\qquad \rangle$

$\equiv \qquad \{ \qquad$ definition of $\#_a$ and $\#_b$ $\quad \}$

true

$\wedge \ \forall \langle \qquad x, y$

$\qquad\qquad : \qquad \#_a x = \#_b x + 1 \ \wedge \ \#_a y = \#_b y + 1$

$\qquad\qquad : \qquad \#_a x + \#_a y = 1 + \#_b x + \#_b y + 1$

$\qquad \rangle$

$\equiv \qquad \{ \qquad$ arithmetic $\quad \}$

true .

Note that this proof is not a proof by induction on the length of words in L. Introducing the length of words in L into the proof is spurious and only obscures the properties that are truly vital to the proof.

Now let us illustrate the use of the computation rule. The problem we consider is how to write a simple loop that determines whether a given word W is in the language L. At the same time we illustrate one of the most basic elements of the mathematics of program construction, namely the use of loop invariants.

For the purposes of the discussion we need two functions on words, fst and rest. The fst function returns the first symbol of a word of length at least one, and the rest function returns the remainder of the word. For example, $\mathsf{fst}.(aba) = a$ and $\mathsf{rest}.(aba) = ba$. We also use ε to denote the empty word (the word of length zero).

The problem is to determine the truth or falsity of $W \in L$. As L is a *fixed* point of its defining equation, we can expand this requirement as follows:

$$W \in L$$

$$\equiv \qquad \{ \qquad \text{by (45)}, \ L = \{a\} \cup \{b\}{\cdot}L{\cdot}L \qquad \}$$

$$W \ \in \ \{a\} \cup \{b\}{\cdot}L{\cdot}L$$

$$\equiv \qquad \{ \qquad \text{set calculus} \qquad \}$$

$$W = a \ \lor \ (\mathsf{fst}.W = b \land \mathsf{rest}.W \in L{\cdot}L) \ .$$

The two tests $W = a$ and $\mathsf{fst}.W = b$ can, of course, easily be implemented. This then leaves us with the task of implementing the test $\mathsf{rest}.W \in L{\cdot}L$. Were we to repeat the same small calculation beginning with the latter then we would end up with the task of implementing the test $\mathsf{rest}.(\mathsf{rest}.W) \in L{\cdot}L{\cdot}L$. This clearly suggests a generalisation of the original problem, namely, given natural number n and word w determine the truth or falsity of the statement $w \in L^n$ where, by definition, $L^0 = \{\varepsilon\}$ and $L^{n+1} = L{\cdot}L^n$.

With this generalised problem we begin our calculation again. First, by definition of L^0,

$$w \in L^0 \ \equiv \ w = \varepsilon \ . \tag{51}$$

Second,

$$w \in L^{n+1}$$

$$\equiv \qquad \{ \qquad L^{n+1} = L{\cdot}L^n \ \text{and, by (45)}, \ L = \{a\} \cup \{b\}{\cdot}L{\cdot}L \qquad \}$$

$$w \ \in \ (\{a\} \cup \{b\}{\cdot}L{\cdot}L){\cdot}L^n$$

$$\equiv \qquad \{ \qquad \text{concatenation distributes through union,}$$

$$\text{concatenation is associative} \qquad \}$$

$$w \ \in \ \{a\}{\cdot}L^n \cup \{b\}{\cdot}L{\cdot}L{\cdot}L^n$$

$$\equiv \qquad \{ \qquad \text{set calculus} \qquad \}$$

$$(\mathsf{fst}.w = a \land \mathsf{rest}.w \in L^n) \ \lor \ (\mathsf{fst}.w = b \land \mathsf{rest}.w \in L^{n+2}) \ .$$

This calculation provides enough information to construct the required loop. The loop uses two variables, a word w and a natural number k, satisfying the loop invariant

$$W \in L \;\equiv\; w \in L^k \;.$$

This invariant is established by the assignment:

$$w, k \;:=\; W, 1 \;.$$

Also, by the above calculation, it is maintained when $k = n+1$ for some number n by the assignment

$$
\begin{aligned}
&\textsf{if}\quad \textsf{fst.}w = a \;\rightarrow\; w, k \;:=\; \textsf{rest.}w, k-1 \\
&\square\quad \textsf{fst.}w = b \;\rightarrow\; w, k \;:=\; \textsf{rest.}w, k+1 \\
&\textsf{fi}\quad.
\end{aligned}
$$

(Here we make the implicit assumption that the given word W is a string of a's and b's and contains no other characters, thus avoiding stipulating the semantics of the statement when neither of the two tests evaluates to $\textsf{true}$.) This statement also makes progress by reducing the length of w by 1 at each iteration. Finally, if we impose the termination condition $w = \varepsilon \vee k = 0$, then the conjunction of the termination condition and the invariant

$$(w = \varepsilon \vee k = 0) \wedge (W \in L \;\equiv\; w \in L^k)$$

implies, using (51) and the calculation immediately following it, that

$$W \in L \;\equiv\; w = \varepsilon \wedge k = 0 \;.$$

This then is the complete program:

$$
\begin{aligned}
&w, k \;:=\; W, 1 \\
&\{\;\text{Invariant: } W \in L \;\equiv\; w \in L^k\,. \\
&\quad\text{Bound function: length of } w\;\} \\
&;\quad \textsf{do}\;\; \neg(w = \varepsilon \vee k = 0) \;\rightarrow\;\quad \textsf{if}\;\; \textsf{fst.}w = a \;\rightarrow\; w, k \;:=\; \textsf{rest.}w, k-1 \\
&\hspace{10.5cm} \square\;\; \textsf{fst.}w = b \;\rightarrow\; w, k \;:=\; \textsf{rest.}w, k+1 \\
&\hspace{8.8cm} \textsf{fi} \\
&\textsf{od} \\
&\{\;(w = \varepsilon \vee k = 0) \wedge (W \in L \;\equiv\; w \in L^k)\;\} \\
&\{\;W \in L \;\equiv\; w = \varepsilon \wedge k = 0\;\}
\end{aligned}
$$

5.3 Kleene Algebra

The purpose of this section is to provide some practice in the use of the characterising properties of least fixed points, in particular the induction rule. For this purpose we consider an algebraic structure called a "Kleene algebra" by Kozen [15].

A Kleene algebra has two constants 0 and 1, two binary operators $+$ and $\cdot$, and a unary operator $*$. These operators satisfy a number of axioms which we shall give shortly. The name "Kleene algebra" is a tribute to S. C. Kleene [14] who postulated an algebraic structure as a basis for studying the behaviour of finite state machines. He called it the "algebra of regular events", which nowadays is most commonly abbreviated to "regular algebra".

Regular algebra is central to the mathematics of program construction because the three operators capture the essential properties of the three main ingredients of programming languages, choice ($+$), sequencing ($\cdot$) and iteration ($*$). The axioms of a Kleene algebra are not sufficient to capture all the properties of choice, sequencing and iteration in programming languages and we shall need to add to the axioms later on. Any Kleene algebra is thus also a regular algebra but it is not necessarily the case that any regular algebra is a Kleene algebra. See sections 6.3 and 6.4 for further discussion.

The Axioms It is convenient to discuss the axioms of a Kleene algebra in two stages, first the axiomatisation of the $+$ and $\cdot$ operators, and then the axiomatisation of the $*$ operator. In presenting the axioms we use variables a , b , x , y and z to range over the carrier set of the algebra. These variables are universally quantified in the usual way.

The notation " $+$ " and " $\cdot$ " is chosen to suggest a connection with addition and multiplication in ordinary arithmetic. Indeed, the $+$ operator of a Kleene algebra is required to be associative and symmetric and to have 0 as unit element:

$$(x+y)+z = x+(y+z) \ ,$$
$$x+y = y+x \ ,$$
and $\quad x+0 = x = 0+x \ .$

Also, just as in arithmetic, multiplication is required to be associative, to distribute over addition, and to have 1 as unit and 0 as zero element:

$$x\cdot(y\cdot z) = (x\cdot y)\cdot z \ ,$$
$$x \cdot (y+z) = (x\cdot y)+(x\cdot z) \ ,$$
$$(y+z) \cdot x = (y\cdot x)+(z\cdot x) \ ,$$
$$x\cdot 0 = 0 = 0\cdot x \ ,$$
and $\quad 1\cdot x = x = x\cdot 1 \ .$

Use of these rules in calculations will be referred to simply as "arithmetic".

The addition and multiplication operators of a Kleene algebra deviate from the operators of normal arithmetic in two respects. First, multiplication is *not* assumed to be commutative. Second, addition is assumed to be idempotent. That is,

$$x+x = x$$

for all x. (Equivalently, $1+1 = 1$.)

Because addition is idempotent, associative and symmetric, the relation $\leq$ defined by

$$x \leq y \equiv x+y = y$$

is reflexive, transitive and anti-symmetric. In short, it is a partial ordering relation. Moreover, because 0 is the unit of addition, it is the least element in the ordering:

$$0 \leq x$$

for all x. Finally, addition and multiplication are both monotonic with respect to the $\leq$ ordering.

Exercise 52   *Verify all the claims made in the last paragraph. Prove also that $+$ is the binary supremum operator. That is,*

$$x+y \leq z \equiv x \leq z \wedge y \leq z \ .$$

□

The $*$ operator will be the focus of our attention. The axioms for $*$ require that $a^* \cdot b$ be the least prefix point of the (monotonic) function mapping x to $b+a\cdot x$ and that $b \cdot a^*$ be the least prefix point of the (monotonic) function mapping x to $b+x\cdot a$. Formally, $a^* \cdot b$ is a prefix point of the function mapping x to $b+a\cdot x$:

$$b+a\cdot(a^* \cdot b) \leq a^* \cdot b \ , \tag{53}$$

and is the least among all such prefix points:

$$a^* \cdot b \leq x \ \Leftarrow \ b+a\cdot x \leq x \ . \tag{54}$$

That is,

$$a^* \cdot b = \mu\langle x :: b+a\cdot x\rangle \ . \tag{55}$$

Similarly, $b \cdot a^*$ is a prefix point of the function mapping x to $b+x\cdot a$:

$$b+(b\cdot a^*)\cdot a \leq b\cdot a^* \ , \tag{56}$$

and is the least among all such prefix points:

$$b\cdot a^* \leq x \ \Leftarrow \ b+x\cdot a \leq x \ . \tag{57}$$

That is,

$$b\cdot a^* = \mu\langle x :: b+x\cdot a\rangle \ . \tag{58}$$

The axioms (53) and (56) are thus instances of (43) and the axioms (54) and (57) are instances of (44), the two properties characterising least prefix points.

An immediate corollary is that $a^*\cdot b$ and $b\cdot a^*$ are *fixed* points of the relevant functions:

$$b + a\cdot(a^*\cdot b) = a^*\cdot b \ , \tag{59}$$

$$b + (b\cdot a^*)\cdot a = b\cdot a^* \ . \tag{60}$$

This concludes the axiomatisation of a Kleene algebra. There are several interpretations of the operators in a Kleene algebra that fulfill the axioms. Table 5.3 summarises a few. The first interpretation in the table, in which the carrier consists of sets of words over a given, fixed alphabet, is the original application of Kleene algebra. Here the addition operation is set union, the multiplication operation is concatenation of sets of words, 0 is the empty set, 1 is the set whose sole element is the empty word, and a^* is the set of words formed by concatenating together an arbitrary number of words in the set a.

The second interpretation is the one we will return to most often in these lecture notes. In this interpretation the carrier set of the algebra is the set of binary relations over some state space, the addition operator is set union, multiplication is the composition operator on relations, 0 is the empty relation, 1 is the identity relation, and the iteration operator is the reflexive, transitive closure operator on relations.

The remaining three interpretations all concern path-finding problems; in each case the iteration operator (*) is uninteresting. These interpretations only become interesting when one considers graphs with edge labels drawn from these primitive Kleene algebras, the crucial theorem being that it is possible to define a Kleene algebra of graphs given that the edge labels are elements of a Kleene algebra [1,15].

Table 1. Kleene algebras

	carrier	$+$	$\cdot$	0	1	a^*	$\leq$
Languages	sets of words	$\cup$	$\cdot$	ϕ	$\{\varepsilon\}$	a^*	$\subseteq$
Programming	binary relations	$\cup$	$\circ$	ϕ	id	a^*	$\subseteq$
Reachability	booleans	$\vee$	$\wedge$	false	true	true	$\Rightarrow$
Shortest paths	nonnegative reals	max	$+$	∞	0	0	$\geq$
Bottlenecks	nonnegative reals	max	min	0	∞	∞	$\leq$

Reflexive, Transitive Closure It is common to call a^* *the reflexive, transitive closure* of a. This is because a^* is reflexive, in the sense that

$$1 \leq a^* ,$$

transitive, in the sense that

$$a^* = a^* \cdot a^* ,$$

and $*$ is a closure operator, i.e.

$$a \leq b^* \equiv a^* \leq b^* .$$

In this section we shall verify, from the axioms given above, that a^* does indeed have these and other related properties. The main tool will be fixed point induction, i.e. axioms (54) and (57).

The reflexivity of a^* is immediate from (59) or (60). Instantiating b to 1 in both these rules and using $1 \cdot x = x = x \cdot 1$ we get

$$1 + a \cdot a^* = a^* = 1 + a^* \cdot a .$$

Thus, since $+$ is the binary supremum operator, $1 \leq a^*$. It then follows that $a \leq a^*$ since

$$a^* = 1 + a \cdot a^* = 1 + a \cdot (1 + a \cdot a^*) = 1 + a \cdot 1 + a \cdot (a \cdot a^*) = 1 + a + a \cdot a \cdot a^* .$$

Now for the transitivity of a^* we use a ping-pong argument:

$$a^* = a^* \cdot a^*$$

$$\equiv \qquad \{ \qquad \text{antisymmetry} \quad \}$$

$$a^* \leq a^* \cdot a^* \ \wedge \ a^* \cdot a^* \leq a^* .$$

The first inequality does not involve induction:

$$a^* \leq a^* \cdot a^*$$

$$\Leftarrow \qquad \{ \qquad \text{transitivity} \quad \}$$

$$a^* \leq 1 \cdot a^* \leq a^* \cdot a^*$$

$$\equiv \qquad \{ \qquad \text{arithmetic for the first inequality;}$$

$$\qquad \qquad \qquad 1 \leq a^* \text{ and product is monotonic for the second} \quad \}$$

$$\text{true} .$$

The second inequality is where we need to use induction:

$$a^* \cdot a^* \leq a^*$$

$$\Leftarrow \qquad \{ \qquad (54) \text{ with } a,b,x := a, a^*, a^* \quad \}$$

$$a^* + a \cdot a^* \leq a^*$$

$$\equiv \qquad \{ \qquad + \text{ is the binary supremum operator} \qquad \}$$
$$a^* \le a^* \ \wedge \ a \cdot a^* \le a^*$$

$$\equiv \qquad \{ \qquad \text{reflexivity of } \le\, ; \ a^* = 1 + a \cdot a^* \qquad \}$$
$$\text{true} \ .$$

Thus we have established that $a^* = a^* \cdot a^*$.

We establish that * is a closure operator by the following ping-pong argument.

$$a^* \le b^*$$

$$\Leftarrow \qquad \{ \qquad (54) \text{ with } a,b,x := a,a,b^* \qquad \}$$
$$1 + a \cdot b^* \le b^*$$

$$\equiv \qquad \{ \qquad + \text{ is the binary supremum operator} \qquad \}$$
$$1 \le b^* \ \wedge \ a \cdot b^* \le b^*$$

$$\Leftarrow \qquad \{ \qquad b^* = 1 + b \cdot b^*\, , \ b^* = b^* \cdot b^*\, , \ \cdot \text{ is monotonic} \qquad \}$$
$$a \le b^*$$

$$\Leftarrow \qquad \{ \qquad a \le a^* \qquad \}$$
$$a^* \le b^* \ .$$

Exercise 61   *Prove the following properties:*

(a) $a \cdot b^* \le c^* \cdot a \ \Leftarrow \ a \cdot b \le c \cdot a$
(b) $c^* \cdot a \le a \cdot b^* \ \Leftarrow \ c \cdot a \le a \cdot b$
(c) $a \cdot (b \cdot a)^* = (a \cdot b)^* \cdot a$
(d) $(a + b)^* = b^* \cdot (a \cdot b^*)^* = (b^* \cdot a)^* \cdot b^*$
(e) $(a^*)^* = a^*$

Properties (a) and (b) are called *leapfrog* rules (because a "leapfrogs" from one side of a star term to the other). Both have the immediate corollary that * is monotonic (by taking a to be 1). Properties (c) and (d) are called the *mirror* rule and *star decomposition* rule, respectively. Property (e) states that * is idempotent.

□

Exercise 62   The goal of this exercise is to show that a^* is the least reflexive and transitive element of the algebra that is at least a .

Let a^+ denote $a \cdot a^*$. We call a^+ the *transitive closure* of a . *Prove the following properties of* a^+ .

(a) $a \le a^+$
(b) $a^+ = a \cdot a^* = a^* \cdot a$
(c) $a^+ \cdot a^+ \le a^+$
(d) $a^+ \le x \ \Leftarrow \ a + x \cdot x \le x$

Note that the combination of (a), (c) and (d) expresses the fact that a^+ is the least prefix point, and hence the least fixed point, of the function $\langle x:: a + x \cdot x \rangle$. That is, a^+ is the least transitive element that is at least a.

(e) *Show that a^* is the least fixed point of the function $\langle x:: 1 + a + x \cdot x \rangle$.*

□

6   Fixed Point Calculus

The least fixed point of a monotonic function is, as we have seen in theorem 42, characterised by two properties. It is a fixed point, and it is least among all prefix points of the functions. This gives us two calculational rules for reasoning about the least fixed point μf of monotonic function f: the *computation rule*

$$\mu f = f . \mu f$$

and the *induction rule*: for all x,

$$\mu f \sqsubseteq x \Leftarrow f . x \sqsubseteq x \ .$$

In principle these are the only rules one needs to know about least fixed points. Every calculation can be reduced to one involving just these two rules (together with the rules pertaining to the specific problem in hand). This indeed is commonly what happens. Many postulates are verified by induction. But this is often not the most effective way of reasoning about fixed points.

The problem is that this basic characterisation of least fixed points typically invites proof by mutual inclusion. That is, given two expressions, E and F, involving fixed points (or prefix points) the obvious strategy to determine conditions under which they are equal is to determine conditions under which the two inclusions $E \sqsubseteq F$ and $F \sqsubseteq E$ hold. This can lead to long and clumsy calculations. To avoid this we state a number of equational properties of least fixed points. Their proofs, which are mostly straightforward, are left as exercises. We conclude the section with the mutual recursion theorem, which expresses the solution of mutually recursive fixed point equations in terms of the successive solution of individual equations. The proof, which we do include, is a fine illustration of the earlier properties.

Unless otherwise stated, we assume throughout this section that f and g are monotonic endofunctions on the complete lattice $\mathcal{A} = (A, \sqsubseteq)$. (The assumption of completeness can be avoided but is convenient and practical.) The set of such functions also forms a complete lattice under the *pointwise ordering* $\dot{\sqsubseteq}$ defined by

$$f \mathbin{\dot{\sqsubseteq}} g \equiv \forall \langle x:: f . x \sqsubseteq g . x \rangle \ .$$

The set of prefix points of f is denoted by $\mathsf{Pre}.f$ and its set of postfix points is denoted by $\mathsf{Post}.f$. The set $\mathsf{Pre}.f$ is also a complete lattice, as is $\mathsf{Post}.f$.

6.1 Basic Rules

The most basic fixed point rule is that the least-fixed-point operator is monotonic:

$$\mu f \sqsubseteq \mu g \Leftarrow f \mathbin{\dot\sqsubseteq} g \ . \tag{63}$$

The second rule is called the *rolling rule*:

$$g.\mu(f \bullet g) = \mu(g \bullet f) \tag{64}$$

(where $f \in (A, \sqsubseteq) \leftarrow (B, \preceq)$ and $g \in (B, \preceq) \leftarrow (A, \sqsubseteq)$ for some posets $(A, \sqsubseteq)$ and $(B, \preceq)$). Note that the rolling rule subsumes the rule that a least prefix point is also a fixed point. Just instantiate f to the identity function. The proof we gave of this fact in the previous section can be adapted to give a proof of the rolling rule.

An immediate corollary of the rolling role is that, for a monotonic endofunction f, $\mu(f^2) = f.\mu(f^2)$ where f^2 denotes $f \bullet f$. This suggests that $\mu(f^2)$ and μf are equal. This is indeed the case, and is called the *square rule*:

$$\mu f = \mu(f^2) \ . \tag{65}$$

Consider now a monotonic, binary function $\oplus$ on the poset $\mathcal{A}$. Then, for each x, the function $(x \oplus)$ (which maps y to $x \oplus y$) is monotonic and so has a least fixed point $\mu(x \oplus)$. Abstracting from x, the function $\langle x :: \mu(x \oplus) \rangle$ is a monotonic endofunction on $\mathcal{A}$ and its least fixed point is $\mu \langle x :: \mu \langle y :: x \oplus y \rangle \rangle$. The *diagonal rule* removes the nesting in this expression:

$$\mu \langle x :: x \oplus x \rangle = \mu \langle x :: \mu \langle y :: x \oplus y \rangle \rangle \ . \tag{66}$$

The diagonal rule is a very important rule because it is the basis of methods for finding fixed points step by step. Suppose one wants to solve a fixed point equation $x :: x = x \oplus x$ where "$x \oplus x$" is a large expression involving several occurrences of the identifier x. The diagonal rule allows one to eliminate the x's one-by-one. This is what happens when one solves a number of equations defining a set of values by mutual recursion (sometimes called a set of "simultaneous equations"). Such a set of equations can be viewed as one equation of the form $\underline{x} = f.\underline{x}$ where $\underline{x}$ is a vector of values. Each occurrence of an element x_i in the set of equations is in fact an occurrence of $\Pi_i.\underline{x}$, where Π_i denotes the function that "projects" the vector $\underline{x}$ onto its ith component. It is thus an occurrence of "$\underline{x}$" itself and the standard practice is to eliminate such occurrences individually. Mutual recursion is discussed further in section 6.5.

Exercise 67   *For arbitrary elements a and b of a Kleene algebra , prove the following properties. Use only equational reasoning. (That is, do not prove any of the properties by mutual inclusion.)* (Hint: Take advantage of exercises 61 and 62.)

(a) $\mu\langle X :: a \cdot X^* \rangle \;=\; a^+$,
(b) $\mu\langle X :: (a+X)^* \rangle \;=\; \mu\langle X :: (a \cdot X)^* \rangle \;=\; \mu\langle X :: a+X^* \rangle \;=\; a^*$,
(c) $\mu\langle X :: a + X \cdot b \cdot X \rangle \;=\; a \cdot (b \cdot a)^*$,
(d) $\mu\langle X :: 1 + a \cdot X \cdot b \cdot X + b \cdot X \cdot a \cdot X \rangle \;=\; \mu\langle X :: 1 + a \cdot X \cdot b + b \cdot X \cdot a + X \cdot X \rangle$.

□

Exercise 68   Verify each of the rules given in this subsection.

□

6.2   Fusion

This section is about perhaps the most important fixed point rule of all, the *fusion* rule. In words, the fusion rule provides a condition under which the application of a function to a least fixed point can be expressed as a least fixed point. The rule is important because many computational problems are initially specified as such a function application, but are solved by computing the (least or greatest) solution to an appropriate fixed point equation.

Several examples arise as path-finding problems. Given a graph with "weighted" edges (formally, a function from the edges to the real numbers), the *length* of a path is defined to be the *sum* of the edge weights, and the *width* of a path is defined to be the *minimum* of the edge weights. The shortest *distance* between two nodes is the *minimum*, over all paths between the nodes, of the length of the path whilst the largest *gap* between two nodes is the *maximum*, over all paths between the nodes, of the width of the path. Thus both the shortest distance and the largest gap are defined as functions applied to the set of all paths between two given nodes; in the case of shortest distance, the function is "minimize the length", and, in the case of the largest gap, the function "maximize the width". However, both these problems are typically solved not by first enumerating all paths (an impossible task in the general case because there are infinitely many of them) but by solving directly recursive equations defining the shortest distance and largest gap functions. The formal justification for this process relies on the fusion theorem below.

The most powerful of the two rules characterising least prefix points is the induction rule. Its power is, however, somewhat limited because it only allows one to calculate with orderings in which the μ operator is the *principal* operator on the *lower* side of the ordering (i.e. orderings of the form $\mu f \sqsubseteq \cdots$). Formally the fusion rule overcomes this restriction on the induction rule by combining the calculation properties of Galois connections with those of fixed points.

Theorem 69 (μ-fusion)   Suppose $f \in A \leftarrow B$ is the lower adjoint in a Galois connection between the posets $(A, \sqsubseteq)$ and $(B, \preceq)$. Suppose also that $g \in (B, \preceq) \leftarrow (B, \preceq)$ and $h \in (A, \sqsubseteq) \leftarrow (A, \sqsubseteq)$ are monotonic functions. Then

(a) $f . \mu g \sqsubseteq \mu h \;\Leftarrow\; f \bullet g \mathbin{\dot{\sqsubseteq}} h \bullet f$,
(b) $f . \mu g = \mu h \;\Leftarrow\; f \bullet g = h \bullet f$.

Indeed, if the condition

$$f \bullet g = h \bullet f$$

holds, f is the lower adjoint in a Galois connection between the posets $(\mathsf{Pre}.h, \sqsubseteq)$ and $(\mathsf{Pre}.g, \preceq)$.

□

We call this theorem μ-"fusion" because it states when application of function, f, can be "fused" with a fixed point, μg, to form a fixed point, μh. (The rule is also used, of course, to "defuse" a fixed point into the application of a function to another fixed point.) Another reason for giving the rule this name is because it is the basis of so-called "loop fusion" techniques in programming: the combination of two loops, one executed after the other, into a single loop. The rule is also called the *transfer* lemma because it states when function f "transfers" the computation of one fixed point (μg) into the computation of another fixed point (μh).

Exercise 70   *Prove the fusion rule.* (Hint: first show that the function $k \in B \leftarrow A$ maps prefix points of h into prefix points of g if $g \bullet k \sqsubseteq k \bullet h$. Use this to show that f is the lower adjoint in a Galois connection between the posets $(\mathsf{Pre}.h, \sqsubseteq)$ and $(\mathsf{Pre}.g, \preceq)$.)

□

Note that in order to apply μ-fusion we do not need to *know* the upper adjoint of function f, we only need to know that it exists. The fundamental theorem of Galois connections is the most commonly used tool to establish the existence of an upper adjoint.

As an aid to memorising the μ-fusion theorems note that the order of f, g, $\sqsubseteq$ or $=$, and h is the same in the consequent and the antecedent, be it that in the antecedent the lower adjoint occurs twice, in different argument positions of $\bullet$.

The conclusion of μ-fusion — $\mu h = f.\mu g$ — involves *two* premises, that f be a lower adjoint, and that $f \bullet g = h \bullet f$. The rule is nevertheless very versatile since being a lower adjoint is far from being uncommon, and many algebraic properties take the form $f \bullet g = h \bullet f$ for some functions f, g and h. The next lemma also combines fixed points with Galois connections. We call it the *exchange rule* because it is used to exchange one lower adjoint for another. Its proof is left as an exercise. (Hint: for part (a) use induction followed by the rolling rule.)

Lemma 71 (Exchange Rule) Suppose f has type $(A, \sqsubseteq) \leftarrow (B, \preceq)$, and g and h both have type $(B, \preceq) \leftarrow (A, \sqsubseteq)$. Then, if g is a lower adjoint in a Galois connection,

(a) $\mu(g \bullet f) \sqsubseteq \mu(h \bullet f) \wedge \mu(f \bullet g) \sqsubseteq \mu(f \bullet h) \;\Leftarrow\; g \bullet f \bullet h \;\dot{\sqsubseteq}\; h \bullet f \bullet g$.

Furthermore, if both g and h are lower adjoints, then

(b) $\mu(g \bullet f) = \mu(h \bullet f) \wedge \mu(f \bullet g) = \mu(f \bullet h) \;\Leftarrow\; g \bullet f \bullet h = h \bullet f \bullet g$.

□

The two conclusions of (b), $\mu(g\bullet f)=\mu(h\bullet f)$ and $\mu(f\bullet g)=\mu(f\bullet h)$, say that g and h can be exchanged within a μ term in which they are composed after or before an arbitrary function f.

Exercise 72   *Prove the exchange rule.*
The two conjuncts in the consequent of 71(b) can be combined into one equation. The resulting lemma states when lower adjoint g can be replaced by lower adjoint h in an arbitrary context. The lemma has four variables rather than three. *Find the lemma and prove its validity.*

□

Applications We mentioned path-finding problems earlier as an example of the use of fusion. Space does not allow us to expand this in detail. Instead, this section illustrates the use of the rule by some examples involving languages.

Shortest Word As explained earlier, a context-free grammar defines a function from languages to languages. The language defined by the grammar is the least fixed point of this function. There is a number of computations that we may wish to perform on the grammar. These include testing whether the language generated is nonempty or not, and determining the length of a shortest word in the grammar. Let us consider the latter problem. (In fact, the problem is intimately related to the shortest path problem on graphs.) For concreteness we will demonstrate how to solve the problem using the grammar with productions

$$S \quad ::= \quad aS \quad | \quad SS \quad | \quad \varepsilon \ .$$

The language defined by the grammar is thus

$$\mu\langle X:: \{a\}\cdot X\cup X\cdot X\cup\{\varepsilon\}\rangle$$

(Of course the problem is very easily solved for a specific example as simple as this one. Try to imagine however that we are dealing with a grammar with a large number of nonterminals and a large number of productions.)
    Given a language L defined in this way, the general problem is to find $\#L$ where the function $\#$ is defined by extending the length function on words to a shortest length function on languages. Specifically, letting length.w denote the length of word w (the number of symbols in the word),

$$\#L \ = \ \Downarrow\langle w: w\in L: \mathsf{length}.w\rangle$$

(where $\Downarrow$ denotes the minimum operator — the minimum over an empty set is defined to be infinity). Now, because $\#$ is the infimum of the length function it is the lower adjoint in a Galois connection. Indeed,

$$\#L\geq k \ \equiv \ L\subseteq\Sigma^{\geq k}$$

where $\Sigma^{\geq k}$ is the set of all words (in the alphabet Σ) whose length is at least k. Noting the direction of the ordering on the left-hand side of this Galois connection, we get that

$$\#(\mu_{\subseteq} f) = \mu_{\geq} g \quad \Leftarrow \quad \# \bullet f = g \bullet \# \quad .$$

Applying this to our example grammar, we fill in f and calculate g:

$$\# \bullet \langle X:: \{a\} \cdot X \cup X \cdot X \cup \{\varepsilon\} \rangle \;=\; g \bullet \#$$

$$\equiv \qquad \{ \qquad \text{definition of composition} \qquad \}$$

$$\forall \langle X:: \#(\{a\} \cdot X \cup X \cdot X \cup \{\varepsilon\}) = g.(\#X) \rangle$$

$$\equiv \qquad \{ \qquad \# \text{ is a lower adjoint and so distributes over } \cup,$$

$$\text{definition of } \# \qquad \}$$

$$\forall \langle X:: \#(\{a\} \cdot X) \downarrow \#(X \cdot X) \downarrow \#\{\varepsilon\} \;=\; g.(\#X) \rangle$$

$$\equiv \qquad \{ \qquad \#(Y \cdot Z) = \#Y + \#Z, \; \#\{a\} = 1, \; \#\{\varepsilon\} = 0 \qquad \}$$

$$(1 + \#X) \downarrow (\#X + \#X) \downarrow 0 \;=\; g.(\#X)$$

$$\Leftarrow \qquad \{ \qquad \text{instantiation} \qquad \}$$

$$\forall \langle k:: (1 + k) \downarrow (k + k) \downarrow 0 \;=\; g.k \rangle \quad .$$

In this way we have determined that, for the language L defined by the above grammar,

$$\#L \;=\; \mu_{\geq} \langle k:: (1 + k) \downarrow (k + k) \downarrow 0 \rangle \quad .$$

That is, the length of a shortest word in the language defined by the grammar with productions

$$S \quad ::= \quad aS \quad | \quad SS \quad | \quad \varepsilon$$

is the greatest value k satisfying

$$k \;=\; (1 + k) \downarrow (k + k) \downarrow 0 \quad .$$

Note how the structure of the equation for k closely follows the structure of the original grammar — the alternate operator has been replaced by minimum, and concatenation of languages has been replaced by addition. What the example illustrates is that the length of the shortest word in the language generated by a context-free grammar can always be computed by determining the *greatest* fixed point (in the usual $\leq$ ordering on numbers — that is, the least fixed point if numbers are ordered by $\geq$) of an equation (or system of simultaneuous equations) obtained by replacing all occurrences of alternation in the grammar by minimum and all occurrences of concatenation by addition. Moreover, the key to the proof of this theorem is the fusion rule.

Membership of a language To illustrate the use of fusion yet further we consider two examples. The first is an example of how the fusion theorem is applied; the second illustrates how the fusion theorem need not be *directly* applicable. We discuss briefly how the second example is generalised in such a way that the fusion theorem does become applicable.

Both examples are concerned with membership of a set. So, let us consider an arbitrary set $\mathcal{U}$. For each x in $\mathcal{U}$ the predicate $(x\in)$ maps a subset P of $\mathcal{U}$ to the boolean value true if x is an element of P and otherwise to false. The predicate $(x\in)$ preserves set union. That is, for all bags $\mathcal{S}$ of subsets of $\mathcal{U}$,

$$x \in \cup\mathcal{S} \equiv \exists\langle P: P\in\mathcal{S}: x\in P\rangle \ .$$

According to the fundamental theorem, the predicate $(x\in)$ thus has an upper adjoint. Indeed, we have, for all booleans b,

$$x\in S \Rightarrow b \quad \equiv \quad S \subseteq \text{if } b\to\mathcal{U} \,\square\, \neg b \to \mathcal{U}\backslash\{x\} \text{ fi} \ .$$

Now suppose f is a monotonic function on sets. Let μf denote its least fixed point. The fact that $(x\in)$ is a lower adjoint means that we may be able to apply the fusion theorem to reduce a test for membership in μf to solving a recursive equation. Specifically

$$(x\in\mu f \equiv \mu g) \quad \Leftarrow \quad \forall\langle S:: x \in f.S \equiv g.(x\in S)\rangle \ .$$

That is, the recursive equation with underlying endofunction f is replaced by the equation with underlying endofunction g (mapping booleans to booleans) if we can establish the property

$$\forall\langle S:: x \in f.S \equiv g.(x\in S)\rangle \ .$$

An example of where this is always possible is testing whether the empty word is in the language defined by a context-free grammar. For concreteness, consider again the grammar with just one nonterminal S and productions

$$S \quad ::= \quad aS \ \mid \ SS \ \mid \ \varepsilon$$

Then the function f maps set X to

$$\{a\}\cdot X \ \cup \ X\cdot X \ \cup \ \{\varepsilon\} \ .$$

We compute the function g as follows:

$$
\begin{aligned}
&\varepsilon \in f.S \\
=\quad & \{ \quad \text{definition of } f \quad \} \\
&\varepsilon \in (\{a\}\cdot S \cup S\cdot S \cup \{\varepsilon\}) \\
=\quad & \{ \quad \text{membership distributes through set union} \quad \} \\
&\varepsilon \in \{a\}\cdot S \ \lor \ \varepsilon \in S\cdot S \ \lor \ \varepsilon \in \{\varepsilon\}
\end{aligned}
$$

$$= \qquad \{ \qquad \varepsilon \in X \cdot Y \ \equiv \ \varepsilon \in X \wedge \varepsilon \in Y \quad \}$$

$$(\varepsilon \in \{a\} \wedge \varepsilon \in S) \ \vee \ (\varepsilon \in S \wedge \varepsilon \in S) \ \vee \ \varepsilon \in \{\varepsilon\}$$

$$= \qquad \{ \qquad \bullet \quad g.b \ = \ (\varepsilon \in \{a\} \wedge b) \vee (b \wedge b) \vee \varepsilon \in \{\varepsilon\} \ ,$$

see below for why the rhs has not been

simplified further $\}$

$$g.(\varepsilon \in S) \ .$$

We have thus derived that

$$\varepsilon \in \mu\langle X :: \{a\} \cdot X \ \cup \ X \cdot X \ \cup \ \{\varepsilon\}\rangle \ \equiv \ \mu\langle b :: (\varepsilon \in \{a\} \wedge b) \vee (b \wedge b) \vee \varepsilon \in \{\varepsilon\}\rangle \ .$$

Note how the definition of g has the same structure as the definition of f. Effectively set union has been replaced by disjunction and concatenation has been replaced by conjunction. Of course, g can be simplified further (to the constant function **true**) but that would miss the point of the example.

Now suppose that instead of taking x to be the empty word we consider any word other than the empty word. Then, repeating the above calculation with "$\varepsilon \in$" replaced everywhere by "$x \in$", the calculation breaks down at the second step. This is because the empty word is the only word x that satisfies the property

$$x \in X \cdot Y \ \equiv \ x \in X \wedge x \in Y$$

for all X and Y. Indeed, taking x to be a for illustration purposes, we have

$$a \in \mu\langle X :: \{a\} \cdot X \ \cup \ X \cdot X \ \cup \ \{\varepsilon\}\rangle \ \equiv \ \mathsf{true}$$

but

$$\mu\langle b :: (a \in \{a\} \wedge b) \vee (b \wedge b) \vee a \in \{\varepsilon\}\rangle \ \equiv \ \mathsf{false} \ .$$

This second example emphasises that the conclusion of μ-fusion — $\mu h = f.\mu g$ — demands *two* properties of f, g and h, namely that f be a lower adjoint, and that $f \bullet g = h \bullet f$. The rule is nevertheless very versatile since being a lower adjoint is far from being uncommon, and many algebraic properties take the form $f \bullet g = h \bullet f$ for some functions f, g and h. In cases when the rule is not immediately applicable we have to seek generalisations of f and/or g that do satisfy both properties. For the membership problem above, this is achieved by generalising the problem of applying the function ($x \in$) to the language but the *matrix* of functions ($u \in$) where u is a segment of x. This is the basis of the Cocke-Younger-Kasami algorithm for general context-free language recognition.

6.3   Uniqueness

An important issue when confronted with a fixed point equation is whether or not the equation has a *unique* solution.

Uniqueness is a combination of there being at least one solution and at most one solution. In a complete lattice every monotonic function has a least and a greatest fixed point, so the question is whether the least and greatest fixed points are equal.

A very important special case is when the equation

$$x:: \ x = a + b \cdot x$$

has a unique solution in a Kleene algebra.

In order to give a general answer to this question, it is necessary to make a further assumption about the partial ordering relation on elements in the algebra. The assumption we make is that the elements in the algebra form a complete lattice under the partial ordering relation and, furthermore, this ordering is such that, for each a, the section $(a+)$ is the upper adoint in a Galois connection. This important property is one that distinguishes a *regular algebra* from a Kleene algebra. The other additional property of a regular algebra (which we do not need to consider until later) is that each section $(b\cdot)$ is a lower adjoint in a Galois connection.

An ordering relation that is complete and is such that sections of the binary supremum operator are upper adjoints in a Galois connection is called a *complete, completely distributive lattice*. (It is called completely distributive because being an upper adjoint is equivalent to being universally distributive over all infima.) A *regular algebra* is thus a Kleene algebra for which underlying poset is a complete, completely distributive lattice and such that each section $(b\cdot)$ is a lower adjoint in a Galois connection.

The assumption of being completely distributive clearly holds for languages and relations, since in both cases the ordering relation is the subset relation and addition is set union and we have the shunting rule:

$$b \subseteq a \cup c \ \equiv \ \neg a \cap b \subseteq c \ .$$

The assumption that $(a+)$ is the upper adoint in a Galois connection allows us to use fusion as follows:

Theorem 73   If $(y+)$ is an upper adjoint, then we have, for all a and b,

$$\nu\langle x:: \ a + x \cdot b\rangle = y + \nu\langle x:: x \cdot b\rangle \ \Leftarrow \ y = a + y \cdot b \ .$$

Proof

$$\nu\langle x:: \ a + x \cdot b\rangle = y + \nu\langle x:: x \cdot b\rangle$$

$\Leftarrow$ $\{$ $(y+)$ is upper adjoint: ν-fusion $\}$

$$\forall\langle x:: \ a + (y+x) \cdot b = y + x \cdot b\rangle$$

$\Leftarrow$ $\{$ $(\cdot b)$ distributes over $+$, associativity of $+$ $\}$

$$a + y \cdot b = y \ .$$

$\square$

As a consequence, in a regular algebra, the *largest* solution of the equation $x:: \ x = a + x \cdot b$ is the sum (i.e. supremum) of an arbitrary solution and the largest solution of the equation $x{::}\ x = x{\cdot}b$. Note that a special choice for y in theorem 73 is $y = a \cdot b^*$.

An immediate corollary of theorem 73 is that if $\nu\langle x{::}\,x{\cdot}b\rangle = 0$, function $\langle x{::}\ a + x{\cdot}b\rangle$ has a unique fixed point. This is the rule we call the *unique extension property* (UEP) of regular algebra.

Theorem 74 (The unique extension property (UEP))   Suppose b is an element of a regular algebra. If $\nu\langle x{::}\,x{\cdot}b\rangle = 0$, then, for all a and x,

$$a + x{\cdot}b = x \;\;\equiv\;\; x = a \cdot b^* \;\;.$$

$\square$

The UEP draws attention to the importance of property $\nu\langle x{::}\,x{\cdot}b\rangle = 0$. In language theory it is equivalent to $\varepsilon \notin b$ since if, on the contrary, x is a non-empty set such that $x = x{\cdot}b$ then the length of the shortest word in x must be equal to the length of the shortest word in b plus the length of the shortest word in x. That is, the length of the shortest word in b is zero. The terminology that is often used is "b does not possess the *empty-word property*". In relation algebra we say "b is well-founded": the property expresses that there are no infinite sequences of b-related elements (thus, if relation b represents a finite directed graph, $\nu\langle x{::}\,x{\cdot}b\rangle = 0$ means that the graph is acyclic).

Exercise 75   Consider the final three instances of a Kleene algebra shown in table 5.3. In each of these instances, suppose b is a square matrix with entries drawn from the carrier set of the relevant instance. (Equivalently, suppose b is a graph with edge labels drawn from the carrier set. If the (i,j)th matrix entry is 0 then there is no edge from i to j in the graph.) *What is the interpretation of $\nu\langle x{::}\,x{\cdot}b\rangle = 0$ in each case?*

$\square$

6.4   Parameterised Prefix Points

Often fixed point equations are parameterised, sometimes explicitly, sometimes implicitly. An example of implicit parameters is the definition of the star operator discussed in section 5.3. In the defining equations given there (see for example equation (53)) a and b are parameters; the equations do not depend on how a and b are instantiated. The equations define the *function* mapping a to a^*. The rules we present in this section are concerned with such parameterised fixed point equations.

The first rule we present, the abstraction rule, is rarely given explicitly although it is very fundamental. The second rule, called the "beautiful theorem" because of its power and generality, is well-known in one particular form —its application to proving continuity properties of functions defined by fixed point equations— but is less well known at the level of generality given here.

The Abstraction Rule The definition of a^* in section 5.3 is a very good example of the "abstraction rule". Recall that a^* is defined to be the least prefix point of the function mapping x to $1 + a \cdot x$. Thus a is a *parameter* in the definition of the star operator. The remarkable, and very fundamental, property is that the star operator is itself a least prefix point. Indeed, suppose we consider the function

$$\langle g{::}\ \langle a{::}\ 1 + a \cdot g.a \rangle \rangle \ .$$

(Note that this function maps an endofunction g on the Kleene algebra to an endofunction on the Kleene algebra and so is a (higher order) endofunction.) Then the star operator is the least fixed point of this function. That is,

$$\langle a{::}\ a^* \rangle \ = \ \mu\langle g{::}\ \langle a{::}\ 1 + a \cdot g.a \rangle \rangle \ .$$

We leave the verification of this fact as an exercise. (We prove a more general theorem shortly.)

The general theorem that this illustrates is obtained in the following way. We begin by making explicit the fact that a is a parameter in the definition of the star operator. This we do by considering the binary operator $\oplus$ defined by

$$a \oplus x = 1 + a \cdot x \ .$$

Then, by definition, $a^* = \mu\langle x{::}\ 1 + a \cdot x \rangle$. So

$$\langle a{::}\ a^* \rangle \ = \ \langle a{::}\ \mu\langle x{::}\ a \oplus x \rangle \rangle \ .$$

This is just a repetition of the definition in section 5.3 but slightly more round-about. But now we consider the function F from functions to functions defined by

$$F \ = \ \langle g{::}\ \langle a{::}\ a \oplus g.a \rangle \rangle \ .$$

(That is, $(F.g).a \ = \ a \oplus g.a$.) So for the particular definition of $\oplus$ given above,

$$F \ = \ \langle g{::}\ \langle a{::}\ 1 + a \cdot g.a \rangle \rangle \ .$$

Then the theorem is that

$$\langle a{::}\ \mu\langle x{::}\ a \oplus x \rangle \rangle \ = \ \mu F$$

for all (monotonic) binary operators $\oplus$ and all F defined as above. That is, for all monotonic binary operators $\oplus$,

$$\langle a{::}\ \mu\langle x{::}\ a \oplus x \rangle \rangle \ = \ \mu\langle g{::}\ \langle a{::}\ a \oplus g.a \rangle \rangle \ . \tag{76}$$

This rule we call the *abstraction rule*.

In order to verify the validity of the rule we have to verify that $\langle a{::}\ \mu\langle x{::}\ a \oplus x \rangle \rangle$ is a prefix point of the function F, and that it is at most any prefix point of F. This turns out to be straightforward. First, it is a prefix point by the following argument:

$$F.\langle a{::}\ \mu\langle x{::}\ a{\oplus}x\rangle\rangle \ \dot{\sqsubseteq}\ \langle a{::}\ \mu\langle x{::}\ a{\oplus}x\rangle\rangle$$

$\equiv$ {   pointwise ordering, definition of $(F.g).a$ }

$$\forall\langle a{::}\ a \oplus \langle a{::}\ \mu\langle x{::}\ a{\oplus}x\rangle\rangle.a \sqsubseteq \mu\langle x{::}\ a{\oplus}x\rangle\rangle$$

$\equiv$ { $\mu\langle x{::}\ a{\oplus}x\rangle$ is a prefix point of $(a\oplus)$ }

true .

Second, it is at most any prefix point. Suppose g is a prefix point of F, i.e. $F.g \ \dot{\sqsubseteq}\ g$. Then

$$\langle a{::}\ \mu\langle x{::}\ a{\oplus}x\rangle\rangle \ \dot{\sqsubseteq}\ g$$

$\equiv$ {   pointwise ordering   }

$$\forall\langle a{::}\ \mu\langle x{::}\ a{\oplus}x\rangle \sqsubseteq g.a\rangle$$

$\Leftarrow$ {   fixed point induction: (44)   }

$$\forall\langle a{::}\ a \oplus g.a \sqsubseteq g.a\rangle$$

$\equiv$ {   pointwise ordering, definition of $(F.g).a$ }

$$F.g \ \dot{\sqsubseteq}\ g$$

$\equiv$ { g is a prefix point of F }

true .

This concludes the proof.

Exercise 77   Suppose the operator $\oplus$ is defined by $x{\oplus}y = f.y$. *What property does one then obtain by instantiating the abstraction rule?*

$\square$

The Beautiful Theorem   A very important application of the abstraction rule in combination with fixed point fusion is a theorem that has been dubbed "beautiful" by Dijkstra and Scholten [4, p. 159].

As observed precisely above, a parameterised least-fixed-point equation defines a function in terms of a binary operator. The beautiful theorem is that this function enjoys any kind of supremum-preserving property enjoyed by the binary operator. Thus supremum-preserving properties are preserved in the process of constructing least fixed points.

Dijkstra and Scholten formulate the "beautiful theorem" in the context of the predicate calculus. In terms of poset theory the theorem is stated as follows. Suppose that $\mathcal{A}=(A,\sqsubseteq)$ and $\mathcal{B}=(B,\preceq)$ are ordered sets and suppose $\oplus \in (\mathcal{A}{\leftarrow}\mathcal{A}){\leftarrow}\mathcal{B}$. (Thus $\oplus$ is a monotonic function mapping elements of the set B into monotonic endofunctions on the set A .) As in section 6.4 denote application of $\oplus$ to x by $x\oplus$. Assume $\mu(x\oplus)$ exists for each x and consider the function $\langle x{::}\ \mu(x\oplus)\rangle$, which we denote by †. The "beautiful theorem" is that † enjoys any type of supremum-preserving property that is enjoyed by the (uncurried binary) function ⊕. More precisely,

$$\forall\langle f :: \sqcup(\dagger \bullet f) = \dagger(\sqcup f)\rangle \;\Leftarrow\; \forall\langle f, g :: \sqcup(f \dot\oplus g) = (\sqcup f) \oplus (\sqcup g)\rangle \;,$$

where, by definition, $f \dot\oplus g$ is the function mapping x to $f.x \oplus g.x$, • denotes function composition and ⊔ denotes the supremum operator on functions of the shape of f and g.

The supremum operator, if it exists for a class of functions of a certain shape, is the lower adjoint in a Galois connection. This is the key to the proof of the beautiful theorem. In order to make this explicit we formulate the theorem yet more abstractly. The theorem is that for arbitrary function G that is the lower adjoint in a Galois connection, and arbitrary function H (G and H having of course appropriate types),

$$\forall\langle f :: G.(\dagger \bullet f) = \dagger(H.f)\rangle \;\Leftarrow\; \forall\langle g :: G.(f \dot\oplus g) = H.f \oplus G.g\rangle \;.$$

The proof is very short. We first note that $(\dagger \bullet f).x = \dagger(f.x) = \mu((f.x)\oplus)$, by definition of †. Thus, by the abstraction rule, $\dagger \bullet f = \mu(f \dot\oplus)$. This is just what we need in order to apply the fusion theorem.

$$G.(\dagger \bullet f) = \dagger.(H.f)$$

$$\equiv \qquad \{ \qquad \text{above} \quad \}$$

$$G.\mu(f \dot\oplus) = \mu((H.f)\oplus)$$

$$\Leftarrow \qquad \{ \qquad \text{by assumption, } G \text{ is a lower adjoint.}$$

$$\text{fusion: theorem 69} \quad \}$$

$$\forall\langle g :: G.(f \dot\oplus g) = H.f \oplus G.g\rangle \;.$$

Cocontinuity of Iteration We conclude the discussion of parameterised fixed points by considering the implications of the beautiful theorem for the iteration operator. Specifically, we show that in a regular algebra the iteration operator is *cocontinuous*[5]. Specifically, this is the property that for an ascending sequence $f.0 \le f.1 \le \ldots \le f.n \le \ldots$

$$(\Sigma\langle n: 0 \le n: f.n\rangle)^* = \Sigma\langle n: 0 \le n: (f.n)^*\rangle \;.$$

A property of a regular algebra that we need to complete the proof is that, for all such sequences f and for all z,

$$z \cdot \Sigma\langle n: 0 \le n: f.n\rangle = \Sigma\langle n: 0 \le n: z \cdot f.n\rangle$$

---

[5] There is a disturbing confusion between the standard terminology in the computing science literature and the literature on category theory in this respect. What is called a "continuity" property in the computing science literature is called a "*cocontinuity*" property in the category theory literature. We use the category theory terminology here.

and $\Sigma\langle n: 0 \leq n: f.n\rangle \cdot z = \Sigma\langle n: 0 \leq n: f.n \cdot z\rangle$

The property of iteration is thus that in a Kleene algebra in which the sections $(\cdot z)$ and $(z\cdot)$ are cocontinuous, for all z, the iteration operator * is also cocontinuous. (This proviso is satisfied in a regular algebra and thus in all Kleene algebras of interest to us.)

   Recalling the discussion in the introduction to this section, the instantiation of the beautiful theorem we wish to consider is as follows: the function $\dagger$ is the operator * (i.e. the function $\langle a:: a^*\rangle$); correspondingly the binary operator $\oplus$ is defined by $a \oplus x = 1 + a \cdot x$. The functions G and H are both taken to be the supremum operator of ascending functions on the natural numbers to the carrier of a regular algebra, which we denote by Σ.

   The instantiation of the beautiful theorem (with $G,H,\dagger := \Sigma,\Sigma,^*$) gives us, for all ascending sequences f:

$$\Sigma\langle n:: (f.n)^*\rangle = (\Sigma f)^* \quad \Leftarrow \quad \forall\langle f,g:: \Sigma\langle n:: 1 + f.n \cdot g.n\rangle = 1 + (\Sigma f)\cdot(\Sigma g)\rangle$$

where the dummies n range over the natural numbers, and the dummies f and g range over ascending sequences. We try to simplify the antecedent of this theorem. First, we have:

$$\Sigma\langle n:: 1 + f.n \cdot g.n\rangle \leq 1 + (\Sigma f)\cdot(\Sigma g)$$

$\equiv$ {   definition of supremum   }

$$\forall\langle n:: 1 + f.n \cdot g.n \leq 1 + (\Sigma f)\cdot(\Sigma g)\rangle$$

$\Leftarrow$ { $+$ is the binary supremum operator   }

$$\forall\langle n:: f.n \cdot g.n \leq (\Sigma f)\cdot(\Sigma g)\rangle$$

$\equiv$ {   property of suprema   }

     true .

So it is the opposite inclusion that is crucial. Now,

$$(\Sigma f)\cdot(\Sigma g)$$

$=$ { $\bullet$ assume, for all z, $(\cdot z)$ is cocontinuous   }

$$\Sigma\langle n:: f.n \cdot (\Sigma g)\rangle$$

$=$ { $\bullet$ assume, for all z, $(z\cdot)$ is cocontinuous   }

$$\Sigma\langle n:: \Sigma\langle m:: f.n \cdot g.m\rangle\rangle .$$

So,

$$\Sigma\langle n:: 1 + f.n \cdot g.n\rangle \geq 1 + (\Sigma f)\cdot(\Sigma g)$$

$\equiv$ { $+$ is the binary supremum operator   }

$$\Sigma\langle n:: 1 + f.n \cdot g.n\rangle \geq 1 \ \wedge \ \Sigma\langle n:: 1 + f.n \cdot g.n\rangle \geq (\Sigma f)\cdot(\Sigma g)$$

$\Leftarrow$ $\qquad$ { $\qquad$ $\Sigma\langle n:: 1{+}c\rangle \geq 1$, for all c,

$\qquad$ and $1 + f.n \cdot g.n \geq f.n \cdot g.n$ $\quad$ }

$\qquad$ $\Sigma\langle n:: f.n \cdot g.n\rangle \geq (\Sigma f)\cdot(\Sigma g)$

$\equiv$ $\qquad$ { $\qquad$ above $\quad$ }

$\qquad$ $\Sigma\langle n:: f.n \cdot g.n\rangle \geq \Sigma\langle n:: \Sigma\langle m:: f.n \cdot g.m\rangle\rangle$

$\equiv$ $\qquad$ { $\qquad$ suprema, dummy change $\quad$ }

$\qquad$ $\forall\langle n, m:: \Sigma\langle p:: f.p \cdot g.p\rangle \geq f.n \cdot g.m\rangle$

$\Leftarrow$ $\qquad$ { $\qquad$ $\Sigma\langle p:: f.p \cdot g.p\rangle \geq f.(n{\uparrow}m) \cdot g.(n{\uparrow}m)$

$\qquad$ where $(n{\uparrow}m)$ denotes the maximum of m and n $\quad$ }

$\qquad$ $\forall\langle n, m:: f.(n{\uparrow}m) \cdot g.(n{\uparrow}m) \geq f.n \cdot g.m\rangle$

$\equiv$ $\qquad$ { $\qquad$ f and g are ascending sequences,

$\qquad$ product is monotonic $\quad$ }

$\qquad$ true .

This completes the proof.

6.5 Mutual Recursion

In all but the simplest cases, recursive functions are defined by *mutual recursion*. For example, the BNF definition of the syntax of a programming language uses mutual recursion to simultaneously define the syntax of expressions, statements, declarations etc. A definition by mutual recursion can be seen as a *single* fixed point equation where there is one unknown —a vector of values— and the function defining the unknown maps a vector to a vector. On the other hand, one also wishes to view a definition by mutual recursion as a collection of individual equations, defining several unknown values, and which may be solved on an individual basis. In this section we show that these two views are compatible with each other. We present one theorem to the effect that least prefix points can be calculated by solving individual equations and back-substituting.

Without loss of generality we can confine ourselves to fixed point equations involving two unknowns: a fixed point equation with $n{+}1$ unknowns can always be viewed as an equation on two unknowns, one of which is a vector of length n.

Any fixed point of a function mapping pairs of values to pairs of values is, of course, a pair. We show how to calculate the individual components of the least fixed point of such a function, given that it is possible to calculate least fixed points of functions mapping single elements to single elements. The fixed-point equation to be dealt with is the following.

$$x, y:: \ x = x \odot y \ \wedge \ y = x \otimes y \quad . \tag{78}$$

We first consider two special cases in which $\odot$ and $\otimes$ depend on one of their arguments only.

Lemma 79

(a) $(\mu f , \mu g) = \mu\langle x, y :: (f.x, g.y)\rangle$
(b) $(\mu(f \bullet g) , \mu(g \bullet f)) = \mu\langle x, y :: (f.y, g.x)\rangle$.

Proof of (a). This is an instance of the abstraction rule. To see this, rename the functions to f_0 and f_1 and their arguments to x_0 and x_1 . Then (76) says that

$$\langle i :: \mu\langle x :: f_i.x\rangle\rangle \;=\; \mu\langle g :: \langle i :: f_i.(g.i)\rangle\rangle$$

Identifying the pair (x_0, x_1) with the function $\langle i :: x.i\rangle$,

$$\mu\langle g :: \langle i :: f_i.(g.i)\rangle\rangle \;=\; \mu\langle x_0, x_1 \;::\; (f_0.x_0 , f_1.x_1)\rangle \;.$$

So

$$\langle i :: \mu\langle x :: f_i.x\rangle\rangle \;=\; \mu\langle x_0, x_1 \;::\; (f_0.x_0 , f_1.x_1)\rangle$$

as required.
Proof of (b)

$$(\mu(f \bullet g) , \mu(g \bullet f)) = \mu\langle x, y :: (f.y, g.x)\rangle$$

$\Leftarrow$ $\{$ (a) on lhs $\}$

$$\mu\langle x, y :: (f.g.x , g.f.y)\rangle = \mu\langle x, y :: (f.y, g.x)\rangle$$

$\equiv$ $\{$ define $\phi : \phi(x,y) = (f.y , g.x)$ $\}$

$$\mu(\phi \bullet \phi) = \mu\phi$$

$\equiv$ $\{$ square rule $\}$

    true .

□

With the aid of lemma (79), we now compute the least solution of (78), viz. we prove

Theorem 80

$$(\mu\langle x :: x \odot p.x\rangle , \mu\langle y :: q.y \otimes y\rangle) = \mu\langle x, y :: (x \odot y, x \otimes y)\rangle$$

where $p.x = \mu\langle v :: x \otimes v\rangle$ and $q.y = \mu\langle u :: u \odot y\rangle$, i.e. $p.x$ and $q.y$ are the least fixed points of the individual equations.

Proof

$$\mu\langle x, y :: (x \odot y, x \otimes y)\rangle$$

$=$ $\{$ diagonal rule (66) $\}$

$$\mu\langle x, y :: \mu\langle u, v :: (u \odot y, x \otimes v)\rangle\rangle$$

$=$ $\{$ lemma (79a) and definition of p and q $\}$

$$\mu\langle x, y:: (q.y, p.x)\rangle$$

$$=\qquad\{\qquad\text{lemma (79b)}\quad\}$$

$$(\ \mu\langle x:: q.(p.x)\rangle\ ,\ \mu\langle y:: p.(q.y)\rangle\ )$$

$$=\qquad\{\qquad\text{definition}\ q\ ,\ p\quad\}$$

$$(\ \mu\langle x:: \mu\langle u:: u\odot p.x\rangle\rangle\ ,\ \mu\langle y:: \mu\langle v:: q.y\otimes v\rangle\rangle\ )$$

$$=\qquad\{\qquad\text{diagonal rule (66) twice:}\ u:=x\ ,\ v:=y\quad\}$$

$$(\ \mu\langle x:: x\odot p.x\rangle\ ,\ \mu\langle y:: q.y\otimes y\rangle\ )\ \ .$$

□

This concludes the presentation of the calculus. The corresponding calculus of greatest fixed points is obtained by the interchanges $\mu\leftrightarrow\nu$, $\sqsubseteq\leftrightarrow\sqsupseteq$, and lower adjoint $\leftrightarrow$ upper adjoint.

Exercise 81   Suppose f is a (unary) function and $\otimes$ is a binary operator. Prove the following:

(a) $\mu\langle x, y:: (f.x\ ,\ x\otimes y)\rangle\ =\ (\mu f\ ,\ \mu\langle y:: \mu f\otimes y\rangle\ )$
(b) $\mu\langle x, y:: (f.y\ ,\ x\otimes y)\rangle\ =\ \mu\langle x, y:: (f.(x\otimes y)\ ,\ x\otimes y)\rangle\ \ .$

Hint: Use theorem 80 for (a). Use the diagonal rule and lemma 79 for (b).

□

6.6   An Illustration — Arithmetic Expressions

The Algol 60 definition of arithmetic expressions, restricted to just multiplication and addition, has the following form. The nonterminals $\langle Term\rangle$ and $\langle Factor\rangle$ serve to introduce a precedence of multiplication over addition, and the use of left recursion (for example, "$\langle Expression\rangle$" is repeated as the leftmost symbol on the right of the production $\langle Expression\rangle\ ::=\ \langle Expression\rangle + \langle Term\rangle$) serves to define a left-to-right evaluation order on repeated occurrences of the same operator.

$$\langle Expression\rangle ::= \langle Expression\rangle + \langle Term\rangle\quad|\quad \langle Term\rangle$$
$$\langle Term\rangle\qquad ::= \langle Term\rangle \times \langle Factor\rangle\quad|\quad \langle Factor\rangle$$
$$\langle Factor\rangle\qquad ::= (\ \langle Expression\rangle\ )\quad|\quad \langle Variable\rangle$$

A much simpler grammar for such arithmetic expressions takes the following form.

$$\langle Expression\rangle ::= \langle Expression\rangle + \langle Expression\rangle$$
$$|\quad \langle Expression\rangle \times \langle Expression\rangle$$
$$|\quad (\ \langle Expression\rangle\ )$$
$$|\quad \langle Variable\rangle$$

This grammar imposes no precedence of multiplication over addition and is ambivalent about the order in which repeated additions or multiplications are evaluated. (The former is clearly undesirable but the latter is of no consequence because addition and multiplication are associative.)

We want to prove that the languages defined by $\langle Expression \rangle$ in the two grammars above are equal. The proof is a combination of the fixed point calculus presented in this section and Kleene algebra presented in chapter 5.3.

To avoid confusion, let us rename the nonterminal and terminal symbols in the grammars. (We need to rename the nonterminals in order not to confuse the two instances of $\langle Expression \rangle$; we need to rename the terminal symbols because of the use of " $+$ " and the parentheses "(" and ")" in both regular expressions (the meta language) and in arithmetic expressions (the object language).)

Choosing letters a, b, c, d and e for " $+$ ", " $\times$ ", "(", ")" and $\langle Variable \rangle$, and renaming $\langle Expression \rangle$, $\langle Term \rangle$ and $\langle Factor \rangle$ as E, T and F, respectively, the first grammar is transformed to the following.

$$
\begin{aligned}
E &::= E \, a \, T \quad | \quad T \\
T &::= T \, b \, F \quad | \quad F \\
F &::= c \, E \, d \quad | \quad e
\end{aligned}
$$

Using the same renaming for the terminal symbols but renaming $\langle Expression \rangle$ as D, we get the following for the second grammar.

$$
D ::= D \, a \, D \quad | \quad D \, b \, D \quad | \quad c \, D \, d \quad | \quad e
$$

The task is now to prove that the languages generated by E and D are equal. Note that the proof does not rely on a, b, c, d and e being terminal symbols. They may denote arbitrary languages.

We begin with an informal calculation. Then we show how the informal calculation is justified using the rules of the fixed point calculus.

The informal calculation treats the grammars as systems of simultaneous equations. We have four equations:

$$
E \;=\; E{\cdot}a{\cdot}T + T \;, \tag{82}
$$

$$
T \;=\; T{\cdot}b{\cdot}F + F \;, \tag{83}
$$

$$
F \;=\; c{\cdot}E{\cdot}d + e \;, \tag{84}
$$

$$
D \;=\; D{\cdot}a{\cdot}D + D{\cdot}b{\cdot}D + c{\cdot}D{\cdot}d + e \;. \tag{85}
$$

The first step is to "solve" the equations for E and T. That is, we eliminate E and T from, respectively, the right sides of equations (82) and (83). We get:

$$
E \;=\; T{\cdot}(a{\cdot}T)^* \tag{86}
$$

and

$$
T \;=\; F{\cdot}(b{\cdot}F)^* \;. \tag{87}
$$

Now we substitute the right side of the equation for T in the right side of the equation for E. We get:

$$E \ = \ F \cdot (b \cdot F)^* \cdot (a \cdot F \cdot (b \cdot F)^*)^*$$

which can be simplified using star decomposition (exercise $61(e)$) to

$$E \ = \ F \cdot (b \cdot F + a \cdot F)^* \quad .$$

This can in turn be simplified, using the "arithmetic" rules of Kleene algebra, to

$$E \ = \ F \cdot ((a+b) \cdot F)^* \quad .$$

So, applying exercise $67(c)$,

$$E = \mu \langle X :: \ F + X \cdot (a+b) \cdot X \rangle \quad .$$

Now we substitute the right side of equation (84) into this last equation, in order to eliminate F. We obtain

$$E = \mu \langle X :: \ c \cdot E \cdot d + e + X \cdot (a+b) \cdot X \rangle \quad .$$

"Solving" this equation by eliminating E on the right side:

$$E = \mu \langle Y :: \ \mu \langle X :: \ c \cdot Y \cdot d + e + X \cdot (a+b) \cdot X \rangle \rangle \quad .$$

The last step is to apply the diagonal rule, together with a little "arithmetic":

$$E = \mu \langle X :: \ X \cdot a \cdot X + X \cdot b \cdot X + c \cdot X \cdot d + e \rangle \quad .$$

That is, E solves the equation (85) for D.

Let us now conduct this calculation formally using the fixed point calculus. The first two steps combine the use of the diagonal rule with exercise $81(a)$ to justify the derivation of equations (86) and (87). The third step uses exercise $81(b)$ to justify the substitution of $F \cdot (b \cdot F)^*$ for T in the informal proof.

$$\mu \langle E, T, F :: \ (E \cdot a \cdot T + T \ , \ T \cdot b \cdot F + F \ , \ c \cdot E \cdot d + e) \rangle$$

$$= \qquad \{ \qquad \text{diagonal rule} \quad \}$$

$$\mu \langle E, T, F :: \ \mu \langle X, Y, Z :: \ (X \cdot a \cdot T + T \ , \ Y \cdot b \cdot F + F \ , \ c \cdot E \cdot d + e) \rangle \rangle$$

$$= \qquad \{ \qquad \text{exercise } 81(a) \text{ and definition of } ^* \ (\text{twice}) \quad \}$$

$$\mu \langle E, T, F :: \ (T \cdot (a \cdot T)^* \ , \ F \cdot (b \cdot F)^* \ , \ c \cdot E \cdot d + e) \rangle$$

$$= \qquad \{ \qquad \text{exercise } 81(b) \quad \}$$

$$\mu \langle E, T, F :: \ ((F \cdot (b \cdot F)^* \cdot (a \cdot F \cdot (b \cdot F)^*)^*) \ , \ F \cdot (b \cdot F)^* \ , \ c \cdot E \cdot d + e) \rangle \quad .$$

The remaining steps in the calculation do not alter the subexpressions "$F \cdot (b \cdot F)^*$" and "$c \cdot E \cdot d + e$". We therefore introduce abbreviations for these subexpressions. Note how formally all elements of the system of equations being solved have to be carried along whereas it is only the equation for E that is being manipulated, just as in the informal calculation.

$$\mu\langle E,T,F:: ((F\cdot(b\cdot F)^*\cdot(a\cdot F\cdot(b\cdot F)^*)^*)\ ,\ F\cdot(b\cdot F)^*\ ,\ c\cdot E\cdot d+e)\rangle$$

$=$ { introduce the abbreviation Φ for $F\cdot(b\cdot F)^*$

and Ψ for $c\cdot E\cdot d+e$ }

$$\mu\langle E,T,F:: (F\cdot(b\cdot F)^*\cdot(a\cdot F\cdot(b\cdot F)^*)^*\ ,\ \Phi\ ,\ \Psi)\rangle$$

$=$ { star decomposition (exercise 61(e)), arithmetic }

$$\mu\langle E,T,F:: (F\cdot((a+b)\cdot F)^*\ ,\ \Phi\ ,\ \Psi)\rangle$$

$=$ { exercise 67(c) }

$$\mu\langle E,T,F:: (\mu\langle X:: F+X\cdot(a+b)\cdot X\rangle,\Phi,\Psi)\rangle$$

$=$ { exercise 81(b), definition of Ψ }

$$\mu\langle E,T,F:: (\mu\langle X:: c\cdot E\cdot d+e+X\cdot(a+b)\cdot X\rangle,\Phi,\Psi)\rangle\ .$$

In the final part of the calculation, we again use exercise 81(a) in combination with the diagonal rule.

$$\mu\langle E,T,F:: (\mu\langle X:: c\cdot E\cdot d+e+X\cdot(a+b)\cdot X\rangle,\Phi,\Psi)\rangle$$

$=$ { exercise 81(a) }

$$\mu\langle E,T,F:: \mu\langle X,Y,Z:: (X\cdot a\cdot X+X\cdot b\cdot X+c\cdot E\cdot d+e\ ,\ \Phi\ ,\ \Psi)\rangle\rangle$$

$=$ { diagonal rule }

$$\mu\langle E,T,F:: (E\cdot a\cdot E+E\cdot b\cdot E+c\cdot E\cdot d+e\ ,\ \Phi\ ,\ \Psi)\rangle$$

$=$ { exercise 81(a)

where $\Theta=\mu\langle E:: E\cdot a\cdot E+E\cdot b\cdot E+c\cdot E\cdot d+e\rangle$ }

$$(\mu\langle E:: E\cdot a\cdot E+E\cdot b\cdot E+c\cdot E\cdot d+e\rangle,\ \mu\langle T,F:: (F\cdot(b\cdot F)^*\ ,\ c\cdot\Theta\cdot d+e)\rangle)\ .$$

No use has been made of the mutual recursion rule, theorem 80, in this calculation although it is applicable to several steps. This is often the case. Theorem 80 is a combination of the diagonal rule and lemma (79) and exercise 81 is another combination. Often it is easier to use the simpler rules, or some straightforward combination of them, than it is to apply the more complicated rule.

7   Further Reading

In spite of the name, the general concept of a "Galois" connection was not invented by the famous mathematician Évariste Galois, but an instance of a "Galois connection" is *the* "Galois correspondence" between groups and extension fields to which Galois owes his fame. The term "adjoint function" used here (and in category theory texts) is derived from the original terminology used by Galois. (Extending a field involves "adjoining" new values to the field.) Detailed discussion of the Galois correspondence can be found in [21,6].

Feijen [5] has written a delightful article on the Galois connection defining the maximum of two numbers. The source of several of the properties of the floor and ceiling functions discussed in section (2) is [9]. The Galois connections defining the floor and ceiling function are mentioned in [9] but never used because the authors "can never remember which inequality to use"! Further elementary examples of Galois connections can be found in [17].

The idea of extracting a Galois connection from a relation would appear to be due to Hartmanis and Stearns [12,13]. The same idea appears in [16]. In that paper Lambek gives several mathematical examples of polarities. Further examples in the areas of geometry and the theory of rings and groups can be found in Birkhoff's classic text [2]. The notion of *concept analysis* is discussed in detail in [10]. Conditional correctness assertions were introduced Hoare in [11] and are called *Hoare triples*.

References

1. R. C. Backhouse and B. A. Carré. Regular algebra applied to path-finding problems. *Journal of the Institute of Mathematics and its Applications*, 15:161–186, 1975. 124

2. Garrett Birkhoff. *Lattice Theory*, volume 25 of *American Mathematical Society Colloquium Publications*. American Mathematical Society, Providence, Rhode Island, 3rd edition, 1967. 147

3. B. A. Davey and H. A. Priestley. *Introduction to Lattices and Order*. Cambridge Mathematical Textbooks. Cambridge University Press, first edition, 1990. 112

4. E. W. Dijkstra and C. S. Scholten. *Predicate Calculus and Program Semantics*. Springer-Verlag, Berlin, 1990. 138

5. W. H. J. Feijen and Lex Bijlsma. Exercises in formula manipulation. In E. W. Dijkstra, editor, *Formal Development of Programs and Proofs*, pages 139–158. Addison-Wesley Publ. Co., 1990. 147

6. Maureen H. Fenrick. *Introduction to the Galois Correspondence*. Birkhaüser Boston, 1991. 146

7. G. Gentzen. Investigations into logical deduction. In M. E. Szabo, editor, *The Collected Papers of Gerhard Gentzen*, pages 68–213. North-Holland, Amsterdam, 1969. 103

8. G. Gierz, K. H. Hofmann, K. Keimel, J. D. Lawson, M. Mislove, and D. S. Scott. *A Compendium of Continuous Lattices*. Springer-Verlag, 1980. 94

9. Ronald L. Graham, Donald E. Knuth, and Oren Patashnik. *Concrete Mathematics: A Foundation for Computer Science*. Addison-Wesley Publishing Company, 1989. 147

10. Bernhard Ganter and Rudolf Wille. *Formal Concept Analysis. Mathematical Foundations*. Springer-Verlag Berlin Heidelberg, 1999. Translated from the German by Cornelia Franzke. Title of the original German edition: Formale Begriffsanalyse – Mathematische Grundlagen. 112, 147

11. C. A. R. Hoare. An axiomatic basis for computer programming. *Communications of the ACM*, 12(10):576–580, 1969. 147

12. J. Hartmanis and R. E. Stearns. Pair algebras and their application to automata theory. *Information and Control*, 7(4):485–507, 1964. 147

13. J. Hartmanis and R. E. Stearns. *Algebraic Structure Theory of Sequential Machines*. Prentice-Hall, 1966. 147

14. S. C. Kleene. Representation of events in nerve nets and finite automata. In Shannon and McCarthy, editors, *Automata Studies*, pages 3–41. Princeton Univ. Press, 1956. 122

15. Dexter Kozen. A completeness theorem for Kleene algebras and the algebra of regular events. *Information and Computation*, 110(2):366–390, 1994. 122, 124

16. J. Lambek. The influence of Heraclitus on modern mathematics. In J. Agassi and R. S.Cohen, editors, *Scientific Philosophy Today*, pages 111–121. D. Reidel Publishing Co., 1981. 147

17. J. Lambek. Some Galois connections in elementary number theory. *J. of Number Theory*, 47(3):371–377, June 1994. 147

18. P. (Ed.) Naur. Revised report on the algorithmic language ALGOL 60. *Comm. ACM*, 6:1–20, Also in *The Computer Journal*, 5: 349–67 (1963); *Numerische Mathematik*, 4: 420–52 (1963) 1963. 89

19. Oystein Ore. Galois connexions. *Transactions of the American Mathematical Society*, 55:493–513, 1944. 93, 101

20. J. Schmidt. Beitrage für Filtertheorie. II. *Math. Nachr.*, 10:197–232, 1953. 94, 101

21. Ian Stewart. *Galois Theory*. Chapman and Hall, 2nd edition, 1989. 146

Chapter 5
Calculating Functional Programs

Jeremy Gibbons

Computing Laboratory, University of Oxford

Abstract. Functional programs are merely equations; they may be manipulated by straightforward equational reasoning. In particular, one can use this style of reasoning to *calculate* programs, in the same way that one calculates numeric values in arithmetic. Many useful theorems for such reasoning derive from an *algebraic* view of programs, built around datatypes and their operations. Traditional algebraic methods concentrate on initial algebras, constructors, and values; dual *co-algebraic* methods concentrate on final co-algebras, destructors, and processes. Both methods are elegant and powerful; they deserve to be combined.

1   Introduction

These lecture notes on algebraic and coalgebraic methods for calculating functional programs derive from a series of lectures given at the *Summer School on Algebraic and Coalgebraic Methods in the Mathematics of Program Construction* in Oxford in April 2000. They are based on an earlier series of lectures given at the Estonian Winter School on Computer Science in Palmse, Estonia, in 1999.

1.1   Why Calculate Programs?

Over the past few decades there has been a phenomenal growth in the use of computers. Alongside this growth, concern has naturally grown over the correctness of computer systems, for example as regards human safety, financial security, and system development budgets. Problems in developing software and errors in the final product have serious consequences; such problems are the norm rather than the exception. There is clearly a need for more reliable methods of program construction than the traditional ad hoc methods in use today. What is needed is a *science* of programming, instead of today's *craft* (or perhaps black art). As Jeremy Gunawardena points out [15], computation is inherently more mathematical than most engineering artifacts; hence, practising software engineers should be at least as familiar with the mathematical foundations of software engineering as other engineers are with the foundations of their own branches of engineering.

By 'mathematical foundations', we do not necessarily mean obscure aspects of theoretical computer science. Rather, we are referring to simple properties and laws of computer programs: equivalences between programming constructs,

R. Backhouse et al. (Eds.): Algebraic and Coalgebraic Methods . . . , LNCS 2297, pp. 149–201, 2002.

relationships between well-known algorithms, and so on. In particular, we are interested in *calculating* with programs, in the same way that we calculate with numeric quantities in algebra at school.

1.2 Functional Programming

One particularly appropriate framework for program calculation is functional programming, simply because the absence of side-effects ensures *referential transparency* — all that matters of any expression is the value it denotes, not any other characteristic such as the method by which it computed, the time taken to evaluate it, the number of characters used to express it, and so on. Expressions in a functional programming language behave as they do in ordinary mathematics, in the sense that an expression in a given context may be replaced with a different expression yielding the same value, without changing its meaning in the surrounding context. This makes calculations much more straightforward.

Functional programming is programming with *expressions*, which denote values, as opposed to *statements*, which denote actions. A program consists of a collection of *equations* defining new functions. For example, here is a simple functional program:

```
square x = x * x
```

This program defines the function `square`. The fact that it is written as an equation implies that any occurrence of an expression `square x` is equivalent to the expression `x * x`, whatever the expression `x`.

1.3 Universal Properties

Suppose one has to define a function satisfying a given specification. Two approaches to solving this problem spring to mind. One, the *explicit approach*, is to provide an implementation of the function. The other, the *implicit approach*, is to provide a property that completely characterizes the function. Such a property is known as a *universal property*. The implicit approach is less direct, and requires more machinery, but turns out to be more convenient for calculating with. Universal properties are a central theme of these lectures.

Example: Fork Given two functions $f :: A \to B$ (which from an A computes a B) and $g :: A \to C$ (which from an A computes a C), consider the problem of constructing a function of type $A \to B \times C$ (which from an A computes both a B and a C). We will write this induced function 'fork (f, g)'. We will think of fork itself as a *higher-order* operator, taking functions to functions.

Solution Using Explicit Approach The explicit approach to constructing this function fork consists of providing an implementation

$$\text{fork } (f, g)\, a = (f\, a, g\, a)$$

That is, applying the function $\mathsf{fork}\,(f,g)$ to the argument a yields the pair whose left component is $f\,a$ and whose right component is $g\,a$. Now the existence of a solution to the problem is 'obvious'. (Actually, the existence of solutions to equations like this is a central theme in semantics of functional programming, but that is beyond the scope of these lectures.) However, proofs of properties of the function can be rather laborious, as we show below.

Projections Eliminate Fork We claim that

$$\mathsf{exl} \circ \mathsf{fork}\,(f,g) = f$$
$$\mathsf{exr} \circ \mathsf{fork}\,(f,g) = g$$

where exl and exr are the pair *projections* or *destructors*, yielding the left and right components of a pair respectively. (Here, $\circ$ is function composition; $\mathsf{exl} \circ$ $\mathsf{fork}\,(f,g)$ is the composition of the two functions exl and $\mathsf{fork}\,(f,g)$, so that

$$(\mathsf{exl} \circ \mathsf{fork}\,(f,g))\,a = \mathsf{exl}\,(\mathsf{fork}\,(f,g)\,a)$$

for any a.) The proof of the first property is as follows:

$$
\begin{aligned}
&(\mathsf{exl} \circ \mathsf{fork}\,(f,g))\,a \\
={}& \{ \text{ composition } \} \\
&\mathsf{exl}\,(\mathsf{fork}\,(f,g)\,a) \\
={}& \{ \text{ fork } \} \\
&\mathsf{exl}\,(f\,a, g\,a) \\
={}& \{ \text{ exl } \} \\
&f\,a
\end{aligned}
$$

and so $\mathsf{exl}\circ\mathsf{fork}(f,g) = f$ as required. The proof of the second property is similar.

Any Pair-Forming Function Is a Fork We claim that, for pair-forming h (that is, $h :: \mathsf{A} \to \mathsf{B} \times \mathsf{C}$),

$$\mathsf{fork}\,(\mathsf{exl} \circ h, \mathsf{exr} \circ h) = h$$

To prove this, assume an arbitrary a, and suppose that $h\,a = (b,c)$ for some particular b and c; then

$$
\begin{aligned}
&\mathsf{fork}\,(\mathsf{exl} \circ h, \mathsf{exr} \circ h)\,a \\
={}& \{ \text{ fork, composition } \} \\
&(\mathsf{exl}\,(h\,a), \mathsf{exr}\,(h\,a)) \\
={}& \{ \text{ } h \text{ } \} \\
&(\mathsf{exl}\,(b,c), \mathsf{exr}\,(b,c)) \\
={}& \{ \text{ exl, exr } \} \\
&(b,c) \\
={}& \{ \text{ } h \text{ } \} \\
&h\,a
\end{aligned}
$$

as required.

Identity Function Is a Fork We claim that

> fork (exl, exr) = id

The proof:

> fork (exl, exr) (a, b)
> =   { fork }
> (exl (a, b), exr (a, b))
> =   { exl, exr }
> (a, b)
> =   { identity }
> id (a, b)

Solution Using Implicit Approach The implicit approach to constructing the function fork consists of observing that fork (f, g) is *uniquely determined* by the fact that it returns the pair with components given by f and g. That is, fork (f, g) is the unique solution of the equations

> exl $\circ$ h = f
> exr $\circ$ h = g

in the unknown h. Equivalently, we have the *universal property of fork*

> h = fork (f, g) $\Leftrightarrow$ exl $\circ$ h = f $\wedge$ exr $\circ$ h = g

It is perhaps not immediately obvious that the system of two equations above has a unique solution (we address this problem later). But, once we can justify the universal property, calculations with forks become much more straightforward, as we illustrate below.

Projections Eliminate Fork For the claim

> exl $\circ$ fork (f, g) = f
> exr $\circ$ fork (f, g) = g

we have the proof

> exl $\circ$ fork (f, g) = f $\wedge$ exr $\circ$ fork (f, g) = g
> $\Leftrightarrow$ { universal property, letting h = fork (f, g) }
> fork (f, g) = fork (f, g)

Any Pair-Forming Function Is a Fork For the claim that, for pair-forming h,

> fork (exl $\circ$ h, exr $\circ$ h) = h

we have the proof

> h = fork (exl $\circ$ h, exr $\circ$ h)
> $\Leftrightarrow$ { universal property, letting f = exl $\circ$ h and g = exr $\circ$ h }
> exl $\circ$ h = exl $\circ$ h $\wedge$ exr $\circ$ h = exr $\circ$ h

Identity Function Is a Fork For the claim that

$$\mathsf{fork}\ (\mathsf{exl}, \mathsf{exr}) = \mathsf{id}$$

we have the proof

$$\mathsf{id} = \mathsf{fork}\ (\mathsf{exl}, \mathsf{exr})$$
$$\Leftrightarrow\quad \{\ \text{universal property, letting } f = \mathsf{exl}\ \text{and}\ g = \mathsf{exr}\ \}$$
$$\mathsf{exl} \circ \mathsf{id} = \mathsf{exl}\ \wedge\ \mathsf{exr} \circ \mathsf{id} = \mathsf{exr}$$

The gain is even more impressive for recursive functions, where the explicit approach requires inductive proofs that the implicit approach avoids. We will see many examples of such gains throughout these lectures.

1.4   The Categorical Approach to Datatypes

In these lectures we will be using category theory as an organizing principle. For our purposes, the use of category theory can be summarized in three slogans:

- *A model of computation is represented by a category.*
- *Types and programs in the model are represented by the objects and arrows of that category.*
- *A type constructor in the model is represented by a functor on that category.*

We will not rely on any deep results of category theory; we will only be using the theory to obtain a streamlined notation.

Definition of a Category A *category* $\mathcal{C}$ consists of a collection $\mathsf{Obj}(\mathcal{C})$ of *objects* and a collection $\mathsf{Arr}(\mathcal{C})$ of *arrows*, such that

- each arrow f in $\mathsf{Arr}(\mathcal{C})$ has a *source* $\mathsf{src}(f)$ and a *target* $\mathsf{tgt}(f)$, both objects in $\mathsf{Obj}(\mathcal{C})$ (we write '$f : \mathsf{src}(f) \to \mathsf{tgt}(f)$');
- for every object A in $\mathsf{Obj}(\mathcal{C})$ there is an *identity arrow* $\mathsf{id}_\mathsf{A} : \mathsf{A} \to \mathsf{A}$;
- arrows $g : \mathsf{A} \to \mathsf{B}$ and $f : \mathsf{B} \to \mathsf{C}$ compose to form an arrow $f \circ g : \mathsf{A} \to \mathsf{C}$;
- composition is associative: $f \circ (g \circ h) = (f \circ g) \circ h$;
- the appropriate identity arrows are units: for arrow $f : \mathsf{A} \to \mathsf{B}$, we have $f \circ \mathsf{id}_\mathsf{A} = f = \mathsf{id}_\mathsf{B} \circ f$.

An Example Category: $\mathcal{S}et$ The category $\mathcal{S}et$ of sets and total functions is defined as follows.

- The objects $\mathsf{Obj}(\mathcal{S}et)$ are sets of values, or *types.*
- The arrows $f : \mathsf{A} \to \mathsf{B}$ in $\mathsf{Arr}(\mathcal{S}et)$ are total functions equipped with domain A and range B.
- The identity arrows are the identity functions $\mathsf{id}_\mathsf{A}\ a = a$.
- Composition of arrows is functional composition: $(f \circ g)\ a = f\ (g\ a)$.

For example, addition is an arrow from the object $\mathsf{Int} \times \mathsf{Int}$ (the set of pairs of integers) to the object Int (the set of integers).

Definition of a Functor An *(endo)-functor* F is an operation on the objects and arrows of a category:

- F A is an object of $\mathcal{C}$ when A is an object of $\mathcal{C}$;
- F f is an arrow of $\mathcal{C}$ when f is an arrow of $\mathcal{C}$.

which respects source and target:

$$F f : F (\operatorname{src}(f)) \rightarrow F(\operatorname{tgt}(f))$$

respects composition:

$$F (f \circ g) = F f \circ F g$$

and respects identities:

$$F \operatorname{id}_A = \operatorname{id}_{F A}$$

An Example Functor in *Set*: Pair The *Set* functor Pair is defined as follows.

- On objects, Pair A $= \{(a_1, a_2) \mid a_1 \in A, a_2 \in A\}$.
- On arrows, $(\text{Pair } f) (a_1, a_2) = (f \, a_1, f \, a_2)$.

We should check that the properties are satisfied (Exercise 1.7.1):

- source and target: Pair f : Pair A $\rightarrow$ Pair B when $f : A \rightarrow B$;
- composition: Pair $(f \circ g) = $ Pair $f \circ$ Pair g;
- identities: Pair $\operatorname{id}_A = \operatorname{id}_{\text{Pair A}}$.

More Functors See Exercise 1.7.2 for the proofs that the following are functors.

Identity functor: The simplest functor Id is defined by

$$\text{Id } A = A$$
$$\text{Id } f = f$$

Constant functor: The next most simple is the constant functor $\underline{B}$ for object B, defined by

$$\underline{B} A = B$$
$$\underline{B} f = \operatorname{id}_B$$

List functor: On an object A, this functor yields List A, the type of finite sequences of values all of type A; on arrows, List f : List A $\rightarrow$ List B when $f : A \rightarrow B$ 'maps' f over a sequence.

Composition of functors: For functors F and G, functor F $\circ$ G is defined by

$$(F \circ G) A = F (G A)$$
$$(F \circ G) f = F (G f)$$

Binary Functors The notion of a functor may be generalized to functors of more than one argument. A *bifunctor* F is a binary operation on the objects and arrows of a category which respects source and target:

$$F(f,g) : F(\mathsf{src}(f), \mathsf{src}(g)) \to F(\mathsf{tgt}(f), \mathsf{tgt}(g))$$

respects composition:

$$F(f \circ g, h \circ k) = F(f, h) \circ F(g, k)$$

and respects identities:

$$F(\mathsf{id}_A, \mathsf{id}_B) = \mathsf{id}_{F(A,B)}$$

Examples of Bifunctors See Exercise 1.7.3 for the proofs that the following are bifunctors.

Product: (a generalization of Pair)

$$A \times B \qquad = \{(a, b) \mid a \in A, b \in B\}$$
$$(f \times g)(a, b) = (f\,a, g\,b)$$

Projection functors:

$$A \ll B = A$$
$$f \ll g = f$$

Making Monofunctors Out of Bifunctors Here are two ways of constructing a monofunctor (that is, a functor of a single argument) from a bifunctor.

Sectioning: for bifunctor $\oplus$ and object A, functor $(A\oplus)$ is defined by

$$(A\oplus)\,B = A \oplus B$$
$$(A\oplus)\,f = \mathsf{id}_A \oplus f$$

(so $(A\ll) = \underline{A}$, for example), and similarly in the other argument.

Lifting: for bifunctor $\oplus$ and monofunctors F and G, functor $F \hat{\oplus} G$ is defined by

$$(F \hat{\oplus} G)\,A = F\,A \oplus G\,A$$
$$(F \hat{\oplus} G)\,f = F\,f \oplus G\,f$$

See Exercise 1.7.4 for the proofs that these do indeed define functors.

1.5   The Pair Calculus

The pair calculus is an elegant theory of operators on pairs. We have already seen the product bifunctor, one of the two main ingredients of the calculus. The other main ingredient is the *coproduct* bifunctor, the dual of the product, obtained by 'turning all the arrows around' in the definition of product. Along with universal properties, duality is another central theme of these lectures.

Product Bifunctor As we saw above, product $\times$ forms a bifunctor; in Set, for types A and B, the type $A \times B$ consists of pairs (a, b) where $a :: A$ and $b :: B$. We saw earlier the product destructors $exl :: A \times B \to A$ and $exr :: A \times B \to B$. We also saw the product *morphisms* ('forks') $f \triangle g :: A \to B \times C$ when $f :: A \to B$ and $g :: A \to C$, defined by the *universal property*

$$h = f \triangle g \Leftrightarrow exl \circ h = f \wedge exr \circ h = g$$

(Some would write '$\langle f, g \rangle$' where we now write '$f \triangle g$'.) Now we can define product *map* (that is, the action of the product bifunctor on arrows) using fork:

$$f \times g = (f \circ exl) \triangle (g \circ exr)$$

Here are some properties of fork and product:

$$
\begin{aligned}
exl \circ (f \triangle g) &= f \\
exr \circ (f \triangle g) &= g \\
(exl \circ h) \triangle (exr \circ h) &= h \\
exl \triangle exr &= id \\
(f \times g) \circ (h \triangle k) &= (f \circ h) \triangle (g \circ k) \\
id \times id &= id \\
(f \times g) \circ (h \times k) &= (f \circ h) \times (g \circ k) \\
(f \triangle g) \circ h &= (f \circ h) \triangle (g \circ h)
\end{aligned}
$$

The proofs are simple consequences of the universal property. We have seen some proofs already; see also Exercise 1.7.5.

Coproduct Bifunctor We define the Set bifunctor $+$ on objects by

$$A + B = \{inl\ a \mid a \in A\} \cup \{inr\ b \mid b \in B\}$$

The intention here is that inl and inr are injections such that $inl\ a$ and $inr\ b$ are distinct, even when $a = b$; thus, coproduct gives a disjoint union. (For example, one might define inl and inr by

$$
\begin{aligned}
inl\ a &= (0, a) \\
inr\ b &= (1, b)
\end{aligned}
$$

but we will not assume any particular definition.) The coproduct *constructors* are the functions $inl :: A \to A + B$ and $inr :: B \to A + B$. We define the coproduct *morphisms* ('joins') $f \triangledown g :: A + B \to C$ when $f :: A \to C$ and $g :: B \to C$, by the *universal property*

$$h = f \triangledown g \Leftrightarrow h \circ inl = f \wedge h \circ inr = g$$

(Some would write '$[f, g]$' where we write '$f \triangledown g$'.) We can now define coproduct map using a join:

$$f + g = (inl \circ f) \triangledown (inr \circ g)$$

Here are some properties of join and coproduct:

$$(f \bigtriangledown g) \circ \mathsf{inl} \quad\quad = f$$
$$(f \bigtriangledown g) \circ \mathsf{inr} \quad\quad = g$$
$$(h \circ \mathsf{inl}) \bigtriangledown (h \circ \mathsf{inr}) = h$$
$$\mathsf{inl} \bigtriangledown \mathsf{inr} \quad\quad = \mathsf{id}$$
$$(f \bigtriangledown g) \circ (h + k) \quad = (f \circ h) \bigtriangledown (g \circ k)$$
$$\mathsf{id} + \mathsf{id} \quad\quad\quad = \mathsf{id}$$
$$(f + g) \circ (h + k) \quad = (f \circ h) + (g \circ k)$$
$$h \circ (f \bigtriangledown g) \quad\quad = (h \circ f) \bigtriangledown (h \circ g)$$

See Exercise 1.7.5 for the proofs.

Duality Notice that each of the above properties of join and coproduct is the dual of a property of fork and product, obtained by reversing the order of composition and by exchanging products, forks, and destructors for coproducts, joins and constructors. Duality gives a 'looking-glass world', in which everything is the mirror image of something in the 'everyday' world.

Exchange Law Here is a law relating products and coproducts, a bridge between the everyday world and the looking-glass world:

$$(f \vartriangle g) \bigtriangledown (h \vartriangle j) = (f \bigtriangledown h) \vartriangle (g \bigtriangledown j)$$
$$\Leftrightarrow \quad \{ \text{ universal property of } \vartriangle \}$$
$$\mathsf{exl} \circ ((f \vartriangle g) \bigtriangledown (h \vartriangle j)) = f \bigtriangledown h \ \wedge$$
$$\mathsf{exr} \circ ((f \vartriangle g) \bigtriangledown (h \vartriangle j)) = g \bigtriangledown j$$
$$\Leftrightarrow \quad \{ \text{ composition distributes over join } \}$$
$$(\mathsf{exl} \circ (f \vartriangle g)) \bigtriangledown (\mathsf{exl} \circ (h \vartriangle j)) = f \bigtriangledown h \ \wedge$$
$$(\mathsf{exr} \circ (f \vartriangle g)) \bigtriangledown (\mathsf{exr} \circ (h \vartriangle j)) = g \bigtriangledown j$$
$$\Leftrightarrow \quad \{ \text{ projections eliminate forks } \}$$
$$\mathsf{true}$$

In fact, there is also a dual proof, using the universal property of joins (Exercise 1.7.6); one might think of it as a proof from the other side of the looking-glass.

Distributivity In *Set*, the objects $A \times (B + C)$ and $(A \times B) + (A \times C)$ are isomorphic. We say that *Set* is a *distributive category*. The isomorphism in one direction,

$$\mathsf{undistl} :: (A \times B) + (A \times C) \to A \times (B + C)$$

is easy to write, in two different ways (Exercise 1.7.7):

$$\mathsf{undistl} = (\mathsf{exl} \bigtriangledown \mathsf{exl}) \vartriangle (\mathsf{exr} + \mathsf{exr})$$
$$= (\mathsf{id} \times \mathsf{inl}) \bigtriangledown (\mathsf{id} \times \mathsf{inr})$$

We could also have defined it in a pointwise style:

> undistl (inl (a, b)) = $(a, \text{inl } b)$
> undistl (inr (a, c)) = $(a, \text{inr } c)$

The inverse operation

> distl :: A × (B + C) → (A × B) + (A × C)

is straightforward to define in a pointwise style:

> distl $(a, \text{inl } b)$ = inl (a, b)
> distl $(a, \text{inr } c)$ = inr (a, c)

Moreover, these two functions are indeed inverses, as is easy to verify.

However, this inverse cannot be defined in a pointfree style in terms of the product and coproduct operations alone. (Indeed, some categories have products and coproducts, and hence a function undistl as defined above, but no inverse function distl, and so are not distributive categories. Typically, such categories do not support definitions in a pointwise style. The category $\mathcal{R}el$ of sets and binary relations is an example.)

Booleans and Conditionals In a distributive category, we can model the datatype of booleans by

> Bool = 1 + 1
> true = inl ()
> false = inr ()

where () is the unique element of the unit type 1. For predicate $p :: A \rightarrow \text{Bool}$, we define the *guard*

> $p? :: A \rightarrow (A + A)$
> $p? = (\text{exl} + \text{exl}) \circ \text{distl} \circ (\text{id} \bigtriangleup p)$

or, in an equivalent pointwise form,

> $p? \, x = \text{inl } x, \text{ if } p \, x$
> $\quad\quad = \text{inr } x, \text{ otherwise}$

We can then define the conditional

> IF p THEN f ELSE $g = (f \bigtriangledown g) \circ p?$

1.6   Bibliographic Notes

The *program calculation* field is a flourishing branch of programming methodology. One recent textbook (based on a theory of relations rather than functions, but similar in spirit to the material presented in these lectures) is [4]. Also relevant are the proceedings of the *Mathematics of Program Construction* conferences [39,2,30,21]. There are many good books on *functional programming*; we recommend [5] in particular. The classic reference for *category theory* is [23], but this is rather heavy going for non-mathematicians; for a computing perspective, we recommend [8,9,31,45].

The observation that *universal properties* are very convenient for calculating programs was made originally by Backhouse [1]. The *categorical approach to datatypes* dates back to the ADJ group [13,14] in the 1970's, but was brought back into fashion by Hagino [16,17] and Malcolm [24,25]. The *pair calculus* is probably folklore, but our presentation of it was inspired by Malcolm's thesis. The claim that *distributive categories* are the appropriate venue for discussing datatypes is championed mainly by Walters [44,45,46].

1.7 Exercises

1. Check that Pair (as defined in §1.4) does indeed satisfy the properties required of a functor.
2. Check that operations claimed in §1.4 to be functors (identity, constant, list, composition) satisfy the necessary properties.
3. Check that operations claimed in §1.4 to be bifunctors ($\times$, $\ll$) satisfy the necessary properties.
4. Check that sectioning and lifting operations claimed in §1.4 to construct monofunctors from bifunctors satisfy the necessary properties.
5. Prove the properties of product (from §1.5) and of coproduct (from §1.5) using the corresponding universal properties.
6. Prove the exchange law from §1.5

$$(f \triangle g) \triangledown (h \triangle j) = (f \triangledown h) \triangle (g \triangledown j)$$

using the universal property of joins (instead of the universal property of forks).

7. Prove the equivalence of the two characterizations of undistl from §1.5:

$$(\mathsf{exl} \triangledown \mathsf{exl}) \triangle (\mathsf{exr} + \mathsf{exr}) = (\mathsf{id} \times \mathsf{inl}) \triangledown (\mathsf{id} \times \mathsf{inr})$$

In fact, there are two different proofs, one for each universal property.

8. Prove the following properties of conditionals:

$$
\begin{aligned}
h \circ \text{IF } p \text{ THEN } f \text{ ELSE } g &= \text{IF } p \text{ THEN } h \circ f \text{ ELSE } h \circ g \\
(\text{IF } p \text{ THEN } f \text{ ELSE } g) \circ h &= \text{IF } p \circ h \text{ THEN } f \circ h \text{ ELSE } g \circ h \\
\text{IF } p \text{ THEN } f \text{ ELSE } f &= f \\
\text{IF } \mathsf{not} \circ p \text{ THEN } f \text{ ELSE } g &= \text{IF } p \text{ THEN } g \text{ ELSE } f \\
\text{IF } \mathsf{const}\ \mathsf{true} \text{ THEN } f \text{ ELSE } g &= f \\
\text{IF } p \text{ THEN } (\text{IF } q \text{ THEN } f \text{ ELSE } g) &= \text{IF } q \text{ THEN } (\text{IF } p \text{ THEN } f \text{ ELSE } h) \\
\text{ELSE } (\text{IF } q \text{ THEN } h \text{ ELSE } j) & \text{ELSE } (\text{IF } p \text{ THEN } g \text{ ELSE } j)
\end{aligned}
$$

(Here, not is negation of booleans, and const is the function such that const $a\ b = a$ for any b.)

2   Recursive Datatypes in the Category *Set*

The pair calculus is elegant, but not very powerful; descriptive power comes with recursive datatypes. In this section we will discuss a simple first approximation to what we really want, namely recursive datatypes in the category *Set*. We will construct monomorphic and polymorphic datatypes, and their duals. However, there are inherent limitations in working within the category *Set*, which we will remedy in Section 3.

2.1   Overview

The Haskell-style recursive datatype definitions

```
data IntList = Nil | Cons Int IntList
data List a  = Nil | Cons a (List a)
```

(one monomorphic, one polymorphic) give for free:

- a 'map' operator;
- a 'fold' (like join for coproducts), to consume a data structure;
- an 'unfold' (like fork for products), to generate a data structure;
- universal properties for fold and unfold;
- a number of theorems about fold and unfold.

Actually, we will discover that we cannot simultaneously achieve all of these goals in *Set*, which will motivate the move to another category, *Cpo*, in Section 3.

2.2   Monomorphic Datatypes

We consider first the case of monomorphic datatypes. The first problem is to identify a common form, encompassing all the datatype declarations in which we are interested. Consider the Haskell-style datatype definition

```
data IntList = Nil | Cons Int IntList
```

This defines two constructors

Nil :: IntList
$Cons$ :: Int $\rightarrow$ (IntList $\rightarrow$ IntList)

Different datatype definitions, of course, will introduce different constructors. This raises some problems for a general theory:

- there may be arbitrarily many constructors;
- the constructors may be constants or functions;
- the constructor functions may be of arbitrary arities.

How can we circumvent these problems, and unify all datatype definitions into a common form?

Unifying Constructors The third problem identified above, constructors of arbitrary arities, can be resolved by 'uncurrying' the constructor functions; that is, by tupling the arguments together using products. For example, the binary *Cons* constructor for lists introduced above is equivalent to the unary constructor

$Cons :: \mathsf{Int} \times \mathsf{IntList} \rightarrow \mathsf{IntList}$

The second problem, that some constructors may be constants rather than functions, can be resolved by treating a constant constructor such as *Nil* as a function from the unit type 1:

$Nil :: 1 \rightarrow \mathsf{IntList}$

Now the first problem, of an arbitrary number of constructors, may be resolved by taking the join of the existing collection of unary constructor functions (because they all share a common target, the defined type):

$Nil \bigtriangledown Cons :: 1 + (\mathsf{Int} \times \mathsf{IntList}) \rightarrow \mathsf{IntList}$

This yields a single constructor $Nil \bigtriangledown Cons$. Being a constructor for the defined type IntList, its target type is that type. Its source type $1 + (\mathsf{Int} \times \mathsf{IntList})$ is some type expression involving the target type IntList — in fact, some functor applied to IntList.

Datatype Definitions Therefore, it suffices to consider datatypes T with a single unified constructor $\mathsf{in_T} :: \mathsf{F}\,\mathsf{T} \rightarrow \mathsf{T}$ for some functor F. We write

$\mathsf{T} = \textsc{data}\ \mathsf{F}$

For example, for IntList, the functor is $\mathsf{F_{IntList}}$, where

$\mathsf{F_{IntList}}\ \mathsf{X} = 1 + (\mathsf{Int} \times \mathsf{X})$

That is,

$\mathsf{F_{IntList}} = \underline{1}\ \hat{+}\ (\underline{\mathsf{Int}}\ \hat{\times}\ \mathsf{Id})$

so we could define

$\mathsf{IntList} = \textsc{data}\ (\underline{1}\ \hat{+}\ (\underline{\mathsf{Int}}\ \hat{\times}\ \mathsf{Id}))$

2.3 Folds

We have identified a common form for all monomorphic datatype definitions. However, datatypes are not much use without functions over them. It is now widely accepted that program structure should, where possible, reflect data structure [18]. Accordingly, we should identify a program structure that reflects the data structure of monomorphic datatypes. It turns out that the right kind of structure is one of *homomorphisms* between *algebras*, which we explore in this section.

Fixpoints The definition 'T = DATA F' defines T to be a *fixpoint* of the functor F; that is, T is isomorphic to F T. In one direction, the isomorphism is given by in_T :: F T → T. In the other direction, we suppose an inverse out_T :: T → F T. (In fact, we see how to define out_T shortly.)

However, to say that the datatype definition 'T = DATA F' defines T to be a fixpoint of the functor F does not completely determine T, as a functor may have more than one fixpoint. For example, the types 'finite sequences of integers' and 'finite and infinite sequences of integers' are both fixpoints of the functor $F_{IntList}$ (Exercise 2.9.3). Informally, what we want is the 'least fixpoint', that is, the 'smallest such type' — finite rather than finite-and-infinite sequences of integers. How can we formalize this idea?

Algebras We define an F-*algebra* to be a pair (A, f) such that f :: F A → A. Thus, the datatype definition T = DATA F defines (T, in_T) to be an F-algebra. For example, (IntList, $Nil \bigtriangledown Cons$) is an $F_{IntList}$-algebra. However, F-algebras are not unique either. For example, (Int, $zero \bigtriangledown plus$) is another $F_{IntList}$-algebra (Exercise 2.9.4), where $zero$ :: 1 → Int and $plus$ :: Int × Int → Int; that is, $zero \bigtriangledown plus$ :: 1 + (Int × Int) → Int.

Homomorphisms A *homomorphism* between F-algebras (A, f) and (B, g) is a function h :: A → B such that

$$h \circ f = g \circ F\,h$$

Pictorially,

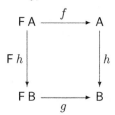

For example, the function sum :: IntList → Int, which sums an IntList,

$$sum\,(Nil\,()) \quad = 0$$
$$sum\,(Cons\,(a, x)) = a + sum\,x$$

is a homomorphism from (IntList, $Nil \bigtriangledown Cons$) to (Int, $zero \bigtriangledown plus$), because

$$sum \circ (Nil \bigtriangledown Cons) = (zero \bigtriangledown plus) \circ F_{IntList}\,sum$$

(see Exercise 2.9.5).

Initial Algebras We say that an F-algebra (A, f) is *initial* if, for any F-algebra (B, g), there is a unique homomorphism from (A, f) to (B, g). Then the datatype definition 'T = DATA F' defines (T, in_T) to be 'the' initial F-algebra. There may be more than one initial algebra, but all initial algebras are equivalent (Exercise 2.9.6); thus, it does not really matter which one we pick.

Existence of Initial Algebras It is well-known that for *polynomial* F (built out of identity and constant functors using product and coproduct) on many categories including *Set* and *Rel*, initial algebras always exist. Malcolm [24] shows existence also for *regular* F (adding fixpoints), allowing us to define *mutually recursive* datatypes such as

```
data IntTree   = Node Int IntForest
data IntForest = Empty | ConsF IntTree IntForest
```

Definition of Folds Suppose that (T, in_T) is the initial F-algebra. Then there is a unique homomorphism to any F-algebra (B, f) — that is, for any such f, there exists a unique h such that $h \circ in_T = f \circ F\, h$. We would like a notation for 'the unique solution h of this equation involving f'; we write 'fold$_T$ f' for this unique solution. Thus, fold$_T$ f has type $T \to B$ when $f :: F\, B \to B$. Pictorially,

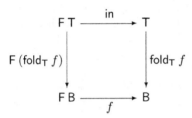

Uniqueness provides the universal property

$$h = \text{fold}_T\, f \Leftrightarrow h \circ in_T = f \circ F\, h$$

2.4   Polymorphic Datatypes

The type IntList has the 'base type' Int built in: it cannot be used for lists of booleans, lists of strings, and so on. We would like *polymorphic* datatypes, parameterized by an arbitrary base type A: lists of As, trees of As, and so on. For example, the Haskell-style type definition

```
data List a  = Nil | Cons a (List a)
```

defines a type List A for each type A; now List is a type *constructor*, whereas IntList is just a type.

Using Bifunctors The essential idea in constructing polymorphic datatypes is to use a bifunctor $\oplus$. A polymorphic type T is then defined by sectioning $\oplus$ with the type parameter as one argument, and then taking the fixpoint:

$$T\, A = \text{DATA}\, (A\oplus)$$

Now the constructor has type

$$in_{T\, A} :: A \oplus T\, A \to T\, A$$

though usually we will write just 'in$_T$' as a polymorphic function, omitting the A. For example, we can define a polymorphic list type by

List A = DATA (A⊕)

where

A ⊕ B = 1 + (A × B)

Equivalently, we could write

List A = DATA ($\underline{1}$ $\hat{+}$ ($\underline{A}$ $\hat{\times}$ Id))

without naming the bifunctor.

Polymorphic Folds Folds over monomorphic datatypes generalize in a straightforward fashion to polymorphic datatypes. The datatype definition

T A = DATA (A⊕)

defines (T A, in$_T$) to be the initial (A⊕)-algebra; therefore there exists a unique homomorphism fold$_T$ A f to any other (A⊕)-algebra (B, f). (Again, we will usually write just 'fold$_T$ f', leaving the fold operator polymorphic in A.) The fold fold$_T$ f has type T A → B when f :: A ⊕ B → B; pictorially,

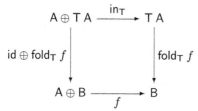

Uniqueness gives the universal property

$h = \text{fold}_T\ f \Leftrightarrow h \circ \text{in}_T = f \circ (\text{id} \oplus h)$

Making It a Functor: Map The datatype definition T A = DATA (A⊕) makes T a type constructor, an operation on types. This suggests that perhaps we can make T a functor: all we need is a corresponding operation on functions T f with type T A → T B when f :: A → B (satisfying the functor laws). We define T f = fold$_T$ A (in$_T$ B ∘ (f ⊕ id)). Pictorially,

$$
\begin{array}{ccc}
A \oplus T A & \xrightarrow{\ \text{in}_T\ A\ } & T A \\
{\scriptstyle \text{id} \oplus T f}\big\downarrow & & \big\downarrow{\scriptstyle T f} \\
A \oplus T B \xrightarrow[{f \oplus \text{id}}]{} B \oplus T B \xrightarrow[{\text{in}_T\ B}]{} & & T B
\end{array}
$$

(We should check that this does indeed satisfy the requirements for being a functor; see Exercise 2.9.7.) For historical reasons, we will write 'map$_T$ f' rather than 'T f'.

2.5   Properties of Folds

There are a number of general theorems about folds that arise as simple consequences of the universal property. These include: an *evaluation rule*, which shows 'one step of evaluation' of a fold; an exact *fusion law*, which states when a function can be fused with a fold; a *weak fusion law*, a simpler but weaker corollary of the exact fusion law; the *identity law*, which states that the identity function is a fold; and a definition of the *destructor* of a datatype as a fold.

Evaluation Rule The evaluation rule describes the composition of a fold and the constructors of its type; informally, it gives 'one step of evaluation' of the fold.

$$\mathsf{fold_T}\ f \circ \mathsf{in_T}$$
$$=\quad \{\text{ universal property, letting } h = \mathsf{fold}\ f\ \}$$
$$f \circ \mathsf{F}\ (\mathsf{fold_T}\ f)$$

Fusion (Exact Version) *Fusion laws* for folds are of the form

$$h \circ \mathsf{fold_T}\ f = \mathsf{fold_T}\ g \Leftrightarrow \dots$$

(or sometimes with the composition the other way around). They give conditions under which one can *fuse* two computations, one a fold, to yield a single monolithic computation. In this case, we have

$$h \circ \mathsf{fold_T}\ f = \mathsf{fold_T}\ g$$
$$\Leftrightarrow\quad \{\text{ universal property }\}$$
$$h \circ \mathsf{fold_T}\ f \circ \mathsf{in_T} = g \circ \mathsf{F}\ (h \circ \mathsf{fold_T}\ f)$$
$$\Leftrightarrow\quad \{\text{ functors }\}$$
$$h \circ \mathsf{fold_T}\ f \circ \mathsf{in_T} = g \circ \mathsf{F}\ h \circ \mathsf{F}\ (\mathsf{fold_T}\ f)$$
$$\Leftrightarrow\quad \{\text{ evaluation rule }\}$$
$$h \circ f \circ \mathsf{F}\ (\mathsf{fold_T}\ f) = g \circ \mathsf{F}\ h \circ \mathsf{F}\ (\mathsf{fold_T}\ f)$$

Fusion (Weaker Version) The above fusion law is an equivalence, so it is as strong as possible. However, it is a little unwieldy, because the premise (the last line in the calculation above) is rather long. Here is a fusion law with a simpler but stronger premise (which therefore is a weaker law).

$$h \circ \mathsf{fold_T}\ f = \mathsf{fold_T}\ g$$
$$\Leftrightarrow\quad \{\text{ exact fusion }\}$$
$$h \circ f \circ \mathsf{F}\ (\mathsf{fold_T}\ f) = g \circ \mathsf{F}\ h \circ \mathsf{F}\ (\mathsf{fold_T}\ f)$$
$$\Leftarrow\quad \{\text{ Leibniz }\}$$
$$h \circ f = g \circ \mathsf{F}\ h$$

Identity The identity function id is a fold:

$$\mathsf{id} = \mathsf{fold_T}\ f$$
$$\Leftrightarrow \quad \{\text{ universal property }\}$$
$$\mathsf{id} \circ \mathsf{in_T} = f \circ \mathsf{F}\ \mathsf{id}$$
$$\Leftrightarrow \quad \{\text{ identity }\}$$
$$f = \mathsf{in_T}$$

That is, $\mathsf{fold_T}\ \mathsf{in_T} = \mathsf{id}$.

Destructors Also, the destructor out_T of a datatype, the inverse of the constructor $\mathsf{in_T}$, can be written as a fold; this is known as *Lambek's Lemma*.

$$\mathsf{in_T} \circ \mathsf{fold_T}\ f = \mathsf{id}$$
$$\Leftrightarrow \quad \{\text{ identity as a fold }\}$$
$$\mathsf{in_T} \circ \mathsf{fold_T}\ f = \mathsf{fold_T}\ \mathsf{in_T}$$
$$\Leftarrow \quad \{\text{ weak fusion }\}$$
$$\mathsf{in_T} \circ f = \mathsf{in_T} \circ \mathsf{F}\ \mathsf{in_T}$$
$$\Leftarrow \quad \{\text{ Leibniz }\}$$
$$f = \mathsf{F}\ \mathsf{in_T}$$

Therefore we can define

$$out_\mathsf{T} = \mathsf{fold_T}\ (\mathsf{F}\ \mathsf{in_T})$$

We should check that this also makes *out* the inverse of in when the composition is reversed:

$$out_\mathsf{T} \circ \mathsf{in_T}$$
$$= \quad \{\text{ above }\}$$
$$\mathsf{fold_T}\ (\mathsf{F}\ \mathsf{in_T}) \circ \mathsf{in_T}$$
$$= \quad \{\text{ evaluation rule }\}$$
$$\mathsf{F}\ \mathsf{in_T} \circ \mathsf{F}\ out_\mathsf{T}$$
$$= \quad \{\text{ functors }\}$$
$$\mathsf{F}\ (\mathsf{in_T} \circ out_\mathsf{T})$$
$$= \quad \{\text{ in} \circ out = \mathsf{id} \ \}$$
$$\mathsf{id}$$

Lambek's Lemma is a corollary of the more general theorem that an injective function (that is, a function with a post-inverse) on a recursive datatype is a fold (Exercise 2.9.8). Since the destructor is by assumption the inverse of the constructors, it is injective.

2.6   Co-datatypes and Unfolds

All of this theory of datatypes dualizes, to give a theory of *co-datatypes* and *unfolds*. The dualization is quite straightforward; nevertheless, we present the facts here for completeness.

Co-algebras and Homomorphisms An F-*co-algebra* is a pair (A, f) such that $f :: A \to F A$. A *homomorphism* between F-co-algebras (A, f) and (B, g) is a function $h :: A \to B$ such that

$$F h \circ f = g \circ h$$

Pictorially,

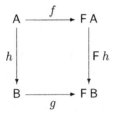

An F-co-algebra (A, f) is *final* if, for any F-co-algebra (B, g), there is a unique homomorphism from (B, g) to (A, f). The datatype definition $T = \textsc{codata}\ F$ defines $(T, \mathsf{out_T})$ to be 'the' final F-co-algebra.

Unfolds Suppose that $(T, \mathsf{out_T})$ is the final F-co-algebra. Then there is a unique homomorphism to $(T, \mathsf{out_T})$ from any F-co-algebra (B, f) — that is, there exists a unique h such that $\mathsf{out_T} \circ h = F h \circ f$. We write '$\mathsf{unfold_T}\ f$' for this homomorphism. The unfold $\mathsf{unfold_T}\ f$ has type $B \to T$ when $f :: B \to F B$:

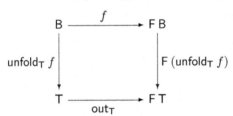

Uniqueness provides the universal property

$$h = \mathsf{unfold_T}\ f \Leftrightarrow \mathsf{out_T} \circ h = F h \circ f$$

Polymorphic Co-datatypes In the same way,

$$T A = \textsc{codata}\ (A \oplus)$$

defines a polymorphic co-datatype, with destructor

$$\mathsf{out_{T A}} :: T A \to A \oplus T A$$

This induces a polymorphic unfold with universal property

$$h = \mathsf{unfold_{T A}}\ f \Leftrightarrow \mathsf{out_T} \circ h = (\mathsf{id} \oplus h) \circ f$$

The typing is $\mathsf{unfold_T}\ f :: B \to T A$ when $f :: B \to A \oplus B$; pictorially,

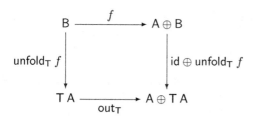

Co-datatypes too form functors; the map for $f :: A \to B$ is given by

$$\mathrm{map}_{T\,A}\ f = \mathrm{unfold}_{T\,B}\ ((f \oplus \mathrm{id}) \circ \mathrm{out}_{T\,A})$$

An Example: Streams The polymorphic datatype of streams (infinite lists) is defined

$$\mathsf{Stream\ A} = \textsc{codata}\ (\mathsf{A}\times)$$

Thus, the destructor for this type is $\mathrm{out}_{\mathsf{Stream}} :: \mathsf{Stream\ A} \to \mathsf{A} \times \mathsf{Stream\ A}$. The unfold $\mathrm{unfold}_{\mathsf{Stream}}\ f$ has type $\mathsf{A} \to \mathsf{Stream\ B}$ for $f :: \mathsf{A} \to \mathsf{B} \times \mathsf{A}$. For example,

$$from = \mathrm{unfold}_{\mathsf{Stream\ Int}}\ (\mathrm{id} \triangle (1+))$$

yields increasing streams of naturals: $from\ n = n, n+1, n+2, \ldots$. For another example,

$$fibs = (\mathrm{unfold}_{\mathsf{Stream\ Int}}\ (\mathrm{exl} \triangle (\mathrm{exr} \triangle plus)))\ (0, 1)$$

defines the Fibonacci sequence $0, 1, 1, 2, 3, 5, 8, \ldots$.

Properties of Unfolds The theorems dualize too, of course. See Exercise 2.9.10 for the proofs.

Evaluation rule:

$$\mathrm{out}_T \circ \mathrm{unfold}_T\ f = \mathsf{F}\ (\mathrm{unfold}_T\ f) \circ f$$

Exact and weak fusion:

$$\mathrm{unfold}_T\ f \circ h = \mathrm{unfold}_T\ g$$
$$\Leftrightarrow \mathsf{F}\ (\mathrm{unfold}_T\ f) \circ f \circ h = \mathsf{F}\ (\mathrm{unfold}_T\ f) \circ \mathsf{F}\ h \circ g$$
$$\Leftarrow f \circ h = \mathsf{F}\ h \circ g$$

Identity:

$$\mathrm{unfold}_T\ \mathrm{out}_T = \mathrm{id}$$

Constructors: (the dual of the 'destructor' law for folds)

$$in_T = \mathrm{unfold}_T\ (\mathsf{F}\ \mathrm{out}_T)$$

Again, this dual is a corollary of a more general law (Exercise 2.9.11), that any surjective function (one with a pre-inverse) to a recursive datatype is an unfold.

Example: Insertion Sort Given the datatype $\mathsf{List\ A} = \mathrm{DATA}\ (\underline{1}\ \hat{+}\ (\underline{\mathsf{A}}\ \hat{\times}\ \mathsf{Id}))$, suppose we have an insertion operation

$$ins :: 1 + (\mathsf{A} \times \mathsf{List\ A}) \to \mathsf{List\ A}$$

that gives an empty list, or inserts an element into a sorted list. Then insertion sort is defined by

$$insertsort = \mathsf{fold}_{\mathsf{List}}\ ins$$

Example: Selection Sort Given the codatatype $\mathsf{CList\ A} = \mathrm{CODATA}\ (\underline{1}\ \hat{+}\ (\underline{\mathsf{A}}\ \hat{\times}\ \mathsf{Id}))$, suppose we have an operation

$$del :: \mathsf{CList\ A} \to 1 + (\mathsf{A} \times \mathsf{CList\ A})$$

that finds and removes the minimum element of a non-empty list. Then selection sort is defined by

$$selectsort = \mathsf{unfold}_{\mathsf{CList}}\ del$$

2.7 ... and Never the Twain Shall Meet

Unfortunately, this elegant theory is severely limited when it comes to actual programming. Datatypes and co-datatypes are different things, so one cannot combine them. For example, one cannot write programs of the form 'unfold then fold'; one instance of this scheme is quicksort, which builds a binary search tree (an unfold) then flattens it to a list (a fold), and another is mergesort, which repeatedly halves a list (unfolding to a tree) then repeatedly merges the fragments (folding the tree). This pattern of computation is known as a *hylomorphism*, and is very common in programming.

Moreover, $\mathcal{S}et$ is not a good model of programs. As it contains only total functions, it necessarily suffers from some lack of power, and corresponds only vaguely to most programming languages. (Indeed, the selection sort given in §2.6 does not really work: the function *del* is necessarily partial, as it makes no sense on an infinite list, and so neither *del* nor *selectsort* are arrows in $\mathcal{S}et$.)

The solution to both problems is to move to the category $\mathcal{C}po$, imposing more structure on the objects and arrows of the category than there is in $\mathcal{S}et$.

2.8 Bibliographic Notes

As mentioned in the bibliographic notes for the previous section, the categorical approach to datatypes is due originally to the ADJ group [13,14] and later to Hagino [16,17]. However, the presentation in these notes owes more to Malcolm [24,25]. The proof that, for the kinds of functor that interest us, initial algebras and final coalgebras always exist, is (a corollary of a more general theorem) due to Smyth and Plotkin [34]. The term 'hylomorphism' is due to Meijer [27].

2.9 Exercises

1. Translate the following Haskell-style definition of binary trees with boolean external labels into the categorical style:

   ```
   data BoolTree = Tip Bool | Bin BoolTree BoolTree
   ```

2. Translate the following categorical-style datatype definition

   $$\mathsf{StringTree} = \text{DATA} \ (\underline{1} \ \hat{+} \ (\mathsf{Id} \ \hat{\times} \ \underline{\mathsf{String}} \ \hat{\times} \ \mathsf{Id}))$$

   into your favourite programming languages (for example, Haskell, Modula 2, Java).

3. Show that the types 'finite sequences of integers' and 'finite and infinite sequences of integers' are both fixpoints of the functor $\underline{1} \ \hat{+} \ (\underline{\mathsf{Int}} \ \hat{\times} \ \mathsf{Id})$.

4. Check that $(\mathsf{IntList}, Nil \bigtriangledown Cons)$ and $(\mathsf{Int}, zero \bigtriangledown plus)$ are $\mathsf{F_{IntList}}$-algebras, where

   $$\begin{aligned} zero\,() \quad &= 0 \\ plus\,(m,n) &= m+n \end{aligned}$$

5. Check that sum, the function which sums an $\mathsf{IntList}$,

   $$\begin{aligned} sum\,(Nil\,()) \qquad &= 0 \\ sum\,(Cons\,(a,x)) &= a + sum\,x \end{aligned}$$

   is an $\mathsf{F_{IntList}}$-homomorphism from $(\mathsf{IntList}, Nil \bigtriangledown Cons)$ to $(\mathsf{Int}, zero \bigtriangledown plus)$.

6. Show that any two initial F-algebras are isomorphic. (Hint: the identity function is a homomorphism from an F-algebra to itself; use uniqueness.) So, given the existence of an initial algebra, we are justified in talking about 'the' initial algebra.

7. Check that defining

   $$\mathsf{T}\,f = \mathsf{fold_{T\,A}}\,(\mathsf{in_{T\,B}} \circ (f \oplus \mathsf{id}))$$

   does indeed make T a functor.

8. Show that if $g \circ h = \mathsf{id_T}$ for recursive datatype T, then h is a fold. Thus, any injective function on a recursive datatype is a fold.

9. In fact, one can say something stronger. Show that h is a fold for recursive datatype DATA F if and only if KER $(\mathsf{F}\,h) \subseteq$ KER $(h \circ \mathsf{in})$, where the kernel KER f of a function $f :: \mathsf{A} \to \mathsf{B}$ is the set of pairs $\{\,(a,a') \in \mathsf{A} \times \mathsf{A} \mid f\,a = f\,a'\,\}$. Use this to solve Exercise 2.9.8.

10. Prove the properties of unfolds from §2.6, using the universal property.

11. Dually to Exercise 2.9.8, show that any surjective function to a recursive datatype is an unfold.

12. Dually to Exercise 2.9.9, show that h is a unfold for recursive codatatype CODATA F if and only if IMG $(\mathsf{F}\,h) \supseteq$ IMG $(\mathsf{out} \circ h)$, where the image IMG f of a function $f :: \mathsf{A} \to \mathsf{B}$ is the set $\{\,b \in \mathsf{B} \mid \exists a \in \mathsf{A}.\ f\,a = b\,\}$. Use this to solve Exercise 2.9.11.

13. Prove that the fork of two folds is a fold:

$$\mathsf{fold_T}\ f \vartriangle \mathsf{fold_T}\ g = \mathsf{fold_T}\ ((f \circ \mathsf{F}\ \mathsf{exl}) \vartriangle (g \circ \mathsf{F}\ \mathsf{exr}))$$

(This is known fondly as the 'banana split theorem', by those who know the fork operation as 'split' and write folds using 'banana brackets'.)

14. Prove the special cases *fold-map fusion*

$$\mathsf{fold_T}\ f \circ \mathsf{map_T}\ g = \mathsf{fold_T}\ (f \circ (g \oplus \mathsf{id}))$$

of the fusion law for folds, and *map-unfold fusion*

$$\mathsf{map_T}\ g \circ \mathsf{unfold_T}\ f = \mathsf{unfold_T}\ ((g \oplus \mathsf{id}) \circ f)$$

of the fusion law for unfolds.

15. For datatype $\mathsf{T} = \textsc{data}\ \mathsf{F}$, Meertens [26] defines the notion of a *paramorphism* $\mathsf{para_T}\ f :: \mathsf{T} \to \mathsf{C}$ when $f :: \mathsf{F}\ (\mathsf{C} \times \mathsf{T}) \to \mathsf{C}$ as follows:

$$\mathsf{para_T}\ f = \mathsf{exl} \circ \mathsf{fold_T}\ (f \vartriangle (\mathsf{in_T} \circ \mathsf{F}\ \mathsf{exr}))$$

It enjoys the universal property

$$h = \mathsf{para_T}\ f \Leftrightarrow h \circ \mathsf{in_T} = f \circ \mathsf{F}\ (h \vartriangle \mathsf{id})$$

Informally, a paramorphism is a generalization of a fold: the result on a larger structure may depend on results on substructures, but also on the substructures themselves. For example, the factorial function is a paramorphism over the naturals:

$$fact = \mathsf{para_{Nat}}\ (\mathsf{const}\ 1 \triangledown (mult \circ (\mathsf{id} \times succ)))$$

where $\mathsf{const}\,ab = a$ and $mult$ multiplies a pair of numbers. That is, $fact0 = 1$, and $fact\ (succ\ n) = mult\ (fact\ n, succ\ n)$.

(a) Show that the second component of the above fold is merely the identity function:

   $\mathsf{exr} \circ \mathsf{fold_T}\ (f \vartriangle (\mathsf{in_T} \circ \mathsf{F}\ \mathsf{exr})) = \mathsf{id}$

   Hence $\mathsf{fold_T}\ (f \vartriangle (\mathsf{in_T} \circ \mathsf{F}\ \mathsf{exr})) = \mathsf{para_T}\ f \vartriangle \mathsf{id}$.

(b) Show that the identity function is a paramorphism:

   $\mathsf{id} = \mathsf{para}\ (\mathsf{in} \circ \mathsf{F}\ \mathsf{exl})$

(c) Prove the (weak) fusion law for paramorphisms:

   $h \circ \mathsf{para}\ f = \mathsf{para}\ g \Leftarrow h \circ f = g \circ \mathsf{F}\ (h \times \mathsf{id})$

(d) Show that any fold is a paramorphism:

   $\mathsf{fold}\ f = \mathsf{para}\ (f \circ \mathsf{F}\ \mathsf{exl})$

   (This is a generalization of Exercise 2.9.15b.)

(e) Show that *any* function on a recursive datatype can be written as a paramorphism:

   $h = \mathsf{para}\ (h \circ \mathsf{in} \circ \mathsf{F}\ \mathsf{exr})$

   Thus, paramorphisms are extremely general.

16. On the codatatype of lists from §2.6, define as an unfold the function *interval*, such that

   $interval\ (1, 5) = [1, 2, 3, 4, 5]$
   $interval\ (5, 5) = [5]$
   $interval\ (6, 5) = []$

17. On the codatatype $\mathsf{Stream}\,A = \mathrm{CODATA}\,(A\times)$, the function *iterate* is defined by

$$iterate\ f = \mathsf{unfold}_{\mathsf{Stream}}\ (\mathsf{id}\ \triangle\ f)$$

Using unfold fusion, prove that

$$\mathsf{map}\ f \circ iterate\ f = iterate\ f \circ f$$

18. For codatatype $\mathsf{T} = \mathrm{CODATA}\ \mathsf{F}$, Uustalu and Vene [40,38] dualize paramorphisms to get *apomorphisms* $\mathsf{apo}_{\mathsf{T}}\ f :: \mathsf{C} \to \mathsf{T}$ when $f :: \mathsf{C} \to \mathsf{F}\,(\mathsf{C} + \mathsf{T})$ as follows:

$$\mathsf{apo}_{\mathsf{T}}\ f = \mathsf{unfold}_{\mathsf{T}}\ (f\ \triangledown\ (\mathsf{F}\ \mathsf{inr} \circ \mathsf{out}_{\mathsf{T}})) \circ \mathsf{inl}$$

They enjoy the universal property

$$h = \mathsf{apo}_{\mathsf{T}}\ f \Leftrightarrow \mathsf{out}_{\mathsf{T}} \circ h = \mathsf{F}\ (h\ \triangledown\ \mathsf{id}) \circ f$$

Informally, an apomorphism is a generalization of an unfold: a larger structure may be generated recursively from new seeds, but may also be generated 'all at once' without recursion. For example, on the codatatype $\mathsf{CList}\,A = \mathrm{CODATA}\,(\underline{1}\ \hat{+}\ (\underline{A}\ \hat{\times}\ \mathsf{Id}))$ of lists, the append function is an apomorphism:

$$append = \mathsf{apo}_{\mathsf{Clist}}\ f$$

where

$$
\begin{aligned}
f\ (x,y) &= \mathsf{inl}\ (), & &\text{if } null\ x \wedge null\ y \\
&= \mathsf{inr}\ (head\ y, \mathsf{inr}\ (tail\ y)), & &\text{if } null\ x \wedge \mathsf{not}\ (null\ y) \\
&= \mathsf{inr}\ (head\ x, \mathsf{inl}\ (tail\ x, y)), & &\text{if } \mathsf{not}\ (null\ x)
\end{aligned}
$$

That is, $append(x,y)$ is the empty list if both are empty, $cons\,(head\,y, tail\,y)$ (which is just y) if only x is empty, and $cons\,(head\,x, append\,(tail\,x,y))$ if neither x nor y is empty. This definition copies just the first list; in contrast, the simple unfold characterization of append

$$append = \mathsf{unfold}_{\mathsf{CList}}\ g$$

where

$$
\begin{aligned}
g\ (x,y) &= \mathsf{inl}\ (), & &\text{if } null\ x \wedge null\ y \\
&= \mathsf{inr}\ (head\ y, (x, tail\ y)), & &\text{if } null\ x \wedge \mathsf{not}\ (null\ y), \\
&= \mathsf{inr}\ (head\ x, (tail\ x, y)), & &\text{if } \mathsf{not}\ (null\ x)
\end{aligned}
$$

copies both lists.

(a) Show that on the second summand the above unfold acts merely as the identity function:
$$\mathsf{unfold}_{\mathsf{T}}\ (f\ \triangledown\ (\mathsf{F}\ \mathsf{inr} \circ \mathsf{out}_{\mathsf{T}})) \circ \mathsf{inr} = \mathsf{id}$$
Hence $\mathsf{unfold}_{\mathsf{T}}\ (f\ \triangledown\ (\mathsf{F}\ \mathsf{inr} \circ \mathsf{out}_{\mathsf{T}})) = \mathsf{apo}_{\mathsf{T}}\ f\ \triangledown\ \mathsf{id}$.

(b) Show that the identity function is an apomorphism:
$$\mathsf{id} = \mathsf{apo}\ (\mathsf{F}\ \mathsf{inl} \circ \mathsf{out})$$

(c) Prove the (weak) fusion law for apomorphisms:

$$\text{apo } f \circ h = \text{apo } g \Leftarrow f \circ h = \mathsf{F}\,(h + \mathsf{id}) \circ g$$

(d) Show that any unfold is an apomorphism:

$$\text{unfold } f = \text{apo }(\mathsf{F}\,\mathsf{inl} \circ f)$$

(This is a generalization of Exercise 2.9.18b.)

(e) Show that any function yielding a recursive datatype can be written as an apomorphism:

$$h = \text{apo }(\mathsf{F}\,\mathsf{inr} \circ \mathsf{out} \circ h)$$

(f) Write $ins :: \mathsf{A} \times \mathsf{CList}\,\mathsf{A} \to \mathsf{CList}\,\mathsf{A}$, which inserts a value into a sorted list, as an apomorphism.

19. Datatypes and codatatypes for the same functor are different structures, but they are not unrelated. Suppose we have the datatype definitions

$$\mathsf{T} = \text{DATA } \mathsf{F}$$
$$\mathsf{U} = \text{CODATA } \mathsf{F}$$

Lambek's Lemma shows how to write $out_\mathsf{T} :: \mathsf{T} \to \mathsf{F}\,\mathsf{T}$, giving an F-coalgebra $(\mathsf{T}, out_\mathsf{T})$ and hence a function $\mathsf{unfold}_\mathsf{U}\, out_\mathsf{T} :: \mathsf{T} \to \mathsf{U}$. This function 'coerces' an element of T to the type U. Give the dual construction, expressing this coercion as a fold. Prove (in two different ways) that these two coercions are equal. Thus, we have two ways of writing the coercion from the datatype T to the codatatype U, and no way of going back again. This is what one might expect: embedding finite lists into finite-or-infinite lists is easy, but the opposite embedding is more difficult. In the following section we move to a setting in which the two types coincide, and so the coercions become the identity function.

3 Recursive Datatypes in the Category *Cpo*

As we observed above, the simple and elegant model of datatypes and the corresponding characterization of the 'natural patterns' of recursion over them in the category *Set* has a number of problems. We solve these problems by moving to the category *Cpo*. This category is a refinement of the category *Set*. Some structure is imposed on the objects of the category, so that they are no longer merely sets of unrelated elements, and correspondingly some structure is induced on the arrows. Some things become neater (for example, we will be able to compose unfolds and folds) but some things become messier (specifically, strictness conditions have to be attached to some of the laws).

3.1 The Category *Cpo*

The category *Cpo* has as objects *pointed complete partial orders*: sets equipped with a partial order on the elements, with a least element and closed under limits of ascending chains. The arrows are *continuous* functions on these structured sets: functions which distribute over limits of ascending chains. (We will explain these notions below.)

Intuitively, we will use the partial order to represent 'approximations' in a 'definedness' or 'information' ordering: $x \sqsubseteq y$ will mean that element x is an approximation to (or less well defined than, or provides less information than) element y. Closure under limits means that we can consider complex, perhaps infinite, structures as the limit of their finite approximations, and be assured that such limits always exist. Continuity means that computations (that is, arrows) respect these limits: the behaviour of a computation on the limit of a chain of approximations can be understood purely in terms of its behaviour on each of the approximations.

Posets A poset is a pair $(A, \sqsubseteq)$, where A is a set and $\sqsubseteq$ is a *partial order* on A. That is, the following properties hold of $\sqsubseteq$:

reflexivity: $a \sqsubseteq a$
transitivity: $a \sqsubseteq b$ and $b \sqsubseteq c$ imply $a \sqsubseteq c$
antisymmetry: $a \sqsubseteq b$ and $b \sqsubseteq a$ imply $a = b$

The *least element* of a poset $(A, \sqsubseteq)$ is the $a \in A$ such that $a \sqsubseteq a'$ for all $a' \in A$, if this element exists. By antisymmetry, a poset has at most one least element. The *upper bounds* in A of the poset $(B, \sqsubseteq)$ where $B \subseteq A$ are the elements $\{a \in A \mid b \sqsubseteq a \quad \text{for all } b \in B\}$; note that they are elements of A, and not necessarily of B. The *least upper bound* (lub) $\bigsqcup B$ in A of the poset $(B, \sqsubseteq)$ where $B \subseteq A$ is the least element of the upper bounds in A of $(B, \sqsubseteq)$, if this least element exists.

Cpos and Pcpos A *chain* $\langle a_i \rangle$ in a poset $(A, \sqsubseteq)$ is a sequence $a_0, a_1, a_2 \ldots$ of elements in A such that $a_0 \sqsubseteq a_1 \sqsubseteq a_2 \sqsubseteq \cdots$. The lub of the chain $\langle a_i \rangle$, if it exists, is denoted $\bigsqcup_i \langle a_i \rangle$. A poset $(A, \sqsubseteq)$ is a *complete partial order* (cpo) if every chain of elements in A has a lub in A. A cpo is a *pointed cpo* (pcpo) if it has a least element (which is denoted $\perp_A$). From now on, we will often write just 'A' instead of '$(A, \sqsubseteq)$' for a pcpo.

Strictness, Monotonicity and Continuity A function $f :: A \to B$ between pcpos A and B is *strict* if

$$f \perp_A = \perp_B$$

A function $f :: A \to B$ between pcpos $(A, \sqsubseteq_A)$ and $(B, \sqsubseteq_B)$ is *monotonic* if

$$a \sqsubseteq_A a' \Rightarrow f a \sqsubseteq_B f a'$$

A monotonic function between pcpos A and B is *continuous* if

$$f \left(\bigsqcup_i \langle a_i \rangle \right) = \bigsqcup_i \left(\langle f a_i \rangle \right)$$

Examples of Pcpos The following are all pcpos:

- for set A such that $\bot \notin A$, the *lifted discrete* set $\{\bot\} \cup A$ with ordering

$$a \sqsubseteq b \Leftrightarrow a = \bot \vee a = b$$

- for pcpos A and B, the *cartesian product* $\{(a, b) \mid a \in A \wedge b \in B\}$ with ordering

$$(a, b) \sqsubseteq (a', b') \Leftrightarrow a \sqsubseteq_A a' \wedge b \sqsubseteq_B b'$$

(so the least element is $(\bot_A, \bot_B)$);
- for pcpos A and B, the *separated sum* $\{\bot\} \cup \{(0, a) \mid a \in A\} \cup \{(1, b) \mid b \in B\}$ with ordering

$$\begin{aligned} x \sqsubseteq y \Leftrightarrow (x = \bot) \qquad\qquad\qquad\qquad\qquad \vee \\ (x = (0, a) \wedge y = (0, a') \wedge a \sqsubseteq_A a') \vee \\ (x = (1, b) \wedge y = (1, b') \wedge b \sqsubseteq_B b') \end{aligned}$$

- for pcpos A and B, the set of continuous functions from A to B, with ordering

$$f \sqsubseteq g \Leftrightarrow (f\, a \sqsubseteq_B g\, a \text{ for all } a \in A)$$

(so the least element is the function f such that $f\, a = \bot_B$ for any a).

Modelling Datatypes in *Cpo* As suggested above, the idea is that we will use pcpos to model datatypes. The elements of a pcpo model (possibly partially defined) values of that type. The ordering $\sqsubseteq$ models 'is no more defined than' or 'approximates'. For example, $(\bot, \bot) \sqsubseteq (1, \bot) \sqsubseteq (1, 2)$ and $(\bot, \bot) \sqsubseteq (\bot, 2) \sqsubseteq (1, 2)$, but $(1, \bot)$ and $(\bot, 2)$ are unrelated. 'Completely defined' values are the lubs of chains of approximations. All 'reasonable' functions are continuous, so we are justified in restricting attention just to continuous functions.

The Category We move from the category *Set* to the category *Cpo*. The objects Obj(*Cpo*) are pcpos; the arrows Arr(*Cpo*) are continuous functions between pcpos. Later, we will also use the category *Cpo*$_\bot$, which has the same objects, but only the *strict* continuous functions as arrows.

3.2   Continuous Algebras

Fokkinga and Meijer [11] have generalized the *Set*-based definitions of datatypes and their morphisms to *Cpo*. This provides a number of advantages over *Set*:

- we can now model *partial* functions, because all types have a least-defined element that can be used as the 'meaning' of an undefined computation;
- unfolds generate and folds consume the same kind of entity, so they can be composed to form hylomorphisms;
- we can give a meaning to arbitrary recursive definitions, not just to folds and unfolds.

(However, these advantages come at the cost of a more complex theory.) In these lectures we will only use the middle benefit of the three.

The Main Theorem A functor F is *locally continuous* if, for all objects A and B, the action of F on functions of type $A \rightarrow B$ is continuous. All functors that we will be using are locally continuous.

Suppose F is a locally continuous functor on Cpo. Suppose also that F preserves strictness, that is, $F\ f$ is strict when f is strict; so F is also a functor on $\mathit{Cpo}_{\perp}$. Then there exists an object T, and strict functions $\mathrm{in}_T :: F\ T \rightarrow T$ and $\mathrm{out}_T :: T \rightarrow F\ T$, each the inverse of the other; hence T is isomorphic to F T. The functor F determines T up to isomorphism, and T uniquely determines in_T and out_T. We write

$$T = \textsc{fix}\ F$$

The pair (T, in_T) is the initial F-algebra in $\mathit{Cpo}_{\perp}$; that is, for any type A and strict function $f :: F\ A \rightarrow A$, there is a unique strict h satisfying the equation

$$h \circ \mathrm{in}_T = f \circ F\ h$$

We write $\mathrm{fold}_T\ f$ for this unique solution. It has the universal property that

$$h = \mathrm{fold}_T\ f \Leftrightarrow h \circ \mathrm{in}_T = f \circ F\ h \qquad \text{for strict } f \text{ and } h$$

(The strictness condition on f is necessary; see Exercise 3.6.1.)

Also, the pair (T, out_T) is the final F-co-algebra in Cpo; that is, for any type A and (not necessarily strict) function $f :: A \rightarrow F\ A$, there is a unique h satisfying

$$\mathrm{out}_T \circ h = F\ h \circ f$$

We write $\mathrm{unfold}_T\ f$ for this unique solution. It has the universal property (without any strictness conditions)

$$h = \mathrm{unfold}_T\ f \Leftrightarrow \mathrm{out}_T \circ h = F\ h \circ f$$

(Apparently the strictness requirements of folds and unfolds are asymmetric. Exercise 3.6.2 shows that this apparent asymmetry is illusory.)

3.3   The Pair Calculus Again

The cool, clear waters of the pair calculus are muddied slightly by the presence of $\perp$ and the possibility of non-strict functions. The cartesian product works fine, as before; all the same properties hold. Unfortunately, the separated sum is no longer a proper coproduct, because the injections inl and inr are non-strict, and so the equations

$$h \circ \mathrm{inl} = f \wedge h \circ \mathrm{inr} = g$$

no longer have a unique solution (because they do not specify $h\ \perp$). However, there is a unique *strict* solution, which is the one we take for join:

$$h = f \bigtriangledown g \Leftrightarrow h \circ \mathrm{inl} = f \ \wedge\ h \circ \mathrm{inr} = g \ \wedge\ h \text{ strict}$$

Such strictness conditions are the price we pay for the extra power and flexibility of Cpo. In view of this, we use the term 'sum' instead of 'coproduct' from now on.

Distributivity Even worse than the extra strictness conditions, we no longer have a distributive category: product no longer distributes over sum. Because the function distl takes $(a, \bot)$ to $\bot$, there is no way of inverting it to retrieve the a. There is more information in $A \times (B + C)$ than in $(A \times B) + (A \times C)$; now distl $\circ$ undistl $=$ id but undistl $\circ$ distl $\sqsubseteq$ id. Nevertheless, we continue to use the guard $p?$, but with care: for example, the equation

$$\text{IF } p \text{ THEN } f \text{ ELSE } f = f$$

now holds only for total p (more precisely, when $p\, x = \bot$ implies $f\, x = \bot$).

3.4 Hylomorphisms

So much for the disadvantages. To compensate, we can now express the common pattern of computation of an unfold followed by a fold, because now unfolds produce and folds consume the same kind of datatype. We present two examples here: quicksort and mergesort.

Lists We use the datatype

$$\text{List } A = \text{FIX } (\underline{1} \,\hat{+}\, (\underline{A} \,\hat{\times}\, \text{Id}))$$

of possibly-empty lists. For brevity, we define separate constructors

$$
\begin{aligned}
nil &= \text{in (inl ())}\\
cons\,(a, x) &= \text{in (inr }(a, x))
\end{aligned}
$$

and destructors

$$
\begin{aligned}
isNil &= (\text{const true} \,\triangledown\, \text{const false}) \circ \text{out}\\
head &= (\bot \,\triangledown\, \text{exl}) \circ \text{out}\\
tail &= (\bot \,\triangledown\, \text{exr}) \circ \text{out}
\end{aligned}
$$

We introduce the following syntactic sugar for folds on this type:

$$
\begin{aligned}
foldL &:: (\mathsf{B} \times (\mathsf{A} \times \mathsf{B} \to \mathsf{B})) \to \text{List A} \to \mathsf{B}\\
foldL\,(e, f) &= \text{fold}_{\text{List}}\,(\text{const } e \,\triangledown\, f)\\
unfoldL &:: ((\mathsf{B} \to \text{Bool}) \times (\mathsf{B} \to \mathsf{A} \times \mathsf{B})) \to \mathsf{B} \to \text{List A}\\
unfoldL\,(p, f) &= \text{unfold}_{\text{List}}\,((\text{const ()} + f) \circ p?)
\end{aligned}
$$

For example, concatenation on these lists is given by

$$cat\,(x, y) = foldL\,(y, cons)\,x$$

Flatten We also use the datatype

$$\text{Tree A} = \text{FIX} \; (\underline{1} \; \hat{+} \; (\underline{A} \; \hat{\times} \; (\text{Id} \; \hat{\times} \; \text{Id})))$$

of internally-labelled binary trees, for which the fold may be sweetened to

$$foldT :: (B \times (A \times (B \times B) \to B)) \to \text{Tree A} \to B$$
$$foldT \; (e, f) = \text{fold}_{\text{Tree}} \; (\text{const} \; e \; \triangledown \; f)$$

The function $flatten$ turns one of these trees into a possibly-empty list:

$$flatten :: \text{Tree A} \to \text{List A}$$
$$flatten \qquad = foldT \; (nil, glue)$$
$$glue \; (a, (x, y)) = cat \; (x, cons \; (a, y))$$

Partition The function $filter$ takes a predicate p and a list x, and returns a pair of lists: those elements of x that satisfy p, and those elements of x that do not.

$$filter :: (A \to \text{Bool}) \to \text{List A} \to \text{List A} \times \text{List A}$$
$$filter \; p \qquad = foldL \; ((nil, nil), step)$$
$$step \; (a, (x, y)) = (cons \; (a, x), y), \text{ if } p \; a$$
$$\qquad \qquad \qquad = (x, cons \; (a, y)), \text{ otherwise}$$

An alternative, point-free but perhaps less clear, definition of $step$ is

$$step = \text{IF } p \text{ THEN } (cons \circ (\text{id} \times \text{exl})) \; \triangle \; (\text{exr} \circ \text{exr})$$
$$\qquad \qquad \text{ELSE } \; (\text{exl} \circ \text{exr}) \; \triangle \; (cons \circ (\text{id} \times \text{exr}))$$

For example, we can partition a non-empty list into those elements of the tail that are less than the head, and those elements of the tail that are not:

$$partition :: \text{List A} \to \text{List A} \times \text{List A}$$
$$partition \; x = filter \; (< head \; x) \; (tail \; x)$$

Quicksort The unfold on our type of trees is equivalent to

$$unfoldT :: ((B \to \text{Bool}) \times (B \to A) \times (B \to B \times B)) \to B \to \text{Tree A}$$
$$unfoldT \; (p, f, g) = \text{unfold}_{\text{Tree}} \; ((\text{const} \; () + (f \; \triangle \; g)) \circ p?)$$

Now we can build a binary search tree from a list:

$$buildBST :: \text{List A} \to \text{Tree A}$$
$$buildBST = unfoldT \; (isNil, head, partition)$$

(Note that $partition$ is applied only to non-empty lists.) Then we can sort by building then flattening a tree:

$$quicksort :: \text{List A} \to \text{List A}$$
$$quicksort = flatten \circ buildBST$$

This is a fold after an unfold.

Merge For this example, we define the datatype

$$\mathsf{PList}\ A = \mathrm{FIX}\ (\underline{A}\ \hat{+}\ (\underline{A}\ \hat{\times}\ \mathsf{Id}))$$

of non-empty lists. Again, for brevity, we define separate destructors

$$
\begin{aligned}
isSing &= (\mathsf{const\ true}\ \triangledown\ \mathsf{const\ false}) \circ \mathsf{out} \\
hd &= (\mathsf{id}\ \triangledown\ \mathsf{exl}) \circ \mathsf{out} \\
tl &= (\bot\ \triangledown\ \mathsf{exr}) \circ \mathsf{out}
\end{aligned}
$$

We also specialize the unfold to

$$
\begin{aligned}
&unfoldPL :: ((B \to \mathsf{Bool}) \times (B \to A) \times (B \to B)) \to B \to \mathsf{PList}\ A \\
&unfoldPL\ (p, f, g) = \mathsf{unfold_{PList}}\ ((f + (f\ \triangle\ g)) \circ p?)
\end{aligned}
$$

Then the function *merge*, which merges a pair of sorted lists into a single sorted list, is

$$
\begin{aligned}
&merge :: \mathsf{PList}\ A \times \mathsf{PList}\ A \to \mathsf{PList}\ A \\
&merge = unfoldPL\ (p, f, g) \circ \mathsf{inl}
\end{aligned}
$$

where

$$
\begin{aligned}
p &= \mathsf{const\ false}\ \triangledown\ isSing \\
f &= (min \circ (hd \times hd))\ \triangledown\ hd \\
g\ (\mathsf{inl}\ (x, y)) &= \mathsf{inr}\ y, & \text{if } hd\ x \le hd\ y \wedge isSing\ x \\
&= \mathsf{inl}\ (tl\ x, y), & \text{if } hd\ x \le hd\ y \wedge \mathsf{not}\ (isSing\ x) \\
&= \mathsf{inr}\ x, & \text{if } hd\ x > hd\ y \wedge isSing\ y \\
&= \mathsf{inl}\ (x, tl\ y), & \text{if } hd\ x > hd\ y \wedge \mathsf{not}\ (isSing\ y) \\
g\ (\mathsf{inr}\ x) &= \mathsf{inr}\ (tl\ x)
\end{aligned}
$$

and *min* is the binary minimum operator. Note that the 'state' for the unfold is either a pair of lists (which are to be merged) or a single list (which is simply to be copied). Exercise 3.6.9 concerns the characterization of *merge* as an apomorphism, whereby the single list is copied to the result 'all in one go' rather than element by element.

Split Similarly, we define separate constructors

$$
\begin{aligned}
wrap\ a &= \mathsf{in}\ (\mathsf{inl}\ a) \\
cons\ (a, x) &= \mathsf{in}\ (\mathsf{inr}\ (a, x))
\end{aligned}
$$

and specialize the fold to

$$
\begin{aligned}
&foldPL :: ((A \to B) \times (A \times B \to B)) \to \mathsf{PList}\ A \to B \\
&foldPL\ (f, g) = \mathsf{fold_{PList}}\ (f\ \triangledown\ g)
\end{aligned}
$$

Then non-singleton lists can be split into two roughly equal halves:

$$
\begin{aligned}
&split :: \mathsf{PList}\ A \to \mathsf{PList}\ A \times \mathsf{PList}\ A \\
&split\ x = foldPL\ (step, start\ (hd\ x))\ (tl\ x) \qquad \text{where} \\
&\qquad\qquad start\ a\ b = (wrap\ a, wrap\ b) \\
&\qquad\qquad step\ (a, (y, z)) = (cons\ (a, z), y)
\end{aligned}
$$

Mergesort We also define the datatype

$$\mathsf{PTree}\,A = \mathrm{FIX}\,(\underline{A}\,\hat{+}\,(\mathsf{Id}\,\hat{\times}\,\mathsf{Id}))$$

of non-empty externally-labelled binary trees. We use the specializations

$$foldPT :: ((A \to B) \times (B \times B \to B)) \to \mathsf{PTree}\,A \to B$$
$$foldPT\,(f, g) = \mathsf{fold}_{\mathsf{PTree}}\,(f \,\triangledown\, g)$$

of fold, and

$$unfoldPT :: ((B \to \mathsf{Bool}) \times (B \to A) \times (B \to B \times B)) \to B \to \mathsf{PList}\,A$$
$$unfoldPT\,(p, f, g) = \mathsf{unfold}_{\mathsf{PTree}}\,((f + g) \circ p?)$$

of unfold. Then mergesort is

$$foldPT\,(wrap, merge) \circ unfoldPT\,(isSing, hd, split)$$

(Note that *split* is applied only to non-singleton lists.)

3.5   Bibliographic Notes

Complete partial orders are standard material from denotational semantics; see for example [10] for a straightforward algebraic point of view, and [33,35] for the specifics of the applications to denotational semantics. Meijer, Fokkinga and Paterson [27] argue for the move from *Set* to *Cpo*. The *Main Theorem* above is from [11], where it is in turn acknowledged to be another corollary of the results of Smyth and Plotkin [34] and Reynolds [32] mentioned earlier.

3.6   Exercises

1. Show that, even for strict f, the equation

$$h \circ \mathsf{in}_\mathsf{T} = f \circ \mathsf{F}\,h$$

   may have non-strict solutions for h as well as the unique strict solution. Thus, the strictness condition on the universal property of fold in §3.2 is necessary.
2. Show that the categorical dual of the notion of 'strictness' vacuously holds of any function. Therefore there really is no asymmetry between the universal properties of fold and unfold in §3.2.
3. Show that the definitions of map as a fold (§2.4) and as an unfold (§2.6) are equal in *Cpo*.
4. Suppose $\mathsf{T} = \mathrm{FIX}\,\mathsf{F}$. Let functor G be defined by $\mathsf{G}\,\mathsf{X} = \mathsf{F}\,(\mathsf{X} \times \mathsf{T})$, and let $\mathsf{U} = \mathrm{FIX}\,\mathsf{G}$. Show that any paramorphism (Exercise 2.9.15) on T can be written as a hylomorphism, in the form of a fold (on U) after $\mathsf{preds}_\mathsf{T}$, where

$$\mathsf{preds}_\mathsf{T} = \mathsf{unfold}_\mathsf{U}\,(\mathsf{F}\,(\mathsf{id}\,\triangle\,\mathsf{id}) \circ \mathsf{out}_\mathsf{T})$$

5. The datatype of natural numbers is $\mathsf{Nat} = \text{FIX}\ (\underline{1}+)$. (Actually, this type necessarily includes also 'partial numbers' and one 'infinite number' as well as all the finite ones.) We can define the following syntactic sugar for the folds and unfolds:

$$foldN \qquad\qquad :: (\mathsf{A} \times (\mathsf{A} \to \mathsf{A})) \to \mathsf{Nat} \to \mathsf{A}$$
$$foldN\ (e, f) \quad = \mathsf{fold}_{\mathsf{Nat}}\ (\mathsf{const}\ e \bigtriangledown f)$$
$$unfoldN \qquad\quad :: ((\mathsf{A} \to \mathsf{Bool}) \times (\mathsf{A} \to \mathsf{A})) \to \mathsf{A} \to \mathsf{Nat}$$
$$unfoldN\ (p, f) = \mathsf{unfold}_{\mathsf{Nat}}\ ((\mathsf{const}\ () + f) \circ p?)$$

Informally, $foldN\ (e, f)\,n$ computes $f^n\,e$, by n-fold application of f to e, and $unfoldN\ (p, f)\,x$ returns the least n such that $f^n\,x$ satisfies p. Write addition, subtraction, multiplication, division, exponentiation and logarithms on naturals, using folds and unfolds as the only form of recursion. (Hint: define a 'predecessor' function using the destructor $\mathsf{out}_{\mathsf{Nat}}$, but make it total, taking zero to zero. You may find it easier to make division and logarithms round up rather than down.)

6. Using the datatype of lists from §3.4, write the insertion function

$$ins :: 1 + (\mathsf{A} \times \mathsf{List}\ \mathsf{A}) \to \mathsf{List}\ \mathsf{A}$$

as an unfold. Hence write *insertsort* using folds and unfolds as the only form of recursion.

7. Using the same datatype as in Exercise 3.6.6, write the deletion function

$$del :: \mathsf{List}\ \mathsf{A} \to 1 + (\mathsf{A} \times \mathsf{List}\ \mathsf{A})$$

as a fold. Hence write *selectsort* using folds and unfolds as the only form of recursion.

8. *Eratosthenes' Sieve* is a method for generating primes. It maintains a collection of 'candidates' as a stream, initially containing $[2, 3, \ldots]$. The first element of the collection is a prime; a new collection is obtained by deleting all multiples of that prime. Write this program using folds and unfolds on streams as the only form of recursion. (You can use *mod* on natural numbers.)

9. Write *merge* from §3.4 as an apomorphism rather than an unfold.

10. Show that if

$$h = \mathsf{fold}_\mathsf{T}\ g \circ \mathsf{unfold}_\mathsf{T}\ f$$

then

$$h = g \circ \mathsf{F}\ h \circ f$$

(Indeed, this is an equivalence, not just an implication; but the proof in the opposite direction requires some machinery that we have not covered.) This is a fusion law for hylomorphisms, sometimes known as *deforestation*: instead of separate unfold and fold phases, the two can be combined into a single monolithic recursion, which does not explicitly construct the intermediate data structure. The now absent datatype T is sometimes known as a *virtual data structure* [36].

11. On Stream $A = $ FIX $(A \times)$, define as an unfold a function

$$do :: (A \to A) \to A \to \text{Stream } A$$

such that $do\,s\,a$ returns the infinite stream a, sa, $s(sa)$ and so on. Also define as a fold a function $while :: (A \to \text{Bool}) \to \text{Stream } A \to A$ such that $while\,p\,x$ yields the first element of stream x that satisfies p. Now $while\,p\circ do\,s$ models a while loop in an imperative language. Use deforestation (Exercise 3.6.10) to calculate a function $whiledo$ such that $whiledo\,(p, s) = while\,p \circ do\,s$, but which does not generate the intermediate stream.

12. Write the function $whiledo$ from Exercise 3.6.11 using the folds and unfolds on naturals (Exercise 3.6.5) instead of on streams. (Hint: $whiledo\,(p, s)\,x$ applies s a certain number n of times; the number n is the least such that $s^n x$ fails to satisfy p.)

13. Folds and unfolds on the datatype of streams are sufficient to compute arbitrary fixpoints, so give the complete power of recursive programming. The fixpoint-finding function fix is defined using explicit recursion by

$$\begin{aligned} fix \quad &:: (A \to A) \to A \\ fix\,f &= f\,(fix\,f) \end{aligned}$$

Equivalently, given the function $apply :: (A \to B) \times A \to B$, it may be defined

$$fix\,f = apply\,(f, fix\,f)$$

Show that fix may also be defined as the composition of a stream fold (using $apply$) and a stream unfold (generating infinitely many copies of a value). Use deforestation (Exercise 3.6.10) to remove the intermediate stream, and show that this yields the explicitly recursive characterization of fix. (This exercise is due to Graham Hutton [20].)

14. Under certain circumstances, the post-inverse of a fold is an unfold, and the pre-inverse of an unfold is a fold:

$$\text{unfold}_T\,f \circ \text{fold}_T\,g = \text{id} \Leftarrow f \circ g = \text{id}$$

Prove this law.

15. The function $cross$ takes two infinite streams of values, and returns an infinite stream containing every possible pair of values, the first component drawn from the first list and the second component drawn from the second list. The difficulty is in enumerating this two-dimensional collection in a suitable order; the standard approach is diagonalization. Define

$$cross = concat \circ diagonals$$

where

$$\begin{aligned} diagonals &:: \text{Stream } A \times \text{Stream } B \to \text{Stream } (\text{List } (A \times B)) \\ concat \quad &:: \text{Stream } (\text{List } (A \times B)) \to \text{Stream } (A \times B) \end{aligned}$$

Express *cross* as a hylomorphism (that is, express *diagonals* as an unfold, and *concat* as a fold). (Hint: first construct the obvious stream of streams incorporating all possible pairs. Then the 'state' of the iteration for *diagonals* consists of a pair, a finite list of those streams seen so far and a stream of streams not yet seen. At each step, strip another diagonal off from the streams seen so far, and include another stream from those not yet seen.) This example is due to Richard Bird [3].

4   Applications

We conclude these lecture notes with three more substantial examples of the concepts we have described: a simple compiler for arithmetic expressions; laws for monads and comonads; and efficient programs for breadth-first traversal of trees.

4.1   A Simple Compiler

In this example, we define a datatype of simple (arithmetic) expressions. We present the obvious recursive algorithm for evaluating such expressions; it turns out to be a fold. We also develop a compiler to translate such expressions into code for a stack machine; this too turns out to be a fold. Clearly, running the compiled code should be equivalent to evaluating the original expression. The proof of this fact turns out to be a straightforward application of the universal properties concerned.

Expressions and Evaluation   We assume a datatype Op of operators. The arities of the operators are given by a function $arity :: \mathsf{Op} \to \mathsf{Nat}$. We also assume a datatype Val of values, and a function $apply :: \mathsf{Op} \times \mathsf{List\,Val} \to \mathsf{Val}$ (where List is as in §3.4) to characterize the operators. Operator application is partial: $apply\,(op, args)$ is defined only when $arity\ op = \mathsf{length}\ args$, where length computes the length of a list. Now we can define a datatype of expressions

$$\mathsf{Expr} = \text{FIX}\,(\underline{\mathsf{Op}}\ \hat{\times}\ \mathsf{List})$$

on which evaluation, which provides the 'denotational semantics' of an expression, is simply a fold:

$$eval = \mathsf{fold}_{\mathsf{Expr}}\ apply :: \mathsf{Expr} \to \mathsf{Val}$$

Compilation   For the 'operational semantics', we assume a datatype Instr of instructions, and an encoding $code :: \mathsf{Op} \to \mathsf{Instr}$ of operators as instructions. Then compilation is also a fold:

$$compile :: \mathsf{Expr} \to \mathsf{List\,Instr}$$
$$compile = \mathsf{fold}\,(cons \circ (code \times concat))$$

Here, $concat :: \mathsf{List\,(List\,A)} \to \mathsf{List\,A}$, and $cons :: \mathsf{A} \times \mathsf{List\,A} \to \mathsf{List\,A}$.

An Example For example, we might want to manipulate expressions like

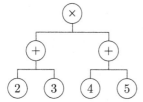

We could define in Haskell

```
> data Op = Sum | Product | Num Int
> type Val = Int

> arity Sum      = 2
> arity Product = 2
> arity (Num x) = 0

> apply (Sum, [x,y])   = x+y
> apply (Product, [x,y]) = x*y
> apply (Num x, [])    = x

> data Instr = Bop ((Val,Val)->Val) | Push Val

> code Sum     = Bop (uncurry (+))
> code Product = Bop (uncurry (*))
> code (Num x) = Push x
```

and so the compiled code of the example expression will be

```
[Bop mul, Bop add, Push 2, Push 3, Bop add, Push 4, Push 5]
   where add = uncurry (+)
         mul = uncurry (*)
```

Execution Steps We assume also a single-step execution function

$$exec :: \mathsf{Instr} \to \mathsf{List\ Val} \to \mathsf{List\ Val}$$

such that

$$exec\,(code\,op)\,(cat\,args\,vals) = cons\,(apply\,(op, args), vals)$$

when $arity\,op = \mathsf{length}\,args$. Continuing the example, we might have

```
> exec (Bop f) (x:y:xs) = f (x,y) : xs
> exec (Push x) xs   = x : xs
```

Complete Execution Now, running the program may be defined as follows:

> run :: List Instr $\rightarrow$ List Val $\rightarrow$ List Val
> $run\ nil\ vals$ $\qquad\qquad$ $=\ vals$
> $run\ (cons\ (instr, prog))\ vals = exec\ instr\ (run\ prog\ vals)$

Equivalently, discarding the last variable:

> $run\ nil$ $\qquad\qquad\qquad$ $=$ id
> $run\ (cons\ (instr, prog)) = exec\ instr \circ run\ prog$

Define $comp\ (f, g) = f \circ g$, and its curried version $comp'\ f\ g = comp\ (f, g)$; then

> $run = foldL'\ (\text{id}, comp' \circ exec)$

(where $foldL' :: (\mathsf{B} \times (\mathsf{A} \rightarrow \mathsf{B} \rightarrow \mathsf{B})) \rightarrow \mathsf{List\ A} \rightarrow \mathsf{B}$, using a curried function as one of its arguments). Equivalently again

> $run = compose \circ \mathsf{map}\ exec$

where

> $compose$ :: List $(\mathsf{A} \rightarrow \mathsf{A}) \rightarrow (\mathsf{A} \rightarrow \mathsf{A})$
> $compose = foldL'\ (\text{id}, comp')$

The Correctness Criterion We assume that expressions are well-formed, each operator having exactly the right number of arguments. Then compiling an expression and running the resulting code on a given starting stack should have the effect of prefixing the value of that expression onto the stack:

> $run\ (compile\ expr)\ vals = cons\ (eval\ expr, vals)$

Equivalently, discarding the last two variables,

> $run \circ compile = cons' \circ eval$

where $cons'$ is the curried version of $cons$.

Strategy The universal property of fold on expressions is

> $h = \mathsf{fold}\ f$
> $\Leftrightarrow$
> $h \circ \mathsf{in} = f \circ (\text{id} \times \mathsf{map}\ h)$

We will use this universal property to show that both operational semantics $run \circ compile$ and denotational semantics $cons' \circ eval$ above are folds. We want to find an f such that

> $run \circ compile \circ \mathsf{in} = f \circ (\text{id} \times \mathsf{map}\ (run \circ compile))$

so that $run \circ compile = \mathsf{fold}\ f$. Then to complete the proof, we need only show that, for the same f,

> $cons' \circ eval \circ \mathsf{in} = f \circ (\text{id} \times \mathsf{map}\ (cons' \circ eval))$

Operational Semantics as a Fold Now,

$$
\begin{aligned}
&run \circ compile \circ \mathsf{in} \\
=\ &\{\ compile = \mathsf{fold}\,(cons \circ (code \times concat))\ \} \\
&run \circ cons \circ (code \times concat) \circ (\mathsf{id} \times \mathsf{map}\,compile) \\
=\ &\{\ run \circ cons = comp \circ (exec \times run)\ \} \\
&comp \circ (exec \times run) \circ (code \times concat) \circ (\mathsf{id} \times \mathsf{map}\,compile) \\
=\ &\{\ \mathrm{pairs}\ \} \\
&comp \circ ((exec \circ code) \times (run \circ concat \circ \mathsf{map}\,compile)) \\
=\ &\{\ run \circ concat = compose \circ \mathsf{map}\,run\ \} \\
&comp \circ ((exec \circ code) \times (compose \circ \mathsf{map}\,run \circ \mathsf{map}\,compile))
\end{aligned}
$$

and so

$$run \circ compile = \mathsf{fold}\,(comp \circ ((exec \circ code) \times compose))$$

Denotational Semantics as a Fold We have

$$
\begin{aligned}
&(cons' \circ eval \circ \mathsf{in})\,(op, exprs) \\
=\ &\{\ eval = \mathsf{fold}\,apply\ \} \\
&cons'\,(apply\,(op, \mathsf{map}\,eval\,exprs)) \\
=\ &\{\ arity\,op = \mathsf{length}\,exprs;\ \text{requirement of } exec\ \} \\
&exec\,(code\,op) \circ cat\,(\mathsf{map}\,eval\,exprs) \\
=\ &\{\ cat = compose \circ \mathsf{map}\,cons'\ \} \\
&exec\,(code\,op) \circ compose\,(\mathsf{map}\,(cons' \circ eval)\,exprs) \\
=\ &\{\ \mathrm{pairs}\ \} \\
&(comp \circ ((exec \circ code) \times (compose \circ \mathsf{map}\,(cons' \circ eval))))\,(op, exprs)
\end{aligned}
$$

and so

$$cons' \circ eval = \mathsf{fold}\,(comp \circ ((exec \circ code) \times compose))$$

too, completing the proof.

4.2   Monads and Comonads

Monads and comonads are categorical concepts; each consists of a type functor and a couple of operations that satisfy certain laws. They turn out to have useful applications in the semantics of programming languages. A monad can be used to model a *notion of computation*; in a sense, monads correspond to operational semantics. Dually, comonads correspond to denotational semantics of programming languages. But we will not get into that here. Rather, we simply observe that many constructions in functional programming are either monads or comonads, and that the proofs of the monad and comonad laws are often simple applications of the universal properties of the functors concerned. We present two simple examples, one a monad and the other a comonad.

Monads A *monad* is a functor M together with two operations

$$\text{unit} :: A \rightarrow M\,A$$
$$\text{mult} :: M\,(M\,A) \rightarrow M\,A$$

The two operations should be *natural transformations*, which is to say that the laws

$$\text{unit} \circ f \qquad = M\,f \circ \text{unit}$$
$$\text{mult} \circ M\,(M\,f) = M\,f \circ \text{mult}$$

should be satisfied. Moreover, the following 'coherence laws' relating the two operations should hold:

$$\text{mult} \circ \text{unit} \quad = \text{id}$$
$$\text{mult} \circ M\,\text{unit} = \text{id}$$
$$\text{mult} \circ \text{mult} \quad = \text{mult} \circ M\,\text{mult}$$

The List Monad Ordinary lists are one example of a monad. The datatype is defined in §3.4. We define the two functions

$$wrap\;a = cons\,(a, nil)$$
$$concat = foldL\,(nil, cat)$$

We claim that List is a monad, with unit *wrap* and multiplication *concat*.

Laws We must verify the following five laws:

$$wrap \circ f \qquad\qquad = \text{map}\,f \circ wrap$$
$$concat \circ \text{map}\,(\text{map}\,f) = \text{map}\,f \circ concat$$
$$concat \circ wrap \qquad\quad = \text{id}$$
$$concat \circ \text{map}\,wrap \quad = \text{id}$$
$$concat \circ concat \qquad\; = concat \circ \text{map}\,concat$$

We address them one by one.

Naturality of Unit

$$\begin{aligned}
&(\text{map}\,f \circ wrap)\,a\\
=\;& \{\;wrap\;\}\\
&\text{map}\,f\,(cons\,(a, nil))\\
=\;& \{\;\text{map}\;\}\\
&cons\,(f\,a, nil)\\
=\;& \{\;wrap\;\}\\
&(wrap \circ f)\,a
\end{aligned}$$

Naturality of Mult

$\quad$ map $f \circ concat$
$=\quad$ { $concat$ }
$\quad$ map $f \circ foldL\,(nil, cat)$
$=\quad$ { fusion: map $f \circ cat = cat \circ ($ map $f \times$ map $f)$ }
$\quad foldL\,(nil, cat \circ ($ map $f \times$ id$))$
$=\quad$ { fold-map fusion (Exercise 2.9.14) }
$\quad foldL\,(nil, cat) \circ$ map (map f)
$=\quad$ { $concat$ }
$\quad concat \circ$ map (map f)

Mult-unit

$\quad (concat \circ wrap)\,x$
$=\quad$ { $wrap$ }
$\quad concat\,(cons\,(x, nil))$
$=\quad$ { $concat$ }
$\quad x$
$=\quad$ { identity }
$\quad$ id x

Mult-map-unit

$\quad concat \circ$ map $wrap$
$=\quad$ { fold-map fusion }
$\quad foldL\,(nil, cat \circ (wrap \times$ id$))$
$=\quad$ { $cat \circ (wrap \times$ id$) = cons$ }
$\quad foldL\,(nil, cons)$
$=\quad$ { identity as a fold }
$\quad$ id

Mult-mult

$\quad concat \circ concat$
$=\quad$ { $concat$ }
$\quad concat \circ foldL\,(nil, cat)$
$=\quad$ { fold fusion: $concat \circ cat = cat \circ (concat \times concat)$ }
$\quad foldL\,(nil, cat \circ (concat \times$ id$))$
$=\quad$ { fold-map fusion }
$\quad concat \circ$ map $concat$

Comonads Dually, a *comonad* is a functor M together with two operations

extr :: M A → A
dupl :: M A → M (M A)

Again, the two operations should be *natural transformations*:

$$f \circ \mathsf{extr} \quad\quad\quad = \mathsf{extr} \circ \mathsf{M} \ f$$
$$\mathsf{M} \ (\mathsf{M} \ f) \circ \mathsf{dupl} = \mathsf{dupl} \circ \mathsf{M} \ f$$

Moreover, the following coherence laws should hold:

$$\mathsf{extr} \circ \mathsf{dupl} \quad\ = \mathsf{id}$$
$$\mathsf{M} \ \mathsf{extr} \circ \mathsf{dupl} = \mathsf{id}$$
$$\mathsf{dupl} \circ \mathsf{dupl} \quad = \mathsf{M} \ \mathsf{dupl} \circ \mathsf{dupl}$$

The Stream Comonad One example of a comonad is the datatype of streams:

$$\mathsf{Stream} \ A = \textsc{fix} \ (\underline{A}\hat{\times})$$

We introduce the separate destructors

$$head = \mathsf{exl} \circ \mathsf{out}$$
$$tail \ = \mathsf{exr} \circ \mathsf{out}$$

Thus, the function *tails*, which turns a stream into the stream of streams of all of its infinite suffices, is an unfold:

$$tails = \mathsf{unfold}_{\mathsf{Stream}} \ (\mathsf{id} \ \triangle \ tail)$$

We claim that **Stream** is a comonad, with extraction *head* and duplication *tails*.

Laws To say that the datatype of streams is a comonad with the above operations is to claim the following five laws:

$$f \circ head \quad\quad\quad\quad = head \circ \mathsf{map} \ f$$
$$\mathsf{map} \ (\mathsf{map} \ f) \circ tails = tails \circ \mathsf{map} \ f$$
$$head \circ tails \quad\quad\quad = \mathsf{id}$$
$$\mathsf{map} \ head \circ tails \quad\ = \mathsf{id}$$
$$tails \circ tails \quad\quad\quad = \mathsf{map} \ tails \circ tails$$

We verify them one by one, below.

Naturality of Extract

$$head \circ \mathsf{map} \ f$$
$$= \quad \{ \ head \ \}$$
$$\mathsf{exl} \circ \mathsf{out} \circ \mathsf{map} \ f$$
$$= \quad \{ \ \mathsf{map} \ \}$$
$$\mathsf{exl} \circ (f \times \mathsf{map} \ f) \circ \mathsf{out}$$
$$= \quad \{ \ \mathsf{pairs} \ \}$$
$$f \circ \mathsf{exl} \circ \mathsf{out}$$
$$= \quad \{ \ head \ \}$$
$$f \circ head$$

Naturality of Duplicate

$\quad$ map (map f) $\circ$ *tails*
$=\quad$ { *tails* }
$\quad$ map (map f) $\circ$ unfold (id $\triangle$ *tail*)
$=\quad$ { map-unfold fusion (Exercise 2.9.14) }
$\quad$ unfold (map $f \triangle$ *tail*)
$=\quad$ { unfold fusion: map $f \circ tail = tail \circ$ map f }
$\quad$ unfold (id $\triangle$ *tail*) $\circ$ map f
$=\quad$ { *tails* }
$\quad$ *tails* $\circ$ map f

Extract-Duplicate

$\quad$ *head* $\circ$ *tails*
$=\quad$ { *head*, *tails* }
$\quad$ exl $\circ$ out $\circ$ unfold (id $\triangle$ *tail*)
$=\quad$ { unfolds }
$\quad$ exl $\circ$ (id $\times$ *tails*) $\circ$ (id $\triangle$ *tail*)
$=\quad$ { pairs }
$\quad$ id

Map-Extract-Duplicate

$\quad$ map *head* $\circ$ *tails*
$=\quad$ { *tails* }
$\quad$ map *head* $\circ$ unfold (id $\triangle$ *tail*)
$=\quad$ { map-unfold fusion }
$\quad$ unfold (*head* $\triangle$ *tail*)
$=\quad$ { identity as unfold }
$\quad$ id

Duplicate-Duplicate

$\quad$ *tails* $\circ$ *tails*
$=\quad$ { *tails* }
$\quad$ unfold (id $\triangle$ *tail*) $\circ$ *tails*
$=\quad$ { unfold fusion: *tail* $\circ$ *tails* = *tails* $\circ$ *tail* }
$\quad$ unfold (*tails* $\triangle$ *tail*)
$=\quad$ { map-unfold fusion }
$\quad$ map *tails* $\circ$ unfold (id $\triangle$ *tail*)
$=\quad$ { *tails* }
$\quad$ map *tails* $\circ$ *tails*

4.3   Breadth-First Traversal

As a final example, we discuss breadth-first traversal of a tree. Depth-first traversal is an obvious program to write recursively, but breadth-first traversal takes a little more thought; one might say that it 'goes against the grain'. We present a number of algorithms, and demonstrate their equivalence.

Lists Once again, we use the datatype of lists from §3.4. We will use the function *concat*, which concatenates a list of lists:

$$concat = foldL\ (nil, cat)$$

Trees Of course, we will also require a datatype of trees:

$$\mathsf{Tree\ A} = \mathrm{FIX}\ (\underline{\mathsf{A}}\ \hat{\times}\ \mathsf{List})$$

for which we introduce the separate destructors

$$root = \mathsf{exl} \circ \mathsf{out}$$
$$kids = \mathsf{exr} \circ \mathsf{out}$$

Now, depth-first traversal is easy to write:

$$df = \mathsf{fold}\ (cons \circ (\mathsf{id} \times concat))$$

but breadth-first traversal is a little more difficult.

Levels The most profitable approach to solving the problem is to split the task into two stages. The first stage computes the *levels* of tree — a list of lists, organized by level:

$$levels :: \mathsf{Tree\ A} \to \mathsf{List\ (List\ A)}$$

The second stage is to concatenate the levels. Thus,

$$bf = concat \circ levels$$

Long Zip The crucial component for constructing the levels of a tree is a function *lzw* (for 'long zip with'), which glues together two lists using a given binary operator:

$$lzw :: (\mathsf{A} \times \mathsf{A} \to \mathsf{A}) \to \mathsf{List\ A} \times \mathsf{List\ A} \to \mathsf{List\ A}$$

Corresponding elements are combined using the binary operator; the remaining elements are merely 'copied' to the result. The length of the result is the greater of the lengths of the arguments. We have

$$lzw\ op = unfoldL\ (p, f)$$

where

$$p\,(x,y) = isNil\,x \wedge isNil\,y$$
$$
\begin{aligned}
f\,(x,y) &= (head\,x, (tail\,x, y)), & \text{if } isNil\,y\\
&= (head\,y, (x, tail\,y)), & \text{if } isNil\,x\\
&= (op\,(head\,x, head\,y), (tail\,x, tail\,y)), & \text{otherwise}
\end{aligned}
$$

(This definition is rather inefficient, as the 'remaining elements' are copied one by one. It would be better to use an apomorphism, which would allow the remainder to be copied all in one go; see Exercise 4.5.8.)

Levels as a Fold Now we can define level-order traversal by

$$levels = \mathsf{fold}\,(cons \circ (wrap \times glue))$$

where $wrap\,a = cons(a, nil)$. Here, the function $glue$ glues together the traversals of the children:

$$glue = foldL\,(nil, lzw\,cat)$$

Levels as a Fold, Efficiently The characterization of $levels$ above is inefficient, because the traversals of children are re-traversed in building the traversal of the parent. We can use an *accumulating parameter* to avoid this problem. We define

$$levels'\,(t, xss) = lzw\,cat\,(levels\,t, xss)$$

and so $levels\,t = levels'\,(t, nil)$. We can now calculate (Exercise 4.5.9) that

$$
\begin{aligned}
levels'\,(\mathsf{in}\,(a, ts), xss) &= cons\,(cons\,(a, ys), foldL\,(yss, levels'))\,ts)\\
&\quad \text{where } (ys, yss) = split\,xss
\end{aligned}
$$

where

$$
\begin{aligned}
split\,xss &= (nil, nil), & \text{if } isNil\,xss\\
&= (head\,xss, tail\,xss), & \text{otherwise}
\end{aligned}
$$

With the efficient apomorphic definition of lzw from Exercise 4.5.8, taking time proportional to the length of the shorter argument, this program for level-order traversal takes linear time. However, it is no longer written as a fold.

Levels as an Unfold A better solution is to use an unfold. We generalize to the level-order traversal of a *forest*:

$$levelsf :: \mathsf{List}\,(\mathsf{Tree\,A}) \to \mathsf{List}\,(\mathsf{List\,A})$$

Again, we can calculate (using the universal property) that $levelsf$ is an unfold:

$$unfoldL\,(isNil, \mathsf{map}\,root \,\triangle\,(concat \circ \mathsf{map}\,kids))$$

See Exercise 4.5.11 for the details.

4.4   Bibliographic Notes

The compiler example was inspired by Hutton [19]. The application of monads to semantics is due to Moggi [28], and of comonads to Brookes [6,7] and Turi [37]; Wadler [43,41,42] brought monads to the attention of functional programmers. The programs for breadth-first tree traversal are joint work with Geraint Jones [12].

4.5   Exercises

1. An alternative definition of compilation is as an unfold, from a list of expressions to a list of instructions. Define *compile* in this way, and repeat the proof of correctness of the compiler.
2. Use fold-map fusion (Exercise 2.9.14) on lists to show that

$$foldL' \ (\mathsf{id}, comp' \circ exec) = foldL' \ (\mathsf{id}, comp) \circ \mathsf{map} \ exec$$

   (so the two definitions of *run* in §4.1 are indeed equivalent).
3. Show that

$$foldL' \ (\mathsf{id}, f) \circ concat = foldL' \ (\mathsf{id}, f) \circ \mathsf{map} \ (foldL' \ (\mathsf{id}, f))$$

   when f is associative. (Hence $run \circ concat = compose \circ \mathsf{map} \ run$).
4. The compiler example would be more realistic and more general if the code for each operation were a list of instructions instead of a single instruction. Repeat the proof for this scenario.
5. The datatype of externally-labelled binary trees from §3.4 forms a monad, with unit operation

   $$leaf = \mathsf{in} \circ \mathsf{inl}$$

   and multiplication operation

   $$collapse = \mathsf{fold} \ (\mathsf{id} \ \triangledown \ (\mathsf{in} \circ \mathsf{inr}))$$

   Prove that the monad laws are satisfied.
6. The datatype $\mathsf{Tree} \ A = \mathrm{FIX} \ (\underline{A} \ \hat{+} \ (\underline{A} \ \hat{\times} \ (\mathsf{Id} \ \hat{\times} \ \mathsf{Id})))$ of homogeneous binary trees forms a comonad, with extraction operation

   $$root = (\mathsf{id} \ \triangledown \ \mathsf{exl}) \circ \mathsf{out}$$

   and duplication operation

   $$subs = \mathsf{unfold} \ ((leaf + (node \ \triangle \ \mathsf{exr})) \circ \mathsf{out})$$

   where *leaf* and *node* are the separate constructors:

   $$leaf = \mathsf{in} \circ \mathsf{inl}$$
   $$node = \mathsf{in} \circ \mathsf{inr}$$

   Prove that the comonad laws are satisfied.

7. On the datatype of lists in §3.4 we defined concatenation of two lists as a fold

$$cat\,(x,y) = \mathsf{fold}\,(\mathsf{const}\,y\bigtriangledown(\mathsf{in}\circ\mathsf{inr}))\,x$$

Calculate a definition as an unfold, using the universal property. Also calculate a definition as an apomorphism.
8. Calculate a definition of $lzw\,f$ (§4.3) as an apomorphism.
9. Calculate the accumulating-parameter optimization of level-order traversal, from §4.3.
10. The program in Exercise 4.5.9 is not a fold. However, if we define instead the curried version $levels''\,t\,xss = levels'\,(t,xss)$, then $levels''$ is a fold. Use the universal property to calculate the f such that $levels'' = \mathsf{fold}\,f$.
11. Calculate the version of level-order traversal from §4.3 as an unfold.
12. The final program for breadth-first traversal of a forest was of the form

$$bff = concat \circ levels f$$

where $concat$ is a list fold and $levels f$ a list unfold. Use hylomorphism deforestation (Exercise 3.6.10) to write this as a single recursion, avoiding the intermediate generation of the list of lists. (This program was shown to us by Bernhard Möller [29]; it is interesting that it arises as a 'mere compiler optimization' from the more abstract program developed here.)
13. To most people, breadth-first traversal is related to queues, but there are no queues in the programs presented here. Show that in fact

$$bff = unfoldL\,(null, step)$$

where $null$ holds precisely of empty forests, and $step$ is defined by

$$step\,(cons\,(t,ts)) = (root\,t, cat\,(ts, kids\,ts))$$

(Hint: the crucial observation is that, for associative operator $\oplus$ with unit e, the equation

$$foldL\,(e,\oplus)\,(lzw\,(\oplus)\,(cons\,(x,xs),ys))$$
$$= x\oplus foldL\,(e,\oplus)\,(lzw\,(\oplus)\,(ys,xs))$$

holds.)

References

1. Roland Backhouse. An exploration of the Bird-Meertens formalism. In *International Summer School on Constructive Algorithmics, Hollum, Ameland.* STOP project, 1989. Also available as Technical Report CS 8810, Department of Computer Science, Groningen University, 1988. 159
2. R. S. Bird, C. C. Morgan, and J. C. P. Woodcock, editors. *LNCS 669: Mathematics of Program Construction.* Springer-Verlag, 1993. 158
3. Richard Bird. Personal communication, 1999. 183

4. Richard Bird and Oege de Moor. *The Algebra of Programming*. Prentice-Hall, 1996. 158
5. Richard S. Bird. *Introduction to Functional Programming Using Haskell*. Prentice-Hall, 1998. 159
6. Stephen Brookes and Shai Geva. Computational comonads and intensional semantics. In M. P. Fourman, P. T. Johnstone, and A. M. Pitts, editors, *Categories in Computer Science*, London Mathematical Society Lecture Notes, pages 1–44. Cambridge University Press, 1992. Also Technical Report CMU-CS-91-190, School of Computer Science, Carnegie Mellon University. 193
7. Stephen Brookes and Kathryn Van Stone. Monads and comonads in intensional semantics. Technical Report CMU-CS-93-140, CMU, 1993. 193
8. Rod Burstall and David Rydeheard. *Computational Category Theory*. Prentice-Hall, 1988. 159
9. Roy L. Crole. *Categories for Types*. Cambridge University Press, 1994. 159
10. B. A. Davey and H. A. Priestley. *Introduction to Lattices and Order*. Mathematical Textbooks Series. Cambridge University Press, 1990. 180
11. Maarten M. Fokkinga and Erik Meijer. Program calculation properties of continuous algebras. Technical Report CS-R9104, CWI, Amsterdam, January 1991. 175, 180
12. Jeremy Gibbons and Geraint Jones. The under-appreciated unfold. In *Proceedings of the Third ACM SIGPLAN International Conference on Functional Programming*, pages 273–279, Baltimore, Maryland, September 1998. 193
13. J. A. Goguen, J. W. Thatcher, E. G. Wagner, and J. B. Wright. An introduction to categories, algebraic theories and algebras. Technical report, IBM Thomas J. Watson Research Centre, Yorktown Heights, April 1975. 159, 169
14. J. A. Goguen, J. W. Thatcher, E. G. Wagner, and J. B. Wright. Initial algebra semantics and continuous algebras. *Journal of the ACM*, 24(1):68–95, January 1977. 159, 169
15. Jeremy Gunawardena. Towards an applied mathematics for computer science. In M. S. Alber, B. Hu, and J. J. Rosenthal, editors, *Current and Future Directions in Applied Mathematics*. Birkhäuser, Boston, 1997. 149
16. Tatsuya Hagino. *A Categorical Programming Language*. PhD thesis, Department of Computer Science, University of Edinburgh, September 1987. 159, 169
17. Tatsuya Hagino. A typed lambda calculus with categorical type constructors. In D. H. Pitt, A. Poigné, and D. E. Rydeheard, editors, *LNCS 283: Category Theory and Computer Science*, pages 140–157. Springer-Verlag, September 1987. 159, 169
18. C. A. R. Hoare. Notes on data structuring. In Ole-Johan Dahl, Edsger W. Dijkstra, and C. A. R. Hoare, editors, *Structured Programming*, APIC studies in data processing, pages 83–174. Academic Press, 1972. 161
19. Graham Hutton. Fold and unfold for program semantics. In *Proceedings of the Third ACM SIGPLAN International Conference on Functional Programming*, Baltimore, Maryland, September 1998. 193
20. Graham Hutton. Personal communication, 1999. 182
21. Johan Jeuring, editor. *LNCS 1422: Proceedings of Mathematics of Program Construction*, Marstrand, Sweden, June 1998. Springer-Verlag. 158
22. Johan Jeuring and Erik Meijer, editors. *LNCS 925: Advanced Functional Programming*. Springer-Verlag, 1995. Lecture notes from the First International Spring School on Advanced Functional Programming Techniques, Båstad, Sweden. 196
23. Saunders Mac Lane. *Categories for the Working Mathematician*. Springer-Verlag, 1971. 159

24. Grant Malcolm. *Algebraic Data Types and Program Transformation.* PhD thesis, Rijksuniversiteit Groningen, September 1990. 159, 163, 169
25. Grant Malcolm. Data structures and program transformation. *Science of Computer Programming,* 14:255–279, 1990. 159, 169
26. Lambert Meertens. Paramorphisms. *Formal Aspects of Computing,* 4(5):413–424, 1992. 171
27. Erik Meijer, Maarten Fokkinga, and Ross Paterson. Functional programming with bananas, lenses, envelopes and barbed wire. In John Hughes, editor, *LNCS 523: Functional Programming Languages and Computer Architecture,* pages 124–144. Springer-Verlag, 1991. 169, 180
28. Eugenio Moggi. Notions of computation and monads. *Information and Computation,* 93(1), 1991. 193
29. Bernhard Möller. Personal communication, 1995. 194
30. Bernhard Möller, editor. *LNCS 947: Mathematics of Program Construction.* Springer-Verlag, 1995. 158
31. Benjamin C. Pierce. *Basic Category Theory for Computer Scientists.* MIT Press, 1991. 159
32. John C. Reynolds. Semantics of the domain of flow diagrams. *Journal of the ACM,* 24(3):484–503, 1977. 180
33. David A. Schmidt. *Denotational Semantics: A Methodology for Language Development.* Allyn and Bacon, 1986. 180
34. M. B. Smyth and G. D. Plotkin. The category-theoretic solution of recursive domain equations. *SIAM Journal on Computing,* 11(4):761–783, November 1982. 169, 180
35. Joseph Stoy. *Denotational Semantics: The Scott-Strachey Approach to Programming Language Theory.* MIT Press, 1977. 180
36. Doaitse Swierstra and Oege de Moor. Virtual data structures. In Bernhard Möller, Helmut Partsch, and Steve Schumann, editors, *LNCS 755: IFIP TC2/WG2.1 State-of-the-Art Report on Formal Program Development,* pages 355–371. Springer-Verlag, 1993. 181
37. Daniele Turi. *Functorial Operational Semantics and its Denotational Dual.* PhD thesis, Vrije Universiteit Amsterdam, June 1996. 193
38. Tarmo Uustalu and Varmo Vene. Primitive (co)recursion and course-of-value (co)iteration. Research Report TRITA-IT R 98:02, Dept of Teleinformatics, Royal Institute of Technology, Stockholm, January 1998. 172
39. J. L. A. van de Snepscheut, editor. *LNCS 375: Mathematics of Program Construction.* Springer-Verlag, 1989. 158
40. Varmo Vene and Tarmo Uustalu. Functional programming with apomorphisms (corecursion). *Proceedings of the Estonian Academy of Sciences: Physics, Mathematics,* 47(3):147–161, 1998. 9th Nordic Workshop on Programming Theory. 172
41. Philip Wadler. Comprehending monads. *Mathematical Structures in Computer Science,* 2(4):461–493, 1992. Earlier version appeared in ACM Conference on Lisp and Functional Programming, 1990. 193
42. Philip Wadler. The essence of functional programming. In *19th Annual Symposium on Principles of Programming Languages,* 1992. 193
43. Philip Wadler. Monads for functional programming. In M. Broy, editor, *Program Design Calculi: Proceedings of the Marktoberdorf Summer School,* 1992. Also in [22]. 193
44. R. F. C. Walters. Datatypes in distributive categories. *Bulletin of the Australian Mathematical Society,* 40:79–82, 1989. 159

45. R. F. C. Walters. *Categories and Computer Science.* Computer Science Texts Series. Cambridge University Press, 1991. 159
46. R. F. C. Walters. An imperative language based on distributive categories. *Mathematical Structures in Computer Science*, 2:249–256, 1992. 159

5   Appendix: Implementation in Haskell

The programs we derive in these lectures are easily translated into a lazy functional programming language such as Haskell. We present one example, the *quicksort* program from §3.4, to illustrate.

5.1   Products

We start by encoding the pair calculus. Here are products:

```
> data Prod a b = Prod a b
> exl (Prod a b) = a
> exr (Prod a b) = b

> fork :: (a -> b) -> (a -> c) -> a -> Prod b c
> fork f g a = Prod (f a) (g a)

> prod :: (a->c) -> (b->d) -> (Prod a b) -> (Prod c d)
> prod f g = fork (f . exl) (g . exr)
```

5.2   Sums

Here are the definitions for sums:

```
> data Sum a b = Inl a | Inr b

> join :: (a -> c) -> (b -> c) -> Sum a b -> c
> join l r (Inl x) = l x
> join l r (Inr y) = r y

> dsum :: (a->c) -> (b->d) -> Sum a b -> Sum c d
> dsum f g = join (Inl . f) (Inr . g)

> query :: (a -> Bool) -> a -> Sum a a
> query p a | p a = Inl a
>           | otherwise = Inr a
```

We include a function `query p` to model *p*? (we cannot use the names `sum` or `guard`, because they are already used in the standard Haskell prelude).

5.3   Functors

Haskell's *type classes* allow us to encode the property of being a functor. This allows us to use the same name `mapf` for the 'map' operation of any type functor. (The standard prelude defines the class `Functor` and the function `fmap` for this purpose; we simply repeat the definition with different names here.)

```
> class TypeFunctor f where
>   mapf :: (a -> b) -> (f a -> f b)
```

Actually, all we can encode is the type of the corresponding map operations; we cannot express the laws that should hold.

5.4   Datatypes

A type functor `f` induces a datatype `Fix f`; the constructor is `In` and the destructor `out`. (The difference in capitalization is an artifact of Haskell's rules for identifiers.)

```
> data TypeFunctor f => Fix f = In (f (Fix f))
```

```
> out :: TypeFunctor f => Fix f -> f (Fix f)
> out (In x) = x
```

5.5   Folds and Unfolds

These are now straightforward translations:

```
> fold :: TypeFunctor f => (f a -> a) -> (Fix f -> a)
> fold f = f . mapf (fold f) . out
```

```
> unfold :: TypeFunctor f => (a -> f a) -> (a -> Fix f)
> unfold f = In . mapf (unfold f) . f
```

5.6   Lists

The encoding of a datatype is almost straightforward. The only wrinkle is that Haskell requires a type constructor identifier (`ListF` below) in order to make something an instance of a type class, so we need to introduce a function to remove this constructor too:

```
> data ListF a b = ListF (Sum () (Prod a b))
> unListF (ListF x) = x

> instance TypeFunctor (ListF a)
>    where
>       mapf f (ListF x) = ListF (dsum id (prod id f) x)
```

Now the datatype itself can be given as a mere synonym:

```
> type List a = Fix (ListF a)
```

We introduce some syntactic sugar for functions on lists:

```
> nil :: List a
> nil = In (ListF (Inl ()))
> cons :: Prod a (List a) -> List a
> cons (Prod a x) = In (ListF (Inr (Prod a x)))

> isNil :: List a -> Bool
> isNil = join (const True) (const False) . unListF . out

> hd :: List a -> a
> hd = join (error "Head of empty list") exl . unListF . out

> tl :: List a -> List a
> tl = join (error "Tail of empty list") exr . unListF . out

> foldL :: Prod b (Prod a b -> b) -> List a -> b
> foldL (Prod e f) = fold (join (const e) f . unListF)

> cat :: Prod (List a) (List a) -> List a
> cat (Prod x y) = foldL (Prod y cons) x
```

(The names head and tail are already taken in the Haskell standard prelude, for the corresponding operations on the built-in lists.)

5.7 Trees

Trees can be defined in the same way as lists:

```
> data TreeF a b = TreeF (Sum () (Prod a (Prod b b)))
> unTreeF (TreeF x) = x

> instance TypeFunctor (TreeF a)
>    where
>       mapf f (TreeF x) = TreeF (dsum id (prod id (prod f f)) x)
> type Tree a = Fix (TreeF a)

> empty :: Tree a
> empty = In (TreeF (Inl ()))
> bin :: Tree a -> a -> Tree a -> Tree a
> bin t a u = In (TreeF (Inr (Prod a (Prod t u))))

> foldT :: Prod b (Prod a (Prod b b) -> b) -> Tree a -> b
> foldT (Prod e f) = fold (join (const e) f . unTreeF)

> unfoldT :: Prod (b -> Bool) (Prod (b -> a) (b -> Prod b b))
>                  -> b -> Tree a
> unfoldT (Prod p (Prod f g))
>   = unfold (TreeF . dsum (const ()) (fork f g) . query p)
```

5.8 Quicksort

The flattening stage of Quicksort encodes simply:

```
> flatten :: Tree a -> List a
> flatten = foldT (Prod nil glue)
>   where glue (Prod a (Prod x y)) = cat (Prod x (cons (Prod a y)))
```

We define filtering as follows (the name **filter** is already taken):

```
> filt :: (a -> Bool) -> List a -> Prod (List a) (List a)
> filt p = foldL (Prod (Prod nil nil) step)
>    where step = join (fork (cons . prod id exl) (exr . exr))
>                      (fork (exl . exr) (cons . prod id exr))
>               . query (p . exl)
```

The definition of **step** here is a point-free presentation of the more perspicuous
definition using variable names and pattern guards:

```
    where step (Prod a (Prod x y))
             | p a        = Prod (cons (Prod a x)) y
             | otherwise = Prod x (cons (Prod a y))
```

Now partitioning a non-empty list is an application of filter:

```
> partition :: Ord a => List a -> Prod (List a) (List a)
> partition x = filt (< hd x) (tl x)
```

(The *context* 'Ord a =>' states that this definition is only applicable to ordered types, namely those supporting the operation <.)

Then the remainder of the Quicksort algorithm translates naturally:

```
> build :: Ord a => List a -> Tree a
> build = unfoldT (Prod isNil (Prod hd partition))

> quicksort :: Ord a => List a -> List a
> quicksort = flatten . build
```

Chapter 6
Algebra of Program Termination

Henk Doornbos [1] and Roland Backhouse [2]

[1] EverMind, Groningen, The Netherlands
[2] School of Computer Science and Information Technology,
University of Nottingham

Abstract. Well-foundedness and inductive properties of relations are
expressed in terms of fixed points. A class of fixed point equations, called
"hylo" equations, is introduced. A methodology of recursive program design based on the use of hylo equations is presented. Current research on
generalisations of well-foundedness and inductive properties of relations,
making these properties relative to a datatype, is introduced.

1   Introduction

Central to computing science is the development of practical programming methodologies. Characteristic of a programming methodology is that it involves a *discipline* designed to maximise confidence in the reliability of the end product. The
discipline constrains the construction methods to those that are demonstrably
simple and easy to use, whilst still allowing sufficient flexibility that the creative
process of program construction is not impeded. A well-established methodology
is the combined use of invariant relations and well-founded relations in the design of iterative algorithms in sequential programming (see sections 2.2 and 2.5),
the constraint being the restriction of the methodology to the design of **while**
statements rather than allowing arbitrary use of **goto** statements.

In this paper we develop an algebra of terminating computations based on
fixed point calculus and relation algebra. We begin by formulating properties of
well-foundedness (of a relation) and admitting induction in terms of fixed points.
This discussion is motivated by the methodology of designing iterative algorithms
mentioned above. We then explore the termination of recursive programs. Here
we argue for a practical discipline of recursive programming based on a class of
recursive fixed-point equations called "hylo" equations (a notion first introduced
by Meijer [20]). The notion of a relation admitting induction is generalised to the
notion of "F-reductivity", where the parameter F captures the data structure
underlying the recursion.

2   Imperative Programming and Well-Founded Relations

An important application of fixed point calculus is in the study of well-founded
relations. Well-founded relations are fundamental to program termination and
to inductive proofs of program properties.

R. Backhouse et al. (Eds.): Algebraic and Coalgebraic Methods . . . , LNCS 2297, pp. 203–235, 2002.
© Springer-Verlag Berlin Heidelberg 2002

Before we can begin to discuss how to express well-foundedness in terms of fixed points we need to introduce relation algebra. In relation algebra, relations are not viewed as sets of pairs but just as values in (the carrier of) an algebraic system. In this way, relation algebra expresses the properties of the most fundamental operations on relations without reference to the elements being related. For example, relation algebra encapsulates the properties of the converse $R^{\cup}$ of relation R without reference to the so-called *pointwise* definition of $R^{\cup}$:

$$(x,y) \in R^{\cup} \equiv (y,x) \in R \quad .$$

Instead the converse operation is given an axiomatic definition, which includes for example the property that it is its own inverse:

$$(R^{\cup})^{\cup} = R \quad .$$

This *point-free* axiomatisation is the key to formulating the notions of well-foundedness and admitting induction in terms of fixed points.

A continuous motivational thread throughout this section will be the formulation of a methodology for the design of iterative programs in terms of relation algebra. We begin in section 2.1 with a brief introduction to relation algebra, just enough to be able to present a concise formulation of the use of invariant properties in section 2.2. This latter discussion raises several issues which motivates the introduction of the domain and division operators in section 2.3.

In section 2.4 we begin with the standard pointwise definition of well-foundedness which we then reformulate in a point-free definition. We then go on to derive an equivalent but more compact definition. The same process is followed for the notion of admitting induction. We recap the standard pointwise definition, reformulate this in a point-free manner and then derive a more compact but equivalent definition. We then discuss the equivalence of admitting induction and being well-founded.

2.1   Relation Algebra

For us, a (non-deterministic) program is an input-output relation. The convention we use when defining relations is that the input is on the right and the output on the left. The convention is thus that used in functional programming and not that used in sequential programming. For example, the relation $<$ on numbers is a program that maps a number into one smaller than itself. The function succ is the relation between natural numbers such that $m\langle\mathsf{succ}\rangle n$ equivales $m = n+1$. It is thus the program that maps a natural number into its successor.

A relation is a set of ordered pairs. In discussions of the theory of imperative programming the "state space" from which the elements of each pair are drawn often remains anonymous. This reflects the fact that type structure is often not a significant parameter in the construction of imperative programs, in contrast to functional programs where it is pervasive. One goal here is to combine the functional and imperative programming paradigms. For this reason, we adopt a typed algebra of relations (formally an "allegory" [11]). A relation is thus a triple consisting of a pair of types I and J, say, and a subset of the cartesian product $I \times J$. We write $R \in I \leftarrow J$ (read R has type I from J), the left-pointing arrow indicating that we view J as the set of all possible inputs and I as the set of possible outputs. I is called the *target* and J the *source* of the relation R, and $I \leftarrow J$ (read I from J) is called its *type*.

We write $x[\![R]\!]y$ if the pair (x, y) is an element of relation R. (As is usual in mathematics, we omit the brackets when R is denoted by a symbol and it is easy to parse the resulting expression — as in, for example, $x < y$.) We use a raised infix dot to denote relational composition. Thus $R \circ S$ denotes the composition of relations R and S (the relation defined by $x[\![R \circ S]\!]z$ equivales $\exists \langle y :: x[\![R]\!]y \wedge y[\![S]\!]z \rangle$). The composition $R \circ S$ is only defined when the source of R equals the target of S. Moreover, the target of $R \circ S$ is the target of R, and the source of $R \circ S$ is the source of S. Thus, $R \circ S \in I \leftarrow K$ if $R \in I \leftarrow J$ and $S \in J \leftarrow K$. The converse of relation R is denoted by $R^{\cup}$. Thus, $x[\![R^{\cup}]\!]y$ equivales $y[\![R]\!]x$. The type rule is that $R^{\cup} \in I \leftarrow J$ equivales $R \in J \leftarrow I$.

Relations of the same type are ordered by set inclusion denoted in the conventional way by the infix $\subseteq$ operator. The relations of a given type $I \leftarrow J$ form a complete lattice under this ordering. The smallest relation of type $I \leftarrow J$ is the empty relation, denoted here by $\perp\!\!\!\perp_{I \leftarrow J}$, and the largest relation of type $I \leftarrow J$ is the universal relation, which we denote by $\top\!\!\!\top_{I \leftarrow J}$. (We use this notation for the empty and universal relations because the conventional notation $\top$ for the universal relation is easily confused with T, a sans serif letter T, particularly in hand-written documents.) The union and intersection of two relations R and S of the same type are denoted by $R \cup S$ and $R \cap S$, respectively.

Because relations are sets, we have the shunting rule

$$R \cap S \subseteq T \equiv S \subseteq \neg R \cup T$$

where $\neg R$ denotes the complement of relation R. The only use we make of this rule here is the fact that relations of type $I \leftarrow I$ form a completely distributive lattice and thus a regular algebra. We use this fact when we exploit the unique extension property of regular algebras in the identification of fixed point equations that define a relation uniquely.

For each set I there is an identity relation on I which we denote by id_I. Thus $\mathrm{id}_I \in I \leftarrow I$. Relations of type $I \leftarrow I$ contained in the identity relation of that type will be called *coreflexives*. (The terminology *partial identity relation* and *monotype* is also used.) By convention, we use R, S, T to denote arbitrary relations and A, B and C to denote coreflexives. A coreflexive A thus has the property that if $x[\![A]\!]y$ then $x = y$. Clearly, the coreflexives of type $I \leftarrow I$ are in one to one correspondence with the subsets of I; we shall exploit this correspondence by identifying subsets of a set I with the coreflexives of type $I \leftarrow I$. Specifically, by an abuse of notation, we write $x \in A$ for $x[\![A]\!]x$ (on condition that A is a coreflexive). We also identify coreflexives with predicates, particularly when discussing induction principles (which are traditionally formulated in terms of predicates rather than sets). So we shall say "x has property A" meaning formally that $x[\![A]\!]x$. Continuing this abuse of notation, we use $\sim A$

to denote the coreflexive having the same type as A and containing just those elements not in A. Thus, $x[\sim A]y$ equivales the conjunction of $x \in I$ (where A has type $I \leftarrow I$) and $x = y$ and not $x[A]x$. We also sometimes write I where id_I is meant. (This fits in with the convention in category theory of giving the same name to that part of a functor which maps objects to objects and that part which maps arrows to arrows.) A final, important remark about coreflexives is that their composition coincides with their intersection. That is, for coreflexives A and B, $A \circ B = A \cap B$.

We use an infix dot to denote function application. Thus $f.x$ denotes application of function f to argument x. Functions are particular sorts of relations; a relation R is *functional* if $y[R]x$ and $z[R]x$ together imply that $y = z$. If this is the case we write $R.x$ for the unique y such that $y[R]x$. Note that functionality of relation R is equivalent to the property $R \circ R^\cup \subseteq \text{id}_I$ where I is the target of R. We normally use f, g and h to denote functional relations.

Dual to the notion of functionality of a relation is the notion of injectivity. A relation R with source J is *injective* if $R^\cup \circ R \subseteq \text{id}_J$. Which of the properties $R \circ R^\cup \subseteq \text{id}_I$ or $R^\cup \circ R \subseteq \text{id}_J$ one calls "functional" and which "injective" is a matter of interpretation. The choice here fits in with the convention that input is on the right and output on the left. More importantly, it fits with the convention of writing $f.x$ rather than say x^f (that is the function to the left of its argument). A sensible consequence is that type arrows point from right to left.

2.2   Imperative Programming

In this section we introduce the derivation of repetitive statements using invariant relations. The section contains just an outline of the methodology expressed in relation algebra. For extensive introductions see (for example) [12,1]. At the end of the section we identify a need to delve deeper into relation algebra, thus motivating the section which follows.

Given a (non-trivial) specification, X, the key to constructing a loop implementing X is the invention of an invariant, Inv. The invariant is chosen in such a way that it satisfies three properties. First, the invariant can be "established" by some initialisation $Init$. Second, the combination of the invariant and some termination $Term$ satisfies the specification X. Third, the invariant is "maintained by" some loop body $Body$ whilst making progress towards termination.

These informal requirements can be made precise in a very concise way. The three components Inv, $Init$ and $Term$ are all binary relations on the state space, just like the specification X. They are so-called input-output relations.

"Establishing" the invariant is the requirement that

$$Init \subseteq Inv \quad .$$

In words, any value w' related to input value w by $Init$ is also related by the invariant relation to w.

That the combination of the termination and invariant satisfies the specification X is the requirement that

$$Term \circ Inv \subseteq X \ .$$

This is the requirement that for all output values w' and input values w,

$$\forall \langle v:\ w' [\![Term]\!] v \wedge v [\![Inv]\!] w:\ w' [\![X]\!] w \rangle$$

(Here we see the convention of placing input values on the right and output values on the left.)

Finally, that the invariant is maintained by the loop body is expressed by

$$Body \circ Inv \subseteq Inv$$

Pointwise this is

$$\forall \langle w', v, w:\ w' [\![Body]\!] v \wedge v [\![Inv]\!] w:\ w' [\![Inv]\!] w \rangle \ .$$

So $Body$ maps values v related by the invariant Inv to w to values w' that are also related by Inv to w.

Together these three properties guarantee that

$$Term \circ Body^* \circ Init \subseteq X \ .$$

That progress is made is the requirement that the relation $Body$ be well-founded. (This we will return to shortly.)

As an example, consider the classic problem of finding the greatest common divisor (abbreviated gcd) of two positive numbers x and y. The state space of the program is $\mathsf{Int} \times \mathsf{Int}$. The specification, invariant, initialisation and termination are thus binary relations on this set. The specification, X, is simply

$$x' = y' = \mathsf{gcd}.(x,y) \ .$$

Here priming x and y is a commonly used convention for abbreviating the definition of a relation between the pair of output values x' and y', and the pair of input values x and y. More formally, X is the relation

$$\{x, y, x', y':\ x' = y' = \mathsf{gcd}.(x,y):\ ((x',y'), (x,y))\} \ .$$

The convention is that the definition

$$\{x, y, x', y': p.(x,y,x',y'):\ ((x',y'), (x,y))\}$$

is abbreviated to

$$p.(x,y,x',y') \ ,$$

the primes indicating the correspondence between input and output variables. Using this convention, the invariant is the relation

$$\mathsf{gcd}.(x',y') = \mathsf{gcd}.(x,y)$$

and the initialisation is the identity relation

$$x' = x \wedge y' = y \ .$$

(The initialisation is thus implemented by skip , the do-nothing statement.) The termination is a subset of the identity relation on the state space. It is the relation

$$x' = x = y' = y \ .$$

The composition of the termination relation and the invariant is thus the relation

$$x' = y' \wedge \mathsf{gcd}.(x',y') = \mathsf{gcd}.(x,y)$$

which, since $\mathsf{gcd}.(x',x')$ equals x' , is identical to the specification X . The loop body in Dijkstra's well-known guarded command solution to this problem is the union of two relations, the relation

$$x < y \wedge x' = x \wedge y' = y - x$$

and the relation

$$y < x \wedge y' = y \wedge x' = x - y \ .$$

Exercise 1   Identify X , Inv , $Init$, $Body$ and $Term$ in the language recognition program discussed in the chapter on Galois Connections and Fixed Point Calculus.

□

2.3   Domains and Division

Domains Our account of invariants is not yet complete. The relationship between the specification X and $Term \circ Body^* \circ Init$ is containment not equality, and may indeed be a proper superset relation. Not every subset of the specification will do, however. An additional requirement is that the input-output relation computed by the program is total on all input values. Formally this is a requirement on the so-called "right domain" of the computed input-output relation. Right domains are also relevant if we are to relate our account of invariants to the implementation of loops by a **while** statement. Recall that $Body$ is the body of the loop, and $Term$ terminates the computation. The implementation of $Term \circ Body^*$ by a **while** statement demands that both of these relations are partial and, more specifically, that their right domains are complementary.

The *right domain* of a relation R is, informally, the set of input values that are related by R to at least one output value. Formally, the right domain $R{>}$ of a relation R of type $I{\leftarrow}J$ is a coreflexive of type $J{\leftarrow}J$ satisfying the property that

$$\forall \langle A:\ A \subseteq \mathsf{id}_J:\ R{\circ}A = R \equiv R{>} \subseteq A \rangle \ .$$

Given a coreflexive A , $A \subseteq \mathsf{id}_J$, the relation $R{\circ}A$ can be viewed as the relation R restricted to inputs in the set A . Thus, in words, the right domain of R

is the least coreflexive A that maintains R when R is restricted to inputs in the set A.

Note that the right domain should not be confused with the source of the relation. The source expresses the set of input values of interest in the context of the application being considered whereas the right domain is the set of input values over which the relation is defined. In other words, we admit the possibility of *partial* relations. Formally, a relation R of type $I \leftarrow J$ is *total* if $R{>}$ is id_J, otherwise it is partial. Similarly the target should not be confused with the left domain of a relation. A relation R of type $I \leftarrow J$ is *surjective* if $R{<}$ is id_I.

Returning to loops, the requirement is that the right domain of $Term$ is the complement of the right domain of $Body$. Letting b denote the right domain of $Body$ and $\sim b$ its complement (thus $b \cup \sim b = \mathsf{id}$ and $b \cap \sim b = \perp\!\!\!\perp$) we thus have

$$Term = Term \circ \sim b \quad \text{and} \quad Body = Body \circ b \ .$$

As a consequence,

$$Term \circ Body^* \circ Init = Term \circ \sim b \circ (Body \circ b)^* \circ Init \ .$$

The statement **while** b **do** $Body$ is the implementation of $\sim b \circ (Body \circ b)^*$ in that the latter is the least solution of the equation

$$X :: \ X = \sim b \cup X \circ Body \circ b$$

and executing this equation is equivalent to executing the program

$$X = \textbf{if } b \textbf{ then } Body; X \ .$$

We continue this discussion in section 2.5.

Division The body of a loop should maintain the loop invariant. Formally, the requirement is that $Body \circ Inv \subseteq Inv$. In general, for relations R of type $I \leftarrow J$ and T of type $I \leftarrow K$ there is a relation $R \backslash T$ of type $J \leftarrow K$ satisfying the Galois connection, for all relations S,

$$R \circ S \subseteq T \equiv S \subseteq R \backslash T \ .$$

The operator $\backslash$ is called a *division* operator (because of the similarity of the above rule to the rule of division in ordinary arithmetic). The relation $R \backslash T$ is called a *residual* or a *factor* of the relation T. Relation $R \backslash T$ holds between output value w' and input value w if and only if

$$\forall \langle v: \ v[\![R]\!]w' : \ v[\![T]\!]w \rangle \ .$$

Applying this Galois connection, the requirement on $Body$ is thus equivalent to

$$Inv \subseteq Body \backslash Inv \ ,$$

the pointwise formulation of which is

$$\forall\langle w', w: \ w'[\![Inv]\!]w: \ \forall\langle w'': w''[\![Body]\!]w': w''[\![Inv]\!]w\rangle\rangle \ .$$

The relation $Body \backslash Inv$ corresponds to what is called the *weakest prespecification* of Inv with respect to $Body$ in the more usual predicate calculus formulations of the methodology [14]. The *weakest liberal precondition* operator will be denoted here by the symbol "$\diagdown$". Formally, if R is a relation of type $I \leftarrow J$ and A is a coreflexive of type $I \leftarrow I$ then $R \diagdown A$ is a coreflexive of type $J \leftarrow J$ characterised by the property that, for all coreflexives B of type $J \leftarrow J$,

$$(R \circ B)^{<} \subseteq A \equiv B \subseteq R \diagdown A \ . \tag{2}$$

(If we interpret the coreflexive A as a predicate p on the type I, then $R \diagdown A$ is the predicate q such that

$$q.w \equiv \forall\langle w': w'[\![R]\!]w: p.w\rangle \ .$$

It is the weakest condition q on input values w that guarantees that all output values w' that are R-related to w satisfy the predicate p.)

The operator $\diagdown$ plays a very significant role in what is to follow. For this reason it is useful to have a full and intimate understanding of its algebraic properties. This, however, is not the place to develop that understanding and we make do with a summary of the most frequently used properties.

First note that the function $(R \diagdown)$, being an upper adjoint, distributes over arbitrary meets of coreflexives. Because meet on coreflexives coincides with composition it follows that $R \diagdown$ distributes over composition: $R \diagdown (A \circ B) = (R \diagdown A) \circ (R \diagdown B)$. This corresponds to the fact that weakest liberal precondition operator associated with a statement R is universally conjunctive. From (2) we obtain the *cancellation* property:

$$(R \circ R \diagdown B)^{<} \subseteq B \ . \tag{3}$$

Often this property is used in a slightly different form, namely:

$$R \circ R \diagdown B \subseteq B \circ R \ . \tag{4}$$

Both (3) and (4) express that program R produces a result from set B when started in a state satisfying $R \diagdown B$. If R is a function then $R \diagdown A$ can be expressed without recourse to the left-domain operator. Specifically, we have for function f:

$$f \diagdown A = f^{\cup} \circ A \circ f \ . \tag{5}$$

A full discussion, including all the properties used here, can be found in [6].

2.4 Well-Foundedness Defined

Expressed in terms of points, a relation R is said to be *well-founded* if there are no infinite chains $x_0, x_1, \ldots$ such that $x_{i+1}[\![R]\!]x_i$ for all i, $i \geq 0$. A relation R is thus *not* well-founded if there is a set A such that

$$A \neq \phi \land \forall\langle x: x \in A: \exists\langle y: y \in A: y[\![R]\!]x\rangle\rangle \ .$$

Noting that $\exists\langle y\colon y{\in}A\colon y[\![R]\!]x\rangle \equiv x\in(A{\circ}R)\!>$ this definition converts directly into the following point-free form.

Definition 6 (Well-founded)   Relation R is said to be *well-founded* if and only if it satisfies

$$\forall\langle A\colon A{\subseteq}I\colon A{\subseteq}{\perp\!\!\!\perp} \Leftarrow A{\subseteq}(A{\circ}R)\!>\rangle \ .$$

□

The connection between well-foundedness and fixed points is the following.

Theorem 7   Relation R is well-founded equivales

$$\nu\langle A\colon A{\subseteq}I\colon (A{\circ}R)\!>\rangle = {\perp\!\!\!\perp} \ .$$

Proof   For arbitrary monotonic function f we have:

$$\nu f = {\perp\!\!\!\perp}$$

$\Leftarrow \qquad \{ \qquad$ reflexivity of $\subseteq$, ${\perp\!\!\!\perp}$ is the least element $\qquad \}$

$$\forall\langle X\colon\colon X{\subseteq}{\perp\!\!\!\perp} \Leftarrow X{\subseteq}\nu f\rangle$$

$\Leftarrow \qquad \{ \qquad$ fixed point induction $\qquad \}$

$$\forall\langle X\colon\colon X{\subseteq}{\perp\!\!\!\perp} \Leftarrow X{\subseteq}f.X\rangle \ .$$

The corollary follows by instantiating f to $\langle A\colon A{\subseteq}I\colon (A{\circ}R)\!>\rangle$.

□

Characteristic of definition 6 is that it is a rule for establishing when a set represented by a coreflexive A , $A{\subseteq}I$, is empty. In the following theorem we replace sets by arbitrary relations. This has the advantage that we can then immediately exploit the unique extension property of a regular algebra.

Theorem 8   For arbitrary relation $R{\in}I{\leftarrow}I$,

$$(\nu\langle X\colon\colon X{\circ}R\rangle)\!> = \nu\langle A\colon A{\subseteq}I\colon (A{\circ}R)\!>\rangle \ .$$

Hence R is well-founded if and only if it satisfies

$$\nu\langle X\colon\colon X{\circ}R\rangle = {\perp\!\!\!\perp} \ .$$

(Here the dummy X ranges over all relations of type $I{\leftarrow}I$.)

Proof   We shall only sketch the proof since we have not discussed the algebraic properties of the right domain operator in sufficient detail to give a completely formal proof. (For such a proof see [9].)

At first sight it would seem that a simple application of the fusion theorem would suffice. This is not the case, however, because the right domain operator is a lower adjoint in a Galois connection, not an upper adjoint as is required to apply fusion.

The key to the proof is to observe that $\nu\langle X::X{\circ}R\rangle$ is a so-called *right condition*. That is,

$$\nu\langle X::X{\circ}R\rangle \;=\; \top{\circ}\nu\langle X::X{\circ}R\rangle \ .$$

(This is easily proved by a mutual inclusion argument.) This suggests the use of the fusion theorem to prove that

$$\iota\,.\,\nu\langle p\colon p{=}\top{\circ}p\colon p{\circ}R\rangle = \nu\langle X::X{\circ}R\rangle$$

where ι denotes the function that embeds the set of right conditions of type $I{\leftarrow}I$ into the set of relations of type $I{\leftarrow}I$. (Embedding functions between complete lattices are both upper and lower adjoints so there is no difficulty in applying the fusion theorem.) The proof is now completed by using the fact that the two functions $\langle p\colon p{=}\top{\circ}p\colon p{>}\rangle$ and $\langle A\colon A{\subseteq}I\colon \top{\circ}A\rangle$ are inverse lattice isomorphisms between the lattice of right conditions and the lattice of coreflexives of type $I{\leftarrow}I$. (This is an application of the unity-of-opposites theorem.) Thus, using the fusion theorem once again,

$$\nu\langle A::(A{\circ}R){>}\rangle = (\nu\langle p::p{\circ}R\rangle){>}$$

and

$$\top{\circ}\nu\langle A::(A{\circ}R){>}\rangle = \nu\langle p::p{\circ}R\rangle \ .$$

From this it follows that

$$(\nu\langle X::X{\circ}R\rangle){>} \;=\; \nu\langle A\colon A{\subseteq}I\colon(A{\circ}R){>}\rangle \ .$$

Now,

$$R \text{ is well-founded}$$

$$\equiv \qquad \{\qquad \text{definition}\quad \}$$

$$\nu\langle A\colon A{\subseteq}I\colon(A{\circ}R){>}\rangle = \bot\!\bot$$

$$\equiv \qquad \{\qquad \text{above}\quad \}$$

$$(\nu\langle X::X{\circ}R\rangle){>} = \bot\!\bot$$

$$\equiv \qquad \{\qquad \text{domains}\quad \}$$

$$\nu\langle X::X{\circ}R\rangle = \bot\!\bot \ .$$

$\square$

Corollary 9   Relation R is well-founded equivales

$$\forall\langle S,T::\ T = S{\cup}T{\circ}R \equiv T = S{\circ}R^*\rangle$$

Proof A relation algebra is a regular algebra. So the unique extension property holds with the product operator instantiated to relational composition and the addition operator instantiated to set union.

$\square$

Having expressed well-foundedness in terms of fixed points it is now possible to apply fixed-point calculus to deduce some of its properties. The following is elementary (even without the use of fixed points!) but needs to be stated because of its frequent use.

Lemma 10   If relation R is well-founded and $S \subseteq R$ then S is well-founded. □

Fixed point calculus gives an easy proof of the following more interesting theorem.

Theorem 11   For all R, that R is well-founded equivales that R^+ is well-founded.

Proof   We prove the stronger theorem that

$$\nu\langle X :: X \circ R\rangle = \nu\langle X :: X \circ R^+\rangle \ .$$

The inclusion $\nu\langle X :: X \circ R\rangle \subseteq \nu\langle X :: X \circ R^+\rangle$ is immediate from monotonicity of ν and the fact that $R \subseteq R^+$. For the other inclusion, we calculate:

$$\nu\langle X :: X \circ R^+\rangle \subseteq \nu\langle X :: X \circ R\rangle$$

$$\Leftarrow \qquad \{ \qquad \text{fixed point induction} \qquad \}$$

$$\nu\langle X :: X \circ R^+\rangle \subseteq \nu\langle X :: X \circ R^+\rangle \circ R$$

$$\equiv \qquad \{ \qquad R^+ = R \circ R^* \qquad \}$$

$$\nu\langle X :: X \circ R^+\rangle \subseteq \nu\langle X :: X \circ R \circ R^*\rangle \circ R$$

$$\equiv \qquad \{ \qquad \text{rolling rule} \qquad \}$$

$$\nu\langle X :: X \circ R^+\rangle \subseteq \nu\langle X :: X \circ R^* \circ R\rangle$$

$$\equiv \qquad \{ \qquad R^+ = R^* \circ R \qquad \}$$

$$\text{true} \ .$$

□

This concludes this section. With dummies A and p ranging over coreflexives and right conditions, respectively, and X, S and T over relations, we have established the equivalence of the properties:

- R is well-founded.
- $\nu\langle A :: (A \circ R)>\rangle = \bot\!\!\!\bot$.
- $\nu\langle p :: p \circ R\rangle = \bot\!\!\!\bot$.
- $\nu\langle X :: X \circ R\rangle = \bot\!\!\!\bot$.
- R^+ is well-founded.
- $\forall\langle S, T :: T = S \cup T \circ R \equiv T = S \circ R^*\rangle$.

Exercise 12   We saw above that $\nu\langle X :: X \circ R\rangle$ is a right condition. *What is the interpretation of this right condition as a set?*
□

Exercise 13   The standard technique for proving termination of a loop statement or a recursive definition in a program is to use a *bound function*. That is,
one defines a function from the state space to a set on which a well-founded
relation is defined. Most commonly the set is the set of natural numbers, and
one proves that the body of the loop statement or recursive definition strictly
reduces the value of the bound function.

Suppose the body of the loop statement is given by relation S, the bound
function is f and the well-founded relation is R. Then the technique amounts
to proving that if $x[\![S]\!]y$ then $f.x\,[\![R]\!]\,f.y$. That is, $S \subseteq f\cup \circ R \circ f$. In view of
lemma 10, the validity of the use of bound functions is justified by the following
theorem: If R is a relation and f a functional relation such that R is well-
founded, then relation $f\cup \circ R \circ f$ is well-founded as well.

Prove this theorem.

Hint: as in the proof of theorem 11 one can make a more general statement
relating $\nu\langle X :: X \circ R\rangle$ and $\nu\langle X :: X \circ f\cup \circ R \circ f\rangle$.

□

Exercise 14   *Show that if R is well-founded then $R^+ \cap I \subseteq \bot\!\!\bot$. (So no non-
empty subset of a well-founded relation is reflexive.)*

*Under what conditions is the well-foundedness of R equivalent to $R^+ \cap I \subseteq
\bot\!\!\bot$? Provide examples where possible.*

□

2.5   Totality of While Statements

We are now in a position to complete our discussion of the construction of **while**
statements using loop invariants.

Recall that *Body* is the body of the loop, and *Term* terminates the computation. The well-foundedness of *Body* guarantees that the execution of the
while statement will always terminate. It also guarantees that the implementation is total, provided that *Term* and *Body* have complementary right domains,
and the initialisation *Init* is total. Specifically, we have:

$$(Term \circ Body^* \circ Init)> = I$$

$\equiv$ {   domain calculus   }

$$((Term \circ Body^*)> \circ Init)> = I$$

$\Leftarrow$ {   by assumption, $Init$ is total, i.e. $Init> = I$ }

$$(Term \circ Body^*)> = I$$

$\equiv$ { $(Term \circ Body^*)>$ is the unique solution of the equation

$A :: A = Term> \cup (A \circ Body)>$ }

$$I = Term> \cup (I \circ Body)>$$

$\equiv$ {   by assumption,

Term and Body have complementary right domains.

In particular, $I = Term_> \cup Body_>$ }

true .

The penultimate step needs further justification. The claim is that the equation

$$A:: \ A = Term_> \cup (A \circ Body)_>$$

has a unique solution provided that Body is well-founded. This is easily derived from (9). Indeed, for all coreflexives A,

$\quad A = Term_> \cup (A \circ Body)_>$

$\equiv$ {   domain calculus.

Specifically, $(\top \circ A)_> = A$ and $\top \circ R = \top \circ R_>$ }

$\quad \top \circ A = \top \circ Term \ \cup \ \top \circ A \circ Body$

$\equiv$ {   Body is well-founded, (9)   }

$\quad \top \circ A = \top \circ Term \circ Body^*$

$\equiv$ {   domain calculus (as above)   }

$\quad A = (Term \circ Body^*)_>$.

That is, $(Term \circ Body^*)_>$ is the unique solution of the above equation in A.

2.6   Induction Principles

Dual to the notion of well-foundedness is the notion of admitting induction. This section formulates the latter notion in terms of fixed points and then shows that well-foundedness and admitting induction are equivalent.

A relation R is said to *admit induction* if the following schema can be used to establish that property P holds everywhere: prove, for all y, that the induction hypothesis $\forall\langle x: x[\![R]\!]y: P.x\rangle$ implies $P.y$. That is, expressed in terms of points, R *admits induction* iff

$$\forall\langle y:: P.y\rangle \Leftarrow \forall\langle y:: \forall\langle x: x[\![R]\!]y: P.x\rangle \Rightarrow P.y\rangle \ .$$

The subterm

$$\forall\langle x: x[\![R]\!]y: P.x\rangle$$

in this formula is called the *induction hypothesis* while the proof of the subterm

$$\forall\langle y:: \forall\langle x: x[\![R]\!]y: P.x\rangle \Rightarrow P.y\rangle$$

the *induction step*. For instance, replacing R by the less-than relation ($<$) on natural numbers and the dummies x and y by m and n, the less-than relation admits induction iff

$$\forall\langle n:: P.n\rangle \Leftarrow \forall\langle n:: \forall\langle m: m < n: P.m\rangle \Rightarrow P.n\rangle \ .$$

This is indeed the case since the above is the statement of the principle of strong mathematical induction. The induction hypothesis is $\forall\langle m: m < n: P.m\rangle$; the induction step is the proof that assuming the truth of the induction hypothesis one can prove $P.n$. That the less-than relation admits induction means that from the proof of the induction step one can infer that $P.n$ holds for all n .

Less directly but nevertheless straightforwardly, replacing R by the predecessor relation on natural numbers, i.e. $x[\![R]\!]y \equiv y = x+1$, and simplifying using the fact that no number is a predecessor of 0 , one obtains the principle of simple mathematical induction: with n ranging over the natural numbers,

$$\forall\langle n:: P.n\rangle \Leftarrow P.0 \wedge \forall\langle n:: P.n \Rightarrow P.(n+1)\rangle \ .$$

Thus the predecessor relation on natural numbers admits induction. Note that in this case the proof of $P.0$ is called the *basis* of the proof by induction and the proof of $P.n \Rightarrow P.(n+1)$, for all n , the induction step.

The pointwise definition of "admits induction" given above is in terms of predicates. Because we want to arrive at a definition in terms of relations we first reformulate it in terms of sets. So we define: relation R *admits induction* if and only if:

$$\forall\langle y:: y \in A\rangle \Leftarrow \forall\langle y:: \forall\langle x: x[\![R]\!]y: x \in A\rangle \Rightarrow y \in A\rangle \ . \tag{15}$$

To arrive at a definition without dummies we first notice that $\forall\langle y:: y \in A\rangle$, the (understood) domain of y being I , can be rewritten as $I \subseteq A$. Furthermore, we see that the expression in the domain of the antecedent, $\forall\langle x: x[\![R]\!]y: x \in A\rangle$, is just $y \in R \backslash A$. So (15) can be drastically simplified to

$$I \subseteq A \Leftarrow R \backslash A \subseteq A \ , \tag{16}$$

for all coreflexives A of type $I \leftarrow I$.

According to the terminology introduced above, $R \backslash A$ is the induction hypothesis, whilst a proof of $R \backslash A \subseteq A$ is the induction step.

This then is the definition of "admits induction".

Definition 17   The relation R is said to *admit induction* if and only if it satisfies

$$\forall\langle A: A \subseteq I: I \subseteq A \Leftarrow R \backslash A \subseteq A\rangle \ .$$

Equivalently, R is said to admit induction if and only if

$$\mu\langle A: A \subseteq I: R \backslash A\rangle = \top \ .$$

□

Just as for well-foundedness, we propose a definition in which the type difference between the variables is removed.

Theorem 18   That relation R admits induction equivales $\mu\langle X:: R \backslash X\rangle = \top$.
□

We omit the proof as it is essentially dual to the proof of theorem 8.

Exercise 19   Definition 17 draws attention to the coreflexive $\mu(R\backslash)$: if relation R admits induction then the set corresponding to $\mu(R\backslash)$ is the universe over which relation R is defined. By restricting the domain of any relation R it is always possible to obtain a relation that admits induction. Specifically, for any relation R, the relation $R \circ \mu(R\backslash)$ admits induction. *Prove this theorem.*

□

2.7   Admits-Induction Implies Well-Founded

Now that we have seen several equivalent definitions of well-founded it is time to explore its relationship to admitting induction. The following lemma is the key insight.

Lemma 20 $\nu\langle T :: T \circ R\rangle \circ \mu\langle T :: R\backslash T\rangle = \bot\!\!\!\bot$.

Proof   The form of the theorem suggests that we try to apply μ-fusion. Of course we then have to find a suitable function f such that $\mu f = \bot\!\!\!\bot$. The identity function is one possibility and, as it turns out, is a good choice. However, since we want to demonstrate how good use of the calculational technique can avoid the need to make guesses of this nature, we construct f. We have, for all X,

$$X \circ \mu\langle T :: R\backslash T\rangle = \bot\!\!\!\bot$$

$\equiv$ $\{$ introduce f such that $\bot\!\!\!\bot = \mu f$ $\}$

$$X \circ \mu\langle T :: R\backslash T\rangle \subseteq \mu f$$

$\Leftarrow$ $\{$ basic fusion theorem $\}$

$$\forall\langle T :: X \circ R\backslash T \subseteq X \circ f.T\rangle$$

$\equiv$ $\{$ choose for f, $f.T = T$, noting that indeed $\bot\!\!\!\bot = \mu\langle T :: T\rangle$.

        factor cancellation: specifically, $R \circ R\backslash T \subseteq T$ $\}$

$$X \subseteq X \circ R$$

$\Leftarrow$ $\{$ definition of $\nu\langle T :: T \circ R\rangle$ $\}$

$$X = \nu\langle T :: T \circ R\rangle \quad .$$

□

Theorem 21   If R admits induction then R is well-founded.

Proof   If R admits induction then, by definition, $\mu\langle T :: R\backslash T\rangle = \top\!\!\!\top$. So, by lemma 20, $\nu\langle T :: T \circ R\rangle \circ \top\!\!\!\top = \bot\!\!\!\bot$. But then, since $I \subseteq \top\!\!\!\top$, $\nu\langle T :: T \circ R\rangle \subseteq \bot\!\!\!\bot$. By theorem 8 we have thus established that R is well-founded.
□

Exercise 22   One might suppose that an argument dual to the above leads to a proof that well-foundedness implies admits-induction. Unfortunately this is not the case: a true inverse, viz. complementation, is needed to do that. To prove the theorem using the techniques developed here it suffices to know that $R \backslash S = \neg(R^\cup \circ \neg S)$. (We haven't given enough information about relation algebra for you to verify this fact within the algebra. A pointwise verification can, of course, be given instead.) This fact can then be used to construct a function f such that $\nu\langle T :: T \circ R\rangle = f.\mu\langle T :: R \backslash T\rangle$. μ-fusion should be used bearing in mind the Galois connection $\neg R \subseteq S \equiv R \supseteq \neg S$ and being particularly careful about the reversal of the ordering relation. Having constructed f it is then straightforward to establish the equivalence between the two notions.

Prove that well-foundedness admits induction along the lines outlined above.

In general, the right condition $\nu\langle T :: T \circ R\rangle$ can be interpreted as the set of all points from which an infinite R-chain begins.

What is the interpretation of $\mu\langle T :: R \backslash T\rangle$?

□

3   Hylo Equations

In this section we introduce a methodology for the design of recursive programs. The methodology is based on constraining the recursion to a particular form of fixed point equation, called a "hylo" equation, rather than allowing arbitrary recursion (which has been called the **goto** of functional programming). The methodology generalises the methodology for designing **while** statements by introducing a datatype as an additional parameter in the design process. (In the case of **while** statements the datatype is just the set of natural numbers, in the case of a divide-and-conquer algorithm the datatype is a tree structure.)

A hylo equation comprises three elements, a "relator" F (which is a function from relations to relations), and two relations, one of which is an "F-algebra" and the other is an "F-coalgebra". The complete definition is given in section 3.1. Section 3.2 gives a number of examples of programs that take the form of a hylo equation. It is shown that programs defined by structural or primitive recursion are instances of hylo programs as well as several standard sorting algorithms and other programs based on a divide-and-conquer strategy. The goal in this section is, of course, to demonstrate that restricting the design methodology to hylo programs still allows sufficient room for creativity. Sections 3.3 and 3.4 introduce an important fixed-point theorem which formally relates hylo equations with the use of an intermediate or "virtual" data structure. Understanding this theorem is crucial to understanding the methodology of designing hylo programs. The final section, section 3.5 is about generalising notions of well-foundedness and inductivity to take into account the intermediate data structure implicit in any hylo program.

3.1   Relators and Hylos

A hylo equation comprises three elements, a so-called "relator" and two relations. The notion of relator plays the same role in relation algebra as the notion of "functor" in the category of functions and sets.

Functors are relevant to functional programming because they correspond to type constructors. The canonical example is List, which is an endofunctor on the category Fun. The object part of the functor List is the mapping from types (sets) to types. (For example List.$\mathbb{N}$, lists of natural numbers, is the result of applying List to $\mathbb{N}$.) The arrow part of the functor List is the function known as map to functional programmers. If $f \in I \leftarrow J$ then map.$f \in$ List.$I \leftarrow$ List.J is the function that applies function f to each element in a list of Js to create a list of Is of the same length. It is a general fact that parameterised datatypes (of which List is an example) define functors. The object part of the functor is the mapping from types to types and the arrow part is the "map" operation that applies a given function to every value stored in an instance of the datatype.

Rather than constrain ourselves to the design of functional programs, we consider programs involving relations as well. (The reasons are obvious: doing so means that we may allow non-determinism in our programs and do not have to make an arbitrary distinction between specifications —which typically involve an element of non-determinism— and implementations. Also, as the theory below shows, there is no good reason for not extending the discussion to include relations.) But the categorical notion of functor is too weak to describe type constructors in the context of a relational theory of datatypes. The notion of an "allegory" [11] extends the notion of a category in order to better capture the essential properties of relations, and the notion of a "relator" [3,6] extends the notion of a functor in order to better capture the relational properties of datatype constructors.

Formally an *allegory* is a category such that, for each pair of objects A and B, the class of arrows of type $A \leftarrow B$ forms an ordered set. In addition there is a converse operation on arrows and a meet (intersection) operation on pairs of arrows of the same type. These are the minimum requirements in order to be able to state the algebraic properties of the converse operation. For practical purposes more is needed. A *locally-complete, tabulated, unitary, division allegory* is an allegory such that, for each pair of objects A and B, the partial ordering on the set of arrows of type $A \leftarrow B$ is complete ("locally-complete"), the division operators introduced in section 2.3 are well-defined ("division allegory"), the allegory has a unit (which is a relational extension of the categorical notion of a unit — "unitary") and, finally, the allegory is "tabulated". We won't go into the details of what it means to be "tabulated" but, basically, it means that every arrow in the allegory can be represented by a pair of arrows in the underlying map category (i.e. by a pair of functions) and captures the fact that relations are subsets of the cartesian product of a pair of sets. (Tabularity is vital because it provides the link between categorical properties and their extensions to relations.)

A suitable extension to the notion of functor is the notion of a "relator". A *relator* is a functor whose source and target are both allegories —remember that an allegory is a category— that is monotonic with respect to the subset ordering on relations of the same type and commutes with converse. Thus, a *relator* F is a function to the objects of an allegory $\mathcal{C}$ from the objects of an allegory $\mathcal{D}$ together with a mapping to the arrows (relations) of $\mathcal{C}$ from the arrows of $\mathcal{D}$ satisfying the following properties:

$$F.R \in F.I \xleftarrow{\mathcal{C}} F.J \quad \text{whenever } R \in I \xleftarrow{\mathcal{D}} J. \tag{23}$$

$$F.R \circ F.S = F.(R \circ S) \quad \text{for each } R \text{ and } S \text{ of composable type,} \tag{24}$$

$$F.\mathsf{id}_A = \mathsf{id}_{F.A} \quad \text{for each object } A, \tag{25}$$

$$F.R \subseteq F.S \;\Leftarrow\; R \subseteq S \quad \text{for each } R \text{ and } S \text{ of the same type,} \tag{26}$$

$$(F.R)^\cup = F.(R^\cup) \quad \text{for each } R. \tag{27}$$

Two examples of relators are List and product. List is a unary relator, and product is a binary relator. If R is a relation of type $I \leftarrow J$ then $\mathsf{List}.R$ relates a list of Is to a list of Js whenever the two lists have the same length and corresponding elements are related by R. The relation $R \times S$ relates two pairs if the first components are related by R and the second components are related by S. List is an example of an inductively-defined datatype; in [2] it was observed that all inductively-defined datatypes are relators.

Now that we have the definition of a relator we may also give the definition of a hylo equation.

Definition 28 (Hylos)   Let R and S be relations and F a relator. An equation of the form

$$X::\quad X = R \circ F.X \circ S \tag{29}$$

is said to be a *hylo equation* or *hylo program*.
□

The identification of the importance of hylo equations is due to Meijer. (See e.g. [20].)

Note that, on typing grounds, if the unknown X in equation (29) is to have type $A \leftarrow B$ then R must have type $A \leftarrow F.A$. We say that R is an F-*algebra with carrier* A. Also S must have type $F.B \leftarrow B$ (equivalently $S^\cup$ must be an F-algebra with carrier B). It is convenient to use the term *coalgebra* for a relation of type $F.B \leftarrow B$ for some B. So a *coalgebra with carrier* B is the converse of an algebra with carrier B.

3.2   Hylo Programs

In this section we show how frequently recursive programs can be rewritten in the form of hylo equations. We consider a variety of classes of recursion: structural recursion, primitive recursion, divide-and-conquer, and so on. In order to show that each of these classes is subsumed by the class of hylo equations some additional notation is introduced as and when necessary. It is not necessay to understand the notation in detail in order to be able to appreciate the examples, and the notation will not be used elsewhere.

Structural recursion The heart of functional programming is the declaration and use of datatypes. This is facilitated by the special purpose syntax that is used. A definition like that of the natural numbers in Haskell:

```
datatype Nat = Zero | Succ Nat
```

introduces two datatype constructors `Zero` and `Succ` of types `Nat` and `Nat -> Nat`, respectively. It also facilitates the definition of functions on natural numbers by pattern matching as in the definition of the function `even`:

```
even Zero = True
even (Succ n) = not (even n)
```

Category theory enables one to gain a proper understanding of such definitions and to lift the level of discussion from particular instances of datatypes to the general case, thus improving the effectiveness of program construction.

Category theory encourages us to focus on function composition rather than function application and to combine the two equations above into one equation, namely:

$$\text{even} \circ (\text{zero} \triangledown \text{succ}) = (\text{true} \triangledown \text{not}) \circ (\mathbb{1} + \text{even}) \ . \tag{30}$$

In this form various important elements are more readily recognised. First, the two datatype constructors `Zero` and `Succ` have been combined into one *algebra* zero$\triangledown$succ. Similarly, `True` and `not` have been combined into the algebra true$\triangledown$not. The general mechanism being used here is the disjoint sum type constructor (+) and the case operator ($\triangledown$). Specifically, given types A and B, their disjoint sum $A+B$ comprises elements of A together with elements of B but tagged to say in which component of the disjoint sum they belong. Application of the function $f \triangledown g$ to a value of type $A+B$ involves inspecting the tag to see whether the value is in the left component of the sum or in the right. In the former case the function f is applied (after stripping off the tag); in the latter case the function g is applied. Thus for $f \triangledown g$ to be correctly typed, f and g must have the same target type. Then, if f has type $A \leftarrow B$ and g has type $A \leftarrow C$, the type of $f \triangledown g$ is $A \leftarrow B+C$.

Another important element of (30) is the *unit type* $\mathbb{1}$ and the term $\mathbb{1}+\text{even}$. The unit type is a type with exactly one element. The term $\mathbb{1}+\text{even}$ is read as the *functor* $\mathbb{1}+$ applied to the function even. As explained earlier, if f has type $A \leftarrow B$ the function $\mathbb{1}+f$ has type $\mathbb{1}+A \leftarrow \mathbb{1}+B$. It is the function that inspects the tag on a value of type $\mathbb{1}+B$ to see if it belongs to the left component, $\mathbb{1}$, or the right component, B. In the former case the value is left unaltered (complete with tag), and in the latter case the function f is applied to the untagged value, and then the tag is replaced. The functor $\mathbb{1}+$ is called the *pattern functor* of the datatype $\mathbb{N}$ (`Nat` in Haskell-speak) [5].

The final aspect of (30) that is crucial is that it uniquely defines the function even. (To be precise, the equation

$$X:: \quad X \circ (\text{zero} \triangledown \text{succ}) = (\text{true} \triangledown \text{not}) \circ (\mathbb{1} + X)$$

has a unique solution.) This is the concept of *initiality* in category theory. Specifically, zero▽succ is an *initial* ($\mathbb{1}+$)-*algebra* which means that for all ($\mathbb{1}+$)-algebras f the equation

$$X:: \quad X \circ (\text{zero} \triangledown \text{succ}) = f \circ (\mathbb{1} + X)$$

has exactly one solution.

In summary, category theory identifies three vital ingredients in the definition (30) of the function even, namely, the functor $\mathbb{1}+$, the initial ($\mathbb{1}+$)-algebra zero▽succ and the ($\mathbb{1}+$)-algebra true▽not.

The general form exemplified by (30) is

$$X \circ \text{in} = f \circ F.X \tag{31}$$

where F is a functor, in is an initial F-algebra and f is an F-algebra. This general form embodies the use of structural recursion in modern functional programming languages like Haskell. The left side embodies pattern matching since, typically, in embodies a case analysis as exemplified by zero▽succ. The right side exhibits recursion over the structure of the datatype, which is represented by the "pattern" functor F.

Here is the formal definition of an initial algebra. The definition is standard —an initial object in the category of F-algebras— but we give it nonetheless in order to introduce some terminology.

Definition 32   Suppose F is an endofunctor on some category $\mathcal{C}$. An arrow f in $\mathcal{C}$ is an F-*algebra* if $f \in A \leftarrow F.A$ for some A, the so-called *carrier* of the algebra. If f and g are both F-algebras with carriers A and B then arrow $\varphi \in A \leftarrow B$ is said to be an F-algebra *homomorphism* to f from g if $\varphi \circ f = g \circ F.\varphi$. The category $F\mathsf{Alg}$ has objects all F-algebras and arrows all F-algebra homomorphisms. Composition and identity arrows are inherited from the base category $\mathcal{C}$. The arrow in $\in I \leftarrow F.I$ is an *initial* F-algebra if for each $f \in A \leftarrow F.A$ there exists an arrow $(\![f]\!) \in A \leftarrow I$ such that for all $h \in A \leftarrow I$,

$$h = (\![f]\!) \quad \equiv \quad h \in f \xleftarrow{\;F\mathsf{Alg}\;} \text{in} \; . \tag{33}$$

So, $(\![f]\!)$ is the unique homomorphism to algebra f from algebra in. We call $(\![f]\!)$ the *catamorphism* of f.

□

The "banana bracket" notation for catamorphisms (as it is affectionately known) was introduced by Malcolm [17,18]. Malcolm was also the first to express the unicity property using an equivalence in this way. It is a mathematically trivial device but it helps enormously in reasoning about catamorphisms. Note that the functor F is also a parameter of $(\![f]\!)$ but the notation does not make this explicit. This is because the functor F is usually fixed in the context of the discussion. Where disambiguation is necessary, the notation $(\![F\,;f]\!)$ is sometimes used. The initial algebra is also a parameter that is not made explicit; this is less of a problem because initial F-algebras are isomorphic and thus catamorphisms are defined "up to isomorphism".

An important property of initial algebras, commonly referred to as Lambek's lemma [16], is that an initial algebra is both injective and surjective. Thus, for example, $\mathsf{zero}\triangledown\mathsf{succ}$ is an isomorphism between $\mathbb{N}$ and $\mathbb{1}+\mathbb{N}$. Lambek's lemma has the consequence that, if in is an initial F-algebra,

$$h \in f \xleftarrow{\;F\mathsf{Alg}\;} \mathsf{in} \;\equiv\; h = f \circ F.h \circ \mathsf{in}^\cup$$

where $\mathsf{in}^\cup$ is the inverse of in. Thus, the characterising property (33) of cata-morphisms is equivalent to, for all h and all F-algebras f,

$$h = (\![f]\!) \;\equiv\; h = f \circ F.h \circ \mathsf{in}^\cup \;. \tag{34}$$

That is, $(\![f]\!)$ is the unique fixed point of the function mapping h to $f \circ F.h \circ \mathsf{in}^\cup$. Equivalently, $(\![f]\!)$ is the unique solution of the hylo equation:

$$h:: \quad h = f \circ F.h \circ \mathsf{in}^\cup \;.$$

In the context of functions on lists the catamorphism $(\![f]\!)$ is known to functional programmers as a *fold* operation. Specifically, for lists of type I the relevant pattern functor F is the functor mapping X to $\mathbb{1}+(I{\times}X)$ (where $\times$ de-notes the cartesian product functor) and an F-algebra is a function of type $A \leftarrow \mathbb{1}+(I{\times}A)$ for some A. Thus an F-algebra takes the form $c \triangledown (\oplus)$ for some function c of type $A \leftarrow \mathbb{1}$ and some function $\oplus$ of type $A \leftarrow I{\times}A$. The characterising property of the catamorphisms is thus

$$h = (\![c \triangledown (\oplus)]\!) \;\equiv\; h = (c \triangledown (\oplus)) \circ (\mathbb{1} + (I{\times}h)) \circ (\mathsf{nil}^\cup \,\text{\tiny$\blacktriangledown$}\, \mathsf{cons}^\cup) \;.$$

Here $\mathsf{nil}^\cup \,\text{\tiny$\blacktriangledown$}\, \mathsf{cons}^\cup$ is the inverse of $\mathsf{nil}\triangledown\mathsf{cons}$. (In general, $R\text{\tiny$\blacktriangledown$}S$ is the converse conjugate of $R\triangledown S$. That is, $(R\text{\tiny$\blacktriangledown$}S)^\cup = R^\cup \triangledown S^\cup$.) It can be read as the pattern matching operator: look to see whether the argument is an empty list or a non-empty list. In the former case $\mathsf{nil}^\cup$ returns an element of the unit type, tagging it so that the result of the test is passed on to later stages; in the latter case $\mathsf{cons}^\cup$ splits the list into a head and a tail, the resulting pair also being tagged for later identification. Using the algebraic properties of case analysis, the characterising property is equivalent to

$$h = (\![c \triangledown (\oplus)]\!) \;\equiv\; h \circ \mathsf{nil} = c \,\wedge\, h \circ \mathsf{cons} = (\oplus) \circ (I{\times}h)$$

the right side of which is a point-free free formulation of the definition of a fold with seed the constant c and binary operator $(\oplus)$. As a concrete example, the function sum that sums the elements of a list is

$$(\![\mathsf{zero} \triangledown \mathsf{add}]\!)$$

where add is the addition function. In Haskell this function would be written

$$\text{fold } 0 \text{ add } .$$

Although catamorphisms (folds) are best known in the context of functional programming many relations are also catamorphisms. For example, the prefix relation on lists is uniquely characterised by the two equations

$$\mathsf{nil}[\![\mathsf{prefix}]\!]\mathsf{nil}$$

and $xs[\![\mathsf{prefix}]\!](y{:}ys) \;\equiv\; xs = \mathsf{nil} \vee \exists(zs{::}\;\; xs = y{:}zs \wedge zs[\![\mathsf{prefix}]\!]ys) \;\;.$

Expressed as one, point-free equation this is

$$\mathsf{prefix} \circ (\mathsf{nil}\triangledown\mathsf{cons}) \;=\; (\mathsf{nil}\triangledown((\mathsf{nil}\circ\top)\cup\mathsf{cons}))\circ(\mathbb{1}+(I\times\mathsf{prefix})) \qquad (35)$$

where I denotes the type of the list elements. Here we recognise a *relator* and two algebras: in this case the relator is $(\mathbb{1}+(I\times))$ and the two $(\mathbb{1}+(I\times))$-algebras are $\mathsf{nil}\triangledown\mathsf{cons}$ and $\mathsf{nil}\triangledown((\mathsf{nil}\circ\top)\cup\mathsf{cons})$. (Note that the second algebra is not a function.) Equivalently, prefix is the unique solution of a hylo equation:

$$\mathsf{prefix} \;=\; (\mathsf{nil}\triangledown((\mathsf{nil}\circ\top)\cup\mathsf{cons}))\circ(\mathbb{1}+(I\times\mathsf{prefix}))\circ(\mathsf{nil}^{\cup}\blacktriangledown\mathsf{cons}^{\cup}) \;\;. \qquad (36)$$

Primitive recursion Structural recursion is useful since many programs that arise in practice have this kind of recursion. However, just as structural induction is not enough to prove all facts that can be proved by induction, structural recursion is not enough to define all programs that can be defined by recursion. As an example of a program that is not structurally recursive, consider the factorial function, the function defined by the two equations

$$\mathsf{fact} \circ \mathsf{zero} = \mathsf{one} \quad\text{and}\quad \mathsf{fact} \circ \mathsf{succ} = \mathsf{times} \circ (\mathsf{fact}\triangle\mathsf{succ}) \;\;,$$

where one is the constant function returning the number 1 and times is the multiplication function. These equations can be combined into the single equation

$$\mathsf{fact} \;=\; (\mathsf{one}\triangledown(\mathsf{times}\circ(\mathsf{succ}\times\mathbb{N})))\circ(\mathbb{1}+(\mathbb{N}\triangle\mathsf{fact}))\circ(\mathsf{zero}^{\cup}\blacktriangledown\mathsf{succ}^{\cup}) \qquad . \qquad (37)$$

Reading from the right, the factorial function first examines its argument to determine whether it is zero or the successor of another number; in the former case a tagged element of the unit type is returned, and in the latter case the predecessor of the input value is returned, suitably tagged. Subsequently, if the input value is $n+1$, the function $\mathbb{N}\triangle\mathsf{fact}$ constructs a pair consisting of the number n and the result of the factorial function applied to n. (As forewarned, $\mathbb{N}$ is used here to denote the identity function on natural numbers.) The calculation of $(n+1)\times n!$ is the result of applying the function $\mathsf{times}\circ(\mathsf{succ}\times\mathbb{N})$ to the (untagged) pair. On the other hand, if the input value is zero then one is returned as result.

To give an example of a relation defined by primitive recursion we need look no further than the suffix relation on lists. It satisfies

$$\text{nil}[\![\text{suffix}]\!]\text{nil}$$

and $xs[\![\text{suffix}]\!](y{:}ys) \;\;\equiv\;\; xs=y{:}ys \;\vee\; xs[\![\text{suffix}]\!]ys$.

Expressed as a fixed point equation this is:

$$\text{suffix} = (\text{nil}\,\triangledown\,((\text{cons}\circ\text{exl})\cup(\text{exr}\circ\text{exr}))) \circ (\mathbb{1} + (I \times (\text{List}.I \,\vartriangle\, \text{suffix}))) \circ (\text{nil}^\cup\, \text{\textbullet}\, \text{cons}^\cup)$$

where I is the type of the list elements and exl and exr project a pair onto its left and right components, respectively. This is a definition by primitive recursion.

When we abstract from the particular functor and initial algebra in factorial program (37) a general recursion scheme is obtained.

$$X \;::\; X = R \circ F.(I \times X) \circ F.(I \vartriangle I) \circ \text{in}^\cup \quad . \tag{38}$$

In the case of the factorial function R is $\text{one}\,\triangledown\,(\text{times}\circ\text{succ}\times\text{id})$, F is $(\mathbb{1}+)$, I is the (identity on) natural numbers and in is $\text{zero}\triangledown\text{succ}$. (Note here that $(W \times X) \circ (I \vartriangle I) = W \vartriangle X$ for all W and X with source I. Therefore we have $F.(I \times X) \circ F.(I \vartriangle I) = F.(I \vartriangle X)$. We have applied this so-called $\times$-$\vartriangle$-fusion law in order to make the term $F.(I \vartriangle I)$ explicit.) A definition of this form is called *primitive recursive*.

This generic formulation of primitive recursion was introduced (for functions) by Meertens [19]. He called such an equation a *para equation* and a solution to the equation a *paramorphism*.

Divide and Conquer As the name suggests, "primitive" recursion is also unsuitable as the basis for a practical methodology of recursive program construction. Divide-and-conquer is a well-known technique that is not easily expressed using primitive recursion.

An example of a divide-and-conquer program is the sorting algorithm known as "quicksort" . Quicksort, here abbreviated to qs, is uniquely defined by the hylo equation:

$$\text{qs} = (\text{nil}\triangledown(\text{join}\circ(I\times\text{cons}))) \circ (\mathbb{1}+(\text{qs}\times(I\times\text{qs}))) \circ (\text{nil}^\cup\,\text{\textbullet}\,\text{dnf}) \tag{39}$$

To see that this is the quicksort program one has to interpret dnf as the well-known "Dutch national flag" relation: the relation that splits a non-empty list into a tuple $(xs,(x,ys))$ formed by a list, an element and a list such that all elements in the list xs are at most x and all elements in ys are greater than x. The results of the recursive calls are assembled to the output list by the operation $\text{join}\circ(I\times\text{cons})$, where join produces the concatenation of two lists.

A typical divide and conquer program is of the form

$$X = (R\triangledown\text{conquer}) \circ (I+(X\times X)) \circ (I+\text{divide}) \circ (A\text{\textbullet}B) \quad . \tag{40}$$

Interpreting this program should not be difficult. A test is made to determine whether the input is a base case (if the input satisfies A), the output then being computed by R. If the input is not a base case (if the input satisfies B)

the input is split into two smaller "subproblems" by divide. Then the smaller problems are solved recursively and finally the two solutions of the subproblems are assembled into an output by conquer.

Of course there are more divide and conquer schemes. For example, the original problem can be split into more than two subproblems. It is also possible that the divide step produces, besides a number of subproblems, a value that is not "passed into the recursion"; then the middle relation of (40) has a form like $I \times (X \times X)$. Quicksort is an example of such a divide and conquer algorithm.

Repetition is an elementary and familiar example of divide and conquer in which the original problem is reduced to a single subproblem. A repetition is a solution of the equation in x:

$$x \quad = \quad \text{if } \neg b \rightarrow \text{skip } [\!] \; b \rightarrow s;x \text{ fi} \quad . \tag{41}$$

Using the fact that skip (do nothing) corresponds to the identity function, I, on the state space and writing B for the coreflexive corresponding to predicate b and S for the relation corresponding to the statement s, we may express (41) using disjoint sum as:

$$X \quad = \quad (I \triangledown I) \circ (I+X) \circ (\sim B \blacktriangledown (S \circ B)) \quad . \tag{42}$$

Here we see how **while** statements are expressed in terms of hylo equations, the relator being $(I+)$.

Parameterised recursion Often recursive programs conform to one of the schemes discussed above but this is obscured by the presence of an additional parameter. Elementary examples are the definitions of addition, multiplication and exponentiation on natural numbers, which are essentially, but not quite, definitions by structural recursion:

$$0+n = n \quad \text{and} \quad (m+1)+n = (m+n)+1 \; ,$$
$$0 \times n = 0 \quad \text{and} \quad (m+1) \times n = m \times n + n \; ,$$
$$n^0 = 1 \quad \text{and} \quad n^{m+1} = n^m \times n \; .$$

All these definitions have the form

$$X.(0, n) = f.n \quad \text{and} \quad X.(m+1, n) = g.(m, h.n)$$

where X is the function being defined and f, g and h are known functions. (We leave the reader to supply the instantiations for f, g and h.) In point-free form, we have yet again a hylo equation:

$$X \quad = \quad k \circ ((\mathbb{1} + X) \times \mathbb{N}) \circ (\text{pass} \vartriangle \text{exr}) \circ ((\text{zero}^{\cup} \blacktriangledown \text{succ}^{\cup}) \times \mathbb{N})$$
$$\text{where} \; k \quad = \quad ((f \circ \text{exr}) \triangledown (g \circ (\text{id} \times h))) \circ \text{distr} \quad .$$

Here distr is a function of type $(H \times K)+(J \times K) \leftarrow (H+J) \times K$ that is polymorphic in H, J and K, and pass is a function of type $\mathbb{1}+(I \times K) \leftarrow (\mathbb{1}+I) \times K$ that is polymorphic in I and K.

Despite the seeming complexity of the underlying algebra and coalgebra, the basic structure is thus a hylo equation.

Another example, with the same structure but defined on a datatype other than the natural numbers, is the program that appends two lists. The standard definition comprises the two equations

$$\mathsf{nil} + ys = ys \quad \text{and} \quad (x : xs) + ys = x : (xs + ys) \ .$$

As a single equation (where we write join instead of $+$):

$$\mathsf{join} = \mathsf{post} \circ ((\mathbb{1} + (I \times \mathsf{join})) \times \mathsf{List}.I) \circ (\mathsf{pass} \vartriangle \mathsf{exr}) \circ ((\mathsf{nil}^\cup \blacktriangledown \mathsf{cons}^\cup) \times \mathsf{List}.I) \ .$$

where $\mathsf{post} = (\mathsf{exr} \triangledown \mathsf{cons}) \circ \mathsf{distr}$. Here distr is as before whereas in this case pass is a function of type $\mathbb{1} + (I \times (J \times K)) \leftarrow (\mathbb{1} + (I \times J)) \times K$ that is polymorphic in I, J and K. Once again we recognise a hylo equation.

3.3   Intermediate Data Structures

At the beginning of section 3.2 we discussed the use of recursion on the structure of a datatype; if R is an F-algebra with carrier A then the catamorphism $(\!|R|\!)$ can be seen as a program that *destructs* an element of an initial F-algebra in order to compute a value of type A. The converse $(\!|R|\!)^\cup$ is thus a program that *constructs* an element of the initial algebra from a value of type A.

Now suppose R and $S^\cup$ are both F-algebras with carriers A and B, respectively. Then the composition $(\!|R|\!) \circ (\!|S^\cup|\!)^\cup$ has type $A \leftarrow B$. It computes a value of type A from a value of type B by first building up an intermediate value which is an element of an initial F-algebra and then breaking the element down. The remarkable theorem is that

$$(\!|R|\!) \circ (\!|S^\cup|\!)^\cup \text{ is the least solution of the hylo equation } (29).$$

This theorem (which we formulate precisely below) gives much insight into the design of hylo programs. It says that executing a hylo program is equivalent to constructing an intermediate data structure, the form of which is specified by the relator F, and then breaking this structure down. The two phases are called the *anamorphism* phase and the *catamorphism* phase. Executing a hylo equation for a specific input value by unfolding the recursion hides this process; it is as if the intermediate data structure is broken down as it is being built up. (A good comparison is with a Unix pipe in which the values in the pipe are consumed as soon as they are produced.) Execution of $(\!|R|\!) \circ (\!|S^\cup|\!)^\cup$ does make the process explicit. For this reason, the relator F is said to specify a *virtual data structure* [21].

Two simple examples of virtual data structures are provided by do-statements and the factorial function. In the case of do-statements (see (42)) the virtual datatype is the carrier set of an initial $(I+)$-algebra, a type which is isomorphic to $I \times \mathbb{N}$ —thus an element of the virtual datatype can be seen as a pair consisting of an element of the state space and a natural number, the latter being a "virtual" count of the number of times the loop body is executed. In the case of the factorial function, definition (37) can be rewritten so as to make the relator F explicit:

$$\mathsf{fact} = (\mathsf{one} \triangledown (\mathsf{times} \circ (\mathsf{succ} \times \mathbb{N}))) \circ (\mathbb{1} + (\mathbb{N} \times \mathsf{fact})) \circ (\mathsf{zero}^{\cup} \mathbin{\blacktriangledown} ((\mathbb{N} \triangle \mathbb{N}) \circ \mathsf{succ}^{\cup})) \ .$$

The "virtual" datatype is thus the type of lists of natural numbers, the carrier set of an initial $\mathbb{1} + (\mathbb{N} \times)$-algebra. The list that is constructed for a given input n is the list of natural numbers from $n - 1$ down to 0 and the hylo theorem states that the factorial of n can be calculated by constructing this list (the anamorphism phase) and then multiplying the numbers together after adding 1 (the catamorphism phase).

Language recognition also illustrates the process well. Let us explain the process first with a concrete example following which we will sketch the generic process. Consider the following grammar:

$$S \quad ::= \quad aSb \mid c$$

where, for our purposes, a, b and c denote some arbitrary sets of words over some fixed alphabet. Associated with this grammar is a data structure: the class of parse trees for strings in the language generated by the grammar. This data structure, Stree, satisfies the equation:

$$\mathsf{Stree} = (a \times \mathsf{Stree} \times b) + c \ .$$

It is an initial F-algebra where F maps X to $(a \times X \times b) + c$. Now the process of *unparsing* a parse tree is very easy to describe since it is defined by induction on the structure of parse trees. Indeed the unparse function is the F-catamorphism $(\!(\mathsf{concat3} \circ (a \times \mathsf{id} \times b)) \triangledown c)\!)$ where $\mathsf{concat3}$ concatenates three strings together, a, b and c are the identity functions on the sets a, b and c, and id is the identity function on all words. Moreover, its left domain is equal to the language generated by the grammar. Since in general the left domain of function f is $f \circ f^{\cup}$ the language generated satisfies

$$S = (\!(\mathsf{concat3} \circ (a \times \mathsf{id} \times b)) \triangledown c)\!) \circ (\!(\mathsf{concat3} \circ (a \times \mathsf{id} \times b)) \triangledown c)\!)^{\cup} \ .$$

This equation defines a (nondeterministic) program to recognise strings in the language. The program is a partial identity on words. Words are recognised by first building a parse tree and then unparsing the tree. By the hylo theorem (or directly from the definition of S) we also have the hylo program

$$S = (\!(\mathsf{concat3} \circ (a \times \mathsf{id} \times b)) \triangledown c)\!) \circ ((a \times S \times b) + c) \circ (((a \times \mathsf{id} \times b) \circ \mathsf{concat3}^{\cup}) \mathbin{\blacktriangledown} c) \ .$$

This is a program that works by (nondeterministically) choosing to split the input word into three segments (using $\mathsf{concat3}^{\cup}$) or to check whether the word is in the language c. In the former case the first segment is checked for membership in a, the third segment is checked for membership in b and the program is called recursively to check the middle segment. Subsequently the three segments are recombined into one. In the latter case the word is left unchanged.

The derivation of a language recogniser in this way can be generalised to an arbitrary context-free grammar. (This is only possible because we base our methodology on relation algebra. The non-determinism present in a typical context-free grammar prohibits the generalisation we are about to make in the context of functional programming.) A context-free grammar defines a type of parse trees in a fairly obvious way. Also an unparse function can always be defined mapping parse trees to strings. This function is a catamorphism. The language generated by the grammar is the left domain of the unparse function, which is unparse ∘ unparse˘. This in turn is the composition of a catamorphism and the converse of a catamorphism, which can be expressed as a hylo program using the hylo theorem.

In practice the process is complicated by the fact that all practical context-free grammars have more than one nonterminal, and nonterminals are linked together via mutual recursion. But the theory we have developed covers this case too. Mutual recursion is modelled by endorelators on a product category.

3.4   The Hylo Theorem

We summarise the previous section with a formal statement of the hylo theorem. The theorem is rather deeper than just the statement that the least solution of a hylo equation is the composition of a catamorphism and an anamorphism. The proof of the theorem has been given in detail elsewhere [4][1].

Recall that we defined the notion of an initial algebra in the context of a category. (See (32).) To all intents and purposes this amounts to defining the notion of an initial algebra in the context of functions between sets. What we need however is the notion of an initial algebra in the context of binary relations on sets, that is, in the context of an allegory. Definition 43 is such a definition. The hylo theorem states that the categorical notion of an initial algebra coincides with the allegorical notion if the allegory is locally complete and tabular.

Definition 43   Assume that F is an endorelator. Then (I, in) is a *relational initial* F-algebra iff in $\in I \leftarrow F.I$ is an F-algebra and there is a mapping $(\![\_]\!)$ defined on all F-algebras such that

$$(\![R]\!) \in A \leftarrow I \quad \text{if } R \in A \leftarrow F.A \ , \tag{44}$$

$$(\![\text{in}]\!) = \text{id}_I \ , \text{ and} \tag{45}$$

$$(\![R]\!) \circ (\![S]\!)^\cup = \mu\langle X :: R \circ F.X \circ S^\cup\rangle \ . \tag{46}$$

---

[1] Actually [4] contains a proof of the dual theorem concerning final coalgebras and is more general than the theorem stated here. Unlike in a category, dualising between initiality and finality is not always straightforward in an allegory because of the lack of duality between intersection and union. However, dualising from a finality property to an initiality property is usually straightforward and it is the other direction that is difficult. That is one reason why [4] chose to present the theorem in terms of coalgebras rather than algebras. The extra generality offered by the theorem in [4] encompasses the relational properties of disjoint sum and cartesian product but at the expense of requiring a more sophisticated understanding of allegory theory which we wanted to avoid in the current presentation.

That is, $(\!(R)\!) \circ (\!(S)\!)^\cup$ is the smallest solution of the equation $X :: R \circ F.X \circ S \cup \subseteq X$.
□

In order to state the hylo theorem we let $Map(\mathcal{A})$ denote the sub-category of functions in the allegory $\mathcal{A}$. For clarity we distinguish between the endorelator F and the corresponding endofunctor defined on $Map(\mathcal{A})$.

Theorem 47 (Hylo Theorem)   Suppose F is an endorelator on a locally-complete, tabular allegory $\mathcal{A}$. Let F' denote the endofunctor obtained by restricting F to the objects and arrows of $Map(\mathcal{A})$. Then in is an initial F'-algebra if and only it is a relational initial F-algebra.

□

3.5   Reducing Problem Size

There are two elements in the design of the body of a **while** statements: it should maintain an invariant relation established by the initialisation procedure, and it should make progress to the termination condition. The latter is guaranteed if the loop body is a well-founded relation on the state space. There are also two elements in the design of hylo equations. The intermediate data structure plays the role of the invariant relation, whilst making progress is achieved by ensuring that each recursive call is "smaller" than the original argument. In this section we formalise this requirement. The notion we introduce, "F-reductivity" due to Henk Doornbos [10], generalises the notion of admitting induction essentially by making the intermediate data structure a parameter. As we shall indicate in section 3.6 this has important ramifications for developing a calculus of program termination.

Informally, for hylo program $X = S \circ F.X \circ R$ we require that all values stored in an output F-structure of R have to be smaller than the corresponding input to R. More formally, with $x[\![\mathsf{mem}]\!]y$ standing for "x is a member of F-structure y" (or, x is a value stored in F-structure y"), we demand that for all x and z

$$\forall \langle y :: x[\![\mathsf{mem}]\!]y \wedge y[\![R]\!]z \Rightarrow x \prec z \rangle \qquad ,$$

for some well-founded ordering $\prec$. If this is the case we say that R is F-reductive.

To make the definition of reductivity completely precise we actually want to avoid the concept of "values stored in an F-structure". (This is because its incorporation into the definition of F-reductivity limits the practicality of the resulting theory.) Fortunately, Hoogendijk and De Moor [13,15] have shown how to characterise membership of a so-called "container" type in such a way that it can be extended to other types where the intuitive notion of "membership" is not so readily apparent.

Hoogendijk and De Moor's characterisation of the membership relation of a relator is the following:

Definition 48 (Membership)   Relation $\mathsf{mem} \in I \leftarrow F.I$ is a membership relation of relator F if and only if it satisfies, for all coreflexives A, $A \subseteq I$:

$$F.A = \mathsf{mem} \backslash A \ .$$

□

When this definition is expressed pointwise it reads:

$$x \in F.A \equiv \forall \langle i: i[\![\mathsf{mem}]\!]x: i \in A \rangle \ .$$

Informally: an F-structure satisfies the property $F.A$ iff all the values stored in the structure satisfy property A. For example, for the list relator mem holds between a point and a list precisely when the point is in the list. For product the relation holds between x and (x,y) and also between y and (x,y).

   This definition of membership leads to a definition of F-reductivity independent of the notion of values stored in an F-structure. To see this we observe that, for coalgebra R with carrier I and for coreflexive A below I, we have:

$$(\mathsf{mem} \circ R) \backslash A$$

$$= \qquad \{ \qquad \text{factors } (2) \quad \}$$

$$R \backslash (\mathsf{mem} \backslash A)$$

$$= \qquad \{ \qquad \text{definition } 48 \quad \}$$

$$R \backslash F.A \ .$$

Now, that $S \in I \leftarrow I$ admits induction is the condition that the least prefix point of the function $\langle A:: S \backslash A \rangle$ is I, and our informal notion of the reductivity of $R \in F.I \leftarrow I$ is that $\mathsf{mem} \circ R$ should be well-founded. Since being well-founded is equivalent to admitting induction, the latter is equivalent to the requirement that the least prefix point of the function $\langle A:: R \backslash F.A \rangle$ is I, which does not involve any appeal to notions of membership of a "container" type. This gives us a precise, generic definition of the notion of F-reductivity:

Definition 49 (F-reductivity)   Relation $R \in F.I \leftarrow I$ is said to be F-*reductive* if and only if it enjoys the property:

$$\mu((R \backslash) \bullet F) = I \ . \tag{50}$$

□

   Obviously F-reductivity generalises the notion of admitting induction. (A relation R admits induction if and only if it is Id-reductive, where Id denotes the identity relator.) An immediate question is whether there is a similar generalisation of the notion of well-foundedness and a corresponding theorem that F-wellfoundedness is equivalent to F-reductivity. As it turns out, there is indeed a generic notion of well-foundedness but this is strictly weaker than F-reductivity.

The definition is given below, the facts just stated are left as exercises in the use of fixed point calculus.

Well-foundedness of relation R is equivalent to the equation $X :: X = X \circ R$ having a unique solution (which is obviously $\bot\!\!\bot$, the empty relation). This is easily generalised to the property that, for all relations S, the equation $X :: X = S \circ X \circ R$ has a unique solution. The generic notion of well-foundedness focusses on this unicity of the solution of equations.

Definition 51 (F-well-founded)   Relation $R \in F.I \leftarrow I$ is F-*well-founded* iff, for all relations $S \in J \leftarrow F.J$ and $X \in J \leftarrow I$,

$$X = S \circ F.X \circ R \quad \equiv \quad X = \mu\langle Y :: S \circ F.Y \circ R \rangle \quad .$$

$\square$

Exercise 52   *Verify the claim made immediately before definition 51. That is, show that R is well-founded equivales*

$$\forall\langle X, S :: X = S \circ X \circ R \quad \equiv \quad X = \mu\langle Y :: S \circ Y \circ R \rangle\rangle \quad .$$

In words, R is well-founded equivales R is Id-well-founded. (Hint: if R is well-founded then $\mu\langle Y :: S \circ Y \circ R \rangle = \bot\!\!\bot$.)

$\square$

Exercise 53   *Prove that an F-reductive relation is F-well-founded.*

$\square$

An example of a relation that is F-well-founded but not F-reductive can be constructed as follows. Define the relator F by $F.X = X \times X$. Suppose $R \in I \leftarrow I$ is a non-empty well-founded relation. Then the relation $R \vartriangle I$ of type $I \times I \leftarrow I$ (which relates a pair of values (x, y) each of type I to a single value z of type I iff x is related by R to z and $y = z$) is F-well-founded but not F-reductive. For a proof see [10].

3.6   A Calculus of F-Reductivity

The introduction of a data structure —the relator F— as a parameter to the notion of reductivity is a significant advance because it admits the possibility of developing a calculus of reductivity and thus of program termination based on the structure of the parameter. A beginning has been made to the development of such a calculus [7,10] sufficient to establish the termination of all the examples given in section 3.2 by a process akin to type checking.

Space only allows us to give a brief taste of the calculus here. The fundamental theorem is the following.

Theorem 54   The converse of an initial F-algebra is F-reductive.

Proof Let in $\in I \leftarrow F.I$ be an initial F-algebra and A an arbitrary coreflexive of type $I \leftarrow I$. We must show that

$$I \subseteq A \quad \Leftarrow \quad \text{in}^\cup \backslash\!\!\!\downarrow F.A \subseteq A \ .$$

We start with the antecedent and derive the consequent:

$\qquad \text{in}^\cup \backslash\!\!\!\downarrow F.A \subseteq A$

$\equiv \qquad\quad \{ \qquad$ for function f and coreflexive B, $f\backslash\!\!\!\downarrow B = f^\cup \circ B \circ f$,

$\qquad\qquad\qquad\quad \text{in}^\cup$ is a function and $F.A$ is a coreflexive $\quad \}$

$\qquad \text{in} \circ F.A \circ \text{in}^\cup \subseteq A$

$\Rightarrow \qquad\quad \{ \qquad$ Hylo theorem: (47) and (43) ,

$\qquad\qquad\qquad\quad$ in is an initial F-algebra $\quad \}$

$\qquad (\!|\text{in}|\!) \subseteq A$

$\equiv \qquad\quad \{$ identity rule: (45), in $\in I \leftarrow F.I$ is an initial F-algebra $\quad \}$

$\qquad I \subseteq A \ .$

$\square$

Theorem 54 has central importance because, if we examine all the programs in section 3.2 we see that the converse of a initial F-algebra is at the heart of the coalgebra in all the hylo equations. In the case, for example, of primitive recursion the generic equation has the form

$$X \ :: \ X = R \circ F.(I \times X) \circ F.(I \vartriangle I) \circ \text{in}^\cup$$

and the coalgebra is $F.(I \vartriangle I) \circ \text{in}^\cup$ where in $\in I \leftarrow F.I$ is an initial F-algebra. For the equation to define a terminating program (and consequently have a unique solution) we must show that the coalgebra is $(F\bullet(I\times))$-reductive. This is done by showing that $F.(I \vartriangle I)$ transforms any F-reductive relation into an $(F\bullet(I\times))$-reductive relation — which is a consequence of the fact that $F.(I \vartriangle I)$ is an instance of a natural transformation of the relator F to the relator $F\bullet(I\times)$.

Acknowledgements

The material in this paper was developed whilst the authors were members of the Mathematics of Program Construction group at Eindhoven University of Technology, particularly during the period 1990–1995. It would not have been possible to write the paper without the wonderfully stimulating and highly productive team effort that went into all we did at that time. The sections on well-foundedness and admitting induction are extracted from [9] written jointly with Jaap van der Woude, the sections on hylomorphisms and reductivity are extracted from Doornbos's thesis [10] (see also [8]), and the hylomorphism theorem in the form presented here is joint work with Paul Hoogendijk [4].

References

1. R. C. Backhouse. *Program Construction and Verification.* Prentice-Hall International, 1986. 206
2. R. C. Backhouse, P. de Bruin, P. Hoogendijk, G. Malcolm, T. S. Voermans, and J. van der Woude. Polynomial relators. In M. Nivat, C. S. Rattray, T. Rus, and G. Scollo, editors, *Proceedings of the 2nd Conference on Algebraic Methodology and Software Technology, AMAST'91,* pages 303–326. Springer-Verlag, Workshops in Computing, 1992. 220
3. R. C. Backhouse, P. de Bruin, G. Malcolm, T. S. Voermans, and J. van der Woude. Relational catamorphisms. In Möller B., editor, *Proceedings of the IFIP TC2/WG2.1 Working Conference on Constructing Programs from Specifications,* pages 287–318. Elsevier Science Publishers B. V., 1991. 219
4. Roland Backhouse and Paul Hoogendijk. Final dialgebras: From categories to allegories. *Theoretical Informatics and Applications,* 33(4/5):401–426, 1999. 229, 234
5. Roland Backhouse, Patrik Jansson, Johan Jeuring, and Lambert Meertens. Generic programming. An introduction. In S. D. Swierstra, editor, *3rd International Summer School on Advanced Functional Programming, Braga, Portugal, 12th-19th September, 1998,* volume LNCS 1608, pages 28–115. Springer Verlag, 1999. 221
6. R. C. Backhouse and J. van der Woude. Demonic operators and monotype factors. *Mathematical Structures in Computer Science,* 3(4):417–433, December 1993. 210, 219
7. Henk Doornbos and Roland Backhouse. Induction and recursion on datatypes. In B. Möller, editor, *Mathematics of Program Construction, 3rd International Conference,* volume 947 of *LNCS,* pages 242–256. Springer-Verlag, July 1995. 232
8. Henk Doornbos and Roland Backhouse. Reductivity. *Science of Computer Programming,* 26(1–3):217–236, 1996. 234
9. H. Doornbos, R. C. Backhouse, and J. van der Woude. A calculation approach to mathematical induction. *Theoretical Computer Science,* (179):103–135, 1997. 211, 234
10. H. Doornbos. *Reductivity arguments and program construction.* PhD thesis, Eindhoven University of Technology, Department of Mathematics and Computing Science, June 1996. 230, 232, 234
11. P. J. Freyd and A. Ščedrov. *Categories, Allegories.* North-Holland, 1990. 204, 219
12. D. Gries. *The Science of Programming.* Springer-Verlag, New York, 1981. 206
13. Paul Hoogendijk and Oege de Moor. Container types categorically. *Journal of Functional Programming,* 10(2):191–225, 2000. 230
14. C. A. R. Hoare and Jifeng He. The weakest prespecification. *Fundamenta Informaticae,* 9:51–84, 217–252, 1986. 210
15. Paul Hoogendijk. *A Generic Theory of Datatypes.* PhD thesis, Department of Mathematics and Computing Science, Eindhoven University of Technology, 1997. 230

16. J. Lambek. A fixpoint theorem for complete categories. *Mathematische Zeitschrift*, 103:151–161, 1968. 223
17. G. Malcolm. *Algebraic data types and program transformation*. PhD thesis, Groningen University, 1990. 222
18. G. Malcolm. Data structures and program transformation. *Science of Computer Programming*, 14(2–3):255–280, October 1990. 222
19. L. Meertens. Paramorphisms. *Formal Aspects of Computing*, 4(5):413–424, 1992. 225
20. Eric Meijer, Maarten Fokkinga, and Ross Paterson. Functional programming with bananas, lenses, envelopes and barbed wire. In *FPCA '91: Functional Programming Languages and Computer Architecture*, number 523 in LNCS, pages 124–144. Springer-Verlag, 1991. 203, 220
21. Doaitse Swierstra and Oege de Moor. Virtual data structures. In Helmut Partsch, Bernhard Möller, and Steve Schuman, editors, *Formal Program Development*, volume 755 of *LNCS*, pages 355–371. Springer-Verlag, 1993. 227

Chapter 7
Exercises in Coalgebraic Specification

Bart Jacobs

Department of Computer Science, University of Nijmegen

Abstract. An introduction to coalgebraic specification is presented via examples. A coalgebraic specification describes a collection of coalgebras satisfying certain assertions. It is thus an axiomatic description of a particular class of mathematical structures. Such specifications are especially suitable for state-based dynamical systems in general, and for classes in object-oriented programming languages in particular. This chapter will gradually introduce the notions of bisimilarity, invariance, component classes, temporal logic and refinement in a coalgebraic setting. Besides the running example of the coalgebraic specification of (possibly infinite) binary trees, a specification of Peterson's mutual exclusion algorithm is elaborated in detail.

1 Introduction

This chapter presents an introduction to the relatively young area of coalgebraic specification, developed in [36,12,14,13,15,16,8,9,3]. It is aimed at a mathematically oriented audience, and therefore it focuses on coalgebraic specifications as axiomatic descriptions of certain mathematical structures, and on how to formulate and prove properties about such structures. The emphasis lies on concrete examples, and not on the meta-theory of coalgebras. Currently, coalgebraic specifications are being used and developed in theoretical computer science, in particular to specify classes in object-oriented languages (such as Java [23]). Much of the motivation, terminology, and many of the examples stem from this area. We shall not emphasise this aspect, and no prior experience in computer science is assumed. It is possible that in the future, coalgebras will find comparable applications in mathematics, for instance in system and control theory. Further, the theory of coalgebras is best formulated and developed using categorical notions and techniques. In this introduction we shall not use any category theory, however, and describe coalgebras at an elementary level. This means that we cover neither homomorphisms of coalgebras, nor the related topic of terminal (also called final) coalgebras.

Coalgebras are simple mathematical structures that can be understood as duals of algebras. We refer to [21] for an introduction to the study of coalgebras. Here we shall simply use coalgebras, without concentrating too much on the difference with algebras, and we hope that readers will come to appreciate their rôle in specification and verification. They are typically used to describe state-based dynamical systems, where the state space (set of states) of the system

R. Backhouse et al. (Eds.): Algebraic and Coalgebraic Methods ..., LNCS 2297, pp. 237–281, 2002.

is considered as a black box, and where nothing is known about the way that the observable behaviour is realised. Coalgebraic specification is thus important for the study of such dynamical systems. In this field one naturally reasons in terms of invariance and bisimilarity. Indeed, these notions are fundamental in the theory of coalgebras[1]. Further, a recent development is the close connection between coalgebras and temporal logic, see [30,17]. The temporal operators $\Box$ for henceforth and $\Diamond$ for eventually can be defined easily in a coalgebraic setting, in terms of invariants. Their use is quite natural in a state-based setting, namely for reasoning about all/some future states in safety/progress formulas. In this chapter we illustrate the use of $\Box$ and $\Diamond$ in coalgebraic specification. We also give an impression of the application of the least and greatest fixed point operators from the μ-calculus [42] in this setting.

As mentioned, coalgebraic specifications give an axiomatic description of mathematical structures. As such they resemble axiomatic descriptions of groups or rings that are common in mathematics. But there are also some differences with standard mathematical approaches, stemming from their use in computer science.

1. Coalgebraic specifications are typically structured, using the object-oriented mechanisms of inheritance (with subclasses inheriting from superclasses) and aggregation (with ambient classes having component classes). This is needed because specifications in computer science tend to become very big, in order to capture all possible scenarios in which a system has to function. Such explicit structuring mechanisms do not exist in axiomatisations in mathematics. Lamport [26, Section 1] writes: "Although mathematicians have developed the science of writing formulas, they haven't turned that science into an engineering discipline. They have developed notations for mathematics in the small, but not for mathematics in the large.".

2. Coalgebraic specifications have a rather precise format. Actually, there is an experimental formal language CCSL, for Coalgebraic Class Specification Language. Specifications in CCSL are thus objects which can be manipulated by a computer. There is a LOOP compiler [9,38] which translates CCSL specifications into logical theories for a proof tool. The latter is a special program that helps in formal reasoning (*e.g.* via built-in tactics and decision procedures). It is like a calculator for reasoning. Such proof tools are useful for proving the correctness of elaborate system descriptions (*e.g.* as complex coalgebraic specifications), involving many different case distinctions. Humans easily make mistakes, by omitting a case or a precondition, but proof tools are very good at such bureaucratism. The specifications in this chapter are presented in a semi-formal style, resembling CCSL. All the results about the examples have been proved with the proof tool PVS [31], using the automatic translation of CCSL specifications into the logic of PVS with (a recent version of) the compiler from [9]. However, here we shall present the proofs of these results in the usual mathematical style.

---

[1] Invariants and bisimilations (or congruences) are also relevant for algebras, see for example [33,35,10], and the end of Section 6.

This introductory chapter is organised as follows. After some explanations about the notation that will be used, an introduction to formal specification is given in Section 3; it contains a slightly unusual specification of vector spaces, meant as preparation for coalgebraic specification. Section 4 introduces the running example of (possibly infinite) binary trees. It is followed by two sections on bisimulations and on invariants. Section 7 introduces temporal logic in a coalgebraic setting, and applies it to binary trees. Subsequently, also the ingredients of a coalgebraic μ-calculus are introduced, and used to describe (in)finiteness for binary trees. Section 9 then introduces the example of Peterson's mutual exclusion algorithm. It is specified in a structured manner, and its correctness is proved. The final section concentrates on refinement in a coalgebraic setting.

2 Mathematical Preliminaries

We will use some standard constructions on sets. For example, the Cartesian product $X \times Y = \{(x, y) \mid x \in X \text{ and } y \in Y\}$, with projection functions $\pi : X \times Y \to X$ and $\pi' : X \times Y \to Y$ given by $\pi(x, y) = x$ and $\pi'(x, y) = y$. We shall frequently make use of the fact that functions $Z \to X \times Y$ correspond to pairs of functions $Z \to X$, $Z \to Y$. We write 1 for an arbitrary singleton set, say $1 = \{*\}$, which can be considered as a degenerate product.

The dual of the product is the coproduct (also called sum or disjoint union): $X + Y = \{(x, 0) \mid x \in X\} \cup \{(y, 1) \mid y \in Y\}$, with coprojection functions $\kappa : X \to X + Y$ and $\kappa' : Y \to X + Y$, given by $\kappa(x) = (x, 0)$ and $\kappa'(y) = (y, 1)$. Sometimes we write $\kappa x = \kappa(x)$ and $\kappa' y = \kappa'(y)$ without brackets $(-)$, like for projections π, π'. Notice that these coprojections are injective functions, and are "disjoint", in the sense that $\kappa(x) \neq \kappa'(y)$, for all $x \in X, y \in Y$. We shall also often use that functions $X + Y \to Z$ correspond to pairs of functions $X \to Z$, $Y \to Z$. For this we use some special notation: given $f : X \to Z$ and $g : Y \to Z$, there is a corresponding function $X + Y \to Z$, which we shall write as:

$$a \longmapsto \textsf{CASES } a \textsf{ OF}$$
$$\kappa x \mapsto f(x)$$
$$\kappa' y \mapsto g(y)$$
$$\textsf{ENDCASES}$$

This function checks for an element $a \in X + Y$ whether it is of the form $\kappa(x) = (x, 0)$, or $\kappa'(y) = (y, 1)$. In the first case it applies the function f to x, and in the second case g to y. We shall apply such $\textsf{CASES}$ functions also when f, g are predicates, since these fit in for $Z = \{0, 1\}$. Thus, for example, the set

$$\{(x, y) \in \mathbb{N} \times (1 + \mathbb{N}) \mid x > 0 \Rightarrow \textsf{CASES } y \textsf{ OF}$$
$$\kappa u \mapsto x = 1$$
$$\kappa' v \mapsto x = y$$
$$\textsf{ENDCASES}\}$$

contains all pairs of the form $(0, \kappa*), (1, \kappa*), (0, \kappa'n), (m, \kappa'm)$, for $n, m \in \mathbb{N}$ with $m > 0$. In general, coproducts are not so frequently used as products, but they play an important rôle for coalgebras, because they occur in many examples.

The empty set will usually be written as 0. Then $X + 0 \cong X$. Note that $X \times 1 \cong X$. We recall that $X \times Y \cong Y \times X$, $X \times (Y \times Z) \cong (X \times Y) \times Z$, and also that $X + Y \cong Y + X$, $X + (Y + Z) \cong (X + Y) + Z$.

We shall further write Y^X for the set of (total) functions from X to Y. There is a one-to-one "Currying" correspondence between functions $Z \to Y^X$ and functions $Z \times X \to Y$. A function $x \mapsto \cdots$ will sometimes be written in lambda notation: $\lambda x. \cdots$.

Finally, $X^\star$ will be the set of finite sequences $\alpha = \langle x_1, \ldots, x_n \rangle$ of elements $x_i \in X$. We shall write $|-|$ for the length, so that $|\alpha| = n$. The empty sequence is $\langle \rangle$, and $x_0 \cdot \alpha$ is $\langle x_0, x_1, \ldots, x_n \rangle$. The set $X^\star$ forms the free monoid on X.

What we shall call a *polynomial functor* is a certain mapping[2] from sets to sets, built from primitive operations. The collection of polynomial functors that we consider in this chapter is the smallest collection satisfying:

1. the identity mapping $X \mapsto X$ is polynomial, and for each set A, the constant mapping $X \mapsto A$ is polynomial;
2. if T_1 and T_2 are polynomial functors, then so are the product $X \mapsto T_1(X) \times T_2(X)$ and coproduct $X \mapsto T_1(X) + T_2(X)$;
3. if T is a polynomial functor, then so is $X \mapsto T(X)^A$, for each set A.

A typical example of a polynomial functor is a mapping

$$X \longmapsto 1 + (A + X)^B + (X \times X)^C.$$

An *algebra* for a polynomial functor T consists of a set X together with a function $T(X) \to X$. A *coalgebra* for T is a set X with a function $X \to T(X)$ in the reverse direction. Polynomial functors describe the "interfaces" of algebras and coalgebras, capturing the types of the operations. This will be illustrated in many examples below. This chapter focuses mostly on coalgebras, assuming that algebras are relatively well-known.

Coalgebras are abstract dynamical systems. A typical example is given by a (deterministic) automaton. Ignoring initial states, such an automaton is usually described as consisting of an alphabet A and a set of states X, together with a transition function $\delta \colon X \times A \to X$ and a subset $F \subseteq X$ of final states. By massaging this structure a bit, using the above correspondences, we can equivalently describe such an automaton as a coalgebra: the subset $F \subseteq X$ can also be described as a "characteristic" function $X \to \{0, 1\}$. Similarly, the transition function $\delta \colon X \times A \to X$ corresponds to a function $X \to X^A$. Combining these two functions $X \to \{0, 1\}$ and $X \to X^A$ we get a coalgebra $X \to \{0, 1\} \times X^A$ capturing the original automaton.

For more introductory information on coalgebras, see [21], and on automata as coalgebras, see [41, 39].

---

[2] These mappings are described here as acting on sets only, but they also act on functions. This "functoriality" aspect will not be relevant in this chapter, and will therefore be ignored. See [21] or Chapter 3 for more information.

Exercises

1. Prove the following "case-lifting" lemma. For functions $f: X \to Z$, $g: Y \to Z$ and $h: Z \to W$, one has for all $a \in X + Y$,

$$h \left(\begin{array}{l} \text{CASES } a \text{ OF} \\ \quad \kappa x \mapsto f(x) \\ \quad \kappa' y \mapsto g(y) \\ \text{ENDCASES} \end{array} \right) = \left(\begin{array}{l} \text{CASES } a \text{ OF} \\ \quad \kappa x \mapsto h(f(x)) \\ \quad \kappa' y \mapsto h(g(y)) \\ \text{ENDCASES} \end{array} \right).$$

This equation is often useful in computing with coproducts.

2. Use the case notation to define the canonical distributivity map $d: (X \times Z) + (Y \times Z) \to (X + Y) \times Z$. Prove that it is an isomorphism, by explicitly constructing a map e in the opposite direction and using the previous exercise to prove that $d \circ e = \text{id}$ and $e \circ d = \text{id}$.

3   Specification of Groups and Vector Spaces

In this section it will be assumed that the reader is (reasonably) familiar with the notions of group, field and vector space. We shall present specifications (or axiomatic descriptions) of (two of) these notions in the same style in which we will specify coalgebras later in this chapter. The intention[3] is to make the mathematically oriented reader feel more comfortable with this style of specification. Therefore, semantical subtleties will be ignored at this stage, since the reader is already assumed to be familiar with the structures that are being specified (*i.e.* with their meaning). We will concentrate on vector spaces because they are fairly familiar and because they involve aspects—like extension and parametrisation—which we shall also see in coalgebraic specification.

We start with groups. Actually, for convenience, we start with Abelian (*i.e.* commutative) groups. Figure 1 presents a specification of Abelian groups, using *ad hoc* notation, which is hopefully self-explanatory. We have used the computer science convention of denoting the operations by explicit names, instead of by mathematical symbols, like 0, + and $(-)^{-1}$. Also, assertions have names (unit, assoc, inv, comm), so that it is easy to refer to them. The specification is presented in a certain (pseudo) format, so that it can (in principle) be processed by a machine. The text after the double slashes (//) serves as comment. Comments are valuable in specifications. The underlying set of the structure that we are specifying is written as X (throughout this chapter).

The use of the unit element zero as a function $1 \to X$ instead of as an element zero $\in X$ is a bit formal. It allows us to treat all operations as functions. Also, it allows us to combine the three operations into a single function:

$$1 + (X \times X) + X \longrightarrow X \tag{1}$$

---

[3] There is no claim whatsoever that this is how groups and vector spaces should be specified; the presentations in this section only serve as preparation.

BEGIN AbelianGroup
// 'AbelianGroup' is the name of the specification
OPERATIONS
    zero: $1 \longrightarrow X$ // recall, 1 is a singleton set $\{*\}$; so we have a constant
    add: $X \times X \longrightarrow X$
    inv: $X \longrightarrow X$
ASSERTIONS   // named requirements that are imposed
    unit: $\left[\forall x \in X.\, \mathsf{add}(x, \mathsf{zero}(*)) = x \wedge \mathsf{add}(\mathsf{zero}(*), x) = x \right]$
    assoc: $\left[\forall x, y, z \in X.\, \mathsf{add}(x, \mathsf{add}(y, z)) = \mathsf{add}(\mathsf{add}(x, y), z) \right]$
    inv: $\left[\forall x \in X.\, \mathsf{add}(x, \mathsf{inv}(x)) = \mathsf{zero}(*) \right]$
    comm: $\left[\forall x, y \in X.\, \mathsf{add}(x, y) = \mathsf{add}(y, x) \right]$
END AbelianGroup

Fig. 1. Specification of Abelian groups

using the bijective correspondences from Section 2. This single function combines the three functions zero, add, inv into an *algebra* of the polynomial functor $\mathcal{G}$ given by $\mathcal{G}(X) = 1 + (X \times X) + X$. Indeed the above specification may be called an "algebraic specification". It describes a collection of algebras of the form (1) satisfying the assertions as in Figure 1. These algebras are the models of the specification, and are of course precisely the Abelian groups. Algebraic specification has developed into a field of its own in computer science, see [2] for an up-to-date source of information. It is used for the description of various kinds of datastructures, like lists and stacks, with associated operations.

We move on to vector spaces, taking the specification of fields for granted[4]. We shall simply write $+, 0, \cdot, 1$ for their operations. Fields are used as parameters in the axiomatic description of vector spaces. Also, the underlying set of vectors of a vector space is an Abelian group. This structure determines the specification in Figure 2.

Notice that the fact that vector spaces are parametrised by fields K is expressed by the addition $[K : \mathrm{FIELD}]$ to the name. Further, we say that vector spaces extend Abelian groups. This means that all the operations and assertions of Abelian groups also exist for vector spaces. Such **EXTENDS** clauses are convenient for structuring specifications. More formally it means that for each field K, the underlying polynomial functor $\mathcal{V}_K$ of the VectorSpace specification contains the polynomial functor $\mathcal{G}$ of the AbelianGroup specification as a coproduct component:

$$\begin{aligned} \mathcal{V}_K(X) &= \mathcal{G}(X) + (K \times X) \\ &= 1 + (X \times X) + X + (K \times X). \end{aligned} \tag{2}$$

---

[4] Such a specification has to deal with partiality, since the division operation of fields is not defined on the zero element.

BEGIN VectorSpace[K: FIELD]
  EXTENDS AbelianGroup   // from Figure 1
  OPERATIONS
    scalar_mult: $K \times X \longrightarrow X$
  ASSERTIONS
    // scalar multiplication and the group structure
    scalar_group_add: $\left[\; \forall a \in K. \forall x, y \in X.\; \text{scalar\_mult}(a, \text{add}(x, y)) \right.$
    $= \text{add}(\,\text{scalar\_mult}(a, x),$
    $\left. \text{scalar\_mult}(a, y)) \;\right]$
    // scalar multiplication and the field structure
    scalar_field_add: $\left[\; \forall a, b \in K. \forall x \in X.\; \text{scalar\_mult}(a + b, x) \right.$
    $= \text{add}(\,\text{scalar\_mult}(a, x),$
    $\left. \text{scalar\_mult}(b, x)) \;\right]$
    scalar_field_mult: $\left[\; \forall a, b \in K. \forall x \in X.\; \text{scalar\_mult}(a \cdot b, x) \right.$
    $\left. = \text{scalar\_mult}(a, \text{scalar\_mult}(b, x)) \;\right]$
    scalar_field_unit: $\left[\; \forall x \in X.\, \text{scalar\_mult}(1, x) = x \;\right]$
END VectorSpace

Fig. 2. Specification of vector spaces

An algebra $\mathcal{V}_K(X) \to X$ of this functor thus combines four operations zero, add, inv and scalar_mult. A model of this specification (for a field K) is such an algebra satisfying the assertions from Figure 2. It is a vector space over K.

Given a specification as above, there are (at least) two things one can do.

1. Describe models of the specification. For example, for an arbitrary field K, one obtains an obvious model by choosing K itself for X, with its own Abelian group structure, and with scalar multiplication given by its multiplication. Similarly, K^n forms a model, for each $n \in \mathbb{N}$. Knowing that a specification has a (non-trivial) model is important, because it shows its consistency.

2. Develop the theory of the specification. For example, one can derive the following well-known consequences of the assertions in the VectorSpace specification:
$$\text{scalar\_mult}(0, x) = \text{zero}(*)$$
$$\text{scalar\_mult}(a, \text{zero}(*)) = \text{zero}(*)$$
$$\text{scalar\_mult}(a, \text{inv}(x)) = \text{scalar\_mult}(-a, x).$$

Theory development often involves further definitions, like basis or dimension for vector spaces.

A third activity is constructing refinements. These may be understood as "relative models", and will be further investigated in Section 10.

Exercises

1. Write down specifications—in the style of this section—for lattices and for Boolean algebras (see *e.g.* [5] or Chapter 2 for details about these notions).

4   A First Coalgebraic Specification: Binary Trees

In the previous section we have seen specifications whose operations could be described as algebras $T(X) \to X$. An obvious step is to consider specifications based on coalgebras $X \to T(X)$. This is what coalgebraic specification is all about. It allows us to describe an entirely new class of structures, having a state space with associated operations. In this coalgebraic context, we shall use 'method' instead of 'operation', in line with object-oriented terminology.

We start with an example. Let us consider certain trees with labels from a fixed set A. The trees we wish to consider are possibly infinite binary trees. This means that each node has a label, and has either no successor trees (also called children), or has two successor trees. The characteristic coalgebraic operations for such trees are $\mathsf{label}\colon X \to A$, giving the label at the top of the tree, and $\mathsf{children}\colon X \to 1 + (X \times X)$ giving the left and right children, if any. Note that these two functions can be combined into a single coalgebra of the form:

$$X \xrightarrow{\langle \mathsf{label}, \mathsf{children} \rangle} A \times (1 + (X \times X))$$

For a "tree" $x \in X$ the result $\mathsf{children}(x)$ is either of the form $\kappa*$ in the left $+$-component 1, telling that x has no children, or of the form $\kappa'(x_1, x_2)$ in the right component $X \times X$, with x_1 as first (or left) and x_2 as second (right) child. From here one can continue unfolding the tree x by inspecting $\mathsf{children}(x_1)$ and $\mathsf{children}(x_2)$ (and their labels). If all of these paths stop at some stage, x behaves like a finite tree, but if one of them continues indefinitely we get an infinite tree. Note that each such tree has at least one label.

For a fixed set A, we say, by analogy with vector space, that a *binary tree space* over A consists of a set U together with a coalgebra $U \to A \times (1 + (U \times U))$, which we shall typically write as a pair of functions $\mathsf{label}\colon U \to A$ and $\mathsf{children}\colon U \to 1 + (U \times U)$. An example of a binary tree space over $A = \{a, b, c\}$ is the set of states $U = \{0, 1, 2, 3, 4\}$ with functions:

$$
\begin{array}{lll}
\mathsf{label}(0) = a & \mathsf{children}(0) = \kappa'(3, 2) & \\
\mathsf{label}(1) = b & \mathsf{children}(1) = \kappa'(1, 2) & \\
\mathsf{label}(2) = a & \mathsf{children}(2) = \kappa* & (3) \\
\mathsf{label}(3) = c & \mathsf{children}(3) = \kappa'(2, 2) & \\
\mathsf{label}(4) = b & \mathsf{children}(4) = \kappa'(4, 2) & \\
\end{array}
$$

The unfoldings (or behaviours) of the states $0 \in U$ and $1 \in U$ then look as follows.

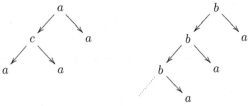

Such binary trees can occur as the (possibly infinite) behaviour of a process, where a process may be understood as a program that is supposed to be running forever, like an operating system on a computer. For terminating processes one gets finite behaviour.

In a next step we like to include a size method in the specification of these binary trees. An immediate problem is that the size of such trees need not yield a natural number. Therefore we choose the "extended natural numbers" $1 + \mathbb{N}$ as range of the size function, where $\kappa*$ denotes infinity. Addition of infinity to an extended natural number always yields infinity. These two methods **children** and **size** form the two main ingredients of our first coalgebraic specification of binary trees in Figure 3.

In this specification we use parametrisation by the type (or set) of labels, like in Figure 2. An important point is that the types of the methods in the specification determines a polynomial functor, which, in this case, is

$$\mathcal{BT}(X) = A \times (1 + (X \times X)) \times (1 + \mathbb{N}).$$

BEGIN BinaryTreeSpace[A: TYPE]
   METHODS   // alternative terminology for operations
     label: $X \longrightarrow A$
     children: $X \longrightarrow 1 + (X \times X)$
     size: $X \longrightarrow 1 + \mathbb{N}$
   ASSERTIONS
     size_def: $\Big[\forall x \in X.\, \text{size}(x) = $ CASES children(x) OF
                   $\kappa* \mapsto \kappa'1$
                   $\kappa'(v_1, v_2) \mapsto$ CASES size(v_1) OF
                            $\kappa* \mapsto \kappa*$
                            $\kappa'n \mapsto$ CASES size(v_2) OF
                                    $\kappa u \mapsto \kappa*$
                                    $\kappa'm \mapsto \kappa'(1 + n + m)$
                                  ENDCASES
                          ENDCASES
           ENDCASES $\Big]$
END BinaryTreeSpace

Fig. 3. Specification of binary trees, version 1

It is obtained by putting a Cartesian product × between the result types of the individual methods. A crucial observation is that the three methods label, children, size correspond to a coalgebra $X \rightarrow \mathcal{BT}(X)$ of the polynomial functor $\mathcal{BT}$. The specification may be understood as describing a collection of coalgebras of $\mathcal{BT}$ satisfying an assertion. Thus, coalgebraic specification is much like algebraic specification as described in the previous section.

The assertion 'size_def' for the size method is non-trivial; it says that empty trees have size 1 (since they do have a label), and that if one of the successors of a non-empty tree has size infinity ($\kappa*$), then the whole tree has size infinity. Otherwise the size is the sum of the sizes of the successors plus one. With this definition we can compute for the earlier example (3) that:

$$
\begin{array}{ll}
\mathsf{size}(2) = \kappa'1 & \text{since } \mathsf{children}(2) = \kappa* \\
\mathsf{size}(3) = \kappa'(1+1+1) = \kappa'3 & \text{since } \mathsf{children}(3) = \kappa'(2,2) \\
\mathsf{size}(0) = \kappa'(1+3+1) = \kappa'5 & \text{since } \mathsf{children}(0) = \kappa'(3,2) \\
\mathsf{size}(1) = \kappa* & \\
\mathsf{size}(4) = \kappa* &
\end{array}
$$

The latter two equations holds since if $\mathsf{size}(1)$ were $\kappa'n$, for some $n \in \mathbb{N}$, then assertion 'size_def' in Figure 3 yields $\kappa'n = \mathsf{size}(1) = \kappa'(n+1+1)$, which is impossible. Hence $\mathsf{size}(1)$ must be $\kappa*$. Similarly for $\mathsf{size}(4)$.

For those readers who are not so familiar with the style of specification as in Figure 3 we shall give a reformulation of the binary tree space specification as an axiomatic description in mathematical style:

Let A be an arbitrary set. A *binary tree space* over A consists of a set X, elements of which will be called (binary) trees, together with three operations label: $X \rightarrow A$, children: $X \rightarrow 1 + (X \times X)$ and size: $X \rightarrow 1 + \mathbb{N}$ satisfying, for all $x \in X$,
1. If $\mathsf{children}(x) = \kappa*$, then $\mathsf{size}(x) = \kappa'1$;
2. If $\mathsf{children}(x) = \kappa'(x_1, x_2)$ and either $\mathsf{size}(x_1) = \kappa*$ or $\mathsf{size}(x_2) = \kappa*$, then $\mathsf{size}(x) = \kappa*$;
3. If $\mathsf{children}(x) = \kappa'(x_1, x_2)$ and $\mathsf{size}(x_1) = \kappa'n_1$ and $\mathsf{size}(x_2) = \kappa'n_2$, then $\mathsf{size}(x) = \kappa'(n_1 + n_2 + 1)$.
In case $\mathsf{children}(x) = \kappa'(x_1, x_2)$ we shall call x_1 and x_2 the successor trees or children of the tree x.

We consider some examples of binary tree spaces (*i.e.* of models of the specification BinaryTreeSpace) over an arbitrary set A.

1. A trivial example is the empty set 0 with obvious operations given by the empty functions. If the set A is non-empty, the singleton set 1 is also a binary tree space.
2. We can turn the set of all infinite trees with labels from A into a binary tree space. This set, call it $\mathsf{InfTree}(A)$, can be defined as the set of functions A^{2^*} of all functions from the free monoid 2^* of finite sequences of elements from

$2 = \{0, 1\}$ to A. For $\phi \in \mathsf{InfTree}(A) = A^{2^*}$ we define

$$\mathsf{label}(\phi) = \phi(\langle\rangle)$$
$$\mathsf{children}(\phi) = \kappa'(\lambda\alpha \in 2^*. \phi(0 \cdot \alpha), \lambda\alpha \in 2^*. \phi(1 \cdot \alpha))$$
$$\mathsf{size}(\phi) = \kappa * .$$

3. Next consider the set of both finite and infinite trees:

$$\mathsf{FinInfTree}(A) \stackrel{\text{def}}{=} \{(a, \phi) : A \times (1 + (A \times A))^{2^*} \mid \forall\alpha \in 2^*. \forall b \in \{0, 1\}.$$
$$\phi(\alpha) = \kappa* \Rightarrow \phi(b \cdot \alpha) = \kappa*\}$$

with operations:

$$\mathsf{label}(a, \phi) = a$$
$$\mathsf{children}(a, \phi) = \mathsf{CASES}\ \phi(\langle\rangle)\ \mathsf{OF}$$
$$\kappa* \mapsto \kappa*$$
$$\kappa'(a_0, a_1) \mapsto \kappa'\big((a_0, \lambda\alpha \in 2^*. \phi(0 \cdot \alpha)),$$
$$(a_1, \lambda\alpha \in 2^*. \phi(1 \cdot \alpha))\big)$$
$$\mathsf{ENDCASES}$$
$$\mathsf{size}(a, \phi) = \ldots$$

The definition of size on $\mathsf{FinInfTree}(A)$ is non-trivial. One can of course say that size is determined by equation 'size_def' from Figure 3, but one has still has to show that such a function exists. One way to go about this is to first define $\mathsf{FinTree}(A) \subseteq \mathsf{FinInfTree}(A)$ to be the smallest subset F satisfying: $(a, \phi) \in F$ if either $\mathsf{children}(a, \phi) = \kappa*$ or $\mathsf{children}(a, \phi) = \kappa'((a_0, \phi_0), (a_1, \phi_1))$ and both $(a_0, \phi_0) \in F$ and $(a_1, \phi_1) \in F$. The elements of $\mathsf{FinTree}(A)$ are the "finite trees", and their size is determined by the computation rules in equation 'size_def' from Figure 3. For elements not in $\mathsf{FinTree}(A)$, the size is $\kappa*$[5].

4. The subset $\mathsf{FinTree}(A) \subseteq \mathsf{FinInfTree}(A)$ defined above (in 3) with inherited operations.

Thus we have seen that binary tree spaces exist as non-trivial mathematical structures. We conclude this section with a warning that coalgebraic specification is a subtle matter.

4.1   Elements of Binary Trees

Suppose that we would like to add to the BinTreeSpace specification in Figure 3 a method

$$\mathsf{elem} : X \times A \longrightarrow \{\mathsf{false}, \mathsf{true}\}$$

---

[5] We will elaborate on this "μ-calculus" style definition in Section 8.

telling whether a tree $x \in X$ contains an element $a \in A$ or not. The associated assertion that probably first comes to mind is:

$$\mathsf{elem\_def} : \big[\, \forall x \in X.\, \forall a \in A.\, \mathsf{elem}(x, a) =$$
$$(\mathsf{label}(x) = a) \vee \mathsf{CASES}\ \mathsf{children}(x)\ \mathsf{OF}$$
$$\kappa\ast \mapsto \mathsf{false}$$
$$\kappa'(v_1, v_2) \mapsto \mathsf{elem}(v_1, a) \vee \mathsf{elem}(v_2, a)$$
$$\mathsf{ENDCASES} \big]$$

But this assertion is not good enough, in the sense that it allows interpretations which are probably unwanted. For example, on the binary tree space $\mathsf{InfTree}(A)$ introduced above, we can define $\mathsf{elem}(\phi) = \mathsf{true}$, for all $\phi \in \mathsf{InfTree}(A)$. Then the assertion $\mathsf{elem\_def}$ holds, although we do not have a meaningful membership method.

Later, in Section 7 we shall introduce a temporal logic for coalgebras which allows us to express an appropriate assertion for the elem method. Then, $\mathsf{elem}(x, a)$ will be equal to: "there is a (not-necessarily direct) successor tree y of x with a as label"[6].

Exercises

1. Check that the subset $\mathsf{FinTree}(A) \subseteq \mathsf{FinInfTree}(A)$ is closed under the children operation defined on $\mathsf{FinInfTree}(A)$.
2. Characterise the subset $\mathsf{InfTree}(A) \subseteq \mathsf{FinInfTree}(A)$ in term of the children operation, by analogy with the above definition of $\mathsf{FinTree}(A) \subseteq \mathsf{FinInfTree}(A)$. (See also the definitions of Fin and Inf in Section 8.)

5   Bisimulations and Bisimilarity

Suppose we have an arbitrary coalgebra $c \colon X \to T(X)$ for a polynomial functor T. At this level of abstraction, we often a call the elements of X *states*, and call X itself the *state space*. The function c provides X with certain operations—like label, children and size in the previous section. These operations give us certain access to the state space X. They may allow us to observe certain things (like the current label, or the size), and they may allow us to "modify states", or to "move to next states" (like the successor trees). Typically for coalgebras, we can observe and modify, but we have no means of constructing new states. The behaviour of a state $x \in X$ is all that we can observe about x, either directly or indirectly (via its successor states).

In this situation it may happen that two states have the same behaviour. In that case we cannot distinguish them with the operations (of the coalgebra) that we have at our disposal. The two states need not be equal then, since the operations may only give limited access to the state space, and certain aspects

---

[6] This definition yields the "smallest" function elem satisfying the above assertion $\mathsf{elem\_def}$ with the first '=' replaced by '⇐'.

may be unobservable. When two states x, y are observationally indistinguishable, they are called *bisimilar*. This is written as $x \leftrightarrow y$. For example, the states 1 and 4 from the binary tree space $U = \{0, 1, 2, 3, 4\}$ in the previous section are bisimilar; they have the same unfoldings.

In this section we shall formally introduce the notion of bisimilarity $\leftrightarrow$, and show how it can be used in (coalgebraic) specification. Therefore we shall first introduce what is called *relation lifting*. Recall that a polynomial functor T is a mapping $X \mapsto T(X)$ of sets to sets. We shall define an associated mapping, called $\mathrm{Rel}(T)$, which maps a relation $R \subseteq X \times X$ to a new relation $\mathrm{Rel}(T)(R) \subseteq T(X) \times T(X)$. This mapping $\mathrm{Rel}(T)$ will be defined by induction on the structure of the polynomial functor T.

1. If T is the identity mapping, then so is $\mathrm{Rel}(T)$.
2. If T is the constant mapping $X \mapsto A$, then $\mathrm{Rel}(T)$ is the constant mapping $R \mapsto =_A$, where $=_A \subseteq A \times A$ is the equality relation consisting of $\{(a, a) \mid a \in A\}$.
3. If T is the product functor $X \mapsto T_1(X) \times T_2(X)$, then

$$\mathrm{Rel}(T)(R) = \{((x_1, x_2), (y_1, y_2)) \mid \mathrm{Rel}(T_1)(R)(x_1, y_1) \wedge \mathrm{Rel}(T_2)(R)(x_2, y_2)\}$$
$$\subseteq \big(T_1(X) \times T_2(X)\big) \times \big(T_1(X) \times T_2(X)\big)$$

4. If T is the coproduct functor $X \mapsto T_1(X) + T_2(X)$, then

$$\mathrm{Rel}(T)(R) = \{(\kappa x_1, \kappa y_1) \mid \mathrm{Rel}(T_1)(R)(x_1, y_1)\}$$
$$\cup \{(\kappa' x_2, \kappa' y_2) \mid \mathrm{Rel}(T_2)(R)(x_2, y_2)\}$$
$$\subseteq \big(T_1(X) + T_2(X)\big) \times \big(T_1(X) + T_2(X)\big)$$

5. If T is the function space functor $X \mapsto T_1(X)^A$, then

$$\mathrm{Rel}(T)(R) = \{(f, g) \mid \forall a \in A. \, \mathrm{Rel}(T_1)(R)(f(a), g(a))\}$$
$$\subseteq \big(T_1(X)^A\big) \times \big(T_1(X)^A\big)$$

For example, for a functor $T(X) = A + (X \times X)$ and a relation $R \subseteq X \times X$, the relation $\mathrm{Rel}(T)(R) \subseteq T(X) \times T(X)$ contains all pairs $(\kappa a, \kappa a)$, for $a \in A$, and all pairs $(\kappa'(x_1, x_2), \kappa'(y_1, y_2))$ with $R(x_1, y_1)$ and $R(x_2, y_2)$. Informally, $\mathrm{Rel}(T)(R)$ contains all pairs $(z, w) \in T(X) \times T(X)$ whose constituents in a constant set are equal, and whose constituents in X are related by R.

Definition 1. *Let T be a polynomial functor, with relation lifting $\mathrm{Rel}(T)$ as defined above. Further, let $c \colon X \to T(X)$ be a coalgebra for T.*

1. *A relation $R \subseteq X \times X$ is a bisimulation (with respect to the coalgebra c) if for all $x, y \in X$,*
$$R(x, y) \implies \mathrm{Rel}(T)(R)(c(x), c(y)).$$

2. *The bisimilarity relation $\leftrightarrow \subseteq X \times X$ (with respect to c) is defined as the greatest bisimulation; that is,*

$$x \leftrightarrow y \iff \exists R \subseteq X \times X. \, R \text{ is a bisimulation, and } R(x, y).$$

Bisimilarity is one of the fundamental notions in the theory of coalgebras. Notice that the above definition is "generic": it gives for each polynomial functor and for each coalgebra thereof an appropriate tailor-made definition of bisimilarity. The definition via relation lifting is convenient in a logical setting, because it is based on induction (on the structure of the polynomial functor). Therefore it can easily be translated in the logical language of proof tools—see the discussion in point 2. in Section 1 (page 238) . One can prove that bisimilarity is an equivalence relation, but this will not be done here. The proof relies on some basic properties of relation lifting, which can be proved by induction on the structure of the functor involved.

The notion of bisimilarity comes alive via examples. Let us return to the binary tree space specification from Figure 3 in the previous section. We have already seen that the functor involved is $BT(X) = A \times (1 + (X \times X)) \times (1 + \mathbb{N})$. We shall elaborate what a bisimulation relation is for an arbitrary coalgebra $c = \langle \text{label}, \text{children}, \text{size} \rangle \colon X \to BT(X)$ of this functor. Therefore we first compute the relation lifting operation $\text{Rel}(BT)$. It turns a relation $R \subseteq X \times X$ into a relation $\text{Rel}(BT)(R) \subseteq BT(X) \times BT(X)$, in the following way. For a pair $((x_1, x_2, x_3), (y_1, y_2, y_3)) \in BT(X) \times BT(X)$,

$$
\begin{aligned}
&\text{Rel}(BT)(R)((x_1, x_2, x_3), (y_1, y_2, y_3)) \\
&\Leftrightarrow \text{Rel}(A)(x_1, y_1) \wedge \text{Rel}(1 + (X \times X))(x_2, y_2) \wedge \text{Rel}(1 + \mathbb{N})(x_3, y_3) \\
&\Leftrightarrow (x_1 = y_1) \wedge \\
&\quad ((x_2 = y_2 = \kappa*) \vee \\
&\quad (x_2 = \kappa'(x_{20}, x_{21}) \wedge y_2 = \kappa'(y_{20}, y_{21}) \wedge R(x_{20}, y_{20}) \wedge R(x_{21}, y_{21}))) \wedge \\
&\quad (x_3 = y_3).
\end{aligned}
$$

Such $R \subseteq X \times X$ is a bisimulation for a coalgebra $c = \langle \text{label}, \text{children}, \text{size} \rangle \colon X \to BT(X)$ if for all $x, y \in X$,

$$
R(x, y) \implies \text{Rel}(BT)(R)(c(x), c(y))
$$

i.e. if,

$$
R(x, y) \implies \begin{cases} \text{label}(x) = \text{label}(y) \wedge \\ ((\text{children}(x) = \text{children}(y) = \kappa*) \vee \\ (\text{children}(x) = \kappa'(x_0, x_1) \wedge \text{children}(y) = \kappa'(y_0, y_1) \wedge \\ R(x_0, y_0) \wedge R(x_1, y_1))) \wedge \\ \text{size}(x) = \text{size}(y) \end{cases}
$$

This means that elements which are related by a bisimulation R have equal labels and sizes, and either both have no children, or both have children, which are again pairwise related by R. Bisimilarity $\leftrightarrow$ for binary trees is the greatest such bisimulation. Since it is an equivalence relation (and is closed under the operations), it behaves very much like an equality relation. In fact, bisimilarity is an important ingredient of assertions in coalgebraic specifications. There, one generally wishes to avoid using actual equality between states, and so one uses bisimilarity instead. The reason for not wanting equality between states is that

```
BEGIN BinaryTreeSpace[A: TYPE]
  METHODS
    label: X ⟶ A
    children: X ⟶ 1 + (X × X)
    size: X ⟶ 1 + ℕ
    mirror: X ⟶ X
  ASSERTIONS
    size_def: [ see Figure 3 ]
    label_mirror: [ ∀x ∈ X. label(mirror(x)) = label(x) ]
    children_mirror: [ ∀x ∈ X. CASES children(x) OF
                         κ∗ ↦ children(mirror(x)) = κ∗
                         κ′(v₁, v₂) ↦ CASES children(mirror(x)) OF
                                        κ∗ ↦ false
                                        κ′(z₁, z₂) ↦ (z₁ ⇌ mirror(v₂)) ∧
                                                      (z₂ ⇌ mirror(v₁))
                                      ENDCASES
                       ENDCASES ]
  END BinaryTreeSpace
```

Fig. 4. Specification of binary trees, version 2

it severely restricts the possible models[7] of the specification. But also, if states are indistinguishable, then they can be considered as equal from the outside.

In Figure 4 we continue the specification of binary tree spaces. What we add is a mirror method which swaps the children of trees (if any), leaving the labels unaffected. The assertion children_mirror uses bisimilarity to express that the left and right children of a mirrored tree with children are bisimilar to the mirrored right and left children.

The reader might have expected an additional assertion stating that mirrorring does not change the size. In fact, this can be derived. Also that mirroring is its own inverse, up to bisimilarity.

Proposition 2. *From the binary tree space assertions in Figure 4 one can derive, for all $x \in X$,*

1. $size(mirror(x)) = size(x)$
2. $mirror(mirror(x)) \leftrightarrow x$.

Proof. We only give a sketch, leaving details to the reader.

1. First, one can prove by well-founded induction,

$$\forall n \in \mathbb{N}.\, size(x) = \kappa'n \Leftrightarrow size(mirror(x)) = \kappa'n$$

The result then follows easily.

---

[7] As a typical example, consider a specification of a system with a "do" and an "undo" operation. The equation $undo(do(x)) = x$ will not hold in "history" models where one internally keeps track of the operations that have been applied.

2. According to the definition of bisimilarity $\underline{\leftrightarrow}$, it suffices to find a bisimulation $R \subseteq X \times X$ with $R(\mathsf{mirror}(\mathsf{mirror}(x)), x)$. Because $\underline{\leftrightarrow}$ is the greatest bisimulation, we then get $R \subseteq \underline{\leftrightarrow}$. One can use

$$R = \{(x, y) \mid x \underline{\leftrightarrow} \mathsf{mirror}(\mathsf{mirror}(y))\}. \qquad \square$$

Exercises

1. Let T be an arbitrary polynomial functor. Prove the following basic properties about the associated relation lifting operation $\mathrm{Rel}(T)$.
   (a) $\mathrm{Rel}(T)(=_X) = {=_{T(X)}}$;
   (b) $\mathrm{Rel}(T)(R^{op}) = \left(\mathrm{Rel}(T)(R)\right)^{op}$, where $R^{op} = \{(y, x) \mid (x, y) \in R\}$;
   (c) $\mathrm{Rel}(T)(R \circ S) = \mathrm{Rel}(T)(R) \circ \mathrm{Rel}(T)(S)$;
   (d) $R \subseteq S$ implies $\mathrm{Rel}(T)(R) \subseteq \mathrm{Rel}(T)(S)$;
   (e) R is symmetric implies $\mathrm{Rel}(T)(R)$ is symmetric;
   (f) For a collection of relations $(R_i \subseteq X \times X)_{i \in I}$ one has $\mathrm{Rel}(T)(\bigcap_{i \in I} R_i) = \bigcap_{i \in I} \mathrm{Rel}(T)(R_i)$.
   Conclude that for a coalgebra $c \colon X \to T(X)$, the union $\underline{\leftrightarrow}$ of all bisimulations on X is itself a bisimulation, and is also an equivalence relation.
2. Prove that the relation R in the proof of Proposition 2 (2) is a bisimulation.
3. Check that the above definition of relation lifting $\mathrm{Rel}(T)$ sending a relation $R \subseteq X \times X$ to $\mathrm{Rel}(T)(R) \subseteq T(X) \times T(X)$ in fact also works on relations $R \subseteq X \times Y$, with different carrier sets, and then yields a relation $\mathrm{Rel}(T)(R) \subseteq T(X) \times T(Y)$. For two coalgebras $X \xrightarrow{c} T(X)$ and $Y \xrightarrow{d} T(Y)$ we then call a relation $R \subseteq X \times Y$ a bisimulation (w.r.t. (c, d)) if $R(x, y) \Rightarrow \mathrm{Rel}(T)(R)(c(x), d(y))$ for all $x \in X$ and $y \in Y$. And we say that a function $f \colon X \to Y$ is a homomorphism (of coalgebras) if its graph $\mathcal{G}(f) = \{(x, f(x)) \mid x \in X\}$ is a bisimulation.
   Prove that the identity function is a homomorphism, and also that the composition of two homomorphisms is again a homomorphism. Thus one can form a category $\mathrm{CoAlg}(T)$ of coalgebras and homomorphisms between them. (Remark: what we present is an alternative to the standard definition, which uses the action of polynomial functors on functions (which we have not mentioned here, see e.g. [21]). It says that a function $f \colon X \to Y$ as above is a homomorphism if and only if the following diagram commutes.

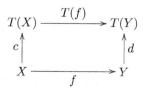

The reader familiar with this '$T(f)$' may wish to prove the equivalence of these two definitions.)

6 Invariants

Bisimulations are binary predicates on the state space of a coalgebra, which are closed under the operations. We will now introduce invariants, which are unary predicates that are closed under the operations. They are important for several reasons.

1. An invariant expresses a property which is maintained by all operations. If it also holds in initial states, then it holds in all reachable states. Thus, intended "safety" properties of a specification—like: the value of the integer (attribute) i will always be positive—are expressed via invariants.
2. Invariants are used for defining the temporal operators $\Box$ (henceforth) and $\Diamond$ (eventually) in a coalgebraic setting, see Section 7.
3. Invariants are crucial for refinements between coalgebraic specifications, see Section 10.

Bisimulations were introduced in Section 5 via relation lifting. Similarly, we shall introduce invariants via what is called predicate lifting. For a polynomial functor T we define a mapping $\mathrm{Pred}(T)$ which sends a predicate $P \subseteq X$ on X to a predicate $\mathrm{Pred}(T)(P)$ on $T(X)$, by induction on the structure of T. This goes as follow.

1. If T is the identity mapping, then so is $\mathrm{Pred}(T)$.
2. If T is the constant mapping $X \mapsto A$, then $\mathrm{Pred}(T)$ is the constant mapping $P \mapsto A$, where A is considered as the "truth" predicate $A \subseteq A$.
3. If T is the product functor $X \mapsto T_1(X) \times T_2(X)$, then

$$\mathrm{Pred}(T)(P) = \{(x,y) \mid \mathrm{Pred}(T_1)(P)(x) \wedge \mathrm{Pred}(T_2)(P)(y)\}$$
$$\subseteq T_1(X) \times T_2(X)$$

4. If T is the coproduct functor $X \mapsto T_1(X) + T_2(X)$, then

$$\mathrm{Pred}(T)(P) = \{\kappa x \mid \mathrm{Pred}(T_1)(P)(x)\} \cup \{\kappa' y \mid \mathrm{Pred}(T_2)(P)(y)\}$$
$$\subseteq T_1(X) + T_2(X)$$

5. If T is the function space functor $X \mapsto T_1(X)^A$, then

$$\mathrm{Pred}(T)(P) = \{f \mid \forall a \in A.\,\mathrm{Pred}(T_1)(P)(f(a))\}$$
$$\subseteq T_1(X)^A$$

For the polynomial functor $T(X) = A + (X \times X)$, a predicate $P \subseteq X$ is lifted to the relation $\mathrm{Pred}(T)(P) \subseteq T(X)$ containing all elements κa and those elements $\kappa'(x_1, x_2)$ where both $P(x_1)$ and $P(x_2)$. In general, $\mathrm{Pred}(T)(P)$ contains all elements from $T(X)$ where P holds on all X-positions in $T(X)$.

Definition 3. *Let $c\colon X \to T(X)$ be a coalgebra of a polynomial functor T, and $P \subseteq X$ be a predicate on its state space.*

1. *A new predicate* $NextTime(c)(P) \subseteq X$ *is defined as*

$$NextTime(c)(P)(x) \Longleftrightarrow Pred(T)(P)(c(x)).$$

It expresses that P *holds for all successor states of* x.
2. *The predicate* $P \subseteq X$ *is then an invariant for* c *if it satisfies, for all* $x \in X$,

$$P(x) \Longrightarrow NextTime(c)(P)(x).$$

The requirement in the definition expresses that if an invariant P holds in a state x, then it holds on each successor state of x. Using some elementary properties of predicate lifting, one can show that invariants are closed under conjunction $\wedge$. Also, the predicate which is always true (or always false) is an invariant. Further, if we have an arbitrary collection $(P_i)_{i \in I}$ of invariants, then $\forall i \in I. P_i$ is an invariant, see the exercises below.

Let us consider the binary tree space specification from Figure 4. The polynomial functor that captures the interface of this specification is:

$$\mathcal{BT}_2(X) = A \times (1 + (X \times X)) \times (1 + \mathbb{N}) \times X.$$

For a predicate $P \subseteq X$, the lifting $Pred(\mathcal{BT}_2)(P) \subseteq \mathcal{BT}_2(X)$ on a 4-tuple $(x_1, x_2, x_3, x_4) \in \mathcal{BT}_2(X)$ is:

$$Pred(\mathcal{BT}_2)(P)(x_1, x_2, x_3, x_4)$$
$$\Leftrightarrow Pred(A)(P)(x_1) \wedge Pred(1 + (X \times X))(P)(x_2) \wedge$$
$$Pred(1 + \mathbb{N})(P)(x_3) \wedge Pred(X)(P)(x_4)$$
$$\Leftrightarrow (x_2 = \kappa* \vee (x_2 = \kappa'(x_{20}, x_{21}) \wedge P(x_{20}) \wedge P(x_{21}))) \wedge P(x_4).$$

An invariant on a coalgebra $c = \langle \mathsf{label}, \mathsf{children}, \mathsf{size}, \mathsf{mirror} \rangle \colon X \to \mathcal{BT}_2(X)$ is a predicate $P \subseteq X$ with

$$P(x) \Longrightarrow Pred(\mathcal{BT}_2)(P)(c(x))$$

i.e. with

$$P(x) \Longrightarrow \begin{cases} (\mathsf{children}(x) = \kappa'(x_0, x_1) \Rightarrow P(x_0) \wedge P(x_1)) \wedge \\ P(\mathsf{mirror}(x)) \end{cases}$$

An invariant P thus holds on all successor states of an $x \in P$, produced either as children of x, or as mirror of x.

A concrete example of an invariant for the binary tree specification is the predicate stating that the size is finite: $FinSize(x) \Leftrightarrow (\mathsf{size}(x) \neq \kappa*)$. Clearly, if $FinSize(x)$, then none of the successor trees can have infinite size; and also $FinSize(\mathsf{mirror}(x))$ holds because mirroring does not change the size, see Proposition 2 (1).

As we have seen, invariants and bisimulations on a coalgebra are unary and binary predicates which are closed under the operations. The more operations the coalgebra has, the more closure requirements there are. The approach that we follow—via predicate and relation lifting—produces tailor-made requirements, following the structure of the interface (as given by a polynomial functor) of a coalgebra. Since these requirements follow from the structure, they can be generated automatically. That is precisely what is done by the LOOP tool (from [9,38]).

As a final remark we add that predicates and relations which are closed under the operations of an algebra (instead of a coalgebra) also make sense, see [33,35,10]. A relation $R \subseteq X \times X$ on the carrier set of an algebra $a \colon T(X) \to X$ is closed under the operations if:

$$\text{Rel}(T)(R)(a(x), a(y)) \Longrightarrow R(x, y).$$

In this case one may call R a *congruence*. But note that such an R need not be an equivalence relation. There is no special name in mathematics for a predicate $P \subseteq X$ which is closed under the operations of an algebra a, *i.e.* which satisfies:

$$\text{Pred}(T)(P)(a(x)) \Longrightarrow P(x).$$

Such a P is called an *inductive predicate* in [10] (since such predicates form the assumptions of induction arguments), but *invariant* would be a reasonable name also in this algebraic case.

Exercises

1. Prove for an arbitrary polynomial functor T that predicate lifting $\text{Pred}(T)$ satisfies:
   (a) $P \subseteq Q$ implies $\text{Pred}(T)(P) \subseteq \text{Pred}(T)(Q)$;
   (b) $\text{Pred}(T)(X \subseteq X) = (T(X) \subseteq T(X))$;
   (c) $\text{Pred}(T)(\bigcap_{i \in I} P_i) = \bigcap_{i \in i} \text{Pred}(T)(P_i)$.
2. Let $c \colon X \to T(X)$ be a coalgebra of a polynomial functor T. Prove that:
   (a) $P \subseteq X$ is an invariant if and only if $\{(x, y) \mid x = y \wedge P(x)\}$ is a bisimulation.
   (b) If R is a bisimulation, then $\pi R = \{x \mid \exists y. R(x, y)\}$ is an invariant.
3. Elaborate what it means for a relation to be a congruence for Abelian groups and vector spaces, using the above formulation (and the interface functors from Section 3).

7   Temporal Logic for Coalgebras

Temporal logic is a formalism for reasoning about assertions whose validity varies with time. Time may be understood here in a loose sense, including situations where one deals with later or earlier stages, or with successor and predecessor states. Typical operators of temporal logic are "henceforth" $\square$ and "eventually" $\diamondsuit$. It was Pnueli [34,29] who first argued that temporal logic could be useful for reasoning about computer systems with potentially infinite behaviour, such as controllers which are meant to be running forever. Hence it comes as no surprise that the operators of temporal logic arise quite naturally for coalgebras, because they abstractly capture dynamical systems, typically with infinite behaviour. In this section we shall define $\Box$ and $\Diamond$ in terms of invariants, and show how to use them in the running example of binary trees.

Let $c: X \to T(X)$ be an arbitrary coalgebra of a polynomial functor T. For a predicate $P \subseteq X$ we shall define two new predicates $\Box(c)(P) \subseteq X$ and $\Diamond(c)(P) \subseteq X$. If the coalgebra c is clear from the context, we often omit it, and simply write $\Box(P)$ and $\Diamond(P)$. For an element $x \in X$, we define the predicate "henceforth P" (with respect to c) as:

$$\Box(c)(P)(x) \Leftrightarrow \exists I \subseteq X. I \text{ is an invariant for } c \text{ and } I \subseteq P \text{ and } I(x). \quad (4)$$

This says that $\Box(c)(P)$ is the greatest invariant contained in P[8]. The associated "eventually" operator $\Diamond$ is defined as $\neg\Box\neg$, or, more precisely as:

$$\Diamond(c)(P)(x) \Leftrightarrow \neg\Box(c)(\{y \in X \mid \neg P(y)\})(x). \quad (5)$$

Here we use $\neg$ for negation on truth values. These temporal operators satisfy the familiar properties from modal logic. Basically they say that $\Box$ is an interior operation: $\Box(P) \subseteq P$, $\Box(P) \subseteq \Box(\Box(P))$, and $P \subseteq Q \Rightarrow \Box(P) \subseteq \Box(Q)$. Invariants are its opens (*i.e.* fixed points).

In the remainder of this section we shall use $\Box$ and $\Diamond$ for binary tree spaces, as described in Figure 4 in the previous section (*i.e.* with mirror operation). There we have already seen what it means for a predicate to be an invariant for binary trees. With the above definitions we thus have $\Box$ and $\Diamond$ for these trees. We will first redescribe these operators concretely. Then we shall show how they can be used in specification and verification (without relying on the concrete description).

7.1   A Concrete Description of $\Box$ and $\Diamond$ for Binary Trees

In order to convince the reader that $\Box(P)$—as defined in (4) above—holds for x if P holds for *all* future states of x, and that $\Diamond(P)$ holds for x if P holds for *some* future state of x, we first have to make explicit what 'future state' means for binary trees. In principle we can proceed to a successor state via left and right children, and via mirroring. A path to a future state of x can thus be described by a finite lists of elements from $\{0, 1, 2\}$, where 0 stands for left child, 1 for right child (if any), and 2 for mirror. But from the way that the children and mirror operations interact, as given by assertion 'children_mirror' in Figure 4, we can simplify such paths into certain normal forms, with at most one mirror operation, right at the beginning, and with paths consisting only of 0's and 1's. Therefore we first introduce the following auxiliary function offspring: $X \times \{0, 1\}^\star \to 1 + X$ producing the successor state offspring(x, α) of a tree $x \in X$ along a path $\alpha \in$

---

[8] More formally, $\Box(c)(P) = \mathsf{gfp}(\lambda Q \in \mathcal{P}X. P \wedge \mathrm{NextTime}(c)(Q))$, using NextTime from Definition 3 and the greatest fixed point operator gfp that will be introduced in the beginning of Section 8.

$\{0,1\}^\star$, if any.

$$
\begin{aligned}
\mathsf{offspring}(x, \langle \rangle) &= \kappa' x \\
\mathsf{offspring}(x, a \cdot \alpha) &= \mathsf{CASES\ offspring}(x, \alpha)\ \mathsf{OF} \\
&\qquad \kappa* \mapsto \kappa* \\
&\qquad \kappa' z \mapsto \mathsf{CASES\ children}(z)\ \mathsf{OF} \\
&\qquad\qquad \kappa* \mapsto \kappa* \\
&\qquad\qquad \kappa'(v_1, v_2) \mapsto \mathsf{IF}\ a = 0 \\
&\qquad\qquad\qquad\qquad\qquad \mathsf{THEN}\ \kappa' v_1 \\
&\qquad\qquad\qquad\qquad\qquad \mathsf{ELSE}\ \kappa' v_2 \\
&\qquad\qquad \mathsf{ENDCASES} \\
&\qquad \mathsf{ENDCASES}
\end{aligned}
$$

First we establish some auxiliary results about this **offspring** function. The last point in the lemma below shows how **offspring** commutes with mirroring.

Lemma 4. *Let x, y be arbitrary tree spaces. Then*

1. *For all lists $\alpha, \beta \in \{0,1\}^\star$,*

$$
\begin{aligned}
\mathit{offspring}(x, \alpha \cdot \beta) = \ &\mathit{CASES\ offspring}(x, \beta)\ \mathit{OF} \\
&\quad \kappa* \mapsto \kappa* \\
&\quad \kappa' w \mapsto \mathit{offspring}(w, \alpha) \\
&\mathit{ENDCASES}
\end{aligned}
$$

   where $\cdot$ is concatenation.

2. *Successor trees along the same path of bisimilar trees are bisimilar again:*

$$
\begin{aligned}
x \leftrightarrow y \implies \forall \alpha \in \{0,1\}^\star.\ &\mathit{CASES\ offspring}(x, \alpha)\ \mathit{OF} \\
&\quad \kappa* \mapsto \mathit{CASES\ offspring}(y, \alpha)\ \mathit{OF} \\
&\qquad\quad \kappa* \mapsto \mathit{true} \\
&\qquad\quad \kappa' v \mapsto \mathit{false} \\
&\qquad \mathit{ENDCASES} \\
&\quad \kappa' w \mapsto \mathit{CASES\ offspring}(y, \alpha)\ \mathit{OF} \\
&\qquad\quad \kappa* \mapsto \mathit{false} \\
&\qquad\quad \kappa' v \mapsto w \leftrightarrow v \\
&\qquad \mathit{ENDCASES} \\
&\mathit{ENDCASES}
\end{aligned}
$$

3. Let $\overline{\alpha} \in \{0,1\}^*$ be obtained from $\alpha \in \{0,1\}^*$ by changing 0's into 1's and vice-versa. Then:

$$\forall \alpha \in \{0,1\}^*. \text{ CASES offspring}(x,\alpha) \text{ OF}$$
$$\kappa* \mapsto \text{ CASES offspring}(\text{mirror}(x),\overline{\alpha}) \text{ OF}$$
$$\kappa* \mapsto \text{true}$$
$$\kappa'v \mapsto \text{false}$$
$$\text{ENDCASES}$$
$$\kappa'w \mapsto \text{ CASES offspring}(\text{mirror}(x),\overline{\alpha}) \text{ OF}$$
$$\kappa* \mapsto \text{false}$$
$$\kappa'v \mapsto \text{mirror}(w) \leftrightarrow v$$
$$\text{ENDCASES}$$
$$\text{ENDCASES}$$

The CASES notation gives a precise way of stating, for example in the last point, that if $\text{offspring}(x,\alpha) = \kappa'w$, then $\text{offspring}(\text{mirror}(x),\overline{\alpha})$ is of the form $\kappa'v$, and this v is bisimilar to $\text{mirror}(w)$.

Proof. By induction on α (in all three cases). □

Proposition 5. *Let $P \subseteq X$ be a predicate on a binary tree space X, which respects bisimilarity, i.e. which satisfies $x \leftrightarrow y \wedge P(x) \Rightarrow P(y)$, for all $x,y \in X$. Then:*

1. $\square(P)(x) \Longleftrightarrow$
$$\forall \alpha \in \{0,1\}^*.$$
$$\begin{pmatrix} \text{CASES offspring}(x,\alpha) \text{ OF} \\ \kappa* \mapsto \text{true} \\ \kappa'w \mapsto P(w) \\ \text{ENDCASES} \end{pmatrix} \wedge \begin{pmatrix} \text{CASES offspring}(\text{mirror}(x),\alpha) \text{ OF} \\ \kappa* \mapsto \text{true} \\ \kappa'w \mapsto P(w) \\ \text{ENDCASES} \end{pmatrix}$$

2. $\lozenge(P)(x) \Longleftrightarrow$
$$\exists \alpha \in \{0,1\}^*.$$
$$\begin{pmatrix} \text{CASES offspring}(x,\alpha) \text{ OF} \\ \kappa* \mapsto \text{false} \\ \kappa'w \mapsto P(w) \\ \text{ENDCASES} \end{pmatrix} \vee \begin{pmatrix} \text{CASES offspring}(\text{mirror}(x),\alpha) \text{ OF} \\ \kappa* \mapsto \text{false} \\ \kappa'w \mapsto P(w) \\ \text{ENDCASES} \end{pmatrix}$$

Proof. The second point follows directly from the first one, since $\lozenge = \neg\square\neg$, and so we concentrate on 1.

($\Rightarrow$) Assume $\square(P)(x)$. Then there is an invariant $Q \subseteq X$ with $Q \subseteq P$ and $Q(x)$. The result follows from the statement:

$$\forall \alpha \in \{0,1\}^*.$$
$$\begin{pmatrix} \text{CASES offspring}(x,\alpha) \text{ OF} \\ \kappa* \mapsto \text{true} \\ \kappa'w \mapsto Q(w) \\ \text{ENDCASES} \end{pmatrix} \wedge \begin{pmatrix} \text{CASES offspring}(\text{mirror}(x),\alpha) \text{ OF} \\ \kappa* \mapsto \text{true} \\ \kappa'w \mapsto \exists y \in X. y \leftrightarrow w \wedge Q(y) \\ \text{ENDCASES} \end{pmatrix}$$

which can be proved by induction on α.

($\Leftarrow$) We have to produce an invariant $Q \subseteq X$ with $Q \subseteq P$ and $Q(x)$. We can take $Q(y)$ as:

$$\forall \alpha \in \{0,1\}^*.$$
$$\left(\begin{array}{l} \text{CASES offspring}(y,\alpha) \text{ OF} \\ \quad \kappa* \mapsto \text{true} \\ \quad \kappa'w \mapsto P(w) \\ \text{ENDCASES} \end{array} \right) \wedge \left(\begin{array}{l} \text{CASES offspring}(\text{mirror}(y),\alpha) \text{ OF} \\ \quad \kappa* \mapsto \text{true} \\ \quad \kappa'w \mapsto P(w) \\ \text{ENDCASES} \end{array} \right)$$

Then $Q(x)$ holds by assumption. The inclusion $Q \subseteq P$ follows easily by taking $\alpha = \langle\rangle$, but invariance is more difficult, requiring Lemma 4. $\qquad\square$

7.2 Using $\square$ and $\diamondsuit$ for Specification and Verification of Binary Trees

Now that we have seen how $\square$ and $\diamondsuit$ (for binary trees) indeed express "for all future states" and "for some future state", we start using these temporal operators in specifications. Subsequently we show how to reason with them (without relying on the concrete descriptions of Proposition 5).

BEGIN BinaryTreeSpace[A: TYPE]
  METHODS
    label: $X \longrightarrow A$
    children: $X \longrightarrow 1 + (X \times X)$
    size: $X \longrightarrow 1 + \mathbb{N}$
    mirror: $X \longrightarrow X$
    elem: $X \times A \longrightarrow \{\text{false}, \text{true}\}$
  ASSERTIONS
    size_def: $\left[\, \text{see Figure 3} \,\right]$
    label_mirror: $\left[\, \text{see Figure 4} \,\right]$
    children_mirror: $\left[\, \text{see Figure 4} \,\right]$
    elem_def: $\left[\, \forall x \in X. \forall a \in A. \, \text{elem}(x,a) = \diamondsuit(\{y \in X \mid \text{label}(y) = a\})(x) \,\right]$
  CONSTRUCTORS
    leaf: $A \longrightarrow X$
    fill: $A \longrightarrow X$
  CREATION
    leaf_def: $\left[\, \forall a \in A. \, \text{label}(\text{leaf}(a)) = a \wedge \text{children}(\text{leaf}(a)) = \kappa * \,\right]$
    fill_def: $\left[\, \forall a \in A. \, \square(\{y \in X \mid \text{label}(y) = a \wedge \text{children}(y) \neq \kappa*\})(\text{fill}(a)) \,\right]$
END BinaryTreeSpace

Fig. 5. Specification of binary trees, version 3

Recall from Subsection 4.1 that the naive assertion for a membership method elem: $X \times A \longrightarrow \{\mathsf{false}, \mathsf{true}\}$ does not work. We are now in a position to express elem(x, a) as "in some future state y of x, label$(y) = a$", namely as $\Diamond(\{y \in X \mid \mathsf{label}(y) = a\})(x)$. This is incorporated in the next version of the binary tree space specification in Figure 5.

Of course one can also define elem(x, a) via the auxiliary function offspring from the previous subsection. But such a definition is too concrete, too verbose, and not at the right level of abstraction. For instance, if we were using ternary trees, with a children operation $X \to 1 + (X \times X \times X)$, instead of binary trees, then the eventually assertion for elem would still work, because $\Diamond$ abstracts from the particular tree structure.

New in this specification are the constructors. These are functions of the form $I \to X$, giving initial states, parametrised by the set I. These initial states are required to satisfy the assertions listed under 'CREATION'. In this case we have two[9] constructors, namely leaf: $A \to X$ and fill: $A \to X$. The intention is that leaf(a) is the tree with a as label and with no children. This is easy to express, see the assertion 'leaf_def' in Figure 5. The other constructor yields a tree fill(a) that has a not only as direct label but also as label for all of its successors, which are all required to exist. This can be expressed conveniently via a $\Box$ formula.

We give an indication of what can be proved about this latest specification in two lemmas. The next section elaborates further on (in)finiteness of behaviour of binary trees.

Lemma 6. *Consider the binary tree specification from Figure 5. The mirror of a tree $x \in X$ has the same elements as x, i.e. for all $a \in A$,*

$$\mathit{elem}(x, a) \Longleftrightarrow \mathit{elem}(\mathit{mirror}(x), a).$$

With this result one can show that mirroring is its own inverse, for binary tree spaces as in Figure 5 (like in Figure 4, see Proposition 2 (2)).

Proof. What we have to prove is, for an arbitrary $x \in X$ and $a \in A$:

$$\exists I \subseteq X. (I \text{ is an invariant}) \wedge (I \subseteq \{y \in X \mid \mathsf{label}(y) \neq a\}) \wedge (I(\mathit{mirror}(x))$$
$$\Longleftrightarrow$$
$$\exists I \subseteq X. (I \text{ is an invariant}) \wedge (I \subseteq \{y \in X \mid \mathsf{label}(y) \neq a\}) \wedge I(x).$$

For the direction ($\Leftarrow$) one can use the same predicate I, but for ($\Rightarrow$) one has to do some work: assume I as in the assumption, and define $I' \subseteq X$ as:

$$I'(x) \Leftrightarrow \exists y \in X. y \leftrightarrow \mathit{mirror}(x) \wedge I(y)$$

Then I' is the required predicate. $\qquad\square$

A next exercise that we set ourselves is to prove that the size of an initial state fill(a), for $a \in A$, is infinite (*i.e.* is $\kappa*$). We do so by first proving a more general statement.

---

[9] These two constructors can be combined into a single one with type $A + A \to X$.

Lemma 7. *Still in the context of the specification in Figure 5,*

1. $\Box(\{y \in X \mid \mathsf{children}(y) \neq \kappa*\})(x) \Rightarrow \mathsf{size}(x) = \kappa*$, *for all $x \in X$.*
2. $\mathsf{size}(\mathsf{fill}(a)) = \kappa*$, *for all $a \in A$.*

Proof. The second point follows immediately from the first one using the definition of $\mathsf{fill}(a)$. For 1 we first prove an auxiliary statement. Assume $\Box(\{y \in X \mid \mathsf{children}(y) \neq \kappa*\})(x)$. Then, for all $n \in \mathbb{N}$,

$$(\mathsf{size}(x) = \kappa'n) \Longrightarrow \forall m \in \mathbb{N}. \Diamond(\{y \in X \mid \mathsf{CASES}\ \mathsf{size}(y)\ \mathsf{OF}$$
$$\kappa* \mapsto \mathsf{false}$$
$$\kappa'v \mapsto v + m \leq n$$
$$\mathsf{ENDCASES}\,\})(x)$$

In words: if the size of x is $\kappa'n$, then for all $m \in \mathbb{N}$ there is a future state y of x whose size is $\kappa'v$ and satisfies $v + m \leq n$. The conclusion of this statement follows by induction on m. This shows that $\mathsf{size}(x)$ cannot be of the form $\kappa'n$—take $m = n + 1$ in that case—and thus that $\mathsf{size}(x)$ must be $\kappa*$. □

Exercises

1. Prove that $\Box(\bigcap_{i \in I} P_i) = \bigcap_{i \in I} \Box(P_i)$.
2. Prove that the predicate I' in the proof of Lemma 6 is an invariant.
3. Prove the following "induction rule of temporal logic":

$$P \cap \Box(P \supset \mathsf{NextTime}(P)) \subseteq \Box(P),$$

where $P \supset Q = \{x \mid P(x) \text{ implies } Q(x)\}$.
4. Consider the specification in Figure 5, and prove, for all $a, b \in A$,

$$\mathsf{elem}(\mathsf{fill}(a), b) \Longrightarrow a = b.$$

5. Note that Lemma 4 (1) describes the function **offspring** as a homomorphism of monoids, when considered as a function $\{0, 1\}^* \to (1+X)^X$ from sequences to partial functions.

8   Towards a μ-Calculus for Coalgebras

We continue the study of binary trees as in Figure 5. In the first point in Lemma 7 in the previous section we have seen a certain property, namely $\Box(\{y \in X \mid \mathsf{children}(y) \neq \kappa*\})(x)$, guaranteeing that $\mathsf{size}(x)$ is infinite. At this stage we wonder: are there formulas expressing finiteness of behaviour, and also infiniteness behaviour, in such a way that a tree has finite behaviour if and only if its size is finite (*i.e.* of the form $\kappa'n$, for some $n \in \mathbb{N}$), and has infinite behaviour if and only if its size is infinite (*i.e.* $\kappa*$)?

In this section we give a positive answer to this question. In order to express such formulas, say $\mathsf{finite}(x)$ and $\mathsf{infinite}(x)$, for a binary tree x, we shall make use of least and greatest fixed points, via operators μ and ν as are standard in what is called the μ-calculus (see [42]). In the μ-calculus one allows μ and ν in the construction of logical formulas, with associated rules for reasoning. Here we shall only illustrate the usefulness of μ and ν in our running example. We proceed at a semantical level, without developing a logic. So first we have to make clear what we mean by these fixed points.

Let Y be an arbitrary set. The set $\mathcal{P}(Y)$ of subsets of Y is partially ordered by inclusion $\subseteq$. A function $F: \mathcal{P}(Y) \to \mathcal{P}(Y)$ is called monotone if it respects inclusions: $P \subseteq Q \Rightarrow F(P) \subseteq F(Q)$. For such an F we define

$$\mathsf{lfp}(F) = \bigcap \{U \subseteq Y \mid F(U) \subseteq U\}$$
$$\mathsf{gfp}(F) = \bigcup \{U \subseteq Y \mid U \subseteq F(U)\}$$

Then it is not hard to prove (using that F is monotone):

$$F(P) \subseteq P \Rightarrow \mathsf{lfp}(F) \subseteq P \qquad F(\mathsf{lfp}(F)) = \mathsf{lfp}(F)$$
$$P \subseteq F(P) \Rightarrow P \subseteq \mathsf{gfp}(F) \qquad F(\mathsf{gfp}(F)) = \mathsf{gfp}(F).$$

This says that $\mathsf{lfp}(F)$ is the least fixed point, and $\mathsf{gfp}(F)$ the greatest fixed point of F. The μ-calculus offers a special syntax for the functions lfp and gfp, namely the binding operators μ and ν. Their meaning is:

$$\mu P. F(P) = \mathsf{lfp}(F) \qquad \text{and} \qquad \nu P. F(P) = \mathsf{gfp}(F).$$

We return to binary tree spaces, and define for a subset $P \subseteq X$, two predicates:

$$\mathsf{Fin}(P) = \{y \in X \mid \mathsf{Pred}(1 + (X \times X))(P)(\mathsf{children}(y))\}$$
$$= \{y \in X \mid \mathsf{CASES} \ \mathsf{children}(y) \ \mathsf{OF}$$
$$\kappa* \mapsto \mathsf{true}$$
$$\kappa'(v_1, v_2) \mapsto P(v_1) \wedge P(v_2)$$
$$\mathsf{ENDCASES}\}$$
$$\mathsf{Inf}(P) = \{y \in X \mid \neg\mathsf{Pred}(1 + (X \times X))(\neg P)(\mathsf{children}(y))\}$$
$$= \{y \in X \mid \mathsf{CASES} \ \mathsf{children}(y) \ \mathsf{OF}$$
$$\kappa* \mapsto \mathsf{false}$$
$$\kappa'(v_1, v_2) \mapsto P(v_1) \vee P(v_2)$$
$$\mathsf{ENDCASES}\}$$

It is not hard to see that both Fin and Inf are monotone functions[10]. Therefore we can define the following two predicates on X.

$$\mathsf{finite} = \mathsf{lfp}(\mathsf{Fin}) \qquad \text{and} \qquad \mathsf{infinite} = \mathsf{gfp}(\mathsf{Inf})$$

---

[10] The occurrence of predicate lifting in this definition is not accidental. For an arbitrary coalgebra $c: X \to T(X)$ of a polynomial functor, one can define the subset of states with finite behaviour as $\mu P. \mathsf{NextTime}(c)(P) = \mathsf{lfp}(\mathsf{NextTime}(c))$, and the subset of states with infinite behaviour as $\nu P. \neg\mathsf{NextTime}(c)(\neg P)$.

In the μ-calculus one would directly define:

$$\text{finite} = \mu P. \{y \in X \mid \text{CASES children}(y) \text{ OF}$$
$$\kappa* \mapsto \text{true}$$
$$\kappa'(v_1, v_2) \mapsto P(v_1) \wedge P(v_2)$$
$$\text{ENDCASES} \}$$
$$\text{infinite} = \nu P. \{y \in X \mid \text{CASES children}(y) \text{ OF}$$
$$\kappa* \mapsto \text{false}$$
$$\kappa'(v_1, v_2) \mapsto P(v_1) \vee P(v_2)$$
$$\text{ENDCASES} \}$$

Such definitions in μ-calculus style are usually very compact (and elegant), but not so easy to read and understand. In this case we shall first relate the definitions of the predicates finite and infinite to the concrete description in terms of the offspring function using paths (introduced in Subsection 7.1). Subsequently we shall relate these predicates to the size function.

In order to familiarise the reader with reasoning using least and greatest fixed points, we start with the following elementary observations.

Lemma 8. *For binary trees $x, y \in X$ satisfying the specification from Figure 5 we have:*

1. *If $x \leftrightarrow y$, then*

$$\text{finite}(x) \Longleftrightarrow \text{finite}(y) \quad \text{and} \quad \text{infinite}(x) \Longleftrightarrow \text{infinite}(y).$$

2. *Also:*

$$\text{finite}(\text{mirror}(x)) \Longleftrightarrow \text{finite}(x) \quad \text{and} \quad \text{infinite}(\text{mirror}(x)) \Longleftrightarrow \text{infinite}(x).$$

Proof. 1. We shall prove the first part about finiteness. So assume $x \leftrightarrow y$ and finite(x), *i.e.* lfp(Fin)(x). Because lfp(Fin) is the least fixed point of Fin, it suffices to find a predicate P with Fin$(P) \subseteq P$ and $P(x) \Rightarrow$ finite(y). These requirements suggest $P = \{z \in X \mid \forall w \in X. z \leftrightarrow w \Rightarrow \text{finite}(w)\}$.

2. We do the infinite case.

($\Rightarrow$) Assume infinite(mirror(x)), *i.e.* gfp(Inf)(mirror(x)). In order to prove infinite(x) we simply take $P = \{y \in X \mid \text{infinite}(\text{mirror}(y))\}$. The inclusion $P \subseteq \text{Inf}(P)$ follows from 1, and $P(x)$ is obvious. Therefore infinite(x).

($\Leftarrow$) Assume infinite(x). In order to prove gfp(Inf)(mirror(x)) it suffices to produce a predicate P with $P \subseteq \text{Inf}(P)$ and $P(\text{mirror}(x))$. We take $P = \{y \in X \mid \exists z \in X. \text{mirror}(z) \leftrightarrow y \wedge \text{infinite}(z)\}$. □

Proposition 9. *Finiteness and infiniteness of behaviour for binary trees can be expressed in terms of the offspring function from Subsection 7.1 as follows.*

1. $\text{finite}(x) \Longleftrightarrow \exists n \in \mathbb{N}. \forall \alpha \in \{0, 1\}^*. |\alpha| \geq n \Rightarrow \text{offspring}(x, \alpha) = \kappa*.$
2. $\text{infinite}(x) \Longleftrightarrow \forall n \in \mathbb{N}. \exists \alpha \in \{0, 1\}^*. |\alpha| = n \wedge \text{offspring}(x, \alpha) \neq \kappa*.$

Proof. 1. For the direction ($\Rightarrow$) one uses that finiteness is defined as a least fixed point. The predicate P with $\mathsf{Fin}(P) \subseteq P$ that one can use is given by $P = \{y \in X \mid \exists n \in \mathbb{N}. \forall \alpha \in \{0,1\}^{\star}. |\alpha| \geq n \Rightarrow \mathsf{offspring}(y, \alpha) = \kappa*\}$.

For the reverse direction ($\Leftarrow$) assume, for some $n \in \mathbb{N}$ that $\mathsf{offspring}(x, \alpha) = \kappa*$ for all $\alpha \in \{0,1\}^{\star}$ with $|\alpha| \geq n$. Then one can prove, by induction on m, that:

$$\forall m \leq n. \forall \alpha \in \{0,1\}^{\star}. \text{ CASES } \mathsf{offspring}(x, \alpha) \text{ OF}$$
$$\kappa* \mapsto \mathsf{true}$$
$$\kappa'v \mapsto |\alpha| \geq n - m \Rightarrow \mathsf{finite}(v)$$
$$\text{ENDCASES}$$

But then we are done by taking $m = n$ and $\alpha = \langle\rangle$.

2. The implication ($\Leftarrow$) can be proved using that infinity is introduced via a greatest fixed point. An appropriate predicate P with $P \subseteq \mathsf{Inf}(P)$ is: $P = \{y \in X \mid \forall n \in \mathbb{N}. \exists \alpha \in \{0,1\}^{\star}. |\alpha| = n \wedge \mathsf{offspring}(y, \alpha) \neq \kappa*\}$.

For the other implication ($\Rightarrow$), assume $\mathsf{infinite}(x)$. By induction on n we can prove a slightly stronger statement:

$$\forall n \in \mathbb{N}. \exists \alpha \in \{0,1\}^{\star}. \text{ CASES } \mathsf{offspring}(x, \alpha) \text{ OF}$$
$$\kappa* \mapsto \mathsf{false}$$
$$\kappa'v \mapsto |\alpha| = n \wedge \mathsf{infinite}(v)$$
$$\text{ENDCASES} \qquad \square$$

In a next step we show that both finiteness and infinity can be expressed in terms of size.

Proposition 10. *For a binary tree space x as in Figure 5 we have*

1. *$\mathsf{finite}(x) \Longleftrightarrow \mathsf{size}(x) \neq \kappa*$.*
2. *$\mathsf{infinite}(x) \Longleftrightarrow \mathsf{size}(x) = \kappa*$.*

Proof. 1. The direction ($\Rightarrow$) follows from finite being a least fixed point. For ($\Leftarrow$) we prove by well-founded induction (on the natural numbers) that:

$$\forall n \in \mathbb{N}. \mathsf{size}(x) = \kappa'n \Rightarrow \mathsf{finite}(x).$$

2. The greatest fixed point property of $\mathsf{infinite}$ takes care of the implication ($\Leftarrow$). For ($\Rightarrow$), assume $\mathsf{infinite}(x)$ and $\mathsf{size}(x) = \kappa'n$. The statement

$$\forall m \in \mathbb{N}. \Diamond(\{y \in X \mid \mathsf{infinite}(y) \wedge \text{ CASES } \mathsf{size}(y) \text{ OF}$$
$$\kappa* \mapsto \mathsf{false}$$
$$\kappa'v \mapsto n \geq v + m$$
$$\text{ENDCASES}\})(x)$$

can be proved by induction on m. But then we get a contradiction by taking $m = n + 1$. Hence $\mathsf{size}(x) = \kappa*$. $\square$

This concludes our brief tour of a μ-calculus in a coalgebraic setting. It also concludes our discussion of binary trees. We only mentioned a few operations that can be used for binary trees, leaving out many others. Typically, one also has operations for inserting and deleting labels, and for extracting (possibly infinite) sequences of labels, using for example pre-order, in-order, or post-order tree traversal. Insertion and deletion are usually defined for so-called *binary search trees* where all labels appear in an ordered fashion (assuming the set A of labels is totally ordered): labels in a left child are below the current label, which is below labels in the right child. Such properties typically appear as invariants. Here we did not include these additional operations in our discussion because our sole aim is to illustrate coalgebraic specification and verification techniques (especially using temporal and fixed point operators), and not to be in any sense complete[11].

Exercises

1. Prove that $\Box(P) = \mathsf{gfp}(\lambda Q. P \cap \mathsf{NextTime}(Q))$.

9   A Case Study: Peterson's Mutual Exclusion Algorithm

In this section we present a non-entirely-trivial application in coalgebraic specification and verification: Peterson's mutual exclusion algorithm. It provides a well-known mechanism for regulated access to what are called critical regions (or critical sections): often in computer science there are situations with two (or more) processes (running programs) which share certain resources, such as computing devices or data in memory (or in files or on disks). In such cases it is important that access is well-regulated, so that no corruption can take place. This issue is called the mutual exclusion problem. What one needs is some mechanism which grants access to a critical region only to one process at a time. This should be done in such a way that all requests for access will be granted at some stage, in a reasonably fair manner. This issue is often discussed at length in books on operating systems, like [43].

9.1   Peterson's Solution for Mutual Exclusion

A particularly nice and easy way to achieve mutual exclusion was developed by Peterson [32], see also [43, 2.2.3], [6, 7.2], [1, 6.5] or [27, 10.5.1]. The latter three references also contain correctness proofs: in [6] the algorithm is presented as a parallel composition of two automata, and its correctness is proved in temporal logic; in [1] the algorithm is described as a parallel composition of two programs, whose (safety only) correctness is established using (the Owicki-Gries extension

---

[11] Also, the way we have set up our binary trees is probably not optimal for storage, because, as is not hard to see, a finite binary tree will always have an odd size. Hence adding single elements is problematic.

of) Hoare logic; and in [28] state machines are used with a precondition-effect notation. Here we shall describe the algorithm in coalgebraic specification, making use of structuring techniques in object-oriented style. We shall return to this example in the next section on refinement.

A first, intuitive impression of Peterson's algorithm can be obtained from the automata theoretic description used in [6]. It consists of two essentially identical automata, put in parallel, see Figure 6. They both have a critical section, indicated by the locations ℓ_3 and m_3 with double circles. They share a variable t, which indicates whose turn it is (to proceed to the critical section), with true for automaton 1 on the left, false for automaton 2 on the right. Both automata can read and change the value of t. Reading is indicated by the question mark '?', and writing by the assignment symbol ':='. There are two additional variables y_i, for $i \in \{1, 2\}$, indicating whether automaton i is interested in becoming critical. Automaton i can read both y_1 and y_2, but change only y_i. Through a subtle interaction of these variables t, y_1, y_2 it is prevented that the automata are both in their critical sections (i.e. at ℓ_3 and m_3) at the same time.

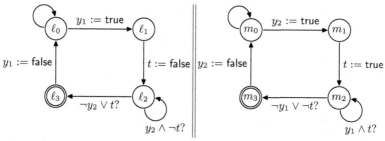

Fig. 6. Peterson's algorithm, described as composition of two parallel automata (from [6])

Of course, this statement needs a rigorous proof. First of all, such a proof requires a precise formalisation of the algorithm. As such, the automata theoretic description from Figure 6 is not ideal. For example, it is somehow implicit that transitions $\ell_1 \rightarrow \ell_2$ and $m_1 \rightarrow m_2$ cannot happen at the same time, because they involve an incompatible assignment to t. Also, in the transitions $\ell_2 \rightarrow \ell_3$, $m_2 \rightarrow m_3$ the turn variable t does not change. Such facts are crucial in verification[12]. Therefore we seek an alternative, purely assertional formalisation, in which all these points will be written explicitly. Necessarily, such a description will be much more verbose. It will be given as a coalgebraic specification below (in Figure 13). Before presenting it, we have to deal with some new aspects that are used in this specification.

---

[12] All these aspects can be made precise in an automata theoretic framework, by defining appropriate notions of behaviour and composition. But doing so is not our aim. The description in Figure 6 only serves as a first introduction.

9.2   Dealing with Time in Coalgebraic Specification

We shall briefly discuss a way of handling time in a coalgebraic setting, following [18]. We concentrate on discrete time, as this will be used in the specification of Peterson's algorithm. But continuous time will also be mentioned.

> **BEGIN** DiscreteTime
> **METHODS**
>   tick: $X \longrightarrow X$
> **END** DiscreteTime

Fig. 7. Discrete time

Discrete time can be modelled via a single operation tick: $X \to X$, see Figure 7. The idea is that every unit of time, this function is called. How this happens is not relevant, but one can think of it as resulting from the clock of a computer system. So for a state $x \in X$, the state after two units of time is tick(tick(x)). It is convenient to have suitable notation, like tick^n, for iteration, where:

$$\text{tick}^0(x) = x \qquad \text{and} \qquad \text{tick}^{n+1}(x) = \text{tick}(\text{tick}^n(x)).$$

> **BEGIN** Timer[$N : \mathbb{N}$]
>   **INHERIT FROM** DiscreteTime   // yields tick
>   **METHODS**
>   set: $X \longrightarrow X$
>   status: $X \longrightarrow \{\text{on}, \text{off}\}$
>   **ASSERTIONS**
>   off_remains: $\left[\forall x \in X. \forall n \in \mathbb{N}. \text{status}(x) = \text{off} \Rightarrow \text{status}(\text{tick}^n(x)) = \text{off} \right]$
>   off_happens: $\left[\forall x \in X. \forall n \in \mathbb{N}. n \geq N \Rightarrow \text{status}(\text{tick}^n(x)) = \text{off} \right]$
>   status_set: $\left[\forall x \in X. \forall n \in \mathbb{N}. n < N \Rightarrow \text{status}(\text{tick}^n(\text{set}(x))) = \text{on} \right]$
> **END** Timer

Fig. 8. A simple parametrised timer

Figure 8 presents a timer which can be set by the user, and then goes off "automatically" after N units of time (given as parameter). We have used **INHERIT FROM** to indicate that this specification also has a method tick: $X \to X$. The polynomial functor T underlying the Timer specification then contains the polynomial functor $\mathcal{DT}$ of the DiscreteTime specification as $\times$-component[13]:

$$T(X) = \mathcal{DT}(X) \times X \times \{\text{on}, \text{off}\} = X \times X \times \{\text{on}, \text{off}\}.$$

The assertion 'off_remains' tells that once the timer is off, it does not "spontaneously" become on by passage of time. This could be expressed via temporal operators—see below—but here we choose to write it explicitly via iteration. The next assertion 'off_happens' expresses that no matter in which state the timer is, it will be off after at least N units of time. Finally, the first N ticks after an invocation of set the timer will be on, as expressed by the third assertion 'status_set'.

This specification has many models. For example, one can take for X the set $[0, N] \subseteq \mathbb{N}$ with functions $\text{tick}, \text{set}: [0, N] \to [0, N]$ and $\text{status}: [0, N] \to \{\text{on}, \text{off}\}$ given on $x \in [0, N]$ as:

$$\text{tick}(x) = \begin{cases} 0 & \text{if } x = 0 \\ x - 1 & \text{otherwise} \end{cases} \quad \text{set}(x) = N \quad \text{status}(x) = \begin{cases} \text{off if } x = 0 \\ \text{on otherwise} \end{cases}$$

A state $x \in [0, N]$ thus represents the number of time units until the timer's status will be off.

The tick function in the specification of discrete time describes the passage to a next state through the passage of time. It can thus be used to described so-called primed versions of attributes: for a method (or attribute) $a: X \to A$, one sometimes sees in the computer science literature the notation $a': X \to A$ for "the attribute a evaluated in the next state". Thus we can understand a' as $a \circ \text{tick}$. In such a way one can translate specifications in the Temporal Logic of Actions (TLA), see [25,26], into coalgebraic specifications. Actions in TLA are predicates, which become methods $X \to \text{bool}$. They describe the preconditions and postconditions in a single conjunction, such as: $(a(x) > 0) \wedge (a'(x) = a(x) - 1)$. The temporal logic of TLA is linear temporal logic, and its $\square$ and $\lozenge$ operators are the ones that are associated with the DiscreteTime specification from Figure 7 (following Section 7):

$$\begin{aligned} \square(P)(x) &\iff \forall n \in \mathbb{N}. P(\text{tick}^n(x)) \\ \lozenge(P)(x) &\iff \exists n \in \mathbb{N}. P(\text{tick}^n(x)). \end{aligned} \quad (6)$$

because $\{y \in X \mid \forall n \in \mathbb{N}. P(\text{tick}^n(y))\}$ is the greatest DiscreteTime-invariant contained in P.

Notice that iteration yields a function $\text{ticks}: X \times \mathbb{N} \to X$, namely $\text{ticks}(x, n) = \text{tick}^n(x)$. This forms an *action* for the natural number monoid $(\mathbb{N}, +, 0)$, since

$$\text{ticks}(x, 0) = x \quad \text{and} \quad \text{ticks}(x, n + m) = \text{ticks}(\text{ticks}(x, m), n).$$

This action aspect is taken as fundamental in handling continuous time, see Figure 9. There we have an action flow: $X \times \mathbb{R}_{\geq 0} \to X$ with respect to the monoid

---

[13] And not as +-component, like in algebraic specification, see the functor for the vector space example (2).

BEGIN ContinuousTime
  METHODS
    flow: $X \times \mathbb{R}_{\geq 0} \longrightarrow X$ // $\mathbb{R}_{\geq 0} = \{s \in \mathbb{R} \mid s \geq 0\}$
  ASSERTIONS
    flow_zero: $\left[\; \forall x \in X. \, \mathsf{flow}(x, 0) = x \; \right]$
    flow_plus: $\left[\; \forall x \in X. \, \forall s, t \in \mathbb{R}_{\geq 0}. \, \mathsf{flow}(x, s + t) = \mathsf{flow}(\mathsf{flow}(x, t), s) \; \right]$
END ContinuousTime

Fig. 9. Continuous time

$(\mathbb{R}_{\geq 0}, +, 0)$ of non-negative real numbers. Such flows are fundamental in system theory (see *e.g.* [24]) and are also known as motions, trajectories or solutions. Indeed, unique solutions to differential equations give such flows, see *e.g.* [11, 8.7]. The temporal operators associated with the ContinuousTime specification of Figure 9 are:

$$\square(P)(x) \Longleftrightarrow \forall s \in \mathbb{R}_{\geq 0}. \, P(\mathsf{flow}(x, s))$$
$$\lozenge(P)(x) \Longleftrightarrow \exists s \in \mathbb{R}_{\geq 0}. \, P(\mathsf{flow}(x, s)).$$

since the predicate $\{y \in X \mid \forall s \in \mathbb{R}_{\geq 0}. \, P(\mathsf{flow}(y, s))\}$ is the greatest Continuous-Time-invariant contained in P. We shall not use these flows in this chapter. For more information, see [18].

9.3 Class-Valued Methods

So far we have seen methods that return a value, like size $\to 1 + \mathbb{N}$ or label: $X \to A$ in Figure 3. Such methods simply describe functions. The question arises whether one can also have "class-valued" methods such as tree: $X \to$ BinaryTreeSpace[$\mathbb{N}$] in coalgebraic specifications, yielding values in classes (also called objects). For each state $x \in X$, tree(x) should then be a binary tree with natural numbers as labels. Such methods are convenient because they allow us to incrementally build structured specifications from smaller components (*i.e.* classes).

    The question is: what kind of functions are such class-valued methods like tree? They should return elements of a model[14] of the tree specification. But which model? We have seen several models in Section 4, but there seems to be no canonical choice. Actually there is a canonical choice here, namely the so-called *terminal* (or *final*) model. It is defined as the model F such that for an arbitrary model M there is a unique homomorphism $M \to F$, see [21] or Chapter 3 for more information. Terminality is useful when casting is required, *i.e.* when elements of classes which inherit from a class C must be regarded as elements of C. This can be done via the unique homomorphism just mentioned, see [13]. But this is beyond scope.

---

[14] Even this condition can be relaxed: one can just require elements of the state space of a coalgebra providing the binary tree space methods, without requiring that the coalgebra also satisfies the assertions. In such a way one can model "casting with late binding". But that is beyond the scope of the present chapter.

For many purposes, it really does not matter which model is used for class-valued attributes. In such a situation one can use an arbitrary model—assuming there is one[15]. Since the chosen model is arbitrary, there is nothing specific that can be used about it. This is called *loose* semantics. It is what we shall use below.

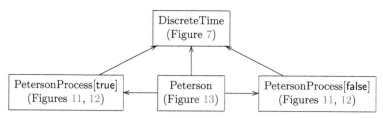

Fig. 10. The structure between specifications in Peterson's algorithm

9.4   Peterson's Algorithm in Coalgebraic Specification

We can finally describe Peterson's mutual exclusion algorithm in coalgebraic specification. The specification as a whole will be built up from smaller specifications, see Figure 10. The central specification is called Peterson. The arrows going upwards point to superclasses (using inheritance), the horizontal ones to component classes (via class-valued methods). The PetersonProcess is parametrised by the set bool = {false, true}, so that the two versions (like in Figure 6) can be described together.

We shall explain the main specifications PetersonProcess (Figures 11, 12) and Peterson (Figure 13) in some more detail. Basically, it follows the automata-theoretic description from Figure 6. In the PetersonProcess specification the real work is done. There are Boolean-valued attributes critical, for describing whether this process is in its critical section, own_interest, telling whether this process is interested in becoming critical (corresponding to y_1 or y_2 in Figure 6), other_interest, telling whether the other process is interested (corresponding to y_2 or y_1), turn, describing whose turn it is (like t does in Figure 6), and pre_critical, indicating whether this process is in the waiting state before becoming critical (corresponding to locations ℓ_2 and m_2 in Figure 6). Finally, there is a method interest which can be used to indicate that a process is interested in becoming critical, as expressed by the assertion 'interest' in Figure 11. The other assertions tell how the system changes under the influence of time: they describe the effect of the tick method under various circumstances. These assertions precisely describe the behaviour, by listing the values of various attributes before and after a tick. One can notice that nothing is stated about the other_interest attribute after a tick, since this attribute is not under the control of this process and can be changed at any time by the other process. The turn attribute is under control of both processes. Hence

---

[15] It is good practice to construct a model after introducing a new specification.

BEGIN PetersonProcess[ident: bool]   // where bool = {false, true}
  INHERIT FROM DiscreteTime   // see Figure 7
  METHODS
    critical: $X \longrightarrow$ bool
    own_interest: $X \longrightarrow$ bool
    other_interest: $X \longrightarrow$ bool   // describes interest of other process
    turn: $X \longrightarrow$ bool   // will be shared
    pre_critical: $X \longrightarrow$ bool   // describes waiting state
    interest: $X \longrightarrow X$ // enables a user to indicate interest
                       // to proceed to critical section
  ASSERTIONS

$$\text{interest:} \left[\begin{array}{l} \text{own\_interest(interest}(x)) \wedge \text{turn(interest}(x)) = \text{turn}(x) \wedge \\ \text{other\_interest(interest}(x)) = \text{other\_interest}(x) \wedge \\ \neg\text{pre\_critical(interest}(x)) \wedge \neg\text{critical(interest}(x)) \end{array} \right]$$

$$\text{remain\_not\_interested:} \left[\begin{array}{l} \neg\text{own\_interest}(x) \Rightarrow \Big(\neg\text{own\_interest(tick}(x)) \wedge \\ \neg\text{critical(tick}(x)) \wedge \neg\text{pre\_critical(tick}(x)) \Big) \end{array} \right]$$

$$\text{become\_pre\_critical:} \left[\begin{array}{l} \Big(\text{own\_interest}(x) \wedge \neg\text{pre\_critical}(x) \wedge \neg\text{critical}(x) \Big) \\ \Rightarrow \Big(\text{own\_interest(tick}(x)) \wedge \text{pre\_critical(tick}(x)) \wedge \\ \neg\text{critical(tick}(x)) \wedge \\ \text{// turn cannot remain ident:} \\ (\text{turn}(x) = \text{ident} \Rightarrow \text{turn(tick}(x)) \neq \text{ident}) \Big) \end{array} \right]$$

$$\text{remain\_pre\_critical:} \left[\begin{array}{l} \Big(\text{own\_interest}(x) \wedge \text{pre\_critical}(x) \wedge \neg\text{critical}(x) \wedge \\ \text{other\_interest}(x) \wedge \text{turn}(x) \neq \text{ident} \Big) \\ \Rightarrow \Big(\text{own\_interest(tick}(x)) \wedge \text{pre\_critical(tick}(x)) \wedge \\ \neg\text{critical(tick}(x)) \Big) \end{array} \right]$$

        $\cdots$ // see Figure 12
END PetersonProcess

Fig. 11. Specification of a (parametrised) Peterson process, part I

changes to turn must be expressed in a careful manner, to avoid clashes (leading to inconsistencies) with possible changes by the other process, see assertions 'become_pre_critical', 'become_critical' and 'critical_remains_or_stops' where restrictions occur which do not block changes by the other process. Notice how the assertion 'become_pre_critical' can be used for both processes at the same time—corresponding to transitions $\ell_1 \rightarrow \ell_2$, $m_1 \rightarrow m_2$ in Figure 6—but that only one "assignment" to turn can take place. The final assertion 'critical_stops' uses the eventually operator $\Diamond$(super). It refers to $\Diamond$ for the superclass DiscreteTime, which can be expressed in terms of iteration, see the equivalences (6). It thus says that the critical section will be left, after an unspecified amount of time. This is needed for fairness: if processes do not leave their critical sections, their competitors will never get access.

BEGIN PetersonProcess[ident: bool]
$\qquad$ $\cdots$ // see Figure 11
$\quad$ **ASSERTIONS**
$\qquad$ $\cdots$ // see Figure 11
$\quad$ become_critical: $\Big[$ $\Big($ own_interest(x) $\wedge$ pre_critical(x) $\wedge$ $\neg$critical(x) $\wedge$
$\qquad\qquad\qquad$ $(\neg$other_interest(x) $\vee$ turn(x) = ident$)$
$\qquad\qquad$ $\Rightarrow$ $\Big($ own_interest(tick(x)) $\wedge$ $\neg$pre_critical(tick(x)) $\wedge$
$\qquad\qquad\qquad$ critical(tick(x)) $\wedge$
$\qquad\qquad\qquad$ // turn cannot change to $\neg$ident:
$\qquad\qquad\qquad$ (turn(x) = ident $\Rightarrow$ turn(tick(x)) = ident$)\Big)$ $\Big]$
$\quad$ critical_remains_or_stops: $\Big[$ $\Big($own_interest(x) $\wedge$ $\neg$pre_critical(x) $\wedge$ critical$(x)\Big)$
$\qquad\qquad$ $\Rightarrow$ $\Big($ $\neg$pre_critical(tick(x)) $\wedge$
$\qquad\qquad\qquad$ (// either remain critical
$\qquad\qquad\qquad$ (own_interest(tick(x)) $\wedge$ critical(tick(x)) $\wedge$
$\qquad\qquad\qquad\quad$ (turn(x) = ident $\Rightarrow$ turn(tick(x)) = ident))
$\qquad\qquad\qquad$ $\vee$ $\quad$ // or stop being critical
$\qquad\qquad\qquad$ ($\neg$own_interest(tick(x)) $\wedge$ $\neg$critical(tick(x)))))$\Big)$ $\Big]$
$\quad$ critical_stops: $\Big[$ critical(x) $\Rightarrow$
$\qquad\qquad$ $\Big($ $\Diamond$(super)($\{y \in X \mid \neg$critical(y) $\wedge$ $\neg$pre_critical(y) $\wedge$
$\qquad\qquad\qquad\qquad$ $\neg$own_interest$(y)\})(x)\Big)$ $\Big]$
END PetersonProcess

Fig. 12. Specification of a (parametrised) Peterson process, part II

We turn to the central specification Peterson in Figure 13. It has two attributes for the two processes, and two methods for indicating interest of these processes[16]. The assertions establish appropriate connections between the two processes ('share_turn' and 'exchange_interest'), and also between the methods tick, interestT, interestF of the Peterson specification and corresponding methods of the processes. Notice that we do not write a requirement ppF(interestT(x)) $\leftrightarrow$ ppF(x), because it is too strong: interestT sets own_interest of ppT to true, and thereby other_interest of ppF to false. Hence it does have an effect on ppF.

---

[16] Actually, using some more expressive language of types, one could combine methods ppF, ppT into pp: $X \rightarrow \prod_{b \in \text{bool}}$ PetersonProcess[b] and interestT, interestF into interest: $X \rightarrow X^{\text{bool}}$.

BEGIN Peterson
  INHERIT FROM DiscreteTime   // see Figure 7
  METHODS
    ppT: $X \longrightarrow$ PetersonProcess[true]
    ppF: $X \longrightarrow$ PetersonProcess[false]
    interestT: $X \longrightarrow X$
    interestF: $X \longrightarrow X$
  ASSERTIONS
    share_turn: $\Big[\ \mathsf{turn}(\mathsf{ppT}(x)) = \mathsf{turn}(\mathsf{ppF}(x))\ \Big]$

    exchange_interest: $\Big[\ \mathsf{own\_interest}(\mathsf{ppT}(x)) = \mathsf{other\_interest}(\mathsf{ppF}(x)) \wedge$
                $\mathsf{other\_interest}(\mathsf{ppT}(x)) = \mathsf{own\_interest}(\mathsf{ppF}(x))\ \Big]$

    interestT: $\Big[\ \mathsf{ppT}(\mathsf{interestT}(x)) \leftrightarrows \mathsf{interest}(\mathsf{ppT}(x)) \wedge$
        $\mathsf{own\_interest}(\mathsf{ppF}(\mathsf{interestT}(x))) = \mathsf{own\_interest}(\mathsf{ppF}(x)) \wedge$
        $\mathsf{pre\_critical}(\mathsf{ppF}(\mathsf{interestT}(x))) = \mathsf{pre\_critical}(\mathsf{ppF}(x)) \wedge$
        $\mathsf{critical}(\mathsf{ppF}(\mathsf{interestT}(x))) = \mathsf{critical}(\mathsf{ppF}(x))\ \Big]$

    interestF: $\Big[\ \mathsf{ppF}(\mathsf{interestF}(x)) \leftrightarrows \mathsf{interest}(\mathsf{ppF}(x)) \wedge$
        $\mathsf{own\_interest}(\mathsf{ppT}(\mathsf{interestF}(x))) = \mathsf{own\_interest}(\mathsf{ppT}(x)) \wedge$
        $\mathsf{pre\_critical}(\mathsf{ppT}(\mathsf{interestF}(x))) = \mathsf{pre\_critical}(\mathsf{ppT}(x)) \wedge$
        $\mathsf{critical}(\mathsf{ppT}(\mathsf{interestF}(x))) = \mathsf{critical}(\mathsf{ppT}(x))\ \Big]$

    synchronise: $\Big[\ \mathsf{ppT}(\mathsf{tick}(x)) \leftrightarrows \mathsf{tick}(\mathsf{ppT}(x)) \wedge$
              $\mathsf{ppF}(\mathsf{tick}(x)) \leftrightarrows \mathsf{tick}(\mathsf{ppF}(x))\ \Big]$
  CONSTRUCTORS
    new: X
  CREATION
    init: $\Big[\ \neg\mathsf{own\_interest}(\mathsf{ppT}(\mathsf{new}) \wedge \neg\mathsf{pre\_critical}(\mathsf{ppT}(\mathsf{new}) \wedge \neg\mathsf{critical}(\mathsf{ppT}(\mathsf{new}) \wedge$
          $\neg\mathsf{own\_interest}(\mathsf{ppF}(\mathsf{new}) \wedge \neg\mathsf{pre\_critical}(\mathsf{ppF}(\mathsf{new}) \wedge \neg\mathsf{critical}(\mathsf{ppF}(\mathsf{new})\ \Big]$
END Peterson

Fig. 13. Specification of Peterson's algorithm

Next we come to correctness, expressed in Theorem 12 below. In our reasoning about the Peterson specification we use the next five predicates: for $x \in X$,

critical_exclusionT(x)
   $= \big(\ \mathsf{critical}(\mathsf{ppT}(x)) \Rightarrow \mathsf{own\_interest}(\mathsf{ppT}(x)) \wedge \neg\mathsf{pre\_critical}(\mathsf{ppT}(x))\ \big)$
critical_exclusionF(x)
   $= \big(\ \mathsf{critical}(\mathsf{ppF}(x)) \Rightarrow \mathsf{own\_interest}(\mathsf{ppF}(x)) \wedge \neg\mathsf{pre\_critical}(\mathsf{ppF}(x))\ \big)$
critical_turnT(x)
   $= \big(\ \mathsf{critical}(\mathsf{ppT}(x)) \wedge \mathsf{pre\_critical}(\mathsf{ppF}(x)) \Rightarrow \mathsf{turn}(\mathsf{ppT}(x))\ \big)$
critical_turnF(x)
   $= \big(\ \mathsf{critical}(\mathsf{ppF}(x)) \wedge \mathsf{pre\_critical}(\mathsf{ppT}(x)) \Rightarrow \neg\mathsf{turn}(\mathsf{ppF}(x))\ \big)$
critical_exclusion(x)
   $= \big(\ $critical_exclusionT$(x) \wedge$ critical_exclusionF$(x) \wedge$
      critical_turnT$(x) \wedge$ critical_turnF$(x) \wedge$
      $\neg(\mathsf{critical}(\mathsf{ppT}(x)) \wedge \mathsf{critical}(\mathsf{ppF}(x)))\ \big).$

Lemma 11. *The following five predicates are invariants for the* Peterson *class specification in Figure 13.*

$$critical\_exclusion\,T, \quad critical\_exclusion F,$$
$$critical\_exclusion\,T \wedge critical\_exclusion F \wedge critical\_turn\,T,$$
$$critical\_exclusion\,T \wedge critical\_exclusion F \wedge critical\_turn F,$$
$$critical\_exclusion.$$

Below we shall only use the last invariant critical_exclusion, but the others are convenient as intermediate steps.

Proof. According to Definition 3 we have to prove for each of the above predicates, say denoted by $Q \subseteq X$, that for all $x \in X$,

$$Q(x) \Longrightarrow \begin{cases} Q(\mathsf{tick}(x)) \\ Q(\mathsf{interest}\mathsf{T}(x)) \\ Q(\mathsf{interest}\mathsf{F}(x)) \end{cases}$$

This is not hard, but a lot of work, because of the many case distinctions that have to be made. Hence a proof tool is useful. □

Theorem 12. *The specification of Peterson's algorithm in Figure 13 satisfies the following two safety and progress properties.*

1. *Mutual exclusion holds in all reachable states:*

$$\Box(\{y \in X \mid \neg(critical(pp\,T(y)) \wedge critical(ppF(y)))\})(new)$$

2. *For both processes, requests to proceed to their critical section will eventually be granted: for all $x \in X$,*

$$\Diamond(\{y \in X \mid critical(pp\,T(y))\})(interest\,T(x))$$
$$\Diamond(\{y \in X \mid critical(ppF(y))\})(interestF(x)).$$

Proof.

1. According to the definition of $\Box$, we have to produce an invariant Q with $Q(y) \Rightarrow \neg(critical(ppT(y)) \wedge critical(ppF(y)))$ and $Q(new)$. We take $Q = critical\_exclusion$ from Lemma 11.
2. The two statements are proved in the same way, so we concentrate on the first one. The following intermediate statement is convenient: for all $x \in X$,

$$\big(\,\mathsf{own\_interest}(ppT(x)) \wedge \mathsf{pre\_critical}(ppT(x)) \wedge \neg critical(ppT(x)) \wedge$$
$$\exists n \in \mathbb{N}.\,\neg\mathsf{own\_interest}(\mathsf{tick}^n(ppF(x))) \vee turn(\mathsf{tick}^n(ppF(x)))\,\big)$$
$$\Longrightarrow$$
$$\exists n \in \mathbb{N}.\,critical(ppT(\mathsf{tick}^n(x)))$$

The proof of this statement proceeds by considering the least n such that $\neg\mathsf{own\_interest}(\mathsf{tick}^n(ppF(x))) \vee turn(\mathsf{tick}^n(ppF(x)))$. For all $m \leq n$, one can show that after m ticks own_interest, pre_critial and $\neg$critical hold for ppT. Hence the assertion 'become_critical' does the job after n ticks. □

10   Refinements between Coalgebraic Specifications

A refinement is a general construction to turn a model of one specification (usually called the concrete one) into a model of another specification (called the abstract specification in this context), using (essentially[17]) the same set of states. Typically, the concrete specification has more structure, and describes a particular way to realise the structure of the abstract specification in terms of its own concrete structure. In computer science a refinement usually adds certain implementation details, reducing the level of underspecification (sometimes called non-determinism), and possibly increasing the use of concurrency.

Constructions to turn a model of one specification into a model of another specification are well-known in mathematics. Typically, one can turn a pointed topological space into its "fundamental" or "Poincaré" group by using as elements homotopy classes of paths with the base point as beginning and end. Also, one can construct the integers from the natural numbers (via a quotient of $\mathbb{N} \times \mathbb{N}$), but in both these cases the state space changes in an essential way. An actual (but trivial) refinement is the construction of a topological space out of a metric space.

In this section we define refinements between coalgebraic specifications, basically as in [16]. Further, we present an abstract Peterson specification, and show how the specification from the previous section forms a refinement.

We now assume two coalgebraic specifications: $\mathcal{A}$ for abstract, and $\mathcal{C}$ for concrete. Let $\mathcal{IA}$ and $\mathcal{IC}$ be the associated polynomial functors capturing the interface of methods. For didactic reasons we first define a "simple refinement" (of $\mathcal{A}$ by $\mathcal{C}$), and postpone the general definition. We assume that both specifications have precisely one initial state[18], written as new. For a coalgebra $c \colon X \to \mathcal{IA}(X)$, we have predicates

$$\mathcal{A}\text{-Assert}(c) \subseteq X \qquad \text{and} \qquad \mathcal{A}\text{-Create}(c) \subseteq X$$

combining all assertions and creation conditions. Similarly for $\mathcal{C}$. How these predicates are obtained can best be seen in Figures 11 and 12 where we have not written quantifiers $\forall x \in X. \cdots$ in assertions. The induced predicate Peterson-Process-Assert(x) is then obtained as conjunction of all seven assertions. The predicate PetersonProcess-Create is obtained by viewing new as a parameter in the creation condition init.

A *simple refinement* of $\mathcal{A}$ by $\mathcal{C}$ consists of a construction which turns an arbitrary model of $\mathcal{C}$, consisting of a coalgebra $c \colon X \to \mathcal{IC}(X)$ and initial state new $\in X$ with $\forall x \in X. \mathcal{C}\text{-Assert}(c)(x)$ and $\mathcal{C}\text{-Create}(c)(\text{new})$, into a model of $\mathcal{A}$, consisting of a coalgebra $c' \colon X \to \mathcal{IA}(X)$ on the same state space, constructed out of c, and an initial state new$'$ $\in X$ constructed out of c and new, in such a way that $\forall x \in X. \mathcal{A}\text{-Assert}(c')(x)$ and $\mathcal{A}\text{-Create}(c')(\text{new}')$.

---

[17] We shall see later what 'essentially' means: a subset of the set of states forming an invariant is also allowed.

[18] And not a parametrised collection of initial states. The definition of refinement can easily be extended to include them as well.

A simple refinement between coalgebraic specifications thus consists of two things (as in TLA [25,26]): a "refinement mapping"

$$(c\colon X \to \mathcal{IC}(X), \mathsf{new} \in X) \longmapsto (c'\colon X \to \mathcal{IA}(X), \mathsf{new}' \in X) \qquad (7)$$

together with an implication

$$\begin{aligned} &\mathcal{C}\text{-Create}(c)(\mathsf{new}) \wedge \forall x \in X.\, \mathcal{C}\text{-Assert}(c)(x) \\ &\Longrightarrow \\ &\mathcal{A}\text{-Create}(c')(\mathsf{new}') \wedge \forall x \in X.\, \mathcal{A}\text{-Assert}(c')(x). \end{aligned} \qquad (8)$$

The definition of refinement says that a concrete model can be turned into an abstract model, in a straightforward way. In practice it usually does not work like this, because the requirement $\forall x \in X.\, \mathcal{A}\text{-Assert}(c')(x)$ cannot be proved for all $x \in X$. Then we often need to restrict the state space X to some subset $P \subseteq X$ for which we can prove $\forall x \in X.\, P(x) \Rightarrow \mathcal{A}\text{-Assert}(c')(x)$. This is good enough if we can additionally prove that P is an invariant (with respect to the constructed coalgebra c'), and that P holds for the constructed initial state new'. Then we know that all states we can reach from new' using c' remain within P. Thus, for a (non-simple) *refinement* the above implication changes into:

$$\begin{aligned} &\mathcal{C}\text{-Create}(c)(\mathsf{new}) \wedge \forall x \in X.\, \mathcal{C}\text{-Assert}(c)(x) \\ &\Longrightarrow \\ &\mathcal{A}\text{-Create}(c')(\mathsf{new}') \wedge \Box(c')(\mathcal{A}\text{-Assert}(c'))(\mathsf{new}'). \end{aligned} \qquad (9)$$

See the definition of $\Box$ in (4).

We turn to an example of a refinement with such an implication.

Proposition 13. *Consider the MutualExclusion specification in Figure 14 describing the essentials of mutual exclusion. The Peterson specification from Figure 13 is a refinement of MutualExclusion.*

Proof. We will construct a refinement mapping as in (7) with an implication (9). Therefore we assume a coalgebra $c = (\mathsf{tick}, \mathsf{ppT}, \mathsf{ppF}, \mathsf{interestT}, \mathsf{interestF})$ and initial state new for the Peterson specification. We get a new coalgebra $c' = (\mathsf{tick}, \mathsf{criticalT}, \mathsf{criticalF}, \mathsf{interestT}, \mathsf{interestF})$ for the MutualExclusion specification by defining $\mathsf{criticalT}(x) = \mathsf{critical}(\mathsf{ppT}(x))$ and $\mathsf{criticalF}(x) = \mathsf{critical}(\mathsf{ppF}(x))$. As new initial state new' we simply take new from Peterson. Then clearly, the (abstract) creation conditions from MutualExclusion hold for new. Further, the predicate critical_exclusion from Lemma 11 is an invariant for c' (since it already is one for c) and implies the abstract assertions, see Theorem 12, and the proof of its first point. $\qquad\Box$

Refinement is a fundamental technique to establish the correctness of larger software (and also hardware) systems: the idea is to first concentrate on an abstract specification of the system—describing the essentials of the required behaviour, without going into any realisation issues—and refine this abstract specification, possibly in several steps, into a concrete specification, coming close to an actual implementation.

BEGIN MutualExclusion
   INHERIT FROM DiscreteTime   // see Figure 7
   METHODS
      criticalT: $X \longrightarrow$ bool
      criticalF: $X \longrightarrow$ bool
      interestT: $X \longrightarrow X$
      interestF: $X \longrightarrow X$
   ASSERTIONS
      exclusion: $\left[\; \neg(\text{criticalT}(x) \wedge \text{criticalF}(x)) \; \right]$
      progressT: $\left[\; \Diamond(\text{super})(\{y \in X \mid \text{criticalT}(y)\})(\text{interestT}(x)) \; \right]$
      progressF: $\left[\; \Diamond(\text{super})(\{y \in X \mid \text{criticalF}(y)\})(\text{interestF}(x)) \; \right]$
      critical_interest: $\left[\begin{array}{l} \neg\text{criticalT}(\text{interestT}(x)) \wedge \\ \text{criticalF}(\text{interestT}(x)) = \text{criticalF}(x) \wedge \\ \text{criticalT}(\text{interestF}(x)) = \text{criticalT}(x) \wedge \\ \neg\text{criticalF}(\text{interestF}(x)) \end{array} \right]$
   CONSTRUCTORS
      new: X
   CREATION
      init: $\left[\; \neg\text{criticalT}(\text{new}) \wedge \neg\text{criticalF}(\text{new}) \; \right]$
END MutualExclusion

Fig. 14. Specification of mutual exclusion

11   Conclusion

We have introduced the subject of specification and verification for coalgebras via several examples, for which we have proved non-trivial results. The area is still under development, but has already reached a certain level of maturity, with its own theory and logic. For further background reading we refer to [21,40,7]. An impression of current research topics in coalgebra can be obtained from the volumes [19,22,37,4] and [20].

Acknowledgements

Thanks are due to the members of the LOOP group at Nijmegen and Dresden (Joachim van den Berg, Marieke Huisman, Erik Poll, Ulrich Hensel and Hendrik Tews) for discussions and collaboration on the development of the LOOP compiler, and also for feedback on a draft version of this chapter. Thanks also to Angelika Mader for discussions on temporal logic and the μ-calculus.

References

1. K. R. Apt and E.-R. Olderog. *Verification of Sequential and Concurrent Programs.* Springer, 2nd revised edition, 1997. 265
2. E. Astesiano, H.-J. Kreowski, and B. Krieg-Brückner, editors. *Algebraic Foundations of Systems Specification.* IFIP State-of-the-Art Reports. Springer, 1999. 242
3. C. Cîrstea. Coalgebra semantics for hidden algebra: parametrised objects and inheritance. In F. Parisi Presicce, editor, *Recent Trends in Data Type Specification*, number 1376 in Lecture Notes in Computer Science, pages 174–189. Springer, Berlin, 1998. 237
4. A. Corradini, M. Lenisa, and U. Montanari, editors. *Coalgebraic Methods in Computer Science (CMCS'01)*, number 44 in Electronic Notes in Theoretical Computer Science. Elsevier, Amsterdam, 2001.
   www.elsevier.nl/locate/entcs/volume44.html. 277
5. B. A. Davey and H. A. Priestley. *Introduction to Lattices and Order.* Math. Textbooks. Cambridge Univ. Press, 1990. 244
6. E. A. Emerson. Temporal and modal logic. In J. van Leeuwen, editor, *Handbook of Theoretical Computer Science*, volume B, pages 995–1072. Elsevier/MIT Press, 1990. 265, 266
7. H. P. Gumm. Elements of the general theory of coalgebras. Notes of lectures given at LUATCS'99: Logic, Universal Algebra, Theoretical Computer Science, Johannesburg. Available as
   www.mathematik.uni-marburg.de/~gumm/Papers/Luatcs.ps, 1999. 277
8. U. Hensel. *Definition and Proof Principles for Data and Processes.* PhD thesis, Techn. Univ. Dresden, Germany, 1999. 237
9. U. Hensel, M. Huisman, B. Jacobs, and H. Tews. Reasoning about classes in object-oriented languages: Logical models and tools. In C. Hankin, editor, *European Symposium on Programming*, number 1381 in Lecture Notes in Computer Science, pages 105–121. Springer, Berlin, 1998. 237, 238, 255
10. C. Hermida and B. Jacobs. Structural induction and coinduction in a fibrational setting. *Information & Computation*, 145:107–152, 1998. 238, 255
11. M. W. Hirsch and S. Smale. *Differential Equations, Dynamical Systems, and Linear Algebra.* Academic Press, New York, 1974. 269
12. B. Jacobs. Mongruences and cofree coalgebras. In V. S. Alagar and M. Nivat, editors, *Algebraic Methodology and Software Technology*, number 936 in Lecture Notes in Computer Science, pages 245–260. Springer, Berlin, 1995. 237
13. B. Jacobs. Inheritance and cofree constructions. In P. Cointe, editor, *European Conference on Object-Oriented Programming*, number 1098 in Lecture Notes in Computer Science, pages 210–231. Springer, Berlin, 1996. 237, 269
14. B. Jacobs. Objects and classes, co-algebraically. In B. Freitag, C. B. Jones, C. Lengauer, and H.-J. Schek, editors, *Object-Orientation with Parallelism and Persistence*, pages 83–103. Kluwer Acad. Publ., 1996. 237
15. B. Jacobs. Behaviour-refinement of coalgebraic specifications with coinductive correctness proofs. In M. Bidoit and M. Dauchet, editors, *TAPSOFT'97: Theory and Practice of Software Development*, number 1214 in Lecture Notes in Computer Science, pages 787–802. Springer, Berlin, 1997. 237
16. B. Jacobs. Invariants, bisimulations and the correctness of coalgebraic refinements. In M. Johnson, editor, *Algebraic Methodology and Software Technology*, number 1349 in Lecture Notes in Computer Science, pages 276–291. Springer, Berlin, 1997. 237, 275

17. B. Jacobs. The temporal logic of coalgebras via Galois algebras. Techn. Rep. CSI-R9906, Computer Science Institute, University of Nijmegen. To appear in *Mathematical Structures in Computer Science*, 1999. 238

18. B. Jacobs. Object-oriented hybrid systems of coalgebras plus monoid actions. *Theoretical Computer Science*, 239:41–95, 2000. 267, 269

19. B. Jacobs, L. Moss, H. Reichel, and J. Rutten, editors. *Coalgebraic Methods in Computer Science (CMCS'98)*, number 11 in Electronic Notes in Theoretical Computer Science. Elsevier, Amsterdam, 1998.
    www.elsevier.nl/locate/entcs/volume11.html. 277

20. B. Jacobs, L. Moss, H. Reichel, and J. Rutten, editors. *Coalgebraic Methods in Computer Science*, volume 260(1/2) of *Theor. Comp. Sci.*, 2001. Special issue on CMCS'98. 277

21. B. Jacobs and J. Rutten. A tutorial on (co)algebras and (co)induction. *EATCS Bulletin*, 62:222–259, 1997. 237, 240, 252, 269, 277

22. B. Jacobs and J. Rutten, editors. *Coalgebraic Methods in Computer Science (CMCS'99)*, number 19 in Electronic Notes in Theoretical Computer Science. Elsevier, Amsterdam, 1999.
    www.elsevier.nl/locate/entcs/volume19.html. 277

23. B. Jacobs, J. van den Berg, M. Huisman, M. van Berkum, U. Hensel, and H. Tews. Reasoning about classes in Java (preliminary report). In *Object-Oriented Programming, Systems, Languages and Applications (OOPSLA)*, pages 329–340. ACM Press, 1998. 237

24. R. E. Kalman, P. L. Falb, and M. A. Arbib. *Topics in Mathematical System Theory*. McGraw-Hill Int. Series in Pure & Appl. Math., 1969. 269

25. L. Lamport. The temporal logic of actions. *ACM Trans. on Progr. Lang. and Systems*, 16(3):872–923, 1994. 268, 276

26. L. Lamport. Specifying concurrent systems with TLA$^+$. In M. Broy and R. Steinbrüggen, editors, *Calculational System Design*, number 173 in Series F: Computer and Systems Sciences, pages 183–247. IOS Press, Amsterdam, 1999. 238, 268, 276

27. N. Lynch. Simulation techniques for proving properties of real-time systems. In J. W. de Bakker, W. P. de Roever, and G. Rozenberg, editors, *A Decade of Concurrency*, number 803 in Lecture Notes in Computer Science, pages 375–424. Springer, Berlin, 1994. 265

28. N. Lynch. *Distributed Algorithms*. Morgan Kaufmann, 1996. 266

29. Z. Manna and A. Pnueli. *The Temporal Logic of Reactive and Concurrent Systems*. Springer-Verlag, Berlin, 1992. 255

30. L. S. Moss. Coalgebraic logic. *Annals of Pure & Applied Logic*, 96(1-3):277–317, 1999. *Erratum* in *Annals of Pure & Applied Logic*, 99(1-3):241–259, 1999. 238

31. S. Owre, J. M. Rushby, N. Shankar, and F. von Henke. Formal verification for fault-tolerant architectures: Prolegomena to the design of PVS. *IEEE Transactions on Software Engineering*, 21(2):107–125, 1995. 238

32. G. L. Peterson. Myths about the mutual exclusion problem. *Information Processing Letters*, 12(3):115–116, 1981. 265

33. G. Plotkin and M. Abadi. A logic for parametric polymorphism. In M. Bezem and J. F. Groote, editors, *Typed Lambda Calculi and Applications*, number 664 in Lecture Notes in Computer Science, pages 361–375. Springer, Berlin, 1993. 238, 255

34. A. Pnueli. The temporal semantics of concurrent programs. *Theor. Comp. Sci.*, 31:45–60, 1981. 255

35. E. Poll and J. Zwanenburg. A logic for abstract data types as existential types. In J.-Y. Girard, editor, *Typed Lambda Calculus and Applications*, number 1581 in Lecture Notes in Computer Science, pages 310–324. Springer, Berlin, 1999. 238, 255

36. H. Reichel. An approach to object semantics based on terminal co-algebras. *Mathematical Structures in Computer Science*, 5:129–152, 1995. 237

37. H. Reichel, editor. *Coalgebraic Methods in Computer Science (CMCS'00)*, number 33 in Electronic Notes in Theoretical Computer Science. Elsevier, Amsterdam, 2000. `www.elsevier.nl/locate/entcs/volume33.html`. 277

38. J. Rothe, H. Tews, and B. Jacobs. The coalgebraic class specification language CCSL. *Journal of Universal Computer Science*, 7(2), 2001. 238, 255

39. J. Rutten. Behavioural differential equations: a coinductive calculus of streams, automata, and power series. Technical report, CWI Report SEN-R0023, 2000. 240

40. J. Rutten. Universal coalgebra: a theory of systems. *Theoretical Computer Science*, 249:3–80, 2000. 277

41. J. J. M. M. Rutten. Automata, power series, and coinduction: Taking input derivatives seriously (extended abstract). In J. Wiedermann, P. van Emde Boas, and M. Nielsen, editors, *International Colloquium on Automata, Languages and Programming*, number 1644 in Lecture Notes in Computer Science, pages 645–654. Springer, Berlin, 1999. 240

42. C. Stirling. Modal and temporal logics. In S. Abramsky, Dov M. Gabbai, and T. S. E. Maibaum, editors, *Handbook of Logic in Computer Science*, volume 2, pages 477–563. Oxford Univ. Press, 1992. 238, 262

43. A. S. Tanenbaum and A. S. Woodhull. *Operating Systems: Design and Implementation*. Prentice Hall, 2nd revised edition, 1997. 265

Table of Contents

Chapter 8
Algebraic Methods for
Optimization Problems

Richard Bird, Jeremy Gibbons, and Shin-Cheng Mu

Computing Laboratory, University of Oxford

Abstract. We argue for the benefits of relations over functions for modelling programs, and even more so for modelling specifications. To support this argument, we present an extended case study for a class of optimization problems, deriving efficient functional programs from concise relational specifications.

1 Introduction

It is very natural to model computer programs as functions from input to output; hence our interest in functional programming, and the approaches to program calculation described in Chapter 5.

However, sometimes the functional view is too concrete, too implementation-oriented. Although functions may be a good model of *programs*, they are not a particularly good model of *specifications*. It is often more natural to specify a problem using features beyond the power of functional programming. Here are some examples.

- It is easy to write the squaring problem *sqr* as a function. A natural specification of the square root problem *sqrt* is as its *converse*: the result of *sqrt x* should be a *y* such that *sqr y = x* (subject to considerations of sign and rounding). A more elaborate application is to specify a parser as the converse of a pretty printer.
- Many problems involve computing a minimal — smallest, cheapest, best — element of a set under some ordering — size, cost, badness. (We will see some examples of such *optimization problems* later in this chapter.) Often the ordering is a preorder rather than a partial order: two different elements may be equivalent under the ordering. Then the problem *minimal r*, which computes a minimal element under ordering *r*, is *non-deterministic*.
- The problem *minimal r* cannot return any result on an empty set. Even on a non-empty set, for there always to be a minimal element the ordering must be *connected* (any two elements must be comparable, one way or the other); for an unconnected ordering there may again be no returnable result. So *minimal r* will in general also be *partial*.
- Many problems involve simultaneously satisfying two requirements *P* and *Q*; for example, sorting a sequence *x* under an ordering *r* involves constructing

R. Backhouse et al. (Eds.): Algebraic and Coalgebraic Methods . . . , LNCS 2297, pp. 281–308, 2002.

a permutation (requirement P) of x that is ordered according to r (requirement Q). One can specify such a problem by sequentially composing two subproblems: first find all elements satisfying requirement P, then discard those that do not satisfy requirement Q. However, doing so inevitably breaks the symmetry in the problem description, thereby introducing a bias towards one kind of solution. A more neutral specification retains the symmetry by simply forming the *conjunction* of the two subproblems.

– Dually, some problems involve satisfying one of two alternative requirements — perhaps two different ways of giving an answer, or perhaps a 'normal' case and an 'exceptional' or 'error' case. Each subproblem is partial, but the two together may be total. Modelling the problem as a function entails entangling the two aspects; a better separation of concerns is obtained by modelling each aspect independently and forming the *disjunction* of the two subproblems.

In summary, many problems are most naturally *specified* using features (converse, non-determinism, partiality, conjunction, disjunction) that are to varying degrees inappropriate for a *programming* language.

The obvious way of resolving this dilemma is to use two languages, one for specification and one for programming. In fact, it is most convenient if the programming language is a sublanguage of the specification language. Then program construction is a matter of reasoning within a single language, namely the wider specification language, and restricting the features used to obtain an acceptable expression in the implementable subset. Moreover, it is then straightforward to have intermediate expressions that are a mixture of program and specification; this is rather harder to achieve if the two are completely separate languages.

What could we choose as a language that encompasses functions and functional programming, but that also provides the expressive power of converse, non-determinism, conjunction, and so on? It is well-known that *relations* have exactly these properties. This chapter, therefore, looks at lifting the results of Chapter 5 from functions to relations. We will carry out an extended case study, illustrating the gain in expressivity provided by the extra features. Our programming methodology will be to *refine* a relational specification to a functional implementation, reducing non-determinism while maintaining the domain of definition. So we will take this case study all the way to code, as a functional program.

There is an added bonus from studying relations as well as functions. Even when a specification and its implementation are both functional, one sometimes can gain greater insight and simpler reasoning by carrying out the calculation of the latter from the former in more general theory of relations. (We see an example in Exercise 2.6.7.) This is analogous to complex numbers and trigonometry in high school mathematics: although trigonometric functions are completely 'real' concepts, it is enlightening to investigate them from the point of view of complex numbers. For example, $\sin\theta$ and $\cos\theta$ are the imaginary and real parts of $e^{\theta i}$, the complex number with 'angle' θ radians and unit 'radius'; so of course

$\sin^2 \theta + \cos^2 \theta = 1$, by Pythagoras' Theorem, and the 'most beautiful theorem of mathematics' $e^{\pi i} = -1$ is easy to visualize.

It turns out that the relational algebra is particularly powerful for specifying and reasoning about optimization problems — informally, problems of the form 'the best data structure constructed in this way, satisfying that condition'. This chapter is structured to lead to exactly this point: Section 2 introduces the algebra of relations, Section 3 develops some general-purpose theory for optimization problems, and Section 4 applies the theory in a case study, which we take all the way to runnable code. There are many interesting diversions en route, some of which are signposted in the exercises; more sources are provided in the bibliographic notes.

1.1   Bibliographic Notes

The relational algebra has been proposed as a basis for program construction by many people; some representative strands of work are by de Roever [10], Hoare [17], Berghammer [3], Möller [24], Backhouse [1,2], Hehner [16], Mili and Desharnais [23], and Bird and de Moor [5]. Indeed, one could argue that relations underlie the entire field of logic programming [22,29].

For more information about the use of relations for program calculation, particularly in the solution of optimization problems, the interested reader is directed towards [5], on which this chapter is based.

2   The Algebra of Relations

2.1   Relations

Like a function, a *relation* is a mapping between a source type and a target type; unlike a function, a relation may be *partial* (mapping a source value to no target value) and/or *non-deterministic* (mapping a source value to multiple target values). We write '$f :: A \rightsquigarrow B$' to denote that relation f is a mapping from source type A to target type B.

Example   For example, consider the datatype PList A of non-empty lists with elements drawn from A. In general, lists xs of this type can be split into a prefix ys and a suffix zs such that $ys \mathbin{+\!\!+} zs = xs$ (here, '$+\!\!+$' denotes list concatenation):

$$split :: \mathsf{PList\ A} \rightsquigarrow \mathsf{PList\ A} \times \mathsf{PList\ A}$$

Most lists can be split in many ways, corresponding to the choice of where to place the division, so *split* is non-deterministic; for example, both $([1, 2], [3])$ and $([1], [2, 3])$ are possible results of *split* $[1, 2, 3]$. Singleton lists can not be split in any way at all, so *split* is partial too.

Pointwise Relational Programming Non-deterministic languages discourage reasoning with variables, because of the care that needs to be taken to retain referential transparency. Basically, one cannot assign to a variable 'the result of running program p on input x', because there may be no or many results. The usual approach, then, is to eschew *pointwise* reasoning with variables representing values, in favour of *pointfree* reasoning with the programs themselves.

Nevertheless, there are times when it is much more convenient to name and reason about particular values. This is especially the case when working on applications rather than general-purpose theory, because one wants to name and capitalize on specific dataflow patterns. The right approach to take to this problem is still not clear; the approach we will follow in this chapter is just one of several, and the details are not yet completely worked out. To be on the safe side, we will not use these 'pointwise relational programming' notations for any formal purpose; rather, we will resort to them only to provide informal but more perspicuous characterizations of sometimes opaque relational expressions.

When we want to refer to the result of 'applying' a relational program, we will avoid using '=', and write instead '$y \leftsquigarrow f\, x$' to mean that y is a possible value of $f\, x$. For example, both

$$([1, 2], [3]) \leftsquigarrow split\,[1, 2, 3]$$

and

$$([1], [2, 3]) \leftsquigarrow split\,[1, 2, 3]$$

In functional programming, we find that it is often convenient to specify a function by *pattern matching*. The function is defined by one or more equations, but the arguments to the function on the left-hand side of the equations are *patterns* rather than simply variables. For example, we might define the factorial function on natural numbers by

$$fact\,0 = 1$$
$$fact\,(n + 1) = (n + 1) \times fact\,n$$

This works for functions because patterns are by definition injective (and usually non-overlapping), and not arbitrary expressions: for any natural argument, exactly one of these two equations applies, and moreover if it is the second equation, the value of n is uniquely determined. Definition by pattern matching is often just as convenient for relations, but with relations we can be more lenient: we can allow non-exhaustive equations (which will lead to partiality) and overlapping equations with non-injective patterns (which will lead to non-determinism). For example, we could define the function *split* above by

$$split\,(ys \mathbin{+\!\!+} zs) \mathrel{\hat{=}} (ys, zs)$$

This pattern is not injective; nevertheless, this equation — together with the type — completely determines the relation *split*. (We decorate the equals sign to emphasize that this is the definition of a relation, rather than a true identity of values; in particular, $=$ is transitive whereas $\,\widehat{=}\,$ is not.)

Non-injective patterns introduce non-determinism implicitly. Explicit non-determinism can be expressed using the choice operator $\square$. For example, here is a more constructive characterization of *split*:

$$split\,(consp\,(x,xs)) = ([x],xs) \;\square\; (consp\,(x,ys),zs)$$
$$\text{where } (ys,zs) \leftsquigarrow split\,xs$$

Here, '*consp*' denotes the prefixing of a single element onto a non-empty list. The pattern is injective — it matches in at most one way for any given list — but still the result is non-deterministic because of the explicit choice.

Composition Relations of appropriate types may be composed; if $f :: A \rightsquigarrow B$ and $g :: B \rightsquigarrow C$, then their composition $g \cdot f :: A \rightsquigarrow C$ is defined by

$$z \leftsquigarrow (g \cdot f)\,x \;\Leftrightarrow\; \exists y.\; y \leftsquigarrow f\,x \wedge z \leftsquigarrow g\,y$$

For every type A, there is an *identity* relation $\mathsf{id}_A :: A \rightsquigarrow A$ mapping each element of A to itself. Identities are the units of composition: for $f :: A \rightsquigarrow B$,

$$f \cdot \mathsf{id}_A = f = \mathsf{id}_B \cdot f$$

We will usually omit the subscript, allowing it to be deduced from the context.

Inclusion One can think of a relation $f :: A \rightsquigarrow B$ as a set of pairs, a subset of $A \times B$ (so $y \leftsquigarrow f\,x$ precisely when $(x,y) \in f$). Unlike functions, different relations of the same type may be comparable under *inclusion*: $f \subseteq g$ precisely when $y \leftsquigarrow f\,x$ implies $y \leftsquigarrow g\,x$ for all x and y.

Composition is monotonic under inclusion:

$$f_1 \subseteq f_2 \,\wedge\, g_1 \subseteq g_2 \;\Rightarrow\; f_1 \cdot g_1 \subseteq f_2 \cdot g_2$$

Moreover, pre- and post-composition have adjoints, called *right division* ('over') and *left division* ('under') respectively:

$$(f \subseteq h\,/\,g) \;\Leftrightarrow\; (f \cdot g \subseteq h) \;\Leftrightarrow\; (g \subseteq f \backslash h)$$

With points,

$$a \leftsquigarrow (h\,/\,g)\,b \;\Leftrightarrow\; \forall c.\,(a \leftsquigarrow h\,c \Leftarrow b \leftsquigarrow g\,c)$$
$$a \leftsquigarrow (f \backslash h)\,c \;\Leftrightarrow\; \forall b.\,(b \leftsquigarrow f\,a \Rightarrow b \leftsquigarrow h\,c)$$

Inclusion of relations is the foundation of our programming method, as equality is for functional programming: we will start with a (presumably non-deterministic) specification g, and manipulate it to construct a (presumably more efficient, or otherwise easier to implement) refinement $f \subseteq g$. Provided that f is still defined everywhere that g was, it is 'at least as good' as g.

Meet and Join Any two relations $f, g :: A \rightsquigarrow B$ have a *meet* $f \cap g :: A \rightsquigarrow B$, defined by the universal property that for all $h :: A \rightsquigarrow B$,

$$h \subseteq f \cap g \Leftrightarrow h \subseteq f \wedge h \subseteq g$$

That is, $f \cap g$ is the greatest lower bound of f and g; it corresponds to intersection of the sets of pairs in the relations. It follows (Exercise 2.6.1) that $\cap$ is associative, commutative and idempotent, and that monotonicity of composition can be re-expressed in terms of $\cap$.

Dually, the join $f \cup g$ of two relations f, g of the same type is defined by the universal property

$$h \supseteq f \cup g \Leftrightarrow h \supseteq f \wedge h \supseteq g$$

Converse Again unlike functions, relations can easily be reversed: if $f :: A \rightsquigarrow B$, then $f^\circ :: B \rightsquigarrow A$, and satisfies

$$y \leftsquigarrow f\, x \Leftrightarrow x \leftsquigarrow f^\circ\, y$$

Converse is:

- its own inverse: $(f^\circ)^\circ = f$;
- order-preserving: $f \subseteq g \Leftrightarrow f^\circ \subseteq g^\circ$;
- contravariant: $(f \cdot g)^\circ = g^\circ \cdot f^\circ$;
- distributive over meet: $(f \cap g)^\circ = f^\circ \cap g^\circ$.

Any *coreflexive* f, that is, one satisfying $f \subseteq \mathrm{id}$, is invariant under converse: $f^\circ = f$. One can think of a coreflexive of type $A \rightsquigarrow A$ as a subset of A, or equivalently as a predicate on A.

2.2 Special Kinds of Relation

Let $f :: A \rightsquigarrow B$; then

- f is *entire* if $\mathrm{id} \subseteq f^\circ \cdot f$, or equivalently if for all $x \in A$ there is at least one $y \in B$ with $y \leftsquigarrow f\, x$;
- f is *simple* if $f \cdot f^\circ \subseteq \mathrm{id}$, or equivalently if for all $x \in A$ there is at most one $y \in B$ with $y \leftsquigarrow f\, x$;
- f is *surjective* if $\mathrm{id} \subseteq f \cdot f^\circ$, or equivalently if for all $y \in B$ there is at least one $x \in A$ with $y \leftsquigarrow f\, x$;
- f is *injective* if $f^\circ \cdot f \subseteq \mathrm{id}$, or equivalently if for all $y \in B$ there is at most one $x \in A$ with $y \leftsquigarrow f\, x$.

A simple relation is also known as a *partial function*, and a simple and entire relation as a *total function*. We write '$f :: A \rightarrow B$' to indicate that f is a total function. Functions enjoy special *shunting rules*:

Lemma 1. *If f is a function, then*

$$f \cdot g \subseteq h \Leftrightarrow g \subseteq f^\circ \cdot h$$
$$g \cdot f^\circ \subseteq h \Leftrightarrow g \subseteq h \cdot f$$

Note that $f \subseteq g \Rightarrow f = g$ if f, g are total functions. For function $p :: \mathsf{A} \to \mathsf{Bool}$, we define the corresponding coreflexive $p? :: \mathsf{A} \rightsquigarrow \mathsf{A}$ by

$$p? = \mathsf{exr} \cdot fsttrue \cdot (p \bigtriangleup \mathsf{id})$$

where the coreflexive $fsttrue$ holds of pairs whose first component is true.

2.3 Breadth

There is a one-to-one correspondence between relations $\mathsf{A} \rightsquigarrow \mathsf{B}$ and set-valued functions $\mathsf{A} \to \mathsf{Set}\,\mathsf{B}$, where Set is the powerset functor ($\mathsf{Set}\,\mathsf{B}$ is the set of all subsets of B). The operator Λ is a witness to this isomorphism, yielding the *breadth* of a relation, that is, the corresponding set-valued function:

$$(\Lambda f)\, x = \{y \mid y \leftsquigarrow f\, x\}$$

For example, $\Lambda split$ is the function that returns the set of all possible splits of a given list.

Note that Λf is an entire and simple relation (a function) for any f. If f itself is a function, then Λf returns singleton sets.

2.4 Folds

Functional folds were discussed in depth in Chapter 5. To summarize, an F-*algebra* (A, f) for a functor F consists of a type A and a function $f :: \mathsf{F}\,\mathsf{A} \to \mathsf{A}$. An F-algebra $(\mathsf{T}, \mathsf{in_T})$ is *initial* if, for every F-algebra (A, f), there is a unique homomorphism $h :: \mathsf{T} \to \mathsf{A}$ such that

$$h \cdot \mathsf{in_T} = f \cdot \mathsf{F}\,h$$

We write $\mathsf{fold_T}\, f$ for this h, giving the universal property

$$h = \mathsf{fold_T}\, f \Leftrightarrow h \cdot \mathsf{in_T} = f \cdot \mathsf{F}\,h$$

Thus, $\mathsf{fold_T}$ has type $(\mathsf{F}\,\mathsf{A} \to \mathsf{A}) \to (\mathsf{T} \to \mathsf{A})$.

The datatype definition

$$\mathsf{T} = \textsc{data}\ \mathsf{F}$$

introduces the initial F-algebra $(\mathsf{T}, \mathsf{in_T})$ and the fold operator $\mathsf{fold_T}$. This was generalized to polymorphic datatypes, using bifunctors rather than functors: the datatype definition

$$\mathsf{T}\,\mathsf{A} = \textsc{data}\ (\mathsf{A}\oplus)$$

introduces the initial $(\mathsf{A}\oplus)$-algebra $(\mathsf{T}\,\mathsf{A}, \mathsf{in_{T\,A}})$ and the fold operator $\mathsf{fold_{T\,A}}$, from which we usually omit the type subscript A, if not the whole of the subscript.

Example: Lists We define the datatype of lists by

$$\text{List } A = \text{DATA } (\underline{1} \mathbin{\hat{+}} (\underline{A} \mathbin{\hat{\times}} \text{Id}))$$

where $\times$ is product, $+$ is coproduct, 1 is the unit type, Id is the identity functor, underlining denotes constant functors and a superscript hat denotes lifting of a bifunctor. This induces a constructor

$$\text{in}_{\text{List}} :: 1 + A \times \text{List } A \to A$$

and a fold operator

$$\text{fold}_{\text{List}} :: (1 + B \times \text{List } A \to B) \to (\text{List } A \to B)$$

We introduce the syntactic sugar

$$\text{const } [\,] \bigtriangledown cons = \text{in}_{\text{List}}$$
$$foldr \; f \; e = \text{fold}_{\text{List}} \, (\text{const } e \bigtriangledown f)$$

where

$$\text{const } a \; b = a$$

This corresponds to the curried Haskell equivalents

```
[]    ::  [a]
(:)   ::  a -> [a] -> [a]
```

for the constructors, and

```
foldr  ::  (a -> b -> b) -> b -> ([a] -> b)
foldr f e []     = e
foldr f e (x:xs) = f x (foldr f e xs)
```

for the fold.

Example: Non-empty Lists In our case study at the end of this chapter, we will also require a datatype of non-empty lists

$$\text{PList } A = \text{DATA } (\underline{A} \mathbin{\hat{+}} (\underline{A} \mathbin{\hat{\times}} \text{Id}))$$

We introduce the syntactic sugar

$$wrap \bigtriangledown consp = \text{in}_{\text{PList}}$$
$$foldrp \; f \; g = \text{fold}_{\text{PList}} \, (g \bigtriangledown f)$$

The Haskell standard prelude has no equivalent, but encourages the reuse of ordinary lists instead, trading notational convenience for lost structure.

Relational Folds The theory from Chapter 5 summarized above is fine in the categories $\mathcal{S}et$ and $\mathcal{C}po$, but turns out not to be appropriate in the category $\mathcal{R}el$ of sets and relations, because too much of the structure collapses there. In particular (Exercise 2.6.4), converses make products and coproducts coincide.

However, any functor in $\mathcal{S}et$ can be extended in a canonical way to a monotonic functor (or *relator*) on $\mathcal{R}el$. In particular, the monotonic extension of cartesian product can be used in place of the true categorical product of $\mathcal{R}el$ (which coincides with disjoint sum).

As a result, folds can be generalized to relations. For monotonically extended functor F, the initial (in $\mathcal{S}et$) F-algebra (T, in) is also initial in $\mathcal{R}el$: we still have the all-important universal property

$$h = \text{fold}_T\, f \Leftrightarrow h \cdot \text{in}_T = f \cdot F\, h$$

only now the fold acts on and yields relations: $\text{fold}_T :: (F\, A \leadsto A) \to (T \leadsto A)$.

Some examples of relational folds on lists that will be used later (Exercises 3.8.5 and 3.8.9) are as follows. Recall Lambek's Lemma (§2.5.5 of Chapter 5), which states that folding with the constructors is the identity function; on lists this becomes $foldr\ cons\ [\,] = \text{id}$. Folding with any subrelation of the constructors gives a coreflexive; for example, the coreflexive *ordered* that holds of ascending lists is given by

$$ordered = foldr\,(cons \cdot ok)\,[\,] \quad \text{where } ok\,(x, xs) = \text{map}\,((x \leq)?)\,xs$$

Using the power of relations in the other direction, namely non-determinism, we can obtain simple characterizations of many combinatorial operations. For example, the relation *prefix* returns an arbitrary prefix of a list:

$$prefix = fold\,(cons \cup \text{const}\,[\,])\,[\,]$$

and the relation *subseq* returns an arbitrary subsequence:

$$subseq = foldr\,(cons \cup \text{exr})\,[\,]$$

Unfolds One might expect now to dualize the relational generalization of folds to get relational unfolds. However, this is not necessary, because converse gives us everything we need: for functor F, the datatype $T = \text{DATA}\ F$ is also a codatatype, and for algebra $f::FA \leadsto A$, the converse $f^\circ::A \leadsto FA$ is a coalgebra, and $(\text{fold}(f^\circ))^\circ$ works as an unfold (Exercise 2.6.6).

Fusion Perhaps the fundamental property of folds, as illustrated at length in Chapter 5, is the fusion theorem: for $T = \text{DATA}\ F$,

$$h \cdot \text{fold}_T\, f = \text{fold}_T\, g \Leftarrow h \cdot f = g \cdot F\, h$$

There are two variants of this fusion theorem for relational folds:

$$h \cdot \text{fold}_T\, f \subseteq \text{fold}_T\, g \Leftarrow h \cdot f \subseteq g \cdot F\, h$$
$$h \cdot \text{fold}_T\, f \supseteq \text{fold}_T\, g \Leftarrow h \cdot f \supseteq g \cdot F\, h$$

Of course, fusion as an equality follows from these two.

2.5 Bibliographic Notes

The relational algebra has a very elegant axiomatic characterization, dating back to Tarski [30], and this is how it is often presented and used [1,2]. Our presentation follows the axiomatization as a (unitary tabular) allegory in [5], and owes more to Freyd and Ščedrov [14] than to Tarski. (In an allegorical setting, the join $\cup$ is actually not the dual of the meet $\cap$ in general; in fact, only *locally complete* allegories have joins, and only in *boolean* locally complete allegories are they dual to meets. We gloss over these details, because we are not directly concerned with the axiomatization here.)

Using either axiomatization leads to *pointfree reasoning*, which is certainly concise, but is often difficult to follow, especially when applied to specific programming problems as opposed to general theory. This is because 'plumbing combinators' must be used to pass values around. In computer programming, we have long realized that variables are important, and that their names clarify programs; the same observation applies to the relational algebra. However, variables interact awkwardly with non-determinism, and finding the right approach is still a matter of ongoing research. The approach taken here is based on [11]; other approaches include [7,13,31,25,26,28].

2.6 Exercises

1. Using the universal property of $\cap$ (§2.1), show that it is associative, commutative and idempotent:

$$f \cap (g \cap h) = (f \cap g) \cap h$$
$$f \cap g = g \cap f$$
$$f \cap f = f$$

   and that monotonicity of composition can be reexpressed as follows:

$$f \cdot (g \cap h) \subseteq (f \cdot g) \cap (f \cdot h)$$
$$(f \cap g) \cdot h \subseteq (f \cdot h) \cap (g \cdot h)$$

   (that is, derive these properties from the original characterization, and vice versa).
2. Prove the shunting rules in Lemma 1.
3. The Λ operation is an isomorphism; there is a one-to-one correspondence between relations $A \rightsquigarrow B$ and set-valued functions $A \rightarrow Set\ B$. What is the inverse operation? That is, given a set-valued function f of type $A \rightarrow Set\ B$, what is the corresponding relation of type $A \rightsquigarrow B$? (Hint: look ahead to §3.1.)
4. A straightforward interpretation in Rel of the standard theory of datatypes from Chapter 5 is inappropriate: products and coproducts coincide, whereas we intend them to be different constructions. Technically, this is because Rel is its own dual, whereas Set and Cpo are not self-dual.
   Categorically speaking, bifunctor $\otimes$ is a product if arrows $f :: A \rightsquigarrow B$ and $g :: A \rightsquigarrow C$ uniquely determine a morphism $h :: A \rightsquigarrow B \otimes C$ with $exl \cdot h = f$

and $\mathsf{exr} \cdot h = g$. Dually, bifunctor $\oplus$ is a coproduct if arrows $f :: \mathsf{A} \rightsquigarrow \mathsf{C}$ and $g :: \mathsf{B} \rightsquigarrow \mathsf{C}$ uniquely determine a morphism $h :: \mathsf{A} \oplus \mathsf{B} \rightsquigarrow \mathsf{C}$ with $h \cdot \mathsf{inl} = f$ and $h \cdot \mathsf{inr} = g$.

(a) Show that cartesian product is not a categorical product in $\mathcal{R}el$.

(b) Show that disjoint sum is a categorical coproduct in $\mathcal{R}el$.

(c) Show that disjoint sum is in fact also a categorical product in $\mathcal{R}el$.

(d) Show, using converses, that any categorical product in $\mathcal{R}el$ is necessarily a coproduct, and vice versa.

5. A *tabulation* of relation $h :: \mathsf{A} \rightsquigarrow \mathsf{B}$ is a pair of functions $f :: \mathsf{C} \rightsquigarrow \mathsf{A}$, $g :: \mathsf{C} \rightsquigarrow \mathsf{B}$ such that $h = g \cdot f^\circ$ and $(f^\circ \cdot f) \cap (g^\circ \cdot g) = \mathsf{id}$. Assuming that every relation has a tabulation, show that for relator F:

(a) when h is a function, so is $\mathsf{F}\, h$, and $(\mathsf{F}\, h)^\circ = \mathsf{F}\, (h^\circ)$;

(b) a functor is a relator iff $(\mathsf{F}\, h)^\circ = \mathsf{F}\, (h^\circ)$ for any (not necessarily functional) h;

(c) if two relators F, G agree on functions, then they agree on all relations.

Thus, functors in $\mathcal{S}et$ can be extended in a canonical way to relators in $\mathcal{R}el$.

6. Show that datatype $\mathsf{T} = \mathsf{DATA}\, \mathsf{F}$ is also a codatatype, with final coalgebra $(\mathsf{T}, \mathsf{in}^\circ)$. That is, for algebra $f :: \mathsf{F}\,\mathsf{A} \rightsquigarrow \mathsf{A}$, show that $(\mathsf{fold}_\mathsf{T}\, (f^\circ))^\circ$ is an unfold:

$$h = (\mathsf{fold}_\mathsf{T}\, (f^\circ))^\circ \;\Leftrightarrow\; \mathsf{in}^\circ \cdot h = \mathsf{F}\, h \cdot f$$

This is another consequence of $\mathcal{R}el$'s self-duality.

7. Using relations, we can give very nice equational proofs of two theorems presented in Exercises 2.9.9 and 2.9.12 of Chapter 5. Despite these being properties of total functions, it seems that their simplest proofs are in terms of relations. For datatype $\mathsf{T} = \mathsf{DATA}\, \mathsf{F}$, show that function $h :: \mathsf{T} \to \mathsf{A}$ is a fold iff $h \cdot \mathsf{in} \cdot \mathsf{F}\, h^\circ$ is simple, and function $g :: \mathsf{A} \to \mathsf{T}$ is an unfold iff $\mathsf{F}\, g^\circ \cdot \mathsf{in}^\circ \cdot g$ is entire. Explain why these conditions are equivalent to those from Chapter 5.

8. Prove the two inclusion fusion theorems

$$h \cdot \mathsf{fold}_\mathsf{T}\, f \subseteq \mathsf{fold}_\mathsf{T}\, g \;\Leftarrow\; h \cdot f \subseteq g \cdot \mathsf{F}\, h$$
$$h \cdot \mathsf{fold}_\mathsf{T}\, f \supseteq \mathsf{fold}_\mathsf{T}\, g \;\Leftarrow\; h \cdot f \supseteq g \cdot \mathsf{F}\, h$$

3 Optimization Problems

Optimization problems are typically of the form 'select the best construct generated by this means, which satisfies that test'. Such a specification is executable, provided that only finitely many constructs are generated, but it is in general too expensive to compute because there still many constructs to consider. The algorithm can be improved by promoting the test and the selection inside the generation, thereby avoiding having to generate and eliminate constructs that cannot possibly contribute to the optimal solution.

Sometimes the improved algorithm has exactly the same extensional behaviour as the original specification, but is faster to execute. More often, however, the specification is non-deterministic (there may be several optimal solutions), and the improved algorithm is a *refinement* of the specification, yielding only a subset of the optimal solutions. The missing solutions are pruned to permit a more efficient algorithm; correctness is maintained by ensuring that for every solution pruned, an equally good one is retained. This refinement characteristic is a strong motivation for the move from functional to relational programming: refinement makes little sense with total functions.

In this chapter we will consider a restricted, but still large, class of optimization problems, of the form

$$\min r \cdot \Lambda(\text{fold } f)$$

The 'test' phase is omitted, and the feasible constructs are generated directly by a (relational) fold. We take the breadth of this fold to get the set of all feasible constructs, and select from this set a minimal element under the preorder r.

We will develop two kinds of improved algorithm for such problems, depending on characteristics of the ingredients f and r. The first embodies a *greedy* approach, building a single optimal solution step by step. The second embodies a *thinning* approach, building up a (hopefully small) collection of representative solutions, some unforeseeable one of which will lead to the optimal solution. The second approach assumes weaker conditions on the ingredients, but yields a less efficient algorithm.

3.1   The Eilenberg-Wright Lemma

Let *choose* :: Set A $\leadsto$ A denote the membership relation for sets, so that

$$x \leftsquigarrow choose \; xs \Leftrightarrow x \in xs$$

Then we have the following lemma:

Lemma 2 (Eilenberg-Wright). *For* $\mathsf{T} = \text{DATA } \mathsf{F}$,

$$\Lambda(\text{fold}_\mathsf{T} \; f) = \text{fold}_\mathsf{T} \; (\Lambda(f \cdot \mathsf{F} \; choose))$$

Informally, the set of results returned by a relational fold can be obtained as a functional fold that at each stage returns the set of all possible partial results.

In particular, we have that

$$\min r \cdot \Lambda(\text{fold}_\mathsf{T} \; f) = \min r \cdot \text{fold}_\mathsf{T} \; (\Lambda(f \cdot \mathsf{F} \; choose))$$

That is, rather than computing a single complete construct in all possible ways and taking the best of the results, we can explore all choices at each step, building up all constructs 'in parallel'.

3.2   Preorders

A preorder $r :: \mathsf{A} \leadsto \mathsf{A}$ is a relation that is

- *reflexive*, that is, id $\subseteq r$, and

— *transitive*, that is, $r \cdot r \subseteq r$.

In addition, preorder $r :: A \rightsquigarrow A$ may or may not be

— *connected*, that is, $r \cup r^\circ = A \times A$.

When we come to translate our results into Haskell, it will be convenient to represent a preorder r by its *characteristic function* $\chi(r)$ of type $A \times A \to Bool$ (or perhaps its curried version $A \to A \to Bool$) such that $x \leftsquigarrow r\, y \Leftrightarrow \chi(r)\,(x,y)$. With this representation, the properties become more long-winded but perhaps more familiar:

— a preorder r is *reflexive*, that is, $\chi(r)\,(x,x)$ for every $x \in A$;
— a preorder r is *transitive*, that is, $\chi(r)\,(x,y) \wedge \chi(r)\,(y,z) \Rightarrow \chi(r)\,(x,z)$ for every $x, y, z \in A$;
— a preorder r may or may not be *connected*, that is, $\chi(r)\,(x,y) \vee \chi(r)\,(y,x)$ for every $x, y \in A$.

3.3 Monotonicity

We say that that an F-algebra $f :: F\,A \rightsquigarrow A$ is *monotonic under a preorder* r if

$$f \cdot F\,r \subseteq r \cdot f$$

Equivalently, in terms of characteristic functions, we have that f is monotonic under r if $\chi(F\,r)\,(x,y)$ and $u \leftsquigarrow f\,x$ together imply that there exists a $v \leftsquigarrow f\,y$ such that $\chi(r)\,(u,v)$. (Note that $F\,r$ is a relation of type $F\,A \rightsquigarrow F\,A$, so its characteristic function $\chi(F\,r)$ has type $F\,A \times F\,A \to Bool$.)

For example, addition of naturals $plus :: Pair\,Nat \to Nat$ is monotonic under leq, the normal linear ordering, because $plus \cdot Pair\,leq \subseteq leq \cdot plus$, or in terms of points, $a \leftsquigarrow leq\,c$ and $b \leftsquigarrow leq\,d$ imply that $plus\,(a,b) \leftsquigarrow leq\,(plus\,(c,d))$.

3.4 Minimum

The function $min :: (A \rightsquigarrow A) \to (Set\,A \rightsquigarrow A)$ is defined by

$$min\,r = choose \cap (r \,/\, choose^\circ)$$

Informally, $min\,r$ takes a set xs and returns a value x that both is an element of xs and satisfies $x \leftsquigarrow r\, y$ for every $y \leftsquigarrow choose\,xs$; in points,

$$x \leftsquigarrow min\,r\,xs \iff (x \in xs) \wedge (\forall y \in xs.\ \chi(r)\,(x,y))$$

Of course, this definition is perfectly symmetric: to obtain the maximum under a preorder r, simply compute the minimum under r°.

If every non-empty set has a minimum under a preorder r, then r is necessarily connected. In general, therefore, we will only be interested in uses of $min\,r$ for connected preorders r.

When it comes to implementing this operator in Haskell, we first must decide how to represent sets. We choose the simplest representation, as an unordered list, but because we will be computing minimum elements of sets, we will stick to non-empty lists; so we define the function $minlist$ as follows:

$$minlist :: (A \times A \rightarrow \mathsf{Bool}) \rightarrow (\mathsf{PList}\ A \rightarrow A)$$

$$minlist\ r = foldrp\ m\ \mathsf{id} \quad \text{where } m\ (x,y) = \text{if } r\ (x,y) \text{ then } x \text{ else } y$$

This implementation breaks ties in favour of the leftmost of two equivalent elements. If r is connected, then

$$minlist\ (\chi(r)) \subseteq \min r \cdot \mathsf{setify}$$

where $\mathsf{setify} :: \mathsf{PList}\,A \rightarrow \mathsf{Set}\,A$ converts a non-empty list to the set of its elements.

3.5   The Greedy Theorem

Greedy algorithms for our class of optimization problems are captured by the following theorem.

Theorem 3 (Greedy Theorem). *Suppose* $\mathsf{T} = \textsc{data}\ \mathsf{F}$, *and* F-*algebra* $f ::$ $\mathsf{F}\,A \rightsquigarrow A$ *is monotonic under the preorder* r°. *Then*

$$\mathsf{fold_T}\ (\min r \cdot \Lambda f) \subseteq \min r \cdot \Lambda(\mathsf{fold_T}\ f)$$

In fact, we have a stronger theorem, of which the above is a simple corollary.

Theorem 4 (Refining Greedy Theorem). *Suppose* $\mathsf{T} = \textsc{data}\ \mathsf{F}$, *and* F-*algebra* $f :: \mathsf{F}\,A \rightsquigarrow A$ *is monotonic under the preorder* q°, *where* $q \subseteq r$. *Then*

$$\mathsf{fold_T}\ (\min q \cdot \Lambda f) \subseteq \min r \cdot \Lambda(\mathsf{fold_T}\ f)$$

Proof (Sketch). Using the Eilenberg-Wright Lemma, it suffices to show

$$\mathsf{fold_T}\ (\min q \cdot \Lambda f) \subseteq \min r \cdot \mathsf{fold_T}\ (\Lambda(f \cdot \mathsf{F}\ choose))$$

This in turn follows, by fusion, from

$$\min q \cdot \Lambda f \cdot \mathsf{F}\ (\min r) \subseteq \min r \cdot \Lambda(f \cdot \mathsf{F}\ choose)$$

Discharging this final proof obligation is left as an exercise for the reader (Exercise 3.8.4).

Informally, to say that f is monotonic under r° is to say that for any 'input' $x :: \mathsf{F}\,A$, any 'worse input' $y \leftsquigarrow \mathsf{F}\ r^{\circ}\ x$, and any result $b \leftsquigarrow f\ y$ of f on this worse input, there corresponds a result $a \leftsquigarrow f\ x$ of f on the original input that is 'better' than b, that is, $b \leftsquigarrow r^{\circ}\ a$. Thus, degrading the inputs to f will always degrade the output, or conversely, it is never beneficial to pick suboptimal intermediate results, as they will only lead to suboptimal final results. Overall, the Greedy Theorem states that a minimal result can be computed by maintaining a single minimal partial result at each stage of the folding process, and so it lies at the other extreme to the Eilenberg-Wright Lemma, which embodies a kind of exhaustive search.

The Refining Greedy Theorem is a little more flexible. It is sometimes the case that f fails to be monotonic under r°, but enjoys monotonicity under a refined ordering q° where $q \subseteq r$. We will see an example in §4.5. Provided that q remains connected, the relation $\min q$ is entire (except for empty sets). The greedy algorithm itself will also be entire (except for empty sets), refining the plain greedy algorithm from Theorem 3: it computes an optimal solution under q, and any optimal solution under q will also be optimal under r — but the converse does not hold. If q is not connected, the theorem still holds, but the resulting algorithm will not be entire (that is, will not always yield a result).

In order to implement the method as a functional program, we have to find some function $step :: \mathsf{F}\,\mathsf{A} \to \mathsf{A}$ such that $step \subseteq \min q \cdot \Lambda f$. We will give an example application of the Greedy Theorem in §4.

3.6   Thinning

Monotonicity under a connected preorder is a strong condition that is satisfied in very few optimization problems; and indeed, few such problems admit greedy solutions. More useful would be something between the two extremes of the Eilenberg-Wright Lemma and the Greedy Theorems, involving maintaining some but not all partial solutions.

For a not necessarily connected preorder q on A, the relation $\mathsf{thin}\,q :: \mathsf{Set}\,\mathsf{A} \rightsquigarrow \mathsf{Set}\,\mathsf{A}$ takes a set xs and returns some subset ys of xs with the property that all elements of xs have a lower bound under q in ys. More precisely,

$$\mathsf{thin}\,q = (choose \setminus choose) \cap ((choose^{\circ} \cdot q) \,/\, choose^{\circ})$$

If $ys \leftsquigarrow \mathsf{thin}\,q\,xs$, then the first conjunct here says that ys is a subset of xs, and the second says that for every $x \leftsquigarrow choose\,xs$, there is a $y \leftsquigarrow choose\,ys$ with $y \leftsquigarrow q\,x$; in points,

$$ys \leftsquigarrow \mathsf{thin}\,q\,xs \ \Leftrightarrow\ (ys \subseteq xs) \wedge (\forall x \in xs.\ \exists y \in ys.\ \chi(q)\,(x,y))$$

The following lemma allows us to introduce applications of thin.

Lemma 5 (Thin introduction). *Provided that q and r are both preorders and $q \subseteq r$, we have*

$$\min r = \min r \cdot \mathsf{thin}\,q$$

That is, any required minimum can be obtained by selecting that minimum from a suitably thinned set. For the proof, see Exercise 3.8.6.

This leads us towards the following *Thinning Theorem*, which entails maintaining a representative collection of partial solutions at each stage of the folding process.

Theorem 6 (Thinning). *Suppose* $\mathsf{T} = \textsc{data}\ \mathsf{F}$, *and* F*-algebra* $f :: \mathsf{F}\,\mathsf{A} \rightsquigarrow \mathsf{A}$ *is monotonic under a (not necessarily connected) preorder* $q°$, *where* $q \subseteq r$. *Then*

$$\min r \cdot \mathsf{fold}_\mathsf{T}\ (\mathsf{thin}\ q \cdot \varLambda(f \cdot \mathsf{F}\ choose)) \subseteq \min r \cdot \varLambda(\mathsf{fold}_\mathsf{T}\ f)$$

Proof (Sketch). We have $\min r = \min r \cdot \mathsf{thin}\ q$, so it suffices to show that

$$\mathsf{fold}_\mathsf{T}\ (\mathsf{thin}\ q \cdot \varLambda(f \cdot \mathsf{F}\ choose)) \subseteq \mathsf{thin}\ q \cdot \varLambda(\mathsf{fold}_\mathsf{T}\ f)$$

Just like the Greedy Theorem, this latter inclusion can be proved (Exercise 3.8.7) by making use of the Eilenberg-Wright Lemma and fusion.

Implementation In order to implement the thinning method as a functional program, we have to implement

$$\mathsf{thin}\ q \cdot \varLambda(f \cdot \mathsf{F}\ choose) :: \mathsf{F}\ (\mathsf{Set}\ \mathsf{A}) \rightsquigarrow \mathsf{Set}\ \mathsf{A}$$

It seems reasonable to represent these sets as lists, sorted by some connected preorder (but not necessarily by q itself); we can capitalize on the list ordering to implement the thinning step efficiently. Therefore, we will actually construct a function

$$step :: \mathsf{F}\ (\mathsf{PList}\ \mathsf{A}) \rightarrow \mathsf{PList}\ \mathsf{A}$$

such that

$$\mathsf{setify} \cdot step \subseteq \mathsf{thin}\ q \cdot \varLambda(f \cdot \mathsf{F}\ choose) \cdot \mathsf{F}\ \mathsf{setify}$$

To do this, we will need a number of ingredients:

- a function

$$sort :: (\mathsf{A} \times \mathsf{A} \rightarrow \mathsf{Bool}) \rightarrow (\mathsf{Set}\ \mathsf{A} \rightarrow \mathsf{PList}\ \mathsf{A})$$

  that sorts a finite set under a given connected preorder;
- a function

$$mergelists :: (\mathsf{A} \times \mathsf{A} \rightarrow \mathsf{Bool}) \rightarrow (\mathsf{PList}\ (\mathsf{PList}\ \mathsf{A}) \rightarrow \mathsf{PList}\ \mathsf{A})$$

  that merges a list of sorted lists into a single sorted list;
- a function

$$thinlist :: (\mathsf{A} \times \mathsf{A} \rightarrow \mathsf{Bool}) \rightarrow (\mathsf{PList}\ \mathsf{A} \rightarrow \mathsf{PList}\ \mathsf{A})$$

  that implements thin:

$$\mathsf{setify} \cdot thinlist\ (\chi(q)) \subseteq \mathsf{thin}\ q \cdot \mathsf{setify}$$

on a suitably sorted list in a reasonably efficient manner, that is, quickly (in linear time) and effectively (yielding a short result), and does so stably:

$$thinlist\ (\chi(q)) \subseteq subseq$$

- a function

$$cp_\mathsf{F} :: \mathsf{F}\,(\mathsf{PList}\,\mathsf{A}) \to \mathsf{PList}\,(\mathsf{F}\,\mathsf{A})$$

that converts an F-structure of lists (possibly of differing lengths) into a list of F-structures (all of the same shape);
- a function *combine* :: F A → PList A satisfying

$$combine \subseteq sort\,(\chi(p)) \cdot \mathsf{thin}\,q \cdot \Lambda f$$

for some connected preorder p.

Given these ingredients, we define

$$step = thinlist\,(\chi(q)) \cdot mergelists\,(\chi(p)) \cdot \mathsf{map}\,combine \cdot cp_\mathsf{F}$$

and claim (Exercise 3.8.8) that

$$minlist\,(\chi(r)) \cdot \mathsf{fold}\,step \subseteq \mathsf{min}\,r \cdot \mathsf{fold}\,(\mathsf{thin}\,q \cdot \Lambda(f \cdot \mathsf{F}\,choose))$$

There is no constraint on p for correctness, but for efficiency a suitable choice will bring related elements together to allow effective thinning with $thinlist\,(\chi(q))$.

3.7 Bibliographic Notes

The Eilenberg-Wright Lemma, and indeed relational folds themselves, were first employed to reason about the equivalence of deterministic and non-deterministic automata [12].

Greedy algorithms are well-known in the algorithm design community; an in-depth study of their properties is in [21], and a more pragmatic description with numerous examples in [8]. Thinning algorithms as an abstraction in their own right are due to Bird and de Moor [4,5]. More results on greedy, thinning and dynamic programming algorithms for optimization problems are given in Curtis' thesis [9]; there the emphasis is on algorithms in which the generation phase is less structured, a simple loop rather than a fold or an unfold.

Cross products (§3.6) and the related zips are investigated in great depth in Hoogendijk's thesis [19].

3.8 Exercises

1. Prove the Eilenberg-Wright Lemma (§3.1), using the universal property of folds.
2. Find an F-algebra $f :: \mathsf{F}\,\mathsf{A} \rightsquigarrow \mathsf{A}$ and a preorder r on A such that f is monotonic under r but not under r°. Prove that when f is a total function, f is monotonic under r iff it is monotonic under r°.
3. Why is connectedness of r necessary for the function *minlist* from §3.4 to be an implementation of min?

4. Complete the proof of the Refining Greedy Theorem (Theorem 4) from §3.5, by showing that

$$\min q \cdot \Lambda f \cdot \mathsf{F} \,(\min r) \subseteq \min r \cdot \Lambda(f \cdot \mathsf{F}\; choose)$$

where f is monotonic under q° with $q \subseteq r$.

5. The function $takewhile :: (A \rightsquigarrow A) \rightarrow (\mathsf{List}\; A \rightsquigarrow \mathsf{List}\; A)$ yields the longest prefix of its second argument, all of whose elements 'satisfy' the coreflexive first argument:

$$takewhile\, p = longest \cdot \Lambda(\mathsf{map}\, p \cdot prefix)$$

where $prefix$ is defined in §2.4, and

$$longest = \min (length^\circ \cdot geq \cdot length)$$

and where $length$ returns the length of a list, and geq is the usual linear ordering on naturals. For example, $takewhile\, prime\, [2, 3, 4, 5] = [2, 3]$. Use fusion to write $\mathsf{map}\, p \cdot prefix$ as a fold, and hence use the Greedy Theorem to derive the standard implementation of $takewhile\, p$ as a fold.

6. Prove that

$$\min r \supseteq \min r \cdot \mathsf{thin}\; q$$

provided that q, r are preorders, and $q \subseteq r$. Because $\mathsf{thin}\; q \supseteq \mathsf{id}$ too, this proves Lemma 5.

7. Complete the proof of the Thinning Theorem from §3.6, by showing that

$$\mathsf{fold_T}\,(\mathsf{thin}\; q \cdot \Lambda(f \cdot \mathsf{F}\; choose)) \subseteq \mathsf{thin}\; q \cdot \Lambda(\mathsf{fold_T}\; f)$$

where $\mathsf{T} = \mathrm{DATA}\; \mathsf{F}$ and f is monotonic under q°.

8. Justify the claim (§3.6) that the thinning algorithm

$$minlist\,(\chi(r)) \cdot \mathsf{fold}\,(thinlist\,(\chi(q)) \cdot mergelists\,(\chi(p)) \cdot \mathsf{map}\; combine \cdot c_{\mathsf{PF}})$$

is indeed a refinement of the optimization problem.

9. The *longest upsequence* problem [15] is to compute the longest ascending subsequence of a list; for example, the longest upsequence of $[1, 6, 5, 2, 4, 3, 3]$ is $[1, 2, 3, 3]$. Formally, the problem is to compute

$$longest \cdot \Lambda(ordered \cdot subseq)$$

where $longest$ is as in Exercise 3.8.5, and $ordered$ and $subseq$ as in §2.4. Derive a thinning algorithm to solve this problem.

10. In a sense, the Thinning Theorem always applies: one can always choose $q = \mathsf{id}$. Prove that this choice satisfies the conditions of Theorem 6, and that the algorithm obtained by applying the theorem is the same as the problem specification $\min r \cdot \Lambda(\mathsf{fold}\; f)$.

11. At the other extreme, the Greedy Theorem is an instance of the Thinning Theorem: choosing $q = r$ in the Thinning Theorem gives 'essentially' the greedy algorithm. More precisely, the thinning algorithm so obtained will still return a set of elements, but all will be optimal; taking the breadth gives the corresponding greedy algorithm. Justify this claim. (Thus, 'thinning' encompasses the whole spectrum from maintaining all partial solutions to maintaining just one.)

4   Optimal Bracketing

To illustrate the foregoing theory, consider the $(A, \leq, \oplus)$ *bracketing problem*, defined as follows. Given a linearly ordered set $(A, \leq)$, an operator $\oplus :: A \times A \rightarrow A$, and a non-empty list $a_1, a_2, \ldots a_n$ of values of type A, it is required to bracket the expression

$$a_1 \oplus a_2 \oplus \cdots \oplus a_n$$

in such a way that the result is as small as possible under the ordering $\leq$. Of course, if $\oplus$ is associative then all bracketings give equally small results.

Example 7. With $a \oplus b = max\,(a, b) + 1$, the $(\mathsf{Nat}, \leq, \oplus)$ bracketing problem corresponds to the task of combining a list of trees (with given heights $a_1, \ldots a_n$) into a single tree of minimum height. For example, given subtrees with heights $[4, 2, 3, 5, 2, 4, 6]$, one optimal tree is

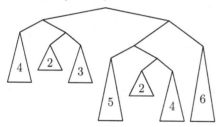

Example 8. Similarly, one interpretation of the $(\mathsf{Nat} \times \mathsf{Nat}, \leq, \oplus)$ bracketing problem, where $\leq$ is the lexical ordering on pairs and

$$(c_1, l_1) \oplus (c_2, l_2) = (c_1 + c_2 + l_1 \times l_2, l_1 + l_2)$$

corresponds to the task of multiplying a list of decimals in the shortest possible time (without exploiting the commutativity of multiplication), where multiplying decimals of lengths l_1 and l_2 costs $l_1 \times l_2$, and yields a decimal of length $l_1 + l_2$.

Example 9. The $(\mathsf{Nat} \times (\mathsf{Nat} \times \mathsf{Nat}), \leq, \oplus)$ bracketing problem, where $\leq$ is the lexical ordering and

$$(c_1, (p, q)) \oplus (c_2, (q, r)) = (c_1 + c_2 + p \times q \times r, (p, r))$$

corresponds to the problem of multiplying a sequence of conformant matrices with minimal cost, where multiplying a $p \times q$ matrix by a $q \times r$ matrix costs $p \times q \times r$, and yields a $p \times r$ matrix.

4.1   Representation

We will represent a single bracketing as a binary tree of type

$$\mathsf{Tree}\ \mathsf{A} = \mathrm{DATA}\ (\underline{\mathsf{A}} \mathbin{\hat{+}} (\mathsf{Id} \mathbin{\hat{\times}} \mathsf{Id}))$$

for which we introduce the syntactic sugar

$$tip\ a = \mathsf{in}\ (\mathsf{inl}\ a)$$
$$fork\ (t, u) = \mathsf{in}\ (\mathsf{inr}\ (t, u))$$

for the constructors, and

$$foldT :: (\mathsf{B} \times \mathsf{B} \rightsquigarrow \mathsf{B}) \rightarrow (\mathsf{A} \rightsquigarrow \mathsf{B}) \rightarrow (\mathsf{Tree}\ \mathsf{A} \rightsquigarrow \mathsf{B})$$
$$foldT\ f\ g = \mathsf{fold}_{\mathsf{Tree}}\ (g \mathbin{\triangledown} f)$$

for the fold.

In particular, the function $flatten :: \mathsf{Tree}\ \mathsf{A} \rightarrow \mathsf{PList}\ \mathsf{A}$ is defined by

$$flatten = foldT\ (+\!\!+)\ wrap$$

The $(\mathsf{A}, \leq, \oplus)$ bracketing problem can now be formalized as one of computing

$$\min r \cdot \Lambda(flatten^{\circ})$$

where $cost = foldT\ (\oplus)\ \mathsf{id}$, and $r = cost^{\circ} \cdot leq \cdot cost$, or in points, $\chi(r)\ (x, y) = cost\ x \leq cost\ y$ (so r is connected). Note that $flatten^{\circ}$ is partial, giving a result only on non-empty lists.

4.2   The Converse-of-a-Function Theorem

One could start by formulating methods for computing

$$\min r \cdot \Lambda((\mathsf{fold}\ f)^{\circ})$$

We will not take this approach (but see [5]); instead, we will make use of the following theorem to express $flatten^{\circ}$ as a fold:

Theorem 10 (Converse of a function). *Suppose $f :: \mathsf{A} \rightarrow \mathsf{T}$ (in particular, f is a total function), where $\mathsf{T} = \mathrm{DATA}\ \mathsf{F}$. Furthermore, suppose $g :: \mathsf{F}\ \mathsf{A} \rightsquigarrow \mathsf{A}$ is surjective and satisfies $f \cdot g \subseteq \mathsf{in} \cdot \mathsf{F}\ f$. Then $f^{\circ} = \mathsf{fold}_{\mathsf{T}}\ g$.*

Use of this theorem is a definite design step in solving an optimization problem: it prescribes the structure of the resulting program, and thereby rules out some potential solutions. It is therefore not always the right step to take; however, it turns out to be a productive one for some instances of the bracketing problem.

4.3   Spines

To express $flatten^\circ$ as a fold, we will represent trees by their *left spines*. The left spine of a tree is a pair consisting of the leftmost tip value and the sequence of right subtrees along the path from the leftmost tip to the root. Thus we define Spine A = A × List (Tree A). For example, the optimal tree in Example 7 has the left spine

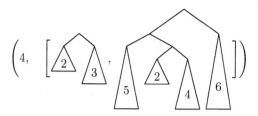

The bijection *roll* takes a spine $(a, [t_1, t_2, \ldots, t_n])$ and returns the tree

$$fork\,(\cdots fork\,(fork\,(tip\,a, t_1), t_2) \cdots, t_n)$$

Formally, we have

$$roll\,(a, ts) = foldl\,fork\,(tip\,a)\,ts$$

where $foldl$ is the natural fold function for *snoc lists*, that is, lists built by adding elements to the end rather than the beginning. On ordinary lists we can simulate $foldl$ by

$$foldl\,f\,e\,[\,] = e$$
$$foldl\,f\,e\,(cons\,(x, xs)) = foldl\,f\,(f\,(e, x))\,xs$$

Using the Converse-of-a-Function Theorem, we can now obtain (Exercise 4.10.1)

$$(flatten \cdot roll)^\circ = foldrp\,add\,one$$

where $one\,a = (a, [\,])$ and $add :: \mathsf{A} \times \mathsf{Spine\,A} \rightsquigarrow \mathsf{Spine\,A}$ is defined (using a non-injective pattern) by

$$add\,(a, (b, xs \mathbin{+\!\!+} ys)) \mathrel{\widehat{=}} (a, cons\,(roll\,(b, xs), ys))$$

For example,

$$foldrp\,add\,one\,[1, 2, 3]$$
$$= add\,(1, add\,(2, one\,3))$$
$$= add\,(1, add\,(2, (3, [\,])))$$
$$= add\,(1, (2, [tip\,3]))$$
$$= (1, [tip\,2, tip\,3]) \;\square\; (1, [fork\,(tip\,2, tip\,3)])$$

That is, both

$$(1, [tip\, 2, tip\, 3]) \leftsquigarrow foldrp\, add\, one\, [1, 2, 3]$$

and

$$(1, [fork\, (tip\, 2, tip\, 3)]) \leftsquigarrow foldrp\, add\, one\, [1, 2, 3]$$

and nothing else is a possible result.

Now we reason, for any r,

$$\min r \cdot \Lambda(flatten^\circ)$$
$$= \quad \{\ roll \text{ is a surjective function}[1], \text{ so } roll \cdot roll^\circ = \text{id}\ \}$$
$$\min r \cdot \Lambda(roll \cdot roll^\circ \cdot flatten^\circ)$$
$$= \quad \{\ \text{claim, with } \chi(rr)\, (x, y) = \chi(r)\, (roll\, x, roll\, y)\ \}$$
$$roll \cdot \min rr \cdot \Lambda(roll^\circ \cdot flatten^\circ)$$
$$= \quad \{\ \text{converse of a function}\ \}$$
$$roll \cdot \min rr \cdot \Lambda(foldrp\, add\, one)$$

The claim above is that computing a minimal tree under r is equivalent to computing a minimal spine under rr, because $roll$ is a bijection between the two types.

So our problem now is to compute $\min rr \cdot \Lambda(foldrp\, add\, one)$, where preorder rr on Spine A is defined by

$$\chi(rr)\, (x, y) = cost\, (roll\, x) \leq cost\, (roll\, y)$$

4.4   An Application of Thinning

For most instances of the bracketing problem, the algebra $one \,\triangledown\, add$ is not monotonic under rr°. For Example 7, for instance, the two trees $fork\, (tip\, 1,$ $fork\, (tip\, 1, tip\, 1))$ and $fork\, (fork\, (tip\, 1, tip\, 1), tip\, 1)$ that can be built from the list of heights $[1, 1, 1]$ are equally good under r (and so their spines are equally good under rr), but only the former can be extended by add to make the unique optimal tree for $cons\, (1, [1, 1, 1])$. So the Greedy Theorem does not apply to Example 7.

However, some instances of the bracketing problem succumb to a thinning algorithm based on the 'pairwise ordering' of the left spines of the trees, defined as follows. Let

$$lspinecosts\, (a, ts) = \text{map}\, (cost'\, a)\, (prefixes\, ts)$$
$$cost'\, a\, us = cost\, (roll\, (a, us))$$

where $prefixes$ returns the prefixes of a list in order of decreasing length — for example,

$$prefixes\, [1, 2, 3] = [[1, 2, 3], [1, 2], [1], []]$$

Then we choose the preorder q such that

$$\chi(q)\,(x,y) = lspinecosts\,x \preccurlyeq lspinecosts\,y$$

where $\preccurlyeq$ is *pairwise* ordering of sequences: $[a_1,\dots,a_m] \preccurlyeq [b_1,\dots,b_n]$ if and only if $m \le n$ and $a_i \le b_i$ for $1 \le i \le m$. Informally, $as \preccurlyeq bs$ when as is no longer than bs, and each element of as is at most the corresponding element of bs. Note that this q is not connected. Note also that $q \subseteq rr$: because $cost\,(roll\,x) = head\,(lspinecosts\,x)$, if $x \leftsquigarrow q\,y$ then certainly $cost\,(roll\,x) \le cost\,(roll\,y)$.

Now we claim that, for Examples 7 and 9, the algebra $one \bigtriangledown add$ is monotonic under this $q°$. We will leave the proof of monotonicity as Exercise 4.10.5 for the energetic reader. We will merely observe here that for the minimum height tree problem, the spines of the two trees $fork\,(tip\,1, fork\,(tip\,1, tip\,1))$ and $fork\,(fork\,(tip\,1, tip\,1), tip\,1)$ introduced above are definitely not equally good under q: the costs of the reverse prefixes of the two spines are $[3,1]$ and $[3,2,1]$, and the former is pairwise strictly less than the latter.

Therefore we conclude that, at least for these two examples,

$$\min r \cdot \Lambda(flatten°)$$
$$= \quad \{\text{ Converse of a Function }\}$$
$$roll \cdot \min rr \cdot \Lambda(foldrn\,add\,one)$$
$$\supseteq \quad \{\text{ thinning }\}$$
$$= roll \cdot \min rr \cdot \mathsf{fold}\,(\mathsf{thin}\,q \cdot \Lambda((one \bigtriangledown add) \cdot \mathsf{F}\,choose))$$

Unfortunately, although the resulting algorithm appears to perform well in practice, its worst-case running time is exponential, and knowing this it is not too difficult to construct pathological inputs. The problem is that too few partial solutions are thinned out in the worst case.

4.5 An Application of Greediness

In fact, for Example 7 we can do a lot better. We have already observed that Theorem 3 does not apply; however, there is a connected preorder q which satisfies the conditions of Theorem 4. We choose the preorder q characterized by

$$\chi(q)\,(x,y) = lspinecosts\,x \trianglelefteq lspinecosts\,y$$

where $\trianglelefteq$ is the *lexicographic* (as opposed to pairwise) ordering on sequences: for sequences $as = [a_1,\dots,a_m]$ and $bs = [b_1,\dots,b_n]$, the ordering $as \trianglelefteq bs$ holds if and only if there exists an i with $0 \le i \le m,n$ such that $a_j = b_j$ for $1 \le j \le i$ and either $i = m$ (in which case as is a prefix of bs) or $i < m,n$ and $a_{i+1} < b_{i+1}$ (in which case as and bs differ first at position $i+1$).

Again, $q \subseteq rr$, for the same reason that the q of §4.4 is included in rr. We leave the proof of monotonicity to Exercise 4.10.6, pausing only to observe as before that the costs of the reverse prefixes of the two spines of the trees constructed from $[1, 1, 1]$ are $[3, 1]$ and $[3, 2, 1]$, and the former is lexicographically (as well as pairwise) strictly less than the latter.

Now, however, q is connected, and so a greedy algorithm works — it suffices to keep a single partial solution at each stage. We have

$$\min r \cdot \Lambda(\text{fold } f)$$
$$\supseteq \quad \{\min r \supseteq \min q \ \}$$
$$\min q \cdot \Lambda(\text{fold } f)$$
$$\supseteq \quad \{ \text{ Refining Greedy Theorem, assuming } f \text{ monotonic under } q^\circ \ \}$$
$$\text{fold } (\min q \cdot \Lambda f)$$

4.6   Refinement of the Greedy Algorithm to a Program

Returning to bracketing problems in general, provided that we can find a connected preorder q under whose converse $one \triangledown add$ is monotonic (as we have seen we can do for the minimum height tree problem, for instance), we have

$$\min r \cdot \Lambda(flatten^\circ)$$
$$= \quad \{ \text{ Converse of a Function } \}$$
$$roll \cdot \min rr \cdot \Lambda(foldrn\, add\, one)$$
$$\supseteq \quad \{ \text{ strengthened preorder } \}$$
$$roll \cdot \min q \cdot \Lambda(foldrn\, add\, one)$$
$$\supseteq \quad \{ \text{ Greedy Theorem } \}$$
$$roll \cdot foldrn\, (\min q \cdot \Lambda add)\, (\min q \cdot \Lambda one)$$

To obtain a deterministic program, we still have to refine $\min q \cdot \Lambda one$ and $\min q \cdot \Lambda add$ to functions. Since one is a function, $\min q \cdot \Lambda one = one$. One can also show (Exercise 4.10.7) that $\min q \cdot \Lambda add \supseteq minadd$, where

$$minadd\,(a, (b, ts)) = (a, cons\,(roll\,(cons\,(b, us)), vs))$$

where $us \mathbin{+\!\!+} vs = ts$, and us is the shortest proper prefix of ts satisfying

$$max\,(a, cost\,(roll\,(cons\,(b, us)))) < cost\,(head\, vs)$$

If no such us exists, then $us = ts$ and $vs = [\,]$.

4.7   Summary

To summarize, the problem of building a tree of minimum height can be solved by computing

$$roll \cdot foldrp\, minadd\, one$$

Moreover, this algorithm takes linear time. The time taken to compute *minadd* is proportional to the length of the *us* chosen, but the length of the resulting spine is reduced by this amount; a standard amortization argument then shows that the total time taken for the algorithm is linear in the length of the given list.

4.8   The Haskell Program

The program in Figure 1 is an implementation in Haskell [20] of the algorithm derived above for the minimum height tree instance of the bracketing problem. To avoid repeated computations, we label trees with their costs.

```
data Tree  = Tip Int | Fork Int Tree Tree
type Spine = (Int, [Tree])

cost :: Tree -> Int
cost (Tip a)     = a
cost (Fork a t u) = a

fork :: Tree -> Tree -> Tree
fork t u = Fork (max (cost t) (cost u) + 1) t u

roll :: Spine -> Tree
roll (a, ts) = foldl fork (Tip a) ts

greedy :: [Int] -> Tree
greedy = roll . foldrp minadd one

one :: Int -> Spine
one a = (a, [])

minadd :: Int -> Spine -> Spine
minadd a (b,ts) = (a, split (Tip b : ts))
  where
    split [t] = [t]
    split (t:u:ts) = if   max a (cost t) < cost u
                      then t:u:ts
                      else split (fork t u : ts)

foldrp  ::  (a -> b -> b) -> (a -> b) -> ([a] -> b)
foldrp f g [x]    = g x
foldrp f g (x:xs) = f x (foldrp f g xs)
```

Fig. 1. Haskell implementation of minimum height tree algorithm

4.9 Bibliographic Notes

The minimum height tree problem comes from [6], where a different greedy solution is presented. This chapter could be thought of as an abstract of Mu's forthcoming DPhil thesis [27], which expands on the approaches discussed here, in particular looking at other thinning algorithms, and exploring the relationship with dynamic programming as well as greedy algorithms.

4.10 Exercises

1. Prove the Converse-of-a-Function Theorem from §4.2.
2. Theorem 10 applies only to total functions f. If f is a partial function (that is, simple buyt not necessarily entire), the corresponding 'Converse of a Partial Function' theorem states, when $\mathsf{T} = \text{DATA } \mathsf{F}$, that $f^\circ = \mathsf{fold}_\mathsf{T}\, g$ provided that $f \cdot g \subseteq \text{in} \cdot \mathsf{F}\, f$ and $\mathsf{dom}\, f = \mathsf{ran}\, g$. Prove this generalization.
3. Verify the application of the Converse-of-a-Function Theorem in §4.3.
4. Show that the Greedy Theorem is not applicable to (that is, $one \bigtriangledown add$ is not monotonic under r° for) Example 9. What can you say about Example 8?
5. Show that for a bracketing problem $(\mathsf{A}, \oplus, \leq)$ such that $\oplus$ is commutative $(a \oplus b = b \oplus a)$, strict $(a \oplus b > a)$ and monotonic in its left argument $(a \leq a' \Rightarrow a \oplus b \leq a' \oplus b)$, the algebra $one \bigtriangledown add$ is monotonic under q°, where q is as introduced in §4.4. Verify that these conditions apply for Examples 7 and 9.
6. Show that $one \bigtriangledown add$ for the minimum height tree problem is monotonic under q°, where q is as introduced in §4.5.
7. Show that $\min q \cdot \Lambda add \supseteq minadd$ for the minimum height tree problem, where $minadd$ is as defined in §4.6.
8. Express as an instance of the bracketing problem the problem of concatenating a list of lists into a single list in the cheapest possible way, when the cost of concatenating two lists is proportional to the length of the lefthand list. Derive a suitable algorithm for solving the problem.

References

1. Roland Backhouse, Peter de Bruin, Grant Malcolm, Ed Voermans, and Jaap van der Woude. A relational theory of datatypes. In *STOP 1992 Summerschool on Constructive Algorithmics*. STOP project, 1992. 283, 290
2. Roland Backhouse and Paul Hoogendijk. Elements of a relational theory of datatypes. In Bernhard Möller, Helmut Partsch, and Steve Schumann, editors, *LNCS 755: IFIP TC2/WG2.1 State-of-the-Art Report on Formal Program Development*, pages 7–42. Springer-Verlag, 1993. 283, 290
3. R. Berghammer and H. Zierer. Relational algebraic semantics of deterministic and non-deterministic programs. *Theoretical Computer Science*, 43(2–3):123–147, 1986. 283
4. Richard Bird and Oege de Moor. Hybrid dynamic programming. Programming Research Group, Oxford, 1994. 297

5. Richard Bird and Oege de Moor. *The Algebra of Programming*. Prentice-Hall, 1996. 283, 290, 297, 300
6. Richard S. Bird. On building trees with minimum height. *Journal of Functional Programming*, 7(4):441–445, 1997. 306
7. A. Bunkenburg. *Expression Refinement*. PhD thesis, Computing Science Department, University of Glasgow, 1997. 290
8. Thomas H. Cormen, Charles E. Leiserson, and Ronald L. Rivest. *Introduction to Algorithms*. MIT Press, 1990. 297
9. Sharon Curtis. *A Relational Approach to Optimization Problems*. PhD thesis, University of Oxford, 1996. Technical Monograph PRG-122. 297
10. J. W. de Bakker and W. P. de Roever. A calculus for recursive program schemes. In M. Nivat, editor, *Automata, Languages and Programming*, pages 167–196. North-Holland, 1973. 283
11. Oege de Moor and Jeremy Gibbons. Pointwise relational programming. In *LNCS 1816: Algebraic Methodology and Software Technology*, pages 371–390, May 2000. 290
12. S. Eilenberg and J. B. Wright. Automata in general algebras. *Information and Control*, 11(4):452–470, 1967. 297
13. Sharon Flynn. *A Refinement Calculus for Expressions*. PhD thesis, University of Glasgow, 1997. 290
14. P. J. Freyd and A. Ščedrov. *Categories, Allegories*. North-Holland, 1990. 290
15. David Gries. *The Science of Programming*. Texts and Monographs in Computer Science. Springer-Verlag, 1981. 298
16. Eric C. R. Hehner. *A Practical Theory of Programming*. Texts and Monographs in Computer Science. Springer-Verlag, 1993. 283
17. C. A. R. Hoare. Programs are predicates. In C. A. R. Hoare and J. C. Shepherdson, editors, *Mathematical Logic and Programming Languages*. Prentice-Hall, 1985. Also Chapter 20 of [18]. 283
18. C. A. R. Hoare. *Essays in Computing Science*. Prentice Hall, 1989. 307
19. Paul Hoogendijk. *A Generic Theory of Datatypes*. PhD thesis, Technische Universiteit Eindhoven, 1997. 297
20. Simon Peyton Jones, John Hughes, Lennart Augustsson, Dave Barton, Brian Boutel, Warren Burton, Joseph Fasel, Kevin Hammond, Ralf Hinze, Paul Hudak, Thomas Johnsson, Mark Jones, John Launchbury, Erik Meijer, John Peterson, Alastair Reid, Colin Runciman, and Philip Wadler. Haskell 98: A non-strict, purely functional language. www.haskell.org/onlinereport, February 1999. 305
21. Bernhard Korte, Laszlo Lovasz, and Rainer Schrader. *Greedoids*. Springer-Verlag, 1991. 297
22. Robert A. Kowalski. Predicate logic as a programming language. In *IFIP Congress*, 1974. 283
23. Ali Mili, Jules Desharnais, and Fatma Mili. *Computer Program Construction*. Oxford University Press, 1994. 283
24. Bernhard Möller. Relations as a program development language. In B. Möller, editor, *IFIP TC2/WG2.1 Working Conference on Constructing Programs from Specifications*, pages 373–397. North-Holland, 1991. 283
25. Joseph M. Morris. Programming by expression refinement: The KMP algorithm. In W. H. J. Feijen, A. J. M. van Gasteren, D. Gries, and J. Misra, editors, *Beauty is our Business*, chapter 37. Springer-Verlag, 1990. 290
26. Joseph M. Morris. Non-deterministic expressions and predicate transformers. *Information Processing Letters*, 61:241–246, 1997. 290

27. Shin-Cheng Mu. *Inverting Programs by Calculation.* DPhil thesis, University of Oxford, in preparation. 306
28. Theo Norvell and Eric Hehner. Logical specifications for functional programs. In R. S. Bird, C. C. Morgan, and J. C. P. Woodcock, editors, *LNCS 669: Mathematics of Program Construction*, pages 269–290. Springer-Verlag, 1993. 290
29. Richard A. O'Keefe. *The Craft of Prolog.* MIT Press, 1990. 283
30. Alfred Tarski. On the calculus of relations. *Journal of Symbolic Logic*, 6(3):73–89, 1941. 290
31. Nigel Thomas Edgar Ward. *A Refinement Calculus for Nondeterministiuc Expressions.* PhD thesis, University of Queensland, February 1994. 290

Chapter 9
Temporal Algebra

Burghard von Karger

University of Kiel

1 Introduction

The complexity of software controlled systems is ever increasing, and so is the need for mathematical theories and tools that help with their design and verification. This need has not been answered by a single grand unified theory; on the contrary the great variety of programming languages and paradigms has led to an equally large number of different and, in most cases, incompatible formalisms. This diversity is of growing concern to academia and industry alike and we have reached the stage where the unification of existing theories should take priority over the invention of new ones.

This tutorial is concerned with two families of programming theories. One of them is the predicate calculus which Dijkstra [14] and Hoare [20] recommend for the design of imperative programs. The other is temporal logic, which was first advocated by Pnueli [35] for reasoning about reactive systems.

Temporal logics have been enormously successful because they combine simplicity and appeal to intuition with practical usefulness. The temporal connectives are easy to grasp, possess nice mathematical properties, and are well suited for specifying properties of concurrent and reactive systems. The powerful decision procedures and model checking algorithms for temporal logic have found many industrial applications, especially in hardware design and telecommunications.

The algebraic approach to program design emphasizes a calculational style based on equational and inequational rewriting. Proofs are guided by the shape of formulae and a few heuristic rules. This style, which is in accordance with familiar mathematical practice, is designed to make proofs easy to conduct and to remember. It is in sharp contrast with many logical deduction schemes that have been invented for theoretical investigations or are geared towards implementation on a digital computer. Consequently, predicate algebras (more commonly known as Boolean algebras) such as relation algebra and the algebra of predicate transformers are especially successful in the *construction* of programs, and many beautiful derivations of algorithms have been published in these notations. Predicate calculi are sometimes denounced as being only pen-and-paper tools, but they certainly exercise a strong influence on the education of computer scientists and on the design of programming languages.

Our goal is to bring the two schools closer together by giving algebraic presentations of the more well-known temporal logics, including linear temporal logic

R. Backhouse et al. (Eds.): Algebraic and Coalgebraic Methods . . . , LNCS 2297, pp. 309–385, 2002.
© Springer-Verlag Berlin Heidelberg 2002

(LTL), interval temporal logic (ITL) and the duration calculus. More specifically, we employ familiar algebraic structures such as complete lattices, Galois connections and the algebra of binary relations for defining temporal operators and exploring their properties. This approach is called *temporal algebra*, because its subject matter are the structures of temporal logic but its tools and methods are those of algebra.

Any attempt at unifying theories is motivated by the twin desires of simplification and generalization. As an example of simplification, we have shown in [45] that all seventeen axioms of Manna and Pnueli's sound and complete proof system for LTL [27] can be derived from just two Galois connections between the 'next' and the 'previous' operator. (We will not, however, reproduce all seventeen proofs in this tutorial.)

Temporal algebra consists of two subdisciplines, which we have called *Galois algebra* and *sequential algebra*. Galois algebra extends the predicate calculus with a pair of conjugate functions which may be interpreted as the 'next' and 'previous' operators. It is the algebraic counterpart of logics such as LTL, CTL and CTL* that are designed for reasoning about runs of reactive systems. Since reactive systems are typically non-terminating, these logics offer no operator for constructing a new system as a sequential composition of two given ones.

On the other hand, sequential composition is the most important combinator of imperative programs. Among the calculi that include it the most well-known is Tarski's algebra of relations [41], which has been remarkably successful in reasoning about possibly non-deterministic systems, provided that their behaviour can be fully characterised by observation of just their initial and final states. Many alternative models have been proposed for reactive systems, whose behaviour between initiation and termination is also of significance. A common feature of these calculi is that past events cannot be cancelled or undone by what comes after. As a consequence, the converse operation of relation algebra must be abandoned. We introduce *sequential algebra* as a common framework of laws applicable to many of these alternative models, including dynamic logic, process algebra, interval temporal logic and the duration calculus.

Temporal algebra emphasises commonalities rather than differences between formalisms. Often two theories are only distinguished by a single axiom. For example, relation algebra is obtained from sequential algebra by postulating an associativity axiom for division, or LTL from CTL by requiring that 'previous' and 'next' form a Galois connection. In either case, both learning and teaching these theories is made easier because large common parts can be factored out.

Further integration is achieved by building models for one theory within another. We will study a number of canonical constructions that yield temporal logics from any given sequential algebra. In this way, we obtain a large number of interesting new models for the previously developed theory, and various properties that a sequential algebra may or may not have (branching, interleaving, confluence, etc.) translate to postulates that one may add to the axioms of Galois algebra, thereby providing additional insight into the hierarchy of temporal logics. Finally, the construction of Galois algebras from sequential ones yields algebras that admit the operators of both signatures. One may well view the temporal connectives as specification constructs and the sequential ones as program operators, so that we have built a mixed calculus which allows the stepwise derivation of an executable program from an abstract specification. The power of this approach has been illustrated in [5] and [6], where we used the mixed calculus for deriving CSP programs from temporal specifications.

Temporal algebra is intended as a link between theories, and there is no suggestion whatsoever that it could be an alternative, let alone a replacement, for temporal logic. Because it is a purely semantic theory, temporal algebra cannot express, much less prove, results about expressivity, completeness and decidability, for these concepts require a syntax for their definition.

Acknowledgements

I am very grateful to Roland Backhouse (and his colleagues at Eindhoven) for teaching me many things about calculations and inviting me to present my ideas in this forum. A special debt is owed to Tony Hoare who started my investigations into temporal algebra with a couple of design exercises for the duration calculus (you can find them in Section 6). His insights have guided my work many times.

This chapter is a revision and expansion of [46].

2 Preliminaries

2.1 Lattices

We describe systems by the set of their possible behaviours; specifications are sets of allowed behaviours. A system P implements a specification S if every behaviour that P can exhibit is allowed by S:

$$P \subseteq S.$$

The implementation relation is a *partial order* on system descriptions. A system is usually required to have many properties:

$$P \subseteq S_1 \ \wedge \ \ldots \ \wedge \ P \subseteq S_n.$$

To express multiple constraints by a single specification, we need *conjunction*:

$$P \subseteq S_1 \cap \ldots \cap S_n.$$

Systems that are built of interactive components typically exhibit non-deterministic behaviour. If a system can behave like P_1 or like P_2, we must show that

$$P_1 \cup P_2 \subseteq S,$$

in order to ensure that the specification S is satisfied. Thus it seems that ordering, disjunction and conjunction are very desirable constituents of a theory of systems and specifications. These operations form the signature of a lattice. We recall the definition.

Definition 1 (Lattice). *A partially ordered nonempty set $\mathcal{G}$ is called a* lattice *when the least upper bound and greatest lower bound of $\{x, y\}$ exist for every $x, y \in \mathcal{G}$. Least upper bounds are also called conjunctions or intersections and greatest lower bounds are referred to as disjunctions or unions. We use the symbols $\subseteq, \cap$ and $\cup$ to denote the lattice ordering and operations.*

2.2   Galois Connections

Whenever an algebraic structure is introduced, attention must be given to structure-preserving maps. An *isomorphism* between two lattices $\mathcal{G}$ and $\mathcal{H}$ is a bijective function $f : \mathcal{G} \to \mathcal{H}$ such that

$$f.x \subseteq y \qquad \Leftrightarrow \qquad x \subseteq f^{-1}.y \quad \text{for all } x \in \mathcal{G} \text{ and } y \in \mathcal{H}.$$

The dot in terms like $f.x$ denotes functional application. It associates to the right, so that $f.g.x = f.(g.x)$. If such an isomorphism exists then $\mathcal{G}$ and $\mathcal{H}$ are essentially the same and every theorem that holds for one of them is also true of the other. A more common and more interesting situation occurs when the two functions relating $\mathcal{G}$ and $\mathcal{H}$ are not each other's inverses. A pair of functions $f : \mathcal{G} \to \mathcal{H}$ and $g : \mathcal{H} \to \mathcal{G}$ is a *Galois connection* if

$$f.x \subseteq y \qquad \Leftrightarrow \qquad x \subseteq g.y \quad \text{for all } x \in \mathcal{G} \text{ and } y \in \mathcal{H}.$$

Galois connections should be thought of as two-way homomorphisms between lattices. The reader may be familiar with the homomorphism theorem for groups, rings, vector spaces, etc: If $f : \mathcal{G} \to \mathcal{H}$ is a homomorphism and $\approx$ the equivalence induced by f then $\mathcal{G}/\approx$ is isomorphic to the image of f (see Figure 1(a)). The corresponding theorem for a Galois connection (f, g) states that f is an isomorphism from the image of g to the image of f, and that g is its inverse.

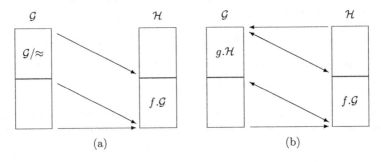

Fig. 1. (a) The usual homomorphism theorem, and (b) the one for Galois connections

Figure 1(b) shows that a Galois connection establishes a very close link between two lattices. The following results are well-known and their proofs can be found in, for example, in [1] or [2].

Definition 2 (Adjoints). *If (f, g) is a Galois connection then we say that f is a lower adjoint (of g) and that g is an upper adjoint (of f). In the preceding figure, the lower adjoint is the one that moves downwards, and the upper adjoint is the one that moves upwards. Adjoints are unique in the sense that each function in a Galois connection determines the other. We use the symbol $\sharp$ for the function that maps a lower adjoint to its upper adjoint and the symbol $\flat$ for its converse. In other words,*

$$(f, g) \text{ is a Galois connection} \quad \Leftrightarrow \quad g = f^{\sharp} \quad \Leftrightarrow \quad f = g^{\flat}.$$

Note that $\sharp$ and $\flat$ are partial functions.

Proposition 3 (Cancellation rule). *Suppose f and g are two functions between complete lattices. Then (f, g) is a Galois connection if and only if*

$$f \circ g \subseteq id \quad and \quad id \subseteq g \circ f.$$

Proposition 4 (Anti-Monotonicity of $\flat$ and $\sharp$). *If f and g are lower adjoints then we have*

$$f \subseteq g \quad \Leftrightarrow \quad g^{\sharp} \subseteq f^{\sharp}.$$

An analogous equivalence holds for upper adjoints.

Proposition 5 (Composition Rule for Galois Connections). *Like homomorphisms, Galois connections may be composed. Suppose that (f_1, g_1) is a Galois connection between $\mathcal{G}$ and $\mathcal{F}$, and that (f_2, g_2) is a Galois connection between $\mathcal{H}$ and $\mathcal{G}$. Then $(f_1 \circ f_2, g_2 \circ g_1)$ is a Galois connection between $\mathcal{H}$ and $\mathcal{F}$. In other words, if $f_1^{\sharp}$ and $f_2^{\sharp}$ exist and $f_1 \circ f_2$ is defined then*

$$(f_1 \circ f_2)^{\sharp} = f_2^{\sharp} \circ f_1^{\sharp}.$$

Definition 6 (Sectioning). *To exploit the calculational properties of Galois connections involving binary operators, such as conjunction, it is frequently necessary to keep one of the arguments fixed. Therefore we define, for any binary infix operator $\diamond$, the functions $(x \diamond)$ and $(\diamond x)$ by*

$$(x \diamond).y =_{df} x \diamond y \quad and \quad (\diamond x).y =_{df} y \diamond x.$$

This process of constructing unary operators from binary ones is known as sectioning and the functions $(x \diamond)$ and $(\diamond x)$ are the sections of $\diamond$.

More detailed accounts of the theory of Galois connections can be found in Chapter 4 and in [1,17,18,29,34].

2.3   Boolean Algebra

Galois connections are very powerful calculation tools. In this section we give a first demonstration by *defining* a Boolean algebra as a lattice with a certain Galois connection and then deriving the familiar laws of Boolean algebra.

Definition 7. *A Boolean algebra is a lattice with a unary operator $\neg$ that satisfies the following law.*

$$p \cap q \subseteq r \qquad \Leftrightarrow \qquad q \subseteq \neg p \cup r.$$

Because it so conveniently allows one to move terms from one side of an inequation to the other, this equivalence is called the *shunting rule*. Using sections, the shunting rule can be expressed more succinctly as

$$(p \cap)^{\sharp} = (\neg p \cup).$$

Throughout the rest of Section 2.3 we assume that $\mathcal{B}$ is a Boolean algebra.

Theorem 8 (Complements). *$\mathcal{B}$ has a least element O and greatest element U. Moreover, we have*

$$p \cap \neg p = \mathsf{O} \quad and \quad p \cup \neg p = U.$$

Proof. Let $p \in \mathcal{B}$. The shunting rule yields

$$p \cap \neg p \subseteq q \quad and \quad q \subseteq \neg p \cup p$$

for every $q \in \mathcal{B}$. It follows that $p \cap \neg p$ and $p \cup \neg p$ are the least and greatest elements of $\mathcal{B}$, respectively.

Theorem 9 (Distributivity). *We have $p \cap (q \cup r) = (p \cap q) \cup (p \cap r)$ for all $p, q, r \in \mathcal{B}$.*

Proof. The following calculation uses the principle of *indirect equality*, which is a standard tool for establishing that two elements of a lattice are the same.

$$p \cap (q \cup r) \subseteq x$$
$$\Leftrightarrow \qquad \{ \text{ Shunt } p \text{ to the right } \}$$
$$q \cup r \subseteq \neg p \cup x$$
$$\Leftrightarrow \qquad \{ \text{ Universal property of } \cup \}$$
$$(q \subseteq \neg p \cup x) \ \wedge \ (r \subseteq \neg p \cup x)$$
$$\Leftrightarrow \qquad \{ \text{ Shunt } p \text{ to the left } \}$$
$$(p \cap q \subseteq x) \ \wedge \ (p \cap r \subseteq x)$$
$$\Leftrightarrow \qquad \{ \text{ Universal property of } \cup \}$$
$$(p \cap q) \cup (p \cap r) \subseteq x.$$

To see that this equivalence chain really proves distributivity, instantiate x first with one, then with the other side of the demonstrandum.

Theorem 10 (Double Negation). $\neg\neg p = p$ *for every* $p \in \mathcal{B}$.

Proof.

$$\neg\neg p$$
$$=$$
$$\neg\neg p \cap U$$
$$=\qquad \{\ \neg p \text{ is a complement of } p\ \}$$
$$\neg\neg p \cap (\neg p \cup p)$$
$$=\qquad \{\ \text{Distributivity}\ \}$$
$$(\neg\neg p \cap \neg p) \cup (\neg\neg p \cap p)$$
$$=\qquad \{\ \neg\neg p \text{ is a complement of } \neg p\ \}$$
$$\text{O} \cup (\neg\neg p \cap p)$$
$$\subseteq$$
$$p.$$

To prove the other inclusion, exchange p and $\neg\neg p$ in the above calculation.

Theorem 11 (Contraposition). *For all* $p, q \in \mathcal{B}$ *we have*

$$p \subseteq q \qquad \Leftrightarrow \qquad \neg q \subseteq \neg p.$$

In particular, negation is anti-monotonic.

Proof.

$$p \subseteq q$$
$$\Leftrightarrow\qquad \{\ \text{By Theorem 10 and Theorem 8}\ \}$$
$$p \subseteq \neg\neg q \cup \text{O}$$
$$\Leftrightarrow\qquad \{\ \text{Shunt } q \text{ to the lhs}\ \}$$
$$\neg q \cap p \subseteq \text{O}$$
$$\Leftrightarrow\qquad \{\ \text{Shunt } p \text{ to the rhs}\ \}$$
$$\neg q \subseteq \neg p \cup \text{O}$$
$$\Leftrightarrow$$
$$\neg q \subseteq \neg p.$$

Remark 12 (The Duality Principle). *Since the dual of a lattice is itself a lattice, every theorem of lattice theory has a dual which is obtained by exchanging* $\cup$ *with* $\cap$, *O with* U, *and* $\subseteq$ *with* $\supseteq$. *Lattices with additional structure, such as Boolean algebras, inherit the duality principle if each new operator has a dual and the set of additional axioms is invariant under duality. Let us define negation to be self-dual. Then dualizing the shunting rule gives*

$$p \cup q \supseteq r \qquad \Leftrightarrow \qquad q \supseteq \neg p \cap r.$$

Since $p = \neg\neg p$ *(as we just have proved), the dualized shunting rule is a consequence of the original shunting rule. It follows that the duality principle carries* over to Boolean algebra. We sometimes call it 'logical duality' or 'de Morgan duality' to distinguish it from the temporal duality that arises from the symmetry of past and future.

Definition 13. *Suppose f is a function between Boolean algebras. Then the de Morgan dual of f is defined by*

$$\tilde{f}.x =_{df} \neg f. \neg x .$$

The de Morgan dual of a binary function is similarly defined by negating both arguments and the result.

The following law states that $\cap$ and $\cup$ are de Morgan duals.

Theorem 14 (De Morgan's Rule). *For all $p, q \in \mathcal{B}$ we have*

$$\neg(p \cap q) \;=\; \neg p \cup \neg q \quad and \quad \neg(p \cup q) = \neg p \cap \neg q .$$

Proof. By the duality principle we need only show the first equation.

$$
\begin{aligned}
& x \;\subseteq\; \neg(p \cap q) \\
\Leftrightarrow \quad & \qquad \{ \text{ Contraposition } \} \\
& \neg x \;\subseteq\; p \cap q \\
\Leftrightarrow \quad & \qquad \{ \text{ Universal property of } \cap \} \\
& (\neg x \subseteq p) \wedge (\neg x \subseteq q) \\
\Leftrightarrow \quad & \qquad \{ \text{ Contraposition } \} \\
& (x \subseteq \neg p) \wedge (x \subseteq \neg q) \\
\Leftrightarrow \quad & \qquad \{ \text{ Universal property of } \cup \} \\
& x \;\subseteq\; \neg p \cup \neg q .
\end{aligned}
$$

Theorem 15 (Complement Rule). *For all $p, q \in \mathcal{B}$ we have*

$$p \cap (\neg p \cup q) \;\subseteq\; q \;\subseteq\; \neg p \cup (p \cap q) .$$

Proof. Apply the cancellation rule (Proposition 3) to the Galois connection $((p\cap), (\neg p\cup))$.

Lemma 16. *Suppose f is a function between Boolean algebras and g is its de Morgan dual. If f distributes over $\cup$ then we have*

$$f.p \cap g.q \;\subseteq\; f.(p \cap q) .$$

Proof. In the following chain of equivalences and implications we start from the demonstrandum. This is the recommended style, because it is consistent with the proof's discovery: the individual steps are natural and in most cases motivated by the desire to simplify the current expression, or, in some cases, to prepare for such a simplification in the next step.

$$f.p \cap g.q \subseteq f.(p \cap q)$$
$\Leftrightarrow$ { Shunting }
$$f.p \subseteq \neg g.q \cup f.(p \cap q)$$
$\Leftrightarrow$ { g is the de Morgan dual of f }
$$f.p \subseteq f.\neg q \cup f.(p \cap q)$$
$\Leftrightarrow$ { f distributes over $\cup$ }
$$f.p \subseteq f.(\neg q \cup (p \cap q))$$
$\Leftarrow$ { Disjunctive functions are monotonic }
$$p \subseteq \neg q \cup (p \cap q)$$
$\Leftrightarrow$ { Complement rule (Theorem 15) }
$$true.$$

Of course, we could have written this chain in the reverse order, deriving the demonstrandum from 'true'. If we had done so, the very first step of the proof (deducing $p \subseteq \neg q \cup (p \cap q)$ from 'true') would have come as a surprise, like the proverbial rabbit from a conjurer's hat, and the reader does not immediately see the reason why this specific deduction is made rather than any one of a hundred other possibilities [42].

Definition 17 (Conjugate functions). *Galois connections are not symmetric: one of the functions is a lower adjoint while the other is an upper adjoint. In a Boolean algebra, symmetry can be forced by replacing the upper adjoint with its de Morgan dual. Assume that f is a lower adjoint and define g by $g.x = \neg f^{\sharp}.\neg x$. Then the Galois connection can be rewritten as*

$$f.x \cap y = 0 \quad \Leftrightarrow \quad x \cap g.y = 0.$$

When this equivalence holds, f and g are said to be conjugate. *If f and g are conjugate functions between Boolean algebras then each of the two functions has an upper adjoint, which is the de Morgan dual of the other function.*

Theorem 18 (Dedekind law). *Suppose f and g are conjugate functions between Boolean algebras. Then we have*

$$f.x \cap y \subseteq f.(x \cap g.y).$$

The Dedekind law was first known in group theory: for subsets O, P, Q of a group one has

$$OP \cap Q \subseteq O(P \cap O^{-1}Q),$$

where $O^{-1} = \{o^{-1} \mid o \in O\}$. In relation algebra it takes the form

$$O;P \cap Q \subseteq O;(P \cap O^{\cup};Q).$$

Since these inequations have the same shape as the defining property of a modular lattice (replace ';' with '$\cup$' and transposition with the identity), Dedekind laws are often called *modular laws*. We will encounter many instances of the Dedekind law in this chapter.

Proof. Let $h =_{df} g^{\sharp}$, the upper adjoint of g. Then f and h are de Morgan duals and we may calculate:

$$f.p \cap q$$
$$\subseteq \qquad \{ \text{ Cancellation rule (Proposition 3) } \}$$
$$f.p \cap h.g.q$$
$$\subseteq \qquad \{ \text{ Lemma 16 } \}$$
$$f.(p \cap g.q) \,.$$

Definition 19 (Implication and Modus Ponens). *As usual, we introduce* $p \to q$ *(p implies q) as an abbreviation for* $\neg p \cup q$. *With this notation, the first inequation in the complement rule becomes the familiar modus ponens*

$$p \cap (p \to q) \subseteq q \,.$$

2.4   Fixed Points

The low popularity of the algebraic approach to temporal logic is partly due to the lack of a convincing presentation. Usually, *modal algebras* are proposed as an algebraic counterpart to temporal (or modal) logic [40,39]. A modal algebra is a Boolean algebra with one or more unary operators that preserve its least element and distribute over finite disjunctions.

We believe that these presentations suffer from excess of generality. All practically relevant Boolean algebras are complete, and most finitely disjunctive operators distribute over infinite disjunctions as well. There is much to be gained from strengthening the assumptions, because every universally disjunctive operator on a complete lattice has an upper adjoint. This fact greatly simplifies the theory because it allows us to *define* the 'past' operators as adjoints of the 'future' operators (whereas, in temporal logics, the 'past' operators are either postulated or omitted). Completeness is also required for the fixed point theorem of Knaster and Tarski. With the aid of recursion and Galois connections, the entire zoo of operators that populate the treatments of LTL can be defined in terms of just the 'next' operator.

Why, then, isn't completeness assumed in most logical treatments of the subject? The most compelling reason against completeness is that it is awkward to state as a logical axiom or inference rule. In a finitary syntactical framework, completeness can only be dealt with indirectly, by postulating the existence of fixed point operators (as one does in the modal μ-calculus). Another reason for not requiring completeness in the first place, is that it can be added a posteriori if necessary, using the perfect extension theorem of Jónsson and Tarski [40] which asserts that any Boolean algebra with finitely disjunctive operators can be embedded in a complete Boolean algebra with universally disjunctive operators. For these reasons, logicians rightly reject the power of completeness. In the context of algebra, completeness is not a complicated postulate at all but a necessary requirement for efficiently calculating with Galois connections and fixed points.

Definition 20 (Completeness). *A lattice* $\mathcal{G}$ *is* complete *if every subset of* G *has a greatest lower bound and a least upper bound. This requirement also pertains to the empty set, so that every complete lattice has a least element (denoted* O *or* F*) and a greatest element (denoted* U*, for universe, or* T*).*

Definition 21 (Disjunctivity and Conjunctivity). *A function between lattices is* disjunctive *if it preserves all binary disjunctions*

$$f.(x \cup y) \;=\; f.x \cup f.y \,.$$

A function between complete lattices $\mathcal{G}$ *and* $\mathcal{H}$ *is* universally disjunctive *if it preserves all disjunctions*

$$f.\bigcup M \;=\; \bigcup_{m \in M} f.m \quad \text{for all } M \subseteq \mathcal{G} \,.$$

Conjunctivity is defined likewise. Every function that is disjunctive or conjunctive is monotonic. Moreover a universally disjunctive (conjunctive) function maps O *to* O *(* U *to* U *).*

Theorem 22 (Existence of Adjoint Functions). *The following two equivalences hold for every function between complete lattices.*

1. f *is universally disjunctive if and only if* f *is a lower adjoint.*
2. f *is universally conjunctive if and only if* f *is an upper adjoint.*

Definition 23 (Fixed Point Operators). *Recursion is the most powerful tool for defining new operators in the calculi we are going to explore, and to determine their properties we must calculate with fixed points. Suppose* f *is a monotonic function on a complete lattice G. Then the theorem of Knaster and Tarski tells us that* f *has a unique least fixed point, denoted* μf*, and a unique greatest fixed point* νf*. Because it is frequently inconvenient to assign names to the functions occurring in fixed point expressions we allow the notations* $\mu_x(f.x)$ *and* $\nu_x(f.x)$ *instead of* μf *and* νf*. For example,* $\mu_x(p \cup \oplus x)$ *denotes the least fixed point of the (anonymous) function that maps* x *to* $p \cup \oplus x$*.*

Fixed points are studied in Chapter 4. We list some rules that we will need. All functions mentioned below are assumed to be monotonic.

Proposition 24 (Fixed Point Rules).

1. *Induction rules*

$$\mu f \subseteq r \quad \Leftarrow \quad f.r \subseteq r \,.$$
$$p \subseteq \nu f \quad \Leftarrow \quad p \subseteq f.p \,.$$

2. *Duality*

$$\mu \tilde{f} = \neg(\nu f) \quad \text{and} \quad \nu \tilde{f} = \neg(\mu f) \,.$$

3. *Fusion. Assume σ is a lower adjoint. Then we have:*

$$\sigma.\mu e \supseteq \mu f \quad \Leftarrow \quad \sigma \circ e \supseteq f \circ \sigma$$
$$\sigma.\mu e \subseteq \mu f \quad \Leftarrow \quad \sigma \circ e \subseteq f \circ \sigma$$
$$\sigma.\mu e = \mu f \quad \Leftarrow \quad \sigma \circ e = f \circ \sigma.$$

4. *Convergence Theorems. If the underlying lattice is a Boolean algebra then*

$$\nu f \cap \mu g \subseteq \mu h \quad \Leftarrow \quad \forall x, y \; : \; f.x \cap g.y \subseteq h.(x \cap y)$$
$$\nu f \subseteq \mu g \cup \nu h \quad \Leftarrow \quad \forall x, y \; : \; f.(x \cup y) \subseteq g.x \cup h.y.$$

2.5   Regular Algebra

Regular algebras are covered in Backhouse's Chapter 4. Here we only give the definition and list the algebraic laws of regular and semiregular algebras that are needed for temporal algebra.

Definition 25. *A regular (semiregular) algebra is a structure $(\mathcal{R}, \diamond, id)$ where $\mathcal{R}$ is a complete lattice, $\diamond$ is a binary operator on $\mathcal{R}$ and id is an element of $\mathcal{R}$. The following axioms are required.*

1. *Associativity:* $(x \diamond y) \diamond z = x \diamond (y \diamond z)$.
2. *Unit element:* $id \diamond x = x = x \diamond id$.
3. *Monotonicity: The operator $\diamond$ is monotonic (in each argument).*
4. *Distributivity:*
   - *(for semiregular algebras) $\diamond$ is universally disjunctive in its left argument, i.e.* $\bigcup_i (a_i \diamond b) = (\bigcup_i a_i) \diamond b$;
   - *(for regular algebras) $\diamond$ is universally disjunctive in both arguments.*

Examples 26. *The set of all binary relations on a fixed set is a regular algebra (with relational composition). The set of all formal languages over a given alphabet is a regular algebra. If $\mathcal{R}$ is a complete lattice, then $Mon(\mathcal{R})$, the set of all monotonic functions on $\mathcal{R}$, is a semiregular algebra (with functional composition as its binary operation).*

2.6   Iteration

This subject is also treated in Backhouse's Chapter 4. We give only definitions and algebraic laws here.

Definition 27 (Iteration of elements). *Let $(\mathcal{R}, \diamond, id)$ be a semiregular algebra and $r \in \mathcal{R}$. Then we define*

$$r^* =_{df} \mu_x (id \cup r \diamond x)$$

For formal languages, this definition coincides with the usual notion of Kleene star. For binary relations the Kleene star is just reflexive and transitive closure. The effect of iteration on functions is less obvious and is explained below.

Proposition 28 (Iteration of functions). *Let $\mathcal{R}$ be a complete lattice. Then $Mon(\mathcal{R})$ is a semiregular algebra, so f^* is defined for every $f \in Mon(\mathcal{R})$, namely*

$$f^* = \mu_g(id \cup f \circ g),$$

where id is the identity function, $\cup$ takes the (element-wise) supremum of its arguments and $\circ$ is functional composition.

Proposition 29 (The Transitivity Rule). *The following law holds in every semiregular algebra*

$$r^{**} = r^* = r^* \circ r^*.$$

Proposition 30 (Leapfrog Rule). *The following law holds in every regular algebra*

$$r \diamond s^* = t^* \diamond r \quad \Leftarrow \quad r \diamond s = t \diamond r.$$

Proposition 31 (Tail Recursion Rule for Functions). *Assume that $\mathcal{R}$ is a complete lattice and $f \in Mon(\mathcal{R})$. The Tail Recursion Rule states that the application of f^* to some $r \in \mathcal{R}$ can be computed as a fixed point in $\mathcal{R}$*

$$f^*.r = \mu_x(r \cup f.x).$$

Proposition 32 (Tail Recursion Rule for Operators). *Let $(\mathcal{R}, \diamond, id)$ be a semiregular algebra. Then we have, for all $r, s \in \mathcal{R}$*

$$s^* \diamond r = \mu_x(r \cup (s \diamond x)).$$

The two tail recursion rules look very similar. Modulo the following theorem, the second one is, in fact, a corollary of the first.

Proposition 33 (Star Fusion). *Let $(\mathcal{R}, \diamond, id)$ be a regular algebra. Then, with each element $r \in R$ we may associate a function $(r\diamond)$ from $\mathcal{R}$ to $\mathcal{R}$ by ruling that $(r\diamond).s = r \diamond s$. If apply is the function that maps $r \to (r\diamond)$ then the star fusion rule states that application and iteration commute:*

$$apply \circ * = * \circ apply$$

which is the same as saying that, for every $s \in \mathcal{R}$

$$(s^* \diamond) = (s\diamond)^*.$$

Proposition 34 (Star Absorption). *Suppose $(\mathcal{R}, \diamond, id)$ is a regular algebra and $e, f \in \mathcal{R}$. If e and f absorb each other, in the sense that $e \diamond f \subseteq id$, then repeated absorptions reduce everything of type $e^i \diamond f^j$ to a composition of only e's or only f's, depending on which kind there were more of to start with. More generally, we have*

$$e^* \diamond f^* = e^* \cup f^* \quad \Leftarrow \quad e \diamond f \subseteq id.$$

The Star Adjunction Theorem below allows us to lift a Galois connection between functions f and g to a Galois connection between their iterates. Because of the skew symmetric nature of Galois connections, a dual form of iteration needs to be applied to the upper adjoint. Iteration is a closure operator; its dual is the interior operator defined below.

Definition 35 (Interior). *If f is a monotonic function on a complete lattice, the interior of f is defined by*

$$f^\circ.g =_{df} \nu_x(g \cap f.x).$$

This is dual to the expression given by the tail recursion rule for f^*, but unlike Kleene star, the interior operator is only defined for functions. This restriction is necessary because the dual of the tail recursion rule for operators is invalid (whereas the one for functions holds).

Proposition 36 (Star Adjunction Theorem). *Assume that f is a universally disjunctive function on a complete lattice. Then the upper adjoint of its closure is the interior of its upper adjoint.*

$$(f^*)^\sharp = (f^\sharp)^\circ.$$

2.7 Repetition

Definition 37. *The repetition operator models an infinite repetition of its operand. Let $(\mathcal{R}, \diamond, id)$ be a semiregular algebra and $r \in \mathcal{R}$. Then we define*

$$r^\infty = \nu_x(r \diamond x).$$

Proposition 38 (Transitivity of Repetition). *Let $(\mathcal{R}, \diamond, id)$ be a regular algebra and $r \in \mathcal{R}$. Then "executing" r first finitely and then infinitely often is the same as "executing" r infinitely often in the first place.*

$$r^* \diamond r^\infty = r^\infty$$

Proposition 39 (Right Absorption Rule). *Let $(\mathcal{R}, \diamond, id)$ be a regular algebra and $r, s \in \mathcal{R}$. Then we have $r^\infty \diamond s \subseteq r^\infty$.*

Proposition 40 (Repetition Rule). *Let $(\mathcal{R}, \diamond, id)$ be a regular algebra and assume that $\mathcal{R}$ is, in fact, a Boolean algebra. Then we have*

$$\nu_x(r \cup s \diamond x) = s^* \diamond r \cup s^\infty.$$

3   Galois Algebra

Temporal logic was originally developed by philosophers to study assertions whose truth is not absolute but depends on the time when they are made. In his seminal paper [35], Pnueli argued that temporal logic could be a useful theory for specifying and verifying reactive computer programs, such as operating systems, controllers, or network protocols. The normal behaviour of a reactive program is a nonterminating computation that continuously or repeatedly interacts with its environment. Such programs cannot be described in terms of initial and final states, and consequently traditional verification techniques such as Hoare logic and the weakest precondition calculus do not apply. The temporal operators such as *sometimes* and *always* are more helpful in describing ongoing computations.

The enormous success of temporal logic is due to the fact that it combines simplicity and appeal to intuition with practical usefulness. The temporal connectives are easy to grasp, possess nice mathematical properties, and are well suited for specifying properties of concurrent and reactive systems. Powerful decision procedures and model checking algorithms exist and have proved their worth in numerous practical applications.

It is known, although not widely, that temporal logic has an algebraic counterpart. This connection has been neglected, perhaps, because all the spectacular results (particularly model checking) were obtained using logical, rather than algebraic, methods. We shall argue that the algebraic presentation deserves more attention. The first argument is simplicity. For example, [27] gives a complete proof system for LTL that requires seventeen axioms (not counting Boolean tautologies). In a complete Boolean algebra, all of these can be deduced from just two Galois correspondences. Secondly, in algebra, concepts can be introduced and understood at a higher and more user-friendly level. For example, we have the following theorem (Proposition 57) that relates the 'Next' and 'Previous' operators of temporal logic to the 'Eventually' and 'Once' operators.

Theorem. *If $(\mathcal{G}, \oplus, \ominus)$ is a Galois algebra, then so is $(\mathcal{G}, \diamondsuit, \diamondsuit)$, where $\diamondsuit = \oplus^*$ and $\diamondsuit = \ominus^*$.*

From that we can infer that every formula valid for $\oplus$ and $\ominus$ also holds for $\diamondsuit$ and $\diamondsuit$. Thirdly, the concise definitions of algebra facilitate the discovery of new models. We have found that the temporal connectives have natural interpretations in a very diverse set of non-standard models, including monotonic predicate transformers, fuzzy relations and prefix-closed sets of traces. None of this can be guessed from reading, say, Manna and Pnueli's book on temporal logic [27] or Emerson's handbook article [16].

Developing the temporal operators from lattice theory and Galois connections yields algebraic theories that correspond to LTL (linear temporal logic) and CTL (computation tree logic); and in both cases our approach is vindicated by the fact that the axioms of a complete proof system appear as theorems of Galois algebra. For a treatment of the full branching logic CTL* see [45].

3.1 Definition and Basic Properties

In this section, Galois algebras are introduced as complete Boolean algebras with a pair of operators like the $\oplus$ and $\ominus$ operators from temporal logic.

Definition 41 (Relational Image and Preimage). *Consider a set M of states and a relation $R \subseteq M \times M$. For any $p \subseteq M$ the relational preimage of p under R is defined by*

$$R \vartriangleleft p =_{df} \{l \in M \mid \exists m : (l, m) \in R \text{ and } m \in p\}.$$

In other words, $R \vartriangleleft p$ consists of all points that have a successor in p. The dual notion can be defined in terms of the relational converse operation which is defined by

$$R^{\cup} =_{df} \{(y, x) \mid (x, y) \in R\}.$$

Now $R^{\cup} \vartriangleleft p$ is the relational image of p under R.

Definition 42 (Next and Previous). *A relation $R \subseteq M \times M$ is often depicted as a directed graph with vertex set M and edge set R. If p is a set of vertices then $R \vartriangleleft p$ is the set of nodes from which a node in p can be reached in one step. Similarly, $R^{\cup} \vartriangleleft p$ is the sets of points from which a point in p can be reached in one backward step. If the relation R is fixed it can be left implicit, and we define*

$$\oplus p =_{df} R \vartriangleleft p \quad \text{and} \quad \ominus p =_{df} R^{\cup} \vartriangleleft p.$$

These operators are pronounced as 'next' and 'previous'.

Remark 43 (on notation). *In CTL one usually writes* EX *or* $\exists \bigcirc$ *instead of our $\oplus$. Since we will later add axioms that make $\oplus$ more like the 'next' operator of LTL, we do not wish to use the heavy notation of CTL here. The plus sign is written inside the 'next' operator in order to stress the symmetry of past and future.*

Theorem 44 (Exchange Rule). *When there is no forward arrow from p to q then there is no backwards arrow from q to p and vice versa. This fundamental connection between $\oplus$ and $\ominus$ is encoded by the following law.*

$$\oplus p \cap q = \mathbf{F} \qquad \Leftrightarrow \qquad \ominus q \cap p = \mathbf{F}.$$

In other words, $\oplus$ and $\ominus$ are conjugate. Since each component of a conjugate pair is determined by its partner, nothing more needs saying about the relationship between $\oplus$ and $\ominus$.

We are now ready for a definition.

Definition 45 ((Classical) Galois Algebra). *A* classical Galois algebra *is a complete Boolean algebra $\mathcal{G}$ with two additional unary operators $\oplus$ and $\ominus$ satisfying the exchange rule (Theorem 44).*

The qualifier 'classical' is employed because Galois algebra, as defined in [22], requires only a Heyting algebra instead of a Boolean algebra. (A Heyting algebra is a boolean without negation but with an implication operator $\rightarrow$ satisfying the Galois connection $(p \cap q) \subseteq r \Leftrightarrow p \subseteq (q \rightarrow r)$; although $\neg p$ can be defined as $p \rightarrow \mathsf{O}$, the double negation rule is generally not valid.) In the rest of this tutorial, however, we will omit the qualifier.

Remark 46 (Duality). *Galois algebra inherits the* logical *duality principle of Boolean algebra: Given any valid equation or inequation, we obtain another one by replacing every operator with its logical dual (and, in the case of an inequation, reversing the inclusion sign). This follows from the fact that the exchange rule (Theorem 44) is self-dual.*

Unlike Boolean algebra, Galois algebra enjoys a second and independent symmetry, the time-wise *duality, which replaces each occurrence of $\oplus$ with $\ominus$ and vice versa. Thus, with every theorem we prove, we obtain three more for free.*

Definition 47 (De Morgan Duals of $\oplus$ and $\ominus$). *In order to write the exchange rule as a Galois connection we introduce the de Morgan duals of $\oplus$ and $\ominus$. Let*

$$\widetilde{\oplus}\, p =_{df} \neg \oplus \neg p \quad and \quad \widetilde{\ominus}\, p =_{df} \neg \ominus \neg p.$$

In the graph-theoretic interpretation, x is an element of $\widetilde{\oplus}\, p$ if every successor of x is in p. For this reason, $\widetilde{\oplus}$ is sometimes called the universal next *operator. Note that we do not necessarily have $\widetilde{\oplus} \subseteq \oplus$ because there may be points without successors.*

Theorem 48 (Galois Connections). *With the aid of the universal next and previous operators, we can restate the exchange rule as a Galois connection, either as*

$$\oplus p \subseteq q \qquad \Leftrightarrow \qquad p \subseteq \widetilde{\ominus}\, q,$$

or as

$$\ominus p \subseteq q \qquad \Leftrightarrow \qquad p \subseteq \widetilde{\oplus}\, q.$$

We have already established the basic laws of Galois algebra in the section on Galois connections. For ease of reference, these laws are repeated here in the new temporal notation.

Theorem 49 (Junctivity). $\oplus$ *and* $\ominus$ *are universally disjunctive. In particular, $\oplus F = F = \ominus F$. By duality, $\widetilde{\oplus}$ and $\widetilde{\ominus}$ are universally conjunctive and preserve* T. *In particular, all four operators are monotonic.*

Proof. By Theorem 22.

Theorem 50 (Cancellation Rule). *In every Galois algebra we have*

$$\oplus \circ \widetilde{\ominus} \subseteq id \subseteq \widetilde{\ominus} \circ \oplus \quad and \quad \ominus \circ \widetilde{\oplus} \subseteq id \subseteq \widetilde{\oplus} \circ \ominus.$$

Proof. Apply the cancellation rule (Proposition 3) to the Galois connections in Theorem 48.

Theorem 51 (Best-of-Both-Worlds). *If some successor (of the current state) enjoys property p, and furthermore every successor enjoys q, then there must be a successor in the 'best of both worlds'.*

$$\oplus p \cap \widetilde{\oplus} q \subseteq \oplus(p \cap q) \quad and \quad \ominus p \cap \widetilde{\ominus} q \subseteq \ominus(p \cap q).$$

Proof. By Lemma 16.

Theorem 52 (Dedekind Law). *In every Galois algebra we have*

$$\oplus p \cap q \subseteq \oplus(p \cap \ominus q) \quad and \quad \ominus p \cap q \subseteq \ominus(p \cap \oplus q).$$

Proof. By the Dedekind law (Theorem 18).

The Best-of-Both-Worlds and Dedekind Rules are illustrated in the proof of the following law.

Exercise 53. *Show that* $\oplus \circ \widetilde{\ominus} \subseteq \oplus \circ \ominus$.

Theorem 54 (Distributivity over Implication).

$$\widetilde{\oplus}(p \to q) \subseteq \widetilde{\oplus}p \to \widetilde{\oplus}q \quad and \quad \oplus(p \to q) \subseteq \widetilde{\oplus}p \to \oplus q.$$

Proof. Shunting $\widetilde{\oplus}p$ to the left hand side, we rewrite the first claim to

$$\widetilde{\oplus}(p \to q) \cap \widetilde{\oplus}p \subseteq \widetilde{\oplus}q,$$

which follows from conjunctivity of $\widetilde{\oplus}$ and modus ponens. To prove the second inequation we shunt $\widetilde{\oplus}p$ to the left hand side and obtain

$$\oplus(p \to q) \cap \widetilde{\oplus}p \subseteq \oplus q,$$

which follows from best-of-both-worlds and modus ponens.

Figure 2 lists the laws of Galois algebra we have established (or postulated) so far. Adding the time-wise and logical duals of these laws we obtain a wealth

$$\ominus \widetilde{\oplus} p \subseteq p \subseteq \widetilde{\oplus} \ominus p$$
$$\oplus F = F = \ominus F$$
$$\oplus(p \cup q) = \oplus p \cup \oplus q$$
$$\oplus p \cap q \subseteq \oplus(p \cap \ominus q)$$
$$\oplus p \cap \widetilde{\oplus} q \subseteq \oplus(p \cap q)$$
$$\widetilde{\oplus}(p \to q) \subseteq \widetilde{\oplus}p \to \widetilde{\oplus}q$$
$$\oplus(p \to q) \subseteq \widetilde{\oplus}p \to \oplus q$$

Fig. 2. Laws of Galois algebra

of useful laws — all derived from the single exchange rule.

3.2   New Algebras from Old

One advantage of algebra over logic is the ease with which new algebras can be defined from old, for example by forming direct products and function spaces. The following proposition shows a simple way to construct a Galois algebra from any complete Heyting algebra. Trivial though they are, these are handy building blocks and we will use them for defining the 'since' and 'until' operators of temporal logic.

Proposition 55 (Sections of Conjunction). *Assume that $\mathcal{G}$ is a complete Heyting algebra and $x \in \mathcal{G}$. Then $(\mathcal{G}, (x\cap), (x\cap))$ is an intuitionistic Galois algebra.*

Proof. By the Shunting Rule, $(x\cap)$ has an upper adjoint, namely $(x \rightarrow)$. The Dedekind law

$$(x\cap).p \cap q \;\subseteq\; (x\cap).(p \cap (x\cap).q)$$

holds trivially.

The following proposition shows how functional composition can be extended to an operator on Galois algebras. Note that the 'previous' operators are composed in reverse order.

Proposition 56 (Composition of Galois Algebras). *If triples $(\mathcal{G}, \oplus_1, \ominus_1)$ and $(\mathcal{G}, \oplus_2, \ominus_2)$ are Galois algebras then so is their composition $(\mathcal{G}, \oplus_1 \circ \oplus_2, \ominus_2 \circ \ominus_1)$.*

Proof. From the composition rule for Galois connections.

Proposition 57 (Iteration of Galois algebras). *If $(\mathcal{G}, \oplus, \ominus)$ is a Galois algebra then so is $(\mathcal{G}, \oplus^*, \ominus^*)$.*

Proof. From the star adjunction theorem (Proposition 36).

3.3   Diamonds and Boxes

The expressions $\oplus p$ and $\widetilde{\oplus} p$ depend only on states that are just one moment removed from the present; for this reason $\oplus$, $\widetilde{\oplus}$, and their past counterparts are sometimes called *immediate* operators. In contrast, *non-immediate* operators, such as $\diamondsuit$, $\boxplus$, and *until* construct expressions that refer to arbitrarily distant points in time. With the aid of iteration, the non-immediate operators can be *defined* in terms of the immediate ones (whereas in most logical treatments their existence is *postulated*). As a consequence, we can calculate their properties without having to introduce any new postulates.

Definition 58 (Operational Definition of $\diamondsuit$). *We have seen in Section 3.1 that every binary relation R on a set M gives rise to a 'next' operator on the powerset of M, defined by*

$$\oplus p =_{df} R \lhd p. \tag{1}$$

In this model, the set $\oplus p$ consists of all elements of M that have a one-step successor in p. A related object of interest is the set of all points from which an element in p can be reached in some arbitrary number of steps. This set is denoted $\diamond p$ (pronounced 'eventually p') and can be defined in terms of the reflexive and transitive closure of R.

$$\diamond p =_{df} R^* \triangleleft p. \tag{2}$$

Remark 59 (Deriving an Algebraic Definition). *We notice that (2) may be seen as an instance of (1). Since a $\oplus$ operator defined by (1) satisfies the axioms of Galois algebra, the same must be true for a $\diamond$ operator defined by (2). However, (2) does not apply to abstract Galois algebra. To make it so, rewrite definitions (1) and (2) to $\oplus = (R \triangleleft)$ and $\diamond = (R^* \triangleleft)$, respectively. By the star fusion theorem (Proposition 33) we have $(R^* \triangleleft) = (R \triangleleft)^*$. Therefore, (1) and (2) imply*

$$\diamond = \oplus^* .$$

Now we do have an equation for $\diamond$ that we can use as a definition.

Definition 60. *In every Galois algebra we define the box and diamond operators by*

$$\diamond = \oplus^* \quad \ominus = \ominus^* \quad \boxplus = \diamond^\sharp \quad \boxminus = \diamond^\sharp .$$

Theorem 61 (Algebraic Laws). *By the iteration rule for Galois algebras, $(\mathcal{G}, \diamond, \ominus)$ is itself a Galois algebra. Therefore, all the calculation rules for the round operators translate into rules for the angular ones. They are captured in Figure 3.*

$$\diamond \boxminus p \subseteq p \subseteq \boxplus \ominus p$$
$$\diamond \mathbf{F} = \mathbf{F} = \ominus \mathbf{F}$$
$$\diamond (p \cup q) = \diamond p \cup \diamond q$$
$$\diamond p \cap q \subseteq \diamond (p \cap \ominus q)$$
$$\diamond p \cap \boxplus q \subseteq \diamond (p \cap q)$$
$$\boxplus (p \to q) \subseteq \boxplus p \to \boxplus q$$
$$\diamond (p \to q) \subseteq \boxplus p \to \diamond q$$

Fig. 3. Laws for non-immediate operators

Proposition 62 (Idempotence). *We have seen that iteration produces a new Galois algebra from a given one. If we play the same trick again we do not get any new results because, unlike the round operators, $\diamond$ and $\boxplus$ are idempotent.*

$$\diamond \circ \diamond = \diamond \quad and \quad \boxplus \circ \boxplus = \boxplus .$$

As a consequence we have $\diamond^* = \diamond$.

Proof. The idempotence of $\diamondsuit$ is a special case of the transitivity rule (Proposition 29). Using the composition rule for Galois connections (Proposition 5), we obtain: $\boxplus \circ \boxplus = \diamondsuit^\sharp \circ \diamondsuit^\sharp = (\diamondsuit \circ \diamondsuit)^\sharp = \diamondsuit^\sharp = \boxplus$.

Theorem 63 (Commutativity of $\oplus$ and $\diamondsuit$). *From the leapfrog rule (Proposition 30) and the composition rule (Proposition 5) we obtain*

$$\diamondsuit \circ \oplus = \oplus \circ \diamondsuit \quad and \quad \boxplus \circ \widetilde{\oplus} = \widetilde{\oplus} \circ \boxplus .$$

Analogous rules apply to the past operators.

Theorem 64 (Fixed Point Definitions). *We can apply the tail recursion rule for functions (Proposition 31) to the defining equations $\diamondsuit = \oplus^*$ and $\diamondsuit = \ominus^*$. This yields the well-known fixed point characterizations for $\diamondsuit$ and $\diamondsuit$*

$$\diamondsuit p = \mu_x(p \cup \oplus x) \quad and \quad \diamondsuit p = \mu_x(p \cup \ominus x) .$$

Theorem 65 (Fixed Point Definitions for $\boxplus$ and $\boxminus$). *The fixed point expressions for the boxes are dual to those for the diamonds.*

$$\boxplus p = \nu_x(p \cap \widetilde{\oplus} x) \quad and \quad \boxminus p = \nu_x(p \cap \widetilde{\ominus} x) .$$

Proof. By the star adjunction theorem (Proposition 36).

These fixed point expressions are sometimes used for defining the diamonds and boxes. But if one does that, it becomes necessary to construct an argument why these definitions are consistent with the usual semantics of $\diamondsuit$ and $\boxplus$. Such an argument being painful, there is a strong temptation to replace it by hand-waving. In contrast, we have started from the 'obviously correct' definition (2) and derived the fixed point expressions by rigorous calculation.

Remark 66 (Logical Duality). *If the underlying lattice $\mathcal{G}$ is Boolean then the duality of ν and μ (see Proposition 24) applied to the above fixed point expressions yields*

$$\boxplus p = \neg \diamondsuit \neg p \quad and \quad \boxminus p = \neg \diamondsuit \neg p .$$

In standard treatments of temporal logic these equations serve as definitions of the box operators. We have departed from tradition and introduced $\boxplus$ and $\boxminus$ as upper adjoints of $\diamondsuit$ and $\diamondsuit$, because that also works in the absence of a negation operator.

Theorem 67 (Temporal Induction Rule). *The fixed point expressions in Theorems 64 and 65 are important because they allow us to prove properties of $\diamondsuit$ and $\boxplus$ by induction. Temporal logic, which does not have the Knaster-Tarski theorem, employs different induction rules, such as the following*

$$\boxplus(p \rightarrow \widetilde{\oplus} p) \subseteq \boxplus(p \rightarrow \boxplus p) .$$

Proof.

$$\boxplus(p \to \widetilde{\oplus}\,p) \;\subseteq\; \boxplus(p \to \boxplus p)$$
$$\Leftarrow \qquad\quad \{\; \boxplus \text{ is monotonic and idempotent } \}$$
$$\boxplus(p \to \widetilde{\oplus}\,p) \;\subseteq\; p \to \boxplus p$$
$$\Leftarrow \qquad\quad \{\; \text{Shunting} \;\}$$
$$p \cap \boxplus(p \to \widetilde{\oplus}\,p) \;\subseteq\; \boxplus p$$
$$\Leftarrow \qquad\quad \{\; \text{Induction rule (Proposition 24) and Theorem 65 } \}$$
$$p \cap \boxplus(p \to \widetilde{\oplus}\,p) \;\subseteq\; p \,\cap\, \widetilde{\oplus}(p \cap \boxplus(p \to \widetilde{\oplus}\,p))$$
$$\Leftrightarrow \qquad\quad \{\; \text{Drop conjunct } p \text{ on the rhs}, \oplus \text{ is conjunctive } \}$$
$$p \cap \boxplus(p \to \widetilde{\oplus}\,p) \;\subseteq\; \widetilde{\oplus}p \,\cap\, \widetilde{\oplus}\boxplus(p \to \widetilde{\oplus}\,p)$$
$$\Leftrightarrow \qquad\quad \{\; \boxplus \subseteq \widetilde{\oplus} \circ \boxplus \;\}$$
$$p \cap \boxplus(p \to \widetilde{\oplus}\,p) \;\subseteq\; \widetilde{\oplus}p$$
$$\Leftrightarrow \qquad\quad \{\; \boxplus \subseteq id, \text{ modus ponens } \}$$
$$true\,.$$

Definition 68 (Strict Operators). *In [27], Manna and Pnueli define so-called strict versions of $\diamondsuit$ and $\boxplus$ by*

$$\widehat{\diamondsuit}p \;=\; \oplus\diamondsuit p \quad and \quad \widehat{\boxplus}p \;=\; \widetilde{\oplus}\boxplus p\,.$$

The strict past operators are defined similarly. We could easily derive the calculational laws for the strict operators from those for the non-strict ones, but the following theorem saves us from going through such a tedious procedure.

Theorem 69. *If $(\mathcal{G}, \oplus, \ominus)$ is a Galois algebra, then so is $(\mathcal{G}, \widehat{\diamondsuit}, \widehat{\diamondsuit})$.*

Proof. The proof of this theorem highlights the difference between algebraic reasoning and logical deduction. Rather than mindlessly checking that the proposed structure satisfies all the axioms, we simply remark that it is the sequential composition of two previously known Galois algebras:

$$(\mathcal{G}\,,\; \oplus \circ \diamondsuit\,,\; \ominus \circ \diamondsuit) \text{ is a Galois algebra}$$
$$\Leftrightarrow \qquad\quad \{\; \text{Commutativity of } \oplus \text{ with } \diamondsuit \text{ (Theorem 63) } \}$$
$$(\mathcal{G}\,,\; \diamondsuit \circ \oplus\,,\; \ominus \circ \diamondsuit) \text{ is a Galois algebra}$$
$$\Leftarrow \qquad\quad \{\; \text{Composition of Galois algebras (Proposition 56) } \}$$
$$(\mathcal{G}, \diamondsuit, \diamondsuit) \text{ and } (\mathcal{G}, \oplus, \ominus) \text{ are Galois algebras}\,.$$

As a consequence, the laws in Figure 3 remain valid when all the temporal operators are decorated with hats.

3.4   'Until' and 'Since'

The diamond operator is useful for specifying that a program must eventually arrive at a certain desirable state, but it does not allow us to constrain the path by which it gets there. Often it is necessary to ensure that some invariant property holds until the desirable state is reached. The 'until' operator of temporal logic has been invented for this very purpose. As with the diamond and box operators, we shall first explain it in terms of a transition relation $R \subseteq M \times M$ and then generalize it to arbitrary Galois algebras.

Definition 70 (Operational Definition of 'Until'). *Assume p and q are subsets of M. Then $x \in (p$ until $q)$ if and only if there is a path from x to some $y \in q$ such that every edge (a, b) in this path satisfies $(a, b) \in R$ and $a \in p$.*

Remark 71 (Deriving an Algebraic Definition). *If we represent p by the diagonal relation*

$$\Delta_p =_{df} \{(y, y) \mid y \in p\},$$

then the two requirements on edges (a, b) can be condensed into the single condition $(a, b) \in \Delta_p \, ; R$. Thus we have

$$p \text{ until } q \; = \; (\Delta_p \, ; R)^* \triangleleft q.$$

Now we can calculate an algebraic expression for the section $(p$ until$)$ as follows.

$$
\begin{aligned}
& (p \text{ until}) \\
= \quad & \{ \text{ Definition } \} \\
& ((\Delta_p \, ; R)^* \triangleleft) \\
= \quad & \{ \text{ Star fusion } \} \\
& ((\Delta_p \, ; R) \triangleleft)^* \\
= \quad & \{ \triangleleft \text{ distributes over composition } \} \\
& ((\Delta_p \triangleleft) \circ (R \triangleleft))^* \\
= \quad & \{ \Delta_p \triangleleft q = p \cap q, \text{ definition of } \oplus \} \\
& ((p \cap) \circ \oplus)^*.
\end{aligned}
$$

We have now derived an expression that can serve as a definition of the 'until' operator. Its dual is the 'since' operator.

Definition 72 ('Until' and 'Since'). *In every Galois algebra, we define*

$$(p \text{ until}) \; = \; ((p \cap) \circ \oplus)^* \quad \text{and} \quad (p \text{ since}) \; = \; ((p \cap) \circ \ominus)^*.$$

The following lemma shows that the 'until' operator gives rise to yet another Galois algebra.

Lemma 73. *If $(\mathcal{G}, \oplus, \ominus)$ is a Galois algebra, then so is $(\mathcal{G}, ((p \cap) \circ \oplus)^*, (\ominus \circ (p \cap))^*)$.*

Proof. From the fact that $(\mathcal{G}, (p\cap), (p\cap))$ is a Galois algebra (by Proposition 55), the composition lemma (Proposition 56) and the iteration lemma (Proposition 57).

Remark 74 (Algebraic Laws). *By the preceding theorem, every law we have established for $\diamondplus$ yields an analogous law for (p until). This includes laws mentioning $\oplus$ if we replace $\oplus$ by $(p\cap)\circ\oplus$. For example, $\oplus\diamondplus q = \diamondplus\oplus q$ translates to the following rolling rule for 'until':*

$$p \cap \oplus(p\ until\ q) \ = \ p\ until\ (p\cap\oplus q).$$

Definition 75 (Fixed Point Definitions for 'Until' and 'Since'). *Using tail recursion, we may rewrite Definition 72*

$$p\ until\ q \ = \ \mu_r(q\cup(p\cap\oplus r)) \quad and \quad p\ since\ q \ = \ \mu_r(q\cup(p\cap\ominus r)).$$

3.5 Confluence

The algebra we have investigated so far works for any pair of operators defined by

$$\oplus p = R\triangleleft p \quad and \quad \ominus p = R^{\cup}\triangleleft p, \tag{3}$$

where $R \subseteq M \times M$ is an arbitrary relation, $R^{\cup}$ is its transposition, and p ranges over subsets of M. In Manna and Pnueli's logic, the relation R is required to have certain linearity properties. We propose to translate these properties into postulates that can be imposed on Galois algebras, so that we may employ the calculus to explore their consequences. As it turns out, a number of these can be proved from a much weaker assumption, namely that the transition relation R be *confluent*. We will therefore look at confluent Galois algebras first.

Definition 76 (Operational Definition of Confluence). *A relation $R \subseteq M \times M$ is called* right-confluent *if its associated directed graph (M, R) has the following property: Any two paths that have the same initial point can be extended (to the right) in such a way that they end up in a common final point. For example, $\circ\!\!\overset{\circ}{\underset{\circ}{\searrow}}\!\!\circ\!\longrightarrow\!\circ$ is right-confluent, whereas $\circ\!\longrightarrow\!\circ\!\!\overset{\circ}{\underset{\circ}{\diagdown}}$ is not. In relational terms, relation R is right-confluent if and only if*

$$(R^{\cup})^*; R^* \ \subseteq \ R^*; (R^{\cup})^*.$$

Remark 77 (Deriving an Algebraic Definition). *If R has this property we may calculate*

$$\ominus\circ\diamondplus$$
$$= \qquad \{\ Definitions\ \}$$
$$\ominus^*\circ\oplus^*$$
$$= \qquad \{\ Definitions\ \}$$
$$(R^{\cup}\triangleleft)^*\circ(R\triangleleft)^*$$

$$= \qquad \{\ \textit{Star Fusion}\ \}$$
$$((R^{\cup})^* \triangleleft) \circ (R^* \triangleleft)$$
$$= \qquad \{\ \textit{Distributivity of} \triangleleft \textit{over composition}\ \}$$
$$((R^{\cup *}; R^*) \triangleleft)$$
$$\subseteq \qquad \{\ \textit{Right Confluence}\ \}$$
$$((R^*; R^{\cup *}) \triangleleft)$$
$$= \qquad \{\ \textit{Unwind first four steps}\ \}$$
$$\Diamond \circ \Diamond .$$

This result motivates the following definition.

Definition 78. *A Galois algebra is called* right confluent *if it satisfies the inequation* $\Diamond \circ \Diamond \subseteq \Diamond \circ \Diamond$. *A Galois algebra in which the dual inequation holds is* left confluent.

Theorem 79 (Weak Commutativity of ⊞ and ⊟). *As expected, the (semi-) commutativity of the diamond operators induces a similar relation between the box operators. In every right-confluent Galois algebra we have*

$$\boxplus \circ \boxminus \ \subseteq \ \boxminus \circ \boxplus .$$

Proof.

$$\boxplus \ \circ \boxminus$$
$$= \qquad \{\ \text{Definitions}\ \}$$
$$\Diamond^{\sharp} \circ \Diamond^{\sharp}$$
$$= \qquad \{\ \text{Composition rule (Proposition 5)}\ \}$$
$$(\Diamond \circ \Diamond)^{\sharp}$$
$$\subseteq \qquad \{\ \Diamond \circ \Diamond \subseteq \Diamond \circ \Diamond,\ \text{anti-monotonicity of } \sharp \text{ (Proposition 4)}\ \}$$
$$(\Diamond \circ \Diamond)^{\sharp}$$
$$= \qquad \{\ \text{Unwind first two steps}\ \}$$
$$\boxminus \circ \boxplus .$$

Theorem 80 (Absorption Laws). *Confluence reduces the number of distinct operators that can be formed from composing boxes and diamonds: in every right-confluent Galois algebra, we have*

$$\boxplus \circ \Diamond \circ \boxplus \ = \ \Diamond \circ \boxplus \quad \textit{and} \quad \Diamond \circ \boxplus \circ \Diamond \ = \ \boxplus \circ \Diamond .$$

Proof. Since $\boxplus \subseteq id$ we certainly have $\boxplus \circ \Diamond \circ \boxplus \subseteq \Diamond \circ \boxplus$. For the other inclusion, we calculate

$$\Diamond \circ \boxplus$$
$$\subseteq \qquad \{\ \text{Cancellation rule (Proposition 3): } id \subseteq \boxplus \circ \Diamond\ \}$$
$$\boxplus \circ \Diamond \circ \Diamond \circ \boxplus$$
$$\subseteq \qquad \{\ \Diamond \circ \Diamond \subseteq \Diamond \circ \Diamond,\ \text{idempotence of } \boxplus\ \}$$

$$\boxplus \circ \Leftrightarrow \circ \ominus \circ \boxplus \circ \boxplus$$
$$\subseteq \qquad \{ \text{ Cancellation rule (Proposition 3): } \Leftrightarrow \circ \boxplus \subseteq id \}$$
$$\boxplus \circ \Leftrightarrow \circ \boxplus .$$

The proof of the second equation is left as an exercise.

Remark 81 (Reverse Induction). *Temporal induction rules are suitable for establishing safety properties (expressions that start with a box). The rule we have seen in Theorem 67 starts from the present and works its way, step by step, into the future (or the past). In the presence of confluence it is also possible to do it the other way round, establishing first the truth of the desired property at the very first (or last) moment in time and working from there towards the present. Since a state is initial if it has no predecessors, we can describe the set of all initial states as follows.*

$$\text{first} =_{df} \widetilde{\ominus} F .$$

The reverse induction rule (Theorem 83) is one of Manna and Pnueli's axioms. The following lemma prepares its proof.

Lemma 82 (Reverse Induction Base). *In every Galois algebra we have* $p \cap \text{first} \subseteq \boxminus p$.

Proof. The claim is easily proved by appealing to the induction rule of fixed point calculus but, as a matter of style, we use this theorem only where it can't be avoided. Instead, we calculate:

$$p \cap \text{first} \subseteq \boxminus p$$
$$\Leftrightarrow \qquad \{ \text{ Galois connection } \}$$
$$\Leftrightarrow (p \cap \text{first}) \subseteq p$$
$$\Leftrightarrow \qquad \{ \Leftrightarrow = id \cup \Leftrightarrow \circ \oplus \}$$
$$\Leftrightarrow \oplus (p \cap \text{first}) \subseteq p$$
$$\Leftarrow \qquad \{ \text{ Monotonicity } \}$$
$$\Leftrightarrow (\oplus p \cap \oplus \text{first}) \subseteq p$$
$$\Leftrightarrow \qquad \{ \text{ first} = \widetilde{\ominus} F, \text{ cancellation rule (Theorem 50) } \}$$
$$\Leftrightarrow (\oplus p \cap F) \subseteq p$$
$$\Leftrightarrow \qquad \{ \Leftrightarrow F = F \}$$
$$true .$$

Theorem 83 (Reverse Induction Rule). *In every left-confluent Galois algebra we have*

$$\text{first} \cap \boxplus (p \rightarrow \widetilde{\ominus} p) \subseteq \boxplus (p \rightarrow \boxminus p) .$$

Proof.

$$\text{first} \cap \boxplus (p \rightarrow \widetilde{\ominus} p)$$
$$\subseteq \qquad \{ \text{ Reverse induction base (Lemma 82) } \}$$
$$\boxminus \boxplus (p \rightarrow \widetilde{\ominus} p)$$

$\subseteq$ { Theorem 79 (dual version) }

$$\boxplus\boxminus(p \to \widetilde{\ominus}\,p)$$

$\subseteq$ { Temporal induction rule (Theorem 67) (dual version) }

$$\boxplus\boxminus(p \to \boxminus p)$$

$\subseteq$ { $\boxminus \subseteq id$ }

$$\boxplus(p \to \boxminus p)\,.$$

We include one more related law, on the grounds that it is also one of Manna and Pnueli's axioms.

Lemma 84. *In every left-confluent Galois algebra we have*

$$\mathsf{first} \cap \boxplus p \;\subseteq\; \boxplus\widetilde{\ominus}\,p\,.$$

Proof.

$$\mathsf{first} \cap \boxplus p$$

$\subseteq$ { Reverse induction base (Lemma 82) }

$$\boxminus\boxplus p$$

$\subseteq$ { Theorem 79 (dual version) }

$$\boxplus\boxminus p$$

$\subseteq$ { $\boxminus \subseteq \widetilde{\ominus}$ }

$$\boxplus\widetilde{\ominus}\,p\,.$$

3.6 Linearity

Definition 85 (Operational Definition of Linearity). *A relation $R \subseteq M \times M$ is called* right-linear *if every node of its associated directed graph has at most one successor (R does not branch to the right). For example, $\circ\!\!\!\nearrow\!\!\!\rightarrow\!\circ\longrightarrow\circ$ is right-linear, whereas $\circ\longrightarrow\circ\!\!\!\nwarrow\!\!\!\searrow\!\!\!\circ$ is not. In relational terms, R is right-linear if*

$$R^{\cup}\,;R \;\subseteq\; id\,,$$

and left-linear *if*

$$R\,;R^{\cup} \;\subseteq\; id\,.$$

Remark 86 (Deriving an Algebraic Definition). *In order to express linearity in terms of the temporal operators, we calculate:*

$$R^{\cup}\,;R \;\subseteq\; id$$

$\Leftrightarrow$

$$\forall p \subseteq M \;:\; (R^{\cup}\,;R)\triangleleft p \;\subseteq\; p$$

$\Leftrightarrow$ { *Distributivity of $\triangleleft$ over composition* }

$$\forall p \subseteq M \;:\; R^{\cup}\triangleleft(R\triangleleft p) \;\subseteq\; p$$

$\Leftrightarrow$ { *Operational definitions of $\oplus$ and $\ominus$* }

$$\forall p \subseteq M \;:\; \ominus\oplus p \;\subseteq\; p\,.$$

Similarly, R is left linear if and only if $\oplus \circ \ominus \subseteq id$. Thus we propose the following definition.

Definition 87 (Linearity). *A Galois algebra is* linear *if*

$$\oplus \circ \ominus \subseteq id \quad and \quad \ominus \circ \oplus \subseteq id.$$

Theorem 88 (Weak Next and Weak Previous). *In LTL, $\widetilde{\ominus}$ is called the 'weak previous' operator. This is because a Galois algebra is linear if and only if*

$$\ominus \subseteq \widetilde{\ominus} \quad and \quad \oplus \subseteq \widetilde{\oplus}.$$

Proof. From the Galois connections in Theorem 48.

Theorem 89 (Linearity Implies Confluence). *Every linear Galois algebra is both left and right confluent, in the sense that*

$$\ominus \circ \oplus \;=\; \oplus \circ \ominus.$$

Proof. By the star absorption theorem (Proposition 34), both sides are equal to $\ominus \cup \oplus$.

Theorem 90 (Distributivity over Implication). *Theorem 54 provides one inclusion (from left to right) of the following distribution law. In a linear Galois algebra the other inclusion holds as well.*

$$\widetilde{\oplus}(p \to q) \;=\; \widetilde{\oplus}p \to \widetilde{\oplus}q.$$

Proof.

$$\widetilde{\oplus}p \to \widetilde{\oplus}q \;=\; \widetilde{\oplus}(p \to q)$$
$\Leftrightarrow$ { By Theorem 54 }
$$\widetilde{\oplus}p \to \widetilde{\oplus}q \;\subseteq\; \widetilde{\oplus}(p \to q)$$
$\Leftrightarrow$ { Galois connection }
$$\ominus(\widetilde{\oplus}p \to \widetilde{\oplus}q) \;\subseteq\; p \to q$$
$\Leftrightarrow$ { Shunting }
$$p \cap \ominus(\widetilde{\oplus}p \to \widetilde{\oplus}q) \;\subseteq\; q$$
$\Leftarrow$ { Dedekind }
$$\ominus(\oplus p \cap (\widetilde{\oplus}p \to \widetilde{\oplus}q)) \;\subseteq\; q$$
$\Leftrightarrow$ { Galois connection }
$$\oplus p \cap (\widetilde{\oplus}p \to \widetilde{\oplus}q) \;\subseteq\; \widetilde{\oplus}q$$
$\Leftrightarrow$ { $\oplus \subseteq \widetilde{\oplus}$ (by Theorem 88) and modus ponens }
$$true.$$

3.7 Infinity

In a linear Galois algebra we have only $\oplus \subseteq \widetilde{\oplus}$, whereas in LTL these two operators coincide. In terms of a transition relation, the identification occurs when every state has precisely one successor, whereas the linearity axiom requires only that there be *at most* one. We say that a Galois algebra is *infinite to the right* if it satisfies

$$\oplus T = T.$$

There are two reasons why we did not introduce this postulate earlier. Firstly, we wished to show that all the hard work is done by the linearity properties, whereas postulating infinity to the right has very little effect. More specifically, we will prove in the next section that a linear Galois algebra which is infinite to the right satisfies all seventeen of Manna and Pnueli's axioms, but sixteen of these axioms can be derived without the infinity postulate.

   Another and even more serious objection to postulating infinity is the violation of time-wise symmetry. On the other hand, there is no reason for disliking infinity if we can also have its time-wise dual, $\ominus T = T$. Then there is an even simpler way to describe the entire situation, namely by

$$\oplus \text{ is an order isomorphism, and } \ominus \text{ is its inverse.}$$

In terms of a transition relation, this means that every state also has precisely one predecessor. This postulate is usually rejected, and rightly so, because every program and every system starts life in some *initial* state, but some do not terminate.

Definition 91 (Perfect Galois Connections). *In [34], a Galois connection (f, g) is called* perfect *if $g \circ f = id$. A Galois connection is perfect if and only if its lower adjoint is injective; for this reason, perfect Galois connections are sometimes called* Galois insertions *[29,30].*

Proposition 92. *Now assume that $(\mathcal{G}, \oplus, \ominus)$ is a Galois algebra. Then the following conditions are mutually equivalent.*

1. *$\ominus \subseteq \widetilde{\ominus}$ and $\widetilde{\oplus} = \oplus$;*
2. *$(\ominus, \oplus)$ is a perfect Galois connection;*
3. *$\ominus \circ \oplus \subseteq id$ and $\oplus \circ \ominus = id$;*
4. *$\ominus \circ \oplus \subseteq id$ and $\oplus \circ \ominus \subseteq id$ and $\oplus T = T$.*

   We omit the proof because it is completely straightforward. Some authors call a pair of functions satisfying these four conditions an injection-projection pair.

4 Sequential Algebra

Galois algebra is an excellent tool for reasoning about the possible behaviours of reactive programs, but its ability to describe a system in term of its constituent parts is very limited. To allow *compositional* reasoning, an algebra must have operations that correspond to the ways larger programs can be built as a combination of smaller ones. For example, the behaviour of a program that is constructed as a non-deterministic choice between, say, P and Q is obtained as the disjunction of the behaviours of P and Q. But apart from disjunction and conjunction, Galois algebra has no operators for combining the meaning of subprograms. The most notable omission is sequential composition. Therefore we shall now investigate Boolean algebras with a binary composition operator. These correspond to a class of programming calculi which is roughly delineated by the following two principles:

- each program or system P is described by a set whose elements represent single observations of a single experiment on P, according to the catch phrase 'Programs are Predicates' [20];
- there is a sequential composition operator that can make a possibly longer observation $x; y$ from subobservations x and y.

The earliest and most well-known such calculus is the calculus of binary relations [41], which has been remarkably successful in reasoning about possibly non-deterministic systems [31,21,4,26,7], provided that their behaviour can be fully characterized by observation of just their initial and final states. Many alternative models have been proposed for reactive systems, whose behaviour between initiation and termination is also of significance.

A common feature of these calculi is that past observations cannot be cancelled or undone by what comes after. As a consequence, the converse operator of relation algebra must be abandoned. We will see that the converse operator can be replaced with left and right division operators, with the effect that much of relation algebra is preserved. Axiomatizing the resulting structure produces the notion of a *sequential algebra*, and its theory is the *sequential calculus*, which provides a set of algebraic laws for many models of programs and reactive systems.

Sequential algebra is the lowest common denominator of a number of formalisms that are built around a sequential composition operator, including relation algebra, regular expressions, dynamic logic, interval temporal logic and the duration calculus. In addition, the temporal logics like LTL and CTL can be modelled inside sequential algebra, which therefore serves as an anchor for combining and unifying theories.

The sequential calculus integrates specification operators like negation and the temporal connectives in a single algebra with programming constructs like conditionals and recursion and thereby allows to move from a specification to a program by stepwise refinement, where each step is justified by an algebraic law. This has been illustrated in [5] and [6], using CSP as the programming language.

The downside of power is complexity. Already Tarski's calculus of relations is very badly behaved, logically speaking: It is undecidable and seriously incomplete (to the point that it cannot be made complete by adding finitely many axioms). Since sequential algebra generalizes relation algebra, it inherits this deficiency. However, neither undecidability nor incompleteness has been considered an impediment for relational reasoning about programs. Also, practitioners are not expected to work directly in abstract sequential algebra, but always in some subtheory suitable to the problem domain, and endowed with additional operators and axioms, which may well be decidable or complete.

4.1   Observations

Before the design of a new system, or the analysis of an existing one, can start we need to determine those properties that are essential to its function. Following established practice in physics and engineering, unnecessary detail is eliminated by restricting attention to observation of relevant data. Choosing the appropriate set of allowed observations is a difficult task, and one with many degrees of freedom. It is a fair assumption that here is one of the reasons why so many competing and often only marginally different theories of programming and system design have emerged.

We aim at a calculus that is applicable to many different kinds of observations. Let us simply say that a system is represented by the set of all observations that could be made on it, and try to develop a calculus of systems from this premise. Any calculus for sets should start from consideration of the properties of their members. What kind of observations we can make depends on the type of experiment we conduct. Typically, such an experiment — or test, as it is more commonly called in computing — is performed by providing some input and then recording the system's reaction, or at least some essential aspect of it.

A simple test is to start a system in some predetermined state and then to measure its final state, if it reaches one. If successful, this test yields a pair (s, t), where s and t are drawn from the same set of states. Axiomatic relation algebra [41,38] formalizes the calculus of sets of such pairs. It has a subtheory, called the interval calculus [9], obtained by requiring s and t to be related by a total ordering $(s \leq t)$.

A different kind of test, often carried out on automata, is to present a system with a sequence of stimuli which it may or may not accept. An observation can then be formalized as a finite sequence, and regular expressions [24] provide a calculus for sets of observations. An interesting variation is Dijkstra's regularity calculus [13] which admits backtracking by giving negative stimuli; this gives the set of observations the structure of a free group. Also the traces and refusals used for describing Communicating Sequential Processes [19] belong in this class.

A more radical approach is to observe the system state at each point in its life-time. In interval temporal logic e.g. [32,43,47], the observations are *timing diagrams*: functions from time intervals to states, where time is a total ordering and may be discrete or continuous, finite or infinite.

A common property of all these observation spaces is the existence of a composition operation which makes a possibly longer observation $x; y$ from sub-observations x and y. For the set of strings over some alphabet this is just concatenation, and for free groups it is the group multiplication. In other cases, composition is a partial operator: in the relational calculus, the pair (r, s) can be composed with (s', t) only if $s = s'$; and when this equality holds, the intermediate state is omitted:

$$(r, s); (s, t) = (r, t).$$

Similarly, for timing diagrams, composition is defined only when the end time and final state of the first operand are the same as the start time and initial state of the second operand. Then the two functions are compatible, so that their union is a function and can be taken as the result of the composition.

We are mainly interested in properties shared by all the observation spaces in question. The first and most important such property is the associativity of composition:

(O_1) $(x; y); z = x; (y; z)$ provided both sides are defined.

To help reasoning about the definedness of composition, we introduce two functions between observations. Each observation x has a left unit $\overleftarrow{x}$ and a right unit $\overrightarrow{x}$, which satisfy the unit properties for composition:

(O_2) $$\overleftarrow{x}; x = x = x; \overrightarrow{x}.$$

For example, in the relational and interval calculi

$$\overleftarrow{(s, t)} = (s, s) \text{ and } \overrightarrow{(s, t)} = (t, t).$$

If x is a timing diagram then $\overleftarrow{x}$ is the initial state and time, whereas $\overrightarrow{x}$ is the final state and time. In both cases, and in all others, we have

(O_3) $$x; y \text{ is defined } \Leftrightarrow \overrightarrow{x} = \overleftarrow{y}.$$

In a space of strings (as in a free group) there is just a single unit for composition, the empty sequence. As a consequence, $\overrightarrow{}$ and $\overleftarrow{}$ are constant functions, and composition is everywhere defined.

The unit functions have two additional properties: they map units to themselves,

(O_4) $$(e = \overleftarrow{x}) \vee (e = \overrightarrow{x}) \quad \Rightarrow \quad (\overleftarrow{e} = e = \overrightarrow{e}).$$

and they depend only on the left or right operands of composition

(O_5) $\overleftarrow{x; y} = \overleftarrow{x}$ and $\overrightarrow{x; y} = \overrightarrow{y}$ provided $x; y$ is defined.

Note that (O_3) and (O_5) allow us to drop the proviso in (O_1), as the definedness of either side now implies the definedness of the other side.

These properties endow the set of observations with the structure of a small category. This gives some hope that our calculus may have even wider applications than those listed. But no acquaintance with category theory is needed for an understanding of this section, or for application of its results.

We assume that an observer will not discard information, once it has been obtained. This postulate is known as *cancellativity*, and it holds in all the observation spaces mentioned so far, and in all that we shall mention later.

(O_6) $(x; y = x'; y) \Rightarrow (x = x')$ and $(x; y = x; y') \Rightarrow (y = y').$

When observations are allowed to take an infinite time, cancellativity is usually lost. For example, in the space of finite and infinite strings we have $a; a^\omega = aa; a^\omega$. We shall later see that the cancellativity postulate may safely be replaced with the following weaker axiom

(O_6) If $(x; y)$ is a unit then so is $y; x$.

For the moment, however, we shall assume cancellativity, because it makes the presentation simpler.

Summing up, an *observation space* is a set equipped with two unary operations $\overleftarrow{}$ and $\overrightarrow{}$, and one (possibly partially defined) binary operation ; satisfying $(O_1–O_6)$.

The observation space that consists of all pairs of states enjoys another characteristic property, namely

(O_7) for all units e and f
                there is an observation x with $\overleftarrow{x} = e$ and $\overrightarrow{x} = f$.

An observation space satisfying (O_7) is said to be *simple*.

The following axiom clearly distinguishes the relational and regularity calculi from all the others. These two calculi apply to systems in which each observation x has an inverse x^{-1}, which cancels its effect:

(O_8) $x^{-1}; x = \overrightarrow{x}$ and $x; x^{-1} = \overleftarrow{x}$.

$(O_1–O_8)$ are the defining properties of a *groupoid* [8,11]. On the other hand, in reactive systems, it is not possible to backtrack or rewrite history by an inverting operation. The only action that can be undone is the trivial action that has not actually done anything, i.e. a unit $\overleftarrow{z}$; all other observations record some real progress. Accordingly, an observation space is said to be an *antigroupoid* if and only if

$(\overline{O_8})$ $x; y = \overleftarrow{z}$ implies $x = y = \overleftarrow{z}$.

The existence of a converse operator is an extremely helpful circumstance; which is why group theory has been so much more successful than semigroup theory. But even in its absence, we may be able to find a substitute. For example, the natural numbers do not have a converse operation with respect to multiplication; the only natural number the converse of which is also a natural number is one. Still we can define a division operator on natural numbers by

$$x \div z = y \quad \text{if and only if } x = yz \ (x, y, z \in \mathbb{N}),$$

which is a useful operation, although it is only partially defined. Similarly we can define the *right quotient* of two observations x and z by

$$x; {-}z = y \quad \text{if and only if } x = y; z.$$

If there is no y with $x = y; z$ then $x\,;\text{-}\,z$ is undefined. The cancellativity axiom (O_6) ensures that there cannot be more than one solution y to the equation $x = y; z$. Unlike integer multiplication, composition of observations is not commutative and so there are two distinct division operations. Cancelling y from the left of x is defined by

$$y\,\text{-};\,x = z \quad \text{if and only if } x = y; z.$$

If observers cannot be distributed in space we may assume that the progress of time is linear within any single observation. Linear observations enjoy a special property. If a linear observation is decomposed in two different ways, then the two transition points can be ordered in time. This concept is formalized easily. First, x is an *initial subobservation* of z if $x; y = z$ for some observation y. Now an observation z is *linear* if the initial subobservations of z are totally ordered in the following sense: For any initial subobservations x and y of z it is true that either x is an initial subobservation of y or y is an initial subobservation of x. An observation space is said to be *locally linear* if all its elements are linear:

(O_9) If $x; y = x'; y'$ then
              there is some r such that either $x' = x; r$ or $x = x'; r$.

All observation spaces mentioned so far satisfy (O_9). However, combining two observation spaces L_1 and L_2 into a composite space $L_1 \times L_2$ models having two independent observers each contributing one component of the overall observation, and in the absence of synchronization, local linearity is lost. Other examples of non-linear observations are bags (with bag union as composition), Mazurkiewicz traces [28] and pomsets [36].

It is sometimes convenient to encode the entire history of an observation into its final state, for example using a history variable. In a deterministic setting we have a dual situation: The entire observation is implicit in its initial state, except that the observer may have a choice when to terminate the experiment. In either case, we obtain a stronger calculus, so it is worthwhile to formalize these notions.

Two observations x and y are *co-initial* (respectively *co-final*) if $\overleftarrow{x} = \overleftarrow{y}$ (respectively $\overrightarrow{x} = \overrightarrow{y}$). An observation space is called *right confluent* if and only if

(O_{10}) For any pair x and y of co-initial observations
                there is an observation z such that
                both x and y are initial subobservations of z.

Symmetrically, an observation space is *left confluent* if any two co-final observations are final subobservations of some common observation z.

Bags, groups and the spaces of pairs or intervals are both left and right confluent, but the spaces of strings or timing diagrams are neither. The observation space consisting of all finite paths through a fixed tree (starting at any node and always moving away from the root) is left confluent but not right confluent.

A locally linear observation space U satisfying $(\overline{O_8})$ may be visualized as a set of lines or curves that may overlay each other and can be concatenated when adjacent. For example, they might be segments of particle trajectories through phase space. In this picture right confluence means that trajectories do not branch. In other words, each trajectory is completely determined by its initial state. For this reason, an observation space that is locally linear and right (left) confluent is said to be *right linear (left linear)*. An observation space is *linear* if it is both left and right linear.

Let us forestall a possible misunderstanding. Linear observation spaces can be quite appropriate for describing non-deterministic systems, as witnessed by the relational calculus. Non-determinacy is modelled by admitting that several different observations can be made on the same system.

4.2 Lifting to Sets

The objective of sequential algebra is to formalize a calculus of sets of observations in the same way that the relational calculus helps in reasoning about sets of ordered pairs. Assume G is a given universe of observations. Our first step is to restore as much as possible of the standard theory of relation algebra. The axioms formalizing a Boolean algebra are obviously inherited by the powerset of any carrier set of observations; we can therefore concentrate on the specifically relational laws, involving composition and units.

Relational composition is just a lifted form of the composition of observations; and our more general composition is defined similarly: For arbitrary $R, S \subseteq G$ let

(G_1) $\qquad R; S \ =_{df} \ \{r; s \mid r \in R \ \wedge \ s \in S \ \wedge \ r; s \text{ is defined}\}.$

This has the advantage of being defined everywhere. We often write RS instead of $R; S$, but we do use the semicolon when it helps visual grouping. In both cases, composition binds more strongly than union and intersection. Composition has a unique identity, which is the set of all unit observations

(G_2) $\qquad\qquad\qquad\qquad I \ =_{df} \ \{\overleftarrow{x} \mid x \in G\}.$

Let us consider first the case where G is a groupoid. Then G has a converse operation, which may also be lifted to the set level

(G_3) $\qquad\qquad\qquad\qquad R^{\cup} \ =_{df} \ \{r^{-1} \mid r \in R\}.$

So the calculus of sets of observations has the same operators, and indeed the same axioms, as the relational calculus.[1] Formally speaking, the powerset of a groupoid, with the operations defined by $(G_1–G_3)$, constitutes a *relation algebra*. We recall the definition:

---

[1] This has been known for long, especially in the case where G is a group. See [23] for historical details. Dijkstra called this fact to the attention of the computer science community by basing his regularity calculus on it [13].

Definition 93 (Relation Algebra). *A relation algebra is a complete Boolean algebra* $(\mathcal{R}, \cap, \cup, \overline{\cdot})$ *with additional operators* ; *and* $^{\cup}$ *satisfying*

1. *composition is associative and has a unit* I*;*
2. *the Exchange law*

$$PQ^{\cup} \cap R = 0 \quad \Leftrightarrow \quad P \cap RQ = 0 \quad \Leftrightarrow \quad R^{\cup}P \cap Q = 0.$$

The second axiom is also called the *Schröder equivalence*; the term 'exchange' is due to Dijkstra. All the familiar equational and inequational laws governing composition and converse of binary relations can be deduced from the above axioms [41,38]. See [25] for a historical review of the research on relation algebras and [10] for its current uses in computing.

Nothing more needs saying about a calculus for subsets of a groupoid G. But the groupoid axiom (O_8) fails in most observation spaces used for modelling reactive systems because the impossibility of backtracking precludes the existence of inverse observations. However, it is often possible to *embed* a given observation space U into a groupoid G. If so, we can continue to use relation algebra for reasoning about sets of observations, and the relational axioms are complemented by additional laws relating U to G. Our starting point is the following proposition.

Proposition 94. *Assume G is a groupoid and U is a subset of G. Then U is an observation space if and only if U is a preorder, in the sense that the following two inequations hold:*

$$(\mathrm{L}_1) \qquad\qquad UU \subseteq U; \qquad\qquad \text{(Transitivity)}$$

$$(\mathrm{L}_2) \qquad\qquad I \subseteq U. \qquad\qquad \text{(Reflexivity)}$$

Now assume that $U \subseteq G$ is indeed transitive and reflexive. Our next goal is to capture other interesting qualities of observation spaces at the set level.

Proposition 95 (Symmetry). *U is a groupoid if and only if*

$$(\mathrm{L}_3) \qquad\qquad U^{\cup} \subseteq U. \qquad\qquad \text{(Symmetry)}$$

Proposition 96 (Antisymmetry). *U is an antigroupoid if and only if*

$$(\mathrm{L}_4) \qquad\qquad U^{\cup} \cap U \subseteq I. \qquad\qquad \text{(Antisymmetry)}$$

Proposition 97 (Simplicity). *U is simple if and only if*

$$(\mathrm{L}_5) \qquad\qquad I \subseteq UPU^{\cup} \quad \text{for all non-empty } P \subseteq U. \quad \text{(Tarski's Rule)}$$

Since Tarski's rule holds for the set of all binary relations on a fixed set, some authors include it in the definition of a relation algebra. Those who do not, call a relation algebra simple if and only if it satisfies Tarski's rule. Since we defined simplicity at the observation level we obtained the equivalence of simplicity with Tarski's rule as a theorem.

Proposition 98 (Local Linearity). *U is locally linear if and only if*

(L$_6$) $$UU^\cup \cap U^\cup U \subseteq U \cup U^\cup. \qquad \text{(Local Linearity)}$$

It is instructive to interpret (L$_6$) in the case where U is a concrete partial order. For better readability let us write $x \leq y$ instead of $(x, y) \in U$. Then (L$_6$) holds if and only if the set of points between any given ordered pair $a \leq b$ forms a linear chain

$$a \leq x, y \leq b \quad \Rightarrow \quad x \leq y \ \vee \ y \leq x.$$

In other word, the Hasse diagram of $\leq$ possesses no diamonds, which is why locally linear orders are sometimes called *poorsets*, or antilattices. Figure 4 shows the smallest partial order which is not locally linear.

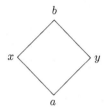

Fig. 4. The smallest non-locally-linear partial order

Proposition 99 (Confluence). *U is right confluent if and only if*

(L$_7$) $$U^\cup U \subseteq UU^\cup. \qquad \text{(Right Confluence)}$$

In the case where U is a concrete preorder $\leq$, (L$_7$) stipulates that every triple $a \leq x, y$ can be completed to a diamond $a \leq x, y \leq b$ as in Figure 4. This is indeed the usual definition of confluence. Similarly, U is left confluent if and only if $UU^\cup \subseteq U^\cup U$.

Proposition 100 (Right Linearity). *Recall that U is right linear if and only if U is locally linear and right confluent. It follows that U is right linear if and only if*

(L$_8$) $$U^\cup U \subseteq U^\cup \cup U. \qquad \text{(Right Linearity)}$$

In the case where U is a partial order $\leq$, right linearity means that for any given x the set of all y with $y \geq x$ forms a linear chain.

The correspondences (L$_3$–L$_8$) capture properties of individual observations at the level of sets, so that they can be exploited in a relational calculus of system descriptions. Of course, this works only for observation spaces that can be embedded into groupoids. The following theorem breathes life into the above correspondence results.

Theorem 101 (Embedding Theorem of Sequential Algebra). *Every locally linear observation space can be embedded into a groupoid.*

Proof. The proof of this theorem is given in [45].

In general the assumption of local linearity cannot be dropped. In the special case where composition is total, the existence of an embedding can be reformulated as: can every cancellative semigroup be embedded into a group? which was believed to be true for many years before Malcev finally discovered a counterexample (see [12], volume 2 for details).

The embedding theorem clarifies the link between the two main classes of observation spaces, namely groupoids and locally linear spaces. A valuable consequence is that we can use the relational calculus for reasoning also about sets of observations that cannot be inverted, simply by postulating the missing inverses. The additional flexibility may be valuable for specification and design, even though any implementation must be confined to sets of proper observations. And finally, the relational calculus, including the converse operator, can be used to define the primitive operations and prove the basic axioms of a more specific calculus for sets of observations. That will be done in the following section.

4.3   Sequential Set Algebras

Let us now confine attention to subsets P, Q, R of an observation space U. Our goal is to define operators on subsets of U which are similar to the relational operators, and to establish a collection of algebraic laws describing their properties. By the embedding theorem (Theorem 101) it is no significant loss of generality to assume that U is a reflexive and transitive subset of some groupoid G.

The main difference between a calculus for U and a calculus for G is the absence of a converse operator. If P is a subset of U, then $P^{\cup}$ is not a subset of U (except in the special case where $P \subseteq I$). We will use the division operators as a substitute. Just like composition, division can be lifted to sets:

(G$_4$) $R\,;\text{-}\,S \;=\; \{r\,;\text{-}\,s \mid r \in R \,\land\, s \in S \,\land\, r\,;\text{-}\,s \text{ is defined}\}$

(G$_5$) $R\,\text{-};\,S \;=\; \{r\,\text{-};\,s \mid r \in R \,\land\, s \in S \,\land\, r\,\text{-};\,s \text{ is defined}\}.$

The powerset of an observation space U equipped with the constant I and the further operations defined by (G$_1$), (G$_4$) and (G$_5$) is called the *sequential set algebra* over U.

Definition 102 (Priorities). *By convention, composition and division bind more tightly than union and intersection. When composition is expressed by juxtaposition, it binds more tightly than division (i.e. $PQ\,;\text{-}\,R = (PQ)\,;\text{-}\,R$).*

When an embedding groupoid G is available, we can use relation algebra to develop the theory of sequential set algebras. This is true because the division operators can be expressed in terms of the relation-algebraic ones.

(L$_9$) $R\,;\text{-}\,S \;=\; RS^{\cup} \cap U\,.$

(L$_{10}$) $R\,\text{-};\,S \;=\; R^{\cup}S \cap U\,.$

The axioms of the relational calculus together with the axioms (L_1-L_2) and equations (L_9-L_{10}) above constitute a calculus for subsets of an observation space. In addition, each of the further axioms (L_3-L_8) may be adopted or rejected individually.

Many laws of this calculus are hedged with side conditions on their free variables, and it turns out to be quite painful to work with two 'universes' G and U, each with their own complement operations. Therefore we plan to eliminate the converse operator completely, so that we can restrict attention to subsets of U. Unlike converse, division does not introduce artificial observations: when R and S are subsets of U then so are $R\,\text{-};S$ and $R\,;\text{-}\,S$. Therefore division is, besides composition, a basic constituent of the new calculus. As a final boon, we will discover that the reduced calculus applies to a wider range of models.

To put our plan into action we replace the axioms and correspondences involving converse by laws that employ division instead. We will use the relational calculus to prove the replacements as theorems of the old calculus before we take them as axioms of the new one. In the remainder of this section, P, Q, and R denote subsets of U.

Proposition 103 (Exchange Axiom). *To translate the exchange law from relation algebra to sequential algebra, we simply replace $PQ^\cup$ with $P\,;\text{-}\,Q$ and $P^\cup Q$ with $P\,\text{-};Q$. Each of the equations states that there are no $p \in P$, $q \in Q$ and $r \in R$ such that $q = p; r$ (see Figure 5).*

$$P\,\text{-};Q \cap R = \mathsf{O} \quad \Leftrightarrow \quad Q \cap PR = \mathsf{O} \quad \Leftrightarrow \quad Q\,;\text{-}\,R \cap P = \mathsf{O}.$$

As an aid to memory note that the first equation is obtained from the second one by cancelling P from the left. If, instead, we cancel R from the right we obtain the last equation. Alternatively, try to remember that composing with P from one side is conjugate to dividing by P from the same side.

$$
\begin{array}{ccc}
\xrightarrow{\;p \in P\;} & \xrightarrow{\;r \in R\;} \\
\xrightarrow{\qquad\quad q \in Q \qquad\quad}
\end{array}
$$

Fig. 5. The exchange law in sequential algebra

Proof. By symmetry, we need only show the first equivalence.

$$
\begin{aligned}
& P\,\text{-};Q \cap R = \mathsf{O} \\
\Leftrightarrow \quad & \{ (L_{10}) \} \\
& P^\cup Q \cap U \cap R = \mathsf{O} \\
\Leftrightarrow \quad & \{ R \subseteq U \} \\
& P^\cup Q \cap R = \mathsf{O} \\
\Leftrightarrow \quad & \{ \text{Exchange law of the relational calculus} \} \\
& Q \cap PR = \mathsf{O}.
\end{aligned}
$$

Proposition 104 (Euclidean Axiom). *A look at Figure 6 reveals an associativity between 'cutting' and 'pasting'. The name of this axiom is motivated by a geometric interpretation which we will not explain here. The interested reader is referred to [37].*

$$P\,(Q\,;\text{-}\,R) \ \subseteq \ PQ\,;\text{-}\,R.$$

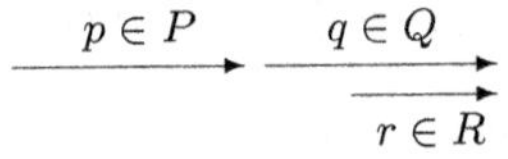

Fig. 6. The Euclidean Axiom

Proof.

$$
\begin{aligned}
&P\,(Q\,;\text{-}\,R)\\
=\quad &\qquad \{\,(\mathrm{L}_9)\,\}\\
&P\,(U \cap QR^{\cup})\\
\subseteq\quad &\qquad \{\text{ Monotonicity of composition }\}\\
&PU \cap PQR^{\cup}\\
\subseteq\quad &\qquad \{\ PU \subseteq UU \subseteq U,\ \text{by transitivity }(\mathrm{L}_1)\,\}\\
&U \cap (PQ)R^{\cup}\\
=\quad &\qquad \{\,(\mathrm{L}_9)\,\}\\
&PQ\,;\text{-}\,R\,.
\end{aligned}
$$

Proposition 105 (Reflection Axiom).

$$I\,;\text{-}\,P \ = \ P\,\text{-};\,I.$$

Proof.

$$I\,;\text{-}\,P = IP^{\cup} \cap U = P^{\cup}I \cap U = P\,\text{-};\,I\,.$$

The reflection axiom is valuable because it allows us to define $I\,;\text{-}\,P$ as the *weak converse* of P without breaking symmetry. The weak converse operator is studied in [45].

The three axioms proved above (Exchange, Euclid and Reflection) are valid in all calculi we have discussed. It now remains to discover axioms that capture additional properties that distinguish the calculi from each other.

Proposition 106 (Symmetry). *Recall that an observation space U is symmetric, $U^{\cup} = U$, if and only if every observation has an inverse. We can express symmetry without using converse:*

$$I\,;\text{-}\,U \ = \ U \qquad \Leftrightarrow \qquad U \text{ is symmetric.}$$

Proof.

> U is symmetric
>
> $\Leftrightarrow$
>
> $U \subseteq U^{\cup}$
>
> $\Leftrightarrow$
>
> $U = U^{\cup} \cap U$
>
> $\Leftrightarrow$
>
> $U = IU^{\cup} \cap U$
>
> $\Leftrightarrow$
>
> $U = I \mathbin{;\text{-}} U$.

Proposition 107 (Antisymmetry). *At the other extreme, an observation space is antisymmetric, $U \cap U^{\cup} = I$, when only unit observations have a converse. Here is a converse-free version of this statement; note the nice contrast to the formula expressing symmetry.*

$$I \mathbin{;\text{-}} U \;=\; I \qquad \Leftrightarrow \qquad U \text{ is antisymmetric.}$$

Proof.

> U is antisymmetric
>
> $\Leftrightarrow$
>
> $U \cap U^{\cup} = I$
>
> $\Leftrightarrow$
>
> $U \cap IU^{\cup} = I$
>
> $\Leftrightarrow$
>
> $I \mathbin{;\text{-}} U = I$.

Proposition 108 (Simplicity). *It is obvious from (L_9) that $I \subseteq UPU^{\cup}$ is equivalent to $I \subseteq UP \mathbin{;\text{-}} U$. Thus we can reformulate Tarski's Rule (the condition for simplicity) as follows:*

$$P \neq 0 \qquad \Rightarrow \qquad I \subseteq UP \mathbin{;\text{-}} U . \qquad \text{(Tarski's Rule)}$$

Proposition 109 (Local Linearity). *Assume that U is locally linear: $UU^{\cup} \cap U^{\cup}U \subseteq U \cup U^{\cup}$. Suppose we take a composite observation $p; q$ and cut r off its right, say $x = (p; q) \mathbin{;\text{-}} r$. Then $x; r = p; q$ and local linearity allows us to order the two cut points in time; the two possibilities are illustrated in Figure 7.*

This suggests the following strengthening of the Euclidean axiom.

$$PQ \mathbin{;\text{-}} R \;=\; P(Q \mathbin{;\text{-}} R) \;\cup\; P \mathbin{;\text{-}} (R \mathbin{;\text{-}} Q)$$

Proof. By Euclid we have $P(Q \mathbin{;\text{-}} R) \subseteq PQ \mathbin{;\text{-}} R$. Less obviously, the Euclidean axiom also implies $P \mathbin{;\text{-}} (R \mathbin{;\text{-}} Q) \subseteq PQ \mathbin{;\text{-}} R$; this will be shown in Proposition 130. Here, we show the inclusion from left to right.

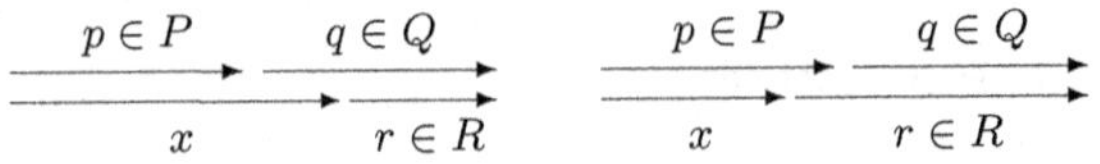

$$\xrightarrow{\;p \in P\;}\xrightarrow{\;q \in Q\;} \qquad \xrightarrow{\;p \in P\;}\xrightarrow{\;q \in Q\;}$$
$$\underset{x}{}\quad \underset{r \in R}{} \qquad \underset{x}{}\quad \underset{r \in R}{}$$

Fig. 7. Local linearity: either $x \in P\,(Q\,;\text{-}\,R)$ or $x \in P\;;\text{-}\,(R\,;\text{-}\,Q)$

$PQ\,;\text{-}\,R$

$=$ $\qquad\{\,(L_9)\,\}$

$U \,\cap\, P(QR^{\cup})$

$\subseteq$ $\qquad\{\,$ Dedekind law of the relational calculus (cf. 18) $\}$

$U \,\cap\, P(P^{\cup}U \cap QR^{\cup})$

$\subseteq$ $\qquad\left\{\begin{array}{l} P^{\cup}U \cap QR^{\cup} \subseteq U^{\cup}U \cap UU^{\cup} \subseteq U \cup U^{\cup}, \\ \text{by local linearity } (L_6) \end{array}\right\}$

$U \,\cap\, P((U \cup U^{\cup}) \cap QR^{\cup})$

$\subseteq$ $\qquad\{\,\cap$ distributes over $\cup\,\}$

$U \,\cap\, P((U \cap QR^{\cup}) \cup (U^{\cup} \cap QR^{\cup}))$

$=$ $\qquad\{\,U^{\cup} \cap QR^{\cup} = (U \cap RQ^{\cup})^{\cup},\ (L_9)\,\}$

$U \,\cap\, P(Q\,;\text{-}\,R \,\cup\, (R\,;\text{-}\,Q)^{\cup})$

$\subseteq$ $\qquad\{\,$ Composition distributes over $\cup$, $(L_9)\,\}$

$P(Q\,;\text{-}\,R) \,\cup\, P\,;\text{-}\,(R\,;\text{-}\,Q).$

Proposition 110 (Confluence). *Suppose U is right confluent, $U^{\cup}U \subseteq UU^{\cup}$, and consider two observations x and y as depicted in Figure 8. Clearly, y extends an initial subobservation of x, but due to confluence we might as well say that y is an initial subobservation of some extension of x.*

This is captured in the following law.

$$(P\,;\text{-}\,U)U \;=\; PU\,;\text{-}\,U.$$

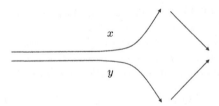

Fig. 8. Right confluence

Proof. The inclusion $PU \mathbin{;-} U \subseteq (P \mathbin{;-} U) U$ can be proved without the axiom of confluence (see Proposition 146). Here we prove the inclusion from left to right using transitivity (L_1) and confluence (L_7).

$$(P \mathbin{;-} U) U$$

$$=$$

$$(PU^{\cup} \cap U) U$$

$$=$$

$$PU^{\cup} U \cap UU$$

$$=$$

$$PUU^{\cup} \cap U$$

$$=$$

$$PU \mathbin{;-} U.$$

Similarly, U is left confluent if and only if

$$U(U \mathbin{-;} P) \;=\; U \mathbin{-;} UP.$$

And, of course, U is confluent when U is both left and right confluent.

Proposition 111 (Right Linearity). *Assume U is right linear, so that we may visualize observations as unbranching trajectories, and let $x = (p \mathbin{;-} q) \mathbin{;} r \in (P \mathbin{;-} Q) \mathbin{;} R$. Then q and r are co-initial, so one must be an initial subobservation of the other. The two possible cases are depicted in Figure 9.*

$$(P \mathbin{;-} Q) R \;\subseteq\; P \mathbin{;-} (R \mathbin{-;} Q) \,\cup\, P(Q \mathbin{-;} R).$$

Proof.

$$(P \mathbin{;-} Q) R$$

$$=\qquad \{\,(L_9)\,\}$$

$$(PQ^{\cup} \cap U) R$$

$$\subseteq\qquad \{\text{ Monotonicity }\}$$

$$PQ^{\cup} R \cap UR$$

$$\subseteq\qquad \{\, R \subseteq U, \text{ transitivity } (L_1)\,\}$$

$$PQ^{\cup} R \cap U$$

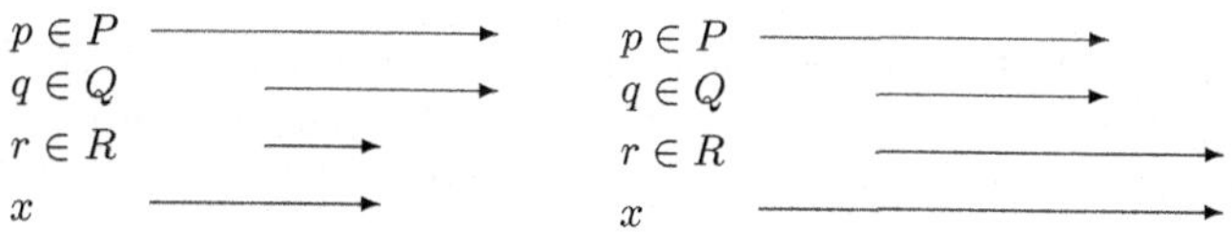

Fig. 9. Right linearity: either $x \in P \mathbin{;-} (R \mathbin{-;} Q)$ or $x \in P; Q \mathbin{-;} R$

$$\subseteq \qquad \{\, Q^{\cup}R \subseteq U^{\cup}U \subseteq U^{\cup} \cup U, \text{ by Right Linearity }\}$$
$$P(Q^{\cup}R \cap (U^{\cup} \cup U)) \cap U$$
$$\subseteq \qquad \{\text{ Relational calculus }\}$$
$$(P(R^{\cup}Q \cap U)^{\cup} \cap U) \cup P(Q^{\cup}R \cap U)$$
$$\subseteq \qquad \{\,(L_9) \text{ and } (L_{10})\,\}$$
$$P \;\text{;-}\; (R\,\text{-;}\; Q) \cup P(Q\,\text{-;}\; R).$$

Proposition 112 (Absence of Branching). *Suppose U is both left and right linear. Then we have the previous inequation and its dual. These two can be combined into a single equation*

$$(P\,\text{;-}\,Q)R \cup (Q\,\text{;-}\,P)\,\text{-;}\, R \;=\; P\,\text{;-}\,(R\,\text{-;}\, Q) \cup P(Q\,\text{-;}\, R).$$

Proof. The two sides of the above equation are mirror images, so it is sufficient to prove, say, the inclusion from left to right. By the axiom of right linearity, $(P\,\text{;-}\, Q)R$ is contained in the left hand side, so it remains to prove that

$$(Q\,\text{;-}\, P)\,\text{-;}\, R \;\subseteq\; P\,\text{;-}\,(R\,\text{-;}\, Q) \cup P(Q\,\text{-;}\, R).$$

This inequation follows from right linearity. We leave the proof as an exercise.

4.4   Abstract Sequential Algebras

Before taking the next abstraction step, let us review what we have achieved so far. We started by embedding an observation space U into a groupoid G, because the subsets of G enjoy the same algebraic properties as binary relations. Then we noticed that U is characterized within G by precisely the same laws that define a preorder.

At this stage we performed our first abstraction. We replaced the powerset of G by an arbitrary relation algebra $\mathcal{R}$, and the observation space U by a reflexive and transitive element of $\mathcal{R}$ (also denoted U). In doing so, we moved to an abstract universe and restricted ourselves to formal axiomatic reasoning.

Within this calculus we defined division operators and derived their fundamental laws, without ever referring to concrete observations. After doing this we are able to drop the converse operator and restrict the calculus to those elements of the underlying relation algebra that represent sets of proper observations.

Now we take a second abstraction step, dropping the assumption that there is an embedding relation algebra in which a converse operation is defined. We do this by taking the operators and laws of the restricted first calculus as an axiomatic definition of a new calculus.

Definition 113. *A sequential algebra is a complete Boolean algebra $(\mathcal{S}, \cap, \cup, \neg)$ with greatest element U and least element O, equipped with three additional binary operators (composition, left division and right division) satisfying the following axioms.*

- $(\mathcal{S},;)$ *is a monoid with an identity* I *(Monoid)*
- $P\,\text{-};Q\cap R = \mathsf{O} \quad\Leftrightarrow\quad Q\cap PR = \mathsf{O} \quad\Leftrightarrow\quad Q\,;\text{-}R\cap P = \mathsf{O}$ *(Exchange)*
- $P(Q\,;\text{-}R) \subseteq PQ\,;\text{-}R$ *(Euclid)*
- $I\,;\text{-}P = P\,\text{-};I$ *(Reflection)*

A sequential algebra is called *symmetric, simple, locally linear, confluent* etc. if the corresponding axiom (Propositions 106 to 112 of Section 4.3) is valid. The elements of a relation algebra are called relations or (in the Dutch school) specs. By analogy, an element of a sequential algebra is called a sequential, or *seq* for short.

Proposition 114 (Correspondences). *Let* U *be an observation space and let* $\mathcal{S}$ *be the sequential set algebra over* U. *Then* $\mathcal{S}$ *satisfies the axioms in Definition 113. Moreover, we have the following correspondences.*

(i) $\mathcal{S}$ *is symmetric* $\Leftrightarrow$ U *is a groupoid;*
(ii) $\mathcal{S}$ *is antisymmetric* $\Leftrightarrow$ U *is an antigroupoid;*
(iii) $\mathcal{S}$ *is simple* $\Leftrightarrow$ U *is simple;*
(iv) $\mathcal{S}$ *is locally linear* $\Leftrightarrow$ U *is locally linear;*
(v) $\mathcal{S}$ *is right (left) confluent* $\Leftrightarrow$ U *is right (left) confluent;*
(vi) Assume that $\mathcal{S}$ *is locally linear. Then we have*
    $\mathcal{S}$ *is right (left) linear* $\Leftrightarrow$ U *is right (left) linear.*

Remark 115 (A Nonstandard Model). *Every sequential set algebra satisfies the four axioms in Definition 113. On the other hand, not every sequential algebra is a sequential set algebra. For example consider a non-cancellative observation space. In the absence of cancellativity we cannot define the quotient of two observations. For when* $x;y = z = x';y$ *then* $z\,;\text{-}\,y$ *must be equal to both* x *and* x'. *But we can still define division on the level of sets:*

$$\text{(G}_4'\text{)} \qquad R\,;\text{-}\,S = \{x \mid \exists r \in R, s \in S : x;s = r\}$$

$$\text{(G}_5'\text{)} \qquad R\,\text{-};S = \{x \mid \exists r \in R, s \in S : r;x = s\}.$$

As an example, consider the set $A^* \cup A^\omega$ *of all finite and infinite strings over* A. *The composition of two strings is defined as concatenation when the first operand is finite, but* $s;t = s$ *when* s *is infinite. Then* $A^* \cup A^\omega$ *is an observation space, except that it is neither left nor right cancellative. Thus the powerset of* $A^* \cup A^\omega$ *is not a sequential set algebra, but the following result shows that it is a sequential algebra.*

Proposition 116. *Assume* U *satisfies* $(O_1\text{–}O_5)$ *and*

$$\text{(O}_6'\text{)} \qquad\qquad \text{If } (x;y) \text{ is a unit then so is } y;x\,.$$

Then the powerset of U *is a sequential algebra, with division defined by* (G_4') *and* (G_5'). *On the other hand, there is no way of embedding the powerset of* $A^* \cup A^\omega$ *into a relation algebra. This shows that sequential algebra is truly more general than relation algebra.*

The assumption (O_6') is necessary for ensuring the reflection axiom (which previously followed from cancellativity). In view of this proposition you might ask why we required cancellativity in the first place. Without cancellation, we could not have defined the quotient of two observations, which would be a pity because the lifted definitions (G_4) and (G_5) are much more intuitive than (G_4') and (G_5'). Even more seriously, it is impossible to embed any non-cancellative space into a groupoid. Of course, we might just have taken Definition 113 as our starting point—that would certainly have saved a lot of work. But such a presentation would not explain our particular choice of axioms, and it would not do justice to the intimate connection between sequential and relational algebra.

4.5   Time-Wise Duality

An apparent flaw in the definition of a sequential algebra is the asymmetry of the Euclidean axiom. Some of the optional axioms also appear to violate symmetry. We shall remove these blemishes now by showing that these axioms do, in fact, imply their mirror images, so that time-wise duality is preserved after all.

Theorem 117 (Euclidean Axiom (dual version)). *In every sequential algebra we have*

$$(P\mathbin{\text{-};} Q)\, R \ \subseteq\ P \mathbin{\text{-};} QR.$$

Proof.

$$(P\mathbin{\text{-};} Q)\, R \cap X \ = \ \mathsf{O}$$
$\Leftrightarrow$ { Exchange (heading for Euclid) }
$$P\mathbin{\text{-};} Q \cap X \mathbin{\text{;-}} R \ = \ \mathsf{O}$$
$\Leftrightarrow$ { Exchange }
$$Q \cap P\,(X \mathbin{\text{;-}} R) \ = \ \mathsf{O}$$
$\Leftarrow$ { Euclid }
$$Q \cap (PX) \mathbin{\text{;-}} R \ = \ \mathsf{O}$$
$\Leftrightarrow$ { Exchange (with the aim to isolate X) }
$$QR \cap PX \ = \ \mathsf{O}$$
$\Leftrightarrow$ { Exchange }
$$P\mathbin{\text{-};} QR \cap X \ = \ \mathsf{O}.$$

Taking $X = \neg(P \mathbin{\text{-};} QR)$ yields the dual Euclid inequation.

Since the Euclidean axiom is the only axiom of sequential algebra that is not obviously self-dual, it follows that sequential algebra enjoys perfect symmetry between left and right (past and future) and that the time-wise dual of any theorem is itself a theorem. Therefore, we will prove only one of each pair of theorems we state.

Exercise 118 (Symmetry and Antisymmetry). *It is immediate from the reflection axiom that the symmetry axiom $I \mathbin{;-} U = U$ and the antisymmetry axiom $I \mathbin{;-} U = I$ each imply their time-wise duals. As an exercise, we invite the reader to prove this self-duality using exchange instead of reflection.*

Proposition 119 (Left and Right Linearity). *Right linearity is independent of left linearity, because there are observation spaces which are right linear but not left linear (and vice versa). The same remark applies to confluence. But the equation in Proposition 112, which subsumes both left and right linearity, is self-dual.*

Proposition 120 (Local Linearity). *The axiom of local linearity also implies its time-wise dual.*

$$P \text{-}; QR \;=\; (P \text{-}; Q)R \;\cup\; (Q \text{-}; P) \text{-}; R.$$

Proof. By indirect equality:

$$P \text{-}; QR \cap X = 0$$
$$\Leftrightarrow \qquad \{ \text{ Exchange, heading for local linearity } \}$$
$$QR \cap PX = 0$$
$$\Leftrightarrow \qquad \{ \text{ Exchange } \}$$
$$QR \text{;-} X \cap P = 0$$
$$\Leftrightarrow \qquad \{ \text{ Local linearity (Proposition 109) } \}$$
$$(Q (R \text{;-} X) \cap P = 0) \;\wedge\; (Q \text{ ;-} (X \text{;-} R) \cap P = 0)$$
$$\Leftrightarrow \qquad \{ \text{ Exchange, with the aim of isolating } X \}$$
$$(R \text{;-} X \cap Q \text{-}; P = 0) \;\wedge\; (Q \cap P(X \text{;-} R) = 0)$$
$$\Leftrightarrow \qquad \{ \text{ Exchange } \}$$
$$(R \cap (Q \text{-}; P) X = 0) \;\wedge\; (P \text{-}; Q \cap X \text{;-} R = 0)$$
$$\Leftrightarrow \qquad \{ \text{ Exchange } \}$$
$$((Q \text{-}; P) \text{-}; R \cap X = 0) \;\wedge\; ((P \text{-}; Q) R \cap X = 0)$$
$$\Leftrightarrow$$
$$((Q \text{-}; P) \text{-}; R \cup (P \text{-}; Q) R) \cap X \;=\; 0.$$

Proposition 121 (Simplicity). *Simplicity is also equivalent to its own dual*

$$(\forall P \neq 0 : I \subseteq UP \text{;-} U) \qquad \Leftrightarrow \qquad (\forall P \neq 0 : I \subseteq U \text{-}; PU).$$

The proof of this result is more difficult, so we postpone it until Proposition 147.

5   Relational Laws of Sequential Algebra

The sequential calculus provides a collection of algebraic laws which apply to many more specialized calculi. This section and the next are intended as a reference and a number of the laws given here have been used without proof in application papers [5,6,44,3]. Section 5 concentrates on re-proving many laws of the relational calculus from the weaker assumptions of sequential algebra whereas the first sections of Section 6 collects algebraic laws with a more distinct temporal flavor.

5.1   Basic Laws

In this section we show the power of division in re-establishing many familiar laws of the relational calculus. The following Dedekind laws are instances of the general Dedekind law for conjugate functions (Theorem 18).

Proposition 122 (Dedekind Law of Composition). *The Dedekind law allows us to factor any expression of the form $(P \cap QR)$, either by pulling Q to the left, or by pulling R to the right:*

$$P \cap QR \subseteq Q\,(Q \mathbin{\text{-;}} P \cap R) \quad and \quad P \cap QR \subseteq (P \mathbin{\text{;-}} R \cap Q)\,R.$$

Exercise 123. *Show that the two Dedekind laws of composition can be combined into the following law.*

$$P \cap QR \ \subseteq\ (P \mathbin{\text{;-}} R \cap Q)(Q \mathbin{\text{-;}} P \cap R).$$

Proposition 124 (Dedekind Law of Division). *We may likewise factor $P \cap Q \mathbin{\text{;-}} R$ by pulling out the 'denominator' R.*

$$P \cap Q \mathbin{\text{;-}} R \ \subseteq\ (PR \cap Q) \mathbin{\text{;-}} R.$$

An analogous rule holds for division from the left.

Exercise 125. *Prove that the Dedekind inequations imply the exchange axiom. Since every inequation $P \subseteq Q$ may be written as an equation $P \cap Q = Q$, it follows that* sequential algebras form a variety (also called an equational class). *The classical reference on varieties of relation algebras is [23].*

Proposition 126 (Eliminate Division). *The following laws are immediate consequences of the exchange axiom:*

$$\neg(P \mathbin{\text{;-}} Q)\,Q \ \subseteq\ \neg P \quad and \quad \neg(PQ) \mathbin{\text{;-}} Q \ \subseteq\ \neg P.$$

Analogous rules apply to division from the left.

Proposition 127 (Associativity of Division). *When cutting something off an observation from both ends, it makes no difference which cut comes first.*

$$P \mathbin{\text{-;}} (Q \mathbin{\text{;-}} R) \ =\ (P \mathbin{\text{-;}} Q) \mathbin{\text{;-}} R.$$

(see Figure 10). This law can be used tacitly by omitting parentheses.

Proof.

$$P \mathbin{\text{-;}} (Q \mathbin{\text{;-}} R) \cap X \ =\ O$$
$$\Leftrightarrow \qquad \{\ \text{Exchange first } P \text{ then } R\ \}$$
$$Q \cap PXR \ =\ O$$
$$\Leftrightarrow \qquad \{\ \text{do it again}\ \}$$
$$(P \mathbin{\text{-;}} Q) \mathbin{\text{;-}} R \cap X \ =\ O.$$

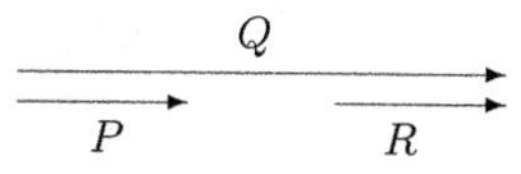

Fig. 10. Associativity of division

Proposition 128 (Identity of Division).

$$I \text{-}; P \ = \ P \ = \ P \text{;-} I.$$

Proof.

$$I \text{-}; P \cap X \ = \ O$$

$$\Leftrightarrow$$

$$P \cap IX \ = \ O$$

$$\Leftrightarrow$$

$$P \cap X \ = \ O.$$

Proposition 129 (Division by a Product). *The relational converse reverses the order of sequential components. So does division: Cutting an observation $q; r$ off p from the right has the same effect as first cutting off r, then q.*

$$PQ \text{-}; R \ = \ Q \text{-}; (P \text{-}; R) \quad and \quad P \text{;-} QR \ = \ (P \text{;-} R) \text{;-} Q.$$

(see Figure 11).

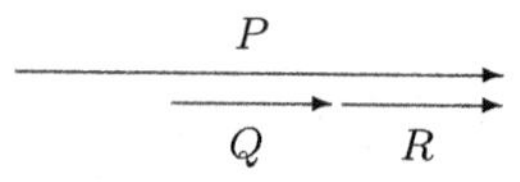

Fig. 11. Division by a product

Proof. Exercise (use indirect equality and repeated application of exchange.)

Proposition 130 (Division by a Quotient). *In the proof of Proposition 109 we claimed that one inclusion of the local linearity axiom followed from Euclid and exchange. Here is the missing law:*

$$P \text{;-} (R \text{;-} Q) \ \subseteq \ PQ \text{;-} R \quad and \quad (Q \text{-}; P) \text{-}; R \ \subseteq \ P \text{-}; QR.$$

(see Figure 12).

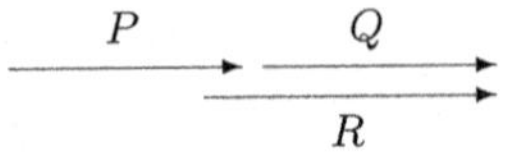

Fig. 12. Division by a quotient

Proof. By indirect inequality.

$$P \; ; \text{-} \; (R \; ; \text{-} \; Q) \cap X \;\; = \;\; 0$$
$$\Leftrightarrow \qquad \{ \text{ Exchange } \}$$
$$P \cap X \, (R \; ; \text{-} \; Q) \;\; = \;\; 0$$
$$\Leftarrow \qquad \{ \text{ Euclid } \}$$
$$P \cap X R \; ; \text{-} \; Q \;\; = \;\; 0$$
$$\Leftrightarrow \qquad \{ \text{ Exchange (twice) } \}$$
$$PQ \; ; \text{-} \; R \cap X \;\; = \;\; 0 \, .$$

Now take $X = \neg (PQ \; ; \text{-} \; R)$.

Remark 131 (A Counterexample). *After we sacrificed the converse operation, which gives the relational calculus its characteristic power and expressiveness, it is gratifying to find that a large part of the relational calculus can be salvaged with the aid of division—which at first sight may seem a poor substitute for converse. However, there are limits. Consider the following theorem of relational calculus*

$$(PQ^{\cup})R \;\; = \;\; P(Q^{\cup}R) \, .$$

Translating into the sequential calculus yields

$$(P \; ; \text{-} \; Q)R \;\; = \;\; P(Q \; \text{-}; R) \, ,$$

which is not a theorem. To see the problem consider Figure 13. At the level of individual observations the equation $(p \; ; \text{-} \; q) \; ; \; r = p \; ; \; (q \; \text{-}; \; r)$ is indeed valid — but only when both sides are defined! If, say, r is 'shorter' than q, then only the left hand side is defined. In a sense, this is the only place where the relational calculus is stronger than the sequential calculus, as shown by the following result.

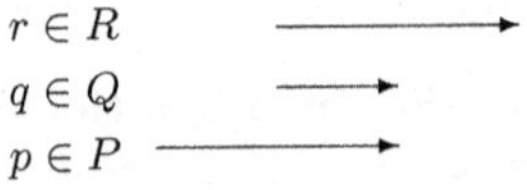

Fig. 13. Relational calculus is stronger than sequential calculus

Theorem 132. *A sequential algebra is a relational algebra (with the converse operator defined by $P^{\cup} =_{df} I\; ;\; \text{-}\,P$) if and only if the following identity is valid.*

$$(P\; ;\; \text{-}\,Q)R \;=\; P(Q\; \text{-};\; R).$$

Proof. Exercise.

5.2   Predicates

In the relational calculus, a state s can be represented by the observation (s, s). So, a *predicate* on states may be given as a set of observations x with $\overleftarrow{x} = x = \overrightarrow{x}$. Generalizing this idea to the sequential calculus, we call P a predicate if $P \subseteq I$. By convention, B and C always denote predicates. The set of all predicates forms a Boolean algebra (where the complement of a predicate B is $I \cap \neg B$).

Predicates can play the rôle of pre- and postconditions. To specify that P must refine Q, whenever precondition B holds, we write

$$BP \subseteq Q.$$

The following formula may be used to state that every execution of P that starts from a state allowed by the precondition B will end in a state allowed by the postcondition C:

$$BP \subseteq PC.$$

The last inequation is traditionally written in Hoare-logic style

$$B\{P\}C.$$

Proposition 133 (Superdistributivity). *Pre- and postconditions distribute over conjunctions, and may be shifted from one conjunct to another*

$$B(P \cap Q) \;=\; BP \cap Q \quad and \quad (P \cap Q)B \;=\; P \cap QB.$$

Proof. By mutual inclusion.

$$BP \cap Q$$
$\subseteq$ { Dedekind law of composition (Proposition 122) }
$$B(P \cap B\,\text{-};\, Q)$$
$\subseteq$ { $B \subseteq I$, identity law of division (Proposition 128) }
$$B(P \cap Q)$$
$\subseteq$ { Monotonicity }
$$BP \cap BQ$$
$\subseteq$ { $B \subseteq I$ }
$$BP \cap Q.$$

Proposition 134 (Predicate Merge Law). *Applying superdistributivity with $P = I$ and $Q = C$ we find that the composition of two predicates is just their conjunction.*

$$BC \;=\; B \cap C.$$

Exercise 135 (Vectors). *We have encoded sets of states as predicates, but that is not the only possibility. Sets of states may also be encoded as vectors [38] (also called left conditions [13]). A seq P is called a vector if there is a predicate B such that $P = BU$. Show the following.*

1. *The set of all vectors forms a Boolean algebra;*
2. *P is a vector if and only if $P = (P\,;\text{-}U)U$.*

Proposition 136 (Division by a Predicate). *Dividing by a predicate has the same filtering effect as multiplying with the same predicate.*

$$B\,\text{-}; P \ = \ BP \quad and \quad P\,;\text{-}B \ = \ PB.$$

Proof.

$$B\,\text{-}; P \cap X \ = \ O$$
$$\Leftrightarrow \qquad \{\ \text{Exchange}\ \}$$
$$P \cap BX \ = \ O$$
$$\Leftrightarrow \qquad \{\ \text{Superdistributivity}\ \}$$
$$BP \cap X \ = \ O.$$

Proposition 137 (Flip Quotient Law). *By cancellativity, $x\,;\text{-}y$ is a unit only when $x = y$, in which case $x\,;\text{-}y = y\,;\text{-}x$. Therefore we have*

$$P\,;\text{-}Q \cap I \ = \ Q\,;\text{-}P \cap I.$$

Proof. By indirect equality.

$$P\,;\text{-}Q \cap I \cap X \ = \ O$$
$$\Leftrightarrow \qquad \{\ \text{Exchange}\ Q\ \}$$
$$P \cap (I \cap X)Q \ = \ O$$
$$\Leftrightarrow \qquad \{\ \text{Division by a predicate (Proposition 136)}\ \}$$
$$P \cap (I \cap X)\,\text{-}; Q \ = \ O$$
$$\Leftrightarrow \qquad \{\ \text{Exchange}\ I \cap X\ \}$$
$$(I \cap X)P \cap Q \ = \ O$$
$$\Leftrightarrow \qquad \{\ \text{Exchange}\ P\ \}$$
$$Q\,;\text{-}P \cap I \cap X \ = \ O.$$

Proposition 138 (Predicate Quotient Laws). *If $x = p\,;\text{-}q \in P\,;\text{-}Q$ then p and q are co-final (see Figure 14). Thus filtering the final state of p has the same effect as filtering the final state of q.*

It follows that a a postcondition can be shifted freely between the 'numerator' and the 'denominator' of a right quotient:

$$PB\,;\text{-}Q \ = \ P\,;\text{-}QB.$$

Moreover, p and x are co-initial, so a precondition may be moved freely from P to $P\,;\text{-}Q$:

$$BP\,;\text{-}Q \ = \ B(P\,;\text{-}Q).$$

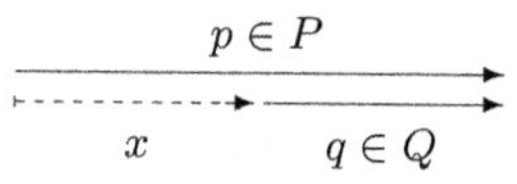

Fig. 14. Filtering final states

Finally, $\vec{x} = \overleftarrow{q}$, so a postcondition on $P \mathbin{;-} Q$ translates to a precondition on Q.

$$P \mathbin{;-} BQ = (P \mathbin{;-} Q)\,B\,.$$

Proof. We prove the first of the above three laws.

$$P \mathbin{;-} QB$$
$$= \qquad \{ \text{ Division by a product (Proposition } 129) \ \}$$
$$(P \mathbin{;-} B) \mathbin{;-} Q$$
$$= \qquad \{ \text{ Division by a predicate (Proposition } 136) \ \}$$
$$PB \mathbin{;-} Q\,.$$

The remaining two equations are left as exercises (hint: use associativity of division, Proposition 127).

5.3   Left and Right Domain

One of the qualities of an effective notation for reasoning about reactive systems is the ability to express assertions about the initial and final state of a program, the start and end of a phase, the transition of a state, or the rise and fall of a waveform. Each of these events occurs at the boundary of an observation such as the very first point in time for which a program is executing, or a system is in a certain phase, or for which a waveform is high.

Every observation has a start point and an end point, and in a sequential set algebra we may define left and right *domain* operators by

$$\overleftarrow{R} =_{df} \{ \overleftarrow{x} \mid x \in R \} \quad \text{and} \quad \overrightarrow{R} =_{df} \{ \overrightarrow{x} \mid x \in R \}\,.$$

Definition 139 (Algebraic Definition). *At the set level, the domain operators may be defined as follows:*

$$\overleftarrow{R} =_{df} I \cap R \mathbin{;-} R = I \cap R \mathbin{;-} U \quad \text{and} \quad \overrightarrow{R} =_{df} I \cap R \mathbin{-;} R = I \cap U \mathbin{-;} R\,.$$

We deduce the nontrivial inclusion of the equation $I \cap R \mathbin{;-} R = I \cap R \mathbin{;-} U$ from the Flip Quotient Law (Proposition 137) and the Dedekind Law of Division (Proposition 124) as follows.

$$I \cap R \mathbin{;-} U = I \cap U \mathbin{;-} R \subseteq (IR \cap U) \mathbin{;-} R = R \mathbin{;-} R\,.$$

Each of the next three laws corresponds directly to one of the axioms of observation spaces. Such laws are especially helpful for translating proofs involving individual observations to the set level.

Proposition 140 (Domain Identity Law). *Observations are required to obey the single-sided unit laws* $\overleftarrow{x}; x = x = x; \overrightarrow{x}$. *At the calculus level we have*

$$\overleftarrow{R} R \;=\; R \;=\; R \overrightarrow{R}.$$

Proof. Using the Dedekind law of composition (Proposition 122) we obtain

$$R \;=\; IR \cap R \;\subseteq\; (I \cap R; -R)R \;=\; \overleftarrow{R} R.$$

The converse inequation is trivial.

Proposition 141 (Domains of a Predicate). *A unit observation e must be equal to its left and right codomain. Since predicates represent sets of unit observations, the postulate* $\overleftarrow{e} = e = \overrightarrow{e}$ *translates to*

$$\overleftarrow{B} \;=\; B \;=\; \overrightarrow{B}.$$

Proof.
$$\overleftarrow{B} = B; -B \cap I = BB \cap I = B.$$

Proposition 142 (Definedness of Composition). *Recall that we originally introduced the domain operators on observations to characterize the definedness of composition:*

$$x; y \text{ is undefined} \quad \Leftrightarrow \quad \overrightarrow{x} \neq \overleftarrow{y}.$$

In the calculus, we have

$$PQ = 0 \qquad \Leftrightarrow \qquad \overrightarrow{P} \cap \overleftarrow{Q} = 0.$$

Proof. Assume first that $\overrightarrow{P} \cap \overleftarrow{Q} = 0$. Then $PQ = P\overrightarrow{P}\overleftarrow{Q}Q = P(\overrightarrow{P} \cap \overleftarrow{Q})Q = 0$ as well. Conversely, assume that $PQ = 0$. Then

$$\overrightarrow{P} \cap \overleftarrow{Q}$$
$$\subseteq \qquad \{ \text{ Definitions } \}$$
$$P\,\text{-}; P \cap Q\,; \text{-}Q$$
$$\subseteq \qquad \{ \text{ Dedekind law of division (Proposition 124) } \}$$
$$P\,\text{-};\, (P(Q\,; \text{-}Q))$$
$$\subseteq \qquad \{ \text{ Euclid } \}$$
$$P\,\text{-};\, (PQ\,; \text{-}Q)$$
$$= \qquad \{ \text{ Assumption } \}$$
$$0.$$

Whenever a new operator is introduced, it is our duty to find out how it distributes over the previously given ones. We already know that the domain operators are disjunctive, and in the remainder of this section we determine the left and right domains of intersections, products and quotients.

Proposition 143 (Domains of an Intersection). *The domain operators do not distribute over conjunctions, but we have the following helpful law:*

$$\overleftarrow{P \cap Q} \;=\; P \,;\text{-}\, Q \cap I \quad and \quad \overrightarrow{P \cap Q} \;=\; P \,\text{-};\, Q \cap I.$$

Proof.

$$P \,;\text{-}\, Q \cap I$$
$$=\qquad \{ \text{ Dedekind law of division (Proposition 124) } \}$$
$$(P \cap Q) \,;\text{-}\, Q \cap I$$
$$=\qquad \{ \text{ Flip quotient (Proposition 137) } \}$$
$$Q \,;\text{-}\, (P \cap Q) \cap I$$
$$=\qquad \{ \text{ Repeat first two steps } \}$$
$$(P \cap Q) \,;\text{-}\, (P \cap Q) \cap I$$
$$=\qquad \{ \text{ Definition } \}$$
$$\overleftarrow{P \cap Q}.$$

Proposition 144 (Left Domain of Quotients).

$$\overleftarrow{P \,;\text{-}\, Q} \;=\; \overleftarrow{P \cap UQ} \quad and \quad \overleftarrow{P \,\text{-};\, Q} \;=\; \overrightarrow{P \cap Q \,;\text{-}\, U}.$$

Proof. Both proofs use Proposition 143.

$$\overleftarrow{P \,;\text{-}\, Q} = (P \,;\text{-}\, Q) \,;\text{-}\, U \cap I = P \,;\text{-}\, UQ \cap I = \overleftarrow{P \cap UQ}.$$

$$\overleftarrow{P \,\text{-};\, Q} = (P \,\text{-};\, Q) \,;\text{-}\, U \cap I = P \,\text{-};\, (Q \,;\text{-}\, U) \cap I = \overrightarrow{P \cap Q \,;\text{-}\, U}.$$

Proposition 145 (Left Domain of a Product).

$$\overleftarrow{PQ} \;=\; \overleftarrow{P \overleftarrow{Q}}.$$

Proof. This is left as an exercise (if you can't solve it, see [45]).

Proposition 146 (Confluence). *Recall that a sequential algebra is confluent if it satisfies* $(P \,;\text{-}\, U)U = PU \,;\text{-}\, U$. *When we established the correspondence between properties of preorders and properties of sequential algebras, we claimed that one inclusion of the confluence axiom was valid in every sequential algebra. It is now time to discharge this proof obligation.*

$$PU \,;\text{-}\, U \;\subseteq\; (P \,;\text{-}\, U)U.$$

Proof.

$$PU \,;\text{-}\, U$$
$$=\qquad \{ \text{ Domain identity law (Proposition 140) } \}$$
$$(\overleftarrow{P} PU) \,;\text{-}\, U$$
$$=\qquad \{ \text{ Predicate quotient law (Proposition 138) } \}$$
$$\overleftarrow{P}(PU \,;\text{-}\, U)$$

$$\subseteq$$
$$\overleftarrow{P} U$$
$$\subseteq \qquad \{ \text{ Definition of } \overleftarrow{P} \}$$
$$(P ;\text{-} U) U .$$

Proposition 147 (Simplicity). *Recall that a sequential algebra S is called* simple *if it obeys Tarski's rule:*

$$P \neq \mathsf{O} \qquad \Rightarrow \qquad I \subseteq UP ;\text{-} U .$$

In the case where S is a relation algebra, this is equivalent to the more familiar law

$$P \neq \mathsf{O} \qquad \Rightarrow \qquad U = UPU .$$

In Proposition 121 we promised to show that Tarski's rule implies its own temporal dual. More precisely, we will now prove that

$$(\forall P \neq \mathsf{O} : I \subseteq U \text{-}; PU) \qquad \Leftrightarrow \qquad (\forall P \neq \mathsf{O} : I \subseteq UP ;\text{-} U).$$

Proof. By symmetry, we need only show one implication, so let $P \in S$ and assume that $I \subseteq U \text{-}; QU$ for all non-zero Q. In the following calculation, B ranges over predicates.

$$P \neq \mathsf{O}$$
$$\Leftrightarrow \qquad \{ \text{ Domain identity law (Proposition 140) } \}$$
$$\overleftarrow{P} \neq \mathsf{O}$$
$$\Rightarrow \qquad \{ \text{ Definedness of composition (Proposition 139) } \}$$
$$\forall B \; : \; I \subseteq \overrightarrow{BU} \quad \Rightarrow \quad BUP \neq \mathsf{O}$$
$$\Rightarrow \qquad \{ \text{ Contraposition } \}$$
$$\forall B \; : \; BUP = \mathsf{O} \quad \Rightarrow \quad \neg(I \subseteq \overrightarrow{BU})$$
$$\Rightarrow \qquad \{ \overrightarrow{BU} \subseteq U \text{-}; BU \text{ by Proposition 139 } \}$$
$$\forall B \; : \; BUP = \mathsf{O} \quad \Rightarrow \quad \neg(I \subseteq U \text{-}; BU)$$
$$\Leftrightarrow \qquad \{ \text{ Assumption } \}$$
$$\forall B \; : \; BUP = \mathsf{O} \quad \Rightarrow \quad B = \mathsf{O}$$
$$\Rightarrow \qquad \{ \text{ Take } B = \neg\overleftarrow{UP} \}$$
$$\neg\overleftarrow{UP} = \mathsf{O}$$
$$\Leftrightarrow$$
$$I = \overleftarrow{UP}$$
$$\Rightarrow \qquad \{ \overleftarrow{UP} \subseteq UP ;\text{-} U \text{ by Proposition 139 } \}$$
$$I \subseteq UP ;\text{-} U .$$

6   Interval Calculi

The previous section emphasized the similarities between the relational calculus and the sequential calculus. We will now turn our attention to temporal phenomena, especially ones that have a duration. Sections 6.1 and 6.2 explain how the sequential calculus is used for reasoning about intervals. Introducing states and durations we successively extend sequential calculus and demonstrate how it may be used in the design of reactive systems.

6.1 Somewhere and Everywhere

Relations are sets of pairs. An interval can also be described as a pair (a, b) but there is the additional constraint that a should be less than or equal to b. The presence of an ordering permits—and requires—the definition of temporal concepts. All of these are related to the notion of *subobservations*. Let u and v be observations. We say that u is a *subobservation* of v if the equation

$$x; u; y = v$$

can be solved. Every relation between observations can be lifted. Let P be a set of observations. Then $\diamond P$ ('somewhere P') is the set of all observations that have a subobservation in P.

$$\diamond P =_{df} \{x; u; y \mid x; u; y \text{ is defined and } u \in P\} = U P U.$$

The definition of $\diamond$ in terms of sequential composition is well-known from interval temporal logic and is used, for example, in [33,47]. The dual modality ('everywhere P') is defined by

$$\boxplus P =_{df} \neg \diamond \neg P,$$

so $x \in \boxplus P$ just when all subobservations of x are in P. The $\boxplus$ and $\diamond$ operators (and their Galois adjoints) are referred to as *interval modalities*. By convention, the interval modalities bind more strongly than composition and division. Applying the above definitions to relations is rather uninteresting, as can be seen from the following restatement of Tarski's rule:

$$\diamond P = U \text{ unless } P = O.$$

This indicates that our decision to abandon the converse operation was necessary for obtaining an interesting and useful temporal calculus. We intentionally use the same symbols $\diamond$ and $\boxplus$ both in Galois algebra and for the interval modalities. This is justified because — in the discrete setting at least — interval algebra is a special case of Galois algebra in the sense that $\diamond = \oplus^*$ where $\oplus$ is defined by $\oplus P = step; P \cup P; step$ where $step = \neg I \cap \neg((\neg I)(\overline{I}))$. Indeed, many laws of interval algebra are familiar from Galois algebra, but the former is distinguished from the latter by the existence of a composition operator. As a consequence, the calculus of intervals is much richer than Galois algebra. The following properties are immediate from the definitions.

Proposition 148 (Basic Properties).

1. $\diamond$ is universally disjunctive and $\boxplus$ is universally conjunctive;

2. $\Diamond$ and $\boxplus$ are idempotent;

3. $\boxplus P \subseteq P \subseteq \Diamond P$.

Definition 149 (Galois Adjoints). *As before, we let* $\Diamond =_{df} \boxplus^{\flat}$ *and* $\boxminus =_{df} \Diamond^{\sharp}$. *Then we have*

$$\Diamond P \;=\; U \mathbin{-;} P \mathbin{;-} U \quad and \quad \boxminus P \;=\; \neg \Diamond \neg P \,.$$

Since the somewhere operator is universally disjunctive, we obtain the usual best-of-both-worlds and Dedekind laws.

Proposition 150 (Dedekind).

$$\Diamond P \cap Q \;\subseteq\; \Diamond(P \cap \Diamond Q) \quad and \quad \Diamond P \cap Q \;\subseteq\; \Diamond(P \cap \Diamond Q)\,.$$

Proposition 151 (Best of Both Worlds). *If* P *holds everywhere and* Q *holds somewhere then they must hold together somewhere.*

$$\boxplus P \cap \Diamond Q \;\subseteq\; \Diamond(P \cap Q)\,.$$

Proposition 152. *Suppose that* $\mathcal{S}$ *is antisymmetric (i.e.* $I \mathbin{;-} U = I = U \mathbin{-;} I$*). Then we have*

$$\boxplus B \;=\; B \quad \text{for every predicate } B.$$

Proof.

$$B = \boxplus B$$

$\Leftrightarrow \qquad \{\ \boxplus B \subseteq B \text{ by Proposition } 148, \text{ definition of } \boxplus\ \}$

$$B \subseteq \neg(U(\neg B)U)$$

$\Leftrightarrow \qquad \{\ \text{Exchange (twice)}\ \}$

$$U \mathbin{-;} B \mathbin{;-} U \subseteq B$$

$\Leftarrow \qquad \{\ \text{Euclid (twice)}\ \}$

$$(U \mathbin{-;} I)B(I \mathbin{;-} U) \subseteq B$$

$\Leftarrow \qquad \{\ \text{Antisymmetry}\ \}$

$$true\,.$$

If the underlying sequential algebra has additional properties (such as antisymmetry, confluence or local linearity) then these can be exploited for the algebra of intervals. Paragraphs 153 to 155 provide some examples. Note that the following absorption laws differ from those of LTL where we have $\boxplus \Diamond \boxplus P = \Diamond \boxplus P$ (see Theorem 80).

Proposition 153 (Absorption Laws). *Assume that* $\mathcal{S}$ *is antisymmetric. Then we have*

$$\Diamond \circ \boxplus \circ \Diamond \;=\; \Diamond \circ \boxplus \quad and \quad \boxplus \circ \Diamond \circ \boxplus \;=\; \boxplus \circ \Diamond \,.$$

Proof. We need two auxiliary calculations. The first is:

$$I \cap \oplus P$$

= $\quad\quad$ { Definition of $\oplus$ }

$$I \cap U P U$$

= $\quad\quad \left\{ \begin{array}{l} \text{Antisymmetry axiom,} \\ \text{importability of } I \text{ (Proposition 165)} \end{array} \right\}$

$$(I \cap U)(I \cap P)(I \cap U)$$

= $\quad\quad$ { Unit of composition }

$$I \cap P.$$

The second auxiliary calculation is as follows

$$I \cap P$$

= $\quad\quad$ { Boolean algebra }

$$I \cap \neg(I \cap \neg P)$$

= $\quad\quad$ { Previous calculation }

$$I \cap \neg(I \cap \oplus \neg P)$$

= $\quad\quad$ { Boolean algebra, $\neg \oplus \neg P = \boxplus P$ }

$$I \cap \boxplus P.$$

We can now prove the first claim in the Absorption Law (Proposition 153). The inclusion from right to left follows immediately from Proposition 148(3). For the other inclusion, we calculate:

$$\oplus \boxplus \oplus P$$

= $\quad\quad$ { $\oplus I = U$ }

$$\oplus(\oplus I \cap \boxplus \oplus P)$$

$\subseteq \quad\quad$ { Best of Both Worlds }

$$\oplus \oplus(I \cap \oplus P)$$

= $\quad\quad$ { $\oplus$ is idempotent }

$$\oplus(I \cap \oplus P)$$

= $\quad\quad$ { Previous two calculations }

$$\oplus(I \cap \boxplus P)$$

$\subseteq \quad\quad$ { Monotonicity }

$$\oplus \boxplus P.$$

The second absorption law follows from (logical) duality.

Remark 154 (Duality). *In Galois algebra the operators $\oplus$ and $\ominus$ are time-wise duals, but in interval algebra the symmetry is fundamentally broken. Here $\oplus$ and $\ominus$ are self-dual, rather than each other's duals. For example, the above absorption laws do not have time-wise duals. The reader may wish to prove that the expression $\boxminus \circ \ominus \circ \boxminus$ cannot be reduced to a composition of only two operators (unless S is confluent).*

Proposition 155 (Confluence). *Assume that S confluent (see Proposition 110 for the definition and explanation of confluence in sequential algebras). Then $\oplus$ and $\ominus$ satisfy the left confluence law (cf. Section 3.5).*

$$\oplus \circ \ominus \ \subseteq \ \ominus \circ \oplus \ .$$

Proof.

$$\oplus \ominus P$$

$=$ { Definitions, Associativity of Division (Proposition 127) }

$U\left(\left(U\text{-};P\right)\text{;- }U\right)U$

$\subseteq$ { Euclid, dual version (Theorem 117) }

$\left(U(U\text{-};P)\ \text{;- }U\right)U$

$=$ { Left Confluence: $U(U\text{-};P) = U\text{-};UP$ }

$\left(\left(U\text{-};UP\right)\ \text{;- }U\right)U$

$=$ { Associativity of Division (Proposition 127) }

$\left(U\text{-};\left(UP\ \text{;- }U\right)\right)U$

$\subseteq$ { Euclid }

$U\text{-};\left(UP\ \text{;- }U\right)U$

$=$ { Right Confluence: $\left(UP\ \text{;- }U\right)U = UPU\ \text{;- }U$ }

$U\text{-};\left(UPU\ \text{;- }U\right)$

$=$ { Definitions, Associativity of Division (Proposition 127) }

$\ominus \oplus P.$

Exercise 156. *Assume that S is confluent. Then we have the absorption laws*

$$\Box \circ \ominus \circ \Box = \ominus \circ \Box \qquad \text{and} \qquad \ominus \circ \Box \circ \ominus = \Box \circ \ominus \ .$$

6.2 Importability

A seq may be regarded as a property of observations; in this section we will study the ways in which properties may be inherited by sub- and superobservations. Inheritable properties abound in temporal algebra, and their identification is useful because they obey additional distribution laws which aid compositional reasoning [33].

Definition 157 (Importability). *A seq P is importable if it is inherited by subobservations*

$$x;y;z \in P \quad \Rightarrow \quad y \in P.$$

which translates, at the set level, to

$$U\text{-};P\,;\text{-}U \subseteq P.$$

It is the latter inequality that we take as the definition of importability in an (abstract) sequential algebra.

Importable properties are extremely common. For example, take observations to be timing diagrams and assume a to be one of the observable variables. Then the set of all observations x satisfying any one given property from the following list is importable:

- the length of x is at most 3.14;
- a is constant;
- a changes at most once;
- a changes continuously with time;
- the derivative of a exists everywhere;
- a increases all the time;
- a is always positive and $\int_x a\, dt < 1.414$.

Note that importability is not a useful concept for relations, because a relation is importable only if it is either empty or universal.

Definition 158 (Safety Properties). *According to Manna and Pnueli's book on temporal logic, P is called a safety property if there is some Q with $P = \boxplus Q$. Since $\boxplus$ is idempotent, every safety property P satisfies $P = \boxplus P$.*

Proposition 159 (Characterizations of Importability). *For any given seq P, the following four statements are equivalent.*

1. *P is a safety property, i.e. $P = \boxplus P$;*
2. *P is importable, i.e. $U\text{-};P\text{;-}U \subseteq P$;*
3. *$\forall Q, R : P \cap QR \subseteq (P \cap Q)(P \cap R)$.*
4. *$\neg P$ is invariant under composition: $U(\neg P)U \subseteq \neg P$;*

Proof. By mutual implication:

'1 $\Rightarrow$ 2' $P = \boxplus Q$

$\Rightarrow$ { $\boxplus$ is idempotent }
          $P \subseteq \boxplus P$

$\Rightarrow$ { $\boxplus P = \neg \Diamond \neg P$, Exchange }
     $U\text{-};P\text{;-}U \subseteq P$.

'2 $\Rightarrow$ 3' $P \cap QR$

$\subseteq$ { Double-sided Dedekind law (Exercise 123) }
     $(P\text{;-}R \cap Q)(Q\text{-};P \cap R)$

$\subseteq$ { Assumption: P is invariant under division }
     $(P \cap Q)(P \cap R)$.

'3 $\Rightarrow$ 4' $U;(\neg P);U \subseteq \neg P$

$\Leftrightarrow$ { Shunting }
     $U(\neg P)U \cap P = \mathsf{O}$

$\Leftrightarrow$ { Assumption (twice) }
     $(P \cap U)(P \cap \neg P)(U \cap P) = \mathsf{O}$

$\Leftrightarrow$

     $true$.

'4 ⇒ 1'   Take the contraposition of statement 4 and choose $Q = P$.

Proposition 160 (Importability of Safety Properties). *Recall that a seq P is importable if $P \cap QR \subseteq (P \cap Q)(P \cap R)$ for all Q and R. The box operator of ITL gives us the following characterization of importability:*

$$P \text{ is importable iff } P = \boxplus P.$$

Proof.

$\qquad P$ is importable
$\Leftrightarrow \qquad\qquad$ { Proposition 159 }
$\qquad U \text{-}; P \text{;-} U \subseteq P$
$\Leftrightarrow \qquad\qquad$ { Galois connection (Definition 149) }
$\qquad P \subseteq \boxplus P$
$\Leftrightarrow \qquad\qquad$ { $\boxplus P \subseteq P$ by Proposition 148 }
$\qquad P = \boxplus P.$

Corollary 161. *Since $\boxplus P = \boxplus\boxplus P$, it follows that $\boxplus P$ is itself importable. Therefore, we have*

$$PQ \cap \boxplus R \subseteq (P \cap \boxplus R)(Q \cap \boxplus R).$$

Definition 162 (Exportability). *A property is called* exportable *if it is inherited by superobservations*

$$x; y \in P \qquad\Leftarrow\qquad x \in P \lor y \in P.$$

In other words, a seq is exportable if and only if its complement is importable.

Definition 163 (Transitivity). *We have seen that a seq P is importable if*

$$P \cap QR \subseteq (P \cap Q)(P \cap R).$$

for all Q, R. A seq P is called transitive *when the converse inequation holds or, more simply put, if $PP \subseteq P$.*

Definition 164 (Compositionality). *A seq that is importable and transitive is said to be* compositional *[33]. In other words, P is compositional if and only if P distributes over composition*

$$P \cap QR = (P \cap Q)(P \cap R).$$

Proposition 165 (Predicates are Compositional). *In an antisymmetric sequential algebra, predicates are compositional.*

$$B \cap PQ = (B \cap P)(B \cap Q) \qquad \text{provided } I \text{;-} U \subseteq I.$$

Proof. Transitivity follows from the predicate merge law (Proposition 134) and importability was proved in Proposition 152.

Exercise 166. *Assume that P is compositional and $I \subseteq P$. Then show that P distributes over iteration:*

$$P \cap Q^* = (P \cap Q)^*.$$

6.3   Engineer's Induction

Safety requirements are best expressed by describing behaviours that may *never* occur (for example, explosions). If Q is the description of a disaster then an implementation X must solve the inequation

$$X \subseteq \neg \diamond Q,$$

Industrial plants are often controlled by looping programs that repeatedly cycle through a fixed set of production steps or alternate between a sensing phase and a correction phase. To ensure that a control program is safe we must therefore verify an inequation of the form

$$P^* \subseteq \neg \diamond Q.$$

There is an old joke about engineers doing induction by just checking the cases $n = 0$, $n = 1$ and $n = 2$. The following theorem provides a criterion for the correctness of this approach, for it reduces the verification of an unbounded number of iterations to the verification of at most two iterations.

Theorem 167 (Engineer's Induction). *Assume that $Q \subseteq \neg \diamond P$. Then we have*

$$P^* \subseteq \neg \diamond Q \qquad \Leftarrow \qquad id \cup P \cup PP \subseteq \neg \diamond Q.$$

The remainder of Section 6.3 is taken up by the proof of this rule. In Section 6.4 we will show that — under mild conditions on P and Q — the same rule can be used to verify infinite loops. Two example applications are described in Section 6.6 and Section 6.7.

Since $\neg \diamond Q = \boxplus \neg Q$ we can apply the Galois correspondence between $\ominus$ and $\boxplus$ and rewrite the conclusion $P^* \subseteq \neg \diamond Q$ to

$$\ominus P^* \subseteq \neg Q.$$

This inequation is more tractable than the previous one because its left hand side allows an application of the local linearity rule. In fact, Theorem 167 follows immediately from the lemma below (with one more application of the Galois connection (Definition 149) between $\ominus$ and $\boxplus$).

Lemma 168. *Assume that S is locally linear. Then we have*

$$\ominus P^* = \ominus id \ \cup \ \ominus P \ \cup \ (U \text{-}; P); P^*; (P; \text{-} U)$$
$$\subseteq \ominus(id \cup P \cup PP) \ \cup \ \diamond P.$$

Proof.

$$\ominus P^*$$
$$= \qquad \{ \text{ Definition of } \ominus \}$$
$$U \text{-}; P^* ; \text{-} U$$

$$= \quad \{ \text{Lemma 169 below} \}$$
$$U\text{-};(id\text{-};U \cup P^*(P\text{-};U))$$
$$= \quad \{ \text{Distributivity, definition of} \diamond \}$$
$$\diamond id \cup U\text{-};(P^*(P\text{-};U))$$
$$= \quad \{ \text{Local linearity} \}$$
$$\diamond id \cup (P^*\text{-};U)\text{-};(P\text{-};U) \cup (U\text{-};P^*)(P\text{-};U)$$
$$= \quad \{ P^*\text{-};U = U, \text{definition of} \diamond \}$$
$$\diamond id \cup \diamond P \cup (U\text{-};P^*)(P\text{-};U)$$
$$= \quad \{ \text{Lemma 169 below} \}$$
$$\diamond id \cup \diamond P \cup (U\text{-};id)(P\text{-};U) \cup (U\text{-};P)P^*(P\text{-};U)$$
$$\subseteq \quad \{ \text{Euclid} \}$$
$$\diamond id \cup \diamond P \cup U\text{-};(id;(P\text{-};U)) \cup (U\text{-};P)P^*(P\text{-};U)$$
$$= \quad \{ \text{Definition of} \diamond \}$$
$$\diamond id \cup \diamond P \cup (U\text{-};P)P^*(P\text{-};U)$$
$$\subseteq \quad \{ P^* \subseteq id \cup \oplus P \}$$
$$\diamond id \cup \diamond P \cup (U\text{-};P)(P\text{-};U) \cup \oplus P$$
$$\subseteq \quad \{ \text{Euclid} \}$$
$$\diamond id \cup \diamond P \cup U\text{-};(P(P\text{-};U)) \cup \oplus P$$
$$\subseteq \quad \{ \text{Euclid, Associativity of converse} \}$$
$$\diamond id \cup \diamond P \cup U\text{-};(PP)\text{-};U \cup \oplus P$$
$$= \quad \{ \text{Definition of} \diamond, \text{Distributivity} \}$$
$$\diamond(id \cup P \cup PP) \cup \oplus P.$$

The following lemma closes the gap in the last proof. It is actually a one-sided version of the same lemma.

Lemma 169. *Suppose that S is locally linear. Then we have the equations*

$$P^*\text{-};U = id\text{-};U \cup P^*(P\text{-};U)$$
$$U\text{-};P^* = U\text{-};id \cup (U\text{-};P)P^*.$$

Proof. By symmetry, it is sufficient to prove the first equation.

$$P^*\text{-};U = id\text{-};U \cup P^*(P\text{-};U)$$
$$\Leftarrow \quad \{ P^* = id \cup \mu_X(P \cup PX), \text{Distributivity} \}$$
$$\mu_X(P \cup PX)\text{-};U = P^*(P\text{-};U)$$
$$\Leftrightarrow \quad \{ \text{Tail recursion rule (Proposition 32)} \}$$
$$\mu_X(P \cup PX)\text{-};U = \mu_X(P\text{-};U \cup PX)$$
$$\Leftarrow \quad \{ \mu\text{-Fusion (Proposition 24)} \}$$
$$\forall X : (P \cup PX)\text{-};U = P\text{-};U \cup P(X\text{-};U)$$
$$\Leftarrow \quad \{ \text{Distributivity, Euclid} \}$$
$$\forall X : PX\text{-};U \subseteq P\text{-};U \cup P(X\text{-};U)$$

$$\Leftrightarrow \qquad \{ \text{ Local linearity } \}$$
$$true .$$

This concludes the proof of Theorem 167.

Lemma 168 has another important corollary. Recall that P is a safety property if $P = \boxplus P$.

Theorem 170. *Assume that $\mathcal{S}$ is locally linear and dense and that $P \in \mathcal{S}$ is a safety property. Then P^* is also a safety property.*

Proof. Since $\mathcal{S}$ is dense, we have $\Leftrightarrow id = id$ (easy exercise). Now assume P is a safety property. Then we have $\Leftrightarrow P \subseteq P$ and Lemma 168 yields $\Leftrightarrow P^* \subseteq \Leftrightarrow id \cup \Leftrightarrow P \cup (\Leftrightarrow P)P^*(\Leftrightarrow P) \subseteq id \cup P \cup PP^*P = P^*$. Thus P^* is also a safety property.

6.4   Finite and Infinite Observations

If we wish to reason about liveness properties (for example fairness), infinite observations must be allowed. A number of authorities, including Hoare and Dijkstra, have argued that fairness is irrelevant to the correctness of software because any violation of fairness takes infinite time and cannot, therefore, be observed. Of course, the same argument would imply that program termination is not an interesting property either. This position is adequate for certain tasks, such as the analysis of real-time software. On the other hand, allowing infinite observations may actually make it easier to specify a system, because it allows us to describe a run of a system with a single observation, rather than an infinite set of approximations. We avoid committing the theory to either point of view by allowing, but not requiring, observation spaces to contain infinite elements.

If infinite observations are allowed then we desire the ability to calculationally distinguish them from finite ones. Let us assume here that observations can only be infinite to the right, into the future. This makes sense from an operational point of view (every program starts at a finite point in time, but some do not terminate)[2]. The following notations are inspired by [15].

Definition 171 (Finity and Infinity). *Infinite observations are characterized by the fact that they cannot be made any longer (to the right). Thus, if E is true of all infinite (or eternal) observations, we should have*

$$E.x$$
$$\Leftrightarrow \quad \forall y, z : x; y = z \quad \Rightarrow \quad id.y$$
$$\Leftrightarrow \quad \neg(\exists y, z : x; y = z \cap \neg id.y)$$
$$\Leftrightarrow \quad \neg(U \; ; \text{-} \; \neg id).x .$$

---

[2] On the negative side, symmetry is destroyed. The infinite iteration operator, too, is inherently asymmetric. A symmetric treatment of infinity would introduce a little extra complexity; we recommend it as an exercise for energetic readers.

Therefore we define

$$F =_{df} U ; \text{-} \neg id \quad and \quad E =_{df} \neg F .$$

Note that, according to this definition, a point at infinity (i.e. the right unit of an infinite observation) counts as an infinite observation. The following two laws are straightforward exercises on the Euclid and exchange laws.

Proposition 172.

$$U; F = F \quad and \quad U; E = E .$$

Definition 173 (Zeno processes). *An infinite number of ever shorter observations does not necessarily consume an infinite amount of time, and $P \subseteq \neg id$ does not, in general, imply that $P^\infty \subseteq E$. Zeno effects are possible. Let us call P Zeno-free if we do have $P^\infty \subseteq E$. We can now formally state and verify our claim that safety properties are finitely refutable.*

Theorem 174 (Finite Refutability of Safety Properties). *Assume that P is Zeno-free and $Q \subseteq F$. Then we have*

$$P^\infty \subseteq \boxplus \neg Q \quad \Leftarrow \quad P^* \subseteq \boxplus \neg Q .$$

Proof.

$$P^\infty \subseteq \boxplus \neg Q$$

$\Leftrightarrow \qquad \{ \text{ Galois connection (Definition 149) } \}$

$$\diamondsuit P^\infty \subseteq \neg Q$$

$\Leftrightarrow \qquad \{ \diamondsuit X = U \text{-}; X ; \text{-} U \}$

$$U \text{-}; P^\infty ; \text{-} U \subseteq \neg Q$$

$\Leftarrow \qquad \{ \text{ Lemma 175 below } \}$

$$U \text{-}; (P^\infty \cup P^* ; \text{-} U) \subseteq \neg Q$$

$\Leftrightarrow \qquad \{ \text{ Disjunctivity and } U \text{-}; P^* ; \text{-} U = \diamondsuit P^* \}$

$$U \text{-}; P^\infty \cup \diamondsuit P^* \subseteq \neg Q$$

$\Leftrightarrow \qquad \{ \text{ Universal property of } \cup \}$

$$U \text{-}; P^\infty \subseteq \neg Q \quad \wedge \quad \diamondsuit P^* \subseteq \neg Q$$

$\Leftrightarrow \qquad \{ \text{ Exchange, Galois connection (Definition 149) } \}$

$$UQ \subseteq \neg P^\infty \quad \wedge \quad P^* \subseteq \boxplus \neg Q$$

$\Leftarrow \qquad \{ \text{ Assumptions } Q \subseteq F \text{ and } P^\infty \subseteq E \}$

$$UF \subseteq \neg E \quad \wedge \quad P^* \subseteq \boxplus \neg Q$$

$\Leftrightarrow \qquad \{ UF = F = \neg E \}$

$$P^* \subseteq \boxplus \neg Q .$$

The following lemma, which is an interesting rule for calculating with infinite loops in its own right, is required to complete the proof of the previous theorem.

Lemma 175.
$$P^\infty \mathbin{;-} U \subseteq P^* \mathbin{;-} U \cup P^\infty .$$

Proof. First we establish a recursive inequation for $P^\infty \mathbin{;-} U$.

$$P^\infty \mathbin{;-} U$$
$$= \qquad \{ \text{ Definition of } P^\infty \}$$
$$(P; P^\infty) \mathbin{;-} U$$
$$= \qquad \{ \text{ Local linearity } \}$$
$$P \mathbin{;-} (U \mathbin{;-} P^\infty) \ \cup \ P; (P^\infty \mathbin{;-} U)$$
$$\subseteq$$
$$P \mathbin{;-} U \ \cup \ P; (P^\infty \mathbin{;-} U) .$$

Now we are ready for the main calculation.

$$P^\infty \mathbin{;-} U$$
$$\subseteq \qquad \{ \text{ Fixed point induction, using the above } \}$$
$$\nu_X (P \mathbin{;-} U \cup P; X)$$
$$= \qquad \{ \text{ Repetition Rule (Proposition } 40) \}$$
$$P^*; (P \mathbin{;-} U) \cup P^\infty$$
$$\subseteq \qquad \{ \text{ Euclid } \}$$
$$(P^*; P) \mathbin{;-} U \cup P^\infty$$
$$\subseteq \qquad \{ P^*; P \subseteq P^* \}$$
$$P^* \mathbin{;-} U \cup P^\infty .$$

6.5   Measuring Time

Most specifications of reactive system involve quantitative timing: for example, a level-crossing barrier must be lowered at least 60 seconds before a train crosses, a gas burner may not leak unburned gas for more than four seconds within any period of 60 seconds, or a lift should never make a customer wait for more than five minutes. A specification is a predicate on observations and we shall now assume that the duration of an observation can be measured: we postulate a real-valued function ℓ on observations that satisfies

$$\ell.x \ \geq \ 0$$
$$\ell.x = 0 \ \Leftrightarrow \ id.x$$
$$\ell.(x; y) \ = \ \ell.x + \ell.y \quad \text{provided } x; y \text{ is defined}$$

We agree to the convention that an expression like $\ell \geq 5$ abbreviates the function $\lambda x.(\ell.x \geq 5)$. This notational trick enriches the calculus with new predicates. For example, $\ell \geq 5$ is a predicate that holds for every observation that takes at least five seconds (or whatever unit of time is agreed to). The new notation also permits us to rewrite the axioms for ℓ in a point-free manner:

$$\ell \geq 0 \quad \text{(Positiveness)}$$
$$(\ell = 0) = id \quad \text{(Definiteness)}$$
$$(\ell = r); (\ell = s) \subseteq (\ell = r + s) \quad \text{for all real numbers } r, s \quad \text{(Additivity)}$$

These postulates are called the *measure axioms*. Note that we are not trying to suppress references to real numbers as measures of interval lengths; we even allow quantification over those. We are just eliminating all references to individual points in time.

The measure operator ℓ is the main innovation of a logic known as the Duration Calculus [47]. It adds considerable expressivity and calculational power to interval logic and sequential algebra. We illustrate the use of a measure operator by proving a synchronization rule. In order to do this, we need the following lemma.

Lemma 176 (Subtractivity).

$$(\ell = r + s) \,;\, \overline{} \, (\ell = s) \; \subseteq \; (\ell = r) \,.$$

Proof.

$$(\ell = r + s) \,;\, \overline{} \, (\ell = s) \; \subseteq \; (\ell = r)$$
$$\Leftarrow \qquad \{ \text{ Predicate calculus } \}$$
$$(\ell = r + s) \,;\, \overline{} \, (\ell = s) \; \subseteq \; \overline{(\ell = t)} \quad \text{for all } t \neq r$$
$$\Leftrightarrow \qquad \{ \text{ Exchange } \}$$
$$(\ell = r + s) \; \subseteq \; \overline{(\ell = t)(\ell = s)} \quad \text{for all } t \neq r$$
$$\Leftrightarrow \qquad \{ \text{ Additivity } \}$$
$$(\ell = r + s) \; \subseteq \; \overline{(\ell = t + s)} \quad \text{for all } t \neq r$$
$$\Leftrightarrow \qquad \{ \text{ Predicate calculus, arithmetic } \}$$
$$true \,.$$

Definiteness is extremely useful in calculations because it permits to distribute composition over conjunction as follows.

Proposition 177 (Synchronization). *If S is locally linear, then we have*

$$P \cup P' \subseteq (\ell = r) \qquad \Rightarrow \qquad PQ \cap P'Q' \; = \; (P \cap P')(Q \cap Q') \,.$$

Proof. Assume $P \cup P' \subseteq (\ell = r)$. The inclusion from right to left follows from monotonicity. To prove the other inclusion, let $s \in \mathbb{R}$. Then we have

$$PQ \cap P'Q' \cap (\ell = s)$$
$$= \qquad \{ \, P \cup P' \subseteq (\ell = r), \text{ definition of measures } \}$$
$$P(Q \cap (\ell = s - r)) \cap P'(Q' \cap (\ell = s - r))$$

$$
\begin{aligned}
&= \qquad \{ \text{ Let } R = Q \cap (\ell = r - s) \text{ and } R' = Q' \cap (\ell = r - s) \} \\
&\quad PR \cap P'R' \\
&\subseteq \qquad \{ \text{ Dedekind law } \} \\
&\quad (P \cap P'R' ;\text{-} R) (R \cap P \text{-}; P'R') \\
&= \qquad \{ \text{ Local linearity } \} \\
&\quad (P \cap (P'(R' ;\text{-} R) \cup P' ;\text{-} (R ;\text{-} R'))); \\
&\quad (R \cap ((P \text{-}; P')R' \cup (P' \text{-}; P) \text{-}; R')) \\
&\subseteq \qquad \{ \text{ Subtractivity } \} \\
&\quad (P \cap (P'(\ell = 0) \cup P' ;\text{-} (\ell = 0))) (R \cap ((\ell = 0)R' \cup (\ell = 0) \text{-}; R')) \\
&= \qquad \{ \text{ Definiteness, } id \text{ is a unit } \} \\
&\quad (P \cap P')(R \cap R') .
\end{aligned}
$$

Since the above calculation works for every $s \in \mathbb{R}$, totality of ℓ yields $PQ \cap P'Q' \subseteq (P \cap P')(Q \cap Q')$, as required.

Note that we are not defining an abstract notion of measure algebras (like we did for sequential algebras). It is possible to give an axiomatic definition for measure algebra, but considerable mathematical plumbing is required for doing it properly, and we ignore the issue here.

6.6   Phase Calculus

The operation of a system is frequently best described in terms of phases into which its execution can be decomposed. A phase is informally defined as a part of an execution during which some predicate B of interest invariantly holds. For example, consider the following automaton fragment.

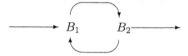

Let us assume that control remains at each node for some non-zero but finite amount of time, and that the outgoing transition must be taken eventually. Taking B_i to be true when control is in state i, we would describe the execution of this small system by the predicate

$$
(\lceil B_1 \rceil; \lceil B_2 \rceil)^*
$$

The predicate $\lceil B \rceil$ is intended to hold for an observation if B holds at almost all (i.e. all but finitely many) points of the observation interval. An observation satisfying $\lceil B \rceil$ is called a B-observation. We do not require B-observations to satisfy B at *every* point of their observation interval because that would beg the very awkward question whether the interval end points should be included in that requirement — and every possible choice has undesirable consequences. Since it is physically impossible to distinguish between time diagrams that agree almost everywhere, we incur no significant loss of generality. Now let us give a formal, axiomatic definition of the phase operator.

Definition 178 (Phase Algebra). *A phase algebra consists of a sequential algebra* $\mathcal{S}$, *a Boolean algebra* $\mathcal{B}$ *and a unary operator that maps every* $B \in \mathcal{B}$ *to some* $\lceil B \rceil \in \mathcal{S}$. *The elements of* $\mathcal{B}$ *are called* state predicates, *and an expression of the form* $\lceil B \rceil$ *is called a* phase. *We require the following laws, which we will call the* phase axioms.

1. *There are no* O*-observations:*

$$\lceil O \rceil = O.$$

2. *Every non-unit observation is a* U*-observation:*

$$\lceil U \rceil = \neg id.$$

3. *Almost everywhere is conjunctive:*

$$\lceil B \rceil \cap \lceil C \rceil = \lceil B \cap C \rceil.$$

4. *The composition of two* B*-observations is itself a* B*-observation:*

$$\lceil B \rceil ; \lceil B \rceil \subseteq \lceil B \rceil.$$

5. *Every restriction of a* B*-observation is either a* B*-observation or a unit:*

$$\ominus \lceil B \rceil \subseteq id \cup \lceil B \rceil.$$

Remark 179 (Phases in Sequential Algebra). *The reader familiar with the relational calculus will know that state predicates correspond to partial identities. The same intuition works for sequential algebras. A predicate* B *is called a* partial identity *(also a* monotype *or* coreflexive*) if* $B \subseteq id$. *Given a sequential algebra* $\mathcal{S}$, *let* $\mathcal{B}$ *denote the set of its partial identities. Clearly,* $\mathcal{B}$ *is a Boolean algebra (with top element* $U_{\mathcal{B}} = id$ *and negation operator* $\neg_{\mathcal{B}} B = \neg B \cap id$*). We first define an auxiliary operator*

$$\llbracket B \rrbracket =_{df} \neg((\neg id)(\neg_{\mathcal{B}} B)(\neg id))$$

Thus $\llbracket B \rrbracket$ *is true of an observation* $x : [a, b] \to \Sigma$ *when* $x.t$ *satisfies* B *for all* t *with* $a < t < b$ *(note the use of strict inequalities here). The phase operator is defined by*

$$\lceil B \rceil =_{df} \neg id \cap \llbracket B \rrbracket^{*}.$$

We now have the following theorem.

Theorem 180. *Suppose* $\mathcal{S}$ *is a locally linear and dense sequential algebra. Then* $\mathcal{S}$ *with* $\mathcal{B}$ *and* $\lceil \cdot \rceil$ *as defined above is a phase algebra.*

Proof. The proofs of phase axioms 1, 2, and 4 are completely straightforward and therefore omitted here. To prove 3 and 5, we first show that, for any state predicate B, the predicate $\llbracket B \rrbracket$ is a safety property.

$\langle\!\langle B\rangle\!\rangle$ is a safety property

$\Leftrightarrow$ { Safety properties (Proposition 159) }

$\langle\!\langle B\rangle\!\rangle \subseteq \boxplus\langle\!\langle B\rangle\!\rangle$

$\Leftrightarrow$ { Contraposition, definition of $\boxplus$ }

$\diamondsuit\neg\langle\!\langle B\rangle\!\rangle \subseteq \neg\langle\!\langle B\rangle\!\rangle$

$\Leftrightarrow$ { Definitions of $\diamondsuit$ and $\langle\!\langle\ \rangle\!\rangle$ }

$U(\neg id)(\neg_{\mathcal{B}} B)(\neg id)U \subseteq (\neg id)(\neg_{\mathcal{B}} B)(\neg id)$

$\Leftarrow$

$U(\neg id) = \neg id = (\neg id)U$

$\Leftrightarrow$ { Density }

$true\,.$

Now we can prove phase axiom 3 like this:

$\lceil B\rceil \cap \lceil C\rceil$

$=$ { Definition of $\lceil\cdot\rceil$ and $\langle\!\langle\cdot\rangle\!\rangle$ }

$\neg id \cap \langle\!\langle B\rangle\!\rangle^* \cap \langle\!\langle C\rangle\!\rangle^*$

$=$ { Theorem 170, using that $\langle\!\langle B\rangle\!\rangle^*$ is a safety property }

$\neg id \cap (\langle\!\langle B\rangle\!\rangle^* \cap \langle\!\langle C\rangle\!\rangle)^*$

$=$ { Theorem 170, using that $\langle\!\langle C\rangle\!\rangle$ is a safety property }

$\neg id \cap (\langle\!\langle B\rangle\!\rangle \cap \langle\!\langle C\rangle\!\rangle)^{**}$

$=$ { Star is idempotent, definition of $\lceil\cdot\rceil$ and $\langle\!\langle\cdot\rangle\!\rangle$ }

$\lceil B\cap C\rceil\,.$

and phase axiom 5 like this:

$\diamondsuit\lceil B\rceil$

$=$ { Definition of $\lceil\cdot\rceil$ and $\langle\!\langle\cdot\rangle\!\rangle$ }

$\diamondsuit(\overline{id} \cap \langle\!\langle B\rangle\!\rangle^*)$

$\subseteq$ { Monotonicity }

$\diamondsuit\langle\!\langle B\rangle\!\rangle^*$

$=$ { Theorem 170, using that $\langle\!\langle B\rangle\!\rangle$ is a safety property }

$\langle\!\langle B\rangle\!\rangle^*$

$\subseteq$ { Boolean algebra }

$id \cup (\overline{id} \cap \langle\!\langle B\rangle\!\rangle^*)$

$=$ { Definition of $\lceil\cdot\rceil$ and $\langle\!\langle\cdot\rangle\!\rangle$ }

$id \cup \lceil B\rceil\,.$

Proposition 181 (More Phase Laws). *The following selection has been made according to what is needed in the unit pulse example below. Their proofs are left as exercises for the reader.*

1. Importability: Assume that $P \subseteq \neg id$ and $Q \subseteq \neg id$. Then we have

$$\lceil B\rceil \cap PQ = (\lceil B\rceil \cap P)(\lceil B\rceil \cap Q)\,.$$

2. *Exclusion property: If $\neg B$ holds on some subinterval then B does not hold on the entire interval*

$$\diamond\lceil\neg B\rceil \;\subseteq\; \neg\lceil B\rceil\,.$$

3. *Initial Exclusion: B and $\neg B$ cannot both be true on an initial interval*

$$\lceil\neg B\rceil;U \;\subseteq\; \neg(\lceil B\rceil;U)\,.$$

4. *No overlap property:*

$$\lceil B\rceil \,\cap\, \diamond(P;\lceil\neg B\rceil;Q) \;\subseteq\; \diamond P \cup \diamond Q\,.$$

Definition 182 (Unit Pulse). *A unit pulse is a Boolean variable B that can only be true for exactly one unit of time. Its specification is*

$$\text{unit-pulse-spec} =_{df} \boxplus Q \quad \text{where} \quad Q =_{df} \lceil B\rceil \;\to\; \diamond((\ell = 1) \cap \lceil B\rceil),$$

i.e., every B-interval must be contained in a B-interval of length one.

Definition 183. *A first step towards an implementation eliminates the modal operator $\boxplus$ and the implication $\xrightarrow{\prime}$, because these are not admitted in any notation for implementation. Instead, we use the iteration operator.*

$$\text{unit-pulse-design} =_{df} P^* \quad \text{where} \quad P =_{df} \lceil\neg B\rceil \;;\; ((\ell = 1) \cap \lceil B\rceil).$$

We claim that this design is correct:

$$\text{unit-pulse-design} \subseteq \text{unit-pulse-spec}$$

Proof.

$$\text{unit-pulse-design} \subseteq \text{unit-pulse-spec}$$
$\Leftrightarrow$ $\qquad$ { Definitions }
$$P^* \subseteq \boxplus Q$$
$\Leftrightarrow$ $\qquad$ { Proof rule for control loops }
$$id \cup P \cup PP \subseteq \boxplus Q \quad \text{and} \quad \diamond P \subseteq Q$$
$\Leftrightarrow$ $\qquad$ { $\diamond P \subseteq Q$ follows from the exclusion property

(Proposition 181.2) }
$$id \cup P \cup PP \subseteq \boxplus Q$$
$\Leftarrow$ $\qquad$ { Galois connection and disjunctivity of $\diamond$ }
$$\diamond\, id \cup \diamond(P \cup PP) \subseteq Q$$
$\Leftrightarrow$ $\qquad$ { $\diamond\, id = id$ holds in every measure algebra }
$$id \cup \diamond(P \cup PP) \subseteq Q$$
$\Leftarrow$ $\qquad$ { $id \subseteq \neg\lceil B\rceil$ }
$$\diamond(P \cup PP) \subseteq Q$$
$\Leftrightarrow$ $\qquad$ { Definition of Q and Boolean algebra (shunting) }
$$\lceil B\rceil \,\cap\, \diamond(P \cup PP) \subseteq \diamond((\ell = 1) \cap \lceil B\rceil)$$
$\Leftrightarrow$ $\qquad$ { No overlap property (Proposition 181.4) (twice) }
$$true\,.$$

6.7 Duration Calculus

Phase Calculus allows us to require that a state predicate B should invariantly hold throughout certain phases. In Duration Calculus we can go one step further, and require that B should hold at least, say, 90% of the time. In the famous gas burner example, there is a state predicate *Leak* which holds whenever the gas valve is open, but no flame is burning. Leaks cannot be totally avoided, because ignition is not instantaneous, and a flame may be blown out. But there must not be too many leaks: it is considered dangerous to have an accumulation of more than four seconds of leakage within any interval of less than thirty seconds.

$$gas\text{-}spec =_{df} \boxplus \neg Q \quad \text{where} \quad Q =_{df} (\ell < 30) \cap (\textstyle\int Leak > 4).$$

We have to explain the predicate $\int Leak > 4$. The intention is that this predicate is satisfied by an observation $x : [a, b] \to \Sigma$ just when $\int_a^b Leak(x.t)\, dt > 4$, where we take *Leak* to be a function on Σ which takes the value 1 when a leak is present and 0 otherwise. The integral $\int_a^b \ldots dt$ is just the Riemann integral.

The formal definition given below is still in terms of observations (i.e. not point-free) but it does not require the observations to be time diagrams.

Definition 184. *Let U be an observation space and $\mathcal{B}$ be a Boolean algebra (whose elements are called state predicates). Then we assume an operator $\int$: $\mathcal{B} \to (U \to \mathbb{R})$ with the following properties*

1. $(\int B).x \geq 0$.
2. *If $x; y$ is defined then* $(\int B).(x; y) = (\int B).x + (\int B).y$.
3. $(\int B \cap C).x + (\int B \cup C).x = (\int B).x + (\int C).x$.
4. $(\int \mathsf{O}).x = 0$.
5. $(\int U).x = 0$ *iff x is a unit*.

Note that, for the purpose of integration, we identify O with 0 and U with 1. The above integral axioms reflect well-known properties of the Riemann integral.

As always, we eliminate points from the calculus: an expression like $\int B \geq 3 \int C$ is taken as a shorthand for the predicate $(\int B).x \geq 3((\int C).x)$. The five integral properties listed above translate to the following point-free postulates.

1. $\int B \geq 0$.
2. $(\int B = r)(\int B = s) \subseteq (\int B = r + s)$.
3. $\int B \cap C + \int B \cup C = \int B + \int C$.
4. $\int \mathsf{O} = 0$.
5. $(\int U = 0) = id$.

To show these axioms at work we prove the monotonicity of the integral operator. Assume B and C are state predicates with $B \subseteq C$. Then we have

$$\int C$$
$$= \qquad \{ \text{Predicate calculus} \}$$

$$\int ((B \cap C) \cup (\neg B \cap C))$$

$= \qquad \{ \text{ Integral axiom 3 } \}$

$$\int (B \cap C) \; + \; \int (\neg B \cap C) \; - \; \int ((B \cap C) \cap (\neg B \cap C))$$

$= \qquad \{ \; B \subseteq C, \text{ predicate calculus } \}$

$$\int B \; + \; \int (\neg B \cap C) \; - \; \int 0$$

$\geq$

$$\int B \, .$$

Given a duration operator with these properties, we can define both a measure operator ℓ and a phase operator $\lceil \cdot \rceil$ as follows.

$$\ell =_{df} \int U \quad \text{and} \quad \lceil B \rceil =_{df} \neg id \cap \left(\int B = \ell \right) .$$

All of the measure and phase axioms can now be proved from the above duration axioms.

Now that we have explained the operators in the specification of the gas burner, we can do an implementation step. Let

$$gas\text{-}design =_{df} P^* \quad \text{where} \quad P =_{df} (\ell = 30) \cap \left(\int Leak \leq 2 \right) .$$

We claim that $gas\text{-}design \subseteq gas\text{-}spec$.

Proof. The proof rule Theorem 167 generates the following two proof obligations

$$\ominus (id \cup P \cup PP) \subseteq \neg Q \quad \text{and} \quad \oplus P \subseteq \neg Q \, .$$

The first claim follows from $\ominus (id \cup P \cup PP) \subseteq \left(\int Leak \leq 4 \right)$ and the second one from $\oplus P \subseteq (\ell \geq 30)$.

7   Conclusion

We have advocated a calculational style for reasoning about temporal propositions, but it would be misguided to suggest that Galois algebra and sequential algebra can replace temporal and interval logic. The logical approach is invaluable for investigating decidability, axiomatizability, expressiveness and related issues. Thanks to the existing decision procedures, temporal logic is also very useful for automatic verification, for example by model checking.

On the other hand, we would like to suggest that algebra is better suited to the human user. Mathematicians (and human beings in general) think in concepts, not in formulae. Rather than storing seventeen axioms in our head—no problem for a computer!—we prefer to remember that $\ominus$ and $\oplus$ are conjugate, and (in the linear case) a perfect Galois connection. Analogies and structural properties like symmetry and duality are more readily recognized and proved in algebra; they form the core of our, human, understanding of what temporal reasoning is about.

Let us contrast the style of algebraic calculation with that of logical deduction. Equational or inequational rewriting is *the* most fundamental technique of mathematics and everybody learns it at school. We have tried to show (as others have before us) that calculations are guided by the shape of the formulae, and proofs flow naturally from the dynamics of the symbols. Rarely, if ever, do we need to make an unexpected step ('pull a rabbit from a hat'). In contrast, logical deductions often build up to the final theorem in a bottom up fashion, giving little pieces at first without saying how they will fit together. In some deduction styles, proofs have little structure; in others the intermediate results form a tree which is hard to write down on paper. It is no accident that chains of (in)equations or implications are in common use throughout the mathematical literature, whereas logical deduction systems are hardly ever employed for convincing readers of theorems (except, of course, in books about logic).

The trade-off between the algebraic and the logical style may be compared to the relation between specification languages and programming languages. The latter are designed for the use of computers, and up to this day they have been far more successful than the former. However, painful experience has taught us that errors occur most easily, and are most costly, in the initial, informal phase of system design. To minimize the risk of error at this stage, specification languages are tailored for human use—often at the price of sacrificing mechanical niceties, such as an LR(1) syntax and automatic executability. The art of turning specifications into implementations is gradually becoming an established engineering craft and as a consequence, specification languages are gaining acceptance steadily. In a similar way, we expect that the calculational and human-oriented method of algebraic calculation will gain its place beside the established machinery of logical deduction.

References

1. C. J. Aarts. Galois connections presented calculationally. Technical report, Eindhoven University of Technology, 1992. Available from `ftp.win.tue.nl/pub/math.prog.construction/galois.dvi.Z`. 313

2. R. C. Backhouse, T. S. Voermans, and J. van der Woude. A relational theory of datatypes. Available via world-wide web at `http://www.win.tue.nl/win/cs/wp/papers`, December 1992. 313

3. Ralf Behnke. *Transformational program derivation in the framework of sequential and relational algebras.* PhD thesis, Christian-Albrechts-Universität Kiel, 1998. In German. 355

4. Rudolf Berghammer, Peter Kempf, Gunther Schmidt, and Thomas Ströhlein. Relation algebra and logic of programs. In *Algebraic Logic*, volume 54 of *Colloquia Mathematica Societatis János Bolyai*. Budapest University, 1988. 338

5. Rudolf Berghammer and Burghard von Karger. Formal derivation of CSP programs from temporal specifications. In Bernhard Möller, editor, *Mathematics of Program Construction*, LNCS 947, pages 180–196. Springer-Verlag, 1995. 311, 338, 355

6. Rudolf Berghammer and Burghard von Karger. Towards a design calculus for CSP. *Science of Computer Programming*, 26:99–115, 1996. 311, 338, 355

7. Richard S. Bird and Oege de Moor. *The Algebra of Programming*. International Series in Computer Science. Prentice Hall, 1996. 338

8. H. Brandt. Über eine Verallgemeinerung des Gruppenbegriffs. *Math. Ann.*, 96:360–366, 1926. 341

9. Stephen M. Brien. A time-interval calculus. In R. S. Bird, C. C. Morgan, and J. C. P. Woodcock, editors, *Mathematics of Program Construction*, LNCS 669. Springer-Verlag, 1992. 339

10. C. Brink, W. Kahl, and G. Schmidt, editors. *Relational Methods in Computer Science*. Advances in Computing Science. Springer, 1997. 344

11. Ronald Brown. From groups to groupoids. *Bull. London Math. Soc.*, 19:113–134, 1987. 341

12. A. H. Clifford and G. B. Preston. *The algebraic theory of semigroups*. Number 7 in Mathematical Surveys. American Mathematical Society, 1961. 346

13. Edsger W. Dijkstra. The unification of three calculi. In Manfred Broy, editor, *Program Design Calculi*, pages 197–231. Springer-Verlag, 1993. 339, 343, 360

14. E. W. Dijkstra and C. S. Scholten. *Predicate Calculus and Program Semantics*. Springer-Verlag, 1990. 309

15. Rutger Dijkstra. Computation calculus: Bridging a formalization gap. *Science of Computer Programming*, 37(1–3):3–36, 2000. 373

16. E. A. Emerson. Temporal and modal logic. In Jan van Leeuwen, editor, *Formal Models and Semantics*, volume B of *Handbook of Theoretical Computer Science*, chapter 16, pages 995–1072. Elsevier, 1990. 323

17. C. J. Everett. Closure operators and Galois theory in lattices. *Trans. Amer. Math. Soc.*, 55:514–525, 1944. 313

18. Horst Herrlich and Miroslav Hušek. Galois connections. In *Proceedings of MFPS*, LNCS 239, pages 122–134. Springer-Verlag, 1985. 313

19. C. A. R. Hoare. *Communicating Sequential Processes*. Series in Computer Sciences. Prentice-Hall, 1985. 339

20. C. A. R. Hoare. Programs are predicates. In C. A. R. Hoare and J. C. Shepherdson, editors, *Mathematical Logic and Programming Languages*, pages 141–155. Prentice-Hall, 1985. 309, 338

21. C. A. R. Hoare and He Jifeng. The weakest prespecification. *Fundamenta Informaticae*, 9:51–84, 217–252, 1986. 338

22. P. T. Johnstone. *Stone Spaces*. Cambridge University Press, 1992. 324

23. B. Jónsson. Varieties of relation algebras. *Algebra Universalis*, 15:273–298, 1982. 343, 356

24. S. C. Kleene. Representation of events in nerve nets and finite automata. In Shannon and McCarthy, editors, *Automata Studies*, pages 3–42. Princeton University Press, 1956. 339

25. R. Maddux. The origin of relation algebras in the development and axiomatization of the calculus of relations. *Studia Logica*, L(3/4):421–456, 1991. 344

26. R. Maddux. A working relational model: The derivation of the Dijkstra-Scholten predicate transformer semantics from Tarski's axioms of the Peirce-Schröder calculus of relations. Manuscript, 1992. 338

27. Zohar Manna and Amir Pnueli. *The Temporal Logic of Reactive and Concurrent Systems—Specification*. Springer-Verlag, 1991. 310, 323, 330

28. Antoni Mazurkiewicz. Traces, histories, graphs: Instances of a process monoid. In M. P. Chytil and V. Koubek, editors, *Mathematical Foundations of Computer Science*, LNCS 176, pages 115–133. Springer-Verlag, 1984. 342

29. Austin Melton, D. A. Schmidt, and George E. Strecker. Galois connections and computer science applications. In David Pitt, Samson Abramsky, Axel Poigné, and David Rydeheard, editors, *Category Theory and Computer Programming*, LNCS 240, pages 299–312. Springer-Verlag, 1986. 313, 337

30. Austin Melton, Bernd S. W. Schröder, and George E. Strecker. Lagois connections—a counterpart to Galois connections. *Theoretical Computer Science*, 136(1):79–108, 1994. 337

31. A. Mili. A relational approach to the design of deterministic programs. *Acta Informatica*, 20:315–328, 1983. 338

32. Ben Moszkowski. A temporal logic for multi-level reasoning about hardware. *IEEE Computer*, 18(2):10–19, 1985. 339

33. Ben Moszkowski. Some very compositional temporal properties. In E. R. Olderog, editor, *Proceedings of the IFIP TC2/WG2.1/WG2.2/WG2.3 Working Conference on Programming Concepts, Methods and Calculi (PROCOMET '94)*, San Miniato, Italy. IFIP Transactions A-56, North-Holland, 1994. 365, 368, 370

34. Oystein Ore. Galois connexions. *Trans. Amer. Math. Soc.*, 55:493–513, 1944. 313, 337

35. Amir Pnueli. The temporal logic of programs. In *18th Ann. IEEE Symp. on Foundations of Computer Science*, pages 46–57, 1977. 309, 322

36. Vaughan Pratt. Modelling concurrency with partial orders. *International Journal of Parallel Programming*, 15:33–71, 1986. 342

37. W. Prenowitz. A contemporary approach to classical geometry. *Amer. Math. Monthly*, 68(1, Part II), 1968. 348

38. Gunther Schmidt and Thomas Ströhlein. *Relations and Graphs*. EATCS Monographs on Theoretical Computer Science. Springer-Verlag, 1991. 339, 344, 360

39. Colin Stirling. Modal and temporal logics. In Samson Abramsky, Dov M. Gabbay, and Thomas S. E. Maibaum, editors, *Background: Computational Structures*, volume 2 of *Handbook of Logic in Computer Science*, pages 478–551. Clarendon Press, 1992. 318

40. A. Tarski and B. Jónsson. Boolean algebras with operators, parts I–II. *Amer. J. Math.*, 73,74:891–939, 127–162, 1951/52. 318

41. Alfred Tarski. On the calculus of relations. *Journal of Symbolic Logic*, 6(3):73–89, 1941. 310, 338, 339, 344

42. A. J. M. van Gasteren. *On the Shape of Mathematical Argument*, volume 445 of *Lecture Notes in Computer Science*. Springer, 1987. 317

43. Yde Venema. A modal logic for chopping intervals. *J. Logic Computat.*, 1(4):453–476, 1991. 339

44. B. von Karger and R. Berghammer. A relational model for temporal logic. *Logic Journal of the IGPL*, 6(2):157–173, 1998. Available from `www.oup.co.uk/igpl/Volume_06/Issue_02`. 355

45. Burghard von Karger. *Temporal Algebra*. PhD thesis, Habilitationsschrift, Christian-Albrechts-Univ. Kiel, 1997. Available from `www.informatik.uni-kiel.de/~bvk/`. 310, 323, 346, 348, 363

46. Burghard von Karger. A calculational approach to reactive systems. *Science of Computer Programming*, 37(1–3):139–161, 2000. 311

47. Chaochen Zhou, C. A. R. Hoare, and Anders P. Ravn. A calculus of durations. *Information Processing Letters*, 40:269–276, 1992. 339, 365, 376

Author Index

Lecture Notes in Computer Science

For information about Vols. 1–2248
please contact your bookseller or Springer-Verlag

Vol. 2284: T. Eiter, K.-D. Schewe (Eds.), Foundations of Information and Knowledge Systems. Proceedings, 2002. X, 289 pages. 2002.

Vol. 2285: H. Alt, A. Ferreira (Eds.), STACS 2002. Proceedings, 2002. XIV, 660 pages. 2002.

Vol. 2286: S. Rajsbaum (Ed.), LATIN 2002: Theoretical Informatics. Proceedings, 2002. XIII, 630 pages. 2002.

Vol. 2287: C.S. Jensen, K.G. Jeffery, J. Pokorny, Saltenis, E. Bertino, K. Böhm, M. Jarke (Eds.), Advances in Database Technology – EDBT 2002. Proceedings, 2002. XVI, 776 pages. 2002.

Vol. 2288: K. Kim (Ed.), Information Security and Cryptology – ICISC 2001. Proceedings, 2001. XIII, 457 pages. 2002.

Vol. 2289: C.J. Tomlin, M.R. Greenstreet (Eds.), Hybrid Systems: Computation and Control. Proceedings, 2002. XIII, 480 pages. 2002.

Vol. 2291: F. Crestani, M. Girolami, C.J. van Rijsbergen (Eds.), Advances in Information Retrieval. Proceedings, 2002. XIII, 363 pages. 2002.

Vol. 2292: G.B. Khosrovshahi, A. Shokoufandeh, A. Shokrollahi (Eds.), Theoretical Aspects of Computer Science. IX, 221 pages. 2002.

Vol. 2293: J. Renz, Qualitative Spatial Reasoning with Topological Information. XVI, 207 pages. 2002. (Subseries LNAI).

Vol. 2295: W. Kuich, G. Rozenberg, A. Salomaa (Eds.), Developments in Language Theory. Proceedings, 2001. IX, 389 pages. 2002.

Vol. 2296: B. Dunin-Kęplicz, E. Nawarecki (Eds.), From Theory to Practice in Multi-Agent Systems. Proceedings, 2001. IX, 341 pages. 2002. (Subseries LNAI).

Vol. 2297: R. Backhouse, R. Crole, J. Gibbons (Eds.), Algebraic and Coalgebraic Methods in the Mathematics of Program Construction. Proceedings, 2000. XIV, 387 pages. 2002.

Vol. 2299: H. Schmeck, T. Ungerer, L. Wolf (Eds.), Trends in Network and Pervasive Computing – ARCS 2002. Proceedings, 2002. XIV, 287 pages. 2002.

Vol. 2300: W. Brauer, H. Ehrig, J. Karhumäki, A. Salomaa (Eds.), Formal and Natural Computing. XXXVI, 431 pages. 2002.

Vol. 2301: A. Braquelaire, J.-O. Lachaud, A. Vialard (Eds.), Discrete Geometry for Computer Imagery. Proceedings, 2002. XI, 439 pages. 2002.

Vol. 2302: C. Schulte, Programming Constraint Services. XII, 176 pages. 2002. (Subseries LNAI).

Vol. 2303: M. Nielsen, U. Engberg (Eds.), Foundations of Software Science and Computation Structures. Proceedings, 2002. XIII, 435 pages. 2002.

Vol. 2304: R.N. Horspool (Ed.), Compiler Construction. Proceedings, 2002. XI, 343 pages. 2002.

Vol. 2305: D. Le Métayer (Ed.), Programming Languages and Systems. Proceedings, 2002. XII, 331 pages. 2002.

Vol. 2306: R.-D. Kutsche, H. Weber (Eds.), Fundamental Approaches to Software Engineering. Proceedings, 2002. XIII, 341 pages. 2002.

Vol. 2307: C. Zhang, S. Zhang, Association Rule Mining. XII, 238 pages. 2002. (Subseries LNAI).

Vol. 2308: I.P. Vlahavas, C.D. Spyropoulos (Eds.), Methods and Applications of Artificial Intelligence. Proceedings, 2002. XIV, 514 pages. 2002. (Subseries LNAI).

Vol. 2309: A. Armando (Ed.), Frontiers of Combining Systems. Proceedings, 2002. VIII, 255 pages. 2002. (Subseries LNAI).

Vol. 2310: P. Collet, C. Fonlupt, J.-K. Hao, E. Lutton, M. Schoenauer (Eds.), Artificial Evolution. Proceedings, 2001. XI, 375 pages. 2002.

Vol. 2311: D. Bustard, W. Liu, R. Sterritt (Eds.), Soft-Ware 2002: Computing in an Imperfect World. Proceedings, 2002. XI, 359 pages. 2002.

Vol. 2312: T. Arts, M. Mohnen (Eds.), Implementation of Functional Languages. Proceedings, 2001. VII, 187 pages. 2002.

Vol. 2313: C.A. Coello Coello, A. de Albornoz, L.E. Sucar, O.Cairó Battistutti (Eds.), MICAI 2002: Advances in Artificial Intelligence. Proceedings, 2002. XIII, 548 pages. 2002. (Subseries LNAI).

Vol. 2314: S.-K. Chang, Z. Chen, S.-Y. Lee (Eds.), Recent Advances in Visual Information Systems. Proceedings, 2002. XI, 323 pages. 2002.

Vol. 2315: F. Arhab, C. Talcott (Eds.), Coordination Models and Languages. Proceedings, 2002. XI, 406 pages. 2002.

Vol. 2316: J. Domingo-Ferrer (Ed.), Inference Control in Statistical Databases. VIII, 231 pages. 2002.

Vol. 2317: M. Hegarty, B. Meyer, N. Hari Narayanan (Eds.), Diagrammatic Representation and Inference. Proceedings, 2002. XIV, 362 pages. 2002. (Subseries LNAI).

Vol. 2318: D. Bošnački, S. Leue (Eds.), Model Checking Software. Proceedings, 2002. X, 259 pages. 2002.

Vol. 2319: C. Gacek (Ed.), Software Reuse: Methods, Techniques, and Tools. Proceedings, 2002. XI, 353 pages. 2002.

Vol. 2322: V. Mařík, O. Štěpánková, H. Krautwurmová, M. Luck (Eds.), Multi-Agent Systems and Applications II. Proceedings, 2001. XII, 377 pages. 2002. (Subseries LNAI).

Vol. 2324: T. Field, P.G. Harrison, J. Bradley, U. Harder (Eds.), Computer Performance Evaluation. Proceedings, 2002. XI, 349 pages. 2002.

Vol. 2329: P.M.A. Sloot, C.J.K. Tan, J.J. Dongarra, A.G. Hoekstra (Eds.), Computational Science – ICCS 2002. Proceedings, Part I. XLI, 1095 pages. 2002.

Vol. 2330: P.M.A. Sloot, C.J.K. Tan, J.J. Dongarra, A.G. Hoekstra (Eds.), Computational Science – ICCS 2002. Proceedings, Part II. XLI, 1115 pages. 2002.

Vol. 2331: P.M.A. Sloot, C.J.K. Tan, J.J. Dongarra, A.G. Hoekstra (Eds.), Computational Science – ICCS 2002. Proceedings, Part III. XLI, 1227 pages. 2002.

Vol. 2332: L. Knudsen (Ed.), Advances in Cryptology – EUROCRYPT 2002. Proceedings, 2002. XII, 547 pages. 2002.